WordPerfect 6.1 for Windows™ ESSENTIALS

NITA HEWITT RUTKOSKY

Pierce College at Puyallup
Puyallup, Washington

Developmental Editor	Lisa McGowan
Proofreader	Susan Capecchi
Cover Designer	Bolger Publications/Creative Printing
Indexer	Nancy Sauro
Text Designer	Joan Silver
Desktop Production	PJ Komar

Microsoft, DOS, and Windows are registered trademarks of Microsoft Corporation. WordPerfect is a registered trademark of Novell, Inc. IBM is a registered trademark of IBM Corporation.

Material for selected documents has been excerpted from *Telecommunications: Systems and Applications* by Robert Hendricks, Leonard Sterry, and William Mitchell, published by Paradigm Publishing Inc., 1993.

The publishing of a book requires the support, encouragement, and assistance of many people. We wish to acknowledge and thank the following reviewers for their time, dedication, and excellent suggestions: Denise Seguin, School of Business, Fanshawe College, London, Ontario; Barbara Crider, Consultant, Centre Hall, PA.

Library of Congress Cataloging-in-Publication Data

Rutkosky, Nita Hewitt
WordPerfect essentials: 6.1 for Windows / Nita Hewitt Rutkosky.
p. cm.
Includes index.
ISBN 1-56118-795-X
1. WordPerfect for Windows (Computer file) 2. Word processing. I. Title.
Z52.5.W655R888 1995
652.5'536--dc20 95-21963
CIP

TEXT + 3.5" DISK: ISBN 1-56118-796-8
Order Number: 05239

TEXT + 5.25" DISK: 1-56118-797-6
Order Number: 10239

Published by: EMC/Paradigm
300 York Ave.
St. Paul, MN 55101
800-535-6865

Printed in the United States of America
10 9 8 7 6 5 4 3 2 1

Contents

Preface v

Getting Started vii

Identifying Computer Hardware vii
Properly Maintaining Disks ix
Using the WordPerfect Template x

Using the Mouse xi

Understanding Mouse Terms xi
Using the Mouse Pointer xi

Executing Commands xii

Using the Menu Bar xii

UNIT 1: PRODUCING BUSINESS CORRESPONDENCE 1

Chapter 1 Starting WordPerfect for Windows 3

Creating a WordPerfect Document 3
Completing Computer Exercises 7
Keying and Saving a WordPerfect Document 7
Chapter Summary* 12
Check Your Understanding* 13
Skill Assessments* 14

Chapter 2 Editing a Document 15

Moving the Insertion Point with the Mouse 15
Moving the Insertion Point with the Keyboard 17
Inserting Text 19
Deleting Text 19
Splitting and Joining Paragraphs 19
Selecting Text 20
Using the Undo, Redo, and Undelete Options 23
Saving Documents 25
Printing a Document 26

Chapter 3 Formatting Characters 31

Creating Text in All Caps 31
Using the Tab Key 31
Formatting Text 32
Using Help 37

Chapter 4 Formatting Lines 45

Centering Text 45
Changing Line Spacing 47
Changing Justification 48
Changing the Viewing Mode 52

Chapter 5 Changing Margins & Indents 59

Changing Margins 59
Indenting Text 62

Chapter 6 Using Writing Tools 73

Using Spell Checker 73
Using Thesaurus 76
Displaying Document Information 79
Using Grammatik 79

Unit 1 Performance Assessment 89

UNIT 2: PRODUCING CUSTOMIZED DOCUMENTS 95

Chapter 7 Changing Fonts 97

Choosing a Typeface 97
Choosing a Type Size 98
Choosing a Type Style 99
Choosing a Font 99
Changing the Default Font 104
Inserting the Date 105
Using WordPerfect Character Sets 105

Chapter 8 Formatting with Special Features 113

Changing the Location of Macro Documents 114
Recording a Macro 114
Playing a Macro 116
Editing a Macro 117
Pausing a Macro 119
Deleting a Macro 121
Using Templates 122
Using WordPerfect's Envelope Feature 124
Creating Mailing Labels 126
Using QuickCorrect 128

Chapter 9 Merging Documents 137

Creating a Data File 137
Creating the Form File 143
Merging Files 144
Creating a Table Data File 145
Canceling a Merge 146
Creating Envelopes 147
Creating a Form File for Labels 148

Chapter 10 Manipulating Tabs 153

Manipulating Tabs with the Ruler Bar 153
Manipulating Tabs with the Tab Set Dialog Box 157

Chapter 11 Printing & Maintaining Documents 167

Printing 167
Maintaining Documents 170

* This feature appears in each chapter.

Displaying File Information 170
Using File Options 170
Opening a Document as a Copy 175
Viewing a Document 176

Unit 2 Performance Assessment 181

UNIT 3: PREPARING MULTI-PAGED DOCUMENTS 187

Chapter 12 Inserting Page Formatting 189
Changing Top and Bottom Margins 189
Turning on Widow/Orphan 190
Inserting Hard Page Breaks 191
Centering Text Vertically on the Page 192
Inserting Page Numbering 193

Chapter 13 Creating Document References 201
Creating Headers and Footers 201
Discontinuing Headers and Footers 205
Creating a Footnote or Endnote 205
Printing Footnotes and Endnotes 208
Editing a Footnote or Endnote 209
Deleting a Footnote or Endnote 209
Changing the Beginning Number 210

Chapter 14 Cutting & Pasting Text 217
Working with Blocks of Text 217
Working with Documents 220
Working with Windows 222
Cutting and Pasting Text between Windows 227

Chapter 15 Conducting a Find and Replace 235
Finding and Replacing Text 235
Customizing Find and Replace 237

Chapter 16 Creating Newspaper & Parallel Columns 247
Creating Newspaper Columns 247
Editing Text in Columns 251
Creating Parallel Columns 252
Changing Column Widths with the Ruler Bar 255

Unit 3 Performance Assessment 261

UNIT 4: CREATING DOCUMENTS WITH GRAPHICS ELEMENTS 265

Chapter 17 Inserting Graphics Images 267
Inserting an Image into a Document 267
Creating a Text Box 269
Creating a Figure Box 270
Creating a Table Box 271
Creating a User Box 272
Creating a Button Box 273
Creating a Watermark 275
Editing a Box 276
Dragging a Box with the Mouse 290
Creating Horizontal and Vertical Lines 291

Chapter 18 Using WordPerfect Draw & TextArt 301
Drawing Shapes 301
Creating Text in WordPerfect Draw 307
Editing an Object 310
Changing Attributes 319
Using TextArt 320

Chapter 19 Creating Tables 333
Creating a Table 333
Entering Text in Cells 336
Changing the Column Width of a Table 338
Selecting Cells 343
Editing a Table 344
Deleting a Table 352

Chapter 20 Creating Charts 361
Creating a Chart 361
Changing Chart Type 368

Unit 4 Performance Assessment 377

Appendix A Formatting Disks 383

Appendix B Proofreaders' Marks 384

Appendix C Formatting Business Documents 385

Appendix D Graphics Images 387

Index 389

Preface

When students prepare for a successful business career, they need to acquire the necessary skills and qualifications essential to becoming a productive member of the business community. Microcomputer systems are prevalent in most business offices, and students will encounter employment opportunities that require a working knowledge of computers and computer software.

Microcomputers, with the appropriate software, are used by businesses in a variety of capacities. One of the most popular uses of a microcomputer system is word processing—the creation of documents.

Word processing certainly belongs in the business office, but it is also a popular application for home computer use. People will want to learn word processing to write personal correspondence, keep personal records, provide support for a home-based business or cottage industry, write term papers and reports, and much more.

This text provides students with the opportunity to learn word processing for employment purposes or home use and to utilize a microcomputer as a word processor. The WordPerfect® for Windows™, Version 6.1, program and an IBM® or IBM-compatible microcomputer system must be available for students to practice the features of the program. WordPerfect needs to be installed on a hard-drive or network system. To properly install the program, please refer to the WordPerfect reference manual.

This textbook instructs students in the theories and practical applications of one of the most popular word processing software programs—WordPerfect. The text is designed to be used in a word processing class and provides approximately 60 to 80 hours of instruction.

The book is divided into four units. Chapters within units each contain a performance objective, material introducing and explaining new concepts and commands, a chapter summary, and a knowledge self-check.

Students and instructors familiar with previous books in the Rutkosky word processing series will notice a significant change in the structure of this text. The guided, step-by-step exercises that formerly appeared at the end of each chapter under the heading "At the Computer" have been integrated within the chapter material so that as students are introduced to each WordPerfect feature, they are immediately given the opportunity to practice using the feature in an exercise. This change was a response to the increasing number of independent lab study courses and the concept that immediate hands-on reinforcement promotes long-term knowledge and understanding.

Also new with this text is the listing of SCANS goals covered in each unit (see the back of the first page of each unit). SCANS (Secretary's Commission on Achieving Necessary Skills) standards emphasize the integration of competencies from the areas of information, technology, basic skills, and thinking skills. The concepts and applications material in each unit of this book has been designed to coordinate with and reflect this important interdisciplinary emphasis. In addition, learning assessment tools implement the SCANS standards. For example, the end-of-chapter exercises called "Skill Assessments" reinforce acquired skills while providing practice in decision-making and problem-solving. A "Performance Assessment" at the end of each unit offers simulation exercises that require students to demonstrate their understanding of the major skills and technical features taught in the unit's chapters within the framework of critical and creative thinking. Also included in the Performance Assessment are three kinds of optional exercises related to SCANS standards: 1) alternative ways to complete specific exercises; 2) a section called "Writing"; and 3) a section called "Research" (this section is included only in selected units).

By the time students have completed the textbook, they have mastered the essential and important features and commands of WordPerfect and are ready to perform on the job. They also will have acquired a solid foundation in the problem-solving and communication abilities so important in the contemporary workplace.

Getting Started

Identifying Computer Hardware

As you work your way through this textbook, you will learn functions and commands for WordPerfect for Windows, Version 6.1. To do this, you will need an IBM PC or an IBM-compatible computer. This computer system should consist of the CPU, monitor, keyboard, disk drives, printer, and mouse. If you are not sure what equipment you will be operating, check with your instructor.

The computer system displayed in figure G.1 consists of six components. Each component is discussed separately in the material that follows.

Figure G.1
IBM Personal Computer System

CPU

CPU stands for Central Processing Unit. The CPU is the intelligence of the computer. All the processing occurs in the CPU. Silicon chips, which contain miniaturized circuitry, are placed on boards that are plugged into slots within the CPU. Whenever an instruction is given to the computer, that instruction is electronically processed through circuitry in the CPU.

Monitor

The monitor is a piece of equipment that looks like a television screen. It displays the information of a program and what is being input at the keyboard.

The quality of display for monitors varies depending on the type of monitor and the type of resolution. Monitors can also vary in the display color. Some monitors are monochrome, displaying only one color, while other monitors display many colors. More than likely, the monitor that you are using is a color monitor.

Keyboard

The keyboard is used to input information into the computer. Keyboards for microcomputers vary in the number and location of the keys. Microcomputers have the alphabetic and numeric keys in the same location as the keys on a typewriter. The symbol keys, however, may be placed in a variety of locations, depending on the manufacturer.

In addition to letters, numbers, and symbols, most microcomputer keyboards contain function keys, arrow keys, and a numeric keypad. Figure G.2 shows an enhanced keyboard.

The 12 keys at the top of the enhanced keyboard, labeled with the letter F followed by a number, are called *function keys*. These keys can be used to perform WordPerfect functions.

To the right of the regular keys is a group of *special* or *dedicated keys*. These keys are labeled with specific functions that will be performed when you press the key. Below the special keys are arrow keys. These keys are used to move the insertion point in the editing window.

In the upper right corner of the keyboard are three mode indicator lights. When certain modes have been selected, a light appears on the keyboard. For example, if you press the Caps Lock key, which disables the lowercase alphabet, a light appears next to Caps Lock. Similarly, pressing the Num Lock key will disable the special functions only on the numeric keypad, which is located at the right side of the keyboard.

Figure G.2
Microcomputer Keyboard

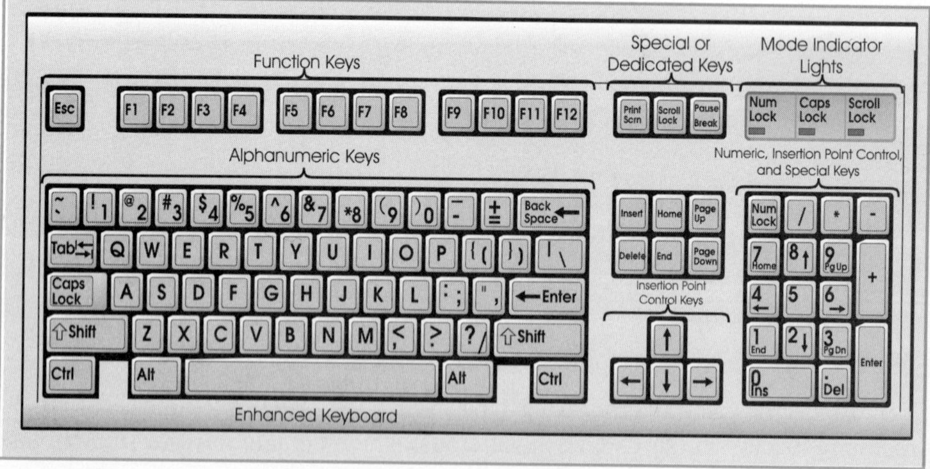

Disk Drives

Depending on the computer system you are using, the WordPerfect program is saved on a hard drive or saved as part of a network system. Whether you are using WordPerfect on a hard-drive or network system, you will need to have a disk drive available for inserting a disk, on which you will save and open documents.

A disk drive spins a disk and reads information from it. There are two sizes of disks—5.25 inches and 3.5 inches. Generally, more information can be saved on a 3.5-inch disk than on a 5.25-inch disk. A 3.5-inch student data disk accompanies this text.

The memory capacity for disks varies depending on the size and the density of the disk. Disk memory is measured in kilobytes (thousands) and megabytes (millions). The following shows the memory capacity for various disks.

5.25-inch, Double Density (DD)	360,000 bytes (360 Kilobytes; written as 360Kb)
5.25-inch, High Density (HD)	1,200,000 bytes (1.2 Megabytes; written as 1.2Mb)
3.5-inch, Double Density (DD)	720,000 bytes (720 Kilobytes; written as 720Kb)
3.5-inch High Density (HD)	1,440,000 bytes (1.44 Megabytes; written as 1.44Mb)

Printer

When you create a document at the editing window, it is considered *soft copy*. If you want a *hard copy* of a document, you need to have it printed on paper. To print documents you will need to access a printer.

Printing methods are either *impact* or *nonimpact*. Impact printers have a mechanism that strikes the paper to create text. Nonimpact printers use a variety of methods—heat, ink-jet, laser—to print characters. These printers are much quieter and faster than impact printers; they are generally also more expensive than impact printers.

Mouse

Some WordPerfect functions are designed to operate more efficiently with a *mouse*. A mouse is a piece of equipment that sits on a flat surface next to the computer and is used with the left or right hand.

If a mouse has been installed with WordPerfect, a mouse pointer will appear in the document window. When the mouse pointer is positioned in the editing window, it appears in the shape of an I-beam (I). This is referred to as the I-beam pointer. When the mouse pointer is moved to the Menu Bar, Toolbar, Power Bar, or Ruler Bar at the top of the document window, or to the scroll bars at the right side and bottom of the document window, the mouse pointer displays as an arrow (↖). This is referred to as the arrow pointer. For specific instructions on using a mouse, please refer to the "Using the Mouse" section at the beginning of this textbook.

Properly Maintaining Disks

To operate WordPerfect for Windows, you will have your own disk on which to save documents. You will be saving and opening documents on the student data disk that accompanies this textbook. You will be using a 3.5-inch disk. To ensure that you will be able to retrieve information from the disk, you need to maintain the disk. To properly maintain a 3.5-inch disk, follow these rules:

1. Do not expose your disk to extreme heat or cold.
2. Keep disks away from magnets and magnetic fields. They can erase the information you have saved.
3. Do not wipe or clean the magnetic surface.
4. Keep the disk away from food, liquids, and smoke.
5. Never remove a disk from the disk drive when the drive light is on.

If you have an opportunity to use a 5.25-inch disk, you would follow these additional rules:

1. Do not touch the exposed surfaces of your disk.
2. Do not use paper clips or rubber bands on the disk.
3. Always keep your disk in the protective envelope when it is not in use.
4. Do not write on the disk with a pencil or ballpoint pen. If you need to write on the disk label, use a felt-tip pen.
5. Store disks in an upright position when they are not being used.

The disk that you will be using for document storage has been formatted and includes several documents. If you use WordPerfect with a blank disk, that disk must be formatted. Formatting is a process that establishes tracks and sectors on which information is stored and prepares the disk to accept data from the disk operating system. The procedure for formatting a disk is presented in appendix A. (Your student data disk has already been formatted—do not format it again.) Many companies sell disks that have been formatted and specify this on the disks or the package containing the disks.

Using the WordPerfect Template

The WordPerfect Corporation includes a template with the WordPerfect program that identifies the commands of the function keys. The template is placed above the function keys to provide a visual aid. The template shown in figure G.3 is from the help screen. A template designed by Paradigm Publishing Inc. is included with this textbook. Use this template as a visual aid to WordPerfect functions.

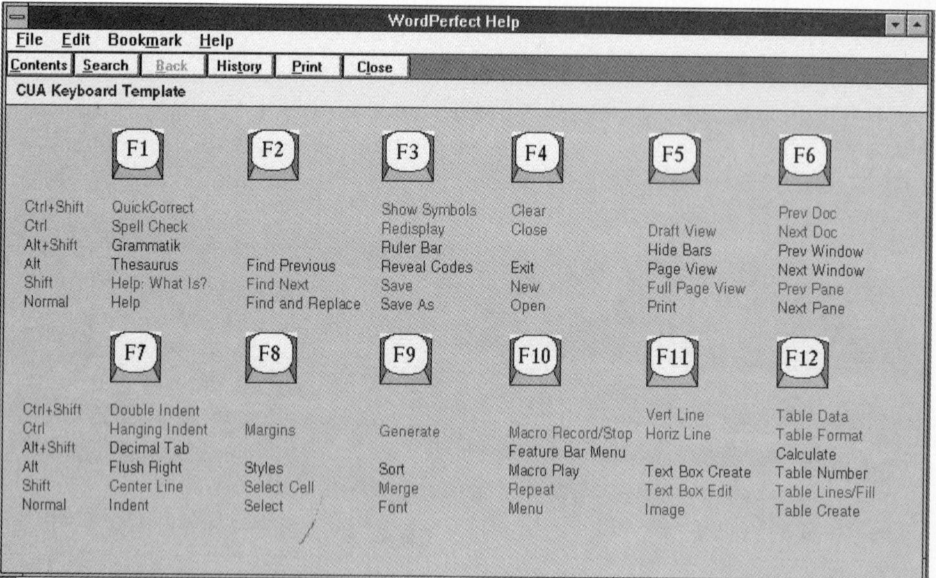

Figure G.3
WordPerfect Help Template

Using the Mouse

The WordPerfect program can be operated using a keyboard or it can be operated with the keyboard and a special piece of equipment called a *mouse*. A mouse is a small device that sits on a flat surface next to the computer. It is operated with one hand and works best if sitting on a mouse pad. On top, the mouse may have two or three buttons, which are pressed to execute specific functions and commands.

To use the mouse, rest it on a flat surface or a mouse pad and put your hand over it with your palm resting on top of the mouse and your wrist resting on the table surface. As you move the mouse on the flat surface, a corresponding pointer moves on the screen.

Understanding Mouse Terms

When using the mouse, there are three terms you should understand—click, double-click, and drag. *Click* means to press a button on the mouse quickly, then release it. *Double-click* means to press the button twice in quick succession. The term *drag* means to press a button, move the pointer to a specific location, then release the button.

Using the Mouse Pointer

The mouse pointer will change appearance depending on the function being performed and its location in the document window. The mouse pointer may appear as one of the following images:

The mouse pointer appears as an I-beam in a document and can be used to move the insertion point or select text.

The pointer appears as an arrow pointing up and to the left when it is moved to the top of the document window or when a dialog box is displayed. For example, to open a new file with the mouse, you would move the arrow pointer to the File option on the Menu Bar. To make a selection, position the tip of the arrow pointer on the File option, then click the left mouse button. Make selections from this drop-down menu by positioning the tip of the arrow pointer on the desired option, then clicking the left mouse button.

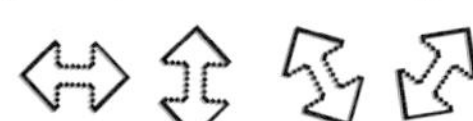

The mouse pointer becomes a double-headed arrow (either pointing left and right, pointing up and down, or pointing diagonally) when performing certain functions such as changing the size of a horizontal or vertical line or a graphics box.

In certain situations, such as moving a graphics box, the mouse pointer becomes a four-headed arrow. The four-headed arrow means that you can move the selected object left, right, up, or down.

When WordPerfect is processing a request, or when the WordPerfect program is being loaded, the mouse pointer appears as an hour glass. This image means "please wait." When the process is completed, the mouse pointer returns to an I-beam pointer or an arrow pointer.

The mouse pointer displays as a hand with a pointing index finger in certain functions such as Help and indicates that there is more information available about the item.

Executing Commands

Using the Menu Bar

The Menu Bar at the top of the document window contains a variety of options that you can use to format a WordPerfect document or complete file management tasks. WordPerfect features are grouped logically into options, which display in the Menu Bar. For example, features to work with WordPerfect files (documents) are grouped in the File option. Either the mouse or the keyboard can be used to make menu selections from the Menu Bar or choose options from a dialog box.

To use the mouse to make a choice from the Menu Bar, position the tip of the arrow pointer on the desired option, then click the left mouse button.

To use the keyboard, press the Alt key to make the Menu Bar active. The Document control box, which is the second gray-shaded box with a hyphen in the middle in the upper left corner of the document window, displays with a darker background. The options from the Menu Bar display with an underline below a letter. To choose an option from the Menu Bar, key the underlined letter of the desired option, or select an option by pressing the left or right arrow keys to select the desired option, then press Enter. This causes a drop-down menu to display.

Selecting from Drop-Down Menus

To make a selection from a drop-down menu with the mouse, position the arrow pointer on the desired option, then click the left mouse button. You can also position the arrow pointer on the desired option in the Menu Bar, such as File, hold down the left mouse button, drag the arrow pointer to the desired option, then release the button. When you position the arrow pointer on an option and hold down the left mouse button, a drop-down menu appears. As you drag the arrow pointer down the menu, the various options in the menu will be selected.

To make a selection from the drop-down menu with the keyboard, key the underlined letter of the desired option. Once the drop-down menu is displayed, you do not need to press Alt with the underlined letter.

Some menu options may be gray shaded (dimmed). When an option is dimmed, that option is currently not available. For example, if you choose the Edit option from the Menu Bar, the Edit drop-down menu displays with several dimmed options including Cut, Copy, and Append. If text is selected before the Edit drop-down menu is displayed, these options are not dimmed because they are available.

Some options from a menu are followed by a right-pointing triangle. This symbol indicates that a cascading submenu will appear when the option is selected. For example, if you choose Format from the Menu Bar and then choose Justification, a cascading submenu displays that contains justification formatting options.

Some menu options are preceded by a check mark. The check mark indicates that the option is currently active. For example, the View drop-down menu will display with check marks before several options.

To make an option inactive (turn it off) using the mouse, position the arrow pointer on the option, then click the left mouse button. To make an option inactive (turn it off) with the keyboard, key the underlined letter of the option.

Selecting from Dialog Boxes

Some of the options in a drop-down menu display with ellipses (...) following the option. The ellipses indicate that a dialog box will display when the option is chosen. A dialog box indicates that WordPerfect needs more information in order to carry out a command and provides a variety of options.

To make selections from a dialog box with the mouse, position the arrow pointer on the desired option, then click the left mouse button. If you are using the keyboard, press the Tab key to move the insertion point forward from option to option. Press Shift + Tab to move the insertion point backward from option to option. You can also hold down the Alt key, then press the underlined letter of the desired option.

When an option is selected, it displays outlined with a dashed box. This dashed box is referred to as a *marquee*. As you move the insertion point from option to option, the marquee moves. The option containing the marquee is the active option.

A dialog box contains one or more of the following elements: text boxes, list boxes, drop-down menus (also called pop-up lists), check boxes, radio buttons, and command buttons.

Text Boxes

Some options in a dialog box require text to be entered. For example, the boxes below the Find and the Replace With options at the Find and Replace Text dialog box, shown in figure G.4, are text boxes.

In a text box, you key text or edit existing text. Edit text in a text box in the same manner as normal text. Use the left and right arrow keys on the keyboard to move the insertion point without deleting text and use the Delete key or Backspace key to delete text. If current text is highlighted, anything you key (type) will replace the current text.

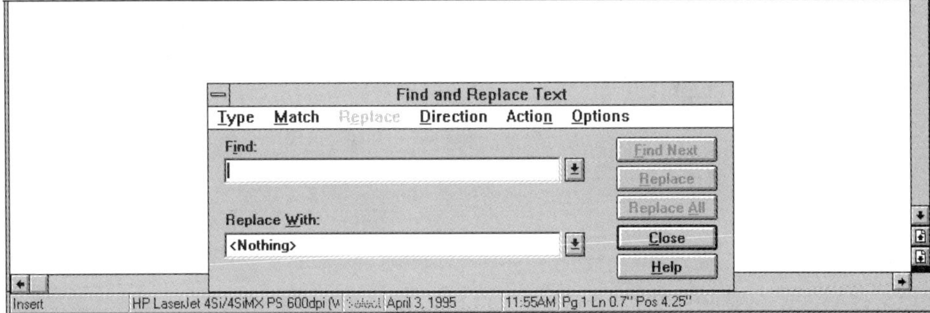

Figure G.4
Find and Replace Text Dialog Box

List Boxes

Some dialog boxes may contain a list box. To make a selection from a list box with the mouse, move the arrow pointer to the desired option, then double-click the left mouse button.

Some list boxes may contain a scroll bar. This scroll bar can be used to move through the list if the list is longer than the box. To move down through the list, position the arrow pointer on the down scroll arrow and hold down the left mouse button. To scroll up through the list, position the arrow pointer on the up scroll arrow and hold down the left mouse button. You can also move the arrow pointer above the scroll box and click the left mouse button to scroll up the list or move the arrow pointer below the scroll box and click the left mouse button to move down the list.

To make a selection from a list using the keyboard, move the insertion point into the box by holding down the Alt key and pressing the underlined letter of the desired option. For some options, you may also need to press the Tab key.

Drop-Down Menus

In some dialog boxes where there is not enough room for a list box, lists of options are inserted in a drop-down menu (also referred to as a pop-up list). Options that contain a drop-down menu display with an up- and down-pointing triangle or just a left-pointing or down-pointing triangle.

Check Boxes

Some dialog boxes contain options preceded by a box called a check box. An X may or may not appear in the check box. If an X appears in the check box, the option is active (turned on). If there is no X in the check box, the option is inactive (turned off).

Any number of check boxes can be active. To make a check box active or inactive with the mouse, position the tip of the arrow pointer in the check box, then click the left mouse button. If you are using the keyboard, press Alt + the underlined letter of the desired option.

Radio Buttons

In the Center Page(s) dialog box, shown in figure G.5, the circles preceding the Current Page, Current and Subsequent Pages, and No Centering options are called *radio buttons* (sometimes referred to as *option buttons*). Only one radio button can be selected at any time. When a radio button is selected, a dark circle appears in the button.

To select a radio button with the mouse, position the tip of the arrow pointer inside the radio button or on the text beside it, then click the left mouse button. To make a selection with the keyboard, hold down the Alt key, then press the underlined letter of the desired option.

Command Buttons

In the Find and Replace Text dialog box, shown in figure G.4, the boxes at the right side of the dialog box are called *command buttons*. A command button is used to execute or cancel a command. Some command buttons contain ellipses (...). A command button that displays with ellipses will open another dialog box.

The default command button will display with the marquee. It can be changed with the mouse by positioning the tip of the arrow pointer on the desired command button, then clicking the left mouse button. To change the command button with the keyboard, press the Tab key until the desired command button contains the marquee, then press the Enter key.

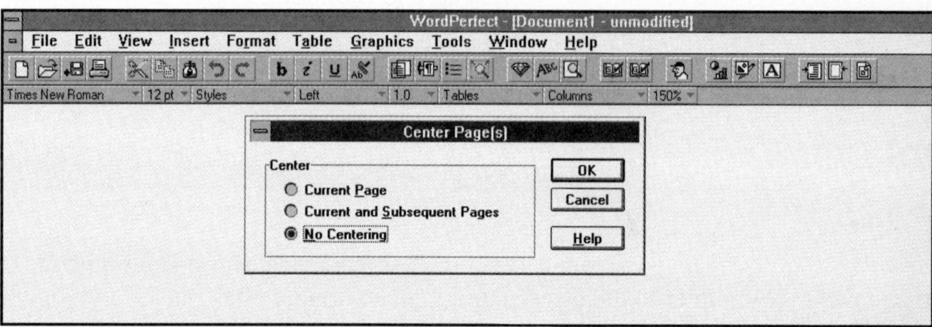

Figure G.5
Center Page(s) Dialog Box

Producing Business Correspondence

In this unit, you will learn to produce business correspondence including memoranda and letters.

SCANS*

* SCANS stands for the Secretary's Commission on Achieving Necessary Skills. The commission was established by the Departments of Labor and Education to help schools plan programs that meet employers' needs. These skills emphasize the performance standards required in the workplace.

Writing

Decision-Making

Technology

- Use computers to process information
- Acquire and evaluate information
- Compose letters and memos
- Correct text for spelling errors

Problem-Solving

Research

Starting WordPerfect for Windows

1

Upon completion of chapter 1, you will be able to create, save, close, and open a WordPerfect document.

This textbook provides you with instructions on a word processing program using a microcomputer system. The program you will learn to operate is the *software*. Software is the program of instructions that tells the computer what to do. The computer equipment you will use is the *hardware*.

In this textbook, you will be learning to operate a software program called WordPerfect for Windows, Version 6.1, on a microcomputer system. WordPerfect for Windows operates within the Windows program.

Creating a WordPerfect Document

Eight basic steps are completed when working with a word processing system to create and revise a document. The steps are:

1. Load the program.
2. Key (type) the information to create the document.
3. Save the document on the disk, then close it.
4. Bring the document back to the editing window.
5. Make any necessary edits (changes).
6. Save the revised document on the disk.
7. Print a hard copy of the document.
8. Exit the program.

In this chapter, you will be provided with the information necessary to complete all the steps except 5 and 7. You will complete several exercises and practice the steps.

Loading WordPerfect

The steps to load WordPerfect may vary depending on the system setup. Generally, to load WordPerfect on a hard-drive system, you would complete the following steps:

1. Turn on the computer. (This may include turning on the CPU, the monitor, and possibly the printer.)
2. At the DOS prompt, load the Windows program by keying **win** (either uppercase or lowercase is acceptable) then pressing Enter.
3. When the Windows program is loaded, you will see a screen that may resemble the one shown in figure 1.1 (your screen display may vary).
4. If you are using a mouse, position the mouse arrow pointer on the WordPerfect program group icon, then double-click the left mouse button. If you are using the keyboard, press the Alt key, the letter F for File, then the letter O for Open.

Operating WordPerfect on your computer system may vary from these instructions. If necessary, ask your instructor for specific steps to load WordPerfect and write the steps here:

____

____

____

____

____

Figure 1.1
Windows Program Manager Screen with WordPerfect Program Group Displayed

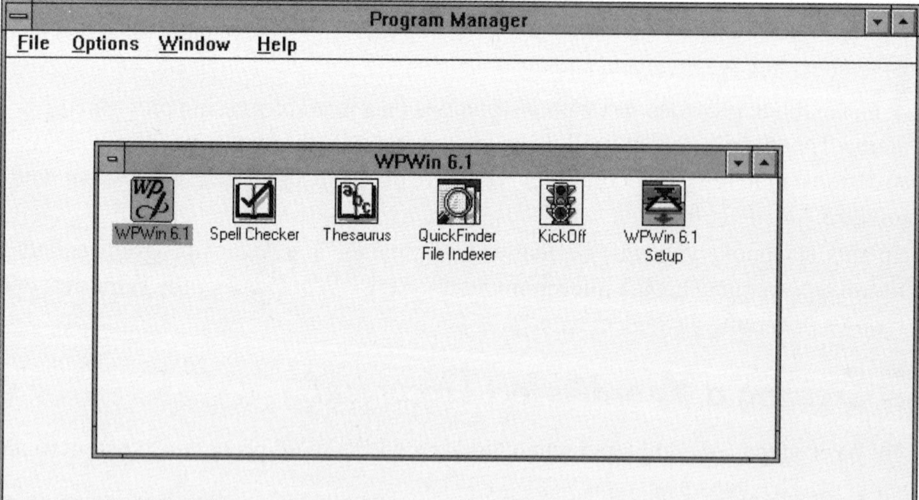

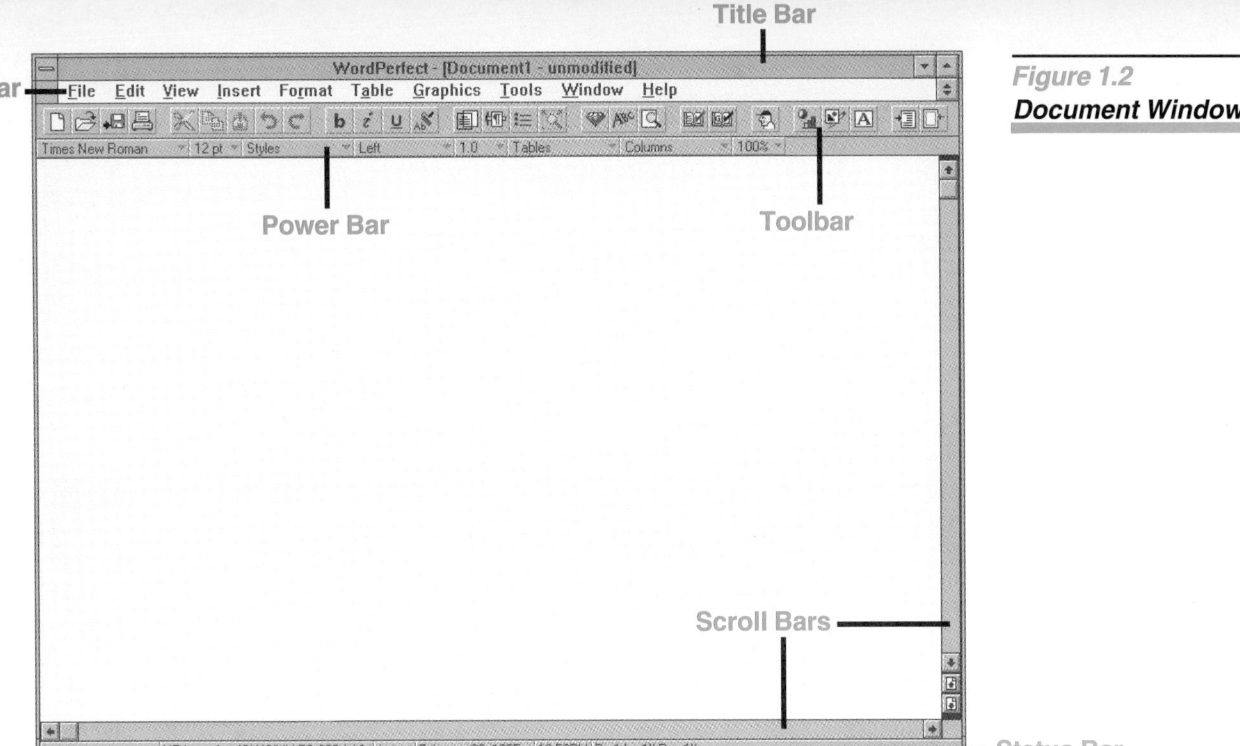

Figure 1.2
Document Window

Identifying the Parts of the Document Window

When you load WordPerfect, you will be presented with a screen that looks similar to the one shown in figure 1.2. This screen is referred to as the *document window.*

Title Bar

The top line of the document window is referred to as the *Title Bar.* When you load WordPerfect, you are given a new document window with the name Document1. The word *unmodified* after the document name indicates that nothing has been entered or modified in the document. As soon as you begin keying text, the word *unmodified* is removed from the Title Bar.

When a document is completed, it can be saved with a new name. If you open a previously saved document to the document window, the document name is displayed in the Title Bar.

The Title Bar also displays information about various parts of the document window. If you position the arrow pointer on a button on the Toolbar or Power Bar, information about the function of the button is displayed in the Title Bar. For example, if you position the arrow pointer on the first button on the Toolbar, the information *Create a blank document in a new window - Ctrl+N* displays in the Title Bar.

Menu Bar

The second line of the document window is called the *Menu Bar.* The Menu Bar contains a list of options that are used to customize a WordPerfect document. WordPerfect functions and features are grouped into menu options located on the Menu Bar. For example, functions to save, close, or open a new document are contained in the File option from the Menu Bar.

Toolbar

WordPerfect includes a *Toolbar* that contains icons of common features, programs, and macros. An *icon* is a picture or image that represents a function. With this Toolbar, located below the Menu Bar, you can use the mouse to execute certain commands quickly. For example, the button with the *b* bolds text, the button with the *i* italicizes text, and the button with the printer displays the Print dialog box. The icons provide representations of the feature.

WordPerfect provides a QuickTip that shows what the button on the Toolbar will perform. To view a QuickTip, position the arrow pointer on a button on the Toolbar. After approximately one second, the QuickTip displays. The QuickTip displays below the button in a yellow box. Figure 1.3 displays the names of each button on the Toolbar.

The Toolbar display is on by default. You can turn off the display of the Toolbar with the Toolbar option from the View option on the Menu Bar.

Figure 1.3
Toolbar Buttons

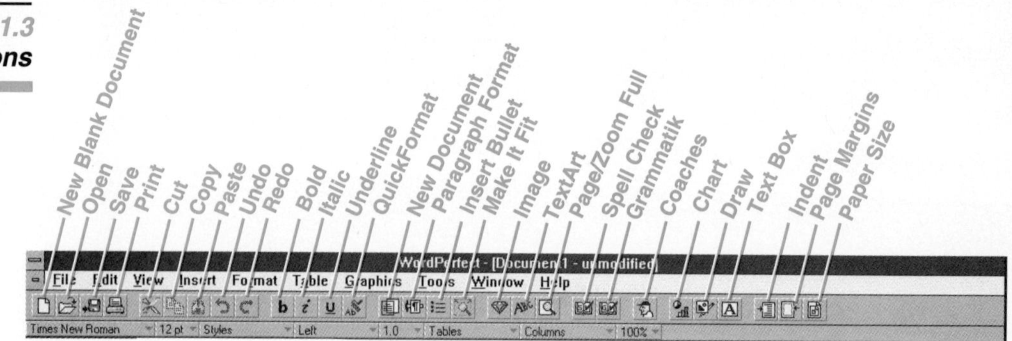

Power Bar

The series of options below the Toolbar is called the *Power Bar*. The options on the Power Bar are used to quickly access text editing and text formatting features. A QuickTip will display when the arrow pointer is positioned on an option (button) on the Power Bar. The display of the Power Bar is on by default. The Power Bar can be turned off with the Power Bar option from the View option on the Menu Bar.

Insertion Point

The blinking vertical bar, located approximately an inch below the Power Bar at the left side of the document window, is called the *insertion point* (also referred to as the *cursor*). The insertion point indicates the location where the next character entered at the keyboard will appear.

The insertion point is positioned in the portion of the document window called the *editing window*. The editing window is the portion of the window where text is entered, edited, and formatted.

In addition to the blinking vertical bar, a mouse pointer will also display in the document window. When the mouse pointer is positioned in the editing window, it displays as an I-beam (I). When the mouse pointer is positioned anywhere else in the document window, it displays as an arrow pointing up and left. For more information on how to use the mouse, please refer to the "Using the Mouse" section at the beginning of this book.

Scroll Bars

The gray shaded bars along the right and bottom of the document window are called *Scroll Bars*. Use the Scroll Bars to view various sections of a document. Additional information on the Scroll Bars is presented in chapter 2.

Status Bar

The gray bar at the bottom of the document window is called the *Status Bar*. The Status Bar displays information about the document and the location of the insertion point.

The word *Insert* displays at the left side of the Status Bar. This indicates that the Insert mode is turned on. The currently selected printer displays to the right of Insert. The word *Select* on the Status Bar displays in gray. This indicates that the Select feature is off. When the Select feature is turned on, the word *Select* displays in black letters. The current date and time are displayed in the Status Bar.

The information at the right side of the Status Bar displays the current location of the insertion point by page number and line and position measurement.

Word Wrap

As you key (type) text, you do not need to press the Enter key at the end of each line as you would on a typewriter. WordPerfect wraps text to the next line. A word is wrapped to the next line if it begins before the right margin and continues past the right margin. The only times you need to press Enter are to end a paragraph, create a blank line, or end a short line.

QuickCorrect

WordPerfect contains a feature called *QuickCorrect*™ that automatically corrects certain words as they are being keyed (typed). For example, if you key the word *adn* instead of *and*, QuickCorrect automatically corrects it when you press the space bar after the word. There are over 120 words that QuickCorrect will automatically correct. You will learn more about this feature in a later chapter.

Completing Computer Exercises

You will be completing hands-on exercises at the end of sections in chapters and at the end of chapters. These exercises will provide you with the opportunity to practice the functions and commands presented.

Exercises in the beginning chapters present text in arranged form. Exercises in later chapters include unarranged text. This provides you with decision-making opportunities. The skill assessment exercises at the end of each chapter include general directions. If you do not remember how to perform a particular function, refer to the text in the chapter.

In the exercises in this chapter, you will be creating and saving several short documents. Press Enter only to end a paragraph or to create a blank line between paragraphs. Otherwise, let the word wrap feature wrap text to the next line within paragraphs.

The WordPerfect editing window displays somewhere between 16 and 19 lines of text at one time. When more lines are entered, the text scrolls off the top of the editing window. The text is not lost or deleted. When the document is saved, all the text is saved, not just the lines you see in the editing window.

Keying and Saving a WordPerfect Document

At the clear WordPerfect editing window, you can begin keying information to create a document. A document is any information you choose; for instance, a letter, a memo, a report, a term paper, or a table.

Saving a Document

When you have created a document, the information will need to be saved on your disk. When a document is keyed (typed) for the first time and is displayed in the editing window, it is only temporary. If you turn off the computer or if the power goes off, you will lose the information and have to rekey it. Only when you save a document on the disk is it saved permanently. Every time you load WordPerfect, you will be able to bring a saved document back to the editing window.

A variety of methods can be used to save a document, such as the following:

- Clicking on the Save button on the Toolbar.
- Clicking on File, then Save.
- Pressing the Alt key, the letter F, then the letter S.

To save a document with the Save button, you would complete the following steps:

1. Position the arrow pointer on the Save button (the third button from the left) on the Toolbar, then click the left mouse button.
2. At the Save As dialog box shown in figure 1.4, key a name for the document.
3. Click on OK.

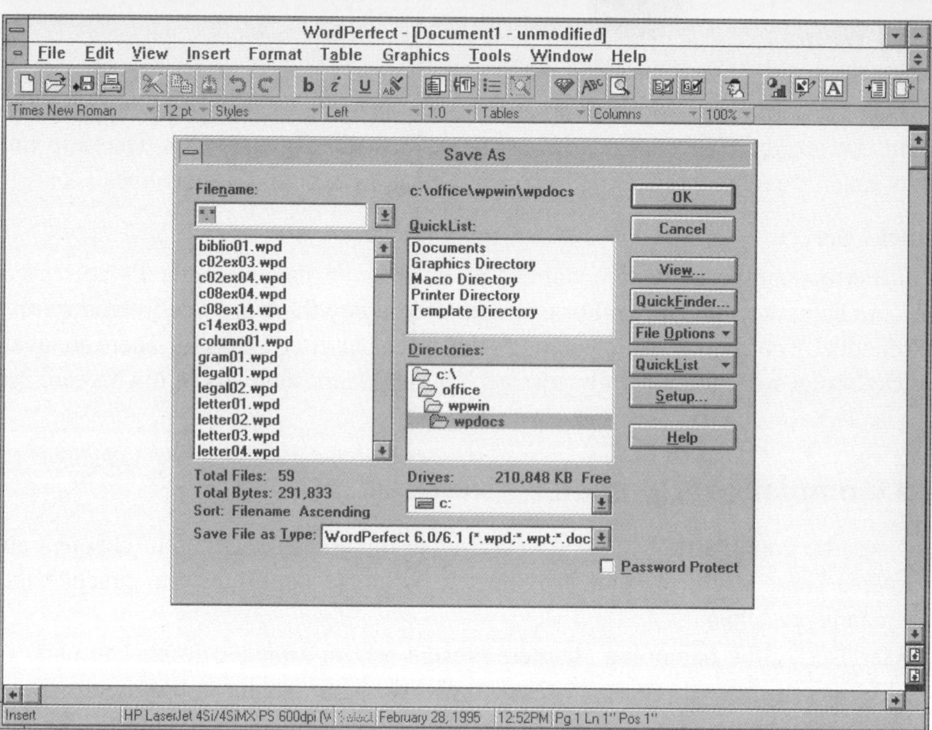

Figure 1.4
Save As Dialog Box

In addition to the Toolbar, a document can be saved by executing a command. There are two methods that can be used. One method uses the Menu Bar with the mouse, the other uses the Menu Bar with the keyboard.

To save a document using the Menu Bar with the mouse, you would complete the following steps:

1. Click on File, then Save.
2. At the Save As dialog box, key a name for the document.
3. Click on OK.

To save a document using the Menu Bar with the keyboard, you would complete the following steps:

1. Press the Alt key, the letter F for File, then the letter S for Save.
2. At the Save As dialog box, key a name for the document.
3. Press the Enter key.

In this text, the steps to execute a command with the Menu Bar and the mouse or keyboard, and the Toolbar (if applicable), are combined. For example, the steps to save a document are written as follows:

1. Choose File, then Save; or click on the Save button on the Toolbar.
2. At the Save As dialog box, key a name for the document.
3. Choose OK or press Enter.

The first part of the first step, "Choose File, then Save," identifies what is selected from the Menu Bar and the menu using either the mouse or the keyboard. The second part of the first step, "click on the Save button on the Toolbar," identifies the button on the Toolbar. The last step identifies the option that is selected to complete the function.

If you are using the mouse, the word *choose* means to click on the menu or option. If you are using the keyboard, the word *choose* means to press the Alt key, press the underlined letter of the desired menu from the Menu Bar, then press the letter of the desired option from the drop-down menu. For more information on executing commands, please refer to the "Executing Commands" section at the beginning of this textbook.

Changing the Default Drive

In this chapter and the remaining chapters in the textbook, you will be saving documents. More than likely, you will want to save documents onto your student data disk. Also, beginning with chapter 2, you will be opening documents that have been saved on your student data disk.

To save and open documents on your data disk, you will need to specify the drive where your disk is located as the default drive. Unless your computer system has been customized, WordPerfect defaults to the hard drive (usually c:) or the network drive. Once you specify the drive where your data disk is located, WordPerfect uses this as the default drive until you exit the WordPerfect program. The next time you load WordPerfect, you will need to specify again the drive where your data disk is located.

You can change the default drive at the Open File dialog box or the Save As dialog box. To change the drive to a: or b: at the Open File dialog box using the mouse, you would complete the following steps:

1. Click on the Open button on the Toolbar (the second button from the left) or click on File, then Open.
2. At the Open File dialog box, position the arrow pointer on the down-pointing arrow next to the Drives text box, hold down the left mouse button, drag the arrow pointer to *a:* or *b:* (depending on where your data disk is located), then release the mouse button.
3. Click on the Cancel button at the right side of the dialog box.

To change the default drive to *a:* or *b:* using the keyboard, you would complete the following steps:

1. Press the Alt key, the letter F, then the letter O.
2. At the Open File dialog box, press Alt + V for Drives.
3. Press the down arrow key, then press the up or down arrow key to select *a:* or *b:*.
4. With the drive selected, press Enter.
5. Press the Tab key until the marquee surrounds the word Cancel on the Cancel button at the right side of the dialog box, then press Enter.

You only need to change the default drive once each time you enter the WordPerfect program.

Naming a Document

A WordPerfect document name can be from one to eight characters in length. It can contain letters, numbers, or both. You can use either uppercase or lowercase letters. Whichever case you use when keying the document name, WordPerfect uses only lowercase letters. The document name cannot contain spaces.

You can extend your document name past eight characters by adding a period to the end of the name. This is called an extension. After the period, you can add up to three more characters.

The following are examples of valid document names:

mathdept.ltr	wilson.doc
chapter1	34522
memo.294	report.wp
3412.888	document.32

The following are examples of invalid document names:

```
chapter 2                    manuscript
collins.memo                 letter* 3
```

The first document name, *chapter 2*, is invalid because of the space. The *manuscript* name is invalid because it is more than eight characters in length. The *collins.memo* document name is invalid because there are more than three characters after the period. The *letter*3* document name is invalid because the asterisk symbol is used.

If you do not include an extension to a document name, WordPerfect automatically adds the extension *.wpd* (for WordPerfect document) to the name.

Canceling a Command

If a drop-down menu is displayed in the editing window, it can be removed with the mouse or the keyboard. If you are using the mouse, position the arrow pointer in the editing window (outside the drop-down menu), then click the left mouse button. If you are using the keyboard, press the Alt key. You can also press the Esc key twice. The first time you press Esc, the drop-down menu is removed but the menu option on the Menu Bar is still selected. The second time you press Esc, the insertion point is returned to the editing window.

Several methods can be used to remove a dialog box from the editing window. To remove a dialog box with the mouse, position the arrow pointer on the Cancel command button, then click the left button. A dialog box can be removed from the editing window with the keyboard by pressing the Esc key. You can also remove a dialog box from the editing window with the keyboard by pressing the Tab key until the Cancel command button is selected, then pressing the Enter key.

Closing a Document

When a document is saved with the Save or Save As options from the File menu, the document is saved on the disk and remains in the editing window. To remove the document from the editing window, use the Close command from the File drop-down menu. To close a document and display a clear editing window, choose File, then Close. If you make changes to a document and then decide to close it without saving the changes, choose File, then Close. At the question asking if you want to save the changes, choose No.

Exercise 1 Creating a Document

1. Follow the instructions in this chapter to load Windows and WordPerfect for Windows.
2. At the clear editing window, change the default drive to the drive where your student data disk is located by completing the following steps. (Depending on your system configuration, this may not be necessary. Check with your instructor before changing the default drive.)
   a. Click on the Open button on the Toolbar or click on File, then Open.
   b. At the Open File dialog box, position the arrow pointer on the down-pointing arrow next to the Drives text box, hold down the left mouse button, drag the arrow pointer to *a:* or *b:* (depending on where your data disk is located), then release the mouse button.
   c. Click on the Cancel button at the right side of the dialog box.
3. At the clear editing window, key (type) the text in figure 1.5. Do not worry about mistakes. You will learn how to correct errors in chapter 2.
4. When you are done keying the text, save the document and name it c01ex01 (for chapter 1, exercise 1) by completing the following steps:
   a. Choose File, then Save; or click on the Save button on the Toolbar.
   b. At the Save As dialog box, key **c01ex01**. (Key a zero when naming documents, not the letter o. In this textbook, the zero, 0, displays thinner and taller than the letter o.)

c. Choose OK or press Enter.
5. Close c01ex01 by choosing File, then Close.

Figure 1.5

The field of telecommunications has been expanding rapidly in the past few decades. In a textbook written by William Mitchell, Robert Hendricks, and Leonard Sterry, the authors state that telecommunications systems are destined to become as common in the workplace of the nineties as typewriters were in the offices of the sixties.

The authors also state that people entering the job market now and in the future will need to understand the basics of telecommunications technology and its applications. This fundamental knowledge will prepare workers to accept and use the new products that result from each advance in technology.

Opening a Document

When a document has been saved, it can be opened with the Open option from the File drop-down menu. To open a previously saved document, you would complete the following steps:

1 At a clear editing window, choose File, then Open; or click on the Open button on the Toolbar.
2 At the Open File dialog box, key the name of the document to be opened.
3 Choose OK or press Enter.

You can also open a document at the Open File dialog box with the mouse by clicking on the document name and then clicking on OK or by double-clicking on the document name. When a document is opened it is displayed in the editing window where you can make changes. Whenever changes are made to a document, save the document again to save the changes.

Exercise 2 Opening and Closing a Document

1. At a clear editing window, open the document named c01ex01 by completing the following steps:
   a. Choose File, then Open; or click on the Open button on the Toolbar.
   b. At the Open File dialog box, key **c01ex01**; or click on c01ex01.
   c. Choose OK or press Enter.
2. Close c01ex01 by choosing File, then Close.

Exiting WordPerfect and Windows

When you are finished working with WordPerfect and have saved all necessary information, exit WordPerfect by choosing File, then Exit. After exiting WordPerfect for Windows, you must exit the Windows program. When you exit WordPerfect, the Program Manager appears on the screen. To exit Windows, choose File, then Exit Windows. At the Exit Windows dialog box, choose OK or press Enter.

Exercise 3 Creating a Document

1. At a clear editing window, key the information shown in figure 1.6.
2. Save the document and name it c01ex03 by completing the following steps:
   a. Choose File, then Save; or click on the Save button on the Toolbar.
   b. At the Save As dialog box, key **c01ex03**.
   c. Choose OK or press Enter.
3. Close the document by choosing File, then Close.

Figure 1.6

> We are living in what is called the "information age." In this age, information is regarded as a company asset or resource. The ability to access information on a timely basis is critical to an organization's ability to be competitive and to operate at a profit. Business information systems that integrate software, hardware, and internal and external communication links are continually being developed and refined.
>
> There are many obstacles to the successful development of integrated systems. First and foremost is how to get people to change the way they communicate information. Other obstacles to improving telecommunications relate to technology.

Exercise 4 Opening and Closing a Document, then Exiting WordPerfect

1. At a clear editing window, open c01ex03 using the mouse by completing the following steps:
   a. Click on the Open button on the Toolbar.
   b. At the Open File dialog box, position the arrow pointer on *c01ex03*, then double-click the left mouse button.
2. Close c01ex03.
3. Exit WordPerfect for Windows and Windows by completing the following steps:
   a. Choose File, then Exit.
   b. At the Windows Program Manager, choose File, then Exit Windows.
   c. At the Exit Windows dialog box, choose OK or press Enter.

CHAPTER SUMMARY

- The Title Bar appears at the top of the screen. It displays the name of the current document as well as information about each button on the Toolbar or Power Bar as you position the arrow pointer on that button.
- The Menu Bar is the second line on the screen. It contains a list of commands used to customize a WordPerfect document.
- The Toolbar is located below the Menu Bar and displays icons of common features, programs, and macros. You can use the mouse and the Toolbar to execute these features quickly.
- The Power Bar is a series of buttons (options) below the Toolbar. These buttons are used to quickly access text editing and text layout features.
- The insertion point appears as a blinking vertical bar and indicates the position of the next character entered at the editing window. If a mouse is being used, the mouse pointer will display as an I-beam or an arrow pointing up and left.
- The Scroll Bars appear as gray shaded bars along the right and bottom of the document window and are used to quickly scroll through a document.
- The Status Bar, the gray bar at the bottom of the document window, displays the current location of the insertion point—page number and line and position measurements. The Status Bar indicates other information such as the current date and time.
- WordPerfect automatically wraps text to the next line as you key information.
- To save and open documents on your data disk, the default drive can be changed at the Open File dialog box or the Save As dialog box.
- Document names can be from one to eight characters long and can contain letters, numbers, or both but no spaces. By adding a period, you can extend the document name by three characters.

- Drop-down menus and dialog boxes can be removed from the editing window with the mouse or the keyboard.
- You should always exit WordPerfect and Windows before turning off the computer.

Loading WordPerfect for Windows

1. Turn on the computer.
2. At the c:\> prompt, key **win**, then press Enter.
3. Position the mouse arrow pointer on the WordPerfect program group icon, then double-click the left mouse button.

Saving a Document

Using the Toolbar with the Mouse

1. Click on the Save button on the Toolbar.
2. At the Save As dialog box, key a name for the document.
3. Click on OK.

Using the Menu Bar with the Mouse

1. Click on File, then Save.
2. At the Save As dialog box, key a name for the document.
3. Click on OK.

Using the Menu Bar with the Keyboard

1. Press the ALT key, press F for File, then press S for Save.
2. At the Save As dialog box, key a name for the document.
3. Press ENTER .

Opening a Document

1. At a clear editing window, choose File, then Open; or click on the Open button on the Toolbar.
2. At the Open File dialog box, double-click on the document to be opened; or key the name of the document to be opened, then choose OK or press ENTER .

Exiting WordPerfect

1. Be sure all needed documents have been saved.
2. Choose File, then Exit.

Exiting Windows

1. Choose File, then Exit Windows.
2. At the Exit Windows dialog box, choose OK or press ENTER .

CHECK YOUR UNDERSTANDING

True/False: Circle the letter T if the statement is true; circle the letter F if the statement is false.

T F 1. The insertion point appears in the editing window as a blinking underline.
T F 2. The mouse pointer appears as a vertical bar.
T F 3. The Title Bar is the second bar on the screen.
T F 4. The Menu Bar contains a list of options that are used to customize a document.
T F 5. The buttons on the Power Bar are used to quickly access text editing and text layout features.
T F 6. The Toolbar contains icons of common features, programs, and macros.
T F 7. The document name *4455.ltr* is a valid name.
T F 8. The document name *memo 4* is a valid name.
T F 9. The document name *medical.docs* is a valid name.

Completion: In the space provided at the right, indicate the correct term.

1. This bar displays at the top of the screen and displays the name of the current document as well as information about each button on the Toolbar and Power Bar. ____________
2. This bar displays at the bottom of the screen and displays the current location of the insertion point. ____________
3. When the arrow pointer is positioned on a button on the Toolbar, this displays after approximately one second. ____________
4. The mouse pointer is referred to as this when positioned in the editing window. ____________
5. The mouse pointer is referred to as this when positioned on the Toolbar or Power Bar. ____________
6. These gray bars display at the right side and bottom of the document window. ____________

SKILL ASSESSMENTS

Assessment 1

1. Load Windows and WordPerfect for Windows.
2. At the clear editing window, change the default drive to the drive where your student data disk is located. (Check with your instructor to determine if this step is necessary.)
3. At the clear editing window, key the text in figure 1.7.
4. Save the document with the Save option from the File menu and name it c01sa01.
5. Close c01sa01.

Figure 1.7

For more than 100 years the U.S. public telephone system has provided the means to transmit information via voice. In the past 30 years, the public telephone system, designed for voice transmission, has also provided the means for transmitting data. Currently, 80 to 85 percent of the traffic over telephone lines is voice. Within the next few years, data traffic over the public telephone system is expected to exceed voice traffic.

Traditionally, the signals sent over the telephone system are sent as analog waves, which are fine for voice transmission. Information transmitted from computers used for business applications transmit signals as digits that have only two values, 0 or 1.

A series of 0s and 1s are used to represent letters, numbers, sounds, values, symbols, and format codes. Since the telephone system transmits information as an analog wave, a modem (MOdulator/DEModulator) is needed to convert digits into analog waves. The modem adds to the cost of transmitting data over the public telephone system.

Assessment 2

1. Open c01sa01.
2. Close c01sa01.
3. Exit WordPerfect for Windows and Windows.

Editing a Document

2

Upon successful completion of chapter 2, you will be able to edit and print a WordPerfect document.

Many documents that are created need to have changes made to them. These changes may include adding text, called *inserting*, or removing text, called *deleting*. To insert or delete text, you need to be able to move the insertion point to certain locations in a document without erasing the text it passes through. For example, if you key three paragraphs and then notice an error in the first paragraph, you need to move the insertion point through lines of text to the location of the error without deleting the lines.

To move the insertion point without interfering with text, you can use the mouse, the keyboard, or the mouse combined with the keyboard.

Moving the Insertion Point with the Mouse

The mouse can be used to move the insertion point quickly to specific locations in the document. To move the insertion point, position the I-beam pointer at the location where you want the insertion point, then click the left mouse button.

Scrolling with the Mouse

In addition to moving the insertion point to a specific location, the mouse can be used to move the display of text in the editing window. Scrolling in a document changes the text displayed but does not move the insertion point. If you want to move the insertion point to a new location in a document, scroll to the location, position the I-beam pointer in the desired location, then click the left mouse button.

You can use the mouse with the *horizontal scroll bar* and/or the *vertical scroll bar* to scroll through text in a document. The horizontal scroll bar displays at the bottom of the document window and the vertical scroll bar displays at the right side. Figure 2.1 displays the document window with the scroll bars and elements of the scroll bars identified.

Figure 2.1
Scroll Bars

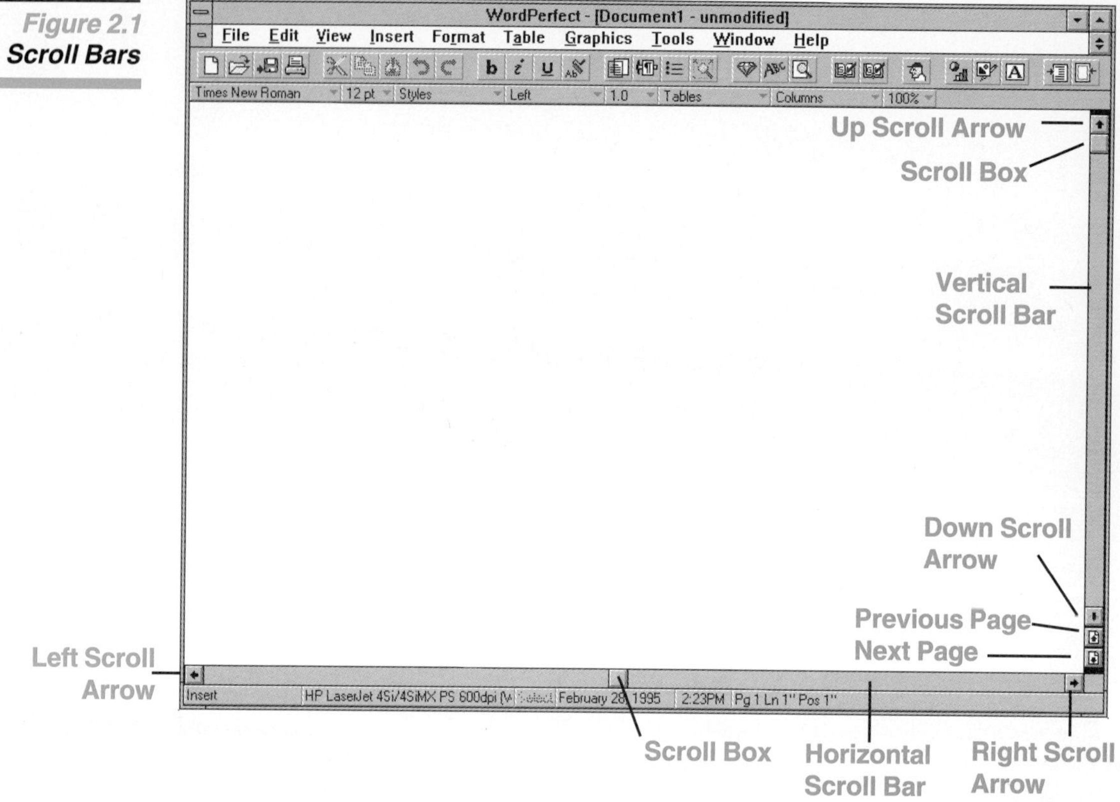

Scrolling with the Vertical Scroll Bar

An up-pointing arrow displays at the top of the vertical scroll bar. This up-pointing arrow is called the *up scroll arrow*. You can scroll up a line in the document by positioning the arrow pointer on the up scroll arrow and clicking the left button. To scroll through the document continuously, position the arrow pointer on the up scroll arrow, then hold down the left button.

The down-pointing arrow at the bottom of the vertical scroll bar is the *down scroll arrow*. Scroll down a line in the document by positioning the arrow pointer on the down scroll arrow then clicking the left button. Hold down the left button if you want continuous action.

When you begin working in longer documents, the scroll bars will be useful in scrolling to certain areas in a document. The small gray box located in the vertical scroll bar is called the *scroll box*. This scroll box indicates the location of the text in the editing window in relation to the document. The scroll box moves along the vertical scroll bar as you scroll through the document. You can scroll up or down through a document one screen at a time by using the arrow pointer on the scroll bar. To scroll up one screen, position the arrow pointer above the scroll box (but below the up scroll arrow), then click the left button. Position the arrow pointer below the scroll box, then click the left button to scroll down a screen. If you hold the left button down, the action becomes continuous. You can also position the arrow pointer on the scroll box, hold down the left mouse button, then drag the scroll box along the scroll bar to reposition text in the editing window. For example, if you want to scroll to the beginning of the document, position the arrow pointer on the scroll box in the vertical scroll bar, hold down the left mouse button, drag the scroll box to the beginning of the scroll bar, then release the mouse button.

Scrolling with the Horizontal Scroll Bar

A left-pointing arrow called the *left scroll arrow* displays at the left side of the horizontal scroll bar. The *right scroll arrow* displays at the right side of the horizontal scroll bar. These scroll arrows operate in the same manner as the up and down scroll arrows on the vertical scroll bar. Click on the left scroll arrow to scroll the text to the right in the editing window. Click on the right scroll arrow to scroll the text to the left in the editing window. To scroll the text to the right, position the arrow pointer to the left of the horizontal scroll box (but after the left scroll arrow), then click the left mouse button. To scroll the text to the left in the editing window, position the arrow pointer to the right of the horizontal scroll box (but before the right scroll arrow), then click the left mouse button. You can also position the arrow pointer on the scroll box, hold down the left mouse button, then drag the scroll box along the horizontal scroll bar to reposition text in the editing window.

Scrolling with Page Icons

Two buttons display at the bottom of the vertical scroll bar. The button with the page and up arrow is the *Previous Page* button. The other with the page and down arrow is the *Next Page* button. Click on the Previous Page button to scroll to the previous page and click on the Next Page button to scroll to the next page in the document.

Exercise 1 Moving the Insertion Point and Scrolling through a Document

1. Load WordPerfect following the instructions in chapter 1.
2. At a clear editing window, open report02. This document is located on your student data disk. (File names will display with the *.wpd* extension.)
3. Practice moving the insertion point and scrolling through the document using the mouse by completing the following steps:
   a. Position the I-beam pointer at the beginning of the first paragraph, then click the left button. This moves the insertion point to the location of the I-beam pointer.
   b. Position the arrow pointer on the down scroll arrow, then click the left mouse button several times. This scrolls down lines of text in the document. With the arrow pointer on the down scroll arrow, hold down the left mouse button and keep it down until the end of the document is displayed.
   c. Position the arrow pointer on the up scroll arrow and hold down the left mouse button until the beginning of the document is displayed.
4. Position the arrow pointer below the scroll box, then click the left mouse button. Continue positioning the arrow pointer below the scroll box and clicking the left mouse button until the end of the document is displayed.
5. Position the arrow pointer on the scroll box in the vertical scroll bar. Hold down the left mouse button, drag the scroll box to the top of the vertical scroll bar, then release the mouse button.
6. Close report02.

Moving the Insertion Point with the Keyboard

To move the insertion point with the keyboard, use the arrow keys located to the right of the regular keyboard. The illustration in figure 2.2 shows arrow keys marked with left, right, up, and down arrows. If you press the up arrow key, the insertion point moves up one line. If you press the other arrow keys, the insertion point moves in the direction indicated on the key. If you hold an arrow key down, it becomes a continuous-action key causing the insertion point to move quickly in the direction indicated. You can also move the insertion point to a specific location in a document by choosing one of the commands shown in figure 2.3.

Figure 2.2
Insertion Point Movement Keys

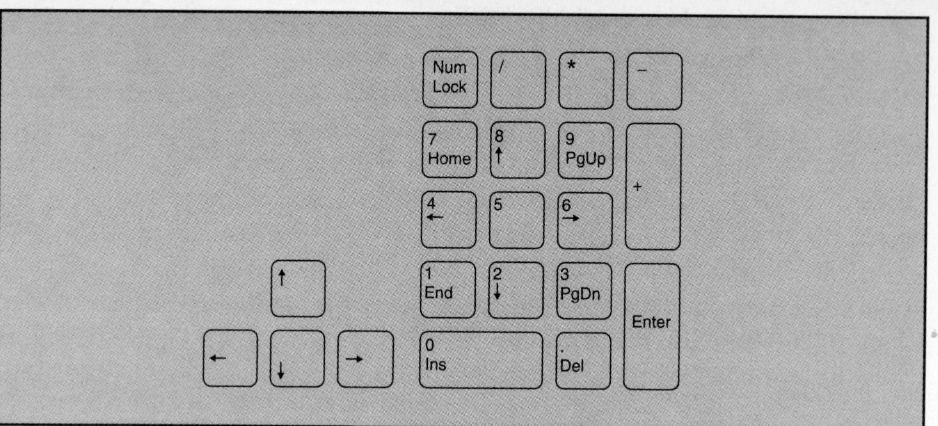

Figure 2.3
Insertion Point Movement Commands

To move insertion point	Press
One character left	left arrow
One character right	right arrow
One line up	up arrow
One line down	down arrow
One word to the left	Ctrl + left arrow
One word to the right	Ctrl + right arrow
To end of a line	End
To beginning of a line	Home
To beginning of current paragraph	Ctrl + up arrow
To beginning of previous paragraph	Ctrl + up arrow twice
To beginning of next paragraph	Ctrl + down arrow
Up one screen	Page Up
Down one screen	Page Down
To top of previous page	Alt + Page Up
To top of next page	Alt + Page Down
To specific page	Edit, Go To, #, Enter
To beginning of document	Ctrl + Home
To end of document	Ctrl + End

Exercise 2 Moving the Insertion Point Using Keys on the Keyboard

1. At a clear editing window, open report03. This document is located on your student data disk.
2. Practice moving the insertion point with the keyboard by completing the following steps:
   a. Press the right arrow key to move the insertion point to the next character to the right. Continue pressing the right arrow key until the insertion point is located at the end of the first paragraph.
   b. Press Ctrl + right arrow key to move the insertion point to the next word to the right. Continue pressing Ctrl + right arrow key until the insertion point is located on the last word of the second paragraph.
   c. Press Ctrl + left arrow key until the insertion point is positioned at the beginning of the document.
   d. Press the End key to move the insertion point to the end of the first line.

e. Press the Home key to move the insertion point to the beginning of the first line.
f. Press Page Down to move the insertion point to the next to last line at the bottom of the editing window.
g. Press Page Up to move the insertion point to the top of the editing window.
h. Press Alt + Page Down to position the insertion point at the beginning of page 2. Press Alt + Page Down again to position the insertion point at the beginning of page 3.
i. Press Alt + Page Up to position the insertion point at the beginning of page 2.
j. Press Alt + Page Up to position the insertion point at the beginning of page 1.
k. Position the insertion point at the beginning of page 3 using the Go To function by completing the following steps:
   (1) Choose Edit, then Go To.
   (2) At the Go To dialog box, key **3**, then press Enter.
l. Press Ctrl + End to move the insertion point to the last character in the document.
m. Press Ctrl + Home to move the insertion point to the first character in the document.

3. Close report03.

Inserting Text

Once you have created a document, you may want to insert information you forgot or have since decided to include. At the default WordPerfect editing window, Insert mode is on. The word *Insert* is displayed at the bottom of the document window in the Status Bar. With Insert on, anything you key will be inserted in the document (rather than taking the place of existing text).

If you want to insert or add something, leave Insert on. However, if you want to key over existing text, turn Insert off by pressing the Insert key. When you press the Insert key, the word *Typeover* (rather than *Insert*) displays in the Status Bar. To turn Insert back on, press the Insert key again.

Deleting Text

When you edit a document, you may want to delete (remove) text. You may want to delete just one character or several lines. WordPerfect offers deletion commands shown in figure 2.4.

Figure 2.4
Deletion Commands

To delete	Press
Character right of insertion point	Delete key
Character left of insertion point	Backspace key
Word where insertion point is positioned	Ctrl + Backspace
Text to the end of the line	Ctrl + Delete

Splitting and Joining Paragraphs

By inserting or deleting, paragraphs of text can be split or joined. To split a large paragraph into two smaller paragraphs, position the insertion point on the first letter that will begin the new paragraph, then press the Enter key twice. The first time you press Enter, the text is moved to the next line. The second time you press Enter, a blank line is inserted between the paragraphs.

To join two paragraphs into one, you need to delete the spaces between them. To do this, position the insertion point on the first character of the second paragraph, then press the Backspace key until the paragraphs join. More than likely, you will need to then press the space bar twice to separate the sentences. You can also join two paragraphs together by positioning the insertion point one space past the period at the end of the first paragraph and then pressing the Delete key until the paragraphs join. When you join the two paragraphs, the new paragraph will be automatically adjusted.

Exercise 3 Editing a Document

1. At a clear editing window, open c02ex03. This document is located on your student data disk.
2. Make the changes indicated by the proofreaders' marks in figure 2.5. (Proofreaders' marks are listed and described in appendix B at the end of this textbook.)
3. Save the document with the same name (c02ex03) by using the Save option from the File menu or clicking on the Save button on the Toolbar.
4. Close c02ex03.

Figure 2.5

One obstacle to smooth communications has to do with standards. As procedure becomes standard through common practice. A person can pick up a phone anywhere and call someone nearly anywhere in the world and if both people speak the same language, they can communicate.

Conversely, not all computers made by manufacturers are able to communicate with each other. This is because they speak different languages. Before communication can occur, special equipment is needed to "translate" the message. Solutions are being developed to correct these and other communication obstacles. There are other operations that depend on a system of telecommunications.

Most major hotel chains, for example, can book reservations from any location in the United States, and increasingly from anywhere in the world. Airlines also use a one-location reservation service. This gives customers the convenience of booking round trip vacations before they ever leave home. These are just a few ways business and industry use telecommunications to gain a sharp competitive edge. To remain competitive, even the smallest businesses are finding themselves entering the telecommunications technology market. Their aim is to increase customer satisfaction and their profit margins.

Selecting Text

The mouse and/or keyboard can be used to select a specific amount of text. Once selected, you can delete the text or perform other WordPerfect functions involving the selected text.

Selecting Text with the Mouse

The mouse can be used to select varying amounts of text. When text is selected it displays in reverse video in the document window as shown in figure 2.6. For example, if the document window displays with a white background and black characters, selected text will display as white characters on a black background.

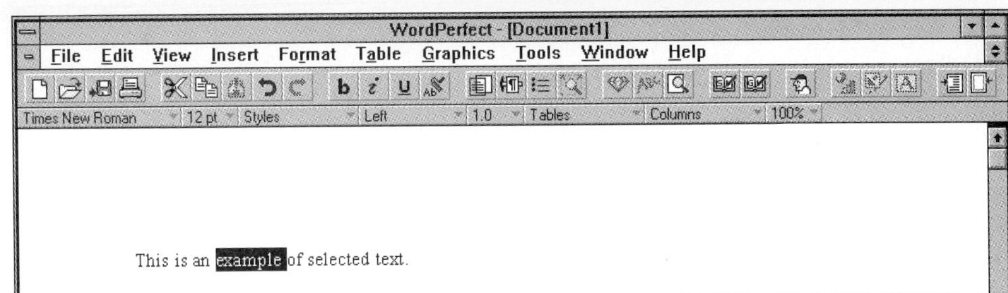

Figure 2.6
Selected Text

You can use the mouse to select a word, sentence, paragraph, or an entire document. Figure 2.7 indicates the steps to follow to select various amounts of text. To select a certain amount of text such as a line, the instructions in the figure tell you to click in the selection bar. The selection bar is the space at the left side of the document window between the left edge of the screen and the text. When the arrow pointer is positioned in the selection bar, the pointer turns into an arrow pointing up and to the right (instead of to the left).

To select	Complete these steps using the mouse
A word	Double-click anywhere in the word.
A sentence	Triple-click anywhere in the sentence.
Multiple sentences	Click and drag in selection bar to left of the sentences.
A paragraph	Double-click in selection bar next to paragraph or quadruple-click anywhere in the paragraph.
Multiple paragraphs	Click and drag in selection bar to the left of the paragraphs.

Figure 2.7
Selecting with the Mouse

To select an amount of text other than word, sentence, or paragraph, position the I-beam pointer on the first character of the text to be selected, hold down the left mouse button, drag the I-beam pointer to the last character of the text to be selected, then release the mouse button.

When text is selected, the word *Select* displays in black in the Status Bar. To delete selected text, press the Delete key. This deletes the selected text and turns off the Select mode. When the Select mode is turned off, the word *Select* displays in gray in the Status Bar. To turn off the Select mode without deleting text, click the left mouse button outside the selected text.

Selecting Text with the Keyboard

To select a specific amount of text using the keyboard, use the Select key, F8, along with the arrow keys. If you press F8, the Select mode is turned on. With the Select mode on, press any of the arrow keys. You can also select text with the keyboard using the commands shown in figure 2.8 without pressing F8.

Figure 2.8
Selecting with the Keyboard

To select	Press
One character to right	Shift + right arrow
One character to left	Shift + left arrow
To end of word	Ctrl + Shift + right arrow
To beginning of word	Ctrl + Shift + left arrow
To end of line	Shift + End
To beginning of line	Shift + Home
One line up	Shift + up arrow
One line down	Shift + down arrow
To beginning of paragraph	Ctrl + Shift + up arrow
To end of paragraph	Ctrl + Shift + down arrow
One screen up	Shift + Page Up
One screen down	Shift + Page Down
To end of document	Ctrl + Shift + End
To beginning of document	Ctrl + Shift + Home
Entire document	Choose Edit, Select, All

With the text selected, press Delete to remove it from the document. When selected text is deleted from the document, the text is removed and the Select mode is turned off. If Select is turned on and you decide to turn it off without deleting any text, press F8 again. This turns off Select and changes the display of Select to gray in the Status Bar.

Selecting Text with the Edit Menu

The Edit menu contains an option that lets you select a sentence, paragraph, page, or the entire document. To use the Edit menu to select a sentence, position the insertion point anywhere in the sentence, then choose Edit, Select, then Sentence. To select a paragraph, choose Edit, Select, then Paragraph. To select a page, choose Edit, Select, then Page. To select the entire document, choose Edit, Select, then All.

Exercise 4 Selecting and Deleting Text

1. At a clear editing window, open c02ex04. This document is located on your student data disk.
2. Delete the name, *Mr. Gerald Koch*, and the department, *CIS Department*, using the mouse by completing the following steps:
   a. Position the I-beam pointer on the *M* in *Mr.* (in the address).
   b. Hold down the left button, then drag the I-beam pointer down until *Mr. Gerald Koch* and *CIS Department* are selected.
   c. Release the left mouse button.
   d. Press the Delete key.
3. With the insertion point positioned at the left margin on the line above *San Mateo Community College*, key the name, **Ms. Aleta Sauter**.
4. Delete the reference line, *Re: Telecommunications Course*, using the Select mode by completing the following steps:
   a. Position the insertion point on the *R* in *Re:*.
   b. Press F8 to turn on the Select mode.

c. Press the down arrow key twice. (This selects the reference line and the blank line below it.)
d. Press the Delete key.

5. Delete the first sentence in the first paragraph using the Edit menu by completing the following steps:
   a. Position the insertion point anywhere in the sentence, *The Western Computer Technology conference we attended last week was very educational for me.*
   b. Choose Edit, Select, Sentence.
   c. Press the Delete key.
6. Delete the first sentence in the second paragraph (the sentence that reads, *The interest in the class has been phenomenal.*) using the Edit menu.
7. Delete the third paragraph in the letter using the Edit menu by completing the following steps:
   a. Position the insertion point anywhere in the third paragraph (the paragraph that begins, *The instructor for the course...*).
   b. Choose Edit, Select, Paragraph.
   c. Press the Delete key.
8. Change the salutation from *Dear Mr. Koch* to *Dear Ms. Sauter*
9. Save the document with the same name (c02ex04) by using the Save option from the File menu or clicking on the Save button on the Power Bar.
10. Close c02ex04.

Using the Undo, Redo, and Undelete Options

If you make a mistake and delete text that you did not intend to delete, or if you change your mind after deleting text and want to retrieve it, you can use the Undo or Undelete options.

The Undo option will undo the last function entered at the keyboard. For example, if you just changed the left and right margins, choosing Edit, then Undo; or clicking on the Undo button on the Toolbar will cause the margin codes to be removed from the document. If you just turned on bold, choosing Edit, then Undo; or clicking on the Undo button on the Toolbar causes the bold codes to be removed from the document. If you just keyed text in the document, choosing Edit, then Undo; or clicking on the Undo button on the Toolbar causes the text to be removed. WordPerfect removes text to the beginning of the document or up to the point where text had been deleted previously in the document. The Redo option will reverse the last Undo action. To do this, click on the Redo button on the Toolbar or choose Edit, then Redo.

You can use the Undelete option from the Edit menu to restore deleted text. WordPerfect retains the last three deletions made in one editing session. If you decide you want to restore text, move the insertion point to the position where you want text inserted, then choose Edit, then Undelete. The Undelete dialog box shown in figure 2.9 displays in the editing window.

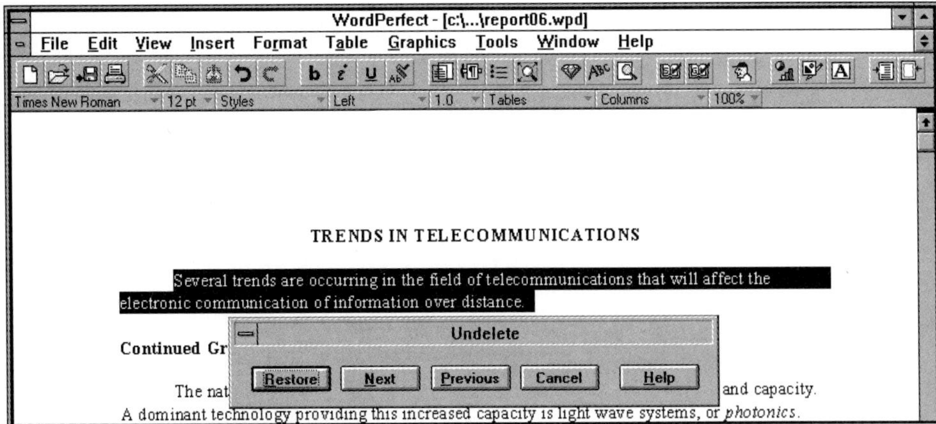

Figure 2.9
Undelete Dialog Box

To restore the text, choose Restore. If you want to see the other two deletions in memory, choose Next or Previous. Choosing Next displays the next deletion in memory and choosing Previous displays the previous deletion in memory. If you want information about the Undelete feature, choose Help. This displays the WordPerfect Help dialog box at the right side of the editing window. This Help screen contains information about the Undelete feature. After reading the information, remove the Help dialog box by choosing File, then Exit at the Help dialog box menu bar. To remove the Undelete dialog box from the editing window without undeleting any text, choose Cancel. The Undelete option restores text at the insertion point while the Undo and Redo options restore information in its original location.

WordPerfect maintains actions in temporary memory. If you want to undo an action performed earlier, choose the Undo/Redo History option from the Edit drop-down menu. With the Undo/Redo History option, you can reverse up to 300 actions in a document. To undo or redo a previous action, choose Edit, then Undo/Redo History. This causes the Undo/Redo History dialog box to display as shown in figure 2.10. The contents of this dialog box will vary depending on what type of action has been performed in the document. Actions that have been performed in the document are displayed at the left side of the dialog box in the Undo list box. Any actions that have been redone are displayed in the Redo list box in the dialog box.

Figure 2.10
Undo/Redo History Dialog Box

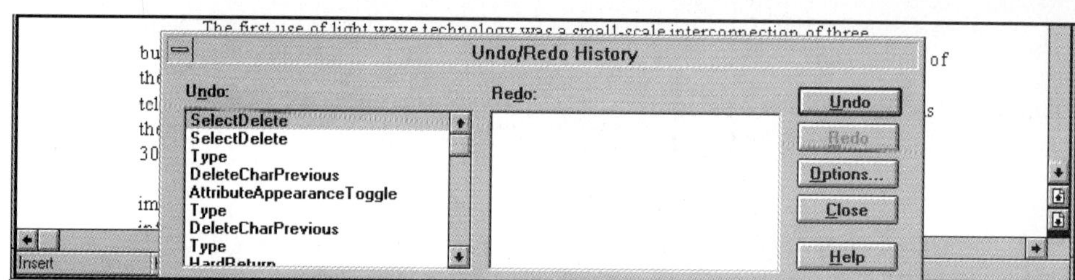

To undo or redo two or more actions, select the item to be undone or redone. This causes any actions listed above the selected item to also be selected. With the items selected, choose Undo or Redo. Choose Options to display the Undo/Redo Options dialog box. At this dialog box, you can specify the number of Undo or Redo items (from 0 to 300) you want to maintain. After selecting items to be undone or redone at the Undo/Redo History dialog box, choose Close to return to the document.

Exercise 5 Deleting and Restoring Text

1. At a clear editing window, open para01. This document is located on your student data disk.
2. Move the insertion point to the end of the document. Press the Backspace key until the last three words of the document (*cluttering your desk.*) are deleted.
3. Undo the deletion by clicking on the Undo button on the Toolbar.
4. Select the first sentence in the first paragraph, then delete it.
5. Select the second paragraph in the document, then delete it.
6. Position the insertion point at the beginning of the document, then insert the paragraph just deleted by completing the following steps:
   a. Choose Edit, then Undelete.
   b. At the Undelete dialog box, choose Restore.
7. Position the insertion point at the end of the second paragraph (one space after the period), then insert the sentence previously deleted by completing the following steps:
   a. Choose Edit, then Undelete.
   b. At the Undelete dialog box, choose Previous until the sentence, *Telecommunications will have a tremendous impact on the office of the twenty-first century.*, is displayed in the document.

c. Choose Restore.
8. Save the document with the same name (para01) by using the Save option from the File menu or clicking on the Save button on the Toolbar.
9. Close para01.

Saving Documents

In chapter 1, you learned to save a document with the Save button on the Toolbar or the Save option from the File drop-down menu. The File drop-down menu also contains a Save As option. The Save As option is used to save a previously created document with a new name.

For example, suppose you created and saved a document named *memo*, then later open it. If you save the document again with the Save button on the Toolbar or the Save option from the File drop-down menu, WordPerfect will save the document with the same name. You will not be prompted to key a name for the document. This is because WordPerfect assumes that when you use the Save option on a previously saved document, you want to save it with the same name. This means that the old copy will be erased. If you open the document named *memo*, make some changes to it, then want to save it with a new name, you must use the Save As option. When you use the Save As option, WordPerfect displays the Save As dialog box where you can key a new name for the document.

To save a document with Save As, choose File, then Save As. In many of the computer exercises in this text, you will be asked to open a document from your student data disk then save it with a new name. You will be instructed to use the Save As option to do this.

Exercise 6 Editing a Document

1. At a clear editing window, open para02. This document is located on your student data disk.
2. Save the document with the name c02ex06 using Save As by completing the following steps:
   a. Choose File, then Save As.
   b. At the Save As dialog box, key **c02ex06**.
   c. Choose OK or press Enter.
3. Make the changes indicated by the proofreaders' marks in figure 2.11.
4. Save the document again with the same name (c02ex06). To do this, choose File, Save; or click on the Save button on the Toolbar.
5. Close c02ex06.

Figure 2.11

A change that is ~~occurring~~ in offices today is the ability to create documents by dictating to ~~your~~ terminal through ~~a feature called~~ voice-activated display. This feature allows you to view dictation on your terminal for editing and revising. You also have the option of ~~dictating or~~ using your hand-manipulated input device to make corrections.

~~Everything~~ you dictate is ~~run through~~ an electronic dictionary and a grammar and syntax validator before the final draft is distributed. If you mistakenly dictate "you is" instead of "you are," the grammar and syntax validator corrects it. Once your document is complete, you control how and when it is distributed. What~~ever~~ you prepare can be sent electronically anywhere within your organization or the world at the touch of a button. ~~In addition,~~ a copy of what you distribute is filed automatically in ~~the~~ optical disk storage system, ~~making~~ storage and retrieval compact and easy.

Printing a Document

The computer exercises you will be completing require that you make a hard copy of the document. (Soft copy is a document displayed in the editing window and hard copy is a document printed on paper.) A document can be printed with the Print button on the Toolbar or the Print option from the File drop-down menu. To print a document, you would complete the following steps:

1 Open the document to be printed.
2 Choose File, then Print; click on the Print button on the Toolbar; or press Ctrl + P.
3 At the Print dialog box, choose Print.

When you choose Print from the Print dialog box, the document is sent to the printer. Before displaying the dialog box, check to make sure the printer is turned on.

Exercise 7 Printing Documents

1. At a clear editing window, print c02ex03 by completing the following steps:
   a. Open c02ex03.
   b. Choose File, then Print; click on the Print button on the Toolbar; or press Ctrl + P.
   c. At the Print dialog box, choose Print.
2. Close c02ex03.
3. At a clear editing window, print c02ex04 by completing steps 1b and 1c.
4. Close c02ex04.

CHAPTER SUMMARY

- The insertion point can be moved throughout the document without interfering with text by using the mouse, the keyboard, or the mouse combined with the keyboard. The insertion point can be moved by character, word, line, screen, or page and from the first to the last character in a document.
- Use the horizontal/vertical scroll bars and the mouse to scroll through a document.
- By default WordPerfect loads with the Insert mode on so text can easily be inserted. The Insert mode can be turned on and off with the Insert key. When Insert has been turned off, the message *Typeover* displays in the Status Bar. When Insert is on, *Insert* displays in the Status Bar.
- Text can be deleted by character, word, line, several lines, or partial page using specific keys or by selecting text using the mouse or the keyboard.
- To split a paragraph into two, position the insertion point on the first letter that will begin the new paragraph, then press Enter twice. To join two paragraphs into one, position the insertion point on the first character of the second paragraph, then press the Backspace key twice.
- A specific amount of text can be selected using the mouse or the keyboard. That text can then be deleted or manipulated in other ways using WordPerfect commands.
- The Undo option will undo the last function entered at the keyboard or delete text that was just entered. The Undelete option will restore one or all of the last three deletions made in the document. WordPerfect retains the last 300 actions in temporary memory. These actions are listed in the Undo/Redo History dialog box.
- The Save As option is used to save a previously created document with a new name.
- A document can be printed with the Print button on the Toolbar, the Print option from the File drop-down menu, or Ctrl + P.

Selecting Text Review

Using the Mouse

Select text	Position the I-beam pointer at the beginning of text to be selected, hold down left mouse button, drag the I-beam pointer to end of text to be selected, then release the button
Select a word	Position the I-beam pointer within the word, double-click the left mouse button
Select a sentence	Position the I-beam pointer within the sentence, triple-click the left mouse button
Select a paragraph	Position the I-beam pointer within the paragraph, quickly click the left mouse button four times or double-click in selection bar

Using the Keyboard

Select text	Press F8, then use arrow keys to select text

Using the Edit Menu

Select a sentence	Position insertion point within the sentence, choose Edit, Select, Sentence
Select a paragraph	Position insertion point within the paragraph, choose Edit, Select, Paragraph
Select a page	Position insertion point within the page, choose Edit, Select, Page
Select entire document	Choose Edit, Selcct, All

Other Commands Review

Undo option	Edit, Undo; or click on Undo button on Toolbar
Undelete option	Edit, Undelete
Undo/Redo History dialog box	Edit, Undo/Redo History
Print	1. Open the document. 2. Choose File, Print; click on the Print button on the Toolbar; or press Ctrl + P 3. At the Print dialog box, choose Print

CHECK YOUR UNDERSTANDING

True/False: Circle the letter T if the statement is true; circle the letter F if the statement is false.

T F 1. To move the insertion point through a document without deleting text, you must use the mouse.

T F 2. Use the Backspace key to delete text to the left of the insertion point.

T F 3. To display *Typeover* in the Status Bar, press the Insert key.

T F 4. The printer produces a soft copy of the document.

T F 5. The Backspace key can be used to combine two paragraphs into one.

T F 6. To select a sentence using the mouse, triple-click the left mouse button.

T F 7. The Undelete option will restore the last four deletions in one editing session.

T F 8. The Save As option is used to save a previously created document with the same name.

Completion: In the space provided at the right, indicate the correct term, command, or number.

1. To delete the character to the right of the insertion point, press this key. ____________
2. When text is selected, this word displays in black in the Status Bar. ____________

Write the name of the key or keys that will accomplish each of the following deletions or insertion point moves.

3. Delete text to the end of the line. ____________
4. Move the insertion point to the beginning of the document. ____________
5. Move the insertion point one word to the right. ____________
6. Move the insertion point to the previous paragraph. ____________
7. Move the insertion point to the end of the document. ____________
8. Move the insertion point to the bottom of the editing window. ____________
9. Delete a word. ____________

SKILL ASSESSMENTS

Assessment 1

1. At a clear editing window, open para03. This document is located on your student data disk.
2. Save the document with Save As and name it c02sa01.
3. Make the changes indicated by the proofreaders' marks in figure 2.12.
4. Save the document again with the same name (c02sa01). To do this, choose File, then Save; or click on the Save button on the Toolbar.
5. Print c02sa01.
6. Close c02sa01.

Figure 2.12

In defending or prosecuting individuals, an attorney must research cases very extensively. This research is based on precedents established in cases having already been resolved before the courts. Many volumes of law books are available to search for the information needed. A number of companies have taken volumes of law manuals and recorded them electronically.

In conventional law practice, hundreds of hours are devoted to checking the indexes for the sources of facts and figures and finding the pages that contain the information.

Being able to access information quickly eliminates wasted time. Attorneys are now able to conduct much of their research electronically by using databases developed for legal research. Attorneys at their law firms pay a monthly fee to access these databases, plus a per-minute charge for the electronic searches.

All the attorney needs is a computer terminal (such as a microcomputer), communication software, and a modem (a device that converts computer signals that travel over a telephone line. To use the electronically stored database of information, the attorney dials the telephone number of the computer that contains the database and as soon as the connection is made, the attorney enters some key words related to the information needed.

In a matter of seconds, the computer electronically searches for the information and sends a message back to the attorney noting the information's location. The attorney can then either direct the computer to display this information on the screen or go back to the hard copy volumes of the law books to complete the research.

Assessment 2

1. At a clear editing window, open para04. This document is located on your student data disk.
2. Save the document with Save As and name it c02sa02.
3. Make the changes indicated by the proofreaders' marks in figure 2.13.
4. Save the document again with the same name (c02sa02).
5. Print c02sa02.
6. Close c02sa02.

Figure 2.13

Imagine yourself in the year 2000. You arrive at your office to meet the challenges of a new day. As you look around at the work stations, you notice that each has a multi-function display terminal for voice, data, and video applications.

You recall that just a short time ago, only selected workers had terminals. They were used primarily for text and data-manipulation functions and activities.

The movement of document and information has also changed. Incoming correspondence that is not transmitted electronically to your work station is converted to a digitized format via laser scanners. This is input into the electronic filing system.

You can access the information from your terminal and choose which to act upon at your convenience. An added bonus is that you don't have a pile of papers sitting around cluttering your desk. Another challenge is the ability to create documents by dictating to your terminal through a feature called voice-activated display. This feature allows you to view dictation on your terminal for editing. You also have the option of dictating or using your hand-manipulated input device to make corrections.

Everything you dictate is run through an electronic dictionary and a grammar and syntax validator before the final draft is distributed. If you mistakenly dictate "you is" instead of "you are," the grammar and syntax validator corrects it.

Assessment 3

1. Open para01.
2. Print para01.
3. Close para01.

3 Formatting Characters

Upon successful completion of chapter 3, you will be able to enhance single-page business documents and reports with character formatting including all caps, bold, underlining, and italics. You will also be able to use WordPerfect's Help and Coaches features.

As you work with WordPerfect, you will learn a number of commands and procedures that affect how the document appears when printed. The appearance of a document in the editing window and how it looks when printed is called the *format*. Formatting may include such elements as all caps, line spacing, margin settings, even or uneven margins, tabs, bolding, underlining, and much more.

Creating Text in All Caps

To key text in all uppercase letters, press Caps Lock. The Caps Lock key is a toggle key—press the key once to activate the Caps Lock feature, and press it again to turn it off. When Caps Lock is turned on, a green mode indicator light appears at the upper right side of the keyboard.

Using the Tab Key

The WordPerfect program contains a variety of default settings. A *default* is a preset standard or value that is established by the program. One default setting in WordPerfect is a Ruler Bar that contains tab settings every one-half inch. In a later chapter, you will learn how to change the default tab settings. For now, use the default tab settings to indent text from the left margin. To indent text, press Tab. The Tab key on a microcomputer keyboard is generally located above the Caps Lock key.

Formatting Text

Text can be formatted to accentuate text, elicit a particular feeling from the text, or draw the reader's eyes to a particular word or words. There are a variety of ways that text can be accentuated such as bolding, italicizing, and underlining. Text can be bolded, italicized, or underlined with buttons on the Toolbar, shortcut commands, or options at the Font dialog box. In this chapter, you will learn to bold, italicize, and underline with buttons on the Toolbar and shortcut commands. The Font dialog box is discussed in chapter 7.

Bolding Text

The Bold button on the Toolbar (the tenth button from the left) or the shortcut command Ctrl + B, can be used to bold text. When text is bolded, it appears darker than surrounding text in the editing window and also on the printed page. Text can be bolded as it is being keyed, or existing text can be bolded.

To bold text as it is being keyed, click on the Bold button on the Toolbar or press Ctrl + B. Key the text to be bolded, then click on the Bold button on the Toolbar again or press Ctrl +B.

In addition to clicking on the Bold button on the Toolbar or pressing Ctrl + B to turn off bold, you can also just press the right arrow key on the keyboard.

Text that has already been keyed in a document can be made bold by selecting the text first, then using the Bold button on the Toolbar or the shortcut command Ctrl + B.

Exercise 1 Bolding Text

Note: In this exercise and other exercises in the text, you will be required to create memoranda. Please refer to appendix C at the end of this text for the correct placement and spacing of a traditional-style memorandum (memo). Unless otherwise instructed by your teacher, use this format when creating memos. The initials of the person keying the memo usually appear at the end of the document. In this text, the initials will appear in the exercises as xx. Key your initials where you see the xx. Identifying document names in correspondence is a good idea because it lets you find and open the document quickly and easily at a future date. In this text, the document name is identified after the reference initials. Before printing any exercise, always proofread the document and correct any errors.

1. At a clear editing window, key the memo shown in figure 3.1 in the traditional memo format. Use Caps Lock to key the memo headings–*DATE*, *TO*, *FROM*, and *SUBJECT*. To align the information after *DATE:*, key **DATE:**, press Tab, then key **November 15, 1996**. (Press Tab after the other headings to align them properly. You will need to press Tab twice after *TO:*.) Bold the money amounts as shown in the memo as it is being keyed by completing the following steps:
   a. Press Ctrl + B.
   b. Key the money amount.
   c. Press Ctrl + B (or press the right arrow key).
2. Save the memo and name it c03ex01.
3. Print c03ex01.
4. With c03ex01 still open, select and bold the words *Maintenance and Operations* in the first paragraph by completing the following steps:
   a. Position the insertion point on the *M* in *Maintenance*.
   b. If you are using the mouse, position the I-beam pointer on the *M* in *Maintenance*, hold down the left button, drag the I-beam pointer to the end of *Operations*, then release the mouse button. If you are using the keyboard, press F8, then move the insertion point immediately past *Operations*.
   c. With *Maintenance and Operations* selected, click on the Bold button on the Toolbar.

5. Select and bold the following text in the memo:
   a. *Assistant Superintendent for Support Services* in the second paragraph.
   b. The heading *DATE:*.
   c. The heading *TO:*.
   d. The heading *FROM:*.
   e. The heading *SUBJECT:*.
6. Save the memo again with the same name (c03ex01).
7. Print c03ex01.
8. Close c03ex01.

Figure 3.1

DATE: November 15, 1996

TO: All School Principals

FROM: Pat Windslow, Superintendent

SUBJECT: BOARD OF EDUCATION MEETING

Two decisions were made at the Board of Education meeting last night that I would like to bring to your attention. The board members passed a recommendation to set a Maintenance and Operations levy for February 1997. The estimated collection for 1997 is **$4,500,000** and the estimated collection for 1998 is **$4,850,000**. These estimates are based on a levy rate of **$4.20** for each **$1,000** assessed value.

The Assistant Superintendent for Support Services reported that the District will save **$9,100** annually if heat pumps are installed in 23 portable buildings. The board members awarded an **$85,450** bid to Gemini Mechanics to install the pumps. You will be notified when portables at your school will be upgraded.

xx:c03ex01

Displaying the Reveal Codes Window

You can identify text that is bolded because it appears darker than surrounding text. There are special codes embedded in the text that are not visible; these codes tell WordPerfect where to start and stop bold. To display the bold codes, you must display a special window called Reveal Codes. At the Reveal Codes window, you can see the format changes that have been made to a document. To display the Reveal Codes window, choose View, then Reveal Codes.

In Reveal Codes a double line is inserted toward the bottom of the screen. Above the double line the text displays normally. Below the double line, the same text displays with formatting codes added. Figure 3.2 shows a document with Reveal Codes displayed.

The insertion point appears above the double line as a blinking vertical bar. Below the double line, the insertion point displays as a red rectangle. The insertion point can be moved through text with the insertion point movement keys.

Codes and text can be deleted in Reveal Codes with the regular deletion commands or with the mouse. For example, the Backspace key will delete the character or code to the left of the insertion point and the Delete key will delete the character or code immediately to the right of the insertion point. You can also use the mouse to "pull" codes out of Reveal Codes.

Figure 3.2
Reveal Codes

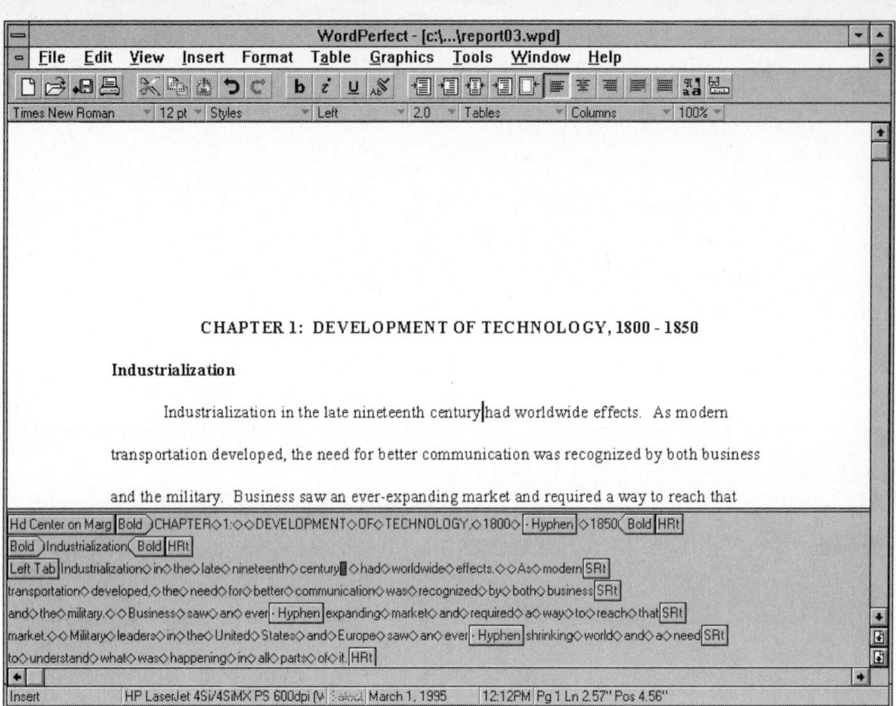

To remove a code with the mouse, position the arrow pointer on the code to be removed, hold down the left mouse button, drag the code into the editing window, then release the mouse button.

Special codes appear in Reveal Codes that identify functions and commands. Some of the lines of text in figure 3.2 end with the code SRt. This code indicates a soft return, which is an end of line created by word wrap. The code HRt identifies a hard return and indicates that the Enter key has been pressed. In Reveal Codes, the code Bold identifies the beginning and the code Bold identifies the end of bold text. If after bolding text you change your mind, display Reveal Codes, then delete one of the bold codes. Because bold codes are paired codes, when one code is deleted its pair is automatically deleted.

Exercise 2 Removing Bold Codes

1. At a clear editing window, open c03ex01.
2. Save the memorandum with Save As and name it c03ex02.
3. Remove the bold codes from the heading *DATE:* by completing the following steps:
   a. Move the insertion point to the *D* in *DATE:*.
   b. Display the Reveal Codes window by choosing View, then Reveal Codes.
   c. Position the insertion point immediately to the right of the Bold code, then press the Backspace key. (This will delete the on code as well as the off code.)
4. Complete similar steps to delete the bold codes from the heading *TO:*.
5. Remove the bold codes from the heading *FROM:* by completing the following steps:
   a. Move the insertion point to the *F* in *FROM*.
   b. Display the Reveal Codes window. (Skip this step if Reveal Codes is already displayed.)
   c. Position the arrow pointer on the Bold code on the left side of *FROM:*.
   d. Hold down the left mouse button.
   e. Drag the arrow pointer into the editing window, then release the mouse button.
6. Complete similar steps to delete the bold codes from the heading *SUBJECT:*.
7. Change the document name after your initials from c03ex01 to c03ex02.
8. Save the memorandum again with the same name (c03ex02).
9. Print c03ex02.
10. Close c03ex02.

Italicizing Text

WordPerfect's italics feature can be used in documents to emphasize specific text such as the names of published works. Text can be italicized using the Italics button on the Toolbar (the eleventh from the left) or the shortcut command Ctrl + I. Text identified with italics will appear in italics on the screen. In Reveal Codes, the code [Italc] identifies the beginning of italicized text and the code [Italc] identifies the end of italicized text.

Exercise 3 Italicizing Text As It Is Keyed

1. At a clear editing window, key the text shown in figure 3.3. Italicize the text shown as it is being keyed by completing the following steps:
   a. Press Ctrl + I.
   b. Key the text.
   c. Press Ctrl + I (or press the right arrow key).
2. Save the document and name it c03ex03.
3. Print c03ex03.
4. Close c03ex03.

Figure 3.3

Collier, Samuel G. (1991). *Educating Our Children* (pp. 56-78). Montpelier, VT: Maple Leaf Publishers.

Fjetland, Brita A. (1992). *Effective Educators* (2nd ed.). Vancouver, British Columbia, Canada: Vancouver Press.

Kitamura, Toshiki. (1990). *Managing the Classroom.* Boston, MA: Atlantic Publishing House.

Mejia, Marianna C. (1994). *Education for the Twenty-first Century.* Spokane, WA: Eastside Publishing and Printing.

Text that has already been keyed in a document can be italicized by selecting the text first.

Exercise 4 Italicizing Previously Keyed Text

1. At a clear editing window, open the document named biblio01 from your student data disk.
2. Save the document with Save As and name it c03ex04.
3. Select and italicize the title, *Telecommunications in Today's Businesses*, by completing the following steps:
   a. If you are using the mouse, position the I-beam pointer on the *T* in *Telecommunications*, hold down the left button, drag the I-beam pointer to the end of *Businesses*, then release the mouse button. If you are using the keyboard, position the insertion point on the *T* in *Telecommunications*, press F8, then move the insertion point immediately past *Businesses*.
   b. With *Telecommunications in Today's Businesses* selected, click on the Italics button on the Toolbar.
4. Select and italicize the following titles in the document:
   a. *Technological Advancements* in the second paragraph.
   b. *Computer Systems and Applications* in the third paragraph.
   c. *The Changing Business Office* in the fourth paragraph.
5. Save the document again with the same name (c03ex04).
6. Print c03ex04.
7. Close c03ex04.

Underlining Text

Text can be underlined using the Underline button on the Toolbar (the twelfth button from the left) or the shortcut command Ctrl + U.

Exercise 5 Underlining Text As It Is Keyed

1. At a clear editing window, key the text shown in figure 3.4. Underline the text shown as it is being keyed by completing the following steps:
   a. Press Ctrl + U.
   b. Key the text.
   c. Press Ctrl + U (or press the right arrow key).
2. Save the document and name it c03ex05.
3. Print c03ex05.
4. Close c03ex05.

Figure 3.4

Caprin, Heidi L. (1993). The Business Educator. Dallas, TX: Longhorn Publishing.

Landeis, Ricardo M. (1994). Total Quality Management in the Educational Environment. Columbus, OH: Midtown Press.

Verdun, Christine L. (1993). The ABCs of Integrated Learning. St. Louis, MO: Riverside Publishing.

Text that has already been keyed in a document can be underlined by selecting the text first, then using the Underline button on the Toolbar or the shortcut command Ctrl + U. In Reveal Codes, the code Und identifies the beginning of underlined text and the code Und identifies the end of underlined text.

Exercise 6 Underlining Previously Keyed Text

1. At a clear editing window, open c03ex04.
2. Save the document with Save As and name it c03ex06.
3. Delete all italics codes from the titles.
4. Select and underline the title *Telecommunications in Today's Businesses* by completing the following steps:
   a. If you are using the mouse, position the I-beam pointer on the *T* in *Telecommunications*, hold down the left button, drag the I-beam pointer to the end of *Businesses*, then release the mouse button. If you are using the keyboard, position the insertion point on the *T* in *Telecommunications*, press F8, then move the insertion point immediately past *Businesses*.
   b. With *Telecommunications in Today's Businesses* selected, click on the Underline button on the Toolbar.
5. Select and underline the title, *Technological Advancements,* in the second paragraph.
6. Select and underline the title, *Computer Systems and Applications,* in the third paragraph.
7. Select and underline the title, *The Changing Business Office*, in the fourth paragraph.
8. Save the document again with the same name (c03ex06).
9. Print c03ex06.
10. Close c03ex06.

Using Help

WordPerfect's Help feature is an on-screen reference manual containing information about all WordPerfect functions and commands. To display the Help dialog box shown in figure 3.5, choose Help, then Contents.

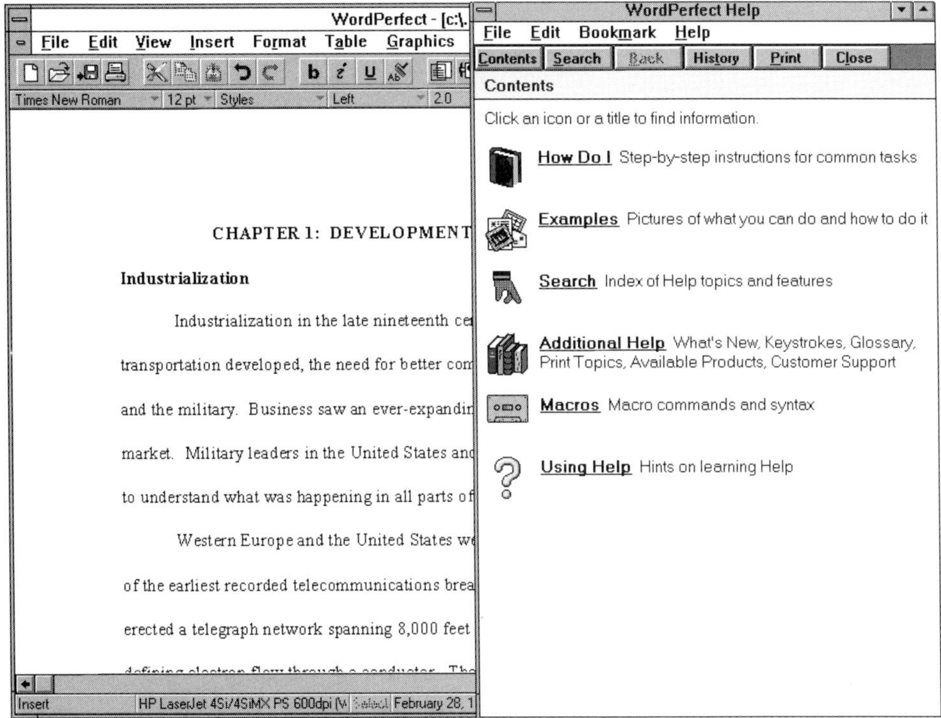

Figure 3.5
Help Dialog Box

The options below Contents in the Help dialog box perform the action described to the right. For example, choose Additional Help then Glossary and WordPerfect will display a list of terms with a definition for each term. Complete exercise 7 to practice using the Help feature.

Exercise 7 Using the Contents Feature in WordPerfect's Help System

1. At a clear editing window, use WordPerfect's Help feature to read about italics by completing the following steps:
   a. Choose Help, then Contents.
   b. At the Help dialog box, choose Search. To do this with the mouse, position the hand pointer on Search, then click the left button. If you are using the keyboard, press the Tab key to select Search, then press Enter.
   c. At the Search dialog box, key **italic**, then press Enter.
   d. Choose Go To. To do this with the mouse, position the arrow pointer on the Go To button, then click the left mouse button. If you are using the keyboard, press Alt + G.
   e. Read the information on the Italic feature. (Press the down arrow key to view all the information.)
   f. To remove the information from the screen and return the insertion point to the document, choose Close. To do this with the mouse, position the arrow pointer on the Close button in the dialog box, then click the left button. If you are using the keyboard, press the Alt + L.
2. Complete the following steps to use the Glossary Option from the Help feature to read the definition for the words *Title Bar* and *Scroll Bar*:
   a. Choose Help, then Contents.
   b. At the Help dialog box, choose Additional Help. To do this with the mouse, position the hand pointer on Additional Help, then click the left mouse button. If

you are using the keyboard, press the Tab key until Additional Help is selected, then press Enter.

c. At the Indexes dialog box, choose Glossary. To do this with the mouse, position the hand pointer on Glossary, then click the left button. If you are using the keyboard, press the Tab key until Glossary is selected, then press Enter.
d. At the Glossary dialog box, select the letter T. To do this with the mouse, position the hand pointer on the letter T button, then click the left mouse button. If you are using the keyboard, press the Tab key until the letter T button is selected, then press Enter.
e. With the list of terms beginning with T displayed, choose title bar. To do this with the mouse, position the hand pointer on the words *title bar*, then click the left mouse button. If you are using the keyboard, press the Tab key until *title bar* is selected (you will need to press Tab several times), then press Enter.
f. Read the definition for *title bar*.
g. Remove the definition from the screen. To do this with the mouse, position the arrow pointer outside the definition box, then click the left mouse button. If you are using the keyboard, press any key on the keyboard (such as the space bar).
h. At the Glossary dialog box, select the letter S.
i. With the list of terms beginning with S displayed, choose *scroll bar*.
j. Read the definition for *scroll bar*.
k. Remove the definition from the screen. To do this with the mouse, position the arrow pointer outside the definition box, then click the left mouse button. If you are using the keyboard, press any key on the keyboard (such as the space bar).
l. Choose Close to remove the Glossary dialog box from the screen. To do this with the mouse, position the arrow pointer on the Close button in the dialog box, then click the left button. If you are using the keyboard, press Alt + L.
m. Close the Indexes dialog box.

Using the Help Menu Options

When you choose Help from the Menu Bar, the drop-down menu shown in figure 3.6 displays on the screen. The first option, Contents, displays the Help dialog box shown in figure 3.5. The Search for Help on option displays the Search dialog box. This is the same dialog box that displays when you choose Search from the Help dialog box.

The How Do I option provides information on WordPerfect functions and how to complete a function.

Figure 3.6
Help Drop-Down Menu

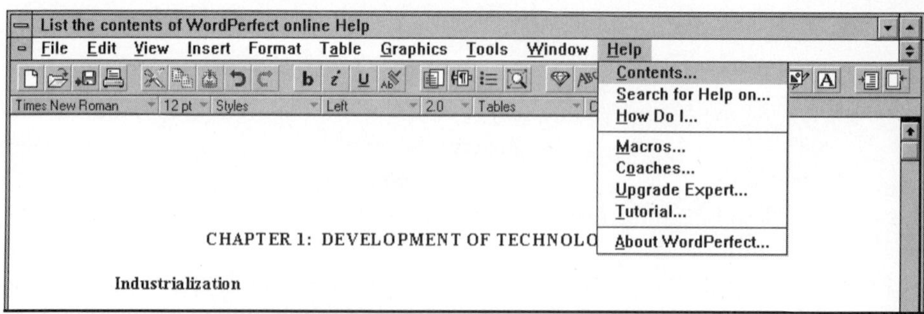

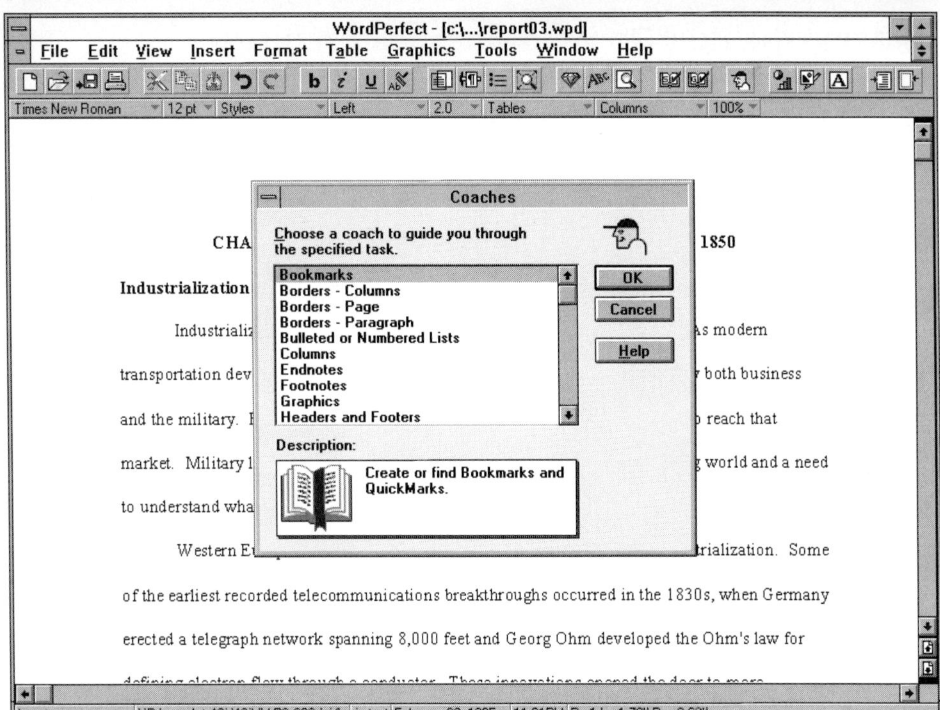

Figure 3.7
Coaches Dialog Box

The Macros option from the Help pull-down menu displays the WordPerfect Online Macros Manual dialog box. At this dialog box, you can select a topic, then read information about that particular topic.

If you choose Coaches from the Help pull-down menu, the Coaches dialog box shown in figure 3.7 displays on the screen. The Coaches feature provides step-by-step instructions on how to perform the newest or most popular WordPerfect functions. The Coaches walk you through the task telling you how to complete the steps. Therefore, when you are done with the Coaches, you have not only read about the feature, but you have also completed the steps.

For people who have used another word processing program or a previous version of WordPerfect, the Help feature provides on-line help for upgrade users. To use the upgrade feature, choose Help, then Upgrade Expert. At the Upgrade Expert dialog box that displays, choose the topic you want to learn more about. WordPerfect will provide information about the topic and, in some cases, will show you how the feature operates.

With the Tutorial option, WordPerfect will teach you the basics of using WordPerfect for Windows, Version 6.1. When you choose Help, then Tutorial, the WordPerfect Tutorial screen displays in the editing window. At this screen, you can choose one of four lessons:

1 Creating a Document
2 Editing Text
3 Formatting Text
4 Finishing Up

To complete a lesson, choose the desired lesson, then follow the steps on the screen. To choose a lesson with the mouse, click on the desired lesson, then click on the Continue button. If you are using the keyboard, press the down arrow key until the desired lesson is selected. Press the Tab key until the Continue button is selected, then press Enter.

The last option, About WordPerfect, displays information about the WordPerfect program including such items as the release date and license number.

Exercise 8 Using the How Do I and Coaches Features in the Help System

1. At a clear editing window, use the Help feature to read about how to save a document by completing the following steps:
   a. Choose Help, then How Do I.
   b. At the How Do I dialog box that displays at the left side of the document window, choose Open and Save Documents. To do this with the mouse, position the hand pointer on Open and Save Documents, then click the left mouse button. If you are using the keyboard, press the Tab key until Open and Save Documents is selected, then press Enter.
   c. From the choices that display below Open and Save Documents, choose Save and Close Documents.
   d. From the choices that display below Save and Close Documents, choose Save Documents.
   e. Read the information about saving documents that displays in the Help dialog box at the right side of the document window. (Press the down arrow key to read all the information.)
   f. After reading the information about saving a document, close the Help dialog box. To do this with the mouse, position the arrow pointer on the Close button in the Help dialog box, then click the left mouse button. If you are using the keyboard, press Alt + L.
   g. Close the How Do I dialog box.
2. Use the Coaches feature to learn about indenting text in a paragraph by completing the following steps:
   a. Choose Help, then Coaches; or click on the Coaches button on the Toolbar.
   b. At the Coaches dialog box choose Indent. To do this with the mouse, position the arrow pointer on the down-pointing arrow to the right of the list box, then click the left mouse button until Indent is visible. Double-click on Indent. If you are using the keyboard, press the down arrow key until Indent is selected, then press Enter.
   c. At the Indenting Lines and Paragraphs menu, choose Continue. To do this with the mouse, click on the Continue button. If you are using the keyboard, press the Tab key until the marquee surrounds the Continue button, then press Enter.
   d. Follow the steps on the screen describing how to indent a line. Complete the steps as described.
3. Close the document without saving it.

CHAPTER SUMMARY

- To key text in all uppercase letters, press the Caps Lock key.
- The default or preset tab setting is one tab set every half inch. Press the Tab key to indent text one-half inch.
- Text is bolded, italicized, or underlined with buttons on the Toolbar, shortcut commands, or options at the Font dialog box. When text has been bolded, italicized, or underlined, special codes are inserted in the document. These codes can be viewed in the Reveal Codes window.
- To bold, italicize, or underline existing text, select the text first. Then use the buttons on the Toolbar or the shortcut commands to change the selected text.
- WordPerfect's Help feature is an on-screen reference manual containing information about WordPerfect functions and commands. The Coaches feature provides step-by-step instructions on how to perform the newest or most popular WordPerfect functions. The Tutorial feature teaches the basics of using WordPerfect for Windows, Version 6.1.

Commands Review

	Mouse (Toolbar)	Keyboard
Uppercase function		CAPS LOCK
Bold	B	CTRL + B
Italics	I	CTRL + I
Underline	U	CTRL + U

	Mouse/Keyboard (Menu Bar)
Reveal Codes	View, Reveal Codes
Help	Help, Contents
Coaches	Help, Coaches
Tutorial	Help, Tutorial

Reveal Codes Symbols Review

Bolded text	Bold text Bold
Italicized text	Italc text Italc
Underlined text	Und text Und
Soft return—end of line created by word wrap	SRt
Hard return—wherever the Enter key has been pressed	HRt

CHECK YOUR UNDERSTANDING

True/False: Circle the letter T if the statement is true; circle the letter F if the statement is false.

T F 1. You can delete an underlining code in Reveal Codes.

T F 2. Before bolding existing text, the text must first be selected.

T F 3. When Reveal Codes is displayed, the insertion point in the editing window displays the same as the insertion point in the Reveal Codes window.

T F 4. When the Enter key is pressed, the code called a hard return is inserted in the document.

T F 5. Paired codes, like Bold and Bold, must both be deleted to turn off the feature.

T F 6. The arrow pointer can be used to remove a code in Reveal Codes.

Completion: In the space provided at the right, indicate the correct term, command, or number.

1. Press this key to indent the insertion point to the first tab setting to the right. ______________
2. This code in Reveal Codes indicates the beginning of underlined text. ______________
3. Existing text can be italicized only if this is done first. ______________
4. This is the shortcut command to underline text. ______________
5. This symbol is inserted in the document each time a line of text is ended by word wrap. ______________
6. This is the name for the on-screen reference manual containing information about all WordPerfect functions and commands. ______________
7. This feature provides step-by-step instructions on how to perform the newest or most popular WordPerfect functions. ______________

SKILL ASSESSMENTS

Assessment 1

1. At a clear editing window, key the memorandum shown in figure 3.8. Bold and underline the text as shown.
2. Save the memorandum and name it c03sa01.
3. Print c03sa01.
4. Close c03sa01.

Assessment 2

1. At a clear editing window, open memo01. This document is located on your student data disk.
2. Save the memorandum with Save As and name it c03sa02.
3. Display Reveal Codes and delete the underline codes from the publication titles, *The ABCs of Integrated Learning* and *Total Quality Management in the Education Environment.*
4. Select and italicize the publication titles, *The ABCs of Integrated Learning* and *Total Quality Management in the Education Environment.*
5. Select and bold the following text:
   a. The headings *DATE:*, *TO:*, *FROM:*, and *SUBJECT:*.
   b. *Tuesday, November 12* in the third paragraph.
   c. *7:00 p.m. to 8:00 p.m.* in the third paragraph.
6. Insert your initials at the end of the document where you see the "xx." Change the document name after your initials from memo01 to c03sa02.
7. Save the document again with the same name (c03sa02).
8. Print c03sa02.
9. Close c03sa02.

Figure 3.8

DATE: November 12, 1996

TO: Rachel Una

FROM: Chris Kuehner

SUBJECT: TELECOMMUNICATIONS

After reviewing a number of telecommunications textbooks, I have chosen Telecommunications: Systems and Applications for use in **CIS 120, Telecommunications**. The bookstore manager has ordered the book for next quarter.

The class was to be held in **Room 310**. Due to computer requirements, the class has been moved to **Room 428**. The classroom can accommodate 25 people. Therefore, the class enrollment has been changed from 30 to 25.

xx:c03sa01

Assessment 3

1. At a clear editing window, open c03sa01.
2. Save the memorandum with Save As and name it c03sa03.
3. Turn on the display of Reveal Codes, delete all the bold and underline codes in the document, then turn off the display of Reveal Codes.
4. Select and italicize the following text:
   a. *Telecommunications: Systems and Applications* in the first paragraph.
   b. *Room 310* in the second paragraph.
   c. *Room 428* in the second paragraph.
5. Select and bold the two occurrences of the number 25 in the second paragraph and the number 30 in the second paragraph.
6. Change the document name after your initials from c03sa01 to c03sa03.
7. Save the document again with the same name (c03sa03).
8. Print c03sa03.
9. Close c03sa03.

Formatting Lines

Upon successful completion of chapter 4, you will be able to enhance business memoranda and letters by changing the alignments of lines and paragraphs of text.

WordPerfect contains a number of features that can be used to change the appearance or layout of a line of text. Three common line features are centering, line spacing, and justification.

Centering Text

Text can be centered between the left and right margins with the shortcut command Shift + F7 or through the Format menu. When you use the command Shift + F7 or the Format menu, the insertion point is moved to the center of the editing window. Text moves left one space for every two characters you key. If you make a mistake while keying text, backspace and rekey it. This will not interfere with the centering process. To center text using the shortcut command, you would press Shift + F7, key the text, then press Enter.

To center text with the Format menu, you would choose Format, Line, then Center, key the text, then press Enter. When you press Enter at the end of the text, the centering feature is deactivated. The next line you key will begin at the left margin. If you want the next line centered, use the Shift + F7 command again or choose Format, Line, then Center.

In Reveal Codes, the code [Hd Center on Marg] identifies the beginning and the code [HRt] identifies the end of centered text. If the words *ADMINISTRATOR'S REPORT* were centered, they would appear as follows in Reveal Codes:

[Hd Center on Marg] **ADMINISTRATOR'S REPORT** [HRt]

Exercise 1 Bolding and Centering Text

1. At a clear editing window, key the text shown in figure 4.1 centered and bolded by completing the following steps:
   a. Key the first line by completing the following steps:
      (1) Press Shift + F7.
      (2) Press Ctrl + B (this turns on bold).
      (3) Key **CIS 120, TELECOMMUNICATIONS**.
      (4) Press Enter twice.
   b. Key the second line by completing the following steps:
      (1) Choose Format, Line, then Center.
      (2) Key **Monday through Thursday**.
      (3) Press Enter twice.
   c. Key the remaining lines following steps similar to those in 1a or 1b.
   d. After keying the last line, **Room 428**, press Ctrl + B to turn off bold.
2. Save the document and name it c04ex01.
3. Print c04ex01.
4. Close c04ex01.

Figure 4.1

CIS 120, TELECOMMUNICATIONS

Monday through Thursday

9:00 - 10:10 a.m.

Room 428

Centering Text at a Specific Position

The Center feature can be used to center text on a specific position on the line other than the center. To center at a specific position, tab or space in to the position on the line where text is to be centered then choose Format, Line, then Center; or press Shift + F7.

When text is centered at a specific position, the code Hd Center on Pos displays in Reveal Codes. The center on position feature can be useful for centering a heading over a column of text.

Exercise 2 Centering Text at a Specific Location

1. At a clear editing window, open column01. This document is located on your student data disk.
2. Save the document with Save As and name it c04ex02.
3. Bold and center the heading, *Directors,* over the text by completing the following steps:
   a. With the insertion point located on the first line in the document, press the space bar until the insertion point is located on *Position 2.6"*. (Check the status line.)
   b. Press Shift + F7 to access the Center command. (This does not move the insertion point. It tells WordPerfect to center text on Position 2.6.)
   c. Press Ctrl + B to turn on bold or click on the Bold button on the Toolbar.
   d. Key **Directors**.
   e. Press Ctrl + B (or click on the Bold button on the Toolbar) to turn off bold.
4. Save the document again with the same name (c04ex02).
5. Print c04ex02.
6. Close c04ex02.

Changing Line Spacing

By default, WordPerfect's word wrap feature single spaces text. Occasionally, you may want to change to another spacing, such as one and a half or double. Line spacing can be changed with the Spacing button on the Power Bar or with the Format menu.

To change line spacing with the Format menu, you would complete the following steps:

1 Choose Format, Line, then Spacing.
2 At the Line Spacing dialog box shown in figure 4.2, key the number of the desired line spacing. Or you can click on the up-pointing triangle to increase the number or click on the down-pointing triangle to decrease the number. If you are using the keyboard, press the up or down arrow keys on the keyboard.
3 Choose OK or press Enter.

When you use the up and down triangles at the Line Spacing dialog box, line spacing is set by one-tenth line increments. You can select settings or key your own measurement. You can enter whole numbers or decimal numbers. You can key up to four numbers after the decimal point; however, WordPerfect will only carry the number to two decimal places.

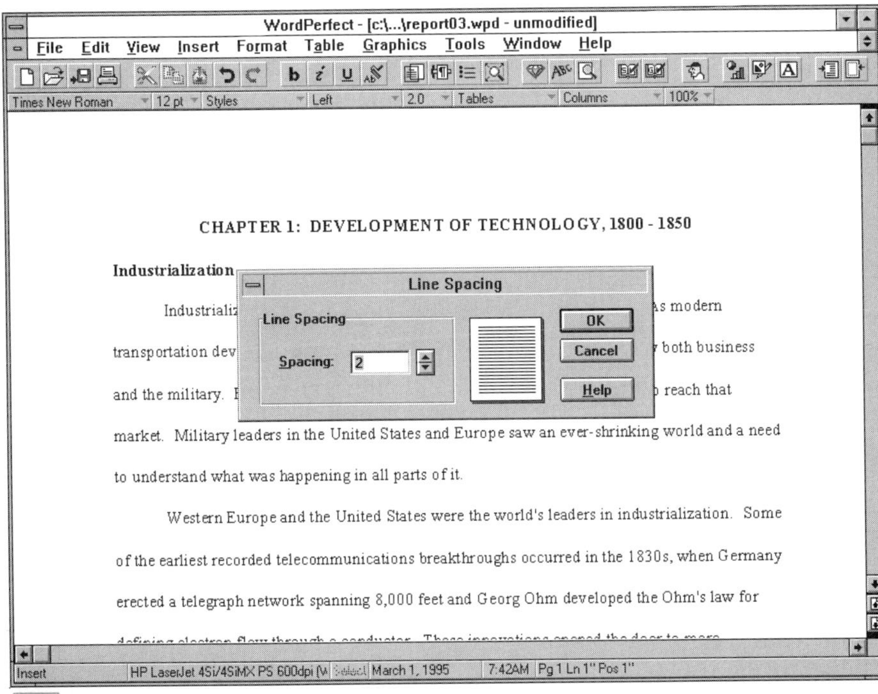

Figure 4.2
Line Spacing Dialog Box

Exercise 3 Changing Line Spacing with the Format Menu

1. At a clear editing window, open para01. This document is located on your student data disk.
2. Save the document with Save As and name it c04ex03.
3. Change the line spacing to 2 (double) by completing the following steps:
   a. Make sure the insertion point is positioned anywhere in the first line.
   b. Choose Format, Line, then Spacing.
   c. At the Line Spacing dialog box, key **2**.
   d. Choose OK or press Enter.
4. Save the document with the same name (c04ex03).
5. Print c04ex03.
6. Close c04ex03.

If you position the arrow pointer on the Line Spacing button on the Power Bar (fifth button from the left), then hold down the left mouse button, a drop-down menu displays with four options: 1.0, 1.5, 2.0, and Other. Drag the arrow pointer to one of the numbers to change the line spacing, then release the mouse button. Or, if you want to change the line spacing to a number not displayed, move the arrow pointer to Other, then release the mouse button. This causes the Line Spacing dialog box shown in figure 4.2 to display. You can also display the Line Spacing dialog box by double-clicking on the Line Spacing button on the Power Bar.

When changes are made to line spacing, a code is inserted in the document that can be seen in Reveal Codes. The line spacing code is inserted at the beginning of the paragraph where the insertion point is located. Line spacing changes affect text from the location of the code to the end of the document or until another line spacing code is encountered. If a line spacing code is deleted, line spacing reverts to the default setting of single spacing or to the setting of a previously placed line spacing code. If line spacing in a document is changed to double, the code would appear in Reveal Codes as Ln Spacing: 2.0. To see the number after Ln Spacing, you must have the insertion point positioned immediately to the left of the code, otherwise the code appears as Ln Spacing. You can also display the number in the code using the mouse. To do this, position the arrow pointer on the code, then click the left mouse button.

In chapter 3 you learned how you could remove codes in Reveal Codes using the mouse. You can also use the mouse together with codes to display dialog boxes. For example, to display the Line Spacing dialog box, position the arrow pointer on a Ln Spacing code in Reveal Codes, then double-click the left mouse button. At the Line Spacing dialog box you can edit the setting as desired.

Exercise 4 Changing Line Spacing with the Spacing Button

1. At a clear editing window, open memo01. This document is located on your student data disk.
2. Save the document with Save As and name it c04ex04.
3. Change the line spacing to *1.5* for the body of the memo by completing the following steps:
   a. Position the insertion point on any character in the first paragraph of the memo.
   b. Position the arrow pointer on the Line Spacing button on the Power Bar.
   c. Hold down the left mouse button.
   d. Drag the arrow pointer to *1.5*, then release the mouse button.
4. Display Reveal Codes. Position the arrow pointer on the Ln Spacing code, then click the left mouse button. (This should expand the code to display the number 1.5.) After viewing the code, turn off the display of Reveal Codes.
5. Save the memo again with the same name (c04ex04).
6. Print c04ex04.
7. Close c04ex04.

Changing Justification

By default, WordPerfect justifies text evenly at the left margin but leaves the text near the right margin uneven. (This is the style that typewriters would produce.) In WordPerfect it is referred to as *left justification*. Justification changes can be made in four ways: (1) shortcut commands, (2) the Justification button on the Power Bar, (3) the Format, Justification drop-down menu, or (4) buttons on the Format Toolbar.

Text in a paragraph can be justified at the left margin, centered between margins, at the right margin, or to the left and right margins. Figure 4.3 illustrates the different paragraph justifications.

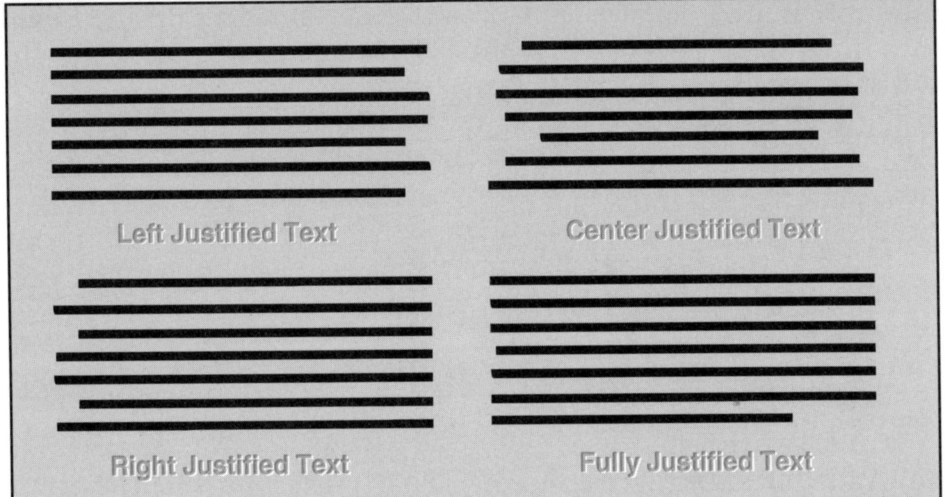

Figure 4.3
Paragraph Justifications

In addition to the four paragraph justifications shown in figure 4.3, you can also justify all lines of text in paragraphs. The difference between Full justification and All justification is that All will justify to both margins all lines of text in a paragraph, including short lines, while Full will not justify the last line of a paragraph to the right margin.

To make changes to justification with the Format menu, choose Format, then Justification. At the drop-down menu that displays as shown in figure 4.4, choose the desired justification.

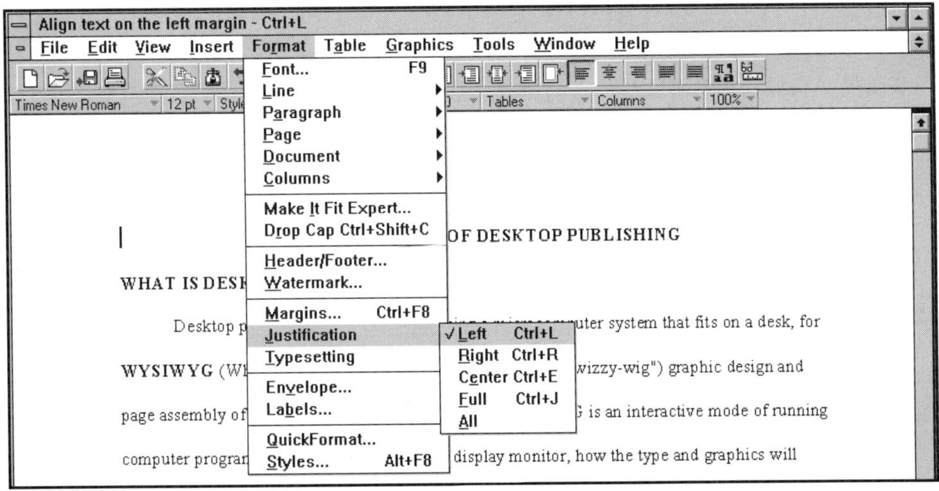

Figure 4.4
Format Justification Drop-Down Menu

Exercise 5 Changing Justification with the Format Menu

1. At a clear editing window, open para03. This document is located on your student data disk.
2. Save the document with Save As and name it c04ex05.
3. Change to center justification using the Format, Justification drop-down menu by completing the following steps:
   a. Position the insertion point on any character in the first paragraph.
   b. Choose Format, then Justification.
   c. At the drop-down menu, choose Center.
4. Save the document again with the same name (c04ex05).
5. Print c04ex05.
6. Close c04ex05.

Justification changes can be made with the Justification button on the Power Bar (the fourth button from the left). To display the justification options shown in figure 4.5, position the arrow pointer on the Justification button, then click the left mouse button.

Figure 4.5
Justification Button Drop-Down Menu

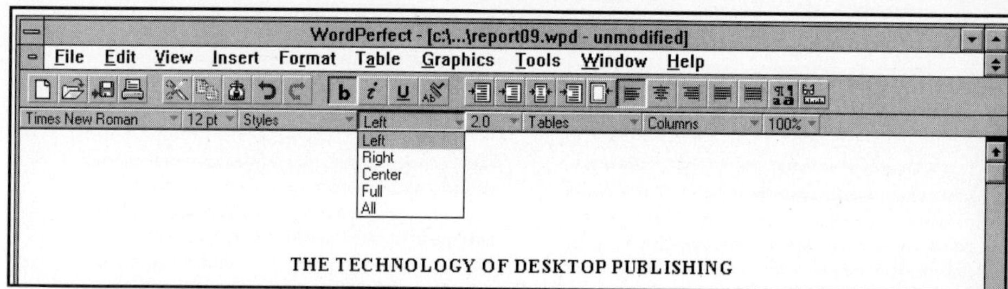

Exercise 6 Changing Justification with the Justification Button

1. At a clear editing window, open para03. This document is located on your student data disk.
2. Save the document with Save As and name it c04ex06.
3. With the insertion point positioned in the first paragraph, change to full justification with the Justification button on the Power Bar by completing the following steps:
   a. Position the arrow pointer on the Justification button on the Power Bar.
   b. Hold down the left mouse button, drag the arrow pointer to Full, then release the mouse button.
4. Save the document again with the same name (c04ex06).
5. Print c04ex06.
6. Close c04ex06.

Shortcut commands can be used to change the justification of text in paragraphs. Use the following shortcut commands to change justification:

Ctrl + L = left justification
Ctrl + R = right justification
Ctrl + E = center justification
Ctrl + J = full justification

There is no shortcut command to fully justify all lines of text (including short lines) in paragraphs.

Exercise 7 Changing Justification with a Shortcut Command

1. At a clear editing window, open para02. This document is located on your student data disk.
2. Save the document with Save As and name it c04ex07.
3. Change the paragraphs in the document to right justification using a shortcut command by completing the following steps:
   a. Position the insertion point on any character in the first paragraph.
   b. Press Ctrl + R.
4. Save the document again with the same name (c04ex07).
5. Print c04ex07.
6. Close c04ex07.

Justification changes can also be made with buttons on the Format Toolbar. By default, the 6.1 WordPerfect Toolbar displays below the Menu Bar and above the Power Bar. WordPerfect provides a variety of other toolbars that can be used to quickly format a document. To view the names of other toolbars, position the arrow pointer on the current Toolbar, then click the *right* mouse button. This causes the drop-down menu shown in figure 4.6 to display.

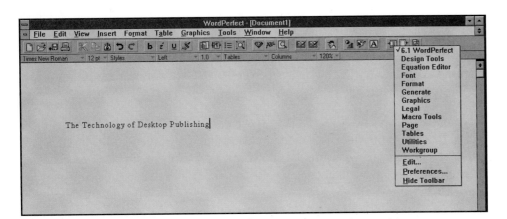

Figure 4.6
Toolbar Drop-Down Menu

To display the Format Toolbar (instead of the 6.1 WordPerfect Toolbar), position the arrow pointer on the Format option at the drop-down menu, then click the left mouse button. This causes the Format Toolbar to display as shown in figure 4.7.

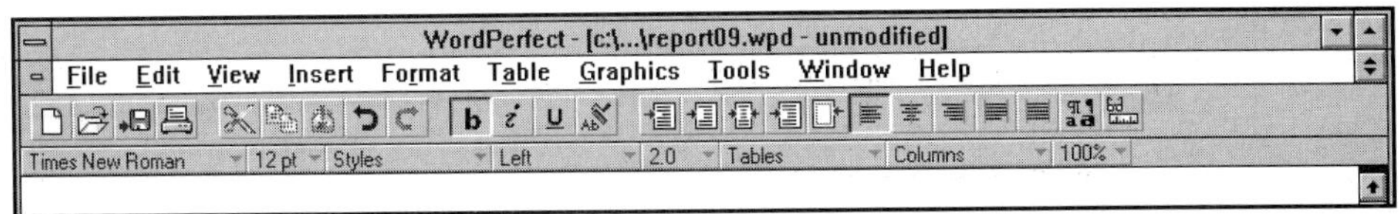

Figure 4.7
Format Toolbar

Exercise 8 Changing Justification with the Format Toolbar

1. At a clear editing window, open para04. This document is located on your student data disk.
2. Save the document with Save As and name it c04ex08.
3. Change to full justification using the Format Toolbar by completing the following steps:
   a. Display the Format Toolbar by positioning the arrow pointer on the current Toolbar, clicking the right mouse button, then clicking on Format. (If the Format Toolbar is already displayed, skip this step.)
   b. Position the arrow pointer on the Justify Full button on the Format Toolbar.
   c. Click the left mouse button.
4. Save the document again with the same name (c04ex08).
5. Print c04ex08.
6. Close c04ex08.
7. Change to the default toolbar (6.1 WordPerfect).

When a change is made to justification, WordPerfect inserts the code at the beginning of the paragraph where the insertion point is positioned. For example, if the insertion point is positioned in the middle of a paragraph and the justification is changed to right, the code is inserted at the beginning of that paragraph. Changes to justification take effect from the location of the code to the end of the document or until another justification code is encountered.

Changing the Viewing Mode

The WordPerfect for Windows 6.1 program has more than one viewing mode. You have been using the default viewing mode, which is Page. You can also change the viewing mode to Draft or Two Page.

Viewing in the Page Mode

The Page mode, which is the default, displays a document in what is considered WYSIWYG (What You See Is What You Get). All aspects of a document display such as headers, footers, page numbers, and watermarks. Because all elements of a document are displayed, the Page mode is slower than the Draft mode. If the viewing mode has been changed and you want to return to the Page mode, choose View, then Page.

Viewing in the Draft Mode

The viewing mode can be changed to the Draft mode by choosing View, then Draft. In the Draft mode, text displays as it will appear when printed; however, special elements such as headers, footers, page numbers, and watermarks will not display. Because special elements are not displayed, the Draft mode is faster than the Page mode.

Viewing in the Two-Page Mode

In addition to the Page and Draft modes, you can change the viewing mode to Two Page. At the Two-Page viewing mode, two pages of a document are displayed side by side as shown in figure 4.8.

The Two-Page mode is useful for viewing the position of elements on pages. You can edit in Two-Page mode but it is not practical to do this. You may want to switch to Two-Page mode to see how elements are positioned, then switch to Draft or Page mode to make any changes.

Figure 4.8
Two-Page Viewing Mode

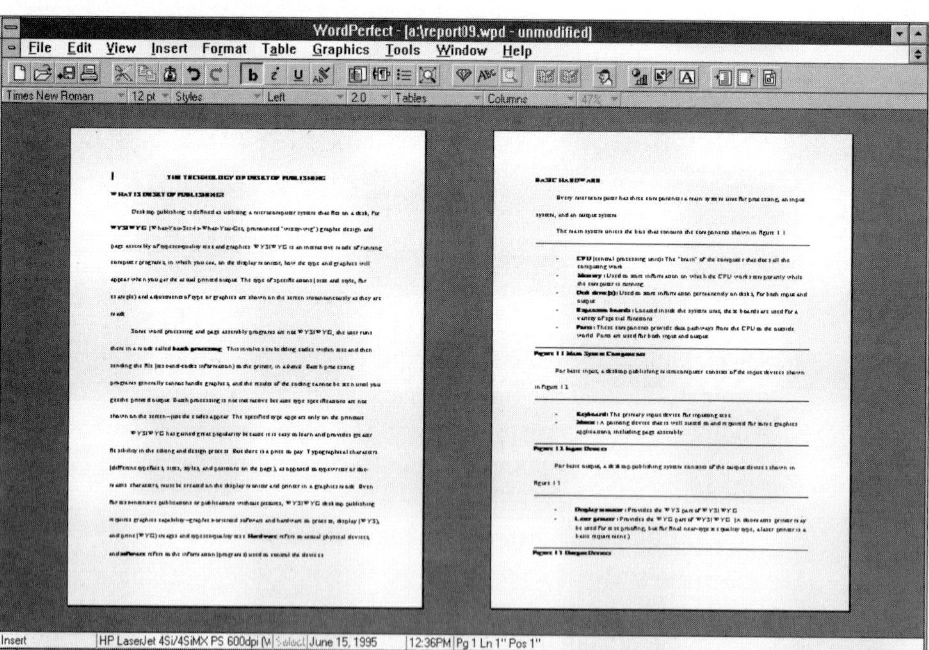

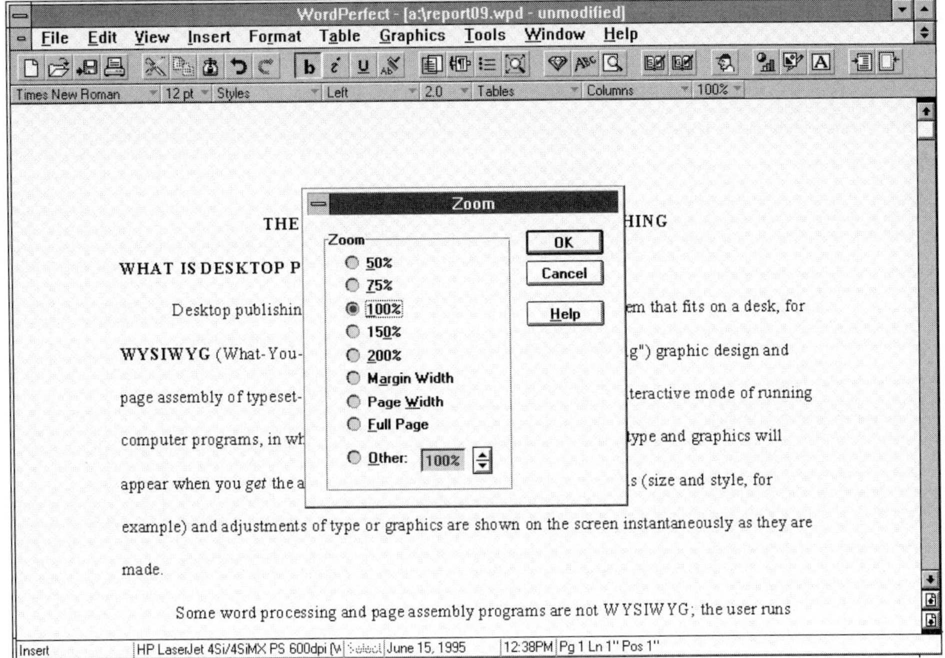

Figure 4.9
Zoom Dialog Box

Changing the Zoom Ratio

In the Draft or Page viewing modes, you can change the size of text and document elements displayed on the screen. By default, the document is displayed at approximately 100% of the size of the document when printed. This ratio can be changed with the Zoom option from the View drop-down menu or with the Zoom button on the Power Bar. When you choose View, then Zoom, the Zoom dialog box shown in figure 4.9 displays.

To decrease the display of the document, choose a percentage lower than 100% such as 50% or 75%. To increase the display, choose a percentage higher than 100% such as 150% or 200%. If you choose Margin Width at the Zoom dialog box, the document displays so that all text and graphics between the left and right margins are visible. Choose Page Width to display the entire document between the left and right edges of the page. If you choose Full Page, the entire current page is displayed. With the Other option from the Zoom dialog box, you can decrease or increase the percentage from 25% to 400%. The same options are available by clicking on the Zoom button on the Power Bar (the last button on the right).

You can also zoom to full page size by clicking on the Page/Zoom Full button on the Toolbar (twentieth button from the left). Click on Page/Zoom Full again to return to the previous viewing mode.

Exercise 9 Changing the Viewing Mode and the Zoom Ratio

1. At a clear editing screen, open report02. This document is located on your student data disk.
2. Change the view to Draft by choosing View, then Draft.
3. Move the insertion point to the end of the document page by page.
4. Move the insertion point to the beginning of the document (Ctrl + Home), then change the view to Two Page by choosing View, then Two Page.
5. Move the insertion point to the end of the document page by page.
6. Move the insertion point to the beginning of the document, then change the view to Draft.

7. Change the Zoom option to 75% by completing the following steps:
   a. Choose View, then Zoom.
   b. At the Zoom dialog box, choose 75%. To do this with the mouse, position the tip of the arrow pointer inside the circle before 75%, then click the left mouse button. If you are using the keyboard, key **7**.
   c. Click on OK or press Enter.
8. Change the Zoom option to Margin Width by completing the following steps:
   a. Choose View, then Zoom.
   b. At the Zoom dialog box, choose Margin Width. To do this with the mouse, position the tip of the arrow pointer inside the circle before Margin Width, then click the left mouse button. If you are using the keyboard, key **A**.
   c. Click on OK or press Enter.
9. Change the Zoom option to Full Page by completing steps similar to those in 8a through 8c.
10. Change the Zoom option back to the default of 100%.
11. Zoom to full page size by clicking on the Page/Zoom Full button on the Toolbar. Click on Page/Zoom Full again to return to the previous viewing mode.
12. Close report02 without saving it.

CHAPTER SUMMARY

- Three common line alignment features are centering, line spacing, and justification.
- Text can be centered between the margins or on a specific position.
- The default line spacing, which is single, can be changed at the Line Spacing dialog box or with the Line Spacing button on the Power Bar. The line spacing code is inserted at the beginning of the paragraph where the insertion point is located.
- Justification determines how text will be aligned when it is printed. The five possible settings are left (which is the default setting); center; right; full; and full, all lines. The justification code is inserted at the beginning of the paragraph where the insertion point is located.
- Three viewing modes are available: Page (the default), Draft, and Two-Page.
- By default, a document is displayed at approximately 100% of the size it will be when printed. This ratio can be increased or decreased with the Zoom option from the View drop-down menu or the Zoom button on the Power Bar.

Commands Review

	Mouse	**Keyboard**
Center text	Format, Line, Center	SHIFT + F7
Change line spacing	Format, Line, Spacing	Format, Line, Spacing
Change line spacing at the Power Bar	Position arrow pointer on Line Spacing button on Power Bar, click left mouse button, click on 1.0, 1.5, 2.0, or Other from the drop-down menu; or double -click on the Line Spacing button to display the Line Spacing dialog box	
Change justification	Format, Justification; or click on Justification button on the Power Bar; or click on a Justify button on the Format Toolbar	CTRL + L (Left) CTRL + R (Right) CTRL + E (Center) CTRL + J (Full)

Change Viewing Mode	View	View
Change the Zoom Ratio	View, Zoom; or click on the Zoom button on the Power Bar	View, Zoom

Reveal Codes Symbols Review

Beginning of centered text between margins	Hd Center on Marg
Beginning of centered text on a specific position	Hd Center on Pos
End of centered text	HRt

CHECK YOUR UNDERSTANDING

True/False: Circle the letter T if the statement is true; circle the letter F if the statement is false.

T F 1. If a line spacing code is inserted at the end of a document, the entire document would change to the new line spacing.

T F 2. The justification code is inserted in the document wherever the insertion point was located when the type of justification was changed.

T F 3. Line spacing can be changed to 2.3.

T F 4. With a left margin of 2 inches and a right margin of 0.5 inches, centered text would still print in the middle of the page.

T F 5. The Draft viewing mode is faster than the other two viewing modes.

T F 6. The shortcut command for full justification is Ctrl + F.

Completion: In the space provided at the right, indicate the correct term, command, or number.

1. This code appears in Reveal Codes before text centered on margins. ____________________
2. At this justification setting, all lines in a paragraph, including short lines, align at the left and right margins. ____________________
3. To view the names of toolbars other than the 6.1 WordPerfect Toolbar, position the arrow pointer on the Toolbar, then click this mouse button. ____________________
4. This is the default justification type. ____________________
5. To see the number after Ln Spacing in Reveal Codes, the insertion point must be on this side of the code. ____________________
6. Increase or decrease the size of the document display at this dialog box. ____________________

SKILL ASSESSMENTS

Assessment 1

1. At a clear editing window, key the memo shown in figure 4.10. Bold the text as shown. Use the Center command, Shift + F7, to center the days.
2. After keying the document, move the insertion point to the beginning of the document, then change justification to full.
3. Save the memo and name it c04sa01.
4. Print c04sa01.
5. Close c04sa01.

Figure 4.10

DATE: January 3, 1997

TO: All College Staff

FROM: James Vaira, Training and Education

SUBJECT: WORDPERFECT CLASSES

Tampa Community College employees will have the opportunity to complete training on WordPerfect for Windows, Version 6.1. This training is designed for current users of WordPerfect who want to become familiar with the changes in the new version.

The WordPerfect classes will be held in Room 200 from 9:00 a.m. to 11:00 a.m. on the following days:

Monday, January 20
Wednesday, January 22
Tuesday, January 27
Thursday, January 29

Room 200 contains fifteen computers; therefore, each training session is limited to fifteen employees. Preregistration is required. To register, please call Training and Education at extension 6552.

xx:c04sa01

Assessment 2

1. At a clear editing window, change the view to Draft mode.
2. Key the memo shown in figure 4.11 with the following specifications:
   a. After keying the headings, press Enter three times, then change the line spacing to 1.5.
   b. Bold and italicize text as indicated.
3. After keying the document, move the insertion point back to the beginning of the document, then change the justification to full.
4. Save the memo and name it c04sa02.
5. Print c04sa02.
6. Close c04sa02.

Figure 4.11

DATE: January 3, 1997

TO: Ronnie Teng

FROM: James Vaira

SUBJECT: WORDPERFECT CLASSES

A memo has been sent to all staff at Tampa Community College advertising the WordPerfect class. I am sure this memo will generate enough interest to fill the sessions. A few days before each session, I will send you a class roster. The *WordPerfect for Windows, Version 6.1* program has been installed on all the computers in **Room 200**. Textbooks and disks will be available for each participant. If you need anything further, call me at extension **6552**.

xx:c04sa02

Assessment 3

Note: In this exercise and other exercises in the text, you will be required to create business letters. Please refer to appendix C at the end of this text for the correct placement and spacing of a block-style business letter.

1. At a clear editing window, key the business letter shown in figure 4.12. Bold, center, and italicize the text as shown.
2. Save the letter and name it c04sa03.
3. Print c04sa03.
4. Close c04sa03.

Figure 4.12

January 15, 1997

Mr. Anthony Maloney
Tampa Community College
6100 Park Drive
Tampa, FL 33610

Dear Mr. Maloney:

The first meeting of the members of the **Outcomes Assessment Project (OAP)** was held yesterday, January 14. As you know from our conversations, the purpose of the project is to determine a process for assessing the success of graduating students as well as determining if college programs are meeting the needs of the business community. At the meeting, the members agreed that the top priority for the project is to develop a survey instrument.

With your expertise in project management, we feel you can provide us with needed information to begin the project. Our next meeting will be held at St. Petersburg College on the following day:

Wednesday, February 5, 1997
1:00 - 3:30 p.m.
Room 104

If you can attend this meeting, please call me at 555-9660, extension 1335, to determine specific topics. The input you can provide the project members will be invaluable.

Very truly yours,

Dawn Perez, Coordinator
Outcomes Assessment Project

xx:c04sa03

Changing Margins & Indents

5

Upon successful completion of chapter 5, you will be able to enhance single-page business memoranda and letters by changing the margins and indentations.

When you begin creating a document with WordPerfect, you have a default left margin of 1 inch and a right margin of 1 inch. When text is keyed and the insertion point reaches the right margin, WordPerfect automatically wraps text down to the next line.

A standard piece of paper is 8.5 inches wide. With the 1-inch default margins, WordPerfect begins the printed text 1 inch from the left edge of the paper and ends 1 inch from the right edge of the paper. Therefore, an actual printed text line is 6.5 inches.

Changing Margins

Even though the 6.5-inch default printed text line may be appropriate for many documents, there will be occasions when you need to shorten or lengthen margins. You can change the left and right margins at the Margins dialog box shown in figure 5.1 or with the Ruler Bar.

Changing Margins with the Margins Dialog Box

To change margins with the Margins dialog box, display the dialog box by choosing Format, then Margins. You can also display the Margins dialog box by clicking on the Page Margins button on the Format Toolbar. (If the Format Toolbar is not displayed, position the arrow pointer on the current Toolbar, click the right button on the mouse, then click on Format from the drop-down menu.)

The Margins dialog box contains options to change the left, right, top, and bottom margins. You will be working with top and bottom margins in chapter 12.

To change the left margin at the Margins dialog box, key the new left margin measurement. You can also position the arrow pointer on the up-pointing triangle beside the Left text box then click the left mouse button to increase the number or click on the down-pointing triangle to decrease the number.

Figure 5.1
Margins Dialog Box

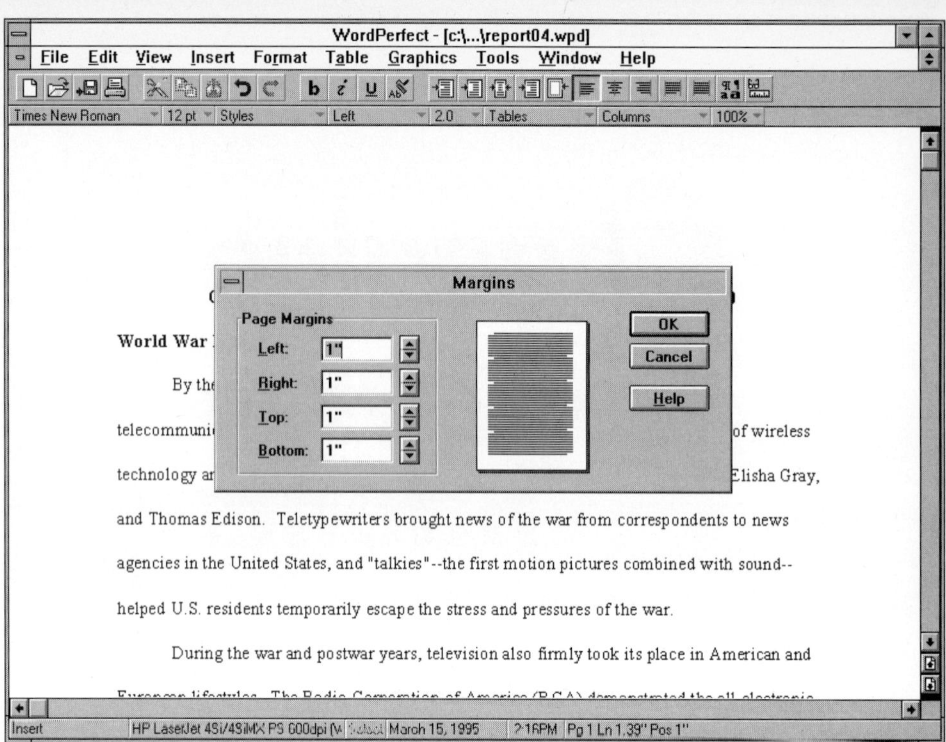

To change the right margin, choose Right, then key the new right margin measurement or click on the up- or down-pointing triangle.

Exercise 1 Changing Margins with the Format Menu

1. At a clear editing window, open para02. This document is located on your student data disk.
2. Save the document with Save As and name it c05ex01.
3. Change the left and right margins to 1.5 inches by completing the following steps:
    a. With the insertion point at the beginning of the document, choose Format, then Margins; or click on the Page Margins button on the Format Toolbar.
    b. At the Margins dialog box, key **1.5** in the Left text box.
    c. Choose Right. To do this with the mouse, select the 1" setting in the Right text box. To do this, position the I-beam pointer immediately left of the 1", hold down the left mouse button, drag the I-beam pointer to the right until 1" is selected, then release the mouse button. If you are using the keyboard, press Alt + R or press the Tab key.
    d. Key **1.5**.
    e. Choose OK or press Enter.
4. Save the document again with the same name (c05ex01).
5. Print c05ex01.
6. Close c05ex01.

When margin settings are changed, a code is inserted in the document at the beginning of the paragraph where the insertion point is positioned. As with justification codes, margin changes take effect from the location of the code to the end of the document or until a subsequent margin code is encountered. The codes can be seen in Reveal Codes. For example, if the left and right margins are changed to 1.5 inches, the codes Lft Mar: 1.5" and Rgt Mar: 1.5" display in Reveal Codes. While in Reveal Codes, you can display the Margins dialog box by positioning the arrow pointer on the margin code then double-clicking the left mouse button.

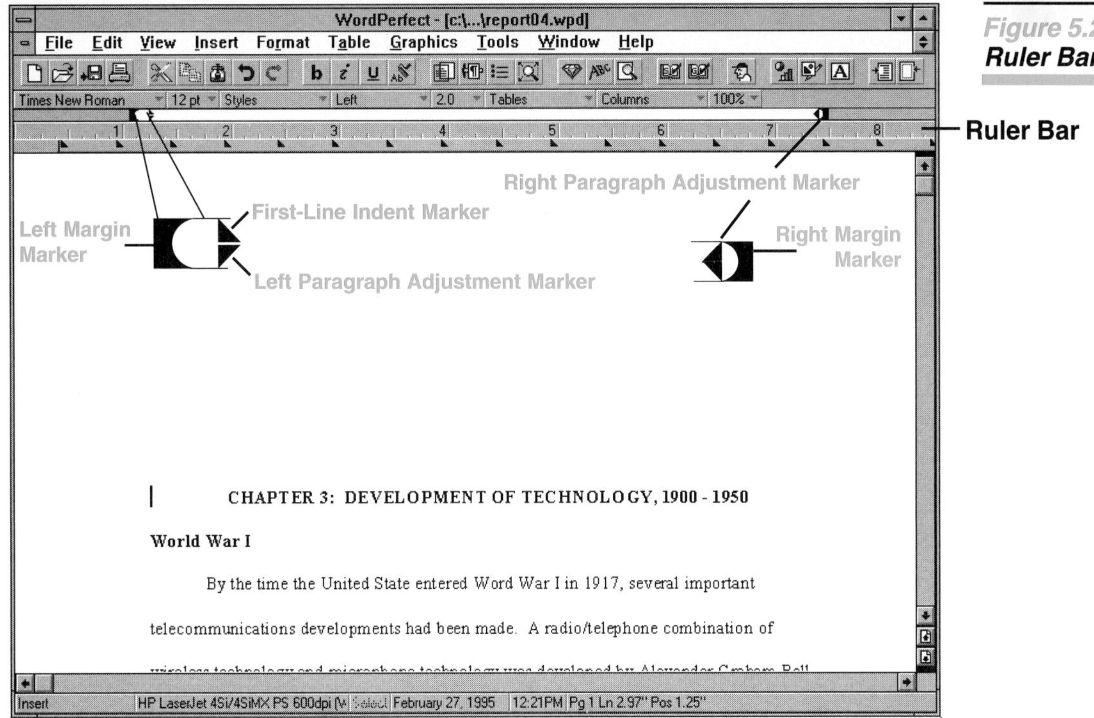

Figure 5.2
Ruler Bar

Changing Margins with the Ruler Bar

WordPerfect provides a Ruler Bar that, together with the mouse, can be used to change margins and tabs. To display the Ruler Bar, choose View, then Ruler Bar. The Ruler Bar displays below the Power Bar as shown in figure 5.2.

The left margin marker displays at the left side of the Ruler Bar above 1 inch as shown in figure 5.2. The right margin marker displays at the right side of the Ruler Bar above 7.5 inches. To change the margin in a document using the Ruler Bar, position the arrow pointer on the left or right margin marker, hold down the left mouse button, drag the marker to the desired location (refer to the Position measurement in the Status Bar), then release the mouse button.

When you position the arrow pointer on a margin marker, then hold down the left mouse button, the margin marker in the original position turns blue and a vertical dashed line appears on the screen. The vertical dashed line is called the ruler guide. Use the ruler guide to position the marker.

When changes are made to the location of the left margin or right margin marker on the Ruler Bar, a margin code is inserted in the document at the beginning of the paragraph where the insertion point is positioned.

Exercise 2 Changing Margins with the Ruler Bar

1. At a clear editing window, open para03. This document is located on your student data disk.
2. Save the document with Save As and name it c05ex02.
3. Change the left and right margins using the Ruler Bar by completing the following steps:
    a. Choose View, then Ruler Bar. (If your Ruler Bar is already displayed, skip this step.)
    b. Position the arrow pointer on the left margin marker.
    c. Hold down the left mouse button, drag the arrow pointer to the right until the Status Bar displays *Left margin: 1.25"*, then release the mouse button.
    d. Position the arrow pointer on the right margin marker.
    e. Hold down the left mouse button, drag the arrow pointer to the left until the Status Bar displays *Right margin: 7.25"*, then release the mouse button.
4. Save the document again with the same name (c05ex02).
5. Print c05ex02.
6. Close c05ex02.

Indenting Text

By now you are familiar with the word wrap feature of WordPerfect, which ends lines and wraps the insertion point to the next line. WordPerfect can force text to wrap to a tab setting instead of the left margin in three ways: (1) indenting all lines of a paragraph from the left margin, (2) indenting all lines of a paragraph on both sides (called double indenting), and (3) indenting all lines except the first line (called a hanging indent). To create these formats use shortcut keys, the Ruler Bar, the Paragraph option from the Format drop-down menu, options from the Paragraph Format dialog box, or buttons on the Format Toolbar.

Indenting the First Line of a Paragraph

When creating certain documents, you may want to indent the first line of a paragraph to identify where a new paragraph begins. You can indent the first line of a paragraph by pressing the Tab key or with an option from the Paragraph Format dialog box.

If you use the Tab key to indent the first line of a paragraph, the insertion point is indented to the first tab setting. By default, WordPerfect contains a tab setting every 0.5 inches. Therefore, if the insertion point is positioned at the left margin and you press the Tab key, the insertion point is moved 0.5 inches from the left margin. When you press the Tab key, the code [Left Tab] is inserted in the document and can be seen in Reveal Codes.

If you want to indent the first line of text to a specific measurement (other than tab settings) or you want the first line of all paragraphs indented, use the Paragraph Format dialog box shown in figure 5.3. Changes made at the Paragraph Format dialog box affect every paragraph in the document from the location of the code to the end of the document or until another indent code is encountered.

Figure 5.3
Paragraph Format Dialog Box

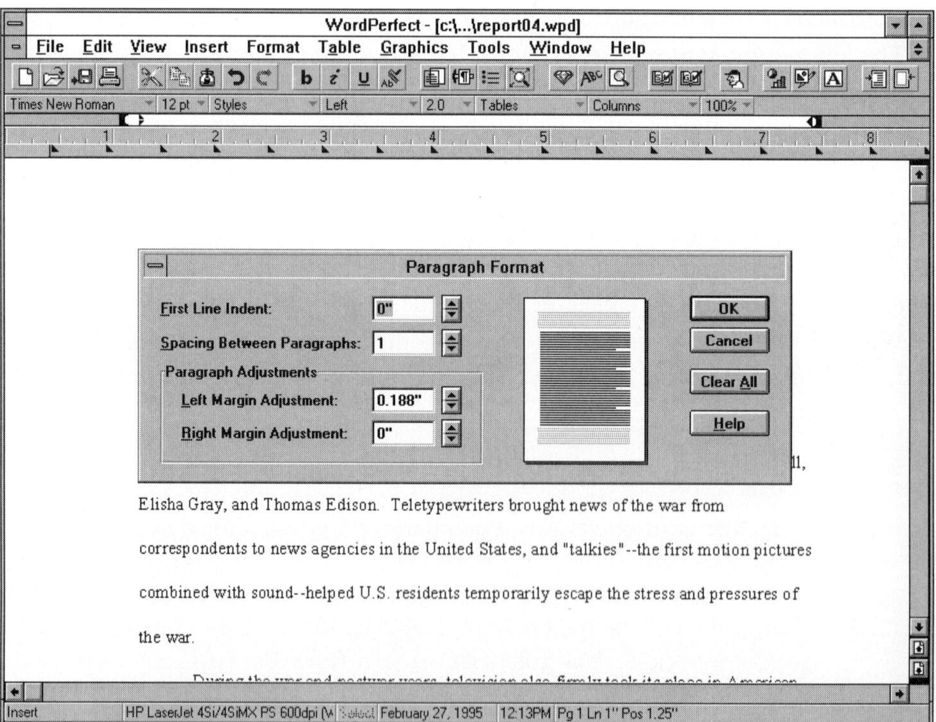

Exercise 3 Indenting a Line to a Specific Measurement

1. At a clear editing window, open para04. This document is located on your student data disk.
2. Save the document with Save As and name it c05ex03.
3. Indent the first line of each paragraph 0.25 inches by completing the following steps:
   a. Position the insertion point at the beginning of the first paragraph.
   b. Choose Format, Paragraph, then Format.
   c. At the Paragraph Format dialog box, key **0.25** in the First Line Indent text box.
   d. Choose OK or press Enter.
4. Save the document again with the same name (c05ex03).
5. Print c05ex03.
6. Close c05ex03.

Indenting Text from the Left Margin

Text in a paragraph can be indented to a tab setting or to a specific measurement from the left margin. When text is indented, all lines in the paragraph are indented to the tab or specific measurement. This is different than the Tab key, which only indents the first line of a paragraph.

To indent all text in a paragraph to a tab setting, use the shortcut command, F7, the Paragraph option from the Format drop-down menu, or the Indent button on the Format Toolbar. With any of these options, all text in a paragraph is indented to the first tab setting. Each of these methods inserts a [Hd Left Ind] code in the document at the beginning of the paragraph where the insertion point is positioned. This code can be seen in Reveal Codes.

The [Hd Left Ind] code only affects the paragraph where the insertion point is positioned. Text in the next paragraph will display at the left margin unless you repeat the steps for indenting.

Use the Paragraph Format dialog box shown in figure 5.3 to indent text in a paragraph and subsequent paragraphs to a specific measurement from the left margin.

The measurement entered at the Left Margin Adjustment option can be a whole number or a decimal number. You can also increase or decrease the Left Margin Adjustment or Right Margin Adjustment at the Paragraph Format dialog box by clicking on the up- or down-pointing triangle after the option.

The left paragraph adjustment marker on the Ruler Bar can be used to indent all lines of text in a paragraph and subsequent paragraphs to a specific measurement. The left paragraph adjustment marker is identified in figure 5.2. To indent all lines of text in a paragraph and subsequent paragraphs from the left margin using the Ruler Bar, position the tip of the arrow pointer on the left paragraph adjustment marker, hold down the left mouse button, drag the arrow pointer to the right to the desired location, then release the mouse button.

If you use the Paragraph Format dialog box or the Ruler Bar to indent text in a paragraph, each paragraph is indented from the location of the code to the end of the document or until another code is encountered.

To remove the indent from a paragraph, display Reveal Codes, position the insertion point immediately left of the Indent code, then press Delete. You can also drag a code out of Reveal Codes using the mouse.

Exercise 4 Indenting Paragraphs

1. At a clear editing window, open memo02. This document is located on your student data disk.
2. Save the document with Save As and name it c05ex04.
3. Indent the second paragraph in the document (containing the book title) to the first tab setting by completing the following steps:
   a. Position the insertion point at the beginning of the second paragraph.
   b. Press F7.
4. Indent the third paragraph in the document following steps similar to those in 3a and 3b.
5. Indent the fourth paragraph in the document to the first tab setting by completing the following steps:
   a. Position the insertion point at the beginning of the fourth paragraph.
   b. Choose Format, Paragraph, then Indent.
6. Indent the fifth paragraph in the document by completing steps similar to those in 5a and 5b.
7. Save the document again with the same name (c05ex04).
8. Print c05ex04.
9. Close c05ex04.

Exercise 5 Changing Margins and Line Spacing; Indenting Paragraphs

1. At a clear editing window, make the following changes:
   a. Change the left and right margins to 1.5 inches.
   b. Change the line spacing to double (2).
2. Key the document shown in figure 5.4. Center and bold the text as indicated. Indent the numbered paragraphs by completing the following steps:
   a. With the insertion point positioned at the left margin of the paragraph to be indented, key the number followed by the period (.).
   b. Press F7.
   c. Key the paragraph.
3. When the document is complete, save it and name it c05ex05.
4. Print c05ex05.
5. Close c05ex05.

Indenting Text from the Left and Right Margins

A paragraph that you want visually set off from other text in a document or a paragraph containing a quotation can be indented from the left as well as the right margin. Indenting from the left and right margins gives a paragraph a balanced look.

Text can be indented 0.5 inches from the left and right margins in three ways: (1) the shortcut command Ctrl + Shift + F7, (2) Format, Paragraph, then Double Indent, or (3) the Double Indent button on the Format Toolbar. By repeating an indent command, text is indented 1 inch from both margins. If text is indented from the left and right margins, a code displays in Reveal Codes.

With the Left Margin Adjustment and Right Margin Adjustment options from the Paragraph Format dialog box, you can indent text a specific amount from the left and right margins. The measurement does not have to be the same for each option.

The left paragraph adjustment marker and the right paragraph adjustment marker on the Ruler Bar can be used to indent all lines of text in a paragraph and subsequent paragraphs to a specific measurement. The markers are identified in figure 5.2.

Figure 5.4

POSITION ACCOUNTABILITIES

REGISTERED NURSE

1. Provides direct and indirect patient care using the nursing process to assess, plan, implement, and evaluate care given.
2. Analyzes the patient's condition and reports changes to the appropriate health care provider.
3. Observes patients for signs and symptoms, collects data on patients, reports and documents results.
4. Evaluates patient response to plan of care and modifies plan. Communicates modifications to other health care professionals.
5. Initiates and participates in patient care conferences.
6. Performs documentation that is timely, accurate, and complete.
7. Documents care that is reflective of patient needs, nursing action, and patient response.

If you use the Paragraph Format dialog box or the Ruler Bar to indent text in a paragraph, each paragraph is indented from the location of the code to the end of the document or until another code is encountered.

Exercise 6 Indenting Text from Both Margins

1. At a clear editing window, open quote. This document is located on your student data disk.
2. Save the document with Save As and name it c05ex06.
3. Indent the second paragraph in the document to the first tab setting from the left and right margins by completing the following steps:
   a. Position the insertion point at the beginning of the second paragraph.
   b. Press Ctrl + Shift + F7.
4. Indent the fourth paragraph in the document to the first tab setting from the left and right margins by completing the following steps:
   a. Position the insertion point at the beginning of the fourth paragraph.
   b. Click on the Double Indent button on the Format Toolbar.
5. Save the document again with the same name (c05ex06).
6. Print c05ex06.
7. Close c05ex06.

Exercise 7 Indenting Paragraphs and Returning to the Default

1. At a clear editing window, open quote.
2. Save the document with Save As and name it c05ex07.
3. Indent the second paragraph 0.75 inches from the left and right margins by completing the following steps:
   a. Position the insertion point at the beginning of the second paragraph.
   b. Choose Format, Paragraph, then Format.
   c. At the Paragraph Format dialog box, choose Left Margin Adjustment.
   d. Key **0.75**.
   e. Choose Right Margin Adjustment.
   f. Key **0.75**.
   g. Choose OK or press Enter.
4. Return the left and right margin adjustments to 0" for the third paragraph by completing the following steps:
   a. Position the insertion point at the beginning of the third paragraph.
   b. Choose Format, Paragraph, then Format.
   c. At the Paragraph Format dialog box, choose Left Margin Adjustment.
   d. Key **0**.
   e. Choose Right Margin Adjustment.
   f. Key **0**.
   g. Choose OK or press Enter.
5. Indent the fourth paragraph 0.75 inches from the left and right margins using the Ruler Bar by completing the following steps:
   a. Choose View, then Ruler Bar. (If the Ruler Bar is already displayed, skip this step.)
   b. Position the insertion point at the beginning of the fourth paragraph.
   c. Position the tip of the arrow pointer on the left paragraph adjustment marker.
   d. Hold down the left mouse button.
   e. Drag the arrow pointer to the right until the Status Bar displays *Left Margin Adjust: 1.75"*, then release the mouse button.
   f. Position the tip of the arrow pointer on the right paragraph adjustment marker.
   g. Hold down the left mouse button.
   h. Drag the arrow pointer to the left until the Status Bar displays *Right Margin Adjust 6.75"*, then release the mouse button.
6. Save the document again with the same name (c05ex07).
7. Print c05ex07.
8. Close c05ex07.

Creating Hanging Indent Paragraphs

With WordPerfect's Hanging Indent feature, you can create paragraphs such as bibliographic entries where the first line begins at the left margin, but second and subsequent lines in the paragraph are indented to the first tab setting. Figure 5.5 shows an example of a hanging indent paragraph.

Figure 5.5
Hanging Indent Paragraph

This is an example of a hanging indent paragraph. Create a hanging indent paragraph with the shortcut command Ctrl + F7, the Paragraph option from the Format drop-down menu, or options from the Paragraph Format dialog box.

To create a hanging indent paragraph with the shortcut command, position the insertion point at the beginning of the paragraph to be indented, then press Ctrl + F7. If you are using the Format Toolbar, position the insertion point at the beginning of the paragraph, then click on the Hanging Indent button. You can also create a hanging indent paragraph by choosing Format, Paragraph, then Hanging Indent.

Exercise 8 Creating Hanging Indents on Single Paragraphs

1. At a clear editing window, open biblio01. This document is located on your student data disk.
2. Save the document with Save As and name it c05ex08.
3. Hang indent the first paragraph by completing the following steps:
   a. Position the insertion point at the beginning of the first paragraph.
   b. Press Ctrl + F7; or click on the Hanging Indent button on the Format Toolbar.
4. Indent the remaining paragraphs in the document by completing steps similar to those in step 3.
5. Save the document again with the same name (c05ex08).
6. Print c05ex08.
7. Close c05ex08.

When you create a hanging indent paragraph with the shortcut command, the Paragraph option from the Format drop-down menu, or the Hanging Indent button on the Format Toolbar, the codes [Hd Left Ind] and [Hd Back Tab] are inserted in the document at the location of the insertion point.

At the Paragraph Format dialog box, the First Line Indent and Left Margin Adjustment options can be used to create a hanging indent paragraph. To create a hanging indent paragraph using the Paragraph Format dialog box, complete Exercise 9. If you use the Paragraph Format dialog box or the Ruler Bar to indent text in a paragraph, each paragraph is indented from the location of the code to the end of the document or until another code is encountered.

Exercise 9 Using the Hanging Indent for All Paragraphs

1. At a clear editing window, open biblio01.
2. Save the document with Save As and name it c05ex09.
3. Hang indent all paragraphs in the document by completing the following steps:
   a. Position the insertion point at the beginning of the first paragraph.
   b. Choose Format, Paragraph, then Format.
   c. At the Paragraph Format dialog box, key **-0.5** in the First Line Indent text box. (If you are using the mouse, you can click on the down-pointing triangle to the right of the First Line Indent text box until -0.500" displays.)
   d. Choose Left Margin Adjustment, then key **0.5**. (If you are using the mouse, you can click on the up-pointing triangle to the right of the Left Margin Adjustment text box until 0.500" displays.)
   e. Choose OK or press Enter.
4. Save the document again with the same name (c05ex09).
5. Print c05ex09.
6. Close c05ex09.

CHAPTER SUMMARY

- The 1-inch default left and right margins can be changed at the Margins dialog box. Margins can be set by inches as well as tenths and hundredths of inches.
- When margin settings are changed, codes like this [Lft Mar: 2"] and [Rgt Mar: 2"] display in Reveal Codes. Margin codes will always appear at the beginning of the paragraph in which the insertion point was located when the margins were changed.

- To indent the first line of a paragraph by a specific measurement (other than tab settings), use the Paragraph Format dialog box or the first-line indent marker on the Ruler Bar.
- The Indent feature will indent text from the left margin to the first tab setting or to a specific measurement.
- You can use the Indent feature to create numbered, indented paragraphs.
- The Double Indent feature will indent text from both the left and right sides of the paragraph. The Double Indent code looks like this [Hd Left Right Ind].
- The first line of a hanging indent paragraph begins at the left margin and the rest of the paragraph is indented. The codes [Hd Left Ind] and [Hd Back Tab] are inserted in the document at the location of the insertion point.

Commands Review

	Mouse	Keyboard
Change margins	Format, Margins; click on Page Margins on the Format Toolbar	Format, Margins
Display the Ruler Bar	View, Ruler Bar	View, Ruler Bar
Display Paragraph Format dialog box	Format, Paragraph, Format	Format, Paragraph, Format
Indent (tab setting)	Format, Paragraph, Indent; or click on Indent button on the Format Toolbar	F7
Double Indent (tab setting)	Format, Paragraph, Double Indent; or click on Double Indent button on the Format Toolbar	CTRL + SHIFT + F7
Hanging Indent (tab setting)	Format, Paragraph, Hanging Indent; or click on the Hanging Indent button on the Format Toolbar	CTRL + F7

CHECK YOUR UNDERSTANDING

Matching: In the space provided at the right, indicate the corresponding letter of each feature described.

A. Indenting first line of a paragraph
B. Indenting text from left margin
C. Indenting text from both margins
D. Hanging indent paragraph

1. Could be used for creating a bibliography. __________
2. Used when inserting long quotations in a document. __________
3. Used when creating numbered paragraphs. __________
4. Used to set off one paragraph from other text in the document. __________
5. Can be used instead of the Tab key. __________

Completion: In the space provided at the right, indicate the correct term, command, or number.

1. The width in inches of a standard piece of paper. ______________
2. The default left and right margin settings. ______________
3. The width of the default line for text. ______________
4. The dialog box where the margins can be changed. ______________

5. If, in Reveal Codes, the reveal codes insertion point was positioned immediately left of a 1.5" right margin code, the code would look like this. ____________________
6. A margin code would be found here in relation to a paragraph. ____________________
7. The keyboard command to indent a paragraph from the left margin. ____________________
8. The keyboard command to indent a paragraph from the left and right margins. ____________________
9. The keyboard command that will create a hanging indent paragraph. ____________________
10. The codes inserted in the document when you create a hanging indent paragraph. ____________________

SKILL ASSESSMENTS

Assessment 1

1. At a clear editing window, change the left and right margins to 1.25 inches, then key the document shown in figure 5.6. Bold and center the text as indicated. Indent the text after each number.
2. After keying the document, move the insertion point back to the beginning of the document, then change the justification to full.
3. Save the document and name it c05sa01.
4. Print c05sa01.
5. Close c05sa01.

Figure 5.6

EXPANSION AND ENHANCEMENT

OF LOCAL AND WIDE AREA NETWORKS

The foundation of the national telecommunications network is the publicly owned telephone network. This network, which was originally designed, installed, and operated by AT&T and local independent telephone companies to provide traditional voice messaging services, now offers a multitude of information services, including:

1. **Electronic Mail/Message Systems.** Individuals have an electronic mailbox in a computer that is accessed via a computer terminal such as a microcomputer.

2. **Voice Mail.** The primary difference in electronic mail/message systems and voice mail is the input/output device, which is a telephone rather than a computer.

3. **Value Added Networks.** These are special services provided by telecommunications companies in addition to transferring information, such as storing information for delivery at a later time, providing security features so that no one is able to intercept the information, and selecting alternative routes for transmitting that help reduce costs.

4. **Expanded Voice Services.** Examples include voice mail, voice responses to answer phones and direct callers to specific departments, and systems that

provide callers with an electronic voice response to questions such as weather information, bank balances, and time of day.

5. **Database Services.** Examples include airline reservation systems so that individuals can reserve seats on flights.

6. **Data Networking.** This includes the connection of computers within a complex, such as a school, or connecting computers at distant sites, such as two schools located in separate areas, for the purpose of exchanging data.

Assessment 2

1. At a clear editing window, make the following changes:
   a. Change the view to Draft mode.
   b. Change the left and right margins to 1.5 inches.
2. Key the memo shown in figure 5.7. Double indent the second paragraph.
3. Save the memo and name it c05sa02.
4. Print c05sa02.
5. Close c05sa02.

Figure 5.7

DATE: December 4, 1996

TO: Diane Tsu, Public Relations Department

FROM: Lee Glidden, CIS Department

SUBJECT: TELECOMMUNICATIONS COURSE

The telecommunications course, CIS 230, was a great success this quarter. The course has been included for the spring quarter. Please include the following description for the course in the spring schedule:

> The fundamental ideas presented in CIS 230 will enable a student to appreciate what telecommunications is and what it encompasses; understand basic telecommunications terminology; know the business applications of telecommunications technology; understand the present status of the technology; understand events that have brought us to the present; and consider trends that will affect future telecommunications.

I would like to see the course advertised not only in the spring schedule but also through the school newspaper. Would you help me write an advertisement for the newspaper? Please let me know. You can contact me at extension 3320.

xx:c05sa02

Assessment 3

1. At a clear editing window, make the following changes:
   a. Change the left and right margins to 1.5 inches.
   b. Change the line spacing to double (2).
2. Key the document shown in figure 5.8. Bold, center, and italicize text as indicated. Hang indent the paragraphs as shown.
3. After keying the document, move the insertion point back to the beginning of the document, then change the justification to full.
4. Save the document and name it c05sa03.
5. Print c05sa03.
6. Close c05sa03.

Figure 5.8

BIBLIOGRAPHY

Brickman, Andrew C. (1992). "Networking Computers." *Power Computing,* (pp. 10-14). Omaha, NE: Myers-Townsend Publishing Company.

Daughtery, Megan A. (1994). "Managing a Local Area Network." *Computer Technologies,* (pp. 19-23). Jacksonville, FL: Macadam Publishers.

Layug, Angela M. (1992). "Wireless LANs." *Business Offices of the 90s,* (pp. 31-45). Denver, CO: Mile-High Publishing International.

Owen, Kerry H. (1995). "Interconnecting Internal LANs." *Network Management,* (pp. 22-31). Fairbanks, AK: Marsh & Monroe Press.

Important: By now you have completed several chapters' worth of exercises, and your student data disk may be filling up. To ensure that you have adequate disk space to continue saving files, you should make a habit of regularly deleting old documents. For example, after you have completed all the exercises for one chapter and have received the graded assignments from your instructor, you should delete the files for those assignments. To delete a file, follow these steps:

1. Display the Open File dialog box.
2. Select the document to be deleted.
3. Choose File Options, then Delete. (You can also use the Delete key.)
4. At the Delete File dialog box, make sure the correct document name is displayed, then choose Delete.
5. Cancel the Open File dialog box.

Follow steps 2-4 for each document you want to delete. Remember to wait until your instructor has graded the exercises.

Using Writing Tools 6

Upon successful completion of chapter 6, you will be able to proof all types of business documents with Spell Checker and Thesaurus tools, and improve the grammar of written documents with Grammatik.

WordPerfect includes writing tools to help create a thoughtful and well-written document. One of these writing tools, Spell Checker, finds misspelled words and offers replacement words. It also finds duplicate words and irregular capitalizations. Another tool, Thesaurus, provides a list of synonyms and antonyms for words. The Grammatik® program checks a document for correct grammar and punctuation.

Using Spell Checker

Spell Checker consists of two dictionaries—a main dictionary (consisting of over 100,000 words) and a supplementary dictionary. In addition to these two dictionaries, a document-specific supplementary dictionary is automatically attached to a document. The words you choose to skip in the current document during a spelling check are added to the document-specific dictionary.

When a spell check is run, Spell Checker first checks the words in the document with words in the supplementary dictionary. If a match is not found, then Spell Checker looks for the word in the main dictionary. Additional supplementary dictionaries can be purchased and used with Spell Checker for specific industries (medical, legal, scientific, etc.).

What Spell Checker Can Do

Spell Checker operates by comparing words in a document with words in the supplementary dictionary and the main dictionary. If there is a match, Spell Checker moves on. If there is no match for the word, Spell Checker will stop and highlight a word for correction if it fits one of the following situations:

- a misspelled word if the misspelling does not match another word that exists in the dictionaries
- typographical errors such as transposed letters
- double word occurrences (such as *and and*)
- irregular capitalization
- some proper names
- jargon and some technical terms

Spell Checker may not stop at all proper names. For example, Spell Checker would assume the first name *Robin* is spelled correctly and pass over it because Robin would appear in the dictionary as a type of bird.

What Spell Checker Cannot Do

A small number of words in the main dictionary are proper names. You will find that many proper names will not appear in this dictionary. Spell Checker will not find a match for these proper names and will highlight the words for correction.

Spell Checker will not identify words that are spelled correctly but used incorrectly. For example, if you want the word *from* in a document but you key it as *form*, it will be passed over. Spell Checker matches *form* with a word in its dictionary and assumes it is spelled correctly.

Spell Checker cannot check grammar usage. For example, if the wrong verb tense is used in a document but the verb is spelled correctly, Spell Checker passes over the verb.

Spell Checker does not eliminate the need for proofreading, but it does provide assistance in editing a document.

Using the Spell Checker Dialog Box

Before operating Spell Checker, save the document currently displayed in the editing window or open a document. To begin Spell Checker choose Tools, then Spell Check; or click on the Spell Check button on the Toolbar (the twenty-first button from the left). The Spell Checker dialog box, shown in figure 6.1, displays on the screen.

When Spell Checker discovers a word in the document that does not match a word in the main or supplementary dictionaries, the word is highlighted and suggestions for spelling are inserted in the Suggestions list box in the Spell Checker dialog box. In addition, the Start button becomes the Replace button during spell checking.

Figure 6.1
Spell Checker Dialog Box

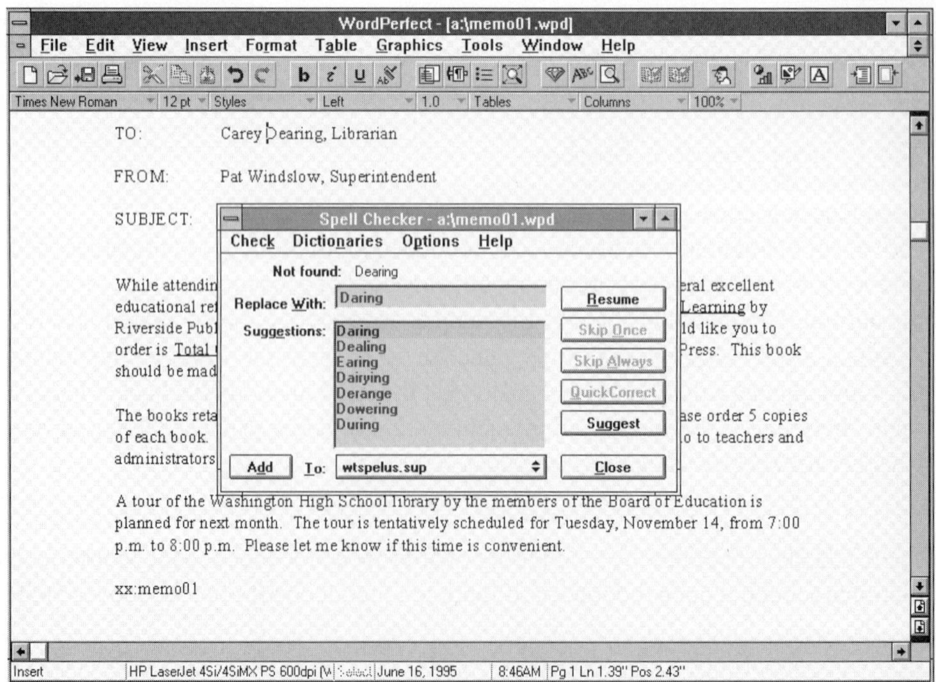

Replace the highlighted word, leave it as written, or edit the highlighted word by choosing one of the command buttons at the right side of the Spell Checker dialog box. The command buttons are explained in figure 6.2.

Figure 6.2
Spell Checker Command Buttons

Replace: When Spell Checker encounters a word that is not in the main or supplementary dictionaries, suggestions for correct spelling are inserted in the Suggestions list box with the first suggestion displayed in the Replace With text box. To replace the highlighted word in the document with one of the suggestions using the mouse, double-click on the correct spelling. If you are using the keyboard, use the arrow keys to select the correct spelling, then press Enter (or press Alt + R for Replace). After correcting a word, Spell Checker automatically corrects all occurrences of the word in the document.

Skip Once and Skip Always: In some situations, Spell Checker will highlight a word for correction that you want to leave alone. Choose Skip Once to tell Spell Checker to skip that occurrence of the word but highlight occurrences in other locations in the document. If the word appears in other locations in the document and you want it skipped in those locations also, choose Skip Always.

QuickCorrect: In chapter 1, you learned that WordPerfect includes a QuickCorrect feature that automatically changes certain words in a document. For example, if you key *teh*, QuickCorrect changes it to *the*. You can add misspelled words and their correct spelling in QuickCorrect. To do this, make sure the proper spelling is inserted in the Replace With text box, then choose QuickCorrect.

Suggest: Spell Checker follows certain rules when looking for possible suggestions for correct spelling. Spell Checker will transpose the characters, make substitutions, and make additions or deletions. The possible suggestions are displayed in the Suggestions list box. Choose Suggest to display additional words or phrases, if there are any.

Add: When WordPerfect is installed, a supplementary dictionary is included. Choose Add to add the highlighted word into Spell Checker's supplementary dictionary.

Close: Choose the Close button to remove the Spell Checker dialog box from the screen.

Editing during a Spell Check

When spell checking a document, you can temporarily leave the Spell Checker dialog box, make corrections in the document, then resume spell checking. For example, suppose while spell checking you notice a sentence that you want to change. To do this move the I-beam pointer to the location in the sentence where the change is to occur, then click the left mouse button. Make changes to the sentence, then choose the Resume command button (previously the Start command button) to resume spell checking the document.

Exercise 1 Completing a Spelling Check

1. At a clear editing window, open memo03. This document is located on your student data disk.
2. Save the memo with Save As and name it c06ex01.
3. Complete a spelling check by completing the following steps:
   a. Choose Tools, then Spell Check; or click on the Spell Check button on the Toolbar.
   b. Spell Checker highlights the word *Mai*. This word is spelled properly (it is a proper name) so choose Skip Always. To do this with the mouse, position the

arrow pointer on Skip Always, then click the left mouse button. If you are using the keyboard, press Alt + A for Skip Always.

c. Spell Checker highlights the word *Ayala*. This name is spelled properly so choose Skip Always.

d. Spell Checker highlights the word *idenified*. The proper spelling is displayed in the Replace With text box so choose Replace. To do this with the mouse, position the arrow pointer on Replace, then click the left mouse button. (You can also double-click on the correct spelling in the Suggestions list box.) If you are using the keyboard, press Alt + R.

e. Spell Checker highlights the word *reqiured*. The proper spelling is displayed in the Replace With text box so choose Replace.

f. Spell Checker highlights *departmnts*. The proper spelling is displayed in the Replace With text box so choose Replace.

g. Spell Checker highlights the word *hte*. Select the correct spelling, *the*, then choose Replace. To do this with the mouse, position the arrow pointer on *the* in the Suggestions list box, click the left mouse button, then click on the Replace button. If you are using the keyboard, press the down arrow key until *the* is selected, then press Alt + R.

h. Spell Checker highlights the word *tmies*. Choose Replace.

i. Spell Checker highlights the word *ncesary* and gives no suggestions. Correct *ncesary* in the Replace With text box by keying the letters **e** and **s** in the appropriate locations in the word.

j. Choose Replace.

k. Spell Checker highlights *xx:memo03*. Choose Skip Once.

l. At the *Spell Check completed. Close Spell Checker?* question, choose Yes or press Enter.

4. Save the memo with the same name (c06ex01).
5. Print c06ex01.
6. Close c06ex01.

Using Thesaurus

WordPerfect offers a Thesaurus program that can be used to find synonyms and antonyms for words. Synonyms are words that have the same or nearly the same meaning. Antonyms are words with opposite meanings. With Thesaurus, the clarity of business communications can be improved.

To use Thesaurus, open the document containing the word for which you want to find synonyms and/or antonyms. Position the insertion point next to any character in the word. Choose Tools, then Thesaurus.

Figure 6.3 displays the Thesaurus dialog box with synonyms and antonyms displayed for the word *document*. Alternatives in Thesaurus are arranged into three categories—headwords, references, and subgroups. A *headword* is a word that can be looked up in Thesaurus.

Words under a headword are called *references* and display in the categories of nouns, verbs, adjectives or adverbs, and antonyms. When the Thesaurus dialog box is displayed, nouns are displayed under the abbreviation (*n*); verbs are displayed below the abbreviation (*v*); and adjectives and adverbs are displayed under the abbreviation (*a*). Antonyms are displayed under the abbreviation (*ant*).

References can be divided into *subgroups*. These subgroups correspond to different meanings of the headword and appear under headwords.

Using Scroll Boxes

The Thesaurus dialog box contains three scroll boxes. In figure 6.3 the first scroll box contains a list of synonyms and antonyms for *document*. You cannot, however, see the entire list. To see the remaining list using the mouse, move the arrow pointer to the down scroll arrow and hold down the left button. To move back through the list, move the arrow pointer to the up scroll arrow and hold down the left button.

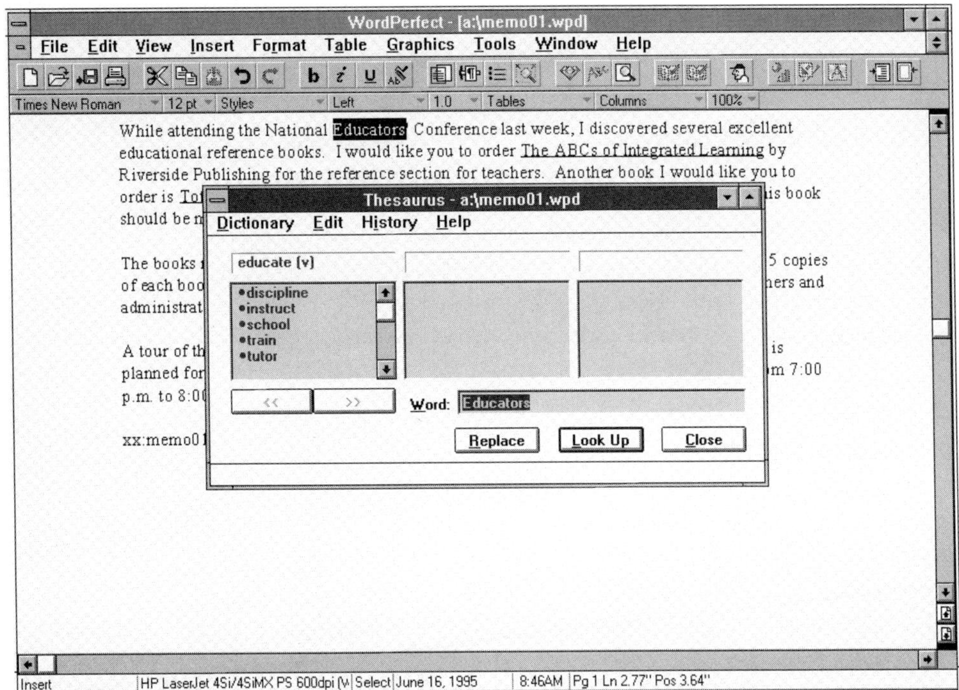

Figure 6.3
Thesaurus Dialog Box

If the list of synonyms displays in more than one scroll box, move the insertion point to the right by clicking on the right-pointing arrow below the scroll boxes at the left side of the dialog box. To move the insertion point to the scroll box on the left, click on the left-pointing arrow below the scroll boxes at the left side of the dialog box.

To view the list using the keyboard, press Alt + L (for Look Up). This moves the insertion point to the scroll box and selects the first word. Press the down arrow key on the keyboard to see the remaining words. Press the up arrow key on the keyboard to move back through the list.

If the list of synonyms displays in more than one scroll box, move the insertion point to the scroll box on the right by pressing the right arrow on the keyboard. Press the left arrow key on the keyboard to move the insertion point to the scroll box on the left.

Using Command Buttons

The Thesaurus dialog box contains three command buttons that display at the bottom of the box. Figure 6.4 explains the Thesaurus command buttons.

Figure 6.4
Thesaurus Command Buttons

Look Up: When Thesaurus displays synonyms and antonyms, certain words in the list are preceded by a bullet (•). This indicates that the word has its own list of synonyms and antonyms. By choosing words with bullets, you can continue looking for a specific synonym or antonym for a word.

The Thesaurus dialog box contains only three scroll boxes. You can, however, look up more than three words. If you look up more than three words, click on the left or right scroll arrow buttons in the lower left corner of the dialog box, or press the left and right arrows on the keyboard to scroll back and forth between scroll boxes.

Replace: If you find a synonym or antonym for a word, you can replace the word in the document with the new word with the Replace command button.

Close: When you replace a word, the Thesaurus dialog box is automatically closed. However, if you look up synonyms and antonyms for a word and then decide not to use any, close the Thesaurus dialog box by choosing Close.

Exercise 2 Using Thesaurus

1. At a clear editing window, complete the following steps:
   a. Key **lugubrious**.
   b. Choose Tools, then Thesaurus.
   c. After viewing the synonyms and antonyms for *lugubrious*, choose Word.
   d. Key **nascent**, then press Enter.
   e. After viewing the synonyms and antonyms for *nascent*, choose Word.
   f. Key **propitious**, then press Enter.
   g. After viewing the synonyms and antonyms for *propitious*, choose Word.
   h. Key **imminent**, then press Enter.
   i. Remove the Thesaurus dialog box from the editing window by choosing Close.
2. Close the document without saving it.

Exercise 3 Replacing Words with Thesaurus

1. At a clear editing window, open memo02.
2. Save the memo with Save As and name it c06ex03.
3. Change the word *several* in the first paragraph to *numerous* using Thesaurus by completing the following steps:
   a. Position the insertion point in the word *several.*
   b. Display the Thesaurus dialog box.
   c. Select *numerous*, then choose Replace.
4. Follow similar steps to make the following changes using Thesaurus:
   a. Change *afford* in the first paragraph to *buy.*
   b. Change the first occurrence of *purchase* in the last paragraph to *buy.*
5. Save the memo with the same name (c06ex03).
6. Print c06ex03.
7. Close c06ex03.

Displaying Document Information

You can display information about the current open document such as the number of characters, words, lines, sentences, and pages with the Document Info option from the File drop-down menu. When you choose File, then Document Info, WordPerfect displays information about the document such as the number of words, lines, sentences, paragraphs, and pages in the document as well as the average word length, the average number of words per sentence, and maximum words per sentence.

Figure 6.5 shows document information for the memo01 document.

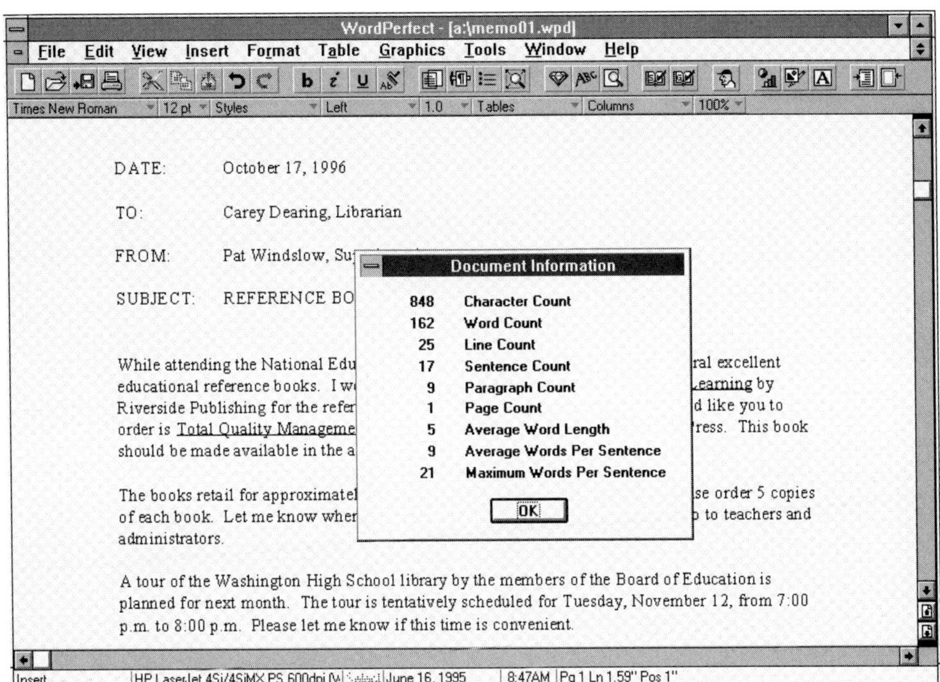

Figure 6.5
Document Information Dialog Box

Exercise 4 Displaying Document Information

1. At a clear editing window, open letter01.
2. Display information about this document by completing the following steps:
   a. Choose File, then Document Info.
   b. At the Document Information dialog box, read the information about letter01.
   c. Choose OK or press Enter.
3. Close letter01.
4. At a clear editing window, open report01.
5. Display information about the report by completing steps 2a through 2c.
6. Close report01.

Using Grammatik

WordPerfect for Windows version 6.1 includes a grammar-checking program called Grammatik (pronounced Gram·mat'·ik). The Grammatik program searches a document for correct grammar, style, punctuation, and word usage. Like Spell Checker, Grammatik does not find every error in a document and may stop at correct phrases. Grammatik can help you create a well-written document but does not replace the need for human proofreading.

To check a document with Grammatik, you would open the document to be checked, then choose Tools, then Grammatik or click on the Grammatik button on the Toolbar (twenty-second button from the left). Grammatik automatically begins checking the document and stops at the first error. When Grammatik highlights an error, you can correct the error or skip the error. When

Grammatik is done checking the document, a dialog box displays with the message *"Grammar check completed. Close Grammatik?"*. At this message, choose Yes.

When you are done checking the document with Grammatik, the open document is displayed on the screen. The changes made during the check are inserted in the document. You can save the document with the same name, overwriting the original; or, you can save the document with a different name, retaining the original.

When you choose Tools, then Grammatik or click on the Grammatik button on the Toolbar, Grammatik begins checking the document. When an error is encountered, Grammatik highlights the error and displays a Grammatik dialog box like the one shown in figure 6.6.

Figure 6.6
Grammatik Dialog Box

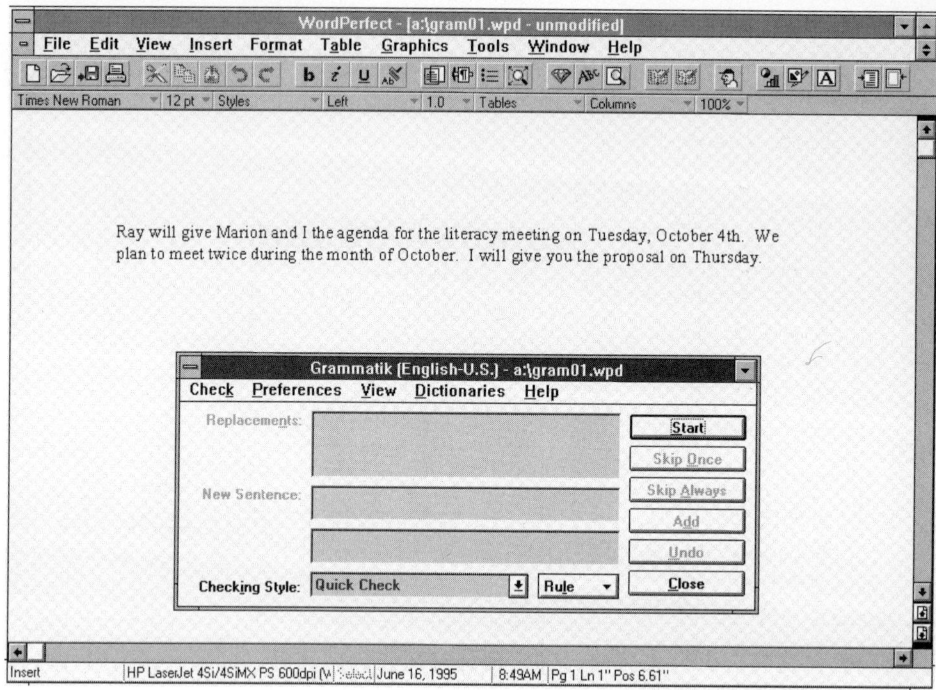

When Grammatik highlights an error, possible replacement words may be inserted in the Replacements section of the Grammatik dialog box. These replacement words can be used to quickly correct the error.

In addition to the Replacements list box, Grammatik may also rewrite the incorrect sentence and place the corrected sentence in the New Sentence text box. If the rewritten sentence is correct, choose Replace and Grammatik will replace the original sentence with the rewritten sentence, then continue searching for errors. If you want Grammatik to use a different word in the Replacements list box when writing the sentence, select the desired word. Grammatik then rewrites the sentence using the selected word and displays it in the New Sentence text box.

When Grammatik highlights an error in a document, the rule class for the error is displayed in the Grammatik dialog box below the New Sentence text box.

At the bottom of the Grammatik dialog box, the Checking Style text box displays the current checking style. The default checking style is *Quick Check*. Later in this chapter, you will learn how to change the checking style.

Making Replacements

When Grammatik detects an error, it tries to include replacement words in the Replacements list box and displays a rewritten sentence in the New Sentence text box. If you want to replace the selected sentence with the suggested sentence, choose Replace. If there is more than one replacement option in the Replacements list box, select the desired replacement option, then choose Replace.

If you want to leave the text as written and not make a correction, choose Skip Once or Skip Always. If you choose Skip Once, Grammatik will ignore the highlighted phrase for the current occurrence only. If you choose Skip Always, Grammatik will ignore the highlighted phrase for the rest of the document.

If Grammatik stops at an error and does not offer a replacement or the offered replacements are not acceptable, you can edit the error. To do this, position the arrow pointer in the editing window at the location of the error, then click the left mouse button. Make necessary corrections, then choose Resume to continue grammar checking.

Grammatik contains its own dictionary of words and will check documents for spelling. The Grammatik dictionary is different than the Speller dictionary. If Grammatik selects a word that is spelled correctly, you can choose Add to add the selected word to the Grammatik dictionary.

Exercise 5 Checking for Errors with Grammatik

1. At a clear editing window, open memo08.
2. Save the document with Save As and name it c06ex05.
3. Complete a check with Grammatik by completing the following steps:
    a. Choose Tools, then Grammatik; or click on the Grammatik button on the Toolbar.
    b. Grammatik highlights *Vanderburg*. This proper name is spelled correctly so choose Skip Always.
    c. Grammatik highlights *Petersen*. This proper name is spelled correctly so choose Skip Always.
    d. Grammatik highlights *likes* and displays the rule class **Incorrect Verb Form** with the advice, **Words like *would* require that the following verb be in the base verb form**. The word *like* is displayed in the Replacements list box, so choose Replace.
    e. Grammatik highlights *a computer literacy programs* and displays the rule class **Noun Phrase** with the advice, ***A* is not usually used with a plural noun such as *programs*.** Grammatik suggests two possible corrections in the Replacements list box. Select *a computer literacy program* in the Replacements list box, then choose Replace.
    f. Grammatik highlights *compare* and displays the rule class **Subject-Verb Agreement** with the advice, **If *it* is the subject of the verb *compare*, try making them agree in number**. The word *compares* is displayed in the Replacements list box, so choose Replace.
    g. At the Grammar check completed. *Close Grammatik?* question, choose Yes.
4. Save the document again with the same name (c06ex05).
5. Print c06ex05.
6. Close c06ex05.

Changing Checking Style

At the bottom of the Grammatik dialog box, the Checking Style option has a default setting of *Quick Check*. Grammatik provides a number of checking styles for various documents. Some checking styles use all Grammatik rules of grammar when checking a document. Other checking styles are less formal and use fewer grammar rules when checking a document.

To change the checking style using the mouse, position the tip of the arrow pointer on the down-pointing arrow to the right of the Checking Style text box, then click the left mouse button. This causes a pop-up menu to display as shown in figure 6.7. To choose a style, click on the desired style.

Figure 6.7
Checking Style Pop-Up Menu

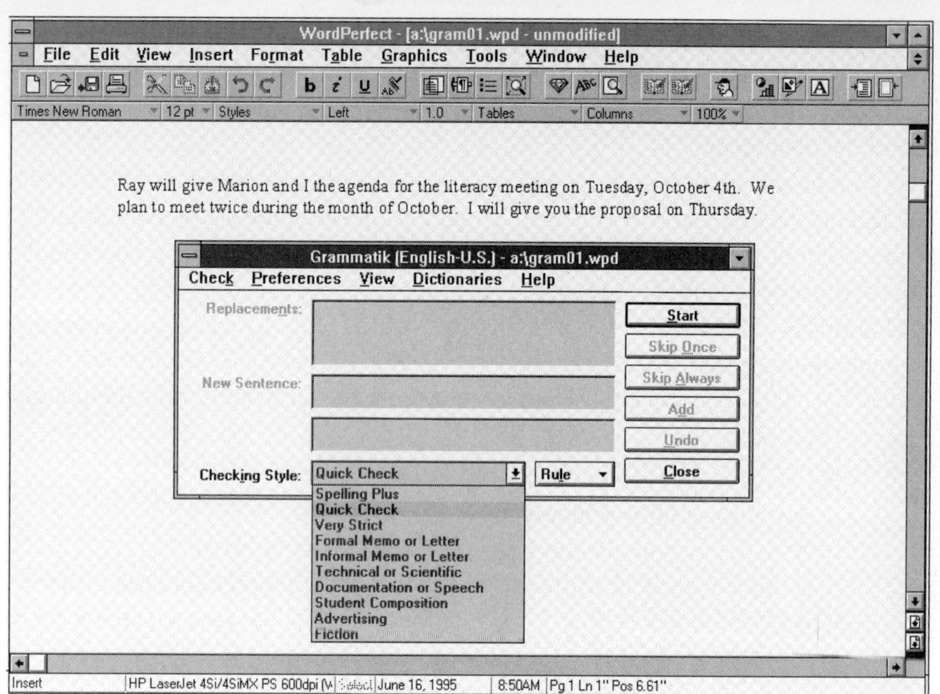

The default checking style is *Quick Check.* This is appropriate for general correspondence targeted to a general population. If you are preparing a formal business letter, choose the *Formal Memo and Letter* style. If you are preparing a technical document, choose the *Technical or Scientific* style. Choose the checking style that matches your document.

Exercise 6 Checking with the Technical or Scientific Style

1. At a clear screen, open report08.
2. Save the document with Save As and name it c06ex06.
3. Change the checking style to *Technical or Scientific* and complete a grammar check on the document by completing the following steps:
   a. Choose Tools, then Grammatik; or click on the Grammatik button on the Toolbar.
   b. When Grammatik highlights *cis*, change the checking style to *Technical or Scientific* by completing the following steps:
      (1) Position the tip of the arrow pointer on the down-pointing arrow to the right of the Checking Style text box, then click the left mouse button.
      (2) From the pop-up menu, click on *Technical or Scientific.*
   c. After changing the checking style, choose Skip Always to tell Grammatik to skip all occurrences of *cis*.
   d. Grammatik highlights *For the purpose of*. Change this to *For* by choosing Replace.
   e. Grammatik highlights *Purpose and Scope*. Choose Skip Always.
   f. Grammatik highlights *SSL*. Choose Skip Always.
   g. Grammatik highlights *in order to*. Change this to *to* by choosing Replace.
   h. Grammatik highlights *configuration*. Choose Skip Always.
   i. Grammatik highlights *utilization*. Change this to *use* by choosing Replace.
   j. Grammatik highlights *are*. Choose Skip Always.
   k. Grammatik highlights the word *The*. Choose Skip Always.
   l. Grammatik highlights *There*. Choose Skip Always.

m. Grammatik highlights *Requirements During Development:*. Choose Skip Always.
n. Grammatik highlights *a CI*. Choose Skip Always.
o. Grammatik highlights *Requirements for Operations/Maintenance*. Choose Skip Always.
p. Grammatik highlights *shall*. Change this to *will* by choosing Replace.
q. Grammatik highlights *shall* (again). Change this to *will* by choosing Replace.
r. At the Grammar check completed. Close Grammatik? question, choose Yes.

4. Save the document again with the same name (c06ex06).
5. Print c06ex06.
6. Close c06ex06.
7. At a clear editing window, change the checking style back to *Quick Check* by completing the following steps:
   a. Choose Tools, then Grammatik; or click on the Grammatik button on the Toolbar.
   b. At the *Grammar check completed. Close Grammatik?* question, choose No.
   c. At the Grammatik dialog box, position the tip of the arrow pointer on the down-pointing arrow to the right of the Checking Style text box, then click the left mouse button. At the pop-up menu, click on *Quick Check.*
   d. Choose Close to close the Grammatik dialog box.

Viewing Rule Class Information

When an error is detected, the rule class for the problem is displayed. If you need further information about the problem or the rule class, choose Rule. (This button is displayed at the bottom of the Grammatik dialog box.) From the drop-down menu that displays, choose Help. Grammatik displays a Help dialog box at the right side of the editing window containing information about the Rule Class. For example, if the writing problem is passive voice, choose Help, then Rule Class and the Help dialog box containing information on Passive Voice shown in figure 6.8 will display in the editing window. After reading the information on passive voice, choose Close to close the Help dialog box.

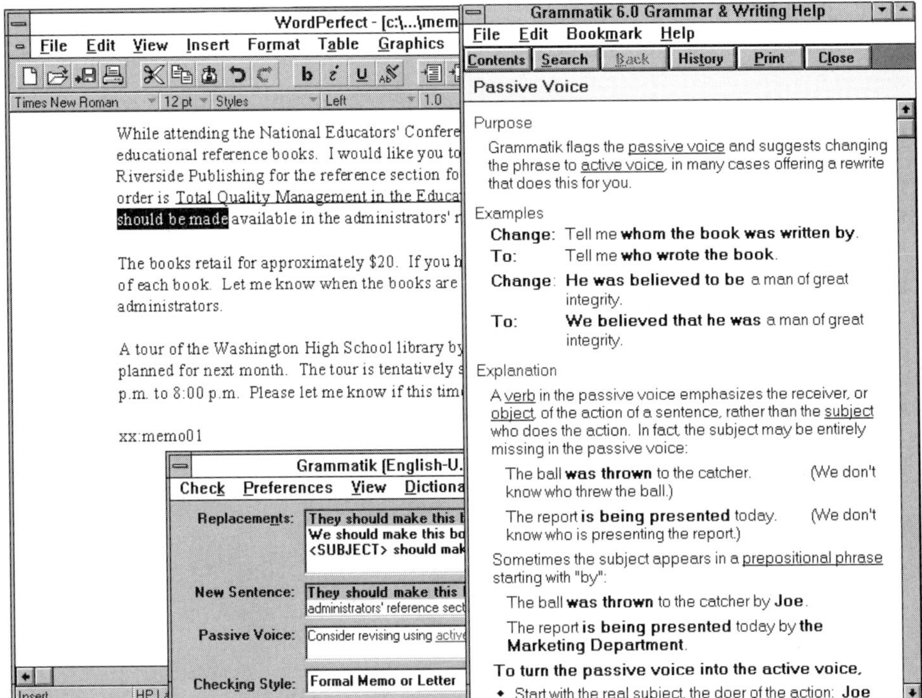

Figure 6.8
Grammatik Help Dialog Box

If you choose Contents from the Help drop-down menu, a Contents dialog box is displayed. At this Contents dialog box the options Grammar Terms, Checking Style, Rule Classes, and Writing are displayed. When you choose one of these options, Grammatik displays information about the option.

Exercise 7 Viewing Rule Class Information

1. At a clear screen, open memo01.
2. Save the document with Save As and name it c06ex07.
3. Change the viewing mode to Draft.
4. Move the insertion point to the end of the document, then press the Enter key ten times. (This provides room at the bottom of the memo for the Grammatik dialog box to display when correcting errors at the end of the memo.)
5. Change the checking style and complete a grammar check by completing the following steps:
   a. Choose Tools, then Grammatik; or click on the Grammatik button on the Toolbar.
   b. When Grammatik highlights *Dearing*, change the checking style to *Formal Memo or Letter*, then choose Skip Always (to tell Grammatik to leave *Dearing* as written.)
   c. Grammatik highlights *Windslow*. This name is correct so choose Skip Always.
   d. Grammatik highlights *of Integrated Learning by Riverside Publishing for the reference section for teachers* and inserts the rule **Consecutive Elements** with the advice, **Avoid using too many prepositional phrases in a row. They can be confusing to follow and may deaden your writing.** View information about consecutive elements, then correct the error by completing the following steps:
      (1) Choose Rule. (This button displays at the bottom of the Grammatik dialog box.)
      (2) Read the information on Consecutive Elements that displays at the right side of the editing window. Press Page Dn or click on the down-pointing arrow in the vertical scroll bar to continue reading text until you reach the end.
      (3) Choose Close.
      (4) Edit the partial sentence so it reads, *of Integrated Learning by Riverside Publishing for the teachers' reference section.* To do this, position the arrow pointer inside the selected text in the document, then click the left mouse button. Delete and/or insert text as needed to edit the sentence.
      (5) After editing the sentence, choose Resume.
   e. Grammatik highlights *This book should be made* and inserts the rule, **Passive Voice** with the advice, **Consider revising using active voice.** View information about passive voice, then correct the error by completing the following steps:
      (1) Choose Rule.
      (2) Read the information on Passive Voice, press Page Dn or click on the down-pointing arrow in the vertical scroll bar, then read the remaining information on Passive Voice.
      (3) Choose Close.
      (4) Edit the partial sentence so it reads, *This book will be available in the administrators' reference section.* To do this, position the arrow pointer inside the selected text in the document, then click the left mouse button. Delete and/or insert text as needed to edit the sentence.
      (5) After editing the sentence, choose Resume.

f. Grammatik highlights *5*, inserts the rule **Number Style** and displays the message **Spell out whole numbers in this range, even as part of larger numbers ("eight million"). If this is part of a fraction standing alone, spell out the fraction ("one-quarter of the class").** The word *five* is displayed in the suggested Replacements text box, so choose Replace.
g. Grammatik highlights *A tour of the Washington High School library by the members of the Board of Education is planned for next month.* Edit this sentence so it reads *The members of the Board of Education will be touring the Washington High School library next month.*
h. Grammatik highlights, *The tour is tentatively scheduled.* Leave this as written so choose Skip Always.
i. At the Grammar check completed. *Close Grammatik?* question, choose Yes.

6. Save the document again with the same name (c06ex07).
7. Print c06ex07.
8. Close c06ex07.
9. At a clear editing window, display the Grammatik dialog box, change the checking style back to *Quick Check*, then close the Grammatik dialog box.

CHAPTER SUMMARY

- Spell Checker is a spell-checking program that consists of two dictionaries—a main dictionary and a supplementary dictionary.
- In addition, a document-specific dictionary is automatically attached to a document. The words you choose to skip during a spelling check are added to this dictionary.
- Spell Checker will not identify words that are spelled correctly but used incorrectly, nor does it identify misspellings that match other words in its dictionaries. Spell Checker cannot check grammar usage.
- After correcting a misspelled word, Spell Checker automatically corrects all future occurrences of that error within the document.
- The Thesaurus program can be used to find synonyms and antonyms for words in your document.
- Use the Document Info option from the File drop-down menu to display information about your document such as the number of characters, words, lines, sentences, and pages.
- WordPerfect for Windows version 6.1 includes a grammar-checking program called Grammatik. With Grammatik you can check the grammar, style errors, and spelling errors in a document.
- When Grammatik detects an error, it tries to include replacement words or sentences in the Replacements list box. You can incorporate these replacements in the document, choose Skip Once or Skip Always, or edit the document yourself.
- When an error is detected, the rule class for the problem is displayed along with advice on how to fix the error. If you need further information about the rule class, choose Rule from the Grammatik dialog box.
- Grammatik uses a default checking style of *Quick Check*. This can be changed with the Checking Style pop-up menu.

Commands Review

	Mouse/Keyboard
Spell Checker dialog box	Tools, Spell Check; or click on Spell Check button on the Toolbar
Thesaurus dialog box	Tools, Thesaurus
Document Information dialog box	File, Document Info
Grammatik dialog box	Tools, Grammatik; or click on the Grammatik button on the Toolbar

CHECK YOUR UNDERSTANDING

True/False: Circle the letter T if the statement is true; circle the letter F if the statement is false.

T F 1. Spell Checker will stop at a correctly spelled word that is used improperly.
T F 2. Spell Checker automatically corrects all occurrences of an error within a document after a word is corrected.
T F 3. Frequently used words not in the main dictionary can be added to the supplementary dictionary.
T F 4. There are no proper names in Spell Checker's main dictionary.
T F 5. You should save a document before checking it with Spell Checker.
T F 6. The WordPerfect Thesaurus is used to find synonyms and antonyms for words in a document.
T F 7. Antonyms are words with similar meanings.
T F 8. You can check grammar usage using the Document Info option from the File drop-down menu.
T F 9. When Grammatik detects an error, advice on correcting the error is provided.
T F 10. The document you want to check must be displayed on the screen in order to use Grammatik.
T F 11. The default checking style for Grammatik is *Formal Memo or Letter*.
T F 12. Click on the Class button at the Grammatik dialog box to view information about the rule class.

Underline the words in the paragraph below that Spell Checker *would* highlight for correction.

Needs assesment will be focused on determining particalar job-specific basic skills that are hindered do to lack of English skills. This will entail developement of both qualitative and quantitative instraments and methodologies. The project coordinator and instructer will analyze basic skills required inn various production area through observation of production processes and teem meetings.

Using the same paragraph above, underline twice the incorrect words that Spell Checker *would not* highlight.

SKILL ASSESSMENTS

Assessment 1

1. At a clear editing window, open memo06.
2. Save the memo with Save As and name it c06sa01.
3. Complete a spell check on the document. You determine whether to skip words or make corrections. (Proper names are spelled correctly.)
4. Proofread the memo.
5. Save the memo with the same name (c06sa01).
6. Print c06sa01.
7. Close c06sa01.

Assessment 2

1. At a clear editing window, open memo07.
2. Save the memo with Save As and name it c06sa02.
3. Complete a spell check on the document. You determine whether to skip words or make corrections. (Proper names are spelled correctly.)
4. After the spell check is completed, proofread the memo and make necessary changes. (There are mistakes that Spell Checker will not highlight.)
5. Save the memo with the same name (c06sa02).
6. Print c06sa02.
7. Close c06sa02.

Assessment 3

1. At a clear editing window, open para04.
2. Save the document with Save As and name it c06sa03.
3. Use Thesaurus to make the following changes:
   a. Change *recall* in the second paragraph to *remember.*
   b. Change *primarily* in the second paragraph to *basically.*
   c. Change *choose* in the fourth paragraph to *select.*
   d. Change *pile* in the fourth paragraph to *mound.*
4. Save the document again with the same name (c06sa03).
5. Print c06sa03.
6. Close c06sa03.

Assessment 4

1. At a clear editing window, open letter03.
2. Save the letter with Save As and name it c06sa04.
3. This letter overuses the words *manage* (in various forms), *efficient* and *efficiently.* Use Thesaurus to make changes to some of the occurrences of *manage*, *manages*, *managed*, and/or *managing* to make the letter read better. Also, use Thesaurus to make changes to one or two of the occurrences of *efficient* and/or *efficiently.*
4. Save the letter again with the same name (c06sa04).
5. Print c06sa04.
6. Close c06sa04.

Assessment 5

1. At a clear editing window, open memo09.
2. Save the document with Save As and name it c06sa05.
3. Change the checking style and check the grammar of the document by completing the following steps:
   a. Choose Tools, then Grammatik; or click on the Grammatik button on the Toolbar.
   b. When Grammatik stops at *Mortensen*, change the checking style to *Formal Memo or Letter*, then choose Skip Always to leave *Mortensen* as written.
   c. When Grammatik highlights *prevelance*, change it to the correct spelling.
   d. When Grammatik highlights *have*, replace it with *has*.
   e. When Grammatik highlights *a moderately high prevalence of latex allergies has been noted*, change it to *We have noted a moderately high prevalence of latex allergies*.
   f. When Grammatik highlights *prevelance*, change it to the correct spelling.
   g. When Grammatik highlights *rate for health care workers is*, change it to *rate for health care workers is*.
   h. When Grammatik highlights *reason for this difference are*, change it to *reason for this diffference is*.
   i. At the *Grammar check completed. Close Grammatik?* question, choose No.
   j. Change the checking style back to the default of *Quick Check*, then close the Grammatik dialog box.
4. Save the document again with the same name (c06sa05).
5. Print c06sa05.
6. Close c06sa05.

Assessment 6

1. At a clear editing window, open memo10.
2. Save the document with Save As and name it c06sa06.
3. Check the grammar in the document. You determine what to leave as written and what to change. (Proper names are spelled correctly.)
4. Save the document again with the same name (c06sa06).
5. Print c06sa06.
6. Close c06sa06.

Unit Performance Assessment

In this unit, you have learned to produce business correspondence including memoranda and letters.

PROBLEM-SOLVING AND DECISION-MAKING

Assessment 1

1. At a clear editing window, key the text shown in figure U1.1 in an appropriate memorandum format with the following specifications:
    a. Change the view to Draft mode.
    b. Change the left and right margins to 1.5 inches.
    c. Double indent the second paragraph.
2. Save the memorandum and name it u01pa01.
3. Print u01pa01.
4. Close u01pa01.

Optional: Rewrite the memo as a letter to the district's attorney.

Figure U1.1

DATE: November 7, 1996
TO: Pat Windslow, Superintendent
FROM: Jocelyn Cook, Assistant Superintendent
SUBJECT: RESERVOIR REPAIR

As you requested, I called Jack Manuel, president of the Alderton Water Company. He explained about the problem with the spring and reservoir that serve Leland Elementary School. During our conversation, he stated:

According to the contract between the District and Alderton Water Company, the District must pay $10,000 toward the repair of the reservoir.

I contacted the District's attorney and asked her to review the documentation referred to by Mr. Manuel. She will call me next week with her impressions.

xx:u01pa01

Assessment 2

1. At a clear editing window, key the document shown in figure U1.2 with the following specifications:
   a. Change the view to Draft mode.
   b. Change the left and right margins to 1.25 inches.
   c. Bold and center the text as indicated.
   d. Indent the text in the numbered paragraphs.
   e. Correct spelling (proper names are spelled correctly).
2. After keying the document, change the justification to Full.
3. Save the document and name it u01pa02.
4. Print u01pa02.
5. Close u01pa02.

Optional: Rewrite the document in paragraph style and format it as a memo.

Figure U1.2

STAFF CHANGES

Update

1. **Food Service Assistants:** Two positions were added to the high scool because of Deli America's success. The assistants are **Marian Muehler** and **Nick Cittadino**.

2. **Bus Drivers:** Sevaral new bus drivers were hired, including **Jon Thach**, **Jesse Casada, Gale Rozine,** and **Douglas Mott**. All were substitute drivers.

3. **Teachers:** At Leland Elementary School, the hiring of **Regina Young** as a third grade teacher will reduce class size. Contracts for **Morrie Lamonte** and **Leslie Bryson** were converted to provisional contracts for the 1995-96 school yaer.

4. **Supplemental Contracts:** Supplimental contracts were isued to **Janine McCall**, Assistant Girl's Basketball Coach; **Ryan Kocar**, Assistant Wrestling Coach; **Daniel Teng**, Head Basketball Coach; and **Anthony Hassart**, Baseball Coach.

5. **Administrators:** Administrative contracts were issued to **Michelle Hayden**, Assistant Principal, McKnight High School; and **Nancy Cameron**, Principal, Dryer Elementary School.

Assessment 3

1. At a clear editing window, key the letter shown in figure U1.3 in an appropriate business letter format. Double indent the paragraphs as indicated.
2. Complete a spell check on the document. (Names are spelled correctly.)
3. Save the letter and name it u01pa03.
4. Print u01pa03.
5. Close u01pa03.

Figure U1.3

November 21, 1996

Mr. and Mrs. Paul Schadt
2311 Northeast 41st Street
St. Charles, MO 65033

Dear Mr. and Mrs. Schadt:

You are invited to partacipate in our morgage life insurance plan that could leave your family a home without house payments. We recomend this program for our home loan customers because it provides important protection at an affordable price.

> While there are many types of insurance, only mortgage life insurance is designed exclusively to pay off the morgage balance if you were to die.

Even if you already have a life insurance plan, you will want to consider morgage life insurance as a low-cost, attractive suppliment.

> Because so many households rely on two wage earners to make mortgage payments, we have selected a plan that can insure a second person at HALF-PRICE.

I think you will agree that this protection is almost a neccessity, but you may be concerned about cost. We have carefully chosen a plan that can fit your budget. We are pleased to offer this important customer service and encourage you to apply today, while it is availible at these attractive rates. To apply, please call 1-800-555-3255.

Sincerely,

Jonathon Baker
Insurance Products Manager

xx:u01pa03

Assessment 4

1. At a clear editing window, change the left and right margins to 1.5 inches, then key the document shown in figure U1.4 in an appropriate business letter format.
2. After keying the letter, save it and name it u01pa04.
3. Print u01pa04.
4. With u01pa04 still open in the editing window, display the Grammatik dialog box, then complete the following steps:
   a. When Grammatik selects *Attorney*, change the checking style to *Formal Memo or Letter.*
   b. Complete a grammar check. You determine what to leave as written and what to change. (Proper names are spelled correctly.)
   c. After checking the grammar, change the checking style back to *Quick Check.*

5. Save the document again with the same name (u01pa04).
6. Print u01pa04.
7. Close u01pa04.

Figure U1.4

April 22, 1997

Ms. Julia Carrick
Attorney at Law
1322 Pine Street
Denver, CO 86441

Dear Ms. Carrick:

Re: Hutton vs. Isham

Enclosed please find the Complaint in the case of Hutton vs. Isham. The Complaint was filed by our legal aide on April 17, 1997, with the Superior Court. I represent the Plaintiff, Benjamin Hutton, in this court action.

Your immediate response to this Complaint will be appreciated. Please respond to Rhonda Howell or I by the date of April 29, 1997. Mr. Hutton is interested in settling this situation as soon as possible.

Very truly yours,

PITTMAN & HOWELL

Robert Pittman
Attorney at Law

xx:u01pa04

WRITING

The following activities give you the opportunity to practice your writing skills along with demonstrating an understanding of some of the important WordPerfect features you have mastered in this unit. In planning the documents, remember to shape the information according to the writing purpose and the audience. Use correct grammar, appropriate word choices, and clear sentence constructions.

Activity 1

Situation: You are Jocelyn Cook, Assistant Superintendent for Omaha City School District. Compose a memo to Jennifer Stanford that includes the following information:

- Her application for a principal internship has been accepted.
- You would like to schedule an interview with her in your office on either of the following dates and times: Tuesday, May 21, 1996, at 3:00 p.m. or Wednesday, May 22, 1996, at 1:30 p.m.

Save the memo and name it u01act01. Print and then close u01act01.

Activity 2

Situation: You are Dione Landers of Landers & Associates. Compose a letter to Steven Ayala, director of the Training and Education Department at Denver Memorial Hospital, that includes the following information:

- Confirmation of a one-day training on telephone systems and techniques to be held on Wednesday, March 20, 1996, from 9:00 a.m. to 4:30 p.m.
- The training topics, which include:

  Handling incoming calls

  Transferring calls

  Telephone etiquette

  Articulation and pronunciation

  Handling stressful calls

Save the letter and name it u01act02. Print and then close u01act02.

RESEARCH

WordPerfect's Help features contains an on-screen reference manual. Use the Help feature to find information on how to select text to make edits. (*Hint: Look for the Create/Edit Text option.*) Write the steps you completed to display this information in the space provided below.

____

____

____

____

____

Producing Customized Documents

In this unit, you will be able to produce business documents with customized features such as fonts and templates.

SCANS

Technology

- Enhance text readability
- Organize and maintain records
- Choose efficient processing techniques
- Generate alternate solutions

Changing Fonts

7

Upon successful completion of chapter 7, you will be able to adjust the style and size of type as well as the appearance of characters in standard business documents.

By default, WordPerfect uses a font that prints text with varying amounts of space. Other fonts may be available depending on the printer you are using. The number of fonts available ranges from a few to several hundred. A font consists of three parts: typeface, type size, and type style.

Choosing a Typeface

A *typeface* is a set of characters with a common design and shape. Typefaces may be decorative, blocked, or plain. Typefaces are either *monospaced* or *proportional*. WordPerfect refers to typeface as font face.

A monospaced typeface allots the same amount of horizontal space for each character. Courier is an example of a monospaced typeface. Proportional typefaces allot a varying amount of space for each character. The space allotted is based on the width of the character. For example, the lowercase *i* will take up less space than the uppercase *M*.

Proportional typefaces are divided into two main categories: *serif* and *sans serif*. A serif is a small line at the end of a character stroke. Traditionally, a serif typeface is used with documents that are text intensive (documents that are mainly text) because the serif helps move the reader's eyes across the page. Figure 7.1 shows examples of serif typefaces.

A sans serif typeface does not have serifs (*sans* is French for *without*). Sans serif typefaces are often used for headlines and advertisements that are not text intensive. Figure 7.2 shows examples of sans serif typefaces.

Figure 7.1
Serif Typefaces

Bookman Light
New Century Schoolbook
Palatino
Times
Century-WP
Times New Roman (TT)
GeoSlab703 Lt BT (TT)

Figure 7.2
Sans Serif Typefaces

Avant Garde Gothic Book
Helvetica
Humanst521 Lt BT (TT)
Arial (TT)

Choosing a Type Size

Type size is divided into two categories: *pitch* and *point size*. Pitch is a measurement used for monospaced typefaces; it reflects the number of characters that can be printed in 1 horizontal inch. (For some printers, the pitch is referred to as *cpi*, or *characters per inch*. For example, the font Courier 10 cpi is the same as 10-pitch Courier.) WordPerfect refers to the type size as font size. The pitch measurement can be changed to increase or decrease the size of the characters. The higher the pitch measurement, the smaller the characters. The lower the pitch number, the larger the characters.

Examples of different pitch sizes in the Courier typeface are shown in figure 7.3.

Figure 7.3
Different Pitch Sizes in Courier

12-pitch Courier
10-pitch Courier
8-pitch Courier

Proportional typefaces can be set in different sizes. The size of proportional type is measured vertically in units called *points*. A point is approximately 1/72 of an inch. The higher the point size, the larger the characters. Examples of different point sizes in the Arial typeface are shown in figure 7.4.

Figure 7.4
Different Point Sizes in Arial

8-point Arial
12-point Arial
18-point Arial
24-point Arial

Choosing a Type Style

Within a typeface, characters may have a varying style. The standard style of the typeface is referred to as *Regular*. There are four main categories of type styles:

1. Regular
2. Bold
3. Italic
4. Bold Italic

Figure 7.5 illustrates the four main type styles in 12 points.

Helvetica (Regular)
Helvetica Bold
Helvetica Italic
Helvetica Bold Italic

Times New Roman
Times New Roman Bold
Times New Roman Italic
Times New Roman Bold Italic

Figure 7.5
Four Main Type Styles

The term *font* describes a particular typeface in a specific style and size. Examples of fonts are *10-pitch Courier*, *10-point Arial*, *12-point Times New Roman Bold*, *12-point Palatino Italic*, and *14-point Bookman Bold Italic*.

Choosing a Font

The printer that you are using has built-in fonts. These fonts can be supplemented with cartridges and/or soft fonts. The types of fonts you have available with your printer depend on the type of printer you are using, the amount of memory installed with the printer, and what supplemental fonts you have.

A font cartridge is inserted directly into the printer and lets you add fonts. To install a font cartridge, refer to the documentation that comes with the cartridge.

Soft fonts are available as software on disk. When soft fonts are installed, specify a directory in WordPerfect for the soft fonts. The WordPerfect for Windows, Version 6.1 program comes with additional fonts that were loaded during installation.

Using the Font Dialog Box

The fonts available with your printer are displayed in the Font Face list box at the Font dialog box shown in figure 7.6. To display the Font dialog box, choose Format then Font; or double-click on the Font Face button on the Power Bar (the first button from the left).

Figure 7.6
Font Dialog Box

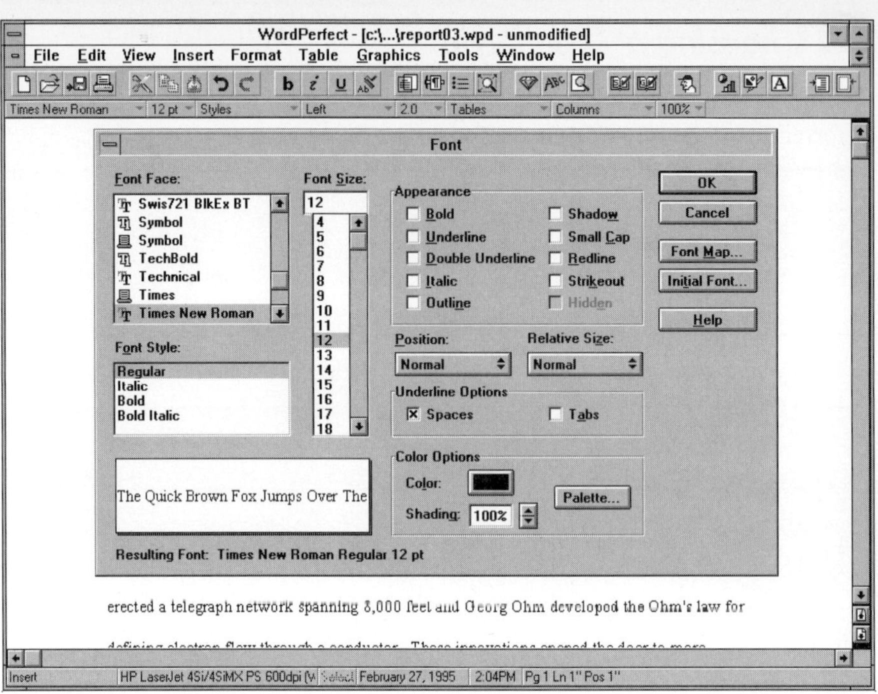

The Font Face list box at the Font dialog box displays the typefaces (font faces) available with your printer. Figure 7.6 shows the typefaces available with a popular laser printer (the fonts displayed with your printer may vary from those shown).

An icon displays before the typefaces in the Font Face list box. The printer icon identifies a built-in font. These are fonts provided with your printer. The V icon and TT icon identify soft fonts. WordPerfect for Windows 6.1 provides a number of True Type soft fonts that are identified with the TT icon. More than likely, these fonts were included during installation. If not, please refer to the WordPerfect documentation for directions on installing the True Type fonts. The fonts preceded by the V indicate Vector typefaces which are generally used with a plotter (a kind of printer). The True Type fonts are *graphically* generated while printer fonts are printer generated. Graphically generated fonts take longer to print than printer generated fonts.

To change to a different typeface, select the desired typeface (font face). The example sentence in the Resulting Font box in the lower left side of the Font dialog box displays in the chosen typeface. After all changes are made to the dialog box, choose OK or press Enter to close it.

Exercise 1 Changing Margins and Typeface

1. At a clear editing window, open para02.
2. Save the document with Save As and name it c07ex01.
3. With the insertion point positioned at the beginning of the document, change the left and right margins to 1.5 inches.
4. Change the typeface to Humanst521 Lt BT by completing the following steps:
   a. With the insertion point positioned at the beginning of the document, display the Font dialog box by choosing Format, then Font; or double-clicking on the Font Face button on the Power Bar.
   b. At the Font dialog box, select Humanst521 Lt BT. To do this with the mouse, click on the up-pointing arrow at the right side of the Font Face list box until Humanst521 Lt BT displays, then click on it. If you are using the keyboard, press the up arrow key until Humanst521 Lt BT is selected.
   c. Choose OK or press Enter.
5. Save the document again with the same name (c07ex01).
6. Print c07ex01.
7. Close c07ex01.

When the typeface (Font Face) is changed, WordPerfect inserts a code in the document at the position of the insertion point. For example, the code to change the typeface to Humanst521 Lt BT would appear as Font: Humanst521 Lt BT.

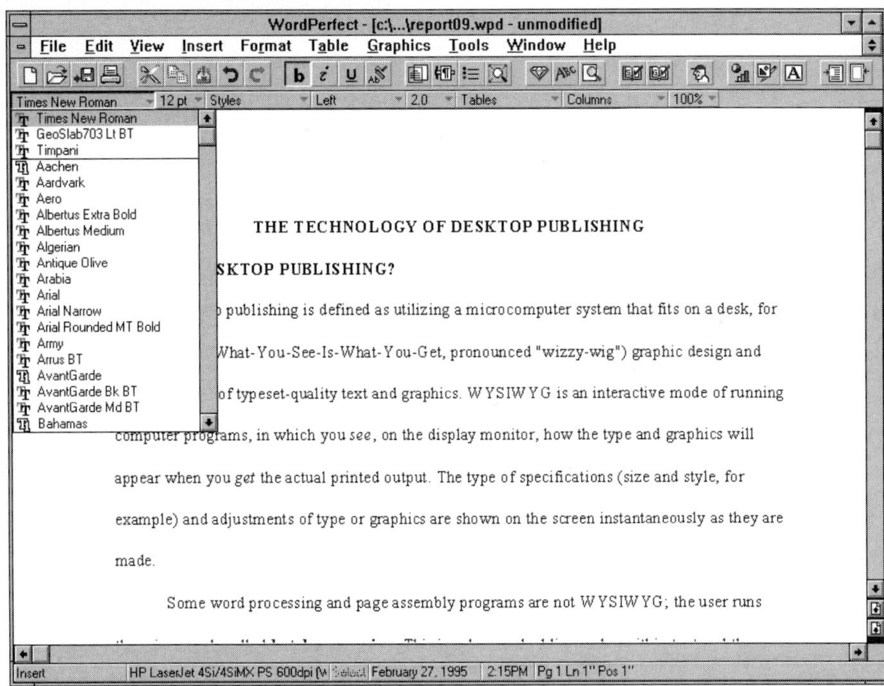

Figure 7.7
Font Face Button Drop-Down Menu

In addition to using the Font dialog box to select a typeface, you can use the Font Face button on the Power Bar. When you position the arrow pointer on the Font Face button on the Power Bar and then click the left mouse button once, a drop-down menu displays as shown in figure 7.7 (your drop-down menu may vary). To select a typeface, position the arrow pointer on the desired typeface, then click the left mouse button.

Exercise 2 Changing the Typeface with the Font Face Button

1. At a clear editing window, open para03.
2. Save the document with Save As and name it c07ex02.
3. With the insertion point positioned at the beginning of the document, change the typeface to Arial using the Power Bar by completing the following steps:
   a. Position the arrow pointer on the Font Face button, then click the left mouse button.
   b. Position the arrow pointer on Arial, then click the left mouse button.
4. Save the document again with the same name (c07ex02).
5. Print c07ex02.
6. Close c07ex02.

The Font Size list box at the Font dialog box displays a variety of common type sizes. Decrease point size to make text smaller or increase point size to make text larger. To select a point size with the mouse, click on the desired point size. If you are using the keyboard, press Alt + S, then press the up or down arrow key until the desired point size is selected.

You can also key a specific point size. To do this with the mouse, position the I-beam pointer on the number immediately below Font Size, click the left button, then key the desired point size. If you are using the keyboard, press Alt + S, then key the desired point size.

Exercise 3 Changing the Typeface and Size

1. At a clear editing window, open para04.
2. Save the document with Save As and name it c07ex03.
3. With the insertion point positioned at the beginning of the document, change the font to 10-point BernhardMod BT using the Font dialog box by completing the following steps:
   a. With the insertion point positioned at the beginning of the document, display the Font dialog box.
   b. At the Font dialog box, select BernhardMod BT. To do this with the mouse, click on the up-pointing arrow at the right side of the Font Face list box until BernhardMod BT displays, then click on it. If you are using the keyboard, press the up arrow key until BernhardMod BT is selected.
   c. Change the Font Size option to 10. To do this with the mouse, position the arrow pointer on the 10 in the Font Size list box, then click the left mouse button. If you are using the keyboard, press Alt + S, then press the up arrow key until 10 is selected.
   d. Choose OK or press Enter.
4. Save the document again with the same name (c07ex03).
5. Print c07ex03.
6. Close c07ex03.

In addition to the Font dialog box, you can use the Font Size button on the Power Bar to change type size. The Font Size button is the second button from the left.

To change the type size with the Font Size button, position the arrow pointer on the button, then click the left mouse button. From the drop-down menu that displays, click on the desired type size.

Exercise 4 Changing Margins, Font, and Type Size

1. At a clear editing window, open para02.
2. Save the document with Save As and name it c07ex04.
3. Change the left and right margins to 1.25 inches.
4. With the insertion point positioned at the beginning of the document, change the font to 10-point GeoSlab703 Lt BT using the Power Bar by completing the following steps:
   a. Position the arrow pointer on the Font Face button, then click the left mouse button.
   b. Position the arrow pointer on GeoSlab703 Lt BT, then click the left mouse button.
   c. Position the arrow pointer on the Font Size button on the Power Bar, then click the left mouse button.
   d. Position the arrow pointer on the 10 in the drop-down menu, then click the left mouse button.
5. Save the document again with the same name (c07ex04).
6. Print c07ex04.
7. Close c07ex04.

The Font Style list box at the Font dialog box displays the styles available with the selected typeface. As you select different typefaces at the Font dialog box, the list of available styles changes in the Font Style list box.

Exercise 5 Changing the Font Style

1. At a clear editing window, open para03.
2. Save the document with Save As and name it c07ex05.
3. Change the typeface to Arrus BT and the style to Bold Italic by completing the following steps:
   a. With the insertion point positioned at the beginning of the document, display the Font dialog box.
   b. At the Font dialog box, select Arrus BT.
   c. Change the Font Style to Bold Italic. To do this with the mouse, position the arrow pointer on Bold Italic in the Font Style list box, then click the left mouse button. If you are using the keyboard, press Alt + O, then press the down arrow key until Bold Italic is selected.
   d. Choose OK or press Enter.
4. Save the document again with the same name (c07ex05).
5. Print c07ex05.
6. Close c07ex05.

The Appearance section of the Font dialog box contains a variety of options that can be used to create different character styles. These appearances are also available on the Font Toolbar. (To display the Font Toolbar, position the arrow pointer on the current Toolbar, click the right mouse button, then click on Font at the drop-down menu.)

Exercise 6 Using the Small Caps Option

1. At a clear editing window, open memo01.
2. Save the document with Save As and name it c07ex06.
3. With the insertion point positioned at the beginning of the document, change the font to 12-point Humanst521 Lt BT.
4. Change the appearance of all the text in the document to Small Caps by completing the following steps:
   a. Select the entire document.
   b. Display the Font Toolbar. To do this, position the arrow pointer on the current Toolbar, click the right mouse button, then click on Font at the drop-down menu.
   c. Click on the Small Caps button on the Font Toolbar.
   d. Click outside the selected text to deselect the text.
5. The date, *October 17, 1996*, needs to be moved to the right. To do this, position the insertion point immediately left of the *O* in *October*, then press the Tab key.
6. Save the document again with the same name (c07ex06).
7. Print c07ex06.
8. Close c07ex06.

Relative Size: The Relative Size option at the Font dialog box contains a drop-down menu with a variety of size options. The size options are used to change the size of the type based on the size of the font in the document. The selections change the size of the current font by the following percentages:

Fine = 60%
Small = 80%
Large = 120%
Very Large = 150%
Extra Large = 200%

If the font in a document is changed to 10-point Arial as shown below, the Fine selection changes the size to 6 points, Small to 8 points, Large to 12 points, Very Large to 15 points, and Extra Large to 20 points.

This text is Fine or 60% of the font

This text is Small or 80% of the font

This text is the default size of the font

This text is Large or 120% of the font

This text is Very Large or 150% of the font

This text is Extra Large or 200% of the font

Some printers support only a few point sizes. If your printer does not support the exact point size selected, WordPerfect tries to choose and print an approximate size.

Changing point size with a Relative Size option from the Font dialog box allows changes to be made easily to text in the document. If the size of the font is changed, any type with relative size options attached is automatically updated. Also, if the typeface is changed, the size options will apply to the new typeface.

Exercise 7 Changing the Font and Relative Size

1. At a clear editing window, open report06.
2. Save the document with Save As and name it c07ex07.
3. Make the following changes to the document:
   a. With the insertion point positioned at the beginning of the document, change the font to 12-point GeoSlab703 Lt BT.
   b. Change the relative size of the title, *TRENDS IN TELECOMMUNICATIONS*, to Very Large by completing the following steps:
      (1) Select the title, *TRENDS IN TELECOMMUNICATIONS.*
      (2) Display the Font dialog box.
      (3) At the Font dialog box, position the arrow pointer in the box below Relative Size (the box containing the word *Normal*), hold down the left mouse button, drag the arrow pointer to Very Large, then release the mouse button.
      (4) Choose OK or press Enter.
   c. Select the heading *Continued Growth of Photonics (Fiber Optics)*, then change the relative size to Large.
   d. Select the heading *Microcomputer Trends in the Nineties*, then change the relative size to Large.
4. Save the document again with the same name (c07ex07).
5. Print c07ex07.
6. Close c07ex07.

Changing the Default Font

By default, WordPerfect uses 12-point Times New Roman as the default font. If you want to use a different font as the default, change the font at the Document Initial Font dialog box. To display this dialog box shown in figure 7.8, choose Format, Document, then Initial Font. At the Initial Font dialog box, change to the desired font, then insert an X in the Set as Printer Initial Font check box located at the bottom of the dialog box. Close the Document Initial Font dialog box by choosing OK. The change made at the Document Initial Font dialog box (if an X was inserted in the Set as Printer Initial Font check box) will remain in effect for all future documents.

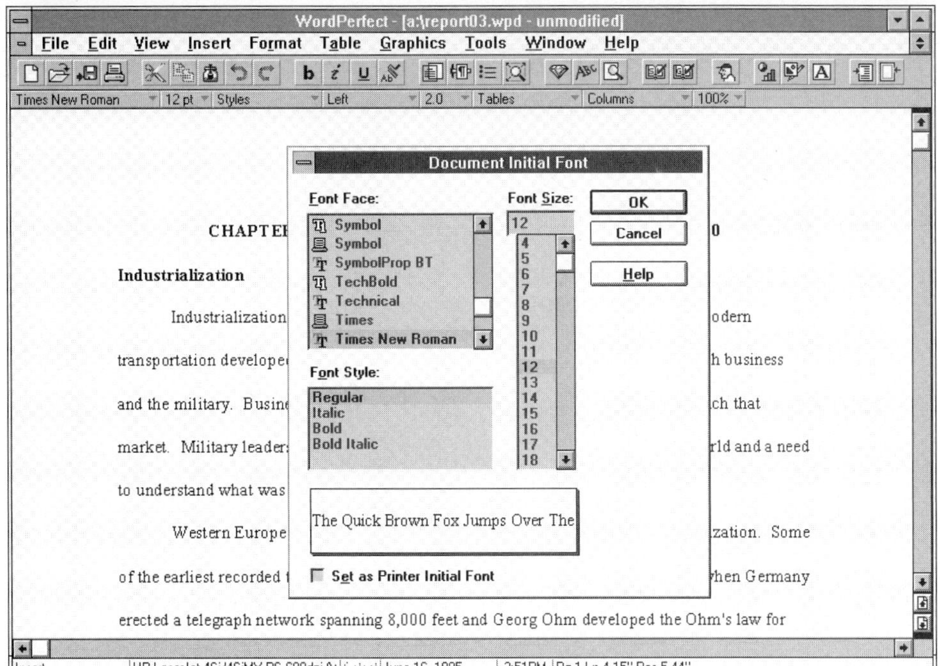

Figure 7.8 Document Initial Font Dialog Box

Inserting the Date

The current date can be inserted in a document as text or a code. To insert the date as text, press Ctrl + D or choose Insert, Date, then Date Text. This date is inserted as month, day, and year. For example, if today's date is May 4, 1996, it will be inserted as *May 4, 1996*. When you insert the date as text, the date is considered text and can be edited.

If you insert the date as code, the date the document is opened is inserted in the document. The date displays as text on the screen, but as a code in Reveal Codes. For example, if you insert the date code in a document created on April 18, 1996, that is the date that will appear. If you open the document on May 2, 1996, the date April 18, 1996, is replaced with May 2, 1996. To insert a date as a code in a document, press Ctrl + Shift + D or choose Insert, Date, then Date Code.

Using WordPerfect Character Sets

The WordPerfect program includes character sets you can use to create special letters and symbols. WordPerfect provides over 1,500 characters and symbols. Depending on the printer you are using, some or all of these symbols will be available. These symbols are grouped into 15 character sets. Each character set contains different types of symbols. For example, character set 4 contains typographic symbols and character set 6 contains mathematic and scientific symbols.

To determine the characters and character sets available, you may want to print the WordPerfect document named *charactr.doc*. Usually this document is found in the WordPerfect *wpc20* subdirectory. Print this document as you would any other document. When printed, the document shows the character set number, the code for the character, and the character itself in each character set.

Inserting a Symbol in a Document

You can insert a symbol in a document with the Character option from the Insert drop-down menu. You can also use the shortcut command Ctrl + W. At the WordPerfect Characters dialog box shown in figure 7.9, use the arrow pointer on the scroll bar to display the desired symbol, then click on the symbol. This inserts a dotted box around the symbol and inserts the character set and symbol number in the Number text box. Choose Insert and Close.

Figure 7.9 WordPerfect Characters Dialog Box

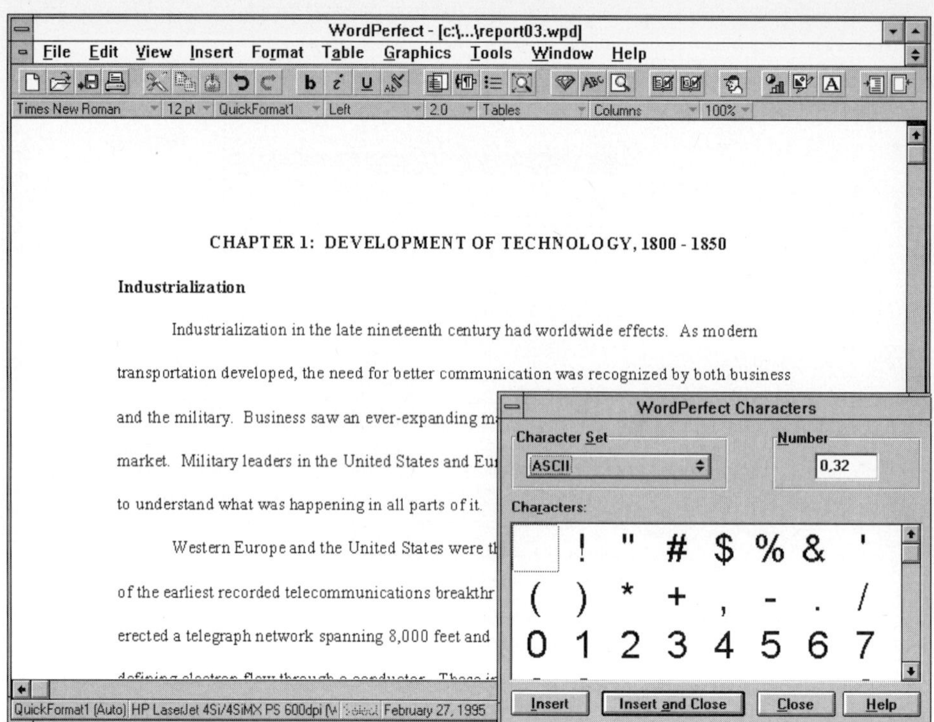

When you choose Insert and Close, the symbol is inserted in the document and the dialog box is closed. A code can be seen in Reveal Codes. For example, if you chose the symbol for a bullet, 4,0, at the WordPerfect Characters dialog box, a round bullet is inserted in the document. The code displays as [• 4,0] in Reveal Codes.

At the WordPerfect Characters dialog box, you can choose Insert to insert the symbol in the document and not close the dialog box. This might be useful if you are inserting more than one symbol in the document at the same time. You can also key the character set number and the symbol number in the Number text box. For example, if you want to insert a copyright symbol in the document and you know the character set number is 4 and the symbol number is 23, you would key 4,23 in the Number text box.

At the WordPerfect Characters dialog box, you can change the character set with the Character Set option. This changes the display of symbols in the viewing box. To do this, select Typographic Symbols from the Character Set option at the WordPerfect characters dialog box. To do this with the mouse, position the arrow pointer in the Character Set text box, hold down the left mouse button, drag the arrow pointer to Typographic Symbols, then release the mouse button. If you are using the keyboard, press Alt + S, press the space bar once, then key T (for Typographic Symbols).

After changing the character set, choose a symbol, then choose Insert and Close to remove the WordPerfect Characters dialog box. This inserts the symbol in the document.

Exercise 8 Creating Special Symbols

1. At a clear editing window, key the memorandum shown in figure 7.10 in an appropriate memorandum format with the following specifications:
   a. Change the left and right margins to 1.5 inches.
   b. Insert the current date after the DATE: heading by choosing Insert, Date, then Date Text; or pressing Ctrl + D.
   c. Change the font to 12-point GeoSlab703 Lt BT.
   d. Complete the following steps to create the special symbols:
      (1) Choose Insert, Character; or press Ctrl + W.

(2) At the WordPerfect Characters dialog box, key the character set number, a comma, the symbol number, then choose Insert and Close. Use the following numbers at the WordPerfect Characters dialog box to create the special symbol:

é	=	1,41
ñ	=	1,57
°	=	6,36
®	=	4,22
•	=	4,3

2. Save the document and name it c07ex08.
3. Print c07ex08.
4. Close c07ex08.

Figure 7.10

DATE: (current date); TO: Maggie Hénédine; FROM: Joni Kapshaw; SUBJECT: DISTRICT NEWSLETTER

The layout for the March newsletter looks great! I talked with Anita Nuñez about the figures. She explained how we can rotate the image inside the box by 90°, 180°, and 270°. As soon as she shows me how to do this, I will pass on the information to you.

Anita plans to offer an informal workshop on some of the graphic capabilities of WordPerfect for Windows®. She plans to address the following topics:

- customizing box borders
- inserting shaded fill
- rotating and scaling images
- creating drop shadow boxes

If you want her to address any other topics, please give me a call by the end of this week.

xx:c07ex08

Inserting Bullets and Numbers

Numbers and commonly used bullets can be easily inserted in a document with the Bullets & Numbers dialog box shown in figure 7.11. To display the Bullets & Numbers dialog box, choose Insert, then Bullets & Numbers.

The Styles list box at the Bullets & Numbers dialog box contains a variety of bullet and numbering options. The second through sixth options can be used to insert a bullet into a document. When a bullet is inserted with this dialog box, the bullet is inserted at the left margin and the insertion point is automatically indented to the first tab setting to the right.

The Numbers option and the last five options in the list box can be used to insert numbers in a document. Like bullets, WordPerfect also automatically indents the insertion point to the first tab setting to the right. If you choose any of the number options, you can identify the beginning value. When a number option is selected, the Starting Value option displays in black. To change the starting value with the mouse, position the arrow pointer in the check box before Starting Value, click the left mouse button, then key the new starting value or click on the up- or down-pointing triangles to increase or decrease the number. If you are using the keyboard, press Alt + V, then key

Figure 7.11
Bullets & Numbers Dialog Box

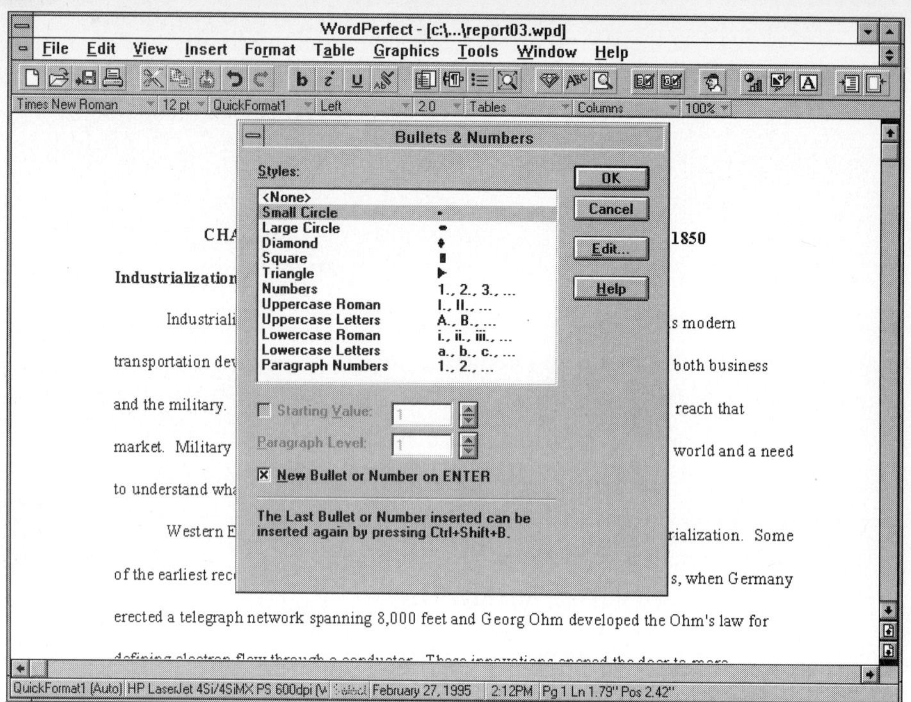

the new starting value. After inserting the first bullet or number in a document, you can insert another bullet or the next number in the document with the shortcut command Ctrl + Shift + B. If you insert an X in the New Bullet or Number on ENTER option, a bullet or the next number in the sequence will be inserted in the document when you press the Enter key. When you are done entering bullets or numbers in a document, display the Bullets & Numbers dialog box, then remove the X from the New Bullet or Number on ENTER option.

The Toolbar contains an Insert Bullet button. When you click on this button, a bullet or number is automatically inserted in the document. What is inserted in the document is determined by what is selected in the Styles list box at the Bullets & Numbers dialog box.

Exercise 9 Inserting Numbers

1. At a clear editing window, key the memorandum shown in figure 7.12 in an appropriate memorandum format with the following specifications:
   a. Change the left and right margins to 1.5 inches.
   b. Insert current date after the DATE: heading.
   c. Complete the following steps to insert the number 6. and indent the insertion point in the first numbered paragraph below the first paragraph of the memorandum:
      (1) Position the insertion point at the left margin where the 6. is to be inserted.
      (2) Choose Insert, then Bullets & Numbers.
      (3) At the Bullets & Numbers dialog box, choose Numbers. To do this with the mouse, click on the Numbers option. If you are using the keyboard, press the up or down arrow key until Numbers is selected.
      (4) Change the starting value to 6. To do this with the mouse, position the arrow pointer in the check box before Starting Value, click the left mouse button, then key **6**. If you are using the keyboard, press Alt + V, then key **6**.
      (5) Make sure an X does not appear in the New Bullet or Number on ENTER check box.
      (6) Choose OK or press Enter.
   d. Complete the following steps to insert the remaining numbers before the numbered paragraphs:

(1) Position the insertion point at the left margin where the next number is to be inserted.
(2) Press Ctrl + Shift + B.

2. After keying the memorandum, save it and name it c07ex09.
3. Print c07ex09.
4. Close c07ex09.

Figure 7.12

DATE: (current date); TO: Maggie Hénédine; FROM: Katherine Brynn; SUBJECT: POSITION DESCRIPTION

At the end of last week, I sent you a position description to be included in the April newsletter. Since that time, the department manager has decided to add the following responsibilities to the list:

6. Skill in interpersonal relationships with emphasis on reaching out and being friendly
7. Ability to be sensitive and show positive regard for fellow employees, patients, and families
8. Ability to set priorities and use good judgment
9. Ability to willingly accept responsibilities

I hope these additional responsibilities can be included in the April newsletter. Please contact me to let me know if you receive this memorandum before the newsletter deadline.

xx:c07ex09

CHAPTER SUMMARY

- A font consists of three parts: typeface, type style, and type size.
- A typeface is a set of characters with a common design and shape. Typefaces are either monospaced or proportional. A monospaced typeface allots the same amount of horizontal space for each character. A proportional typeface allots a varying amount of space for each character.
- Type size is divided into two categories: pitch and point size. Pitch is the number of characters that can be printed in one horizontal inch. The higher the pitch, the smaller the characters. Point size is a vertical measurement used with proportional typefaces. The higher the point size, the larger the characters.
- A type style is a variation of style within a certain typeface. The standard style is Regular. Other type styles include bold, italic, and bold italic.
- At the Font dialog box you can change the typeface, the type size, and see examples of the text as you make each change. You can also create different character styles such as bold, underline, double underline, and italics or a combination of these styles, as well as change the relative size of text.
- The current date can be inserted in a document as text or code.
- The WordPerfect program includes character sets you can use to create special letters and symbols.
- Use the Bullets & Numbers dialog box to easily insert bullets or numbers in a document.

Commands Review

	Mouse	Keyboard
Font dialog box	Format, Font; or double-click on the Font Face button on the Power Bar	Format, Font
Insert date as text	Insert, Date, Date Text	CTRL + D
Insert date as code	Insert, Date, Date Code	CTRL + SHIFT + D
Insert a symbol	Insert, Character	CTRL + W
Insert bullets and numbers	Insert, Bullets & Numbers; or click on the Insert Bullet button on the Toolbar	Insert, Bullets & Numbers
Insert second and succeeding bullets or numbers	Insert, Bullets & Numbers, OK	CTRL + SHIFT + B

CHECK YOUR UNDERSTANDING

Matching: In the space provided at the right, indicate the correct letter or letters that match each description.

A.	Courier	I.	italic
B.	typeface	J.	pitch
C.	type style	K.	font
D.	type size	L.	font face
E.	font size	M.	bold
F.	proportional	N.	regular
G.	serif	O.	book
H.	sans serif	P.	Times New Roman

1. Examples of different type styles. ____________
2. Does not have a small line at the end of each character stroke. ____________
3. A particular typeface in a specific style and size. ____________
4. A set of characters with a common design and shape. ____________
5. Examples of different typefaces. ____________
6. A measure of the number of characters that can be printed in one horizontal inch. ____________
7. The typefaces available with your printer are displayed in this box at the Font dialog box. ____________
8. The common font sizes are displayed in this box at the Font dialog box. ____________
9. A small line at the end of a character stroke. ____________

SKILL ASSESSMENTS

Assessment 1

1. At a clear editing window, open report06.
2. Save the document with Save As and name it c07sa01.
3. Make the following changes to the document:
   a. Change the font for the report to 12-point GeoSlab703 Lt BT.
   b. Change the relative size of the title to Very Large.

c. Change the relative size of the two headings to Large.
d. Change the font style for the last six lines of the report to italic.
e. Insert a round hollow bullet (4,1) before each of the last six lines in the report. (Indent the bullet to the first tab setting. This will cause the lines of text to indent to the second tab setting. The bullets will be italicized.)

4. Save the document again with the same name (c07sa01).
5. Print c07sa01.
6. Close c07sa01.

Assessment 2

1. At a clear editing window, display the Font dialog box, then change the font to 24-point Arrus Blk BT and turn on the Shadow appearance option.
2. Key the text shown in figure 7.13 centered.
3. Save the document and name it c07sa02.
4. Print c07sa02.
5. Close c07sa02.

Figure 7.13

Intensive Care Unit

Respiratory Therapy Techniques

Tuesday, May 13, 1997

1:00 - 3:30 p.m., Room 430

Assessment 3

1. At a clear editing window, create the document shown in figure 7.14 with the following specifications:
   a. Change the font to 12-point GeoSlab703 Lt BT.
   b. Center and bold text as indicated.
   c. Double indent the paragraph below *General Description* and double indent the paragraph below *Distinguishing Features*.
   d. Insert the first triangle bullet and the indent with the Bullets & Numbers dialog box. Make sure an X does not appear in the New Bullet or Number on ENTER check box. Insert the other triangle bullets and indents by pressing Ctrl + Shift + B.
2. After keying the document, select the title, *TECHNICAL SUPPORT PARTNER*, then change the relative size to Large.
3. Change the relative size to Large for the headings, *General Description*, *Distinguishing Features*, *Principal Accountabilities*, and *Minimum Qualifications*.
4. Save the document and name it c07sa03.
5. Print c07sa03.
6. Close c07sa03.

Figure 7.14

TECHNICAL SUPPORT PARTNER

General Description

The Technical Support Partner is a team member working under the direction of a Registered Nurse to provide quality care that is focused on the comfort and well being of the patient and family.

Distinguishing Features

This position requires a service oriented individual with strong interpersonal skills for the purpose of delivering care and services to patients from diverse ethnic and social groups. Independent decision making is expected in the execution of daily routine duties. Decisions regarding patient care or services require the review and approval of the Clinical Partner.

Principal Accountabilities

- Performs direct patient care activities
- Maintains a clean and comfortable environment in assigned patient rooms
- Obtains blood specimens using approved procedures for venipuncture and capillary collection
- Performs simple respiratory therapy functions
- Assists the Clinical Partner in providing patient care as needed
- Assembles and disassembles specialty equipment
- Responds promptly and with caring actions to patient's requests
- Performs other related work as needed or directed by the Clinical Partner

Minimum Qualifications

- High school graduate or equivalent
- Previous work experience in a health care environment as an Aide, Housekeeper, or Transporter preferred
- Previous experience in phlebotomy preferred and/or willingness to train
- Basic knowledge and ability to perform specified tasks
- Knowledge of medical terminology
- Knowledge of communication skills with ability to listen actively
- Ability to work independently and take initiative

Formatting with Special Features

8

Upon successful completion of chapter 8, you will be able to record keystrokes for commands, then play those keystrokes in many different business documents; create business documents such as a letter, sign, and calendar using WordPerfect templates; and create envelopes and labels.

In this chapter, you will learn about two time-saving features—Macros and Templates. With macros, you can automate the formatting of a document. The word *macro* was coined by computer programmers for a collection of commands used to make a large programming job easier and save time. A WordPerfect *macro* is a document containing recorded commands that can accomplish a task automatically and save time.

In WordPerfect, creating a macro is referred to as *recording*. As a macro is being recorded, all the keys pressed and the menus and dialog boxes displayed are recorded and become part of the macro. For example, you can record a macro to change the left and right margins or insert page numbering in a document. In this chapter, you will learn to record and play macros. WordPerfect's macro feature can also be used to write macros. For more information on writing macros, refer to the WordPerfect reference manual.

Every document created in WordPerfect is based on a template. When you create a document at a clear editing window, you are using the default template. This default template establishes the formatting for the document such as margins, tabs, fonts, etc. WordPerfect also includes a number of other templates that can be used to produce a variety of business documents such as memos, business letters, calendars, faxes, and much more.

Additional features WordPerfect provides to format documents include envelopes, labels, and QuickCorrect. These features are also discussed in this chapter.

Changing the Location of Macro Documents

Before learning about recording and playing macros, you may want to change the location of macro documents. By default, a macro document is saved in the **c:\office\wpwin\macros** directory (the drive letter may vary depending on the system you are using). In some situations, you may want to change where WordPerfect saves macro documents. For example, in a school setting, you may want to change the location of macro documents to drive **a:** or drive **b:** (the drive that contains your student disk). This lets you record macros and save them on your disk. Change the location of macro documents at the File Preferences dialog box. To do this, you would complete the following steps:

1. Choose Edit, then Preferences.
2. At the Preferences dialog box, choose File. To do this with the mouse, position the arrow pointer on File, then double-click the left mouse button. If you are using the keyboard, press Alt + F, then press Enter.
3. At the File Preferences dialog box, choose Macros.
4. Choose Default Directory, then key **a:** (or **b:**). (Key the drive letter where your student data disk is located.) To do this with the mouse, select the text in the Default Directory text box, then key **a:** (or **b:**). If you are using the keyboard, press Alt + E, then key **a:** (or **b:**).
5. Choose Supplemental Directory, then key **c:\office\wpwin\macros** (this path may vary).
6. Choose OK or press Enter.
7. At the Preferences dialog box, choose Close.

Changes made to the File Preferences dialog box stay in effect even after you exit WordPerfect. Check with your instructor before completing any exercises in this chapter to see if you need to change the location of macro documents.

Recording a Macro

You can use the Macro option from the Tools drop-down menu to record a macro, or you can use a button on the Macro Tools Toolbar. To display the Macro Tools Toolbar, position the arrow pointer on the current Toolbar, click the right mouse button, then click on Macro Tools. When you click on Macro Tools, the Macro Tools Toolbar displays as shown in figure 8.1.

Figure 8.1 **Macro Tools Toolbar**

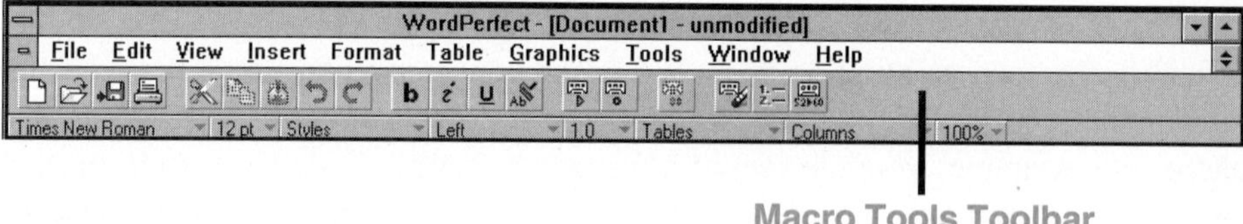

Macro Tools Toolbar

Recording a macro involves four steps. They are:

1. Choose Tools, Macro, then Record; or click on the Record button on the Macro Tools Toolbar (the fifth button from the right).
2. Name the macro.
3. Complete the steps to be recorded in the macro.
4. End the recording of the macro by choosing Tools, Macro, then Record; or clicking on the Record button on the Macro Tools Toolbar.

When you choose Tools, Macro, then Record; or click on the Record button on the Macro Tools Toolbar, the Record Macro dialog box shown in figure 8.2 displays on the screen.

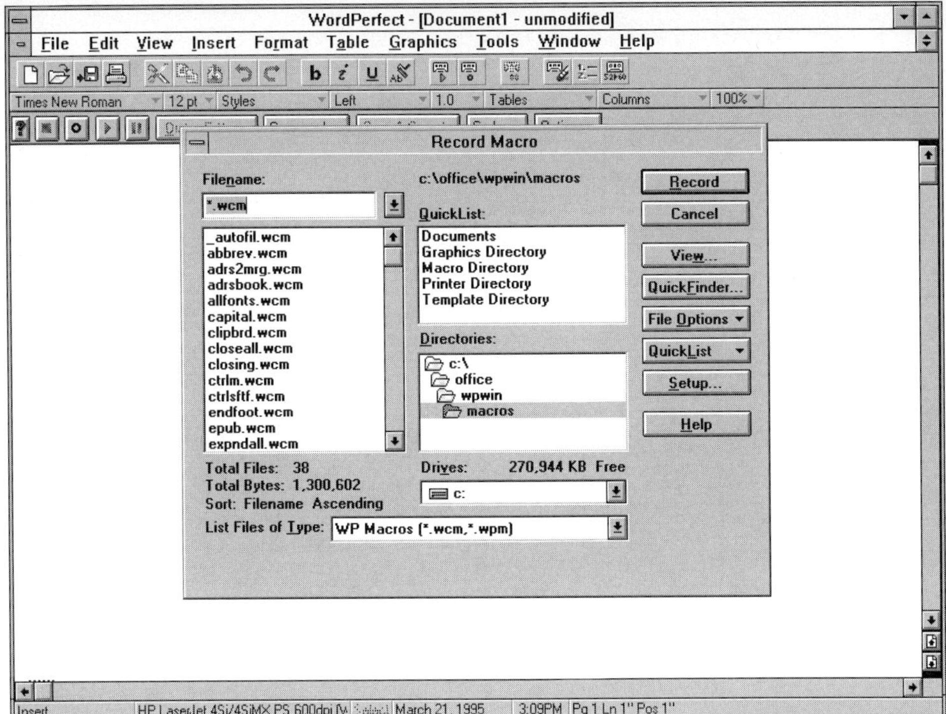

Figure 8.2
Record Macro Dialog Box

Naming a Macro

At the Record Macro dialog box, key a name for the macro. A macro name can be from one to eight characters in length. Use any letter or number. Do not use a space when naming a macro. Symbols can be used in macro names except ^ + = \ / [ ] " ; : ? , . and |. Do not use the period when naming a macro. WordPerfect adds a period and the extension **wcm** (for WordPerfect Corporation Macro) to the macro name. When you name a macro, name it something that is easy to remember and gives you an idea what is saved in the macro.

Exercise 1 Creating Macros

1. At a clear editing window, record a macro named **sig.wcm** that includes the signature information shown in figure 8.3 by completing the following steps:
   a. Display the Macro Tools Toolbar by completing the following steps: (If the Macro Tools Toolbar is already displayed, skip this step.)
      (1) Position the arrow pointer on the current Toolbar, then click the right mouse button.
      (2) At the drop-down menu that displays, click on Macro Tools.
   b. Choose Tools, Macro, then Record; or click on the Record button on the Macro Tools Toolbar (the fifth button from the right).
   c. At the Record Macro dialog box, key **sig**, then choose Record or press Enter.
   d. At the editing window, key the text shown in figure 8.3 (be sure to include the blank lines between the complimentary close and the name as shown in the figure).
   e. After keying the signature information, end the recording of the macro by choosing Tools, Macro, then Record; or clicking on the Record button on the Macro Tools Toolbar.
   f. Close the document without saving it.
2. At a clear editing window, create a macro named margins that changes the left and right margins to 1.5 inches by completing the following steps:
   a. Choose Tools, Macro, then Record; or click on the Record button on the Macro Tools Toolbar.

b. At the Record Macro dialog box, key **margins**, then choose Record or press Enter.
c. At the editing window, complete the necessary steps to change the left and right margins to 1.5 inches.
d. At the editing window, end the recording of the macro by choosing Tools, Macro, then Record; or clicking on the Record button on the Macro Tools Toolbar.
e. Close the document without saving it.

3. Record a macro named **ls.wcm** that changes the line spacing to double. After creating the macro, close the document without saving it.

Figure 8.3

Sincerely yours,

ENERSEN & TALBOTT

Jeanette Enersen
Senior Partner

xx:

Playing a Macro

After a macro has been recorded, it can be played back in a document. To play a macro, you would complete the following steps:

1 Choose Tools, Macro, then Play; or click on the Play button on the Macro Tools Toolbar (the sixth button from the right).
2 At the Play Macro dialog box shown in figure 8.4, select the macro in the Filename list box, then choose Play.

Figure 8.4
Play Macro Dialog Box

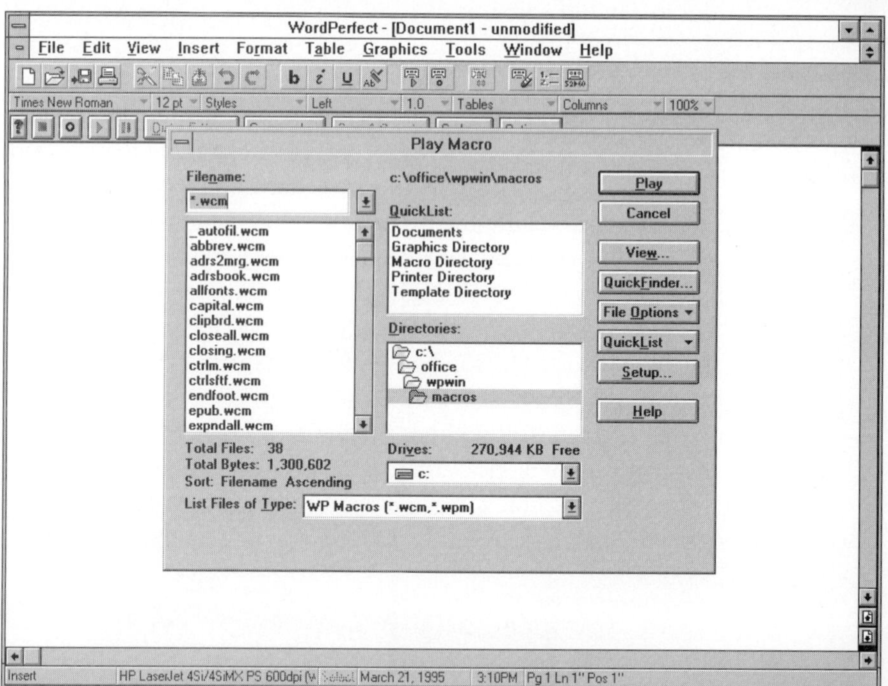

You can also play a macro by double-clicking on the macro name in the Filename list box at the Play Macro dialog box.

 Exercise 2 Playing Macros within a Letter

1. At a clear editing window, complete the following steps:
   a. Play the **margins.wcm** macro by completing the following steps:
      (1) Choose Tools, Macro, then Play; or click on the Play button on the Macro Tools Toolbar (the sixth button from the right).
      (2) At the Play Macro dialog box, double-click on **margins.wcm** in the Filename list box.
   b. Key the letter shown in figure 8.5. Play the **sig.wcm** macro where you see it in the letter.
   c. After you play the **sig.wcm**, add the document name after your initials.
2. Save the letter and name it c08ex02.
3. Print c08ex02.
4. Close c08ex02.

Figure 8.5

October 14, 1996

Mr. Charles Heinz
Chicago Community Hospital
300 Midtown Drive
Chicago, IL 66732

Dear Mr. Heinz:

Re: Victoria Hunt vs. Chicago Community Hospital

Thank you for sending the Complaint in the case of Victoria Hunt vs. Chicago Community Hospital. I have reviewed the Complaint along with the list of allegations. There are some responses to questions that need your input. Please call my office to schedule an appointment.

At first glance, the Complaint seems to lack sufficient evidence for this to go to trial. I will have a clearer idea after I talk with you about the allegations in the Complaint.

sig.wcm

 Editing a Macro

If you have recorded a macro, then decide you want to change it, you can either replace it or edit it. If you replace the macro, you will need to re-record each keystroke. To replace a macro, you would complete the following steps:

1 Choose Tools, Macro, then Record; or click on the Record button on the Macro Tools Toolbar.
2 At the Record Macro dialog box, select an existing macro in the Filename list box, then choose Record.
3 WordPerfect inserts a box saying that the macro already exists. At this box, choose Replace.
4 Complete the steps to be recorded in the macro.
5 End the recording of the macro by choosing Tools, Macro, then Record; or clicking on the Record button on the Macro Tools Toolbar.

There are two methods for opening a macro document for editing. You can open the document as you would a regular document. Or, you can edit a document by completing the following steps:

1 Choose Tools, Macro, then Edit; or click on the Edit Macro button on the Macro Tools Toolbar.
2 At the Edit Macro dialog box, select the macro to be edited in the Filename list box, then choose Edit.
3 The macro document is opened on the screen. Make any changes/revisions, then save and close the macro document in the normal manner.

Exercise 3 Changing Margins in a Macro

1. At a clear editing window, edit the **margins.wcm** macro so it changes left and right margins to 1.25 inches (rather than 1.5 inches) by completing the following steps:
   a. Choose Tools, Macro, then Edit; or click on the Edit Macro button on the Macro Tools Toolbar.
   b. At the Edit Macro dialog box, select **margins.wcm**, then choose Edit.
   c. At the macro document shown in figure 8.6, move the insertion point immediately left of the *5* in the line *MarginLeft (1.5")* then key a 2. (This should make the line display as *MarginLeft (1.25")*.)
   d. Move the insertion point immediately left of the *5* in the line *MarginRight (1.5")* then key a 2. (This should make the line display as *MarginRight(1.25")*.)
   e. Choose Save & Compile from the Macros Feature Bar.
   f. Close the macro by choosing Options from the Macros Feature Bar, then choosing Close Macro.
2. At a clear editing window, play the **margins.wcm** macro and the **ls.wcm** macro.
3. Key the document shown in figure 8.7. Change the line spacing back to single to key the signature line and the information below it.
4. Save the document and name it c08x03.
5. Print c08ex03.
6. Close c08ex03.

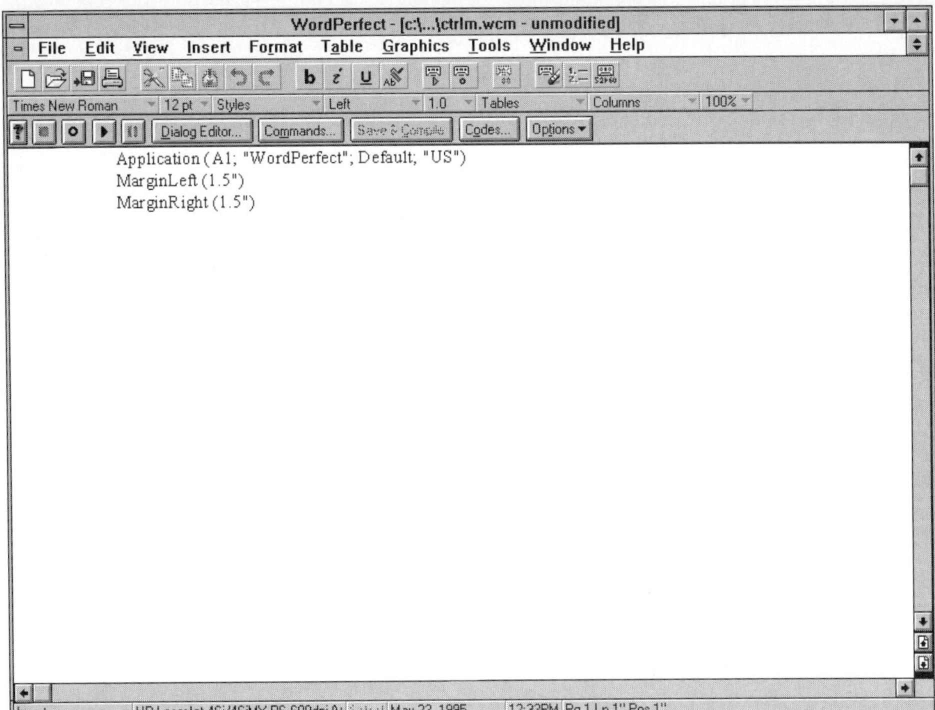

Figure 8.6
margins.wcm Macro Document

Figure 8.7

CLAIM OF LIEN

Chicago Community Hospital, Claimant vs. Ian Sands

Notice is hereby given that the person named below claims a lien pursuant to Chapter 94.23 RCI. In support of this lien, the following information is submitted:

1. Name of Lien Claimant: Chicago Community Hospital

   Telephone Number: (215) 555-4300

   Address: 300 Midtown Drive, Chicago, IL 66732
2. Date claimant performed services: October 15, 1996, through October 30, 1996
3. Name of person indebted to the claimant: Ian Sands
4. Principal amount claimed in the lien: $8,400

JEANETTE ENERSEN
Attorney for Claimant

Pausing a Macro

When recording some macros, you may want to pause the macro to allow keyboard entry. The Pause button on the Macro Tools Toolbar or the Pause option from the Tools, Macro drop-down menu will pause a macro at a specific location. To create a macro with a pause, you would complete the following steps:

1 Choose Tools, Macro, then Record; or click on the Record button on the Macro Tools Toolbar.

2 At the Record Macro dialog box, key a name for the macro, then choose Record.

3 At the clear editing window, record the steps for the macro. As the steps are being recorded, insert a pause where you want keyboard entry to occur by completing the following steps:
   a. Choose Tools, Macro, then Pause; or click on the Pause button on the Macro Tools Toolbar.
   b. Choose Tools, Macro, then Pause; or click on the Pause button on the Macro Tools Toolbar.

4 After recording all steps for the macro, including the pauses, end the recording of the macro. To do this, choose Tools, Macro, then Record; or click on the Record button on the Macro Tools Toolbar.

In steps 3a and 3b, you choose Tools, Macro, then Pause twice; or click twice on the Pause button. (These must be two separate clicks—not a double-click.)

When the macro is played, the macro plays to the first pause. Key the required text, then press Enter. This continues playing the macro.

Exercise 4 Recording a Macro with Pauses

1. At a clear editing window, record a macro named **notary** that contains pauses by completing the following steps:
   a. Choose Tools, Macro, then Record; or click on the Record button on the Macro Tools Toolbar.
   b. At the Record Macro dialog box, key **notary**, then choose Record.
   c. At the editing window, key the text shown in figure 8.8 to the location of the first **(pause)**, then insert a pause by clicking on the Pause button on the Macro Tools Toolbar, then clicking on the Pause button again. (You will not see anything identifying the pause in the editing window.)
   d. Press the space bar once, then continue keying the document. Insert pauses in the macro where you see **(pause)** in the figure. Do not key (pause) in the macro. This is only to identify where the pause is inserted.
   e. When you are done keying the text in figure 8.8, end the recording of the macro by choosing Tools, Macro, then Record; or clicking on the Record button on the Macro Tools Toolbar.
   f. Close the document without saving it.
2. At a clear editing window, record a macro named **heada** (for Heading A) that selects a heading, then changes the relative size to Very Large by completing the following steps:
   a. Key **This is a heading**. (This gives you some text to select when recording the macro.)
   b. Position the insertion point immediately left of the *T* in *This*.
   c. Click on the Record button on the Macro Tools Toolbar.
   d. At the Record Macro dialog box, key **heada**, then choose Record.
   e. At the editing window, complete the following steps:
      (1) Press F8 to turn on Select.
      (2) Press the End key to select text to the end of the line.
      (3) Double-click on the Font Face button on the Power Bar to display the Font dialog box.
      (4) At the Font dialog box, choose Relative Size, then Very Large.

(5) Choose OK to close the font dialog box.
(6) Press F8 to turn off Select.

f. End the recording of the macro by clicking on the Record button on the Macro Tools Toolbar.

3. Close the document without saving it.

Figure 8.8

STATE OF ILLINOIS)
) ss.
COUNTY OF MADISON)

I, the undersigned, duly swear that I am the **(pause)** in this case, have read the foregoing instrument, know the contents thereof, and believe the same to be true and correct.

SUBSCRIBED AND SWORN to before me this **(pause)** day of **(pause)**, 1996.

____

NOTARY PUBLIC in and for the State
of Illinois, residing at Chicago

Exercise 5 Entering Text at Pauses

1. At a clear editing window, open c08ex03.
2. Save the document with Save As and name it c08ex05.
3. Position the insertion point on the *C* in *CLAIM OF LIEN*, then play the **heada** macro.
4. Move the insertion point to the end of the document (a triple space below the lines below Attorney for Claimant, then play the **notary** macro. As the macro stops at a pause, enter the following text (press Enter after entering the text; this causes the macro to continue):

first pause	=	**Claimant**
second pause	=	**6th**
third pause	=	**November**

5. Save the document again with the same name (c08ex05).
6. Print c08ex05.
7. Close c08ex05.

Deleting a Macro

A macro document can be deleted at the Open File dialog box. To delete a macro, you would complete the following steps:

1 Display the Open File dialog box.
2 Select the macro document name in the Filename list box.
3 Choose File Options, then Delete.
4 At the Delete question, choose Yes.
5 Cancel the Open File dialog box.

Using Templates

WordPerfect has included a number of *template* documents that are formatted for specific uses. Each WordPerfect document is based on a template document; the standard template document is the default.

You can create a variety of documents using WordPerfect templates such as business documents, calendars, envelopes, faxes, legal documents, letters, memos, publication documents, reports, and resumes. To display the types of templates available, choose File, then New; or click on the New Document button on the 6.1 WordPerfect Toolbar (the fourteenth button from the left). The New Document button is different than the New Blank Document button on the Toolbar. The New Blank Document button (the first button from the left) opens a new document based on the main template. The New Document button displays the New Document dialog box so you can choose the template on which you want the new document based.

At the New Document dialog box shown in figure 8.9, types of templates are displayed in the Group list box. Select a type of template in the Group list box and WordPerfect displays specific templates in the Select Template list box. For example, if you select *envelope* in the Group list box, WordPerfect displays *Envelope - Contemporary, Envelope - Cosmopolitan, Envelope - Traditional,* and *Envelope - Trimline* in the Select Template list box. To choose a template, select it in the Select Template list box, then choose Select. Depending on the template you choose, you will be presented with a screen or a dialog box requesting specific information.

Figure 8.9
New Document Dialog Box

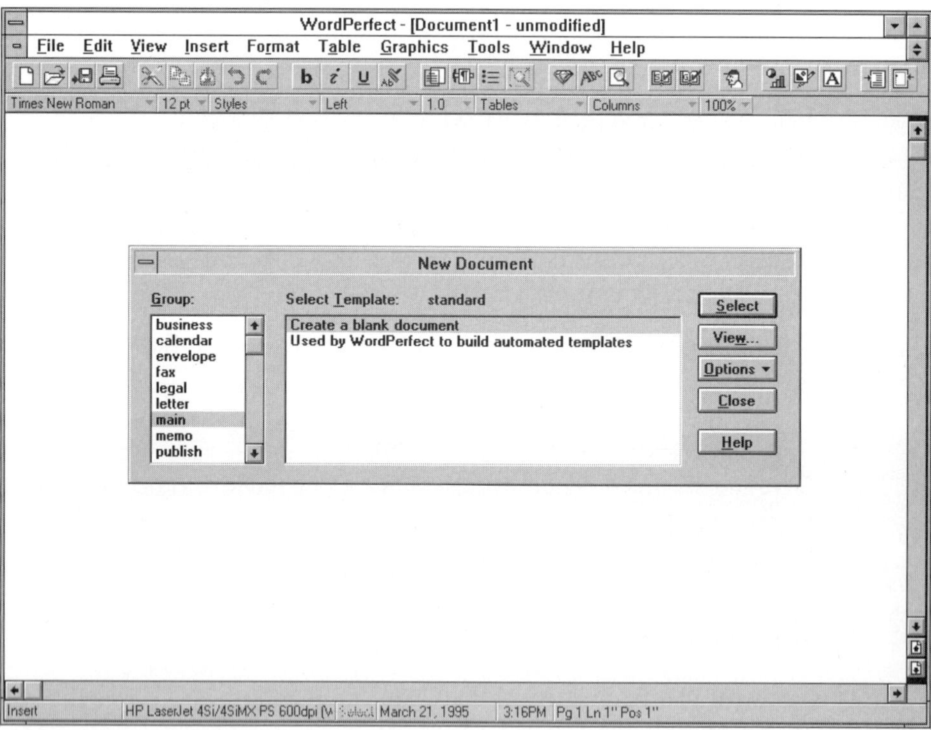

Exercise 6 Creating a Calendar

1. At a clear editing window, create a calendar for the current month using a WordPerfect template by completing the following steps:
   a. Choose File, then New; or click on the New Document button on the Toolbar (fourteenth button from the left).
   b. At the New Document dialog box, select *calendar* in the Group list box.
   c. Select *Monthly Calendar - Portrait orientation* in the Select Template list box, then choose Select.

d. At the Calendar dialog box, make sure the current month and year display, then choose OK.

2. When WordPerfect has completed building the calendar, click on the Page/Zoom Full button to view the calendar on the entire page. After viewing the calendar, click on the Page/Zoom Full button again to return the view to the default.
3. Save the document and name it c08ex06.
4. Print c08ex06.
5. Close c08ex06.

In exercise 6, all you had to do was specify the month and the year. WordPerfect created the calendar without any more input. Other templates, however, require considerable input from you. For example, in exercise 7, you will use a letter template to create a business letter that requires information from you.

The first time you create a document such as a business letter or memo, WordPerfect displays the Enter Your Personal Information dialog box. At this dialog box, you are prompted to enter information such as your name, title, organization, address, city, state, ZIP, telephone number, and fax number. This dialog box displays only the first time you create a document requiring personal information. After that, WordPerfect automatically uses the personal information. Because WordPerfect only prompts you for personal information the first time you create a document requiring it, the steps in exercise 7 may vary.

Exercise 7 Working with the Letter Template

1. At a clear editing window, create a business letter with the text shown in figure 8.10 using a letter template by completing the following steps:
   a. Choose File, then New; or click on the New Document button on the Toolbar.
   b. At the New Document dialog box, select *letter* in the Group list box.
   c. Select *Letter - Contemporary Letterhead* in the Select Template list box, then choose Select.
   d. At the Letter dialog box, key the following information in the Recipient's Name and Address text box:

      Rhea Hollis
      Consultant
      Rodelo & Associates
      4713 North Kelly Drive
      Denver, CO 86422

   e. Choose Salutation, then key **Dear Ms. Hollis:**.
   f. Choose Personal Info. (This button is located at the right side of the Letter dialog box.)
   g. At the Enter Your Personal Information dialog box, key the following text in the specified text box: (After keying text in a text box, press Enter or Tab. This moves the insertion point to the next text box. If the following text is already displayed in the dialog box, skip to step h.)

Name:	=	Cynthia Wagner
Title:	=	Director of Facilities
Organization:	=	Denver Memorial Hospital
Address:	=	900 Colorado Boulevard
City, State ZIP:	=	Denver, CO 86530
Telephone:	=	(303) 555-4400
Fax:	=	(303) 555-4110

   h. When all information is entered, choose OK or press Enter.

i. At the Letter dialog box, choose OK.
j. The Letter Formatting Complete dialog box displays with the message *To insert the letter closing, choose "Letter Closing" from the "Insert" menu.* At this message, choose OK.
k. With the insertion point positioned below the salutation, key the text shown in figure 8.10. (Press the Enter key once after each paragraph. The letter template contains a paragraph spacing code that will move the insertion point down almost a double space.)
l. After keying the body of the letter, create the complimentary close by completing the following steps:
   (1) With the insertion point a double space below the text of the letter, click on Insert, then Letter Closing.
   (2) At the Letter Closing dialog box, choose Typist's Initials, then key your initials.
   (3) Choose OK.

2. Save the completed letter and name it c08ex07.
3. Print c08ex07.
4. Close c08ex07.

Figure 8.10

Two copies of the Traffic Flow Study are attached for your review. After completion of the study, I recommend implementation of one of the following:

1. For a long-range plan, use a single, centrally located information desk with an adjacent area gift delivery.

2. Close the North entrance information desk and leave the West entrance information desk in its current location. Enhance the directional signs.

3. Retain both information desks, but reduce the hours of operation of the North entrance information desk to 12:00 noon to 5:30 p.m.

The first recommendation will be the most costly and will take the most time to implement. The second recommendation can be implemented within a six-month period and will require a modest financial outlay. The third recommendation does not require any financial outlay and could be a transitional step. Please call me at 555-4400 extension 767 to schedule a time to meet and discuss the analysis.

WordPerfect uses True Type fonts to format the specific templates such as the calendar and the business letter. You may find that printing documents containing True Type fonts may take some time.

Using WordPerfect's Envelope Feature

You can use WordPerfect's Envelope feature to create an envelope for a business letter document. The envelope can be created at a clear editing window or can be created with information in a business letter document.

Creating an Envelope at a Clear Editing Window

To create an envelope document at a clear editing window using the Envelope feature, choose Format, then Envelope. At the Envelope dialog box shown in figure 8.11, make sure the correct envelope definition is displayed in the Envelope Definitions text box. Key a return address in the

Return Addresses section of the dialog box and a mailing address in the Mailing Addresses section. The envelope can then be sent directly to the printer by choosing Print Envelope or it can be appended to the document by choosing Append to Doc.

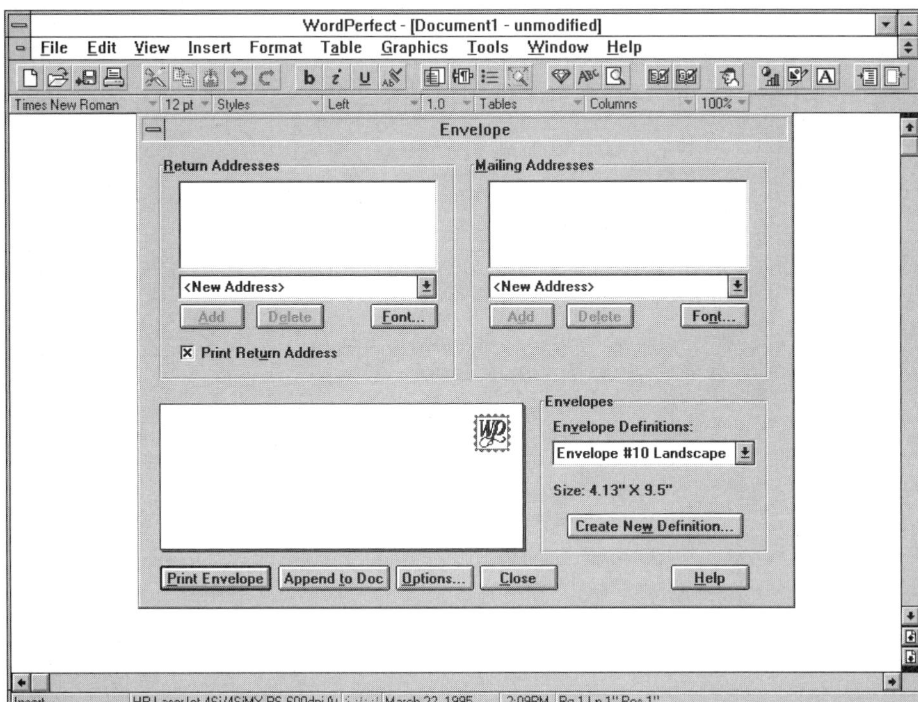

Figure 8.11
Envelope Dialog Box

Exercise 8 Creating an Envelope

1. At a clear editing window, create an envelope using WordPerfect's Envelope feature by completing the following steps:
   a. Choose Format, then Envelope.
   b. At the Envelope dialog box, choose Return Addresses.
   c. Key the return address shown in figure 8.12.
   d. Choose Mailing Addresses.
   e. Key the mailing address shown in figure 8.12.
   f. Choose Append to Doc to insert the envelope in the document.
2. Save the document and name it c08ex08.
3. Print c08ex08. (Depending on the printer you are using, WordPerfect may insert the message, *The Windows driver did not accept the requested paper size. Document will print on paper size the printer did select.* At this message, choose OK or press Enter.)
4. Close c08ex08.

Figure 8.12

Michelle Ching
3320 Westside Drive
San Diego, CA 99432

Mr. Scott Ingram
860 South 52nd Street
San Diego, CA 99567

Creating an Envelope in an Existing Document

If you open the Envelope dialog box in a document containing a letter, the address is automatically inserted in the Mailing Addresses section of the Envelope dialog box. The mailing address in the letter must be inserted at the left margin and there must be two hard returns following the address.

Including a POSTNET Bar Code

You can include a POSTNET (Postal Numeric Encoding Technique) Bar Code in the mailing address at the Envelope dialog box. The bar code speeds mail sorting, increases accuracy of delivery, and reduces postage costs. To create a POSTNET Bar Code, choose POSTNET Bar Code, then key the five-, nine-, or eleven-digit ZIP code. WordPerfect automatically converts the ZIP code into short and tall lines that create the bar code.

The POSTNET Bar Code option displays below the Add, Delete, and Font options in the Mailing Addresses section of the Envelope dialog box. If the POSTNET Bar Code option is not visible, choose Options. At the Envelope Options dialog box, choose Include and Position Above Address or Include and Position Below Address, then choose OK.

Exercise 9 Using Envelope Dialog Box Options

1. At a clear editing window, open letter01.
2. Save the document with Save As and name it c08ex09.
3. Create an envelope for this letter with a POSTNET Bar Code, using WordPerfect's Envelope feature by completing the following steps:
   a. Choose Format, then Envelope.
   b. At the Envelope dialog box, make sure the mailing address is inserted properly in the Mailing Addresses section.
   c. If there is an address in the Return Addresses section, delete it.
   d. Choose Options, then Include and Position Above Address.
   e. Choose OK or press Enter.
   f. Choose Append to Doc.
4. Change the viewing mode to Two Page to see how the address will print on the envelope.
5. Save the document again with the same name (c08ex09).
6. Print only the page containing the envelope. (Depending on the printer you are using, WordPerfect may insert the message, *The Windows driver did not accept the requested paper size. Document will print on paper size the printer did select.* At this message, choose OK or press Enter.)
7. Close c08ex09.

Creating Mailing Labels

Use WordPerfect's Labels feature to print text on mailing labels, file labels, disk labels, or other types of labels. WordPerfect includes approximately 130 definitions for labels that can be purchased at an office supply store. To use a predefined label definition in a document, choose Format, then Labels. At the Labels dialog box shown in figure 8.13, select the desired label type in the Labels list box, then choose Select. As you move the insertion point to different label forms, details of the label form appear below the Labels list box. The label details include the sheet size, label size, number of labels, and the label type.

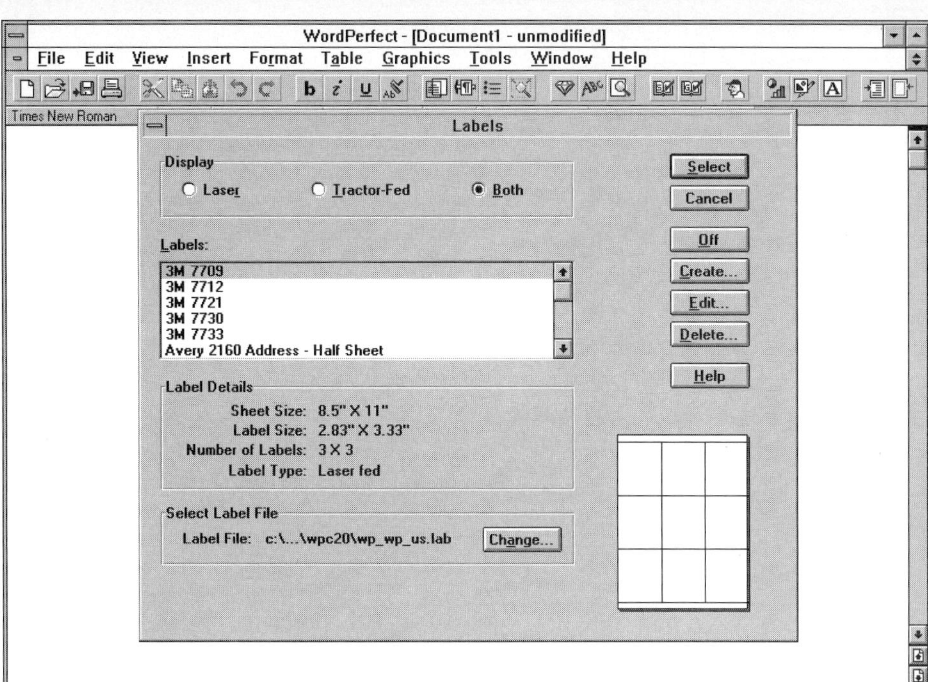

Figure 8.13
Labels Dialog Box

Entering Text in Labels

After inserting a label definition in a document, key the information for the labels. When entering information for labels, use the keys shown in figure 8.14 to perform the action described:

Ctrl + Enter	=	Ends the text of the current label and moves the insertion point to the next label.
Enter	=	Ends a line within a label.
Alt + Page Down	=	Moves the insertion point to the next label.
Alt + Page Up	=	Moves the insertion point to the previous label.

Figure 8.14
Keys for Entering Label Information

When entering text in a label, press Ctrl + Enter to insert a hard page break. The hard page break tells WordPerfect to move to the next label. In a labels form, a page created with Ctrl + Enter is called a *logical page*, while the entire sheet of labels is called the *physical page*. Each label is considered a separate page. Formatting features that affect a page such as page numbering or headers or footers will print on each label.

In a labels document, you may want to change the font to a smaller point size to ensure that all information fits on the label. You may also want to insert a code to center text on the current page and subsequent pages. This will center the text of the label in the middle of the label vertically.

At the Page viewing mode, you will see the label in the editing window. When you press Ctrl + Enter, the insertion point moves to the next label. The labels are outlined in a single gray line. At the Draft viewing mode, you will not see the label. When you press Ctrl + Enter, a double line is inserted in the editing window, and the insertion point is moved below the double line.

Exercise 10 Creating Mailing Labels

1. At a clear editing window, create mailing addresses using a predefined labels definition by completing the following steps:
   a. Choose Format, then Labels.
   b. At the Labels dialog box, position the insertion point on Avery 5160 Address, then choose Select. (This label is quite far down on the labels list. Check with your instructor to see whether your printer will print this label form size. If not, use a different label form size.)
2. At the editing window, key the addresses shown in figure 8.15. Press Ctrl + Enter to end a label and move the insertion point to the next label.
3. Save the document and name it c08ex10.
4. Print c08ex10. (Before printing, check with your instructor to make sure that the printer you are using can print a document with this label definition.)
5. Close c08ex10.

Figure 8.15

Mr. Tony Brewster 903 North Academy Tampa, FL 33543	Dr. Dione Teague Madison Clinic 100 Madison Avenue Tampa, FL 33512	Ms. Lona Schauffer Southside Shipping 9873 Parker Road Tampa, FL 33422
Mrs. Elana Steffan 15403 South 42nd Street Tampa, FL 33541	Mr. Rodney Marlow 6320 South 32nd Tampa, FL 33453	Professor Lea Steele Bayside Community College 2300 North 51st Tampa, FL 33422

Using QuickCorrect

As mentioned in chapter 1, WordPerfect includes a feature called *QuickCorrect* that automatically corrects certain words as they are being keyed. For example, if you key the word *adn* instead of *and*, QuickCorrect automatically corrects it when you press the space bar after the word. There is a large number of automatic corrections that can be seen in the QuickCorrect dialog box. To display the QuickCorrect dialog box shown in figure 8.16, choose Tools, then QuickCorrect. At the QuickCorrect dialog box, use the vertical scroll bar in the list box to view the entire list of words that WordPerfect will correct.

Adding a Word to QuickCorrect

Commonly misspelled words or typographical errors can be added to QuickCorrect. For example, if you consistently key *oopen* instead of *open*, you can add *oopen* to QuickCorrect and tell it to correct it as *open*. To add an entry to QuickCorrect, key the misspelling in the Replace text box, key the correct spelling in the With text box, then choose Add Entry.

Entries in QuickCorrect can be deleted. To delete an entry, select the entry in the list box at the QuickCorrect dialog box, then choose Delete Entry. WordPerfect will insert a dialog box asking if you want to delete the entry. At this dialog box, choose Yes.

By default, QuickCorrect will automatically replace text. You can turn automatic replacement off by removing the X from the Replace Words as You Type check box that displays at the bottom of the QuickCorrect dialog box.

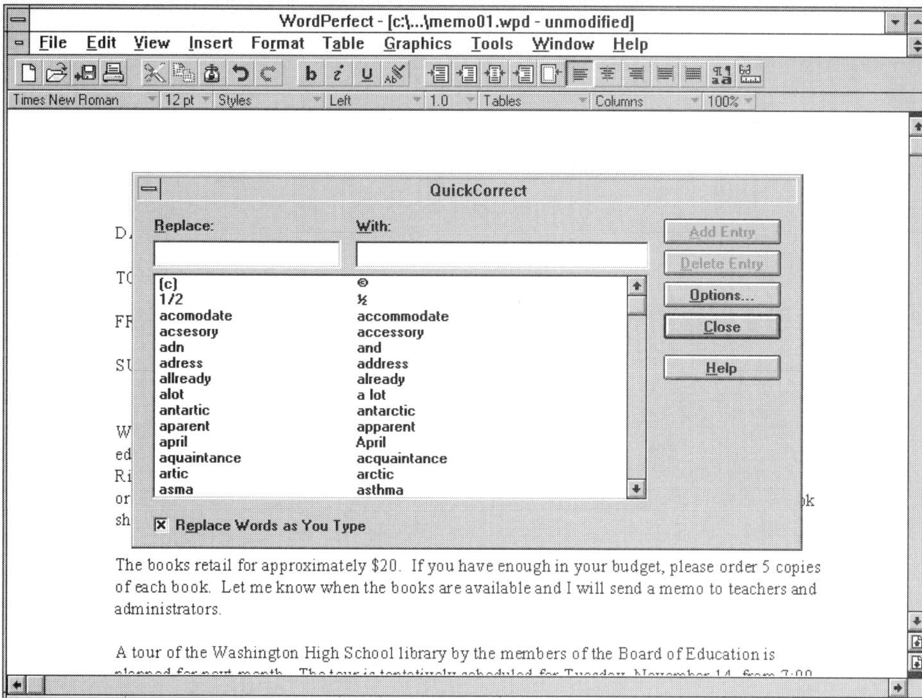

Figure 8.16
QuickCorrect Dialog Box

Changing QuickCorrect Options

The QuickCorrect feature contains a number of options that can be active or inactive. To view QuickCorrect options, choose Options from the QuickCorrect dialog box. At the QuickCorrect Options dialog box shown in figure 8.17, an option is active if an X appears in the check box. An option is also active if a black dot appears in the radio button before it.

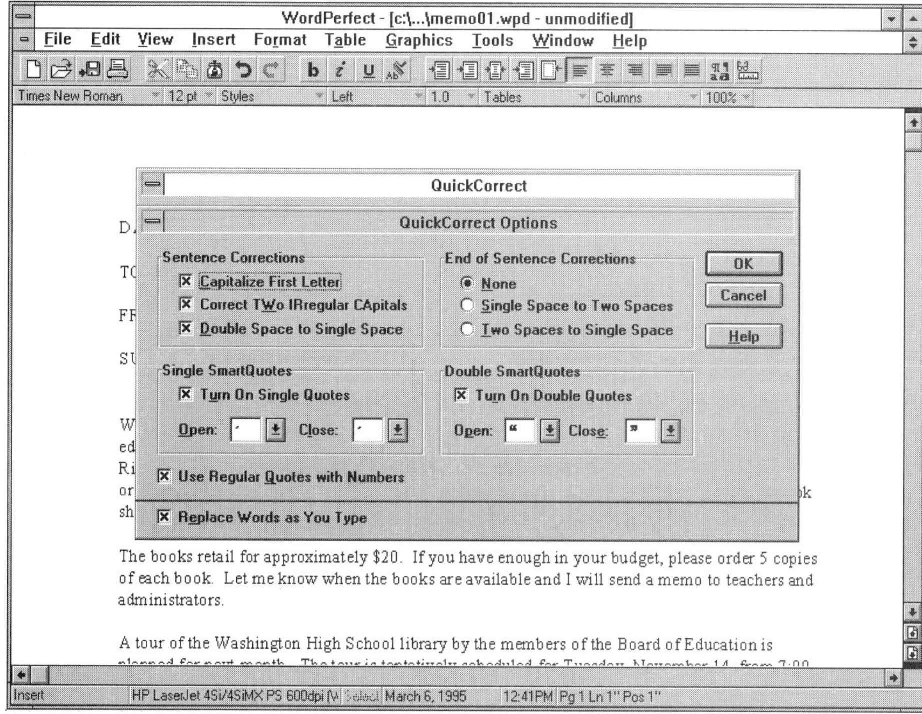

Figure 8.17
QuickCorrect Options Dialog Box

At the QuickCorrect Options dialog box, insert an X for those options you want active and remove the X from those options you want inactive. The End of Sentence Correction box contains three choices: None, Single Space to Two Spaces, and Two Spaces to Single Space. The default is None. Choose one of the other options if you want QuickCorrect to correct how many spaces are inserted after punctuation at the end of a sentence.

After making any changes to the QuickCorrect Options dialog box, choose OK or press Enter. This returns you to the QuickCorrect dialog box. Choose Close to close the QuickCorrect dialog box.

Exercise 11 Editing QuickCorrect Entries

1. At a clear editing window, add words to QuickCorrect by completing the following steps:
   a. Choose Tools, then QuickCorrect.
   b. At the QuickCorrect dialog box, make sure the insertion point is positioned in the Replace text box. (If not, choose Replace.)
   c. Key **efficiancy**.
   d. Choose With.
   e. Choose **efficiency**.
   f. Choose Add Entry.
   g. Choose Replace.
   h. Key **facters**.
   i. Choose With.
   j. Key **factors**.
   k. Choose Add Entry.
   l. Choose Replace.
   m. Key **tele**.
   n. Choose With.
   o. Key **telecommunications**.
   p. Choose Add Entry.
   q. Choose Close.
2. Key the text shown in figure 8.18. (Key the text exactly as shown. QuickCorrect will correct words as you key.)
3. Save the document and name it c08ex11.
4. Print c08ex11.
5. Delete the words you added to QuickCorrect by completing the following steps:
   a. Choose Tools, then QuickCorrect.
   b. At the QuickCorrect dialog box, click on *efficiancy* in the list box. (You will need to scroll down the list box to display *efficiancy*.)
   c. Choose Delete Entry.
   d. At the dialog box asking if you want to delete the entry, choose Yes.
   e. Click on *facters* in the list box. (You will need to scroll down the list box to display *facters*.)
   f. Choose Delete Entry.
   g. Click on *tele* in the list box.
   h. Choose Delete Entry.
   i. Choose Close.
6. Close c08ex11.

Figure 8.18

You consider several important facters before deciding which new tele system management should purchase. You thoroughly study cost, efficiancy, quality, time, and ease of use. You use these facters to evaluate every tele application in terms of how well it solves a specific business problem. Later, you will be asked to rate tele systems using the facters of cost, efficiancy, quality, time, and ease of use.

CHAPTER SUMMARY

- A *macro* is a document containing recorded commands and/or text. This document can be played back at any time to accomplish a task automatically.
- When creating a macro, known as *recording*, all commands and keystrokes pressed are stored in a macro document to be played back later.
- By default, a macro document is saved in the **c:\office\wpwin\macros** directory. This can be changed at the File Preferences dialog box.
- A macro name can be from 1-8 characters and cannot contain spaces. The macro extension, **.wcm**, is added automatically.
- Macros can be played once or several times anywhere in a document, from the Play Macro dialog box.
- To change a macro, it must be either replaced or edited.
- While recording a macro, it can be paused to allow keyboard entry.
- A macro can be deleted at the Open File dialog box.
- A number of template documents that can be used to produce a variety of creative documents are provided by WordPerfect.
- The default template document is the main template.
- Use the Envelope feature to create an envelope at a clear editing window or in an existing document. In an existing document, the address is automatically inserted in the Mailing Addresses section of the Envelope dialog box.
- Use the Labels feature to print text on mailing labels, file labels, disk labels, etc. To use a predefined label definition, display the Labels dialog box.
- The QuickCorrect feature automatically corrects certain words as they are being keyed. At the QuickCorrect dialog box, you can add words to QuickCorrect or change or delete words.

Commands Review

	Mouse/Keyboard
File Preferences dialog box	Edit, Preferences
Macro Tools Toolbar	Position arrow pointer on current Toolbar, click the right mouse button, then click on Macro Tools
Record Macro dialog box	Tools, Macro, Record; or click on the Record button on the Macro Tools Toolbar
Play Macro dialog box	Tools, Macro, Play; or click on the Play button on the Macro Tools Toolbar.
Edit Macro dialog box	Tools, Macro, Edit; or click on the Edit Macro button on the Macro Tools Toolbar
Pause during macro recording	Tools, Macro, Pause twice; or click on the Pause button on the Macro Tools Toolbar twice

New Document dialog box	File, New; or click on the New Document button on the Toolbar
Envelope dialog box	Format, Envelope
Labels dialog box	Format, Labels
QuickCorrect dialog box	Tools, QuickCorrect

CHECK YOUR UNDERSTANDING

True/False: Circle the letter T if the statement is true; circle the letter F if the statement is false.

T F 1. A macro name can contain 1-10 characters.

T F 2. If you define a macro with the name **rm**, it appears in the directory as **rm.mac**.

T F 3. A macro cannot be edited.

T F 4. A macro can be deleted at the Open File dialog box.

T F 5. When a macro is created, it is automatically saved on the drive where the user's documents are located.

T F 6. The default template document is named *Letter - Contemporary*.

T F 7. Use a template document to create a macro.

T F 8. If you open the Envelope dialog box in a document containing a letter, the address is automatically inserted in the Mailing Addresses section of the Envelope dialog box.

T F 9. An entire sheet of labels is referred to as a logical page.

T F 10. Display the QuickCorrect dialog box by choosing Format, then QuickCorrect.

T F 11. Entries can be added or deleted from the QuickCorrect dialog box.

List the steps that are necessary (using either a mouse or the keyboard) to record a macro that changes the top margin to 2 inches. Name the macro **top2**.

____

____

____

____

____

List the steps that are necessary (using either a mouse or the keyboard) to play the **top2** macro recorded above.

____

____

____

____

SKILL ASSESSMENTS

Assessment 1

1. At a clear editing window, record the following macros:
   a. Record a macro named **headb** that selects text, then changes the Relative Size to Large.
   b. Record a macro named **geo12** that changes the font to 12-point GeoSlab703 Lt BT.
2. Close the document without saving it.

Assessment 2

1. At a clear screen, open report01.
2. Save the document with Save As and name it c08sa02.
3. With the insertion point positioned at the beginning of the document, play the following macros:
   a. **geo12.wcm**
   b. **margins.wcm**
4. Position the insertion point on the *T* in *TRENDS IN TELECOMMUNICATIONS*, then play the **heada.wcm** macro.
5. Position the insertion point on the *C* in *Continued Growth of Photonics (Fiber Optics)*, then play the **headb.wcm** macro.
6. Position the insertion point on the *M* in *Microcomputer Trends in the Nineties*, then play the **headb.wcm** macro.
7. Save the document again with the same name (c08sa02).
8. Print c08sa02.
9. Close c08sa02.

Assessment 3

1. At a clear editing window, replace the **heada.wcm** macro so it selects text, changes the selected text to 16-point Humanst521 Lt BT, then turns off Select.
2. Replace the **headb.wcm** macro so it selects text, changes the selected text to 14-point Humanst521 Lt BT, then turns off Select.
3. Close the document without saving it.

Assessment 4

1. At a clear editing window, open report08.
2. Save the document with Save As and name it c08sa04.
3. With the insertion point positioned at the beginning of the document, play the following macros:
   a. **geo12.wcm**
   b. **margins.wcm**
4. Position the insertion point on the *I* in *IDENTIFICATION OF CI*, then play the **heada.wcm** macro.
5. Play the **headb.wcm** macro for each of the following headings:
   Introduction
   Purpose and Scope
   Application
   Requirements
6. Save the document again with the same name (c08sa04).
7. Print c08sa04.
8. Close c08sa04.

Assessment 5

1. At a clear editing window, create a sign using a template document by completing the following steps:
   a. Display the New Document dialog box.
   b. At the New Document dialog box, select *publish* in the Group list box, select *Sign - Seminar announcement* in the Select Template list box, then choose Select.
   c. At the Template Information dialog box, key the following text in the specified field:

Title of Seminar:	=	Managing Stress on the Job
Sponsored By:	=	Denver Memorial Hospital
Name of Speaker:	=	Jillian Youngblood
Speaker's Title:	=	Trainer
Speaker's Organization:	=	ROM Corporation
Date of Seminar:	=	Wednesday, March 19, 1997
Location of Seminar:	=	Room 234, East Wing
Telephone # for Information:	=	(303) 555-4428

   d. After keying the information at the Template Information dialog box, choose OK.
2. When the sign is completed, save it and name it c08sa05.
3. Print c08sa05.
4. Close c08sa05.

Assessment 6

1. At a clear editing window, open letter04.
2. Save the document with Save As and name it c08sa06.
3. Use WordPerfect's Envelope feature to create an envelope for this letter. Make sure the ZIP Code displays in the POSTNET Bar Code text box.
4. Save the document again with the same name (c08sa06).
5. Print only the page containing the envelope.
6. Close c08sa06.

Assessment 7

1. At a clear editing window, create mailing addresses using a predefined labels definition. Choose a labels definition that can be used by your printer. Depending on the label size, you may need to change the font to a smaller point size to ensure that the text fits on each line.
2. At the editing window, key the addresses shown in figure 8.19. Press Ctrl + Enter to end a label and move the insertion point to the next label.
3. Save the document and name it c08sa07.
4. Print c08sa07.
5. Close c08sa07.

Figure 8.19

Mr. Karl Erwin 320 McCutcheon Road Santa Fe, NM 88932	Ms. Patricia Paterno 1008 Valley Avenue Santa Fe, NM 88934	Doug Miyasaki, M.D. Miyasaki & Associates 1102 Lakeridge Drive Santa Fe, NM 88930
Ms. LaDonna Ferraro After-Five Flowers 4302 Third Avenue Santa Fe, NM 88432	Mr. Lloyd Catlin Atwood Fencing 4039 Ridge Street Santa Fe, NM 88043	Mrs. Tamara Butler 9803 Deer Road Santa Fe, NM 88032

Assessment 8

1. At a clear editing window, add the following entries to QuickCorrect:
   a. Enter *dtp* in the Replace text box and *desktop publishing* in the With text box.
   b. Enter *prouduce* in the Replace text box and *produce* in the With text box.
2. Key the text shown in figure 8.20. (Key the text exactly as shown. QuickCorrect will correct words as you key.)
3. Save the document and name it c08sa08.
4. Print c08sa08.
5. Delete *dtp* and *prouduce* from QuickCorrect.
6. Close c08sa08.

Figure 8.20

In the graphic arts world, dtp is considered a prepress technology, that is, the dtp system itself is generally not used to prouduce the final multiple copies of a publication, but rather to prouduce masters for reproduction. Because it is relatively inexpensive and user-friendly, dtp has put the power of professional-quality publishing in the hands of many who are not publishing professionals. Some speak out against this trend and point to the flood of poorly designed publications produced by inexperienced publishers.

Merging Documents

Upon successful completion of chapter 9, you will be able to format and merge separate files to create a series of similar business documents, such as personalized form letters and envelopes.

WordPerfect includes a merge feature that you can use to create letters, envelopes, labels, and much more, all with personalized information.

Generally, there are two documents that need to be created for merging. One document, which WordPerfect calls the *data file*, contains the variable information. The second document contains the standard text along with identifiers showing where variable information (information that changes) is to be inserted. WordPerfect refers to this as the *form file*.

Creating a Data File

Generally, a merge takes two documents—the *data file* and the *form file*. These documents can be created in any order, but you might find it easiest to create the data file first and then the form file.

The data file contains the variable information that will be inserted in the form file. Before creating a data file, you may want to determine what type of correspondence you will be inserting the variable information into. For example, suppose the sales manager of Sealine Products wants to introduce a new sales representative to all customers in the Spokane, Washington, area. The sales manager determines that a personal letter should be sent to all customers in the greater Spokane area. Figure 9.1 shows one way this letter can be written.

The date, body of the letter, and the complimentary close are standard. The variable information—information that will change with each letter—is the name, company name, address, city, state, ZIP Code, and salutation.

Determining Fields

In this letter, the variable information needs to be broken into sections called *fields*. To determine the variable fields, you need to decide how, and in what form, the information will be used.

Figure 9.1
Sample Letter

June 8, 1996

Name
Company name
Street address
City, State ZIP
Dear (Name):

At Sealine Products, we are committed to providing quality products and services to our customers. To provide continuing service to you, a new sales representative has been hired. The new sales representative, Ms. Leanne Guile, began her employment with Sealine Products on May 1. She comes to our company with over 10 years' experience in the food industry.

Ms. Guile will be in the Spokane area during the third week of June. She would like to schedule a time for a visit to your company, and will be contacting you by telephone next week.

Sincerely,

Mark Deveau, Manager
Sales Department

The following is a name and address of a customer of Sealine Products:

Mr. Albert Rausch
Lobster Shoppe
450 Marginal Way
Spokane, WA 98012

The name, *Mr. Albert Rausch*, could be identified as an entire field. However, the salutation for this letter should read *Dear Mr. Rausch.* If the name is left as one field, the salutation will read *Dear Mr. Albert Rausch.* In this example, then, the name should be broken into three fields: title (Mr.), first name, and last name.

There is no need for the company name, *Lobster Shoppe*, to be broken into smaller parts. Therefore, it can be identified as one field. The street address, *450 Marginal Way*, can also remain as one field.

The city, state, and ZIP Code in this example can also be considered as one field. However, if you decide that you need the city, state, or ZIP Code separated, you need to make separate fields for each item.

After all fields have been determined, the next step is to determine field names. (This step is optional. If you do not include field names, WordPerfect numbers fields.) There is no limit to the number of fields a data file can contain. The following shows one way the fields can be named:

title
first name
last name
company name
street address
city, state ZIP

A field name can be up to 80 characters in length and can include spaces. You can use either uppercase or lowercase letters.

Variable information in a data file is saved as a *record*. A record contains all the information for one unit (for example, a person, family, customer, client, or business). A set of fields makes one record, and a set of records makes a data file.

In the data file for the example letter in figure 9.1, each record will contain six fields of information: title; first name; last name; company name; address; and the city, state ZIP. Each record in the data file must contain the same number of fields. If the number of fields is not consistent, information will not be inserted correctly during the merge.

WordPerfect offers two methods for creating a data file. You can create a data file as a normal text file, or you can create a data file in the Table format.

Creating a Data File

Create a data file for the variable information that will be inserted into a form file. When you create a data file, name the fields consistent with the field names in the form file. To create a data file for the example letter in figure 9.1, complete exercise 1.

Exercise 1 Creating a Data File

1. At a clear editing window, create a data file for the customers of Sealine Products shown in figure 9.2 by completing the following steps:
   a. At a clear screen, choose Tools, then Merge.
   b. At the Merge dialog box shown in figure 9.3, choose Data.
   c. At the Create Data File dialog box shown in figure 9.4, key **title**, then press Enter. (This inserts *title* in the Field Name List list box.)
   d. Key **first name**, then press Enter.
   e. Key the other field names—**last name**; **company name**; **street address**; and **city, state ZIP**. Press Enter after each field name.
   f. When all field names have been keyed, choose OK or press Enter.
   g. At the Quick Data Entry dialog box shown in figure 9.5, key **Mr.** in the *title* field, then press Enter.
   h. Continue keying the information in figure 9.2 in the appropriate field.
   i. After keying the last field of information for the last customer, choose Close.
   j. WordPerfect inserts the message *Save the changes to disk?* At this question, choose Yes.
   k. At the Save Data File As dialog box, key **spcust.df**, then choose OK or press Enter.
2. Print spcust.df. (This may be optional. Check with your instructor to see if you should print this document. Each record will print on a separate page.)
3. Close the spcust.df document.

Figure 9.2

title	=	Mr.
first name	=	Darren
last name	=	Judd
company name	=	Chips 'n Chowder
street address	=	2349 Lowell Drive
city, state ZIP	=	Spokane, WA 98031
title	=	Mrs.
first name	=	Kiley
last name	=	Hostkins
company name	=	Kiley's Kitchen
street address	=	903 Fifth Street
city, state ZIP	=	Spokane, WA 98036
title	=	Mr. and Mrs.
first name	=	Tristin
last name	=	Keating
company name	=	The Salmon Cafe
street address	=	332 River Drive
city, state ZIP	=	Spokane, WA 98031

Figure 9.3
Merge Dialog Box

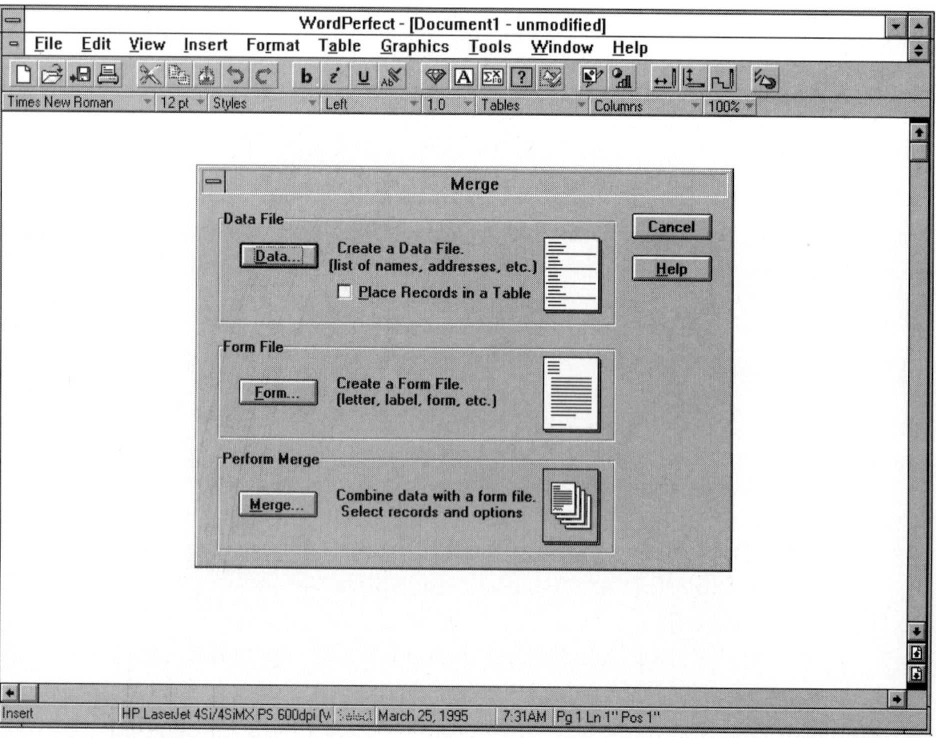

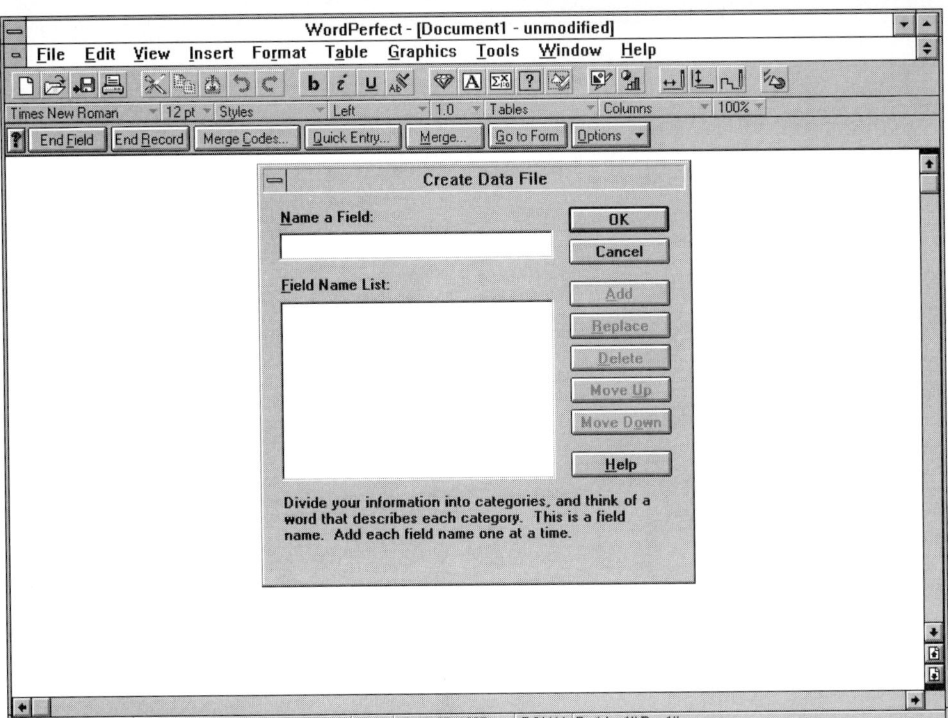

Figure 9.4
Create Data File Dialog Box

When entering text in the Quick Data Entry dialog box, you can use the Tab key to move the insertion point to the next field or press Shift + Tab to move the insertion point to the previous field. These commands are useful for editing text in the fields.

When you save the document in step 1k (before closing the document), the data file displays in the editing window. The Data File Feature Bar displays below the Power Bar. Figure 9.6 shows how the data file will display for customers of Sealine Products.

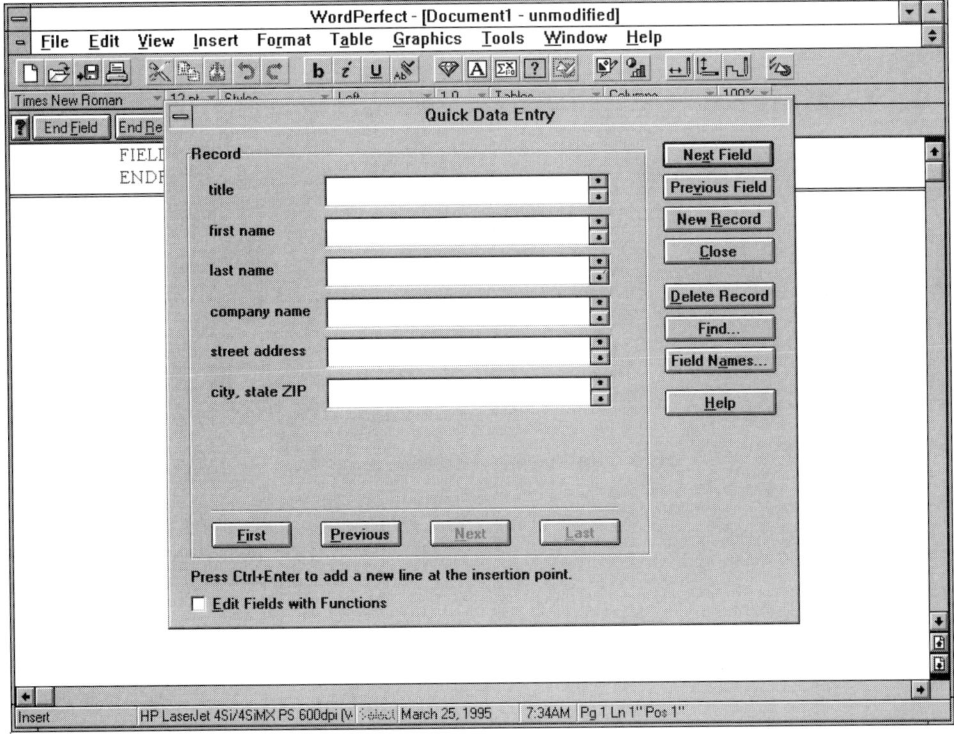

Figure 9.5
Quick Data Entry Dialog Box

Figure 9.6
Sample Text Data File

```
FIELDNAMES(title;first name;last name;company name;
street address;city, state ZIP)ENDRECORD
________________________________________________
Mr.ENDFIELD
DarrenENDFIELD
JuddENDFIELD
Chips 'n ChowderENDFIELD
2349 Lowell DriveENDFIELD
Spokane, WA 98031ENDFIELD
ENDRECORD
________________________________________________
Mrs.ENDFIELD
KileyENDFIELD
HostkinsENDFIELD
Kiley's KitchenENDFIELD
903 Fifth StreetENDFIELD
Spokane, WA 98036ENDFIELD
ENDRECORD
________________________________________________
Mr. and Mrs.ENDFIELD
TristinENDFIELD
KeatingENDFIELD
The Salmon CafeENDFIELD
332 River DriveENDFIELD
Spokane, WA 98031ENDFIELD
ENDRECORD
________________________________________________
```

In the data file shown in figure 9.6 each field takes up less than one line. A field can contain more than one line, however. For example, the record for Mr. and Mrs. Keating could include the following:

Mr. and Mrs.**ENDFIELD**
Tristin**ENDFIELD**
Keating**ENDFIELD**
The Salmon Cafe**ENDFIELD**
332 River Drive
Suite 210**ENDFIELD**
Spokane, WA 98031**ENDFIELD**

When entering the information in the *street address* field at the Quick Data Entry dialog box, key the first line (332 River Drive), then press Ctrl + Enter. This causes the first line to move up in the *street address* field and it does not display. Key the second line of the field, then press Enter. This moves the insertion point to the next field.

Creating the Form File

When you have determined the fields and field names and created the data file, the next step is to create the form file. When the form letter is completed and the fields have been keyed in the proper locations, it will look like the letter in figure 9.7.

Figure 9.7
Example Form File

June 8, 1996

FIELD(title) **FIELD**(first name) **FIELD**(last name)
FIELD(company name)
FIELD(street address)
FIELD(city, state ZIP)

Dear **FIELD**(title) **FIELD**(last name):

At Sealine Products, we are committed to providing quality products and services to our customers. To provide continuing service to you, a new sales representative has been hired. The new sales representative, Ms. Leanne Guile, began her employment with Sealine Products on May 1. She comes to our company with over 10 years' experience in the food industry.

Ms. Guile will be in the Spokane area during the third week of June. She would like to schedule a time for a visit to your company, and will be contacting you by telephone next week.

Sincerely,

Mark Deveau, Manager
Sales Department

To create the form file shown in figure 9.7, complete exercise 2.

Exercise 2 Creating a Form File

1. At a clear editing window, create the form file shown in figure 9.7 by completing the following steps:
   a. Choose Tools, then Merge.
   b. At the Merge dialog box, choose Form.
   c. At the Create Form File dialog box, key **spcust.df**, then choose OK or press Enter.
   d. At the editing window with the Merge Feature Bar displayed as shown in figure 9.8, key the letter to the point where the first field code (the field for *title*) is to be inserted.
   e. Choose Insert Field from the Merge Feature Bar. This causes the Insert Field Name or Number dialog box shown in figure 9.9 to display.
   f. At the Insert Field Name or Number dialog box, make sure the insertion point is positioned on *title*, then choose Insert. (This inserts *FIELD(title)* in the document.)
   g. Press the space bar once, select *first name* in the Insert Field Name or Number dialog box, then choose Insert.

h. Continue creating the fields and text shown in figure 9.7 following steps similar to those in steps f and g. (Leave on the display of the Insert Field Name or Number dialog box until you have inserted all fields in the form file.)
i. When the form file is completed, save it in the normal manner and name it spcust.ff.
2. Print spcust.ff.
3. Close spcust.ff.

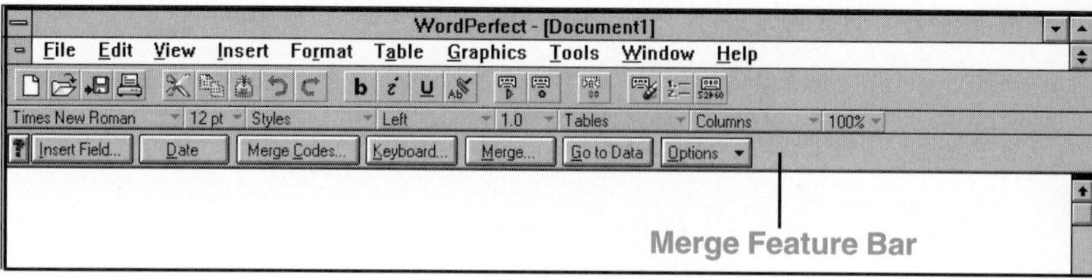

Figure 9.8
Merge Feature Bar

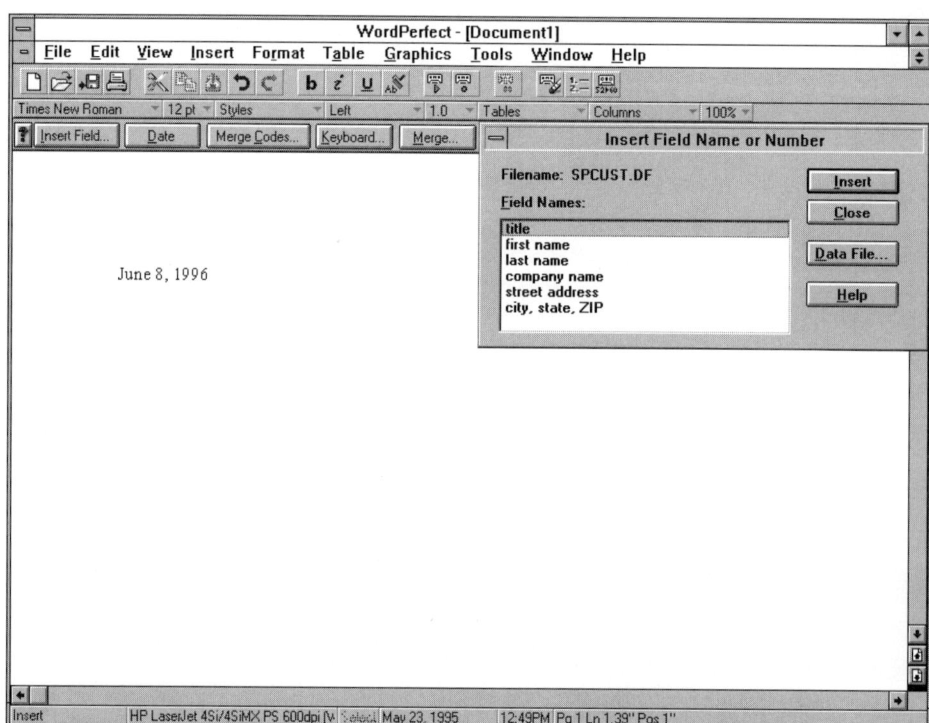

Figure 9.9
Insert Field Name or Number Dialog Box

Notice that in figure 9.7 there is a space between the fields. Spaces are inserted between fields as if there were text; then, when the variable information is inserted, it is spaced correctly. This is also true for punctuation. Insert punctuation in a form file as you would a normal file. For example, place the colon (:) immediately after *FIELD(last name)* in the salutation.

The title and last name fields were used more than once in the form file in figure 9.7. Fields in a form file can be used as often as needed.

Merging Files

Once the data file and the form file have been created and saved, they can be merged. For example, to merge spcust.ff with spcust.df, complete exercise 3.

Exercise 3 Merging a Data File and a Form File

1. At a clear editing window, merge spcust.ff with spcust.df by completing the following steps:
   a. Choose Tools, then Merge.
   b. At the Merge dialog box, choose Merge.
   c. At the Perform Merge dialog box shown in figure 9.10, key **spcust.ff** in the Form File text box.
   d. Choose Data File. (This should insert SPCUST.DF in the Data File text box because it is the associate file.)
   e. Choose OK or press Enter.
2. Save the merged document and name it c09ex03.
3. Print c09ex03.
4. Close c09ex03.

When the merge is complete, the merged letters are displayed on the screen and the insertion point is positioned at the end of the last letter. The number of letters is determined by the number of records in the data file.

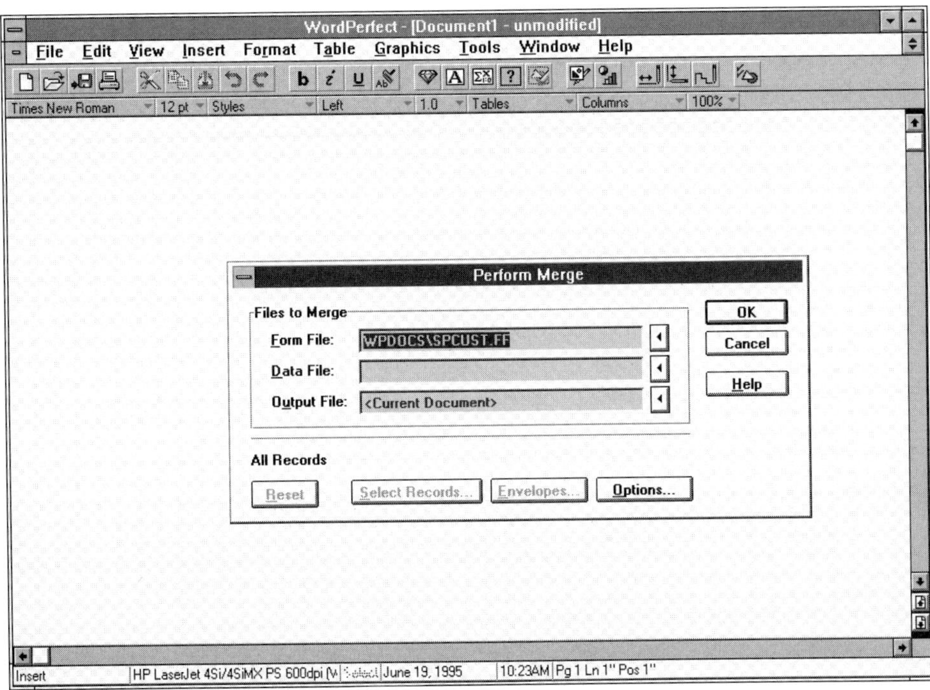

Figure 9.10
Perform Merge Dialog Box

Creating a Table Data File

With WordPerfect's Tables feature, columns and rows of information can be created that are surrounded by horizontal and vertical lines. A table contains cells that are the intersections between rows and columns. Fields in a data file can be entered in *cells* within a table. In this manner, each field in a cell is easily identified. To create a table data file for customers of Sealine Products, complete exercise 4.

Exercise 4 Creating a Table Data File

1. At a clear editing window, change the font to 10-point Times New Roman, then create the table data file shown in figure 9.11 by completing the following steps:
   a. Choose Tools, then Merge.
   b. At the Merge dialog box, choose Place Records in a Table.
   c. Choose Data.
   d. At the Create Merge File dialog box, choose OK or press Enter.
   e. At the Create Data File dialog box, key **title**, then press Enter. (This inserts *title* in the Field Name List list box.)
   f. Key **first name**, then press Enter.
   g. Key the other field names—**last name**; **company name**; **street address**; and **city, state ZIP**. Press Enter after each field name.
   h. When all field names have been keyed, choose OK or press Enter.
   i. At the Quick Data Entry dialog box, key **Mr. and Mrs.** in the *title* field, then press Enter. Continue keying the information in each of the fields identified as shown in figure 9.11.
   j. After keying the last field of information for the last customer, choose Close.
   k. WordPerfect inserts the message *Save the changes to disk?* At this question, choose Yes.
   l. At the Save Data File As dialog box, key **spcust2.df**, then choose OK or press Enter.
2. Print spcust2.df. (This may be optional. Check with your instructor.)
3. Close spcust2.df.

Figure 9.11

title	first name	last name	company name	street address	city, state ZIP
Mr. and Mrs.	Robert	Underwood	Seafood Express	520 South 32nd Avenue	Spokane, WA 98031
Ms.	Victoria	Strauser	Strauser Inn	1325 Spruce Street	Spokane, WA 98036
Mr.	Albert	Fischer	Fischer's Fine Foods	1217 Kapowsin Highway	Spokane, WA 98032

Exercise 5 Merging Two Files

1. At a clear editing window, merge spcust.ff with spcust2.df by completing the following steps:
   a. Choose Tools, then Merge.
   b. At the Merge dialog box, choose Merge.
   c. At the Perform Merge dialog box, key **spcust.ff** in the Form File text box.
   d. Choose Data File, then key **spcust2.df**.
   e. Choose OK or press Enter.
2. Save the merged document and name it c09ex05.
3. Print c09ex05.
4. Close c09ex05.

Canceling a Merge

If, during the merge, you want to stop it, press the Esc key or press Ctrl + Break. To begin the merge again, you will need to repeat the steps for completing a merge.

Creating Envelopes

There are two methods you can use to create envelopes with a data file. You can create a form file to print envelopes, or you can create envelopes while merging a letter or other form file.

Merging Envelopes Only

You can create a form file for printing envelopes that you will merge with a data file. To create an envelope form file to be merged with spcust.df, complete exercise 6.

Exercise 6 Creating an Envelope Form File

1. At a clear editing window, create an envelope form file to be merged with spcust.df by completing the following steps:
   a. Choose Tools, then Merge.
   b. At the Merge dialog box, choose Form.
   c. At the Create Form File dialog box, key **spcust.df** in the Associate a Data File text box, then choose OK or press Enter.
   d. At the clear editing window (with the Merge Feature Bar displayed), choose Format, then Envelope.
   e. At the Envelope dialog box make sure the insertion point is positioned in the Mailing Address section. If it is not, choose Mailing Address.
   f. Choose Field. This causes the Insert Field Name or Number dialog box to display.
   g. At the Insert Field Name or Number dialog box, make sure the insertion point is positioned on *title* in the Field Names list box, then choose Insert. (This inserts the *title* field in the Mailing Address section of the Envelope dialog box.)
   h. Press the space bar once, then choose Field.
   i. At the Insert Field Name or Number dialog box, position the insertion point on *first name* in the Field Names list box, then choose Insert.
   j. Press the space bar once, then choose Field.
   k. At the Insert Field Name or Number dialog box, position the insertion point on *last name* in the Field Names list box, then choose Insert.
   l. Press the Enter key once, then choose Field.
   m. At the Insert Field Name or Number dialog box, position the insertion point on *company name* in the Field Names list box, then choose Insert.
   n. Continue inserting field names in the Mailing Address section of the Envelope dialog box. Insert the field names in the appropriate location.
   o. After all field names have been entered in the Mailing Address section of the dialog box, choose Append to Doc.
   p. At the editing window containing the envelope fields, save the document in the normal manner and name it spenv.ff.
2. Merge spenv.ff with spcust.df.
3. Save the merged document and name it c09ex06.
4. Print c09ex06.
5. Close c09ex06.

Creating Envelopes During Merging

Envelopes can be created for the form file during the merge. When you create envelopes during the merge, you do not have to create a separate form file. To create envelopes while merging spcust.ff with spcust2.df, complete exercise 7.

Exercise 7 Addressing Envelopes during a Merge

1. At a clear editing window, create envelopes when merging spcust.ff with spcust2.df by completing the following steps:
   a. Choose Tools, then Merge.
   b. At the Merge dialog box, choose Merge.
   c. At the Perform Merge dialog box, key **spcust.ff** in the Form File text box.
   d. Choose Data File, then key **spcust2.df**.
   e. Choose Envelopes.
   f. At the Envelope dialog box, insert the fields in the Mailing Address section as described in exercise 6.
   g. After all necessary fields have been inserted in the Mailing Address section, choose OK.
   h. At the Perform Merge dialog box, choose OK or press Enter.
2. When the merge is completed, save the merged document and name it c09ex07.
3. Print c09ex07.
4. Close c09ex07.

Creating a Form File for Labels

In chapter 8, you created forms for labels. A form file can be created for labels and can then be merged with a data file to create the labels. To create labels for the spcust.df data file complete exercise 8.

Exercise 8 Creating a Label Form File

1. At a clear editing window, create a label form file for printing mailing labels by completing the following steps:
   a. Choose Format, then Labels.
   b. At the Labels dialog box, position the insertion point on Avery 5160 Address. (The Avery 5160 Address is in the Labels list box. To display this label with the mouse, click on the down-pointing arrow to the right side of the Labels text box until *Avery 5160 Address* is displayed, then click on it. If you are using the keyboard, press the down arrow key until *Avery 5160 Address* is selected. Check with your instructor to see whether your printer will print this label form size. If not, use a different label form size.)
   c. Choose Select.
   d. At the editing window, display the Merge dialog box.
   e. At the Merge dialog box, choose Form.
   f. At the Create Merge File dialog box, make sure Use File in Active Window is selected, then choose OK or press Enter.
   g. At the Create Form File dialog box, key **spcust.df** in the Associate a Data File text box, then choose OK or press Enter.
   h. At the editing window, choose Insert Field from the Merge Feature Bar.
   i. At the Insert Field Name or Number dialog box, make sure the insertion point is positioned on *title* in the Field Names list box, then choose Insert.
   j. Continue inserting field names in the appropriate location in the label. (The fields may wrap; this is okay.)
   k. When all field names have been inserted, choose Close to close the Insert Field Name or Number dialog box.
   l. Save the labels form in the regular manner and name it labels.ff.

2. Close the labels.ff document.
3. At a clear editing window, merge labels.ff with spcust.df.
4. Save the merged document and name it c09ex08.
5. Print c09ex08.
6. Close c09ex08.

CHAPTER SUMMARY

- Personalized form documents, such as letters and envelopes, can be created with the merge feature.
- The merge feature requires two documents: the *data file* that contains the variable information and the *form file* that contains the standard text.
- A data file contains records. A record contains all the information for one unit (a person, family, or business). To be merged with the form file, the information in one record must be divided into fields.
- When you create a form file, name the fields consistent with the field names in the data file.
- You can create a data file at the Create Data File dialog box. The data for each record can then be entered at the Quick Data Entry dialog box.
- The form file includes standard text along with identifiers showing where variable information is to be inserted. The form file is created at the Create Form File dialog box.
- Once the data file and form file have been created and saved, they can be merged at the Perform Merge dialog box.
- When the merge is complete, the merged letters (or other documents) are displayed in the editing window. These merged letters can then be saved as a separate file.
- Another way to create a data file is to enter the fields of the data file in cells within a table. To use this method, choose Place Records in a Table, then choose Data at the Merge dialog box.
- Create a form file to print envelopes at the Envelope dialog box, or you can create envelopes while merging a letter or other form file.
- A form file can be created for labels at the Labels dialog box and then merged with a data file to create the labels.

Commands Review

	Mouse/Keyboard
Merge dialog box	Tools, Merge
Create Data File dialog box	Tools, Merge, Data
Create Form File dialog box	Tools, Merge, Form
Perform Merge dialog box	Choose Merge at the Merge dialog box

CHECK YOUR UNDERSTANDING

True/False: Circle the letter T if the statement is true; circle the letter F if the statement is false.

T **F** 1. When preparing to use the merge feature, the form file is usually created first.
T **F** 2. A field contains all the information for one unit.
T **F** 3. Envelopes can be printed by creating a form file or during a merge.
T **F** 4. The data file needs to be displayed in the editing window before merging with the form file.
T **F** 5. A form file can be created for printing labels.

Completion: In the space provided at the right, indicate the correct term, command, or number.

1. Creating a personalized form letter with WordPerfect's merge feature usually requires this number of documents. ____________________
2. A data file can be created as a normal text file or in this format. ____________________
3. This code will appear at the end of each *field* created in a data file. ____________________
4. This code will appear at the end of each *record* created in a data file. ____________________
5. Press this key to cancel a merge. ____________________

SKILL ASSESSMENTS

Assessment 1

1. At a clear editing window, look at the letter in figure 9.13 and the records in figure 9.12. Determine the fields you need for the form file, then create a data file for the records in figure 9.12.
2. Save the data file and name it reltr.df.
3. Print reltr.df. (Check with your instructor to see if you should complete this step.)
4. Close reltr.df.

Figure 9.12

Ms. Gayle Waymire
14952 Pioneer Way
Portland, OR 99032

Mr. and Mrs. LeRoy Huse
1450 Willow Street
Gresham, OR 99054

Mr. Douglas Ichikawa
8509 57th Avenue East
Portland, OR 99032

Mrs. Heather Casey
1409 Church Lake Drive
Gresham, OR 99504

Dr. Holly Bartel
348 Seventh Street
Portland, OR 99043

Assessment 2

1. At a clear editing window, create the form file shown in figure 9.13 in an appropriate business letter format. (At the Create Form File dialog box, identify reltr.df as the data file.)
2. Save the form file and name it reltr.ff.
3. Print reltr.ff.
4. Close reltr.ff.

Figure 9.13

(current date)

name
address
city, state ZIP

Dear (name):

If you have considered buying a new home or refinancing your present home, then take a minute to read this letter. Interest rates have fallen and now is the time to refinance. In addition, real estate prices have appreciated tremendously and tax laws have changed to benefit the homeowner.

The decline of interest rates lets you refinance your home loan at a lower interest rate, which could save you thousands of dollars or give you extra money to remodel or pay off bills.

Northwest Brokers is the largest mortgage broker in the state of Oregon. We specialize in FHA, VA, and conventional loans. We have over 50 lenders to choose from to help find you the lowest rates at no extra cost to you.

If you are curious about the options available to you, the amount you qualify for in a new home, or the amount of equity that is accessible in your current home, then please call me at Northwest Brokers. The information is free and I guarantee the best rates and service available.

Sincerely,

NORTHWEST BROKERS

Anthony Masela
Loan Officer

Assessment 3

1. At a clear editing window, merge reltr.ff with reltr.df to the current document.
2. Save the merged document and name it c09sa03.
3. Print c09sa03.
4. Close c09sa03.

Assessment 4

1. Create an envelope form file named env2.ff with fields to create envelopes for the records in reltr.df.
2. Merge env2.ff with reltr.df to the current document.
3. Name the merged document c09sa04.
4. Print c09sa04.
5. Close c09sa04.

Assessment 5

1. Create a label form file named mlabels.ff with fields to create mailing labels for the records in the reltr.df. (Select the Avery 5160 Address or Avery 5151 Address label definition.)
2. Merge mlabels.ff with reltr.df.
3. Name the merged document c09sa05.
4. Print c09sa05.
5. Close c09sa05.

Manipulating Tabs

10

Upon successful completion of chapter 10, you will be able to enhance business memoranda, letters, and generate two- and three-column tables with tab settings including left, right, center, and decimal.

When you work with a document, WordPerfect offers a variety of default settings such as margins and line spacing. One WordPerfect default setting is tab settings every 0.5 inches. In some situations, these default tab settings are appropriate; in others, you may want to create your own tab settings. There are two methods for clearing and setting tabs. Tabs can be cleared and set at the Ruler Bar or at the Tab Set dialog box.

Manipulating Tabs with the Ruler Bar

The Ruler Bar can be used, together with the mouse, to clear, set, and move tabs. To display the Ruler Bar shown in figure 10.1, choose View, then Ruler Bar.

The Ruler Bar, by default, contains left tabs every 0.5 inches. This is indicated by the left triangles below the numbers. At this setting, text aligns at the left edge of the tab as shown in figure 10.2.

The other types of tabs that can be set are Center, Right, and Decimal. You can also set Left, Center, Right, and Decimal tabs with dot leaders (periods). To display the types of tabs available, position the arrow pointer on any tab icon on the Ruler Bar, then hold down the *right* mouse button. This causes a drop-down menu to display as shown in figure 10.3.

Figure 10.1
Ruler Bar

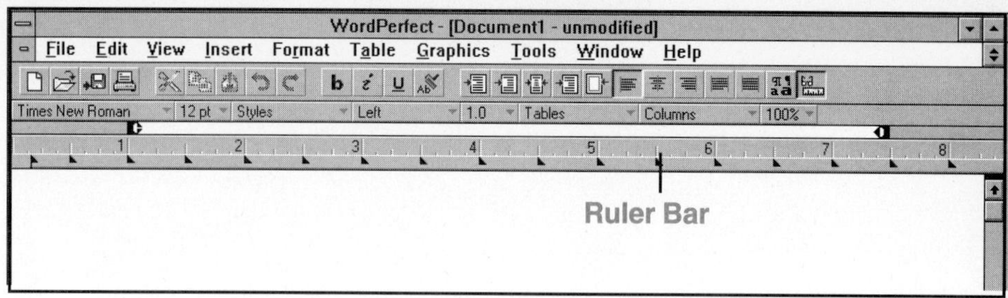

Figure 10.2
Left Align Tab

Robert Freitas
Bethany Mortensen
Laura Culver
Marina Pasquale

Figure 10.3
Tab Drop-Down Menu

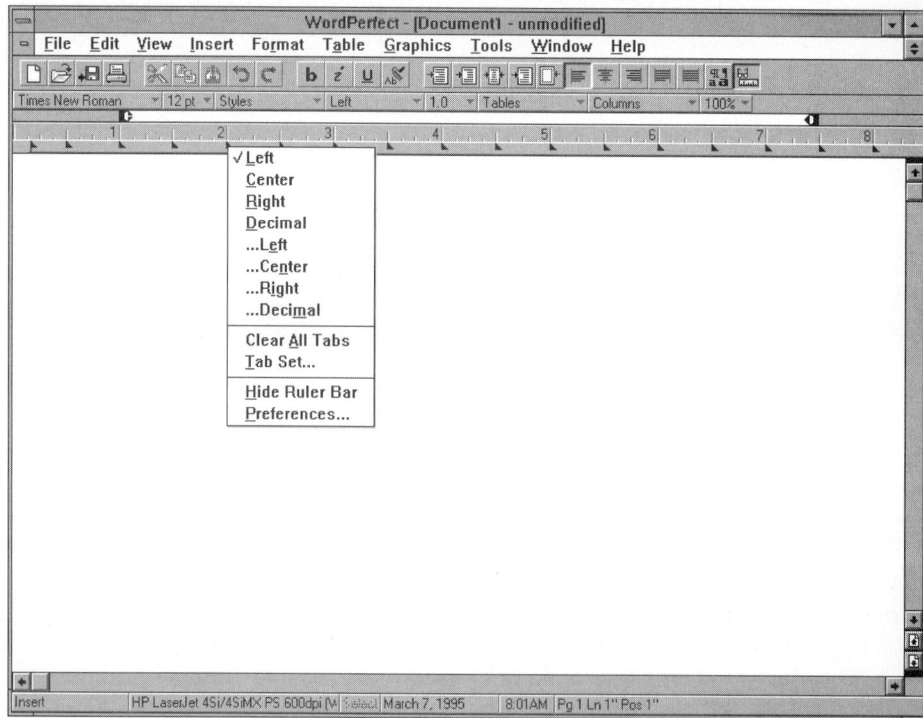

The columns displayed in figure 10.4 show text aligned at different tabs. The text in the first column in figure 10.4 was keyed at a center tab. The second column of text was keyed at a right tab, and the third column was keyed at a decimal tab.

Figure 10.4
Types of Tabs

British Columbia	Victoria	0.235
Saskatchewan	Regina	17.10
Alberta	Edmonton	182.3333

The four types of tabs can also be set with dot leaders. Leaders are useful in a table of contents or other material where you want to direct the reader's eyes across the page. Figure 10.5 shows an example of leaders. The text in the first column was keyed at a left tab. The text in the second column was keyed at a right tab with dot leaders.

British Columbia..	Victoria
Alberta	Edmonton
Saskatchewan..	Regina
Manitoba	Winnipeg
Ontario	Toronto
Quebec	Montreal

Figure 10.5
Leader Tabs

Clearing Tabs

Before setting tabs you will more than likely want to clear the default tabs. You can clear an individual tab, all tabs, or selected tabs. To clear one tab from the Ruler Bar, position the tip of the arrow pointer on the tab icon to be cleared, then hold down the left mouse button. (If the arrow pointer is in the proper position, a vertical dashed line will appear on the screen. This vertical dashed line is called the *ruler guide.*) Drag the tab icon down into the editing window, then release the mouse button.

To clear all tabs from the Ruler Bar, position the tip of the arrow pointer on a tab icon on the Ruler Bar, hold down the *right* mouse button, drag the arrow pointer to Clear All Tabs, then release the mouse button.

Setting Tabs

To set a left tab on the Ruler Bar, position the arrow pointer at the position on the Ruler Bar where you want the tab set, then click the left mouse button.

To set a tab other than a left tab, you must change the type of tab. To do this, position the tip of the arrow pointer on a tab icon, hold down the *right* mouse button, drag the arrow pointer to the desired tab type, then release the mouse button. After changing the tab type, set the tab on the Ruler Bar in the normal manner.

If you change the type of tab at the Tab drop-down menu, the type stays changed until you change it again or you exit WordPerfect.

Exercise 1 Setting Tabs on the Ruler Bar

1. At a clear editing window, create the directory shown in figure 10.6 by completing the following steps:
   a. Key the heading, *FINANCE DEPARTMENT*, centered and bolded.
   b. Press Enter three times.
   c. Set left tabs at the 2.5-inch mark on the Ruler Bar and the 4.75-inch mark by completing the following steps:
      (1) Turn on the display of the Ruler Bar by choosing View, then Ruler Bar.
      (2) Position the arrow pointer on a tab icon on the Ruler Bar, hold down the *right* mouse button, drag the arrow pointer to Clear All Tabs, then release the mouse button. (This clears all tab icons from the Ruler Bar.)
      (3) Position the arrow pointer just below the 2.5-inch mark on the Ruler Bar, then click the left mouse button.
      (4) Position the arrow pointer just below the 4.75-inch mark on the Ruler Bar, then click the left mouse button.
   d. Key the text in columns as shown in figure 10.6. Press the Tab key before keying each column entry. (Make sure you press Tab before keying the text in the first and second columns.)
2. Save the document and name it c10ex01.
3. Print c10ex01.
4. Close c10ex01.

Figure 10.6

FINANCE DEPARTMENT

Patient Accounts	Julius Ramo
Admitting	Simone Watanabe
Medical Records	Marina Pasquale
Payroll	James Fairbanks

Exercise 2 Setting Tabs with Dot Leaders on the Ruler Bar

1. At a clear editing window, key the document shown in figure 10.7 by completing the following steps:
   a. Key the heading, *NURSING DEPARTMENT*, centered and bolded.
   b. Press Enter three times.
   c. Change the line spacing to double (2).
   d. Set a left tab at the 2-inch mark on the Ruler Bar and a decimal tab with dot leaders at the 6.5-inch mark by completing the following steps:
      (1) Turn on the display of the Ruler Bar.
      (2) Position the tip of the arrow pointer on a tab icon, hold down the *right* mouse button, drag the arrow pointer to Clear All Tabs, then release the mouse button.
      (3) Position the arrow pointer just below the 2-inch mark on the Ruler Bar, then click the left mouse button.
      (4) Position the tip of the arrow pointer on a tab icon on the Ruler Bar, hold down the *right* mouse button, drag the arrow pointer to **...Right** in the drop-down menu, then release the mouse button.
      (5) Position the arrow pointer just below the 6.5-inch mark on the Ruler Bar, then click the left mouse button.
   e. Key the text in columns as shown in figure 10.7. Press the Tab key before keying each column entry. (Make sure you press Tab before keying the text in the first and second columns.)
2. Save the document and name it c10ex02.
3. Print c10ex02.
4. Close c10ex02.

Figure 10.7

NURSING DEPARTMENT

Intensive Care Unit .... Terrie Mamaud

Emergency Room .... Kimberly Goetz

Labor and Delivery .... Ola Busching

Coronary Care Unit............................... Thomas Heusers

Surgical Unit.. Bernice Light

Medical Services................................ Bethany Mortensen

Pediatrics .... Tina Vitali

Moving Tabs

After a tab has been set on the Ruler Bar, it can be moved to a new location. To move a tab, position the tip of the arrow pointer on the tab icon to be moved, hold down the left mouse button, drag the icon to the new location on the Ruler Bar, then release the mouse button.

Exercise 3 Moving Tabs to Create More Space between Columns

1. At a clear editing window, open c10ex02.
2. Save the document with Save As and name it c10ex03.
3. Move the tab settings so there is more space between the columns by completing the following steps:
   a. Position the arrow pointer on the left tab icon at the 2-inch mark, hold down the left mouse button, move the arrow pointer to the left until it is located below the 1.5-inch mark, then release the mouse button.
   b. Position the arrow pointer on the right tab icon with dot leaders at the 6.5-inch mark, hold down the left mouse button, drag the arrow pointer to the right until it is located below the 7-inch mark, then release the mouse button.
4. Save the document again with the same name (c10ex03).
5. Print c10ex03.
6. Close c10ex03.

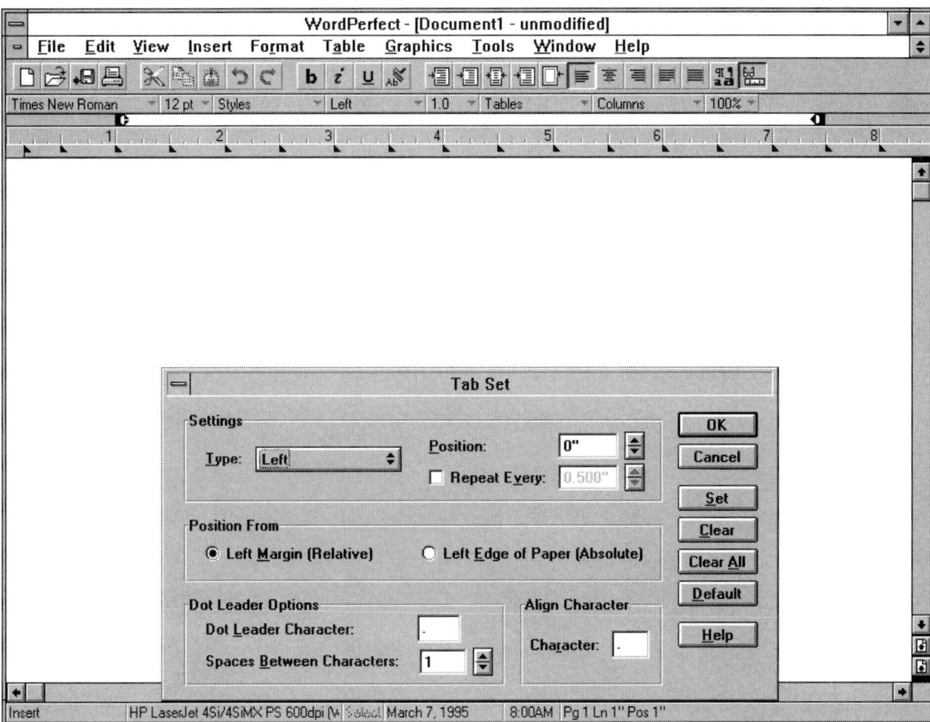

Figure 10.8
Tab Set Dialog Box

Manipulating Tabs with the Tab Set Dialog Box

The Tab Set dialog box shown in figure 10.8 can be used to complete such tasks as clearing a tab or tabs and setting a variety of tabs at precise measurements. There are several methods that can be used to display the Tab Set dialog box including:

- Choose Format, Line, then Tab Set.
- Position the arrow pointer anywhere on the Ruler Bar, click the *right* mouse button, then click on Tab Set.

- Double-click on a tab icon on the Ruler Bar.
- Double-click on any tab code in Reveal Codes.

If the display of the Ruler Bar is on, the Ruler Bar can be seen above the Tab Set dialog box. This is helpful when determining tab settings.

Clearing Tabs

At the Tab Set dialog box, you can clear an individual tab or all tabs. To clear all tabs from the Ruler Bar, choose Clear All. To do this with the mouse, click on the Clear All button in the dialog box. If you are using the keyboard, press Alt + A.

To clear an individual tab, display the Tab Set dialog box, choose Position, then key the measurement of the tab to be cleared. If you are using the mouse, you can click on the up-pointing triangle after Position until the desired measurement displays in the Position text box. Or, you can select the current measurement in the Position text box, then key the desired measurement. With the desired measurement displayed, choose Clear.

Tabs in the Tab Set dialog box are, by default, relative tabs. Relative tabs are measured from the left margin. The Ruler Bar displays absolute tabs, which are measured from the left edge of the page.

With tabs that are measured from the left margin, the left margin is 0 inches. Positions to the right of the left margin are positive numbers and positions to the left of the left margin are negative numbers. With tabs that are measured from the left margin, the distance between tab settings and the left margin remains the same regardless of what changes are made to the document.

With tabs that are measured from the left edge of the page, the left edge of the page is 0 inches. Tabs that are set from the left edge of the page remain at the fixed measurement regardless of what changes are made to the document.

Setting Tabs

All the tab types available with the Tab drop-down menu are available with the Type option from the Tab Set dialog box. To change the type of tab at the Tab Set dialog box, display the dialog box, then choose Type. If you are using the mouse, position the arrow pointer in the Type text box, then hold down the left mouse button. If you are using the keyboard, press Alt + T, then press the space bar. With the Type drop-down menu displayed, choose the desired type of tab.

The Position option from the Tab Set dialog box is used to identify the specific measurement where the tab is to be set. To set a tab, choose Position, key the desired measurement, then choose Set. The measurement that you key is a relative measurement. For example, if you set a tab at 3 inches, the tab will appear at the 4-inch mark on the Ruler Bar (if the left margin is at the default setting of 1 inch). In Reveal Codes, the tab would display as Tab Set: (Rel)+3'L. As an example of how to clear and set tabs at the Tab Set dialog box, complete exercise 4.

Exercise 4 Clearing and Setting Tabs at the Tab Set Dialog Box

1. At a clear editing window, key the document shown in figure 10.9 by completing the following steps:
   a. Key the headings in the memo, the first paragraph, then center and bold the title, *TOP TEN CALORIE BURNING EXERCISES.*
   b. With the insertion point a double space below the title, use the mouse and the Tab Set dialog box to set a left tab 1.25 inches from the left margin and a right tab 5.25 inches from the left margin by completing the following steps:
      (1) Display the Ruler Bar.
      (2) Double-click on a tab icon on the Ruler Bar. (This displays the Tab Set dialog box.)
      (3) At the Tab Set dialog box, click on the Clear All button.
      (4) Select the *0"* in the Position text box.
      (5) Key **1.25**.

(6) Click on the Set button.
(7) Position the arrow pointer in the Type text box, hold down the left mouse button, drag the arrow pointer to *Right*, then release the mouse button.
(8) Select the *1.25"* in the Position text box.
(9) Key **5.25**.
(10) Click on the Set button.
(11) Click on the OK button.

c. Key the text in columns as shown in figure 10.9. Bold the text as indicated. Press the Tab key before keying each column entry. (Make sure you press Tab before keying the text in the first and second columns.)

2. Key the remaining text in the memo.
3. Save the memo and name it c10ex04.
4. Print c10ex04.
5. Close c10ex04.

Figure 10.9

DATE: February 6, 1997

TO: Paula Kerns, Editor, *Hospital Happenings*

FROM: Steve Ayala

SUBJECT: MARCH NEWSLETTER

At the last department meeting, you told us that the theme for the March *Hospital Happenings* newsletter was exercise. Just last week, I ran across this information about the efficiency of common exercises.

TOP TEN CALORIE BURNING EXERCISES

Activity	**Cal. per hr.**
Skiing (cross-country)	1,000
Running	950
Bicycling (stationary)	850
Bicycling (12 m.p.h.)	650
Swimming	640
Rowing machine	600
Tennis	600
Handball/Racquetball	577
Jogging (12-minute mile)	570
Aerobic dance	525

I thought this information would be interesting to the readers of the newsletter. Let me know if you decide to publish it.

xx:c10ex04

When tabs are set, a tab set code is inserted in the document at the beginning of the paragraph where the insertion point is positioned. The tab set code displays the relative measurement of the tab as well as the type of tab. For example, if previous tabs were cleared and a left tab was set at 2.3 inches from the left margin, a center tab 4.5 inches from the left margin, and a right tab 6.4 inches from the left margin, the code [Tab Set: (Rel)+2.3'L, +4.5'C, +6.4'R] would display in Reveal Codes. Tab codes take effect from the location of the code to the end of the document or until another tab set code is encountered.

Exercise 5 Creating a Table of Contents with a Dot Leader Tab

1. At a clear editing window, create the document shown in figure 10.10 by completing the following steps:
   a. Change the font to 12-point Arrus BT.
   b. Change the line spacing to double (2).
   c. Center and bold the title, *TABLE OF CONTENTS*.
   d. With the insertion point a double space below *TABLE OF CONTENTS*, use the keyboard and the Tab Set dialog box to set a left tab 1 inch from the left margin and a right tab with dot leaders 5.5 inches from the left margin by completing the following steps:
      (1) Choose Format, Line, then Tab Set. (This displays the Tab Set dialog box.)
      (2) At the Tab Set dialog box, press Alt + A (for Clear All).
      (3) Press Alt + P (for Position).
      (4) Key **1**.
      (5) Press Alt + S (for Set).
      (6) Press Alt + T (for Type).
      (7) Press the space bar, move the insertion point to *Dot Right*, then press the space bar again.
      (8) Press Alt + P.
      (9) Key **5.5**.
      (10) Press Alt + S.
      (11) Press Enter.
   e. Key the text in columns as shown in figure 10.10. Press the Tab key before keying each column entry. (Make sure you press Tab before keying the text in the first and second columns.)
2. Save the document and name it c10ex05.
3. Print c10ex05.
4. Close c10ex05.

Figure 10.10

TABLE OF CONTENTS

Administration of Employee Survey 2

Calendar of Events 5

Administrative Feedback 6

Clerical Support 7

Team Talk 8

Confidentiality 10

Team Leaders/Members	12
Summary	13
Exhibit A	14
Exhibit B	15
Exhibit C	16

Setting Evenly Spaced Tabs

With the Repeat Every option from the Tab Set dialog box, you can set tabs at regular intervals. First clear all previous tabs, then choose Position. With the insertion point in the Position text box, key the measurement where the first tab set is to occur, then choose Set. Choose Repeat Every, key the measurement of the interval, then choose OK to close the Tab Set dialog box.

Returning to Default Tabs

If you make changes to the tab settings, then want to return to the default tabs, use the Default option from the Tab Set dialog box. This option returns the tabs to the default of a tab set every 0.5 inches.

Changing Tab Type

As mentioned earlier, tabs can be set that are measured from the left margin or the left edge of the page. Tabs that are measured from the left margin are called *relative tabs* and tabs set from the left edge of the page are called *absolute tabs.* By default, tabs are measured from the left margin.

The Tab Set dialog box contains a Left Margin (Relative) option and a Left Edge of Paper (Absolute) option. The default option is Left Margin (Relative).

Exercise 6 Creating Columns with Absolute Tabs

1. At a clear editing window, key the document shown in figure 10.11 by completing the following steps:
   a. Change the line spacing to double (2).
   b. Center and bold the title, *THE ROLE OF TRANSMISSION IN TELECOMMUNICATIONS.*
   c. Press Enter, then bold the heading, *Receiving.*
   d. Press Enter, then key the first paragraph.
   e. After keying the paragraph, press Enter once, then change the line spacing to single (1).
   f. Clear all tabs and set absolute left tabs at 2.8 and 4.5 by completing the following steps:
      (1) Display the Tab Set dialog box.
      (2) At the Tab Set dialog box, click on the Clear All button.
      (3) Click on the radio button before the Left Edge of Paper (Absolute) option.
      (4) Select *0″* in the Position text box.
      (5) Key **2.8**.
      (6) Click on the Set button.
      (7) Select *2.8″* in the Position text box.
      (8) Key **4.5**.
      (9) Click on the Set button.
      (10) Click on the OK button.
   g. Key the text in columns. After keying the last entry in the second column, press Enter twice.

h. Change the line spacing to double.
i. Return the tabs to the default settings by completing the following steps:
   (1) Display the Tab Set dialog box.
   (2) At the Tab Set dialog box, click on the Default button.
   (3) Click on the OK button.
j. Key the remaining paragraphs of the document.

2. Save the document and name it c10ex06.
3. Print c10ex06.
4. Close c10ex06.

Figure 10.11

THE ROLE OF TRANSMISSION IN TELECOMMUNICATIONS

Receiving

Information is sent through the atmosphere as an *electromagnetic* signal (a signal with magnetic properties resulting from being passed through electrical current). At the intended destination, the electromagnetic signal must be recognized and captured by an antenna system. Antenna systems must accept only those signals we want them to receive and ignore the rest. Some common receiving devices include:

TV Antenna	Satellite Dish
Tuner	Amplifier
Modem	VSAT

The typical home satellite earth station has a number of electromagnetic signals that may strike it. These signals may come from AM (amplitude modulation) or FM (frequency modulation) radio towers, a variety of television stations, ham radio operators, CB radio operators, or microwave signals used for telephone or other telecommunications services. One task of the antenna is to sort out which signal to accept and which to ignore.

Receiving Information Sent Through Physical Channels

If we look at the physical channels used for transmitting information, we can see the need to design devices that allow for the physical interconnection of the channel to the transmitter and receiver. This may take a simple form, such as fastening a copper wire to a screw on the back of the receiver, or a quite complicated form, such as splicing a fiber optic cable.

CHAPTER SUMMARY

- By default, left tabs are set every 0.5 inches.
- At the Ruler Bar or the Tab Set dialog box, tabs can be deleted, reset, or moved.
- The four types of tabs are Left (the default), Center, Right, and Decimal. Any type of tab can be set with dot leaders (periods).
- To display the types of tabs available to set on the Ruler Bar, position the arrow pointer on any tab icon on the Ruler Bar, then hold down the *right* mouse button. The tab type can also be changed at the Tab Set dialog box.
- By default, the Tab Set dialog box displays relative tabs—tabs that are measured from the left margin. The Ruler Bar displays absolute tabs—tabs that are measured from the left edge of the page.
- When tabs are set, a tab set code is inserted in the document at the beginning of the paragraph where the insertion point is positioned. Tab codes take effect from the location of the code to the end of the document or until another tab set code is encountered.
- At the Tab Set dialog box you can set new tabs at regular intervals or return to the default tabs.

Commands Review

	Mouse/Keyboard
Ruler Bar	View, Ruler Bar
Tab Set dialog box	Format, Line, Tab Set; position the arrow pointer anywhere on the Ruler Bar, click the *right* mouse button, then click on Tab Set; double-click on any tab code in Reveal Codes

CHECK YOUR UNDERSTANDING

Completion: In the space provided at the right, indicate the correct command, term, or number.

1. How many inches apart are tabs set by default? ____________
2. What are the four types of tabs? ____________ ____________ ____________ ____________
3. Which kind of tab is the default? ____________
4. Tabs can be set at the Tab Set dialog box and here. ____________
5. Relative tabs are measured from here. ____________

6. What is the name for the line of periods that can run between columns? ________________

7. What should be done with the existing tabs before setting new ones? ________________

SKILL ASSESSMENTS

Assessment 1

1. At a clear editing window, key the document shown in figure 10.12. Before keying the text in columns, clear all tabs, then set left tabs on the Ruler Bar at the 2-inch mark, the 4.25-inch mark, and the 5.5-inch mark.
2. Save the document and name it c10sa01.
3. Print c10sa01.
4. Close c10sa01.

Figure 10.12

WELLNESS CLASSES

Personal Wellness	02/04/97	4:30 - 6:30
Counting Calories	02/06/97	4:00 - 5:30
Healthy Exercises	02/11/97	1:30 - 3:30
The Dieting Cycle	02/13/97	2:00 - 4:00

Assessment 2

1. At a clear editing window, key the document shown in figure 10.13. Before keying the text in columns, display the Tab Set dialog box, clear all tabs, then set a left tab 0.5 inches from the left margin and a decimal tab with dot leaders 5.5 inches from the left margin.
2. After keying the memo, save the document and name it c10sa02.
3. Print c10sa02.
4. Close c10sa02.

Figure 10.13

DATE: February 5, 1997

TO: Maxine Paulson, Editor

FROM: Barbara Essex, Investment Coordinator

SUBJECT: PORTFOLIO INFORMATION

Several clients have indicated how the "sample portfolio" helps them understand how and where our company invests their money. Would you please include the following information in the next client newsletter.

PORTFOLIO ACCUMULATION

Direct loans to business .... $ 60,453.20
Public debt securities 87,540.00
Mortgage loans 108,540.32
Real estate investments 55,490.90
All others 9,904.50

If you want more information about this sample portfolio, call me at extension 564.

xx:c10sa02

Assessment 3

1. At a clear editing window, key the table of contents shown in figure 10.14.
2. Save the document and name it c10sa03.
3. Print c10sa03.
4. Close c10sa03.

Figure 10.14

TABLE OF CONTENTS

Telecommunications at Work 4

Factors for Evaluating Systems 7

Technology Defined 10

What Telecommunications Offers 12

Development of Technology 14

Contributions of Historical Events 19

Summary 27

Review 29

Reminder: You may want to delete outdated document files now.

Printing & Maintaining Documents 11

Upon successful completion of chapter 11, you will be able to control printing features for simple business documents and copy, move, or rename documents.

In chapter 2, you learned to print the document displayed on the screen with the Print dialog box, shown in figure 11.1. In this chapter, you will learn to customize a print job with selections from the Print dialog box.

Printing

To display the Print dialog box, choose File, then Print; or click on the Print button on the Toolbar.

Printing Specific Text

The Print Selection section of the Print dialog box contains several options to control printing.

Full Document: The first option in the Print Selection is Full Document. Choose this option to print the document currently displayed in the editing window.

Current Page: The Current Page option in Print Selection is used to print the specific page where the insertion point is located. For example, to print page 4 of a document, position the insertion point in page 4, display the Print dialog box, choose Current Page, then choose Print.

Figure 11.1
Print Dialog Box

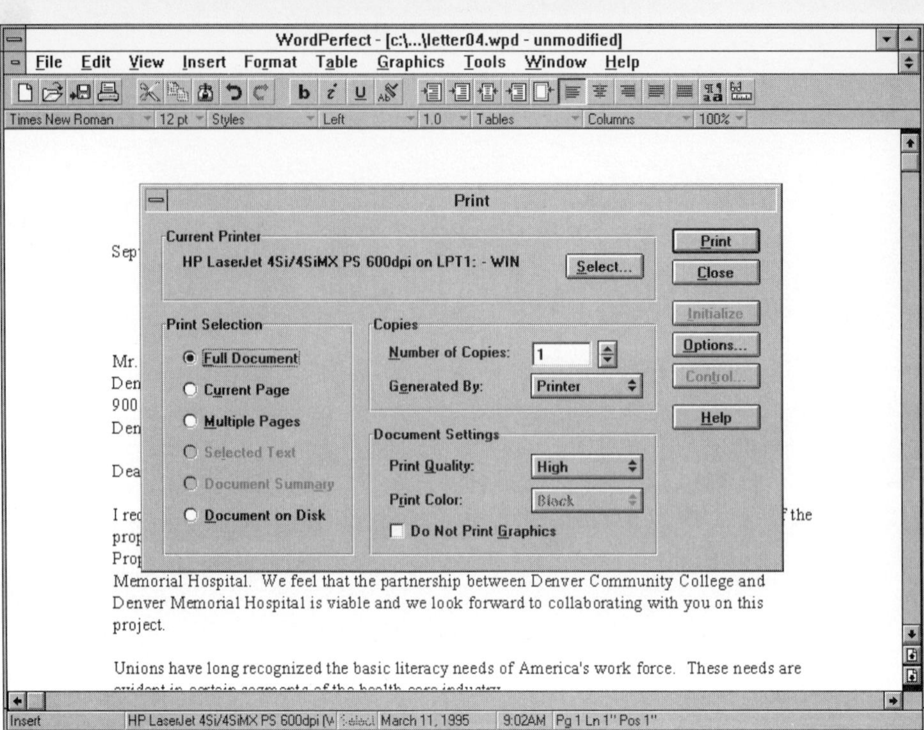

Exercise 1 Printing the Current Page

1. At a clear editing window, open report01.
2. Print page 2 by completing the following steps:
   a. Position the insertion point on page 2.
   b. Display the Print dialog box.
   c. At the Print dialog box, choose Current Page (this will cause a black dot to appear in the radio button).
   d. Choose Print or press Enter.
3. Close report01.

Multiple Pages: The Multiple Pages option in the Print Selection is used to print specific multiple pages of the document currently displayed in the editing window. When you choose Multiple Pages, then Print, the Multiple Pages dialog box, shown in figure 11.2, displays on the screen.

By default, the Page(s) option text box contains the word *all*. At this setting, all pages of the current document will be printed. If you want specific multiple pages printed, use a comma (,) to indicate *and* and use a hyphen (-) to indicate *through*. For example, to print pages 4 and 7, you would key **4,7** in the Page(s) text box. To print pages 4 through 9, you would key **4-9**. The following table illustrates options for printing pages (X, Y, and Z denote page numbers):

Entry	Action
X	Page X printed
X,Y	Pages X and Y printed
X-	Pages X to end of document printed
X-Y	Pages X through Y printed
-X	Beginning of document through page X printed
X-Y,Z	Pages X through Y and page Z printed

As illustrated in the last entry, the hyphen and comma can be used in the same print job. Page numbers must be entered in numerical order. If you do not enter page numbers in numerical order, WordPerfect will print only the first page. For example, if you enter 9,3,4 in the Pages text box, WordPerfect will print only page 9.

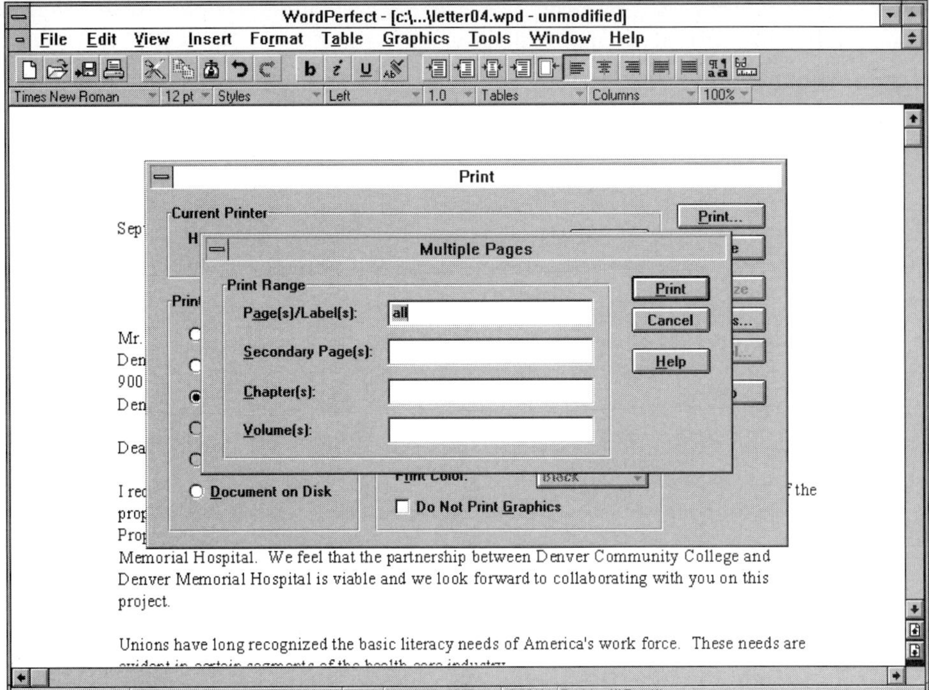

Figure 11.2
Multiple Pages Dialog Box

Exercise 2 Printing Specific Pages

1. At a clear editing window, open report02.
2. Print pages 1 and 3 by completing the following steps:
   a. Display the Print dialog box.
   b. At the Print dialog box, choose Multiple Pages, then Print.
   c. At the Multiple Pages dialog box, key **1,3**.
   d. Choose Print or press Enter.
3. Close report02.

Selected Text: Many print methods limit you to printing an entire document, a page, or specific pages. If you want to print a specific amount of text (such as two paragraphs, half a page, or a page and a half), use the Selected Text option from the Print dialog box. By default, the Selected Text option is dimmed. If you select text in a document, then display the Print dialog box, the Selected text option is available and is automatically selected.

Exercise 3 Printing Selected Text

1. At a clear editing window, open report06.
2. Select and print the last six lines of text in the report by completing the following steps:
   a. Select the last six lines of text in the report.
   b. Display the Print dialog box.
   c. At the Print dialog box, choose Print.
3. Close report06.

Printing Multiple Copies

If you want to print more than one copy of a document or page(s), use the Number of Copies option in the Copies section of the Print dialog box. To print multiple copies, display the Print dialog box. Change the number in the Number of Copies text box. To do this with the mouse, move the arrrow pointer to the up-pointing triangle after Number of Copies, then click the left mouse button until the desired number appears in the box. If you are using the keyboard, press Alt + N, then press the up arrow key until the desired number appears in the box. Choose Print or press Enter.

The number of copies will remain at the new setting until you change it or close the document.

Exercise 4 Printing Multiple Copies

1. At a clear editing window, open notice01.
2. Print three copies of this document by completing the following steps:
   a. Display the Print dialog box.
   b. Change the number in the Number of Copies text box to 3. To do this with the mouse, move the arrow pointer to the up-pointing triangle after Number of Copies, then click the left mouse button until the number 3 appears in the box. If you are using the keyboard, press Alt + N, then press the up arrow key until the number 3 appears in the box.
   c. Choose Print or press Enter.
3. Close notice01.

Maintaining Documents

Almost every company that conducts business maintains a filing system. The system may consist of documents, folders, and cabinets; or it may be a computerized filing system where information is stored on tapes and disks. Whatever kind of filing system a business uses, daily maintenance of files is important to a company's operation. Maintaining files can include such activities as moving and copying documents, and deleting documents. These types of functions can be completed at the Open File, Save As, or Insert File dialog boxes.

Displaying File Information

The Open File, Save As, and Insert File dialog boxes contain many of the same options. The Open File dialog box is shown in figure 11.3. The Save As and Insert File dialog boxes appear in a similar manner.

The first option, Filename, displays the current filename in the text box. Below the Filename option, the Filename list box displays an alphabetic list of the documents in the current directory. Document names with numbers are alphabetized before names with letters. For example, memo01 would be listed before memoa.

Below the Filename list box, WordPerfect displays the total number of files in the current directory and the total number of bytes in the current directory or document. As you select different document names in the Filename list box, WordPerfect displays the day and time the selected document was last saved, as well as the number of bytes for the selected document. This information displays at the bottom left side of the Open File dialog box.

The List Files of Type option at the bottom of the dialog box lets you choose what type of documents you want displayed in the Filename list box. This option is available at the Open File and Insert File dialog boxes but not the Save As dialog box. By default, WordPerfect will display all filenames in the current directory. If you choose this option, a drop-down list displays showing a variety of document extensions. For example, if you choose *WP Documents (*.wpd)* from the drop-down menu, WordPerfect will display in the Filename list box only those documents ending in the extension *.wpd.*

In chapter 1, you learned how to change the default drive with the Drives option. To change the drive, choose Drives, then select the desired drive from the drop-down list.

Using File Options

At the right side of the Open File, Save As, and Insert File dialog boxes, a File Options command button displays. When you choose File Options, the drop-down menu shown in figure 11.4 displays.

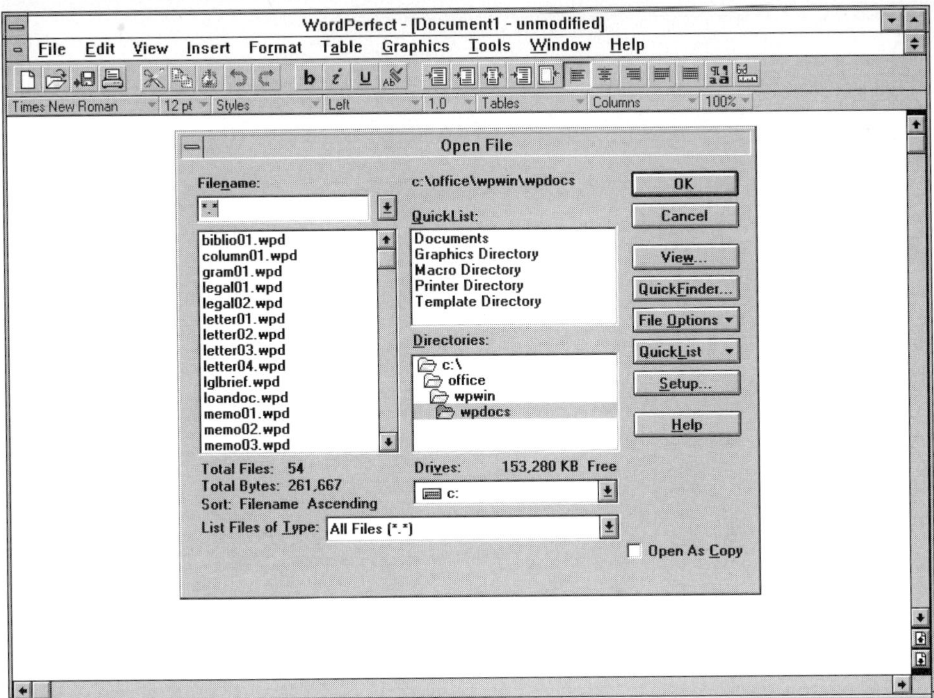

Figure 11.3
Open File Dialog Box

Copying a Document

With the Copy option from the File Options drop-down menu, you can make an exact copy of a document and save it on the same disk, another disk, or into a directory or subdirectory. If you copy a document to the same directory, you must give it a different name than the original. If you copy a document to another directory, drive, or subdirectory, it can retain its original name.

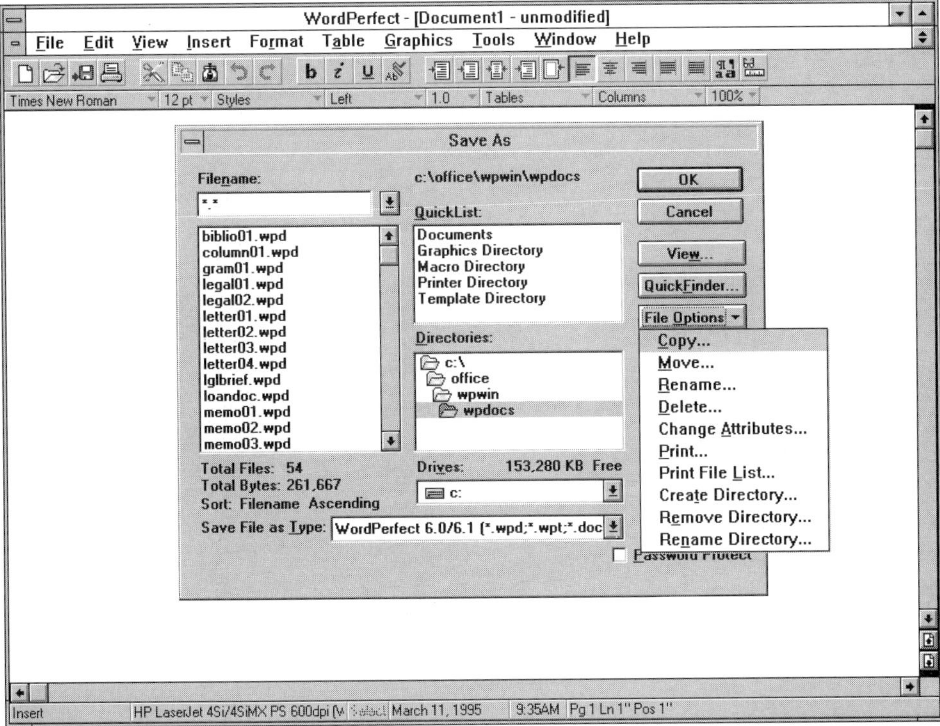

Figure 11.4
File Options Drop-Down Menu

Figure 11.5
Copy File Dialog Box

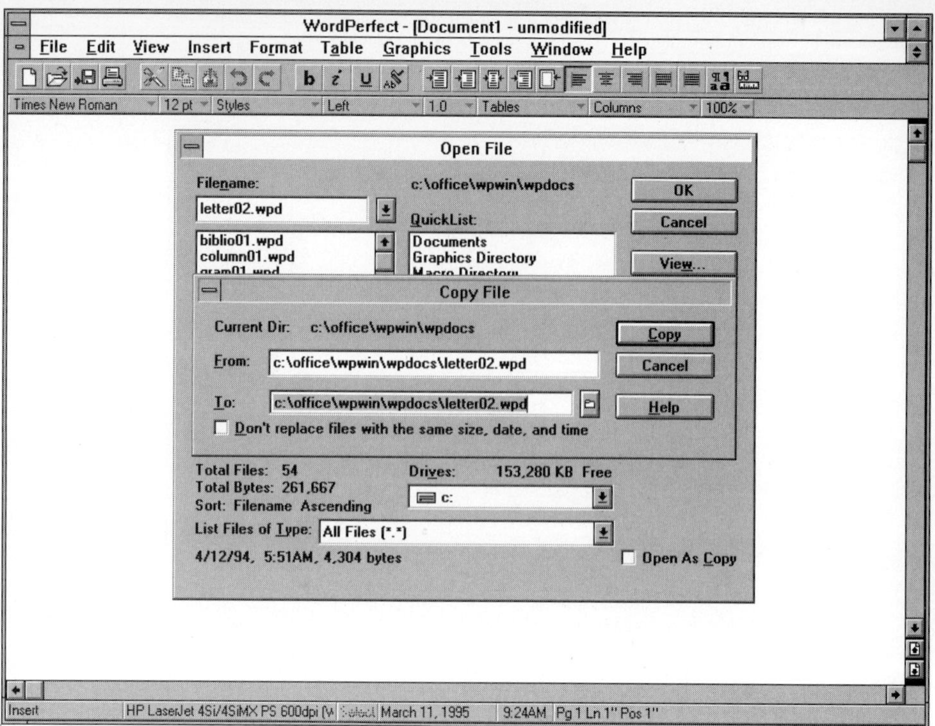

As an example of how to copy a document, complete exercise 5. When a document is copied, the original document is retained and an exact copy is made.

Exercise 5 Copying a Document to the Same Drive

1. Complete the following steps to copy the document named *memo02* and name it *kainu*:
   a. Display the Open File dialog box.
   b. Select the document named *memo02* in the Filename list box.
   c. Choose File Options.
   d. At the File Options drop-down menu, choose Copy.
   e. At the Copy File dialog box (shown in figure 11.5) key **kainu**.
   f. Choose Copy.
2. Complete steps similar to those in step 1 to copy the following documents with the names listed:

memo03	copy to	lam
memo04	copy to	hedegard
memo05	copy to	wep
memo06	copy to	windslow

3. Cancel the Open File dialog box.

Moving a Document

If you decide that a document needs to be moved to a different directory, subdirectory, or drive, use the Move option from the File Options drop-down menu. As an example of how to move a document, complete exercise 6.

Exercise 6 Moving a Document

1. Complete the following steps to move the document named *kainu* to the **c:\office\wpwin\wpdocs** directory. (Before completing this exercise, check with your instructor. If you are working on a network system, you may want to skip this exercise.)

a. Display the Open File dialog box.
b. Select the document named *kainu.*
c. Choose File Options, then Move.
d. At the Move File dialog box, key **c:\office\wpwin\wpdocs**.
e. Choose Move.
2. Cancel the Open File dialog box.

Renaming a Document

Use the Rename option from the File Options drop-down menu to rename a document. As an example of how to use the Rename option, complete exercise 7.

Exercise 7 Renaming a Document

1. Complete the following steps to rename the document *lam* to *firstaid.*
   a. Display the Open File dialog box.
   b. Select the document named *lam.*
   c. Choose File Options, then Rename.
   d. At the Rename File dialog box, key **firstaid**.
   e. Choose Rename.
2. Complete steps similar to those in step 1 to rename the following documents with the names listed:

hedegard	rename to	wepmemo
wep	rename to	wepmeet
windslow	rename to	survmemo

3. Cancel the Open File dialog box.

Deleting a Document

At some point, you may want to delete certain documents on your student data disk. If you work with WordPerfect for Windows on a regular basis, you should establish a system for deleting documents. The system you choose depends on the work you are doing.

To learn how to delete a document, complete exercise 8.

Exercise 8 Deleting a Document

1. Complete the following steps to delete the document named *firstaid*:
   a. Display the Open File dialog box.
   b. Select the document named *firstaid.*
   c. Choose File Options, then Delete.
   d. At the Delete File dialog box, make sure the correct document name is displayed, then choose Delete.
2. Complete steps similar to those in step 1 to delete the following documents:
   wepmemo
   wepmeet
   survmemo
3. Delete the document named *kainu* located in the **c:\office\wpwin\wpdocs** directory (you must have completed exercise 6 for this document to be located in the c:\office\wpwin\wpdocs directory) by completing the following steps:
   a. Display the Open File dialog box.
   b. Choose File Options, then Delete.
   c. At the Delete File dialog box, key **c:\office\wpwin\wpdocs\kainu**.
   d. Choose Delete.
4. Cancel the Open File dialog box.

You can also use the Delete key to delete a file. For example, in step 1c in exercise 8 above you could just press the Delete key (rather than choosing File Options, then Delete).

Printing a Document

In chapter 2 and the beginning of this chapter, you learned a variety of printing methods. In addition to these methods, you can also print a document with the Print option from the File Options drop-down menu.

To print a document with the Print option, complete exercise 9.

Exercise 9 Using the Print Option

1. Complete the following steps to print the document named *memo01*:
   a. Display the Open File dialog box.
   b. Select the document named *memo01*.
   c. Choose File Options, then Print.
   d. At the Print File dialog box, make sure the correct document name is displayed, then choose Print.
2. Cancel the Open File dialog box.

Printing a List

The Filename list box at the Open File, Save As, or Insert File dialog box contains a list of all documents in a particular directory. At times, you may want a hard copy of the directory. To print the list of documents, complete exercise 10.

Exercise 10 Printing a List

1. Complete the following steps to print a list of the documents in the current directory:
   a. Display the Open File dialog box.
   b. Choose File Options, then Print File List.
2. Cancel the Open File dialog box.

Selecting Documents

In the Filename list box, you can copy, move, delete, or print individual documents or a group of documents. To copy, move, delete, or print more than one document, the documents must be selected.

To select a group of adjacent documents in the Filename list box using the mouse, you would complete the following steps:

1 Position the arrow pointer on the first document in the group.
2 Hold down the left mouse button.
3 Drag the mouse to the last document in the group.
4 Release the mouse button.

To select a group of adjacent documents in the Filename list box using the keyboard, you would complete the following steps:

1 Position the insertion point on the first document in the group.
2 Hold down the Shift key, then press the down arrow key until the insertion point is positioned on the last document in the group.
3 Release the Shift key.

You can also select documents that are not adjacent in the Filename list box. To do this with the mouse, you would complete the following steps:

1. Position the arrow pointer on the first document to be selected.
2. Hold down the Ctrl key and the left mouse button.
3. Drag the arrow pointer, selecting the desired document. Release the mouse button on those documents that are not to be selected. Continue pressing and releasing the Ctrl key and the mouse button to select or not select specific documents.
4. When all desired documents are selected, release the Ctrl key and then the left mouse button.

To select documents that are not adjacent in the Filename list box using the keyboard, you would complete the following steps:

1. Position the insertion point on the first document in the group.
2. Hold down the Shift key, then press the down arrow key until the insertion point is positioned on the last document in the group.
3. To remove the selection from specific documents within the group, position the insertion point on the document you do not want selected, then press the space bar. Repeat this for all documents you do not want selected in the group.

Exercise 11 Printing Selected Documents

1. Complete the following steps to select then print *block01*, *memo01,* and *notice01:*
   a. Display the Open File dialog box.
   b. Position the arrow pointer on *block01.*
   c. Hold down the Ctrl key, click the left mouse button, then release the Ctrl key.
   d. Position the arrow pointer on *memo01,* hold down the Ctrl key, click the left mouse button, then release the Ctrl key.
   e. Position the arrow pointer on *notice01,* hold down the Ctrl key, click the left mouse button, then release the Ctrl key.
   f. Choose File Options, then Print.
   g. At the question, *Do you want to print the selected files?*, choose Print.
2. When all documents have printed, cancel the Open File dialog box.

Opening a Document as a Copy

The Open File dialog box contains the option, *Open As Copy*, that can be used to open a document as read only. When a document is opened as read only, it cannot be saved with the same name. Because the file is read only, you cannot accidentally save it with the same name. This is useful in a situation where you want to retain the document in its original form.

To open a document as read only, display the Open File dialog box, insert an X in the Open As Copy check box, then open the desired document. The words *(Read-Only)* will display in the Title Bar after the document name.

Exercise 12 Opening a Document as Read Only

1. At a clear editing window, open *block01.wpd* as read only by completing the following steps:
   a. Click on the Open button on the Toolbar.
   b. At the Open File dialog box, click inside the Open As Copy check box. (This inserts an X.)

c. Double-click on *block01.wpd* in the Filename list box.
2. With *block01.wpd* displayed in the editing window and the insertion point positioned at the beginning of the document, change the font to 18-point GeoSlab703 Lt BT.
3. Save the document and name it *c11ex12* by completing the following steps:
   a. Click on the Save button on the Toolbar.
   b. At the Save As dialog box, key **c11ex12**, then press Enter.
4. Print and then close c11ex12.

Figure 11.6
View Document Window

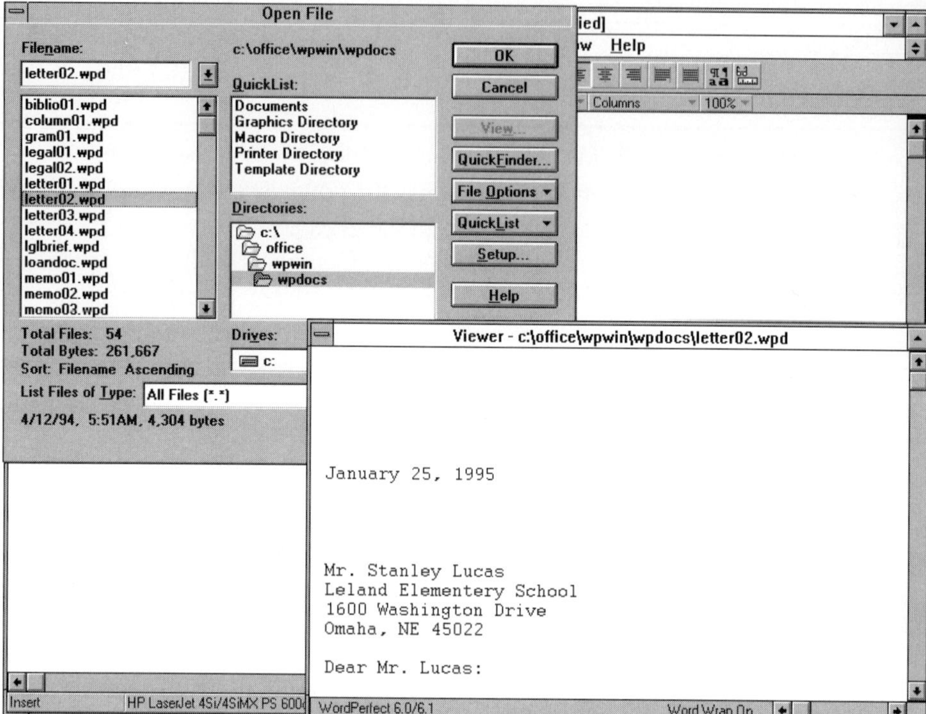

Viewing a Document

With the View option from the Open File, Save As, or Insert File dialog box, you can view a document without bringing it to the editing window. This feature is useful if you are looking for a particular document but cannot remember what it was named. You can check documents with the View option until you find the right one.

When you choose View, the document is inserted in the View window as shown in figure 11.6. You can use the mouse with the up, down, left, or right scroll arrows to view different parts of the document.

To remove the View window, use the Document control button in the View window. To do this with the mouse, position the tip of the arrow pointer on the Document control button in the upper left corner of the View window, click the left mouse button, then click on Close at the drop-down menu. If you want to remove the View window and cancel the dialog box at the same time, just choose Cancel.

Exercise 13 Viewing Documents without Retrieving Them

1. Complete the following steps to view all letter documents:
   a. Display the Open File dialog box.
   b. Select the first document with a name that begins with *letter*.
   c. Choose View.
   d. After viewing the first letter document, position the arrow pointer on the next *letter* document in the Filename list box, then click the left mouse button. This causes the next *letter* document to display in the View window.
   e. Continue clicking on the next *letter* document and viewing the contents in the View window until all *letter* documents have been viewed.
2. Cancel the Open File dialog box.

CHAPTER SUMMARY

- The options available at the Print dialog box can help to customize a print job.
- At the Print dialog box, choose Full Document to print the open document. Choose Current Page to print the page where the insertion point is located. Choose Multiple Pages to print specific pages in the open document. Use the Selected Text option to print selected text in the open document.
- At the Number of Copies option from the Print dialog box, you can choose to print more than one copy of a document or page(s) of a document.
- Some of the activities involved in disk maintenance are moving, copying, and deleting documents.
- Three dialog boxes will allow you to do the activities listed above. These dialog boxes are Open File, Save As, and Insert File; all three contain many of the same options.
- Several useful choices are available at any of the three dialog boxes:
  Copy can make an exact copy of a document and save it on the same disk, another disk, or into another directory.
  Move can place a document in another directory or drive.
  Rename allows the name of a document to be changed.
  Delete will remove unneeded documents.
  The Print option offers an additional method for printing documents.
  Use Print List to print a hard copy of a directory.
- Use the Open As Copy option at the Open File dialog box to open a document as read only. A read only document must be saved with a name other than the original name.
- With the View option from the Open File, Save As, or Insert File dialog box, you can view a document without bringing it to the editing window for editing.

Commands Review

	Mouse/Keyboard
Print dialog box	File, Print; or click on the Print button on Toolbar
Open File dialog box	File, Open
Save As dialog box	File, Save As
Insert File dialog box	Insert, File

CHECK YOUR UNDERSTANDING

True/False: Circle the letter T if the statement is true; circle the letter F if the statement is false.

T F 1. At the Multiple Pages dialog box, the default is page 1.

T F 2. When specifying a range of pages to be printed, a hyphen specifies *and,* a comma means *through.*

T F 3. Selected text can be printed.

T F 4. Two identical documents may exist in the same directory if the filenames are different.

T F 5. A group of documents in the Filename list box can be selected at the same time only if they are adjacent to each other.

T F 6. As you select different document names in the Filename list box, WordPerfect displays the number of words for the selected document.

Completion: In the space provided at the right, indicate the correct term, command, or number.

1. Enter this at the Multiple Pages dialog box to print pages 3, 4, 5, and 8 of the open document. ____________________
2. Enter this at the Multiple Pages dialog box to print pages 7 and 9 of the open document. ____________________
3. Enter this at the Multiple Pages dialog box to print pages 15 to the end of the document of the open document. ____________________
4. Most document maintenance functions can be performed at these three dialog boxes: ____________________

   ____

   ____
5. If you want a hard copy of a directory, choose this from the File Options drop-down menu. ____________________
6. To see a document from the Filename list box without bringing it to the editing window, choose this. ____________________
7. Choose this option at the Open File dialog box to open a document as read only. ____________________

SKILL ASSESSMENTS

Assessment 1

1. Open report03.
2. Select and print the heading *The American Civil War* and the paragraph below it.
3. Close report03.

Assessment 2

1. Open report03.
2. Print pages 1 and 3 of the document.
3. Close report03.

Assessment 3

1. Display the Open File dialog box, then complete the following steps:
   a. Copy letter01 and name it corres01.
   b. Copy letter02 and name it corres02.
   c. Copy letter03 and name it corres03.
   d. Copy letter04 and name it corres04.
   e. Print the directory list.
   f. Rename corres01 to dmh01.
   g. Rename corres02 to les01.
   h. Rename corres03 to dmh02.
   i. Rename corres04 to dmh03.
   j. Print the directory list.
   k. Delete dmh01, les01, dmh02, and dmh03.
2. Cancel the Open File dialog box.

Assessment 4

1. Display the Open File dialog box, then select and print *letter01*, *memo02*, and *memo03*.
2. Cancel the Open File dialog box.

Unit Performance Assessment

In this unit, you have learned to produce business documents with customized features such as fonts and templates.

PROBLEM-SOLVING AND DECISION-MAKING

Assessment 1

1. At a clear editing window, create a certificate using *Certificate of Achievement – Landscape orientation* in the *publish* group. Insert the following text at the Template Information dialog box:

Name of Recipient:	=	**Rebecca Cook**
Description of Achievement:	=	**Employee of the Month**

2. Save the certificate and name it u02pa01.
3. Print u02pa01.
4. Close u02pa01.

Assessment 2

1. At a clear editing window, look at the letter in figure U2.2 and the records in figure U2.1. Determine the fields you need for the form file, then create a data file for the records in figure U2.1.
2. Save the data file and name it nhrc.df.
3. Print nhrc.df. (Check with your instructor to see if you should complete this step.)
4. Close nhrc.df.

Optional: Write a short summary explaining the advantages and any disadvantages to the fields you chose.

Figure U2.1

Mrs. Sheila Goldsmith
33 Rosemont Way
Petersburg, VA 23415

Ms. Susan Benford
201 West Point Drive
Hopewell, VA 22459

Mr. Robert Weisert
29044 East Graham
Hopewell, VA 22459

Mr. Thomas Dircks
2007 East Harris
Hopewell, VA 22459

Dr. Glen Davis
7843 90th Street
Petersburg, VA 23451

Mrs. Donna Rudman
4812 South 191st Place
Petersburg, VA 23415

Assessment 3

1. At a clear editing window, key the letter shown in figure U2.2 in an appropriate business letter format as a form file. (At the Create Form File dialog box, identify nhrc.df as the data file.) You determine the fields and field names.
2. Save the letter and name it nhrc.ff.
3. Print nhrc.ff.
4. Close nhrc.ff.

Optional: Rewrite this letter in a more enthusiastic and personal tone.

Figure U2.2

February 12, 1997

(name)
(address)

Dear (salutation):

The Assisted Living Program and New Hope Retirement Center offers an independent and dignified lifestyle for senior adults with modest needs for physical assistance. There is assistance available to each resident at New Hope Retirement Center according to his or her individual needs. This assistance is provided 24 hours a day by trained staff members. The types of assistance provided include:

- storing prescribed medication
- reminders of medical schedule
- assistance with dressing and grooming
- assistance with bathing and hygiene
- supervision of nutritional intake
- arranging transportation for medical appointments

Assisted Living residents are provided three full meals a day plus snacks. Housekeeping is done weekly unless more frequency is required. There is a full schedule of social activities such as games and crafts to hold the interest of each resident.

New Hope Retirement Center is committed to providing a fulfilling lifestyle for each resident. If you would like an informational brochure on Assisted Living, please call 555-9093. A tour of the New Hope Retirement Center facilities can also be arranged.

Sincerely,

Antoinette Moreno
Director, Assisted Living

Assessment 4

1. At a clear editing window, merge nhrc.ff with nhrc.df.
2. After the records are merged, save the document and name it u02pa04.
3. Print u02pa04.
4. Close u02pa04.

Assessment 5

1. At a clear editing window, key the text shown in figure U2.3 in an appropriate business letter format with the following specifications:
   a. Change the font to 12-point GeoSlab703 Lt BT.
   b. Indent the text after the enumerated items.
   c. Set tabs for the text columns.
   d. After keying the letter, change the justification to Full.
2. Complete a spell check on the letter.
3. Proofread and correct any grammatical errors.
4. Save the letter and name it u02pa05.
5. Print u02pa05.
6. Close u02pa05.

Figure U2.3

March 14, 1997

Mrs. Darlene Frye
City of Tampa
Public Works Department
2105 South 42nd Street
Tampa, FL 33613

Dear Mrs. Frye:

The third meting of the members of the Outcomes Assesment Project (OAP) were held yesterday, march 15. I am sorry you were unable to attend. The following items were discused:

1. Survey: Each member shared the current status of the section of the survey for which he or she is responsible.

2. Survey Instruments: Members modified and prioritized items on the first draft of the survey questionnaire.

3. Meeting Dates and Times: The next three meeting days and times were determined as follows:

Tuesday, April 8	3:00 p.m.	Room 420
Wenesday, April 22	11:30 a.m.	Room 100A
Tusday, May 6	3:00 p.m.	Room 420

Hopefully, these days and times are convenient for your. If you want to discuss this meeting farther, give me a call.

Very truly yours,

Dawn Perez, Coordinator
Outcomes Assesment Project
xx:u02pa05

Assessment 6

1. At a clear editing window, key the text shown in figure U2.4 in an appropriate memorandum format with the following specifications:
   a. Insert the appropriate bullets as indicated.
   b. Set tabs for the text columns.
2. Complete a spell check on the memorandum.
3. Save the memorandum and name it u02pa06.
4. Print u02pa06.
5. Close u02pa06.

Optional: Change the typeface and size to give the document a different look.

Figure U2.4

DATE: October 3, 1996

TO: All Parents

FROM: Pat Windslow, Superintendent

SUBJECT: EMERGENCY WEATHER SCHEDULE

Each family should have a plan covering what to do when children arrive home early due to an emergency situation. Consider the following questions:

- What is the best route home if your child cannot be delivered to the normal bus stop?
- Where could your child go if he or she needed help?
- Who would care for him or her until you arrive?
- Is there someone your child could call to calm any concerns he or she might have?

Please develop an emergency plan for your family and practice it with your child.

Listen to the radio between 6:00 a.m. and 8:00 a.m. if you feel the weather may create hazardous traveling conditions. Radio/TV stations will be announcing schedule changes by district name and number. If the Omaha City School District is not mentioned on the air, assume normal operations will prevail.

The following AM and FM radio stations will broadcast changes in school and bus operations:

KTC 520	KPLC 88.5
KCIT 730	KLCY 93.5
KICS 1100	KUTE 100.0
KJS 1220	KZOS 103.7
KMPS 1350	KVTS 105.5

When you hear "Schools Closed," it means schools will be closed for the day and all after-school and evening activities will be cancelled unless otherwise announced.

xx:u02pa06

WRITING

The following activities give you the opportunity to practice your writing skills along with demonstrating an understanding of some of the important WordPerfect features you have mastered in this unit. In planning the documents, remember to shape the information according to the writing purpose and the audience. Use correct grammar, appropriate word choices, and clear sentence constructions.

Activity 1

Situation: You are Jocelyn Cook, assistant superintendent for the Omaha City School District. Compose a memo to all elementary school principals informing them that the members of the site selection committee will be visiting their schools on the following dates and times:

Carr Elementary School	February 20	10:00 - 11:30 a.m.
Leland Elementary School	February 20	1:30 - 3:00 p.m.
Sahala Elementary School	February 22	9:30 - 11:00 a.m.
Young Elementary School	February 22	1:00 - 2:30 p.m.
Armstrong Elementary School	February 27	10:00 - 11:30 a.m.
Bothell Elementary School	February 27	1:30 - 3:00 p.m.

Print and then close u02act01.

Activity 2

Situation: You are Owen Lindal, administrative assistant for Jocelyn Cook, the assistant superintendent for the Omaha City School District. You have been asked by Ms. Cook to compose a letter to the individuals listed below with the following information: They have been selected by the principal of the school where their child or children attend to serve on the Facilities Planning Committee. This committee will be comprised of school district administrators, staff, and teachers, as well as people with a child or children attending school in the Omaha City School District. The committee will be responsible for establishing short- and long-term priorities for facilities planning for the district. The first meeting of the committee will be held from 7:00-9:30 p.m. on Tuesday, February 13, 1996, in room 106 at the school administration building. Approximately five additional meetings will be scheduled for the remainder of the school year.

Create a form file containing this information and create a data file for the names and addresses listed below. You determine the names for the form file and data file. After creating the data file and the form file, merge the documents. Save the merged document and name it u02act02. Print and then close u02act02.

Mr. Paul Jackson
302 East 40th Street
Omaha, NE 45056

Mrs. Elaine Natario
9932 Montgomery
Omaha, NE 45054

Ms. Josefina Valdes
14503 South Mildred
Omaha, NE 45054

Mr. Vance Blumenthal
3712 Del Monte Drive
Omaha, NE 45056

Ms. Vicki Cates
24113 Rembert Court
Omaha, NE 45054

Ms. Sung Lim
2033 Columbia Avenue
Omaha, NE 45056

Activity 3

Situation: Using the data file created for Activity 2, create mailing labels. Merge the mailing labels document with the data file. Save the merged document and name it u02act03. Print and then close u02act03.

Preparing Multi-Paged Documents

Upon successful completion of Unit 3, you will be able to prepare multi-paged documents with specific formatting including page numbering, headers/footers, footnotes/endnotes, and newspaper and parallel columns.

SCANS

Writing

Decision-Making

Technology

- Reorganize document content
- Compose informative reports
- Rewrite for a different audience
- Research how to solve problems

Problem-Solving

Research

Inserting Page Formatting 12

Upon successful completion of chapter 12, you will be able to adjust page breaks, turn on the widow/orphan feature, and number pages in a document.

WordPerfect assumes that you are using standard-sized paper, which is 8.5 inches wide and 11 inches long. By default, WordPerfect leaves a 1-inch top margin and a 1-inch bottom margin. This allows a total of 9 inches available for text to be printed on a standard page.

As you create a long document, you will notice that when the insertion point nears Line 9.83", a page break is inserted in the document. The page break is inserted at the next line (Line 10"). The line below the page break is the beginning of page 2. In the Page mode, this page break displays as a thick line that is black on top and gray on the bottom. In the Draft mode, the page break displays as a thin black line. The page break occurs at 10 inches because WordPerfect leaves the first inch of the paper blank and prints text on the next 9 inches.

While WordPerfect's default settings break each page near Line 10", there are several features that can affect the location of page breaks.

Changing Top and Bottom Margins

The top and bottom margin defaults are 1 inch. These settings are displayed at the Margins dialog box. To display the Margins dialog box, choose Format, then Margins; or click on the Page Margins button on the Format Toolbar. (To display the Format Toolbar, position the arrow pointer on the current Toolbar, click the right mouse button, then click on Format.)

When top or bottom margin settings are changed, codes are inserted in the document at the beginning of the page where the insertion point is positioned. For example, if the insertion point is located in the middle of page 3 when the top and bottom margins are changed, the code is inserted at the beginning of page 3. Changes to top and bottom margins take effect from the location of the code to the end of the document or until another margin code is encountered. If you want top and bottom margins to affect the entire document, position the insertion point on page 1 before displaying the Margins dialog box.

If you change the top or bottom margins on any page except the first page, WordPerfect inserts the code at the beginning of the page where the insertion point is positioned. This code displays as a Delay code. Additionally, WordPerfect inserts a Delay code at the beginning of the document. For example, if you change the top and bottom margins on page 2, the code Delay Codes: [Bot Mar][Top Mar] displays at the beginning of page 2 and the code Delay: 1 (this number may vary) displays at the beginning of the document. The code at the beginning of the document indicates that formatting has been added to the document that is delayed until the code is encountered. The number after Delay identifies which Delay code it relates to within the document. If you delete either of the Delay codes, the other is removed.

Exercise 1 Changing Margins

1. At a clear editing window, open report01 as a read only document by completing the following steps:
   a. Display the Open File dialog box.
   b. At the Open File dialog box, choose Open As Copy.
   c. Double-click on report01.wpd.
2. Make sure the insertion point is located somewhere on page 1, then change the top and bottom margins to 1.5 inches by completing the following steps:
   a. Choose Format, then Margins; or click on the Page Margins button on the Format Toolbar.
   b. Choose Top.
   c. Key **1.5**.
   d. Choose Bottom.
   e. Key **1.5**.
   f. Choose OK or press Enter.
3. Save the document and name it c12ex01.
4. Print c12ex01.
5. Close c12ex01.

Turning on Widow/Orphan

In a long document, you will want to avoid creating widow or orphan lines. A *widow* is the last line of a paragraph that appears at the top of a page. An *orphan* is the first line of a paragraph that appears at the bottom of a page.

WordPerfect contains a feature that lets you control whether widows or orphans appear in a document. This feature, called Widow/Orphan, is off by default. At this setting, WordPerfect inserts page breaks without considering whether a widow or orphan has occurred. When working with long documents, you will usually want this feature on. WordPerfect then takes the first line of a paragraph to the next page or breaks the page a line sooner so that a minimum of two lines of a paragraph fall at the top or bottom of a page.

To learn how to turn on the Widow/Orphan feature, complete exercise 2.

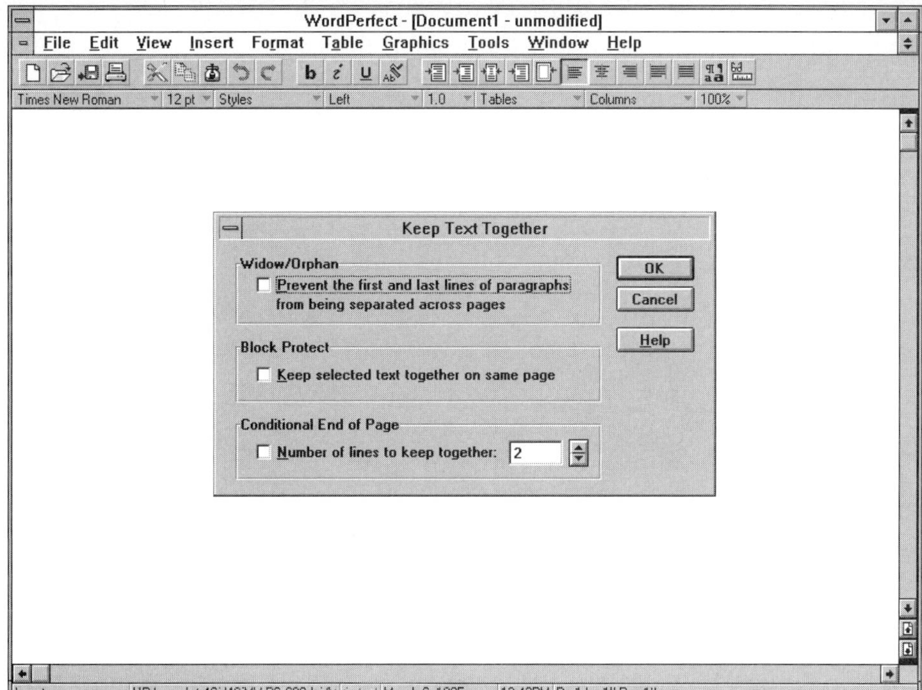

Figure 12.1
Keep Text Together Dialog Box

Exercise 2 Using the Widow/Orphan Feature

1. At a clear editing window, open report01.
2. Save the report with Save As and name it c12ex02.
3. Scroll through the document to see if any widow or orphan lines occur in the document, then move the insertion point to the beginning of the document.
4. Turn on the Widow/Orphan feature by completing the following steps:
   a. Choose Format, Page, then Keep Text Together; or click on the Keep Together button on the Page Toolbar. (To display the Page Toolbar, position the arrow pointer on the current Toolbar, click the right mouse button, then click on Page at the drop-down menu.)
   b. At the Keep Text Together dialog box shown in Figure 12.1, choose Widow/ Orphan. To do this with the mouse, position the arrow pointer in the check box just below Widow/Orphan, then click the left mouse button. If you are using the keyboard, press Alt + P.
   c. Choose OK or press Enter.
5. Save the report again with the same name (c12ex02).
6. Print c12ex02.
7. Close c12ex02.

When Widow/Orphan is on, WordPerfect inserts the code [Wid/Orph: On] at the beginning of the page where the insertion point is positioned. To turn off Widow/Orphan, complete similar steps to remove the X in the Widow/Orphan check box or delete the Widow/Orphan code in Reveal Codes.

Inserting Hard Page Breaks

WordPerfect's default settings break each page after Line 9.83". If you have turned on the Widow/ Orphan feature or changed the top or bottom margins, the page break may vary. Even with these features, however, page breaks may occur in undesirable locations. To remedy these occurrences you can insert your own page break.

In Draft mode, the WordPerfect page break displays as a single line across the screen. The page break you insert displays as a double line across the screen. The default page break is called a *soft page break* and a page break you insert is called a *hard page break*. Soft page breaks automatically adjust if text is added to or deleted from a document. A hard page break does not adjust and is therefore less flexible than a soft page break. If text is added to or deleted from a document with a hard page break, check the break to determine whether it is still in a desirable location.

To insert a page break, move the insertion point to the position where you want the page to break, then choose Insert, then Page Break; or press Ctrl + Enter. Always check page breaks in a document; some require a judgment call that only you can make.

Exercise 3 Inserting Page Breaks

1. At a clear editing window, open report01 as a read only document.
2. Insert a hard page break at the line beginning *The speed at which information...* by completing the following steps:
   a. Position the insertion point at the left margin of the line beginning *The speed at which information...* (toward the end of the first page).
   b. Choose Insert, then Page Break; or press Ctrl + Enter.
3. Insert a hard page break at the left margin of the line beginning *Computing and telecommunications...* (toward the end of the second page).
4. Save the report and name it c12ex03.
5. Print c12ex03.
6. Close c12ex03.

Centering Text Vertically on the Page

WordPerfect's Center Current Page and Center Pages options are used to center text vertically on the page. You may, for example, want to center vertically the title page of a report, a short letter or memo, a table, or an illustration. With options from the Center Page(s) dialog box, shown in figure 12.2, you can center text vertically only on the page where the insertion point is positioned or center text on current and subsequent pages.

Figure 12.2
Center Page(s) Dialog Box

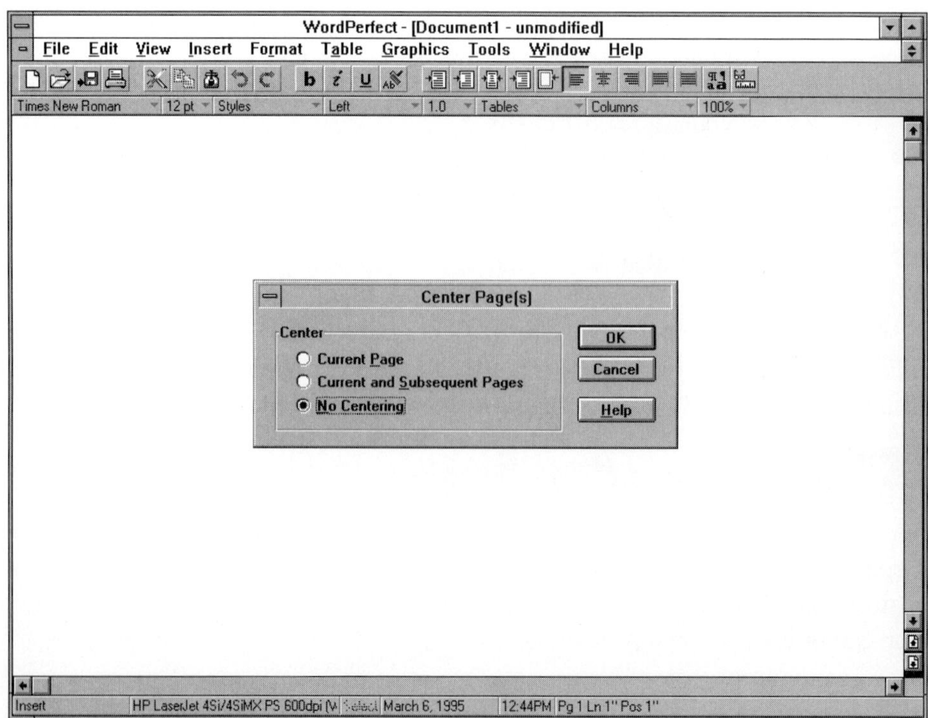

Exercise 4 Centering Text Vertically

1. At a clear editing window, key the text shown in figure 12.3. Center and bold the text as indicated. Press the Enter key the number of times indicated in the brackets. (Do not key the information in brackets.)
2. Center the text vertically on the page by completing the following steps:
   a. With the insertion point positioned anywhere in the page, choose Format, Page, then Center; or click on the Center Page button on the Page Toolbar.
   b. At the Center Page(s) dialog box, choose Current Page.
   c. Choose OK or press Enter.
3. Save the document and name it c12ex04.
4. View the full page to see how the document will look when printed.
5. Print c12ex04.
6. Close c12ex04.

Figure 12.3

HISTORY OF TELECOMMUNICATIONS
[press Enter 15 times]

by Ramona Salas
[press Enter 15 times]

CIS 120
January 17, 1997

WordPerfect inserts the code Cntr Cur Pg: On at the beginning of the page where the insertion point is located.

Inserting Page Numbering

WordPerfect, by default, does not print page numbers on a page. For documents such as memos and letters, this is appropriate. For longer documents, however, page numbers may be needed. WordPerfect includes several options for numbering pages in documents. Page numbers can appear in a variety of locations on the page and can be turned on and off in the same document.

Numbering Pages in a Document

When page numbering is turned on in a document, WordPerfect inserts a page numbering code at the beginning of the page where the insertion point is located. If you want page numbering to appear on all pages of the document, position the insertion point somewhere on page 1, then turn on page numbering.

To turn on page numbering in a document, choose Format, Page, then Numbering; or click on the Page Numbering button on the Page Toolbar. At the Page Numbering dialog box, shown in figure 12.4, choose Position, then choose an option from the Position drop-down menu. Choose OK or press Enter to close the Page Numbering dialog box.

When you choose a page numbering option from the Position drop-down menu, the Page Numbering dialog box displays page numbering in the example pages.

When page numbering is included in a document, a code is inserted in the document that can be seen in Reveal Codes. For example, if page numbering is turned on and numbers are to print at the bottom center of the page, the code Pg Num Pos: Bottom Center displays in Reveal Codes.

When a document includes page numbering, WordPerfect subtracts two lines from the total number of lines printed on a page. One line is subtracted for the page number and the other to separate the page number from the text. The page number is printed one inch from the top or bottom of the page. Page numbers appear on the screen in page and two-page view, but not draft view.

Figure 12.4
Page Numbering Dialog Box

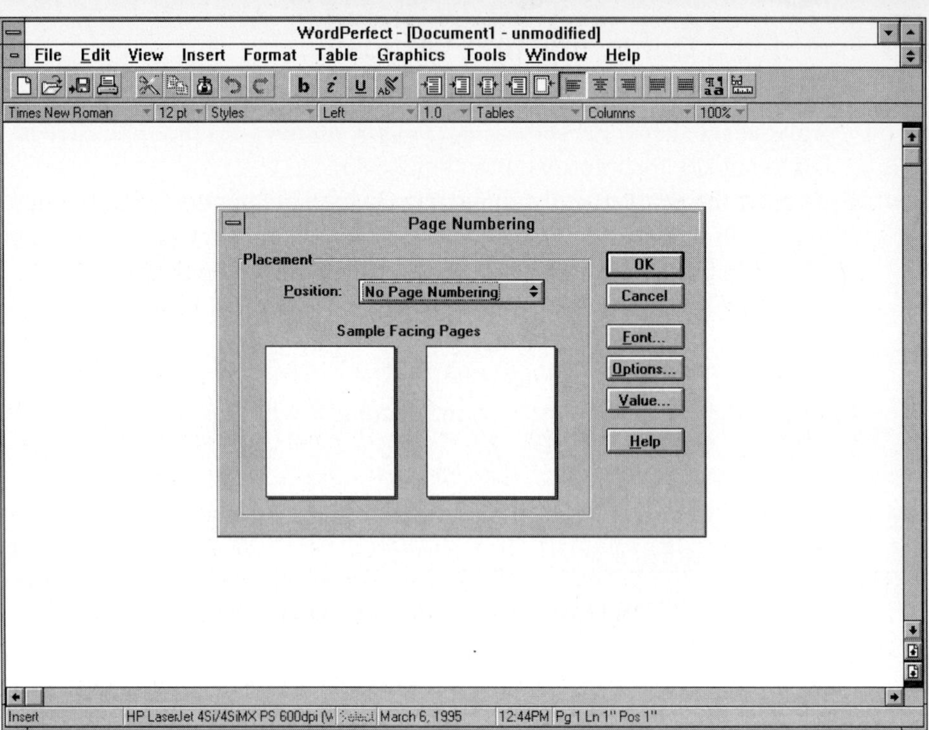

Exercise 5 Numbering Pages at the Bottom Center

1. At a clear editing window, open report01.
2. Save the report with Save As and name it c12ex05.
3. Change the left and right margins to 1.5 inches.
4. With the insertion point positioned anywhere in the first page, turn on the Widow/Orphan feature.
5. With the insertion point positioned anywhere in the first page, turn page numbering on and number pages at the bottom center of the page by completing the following steps:
   a. Choose Format, Page, then Numbering; or click on the Page Numbering button on the Page Toolbar.
   b. At the Page Numbering dialog box choose Position, then Bottom Center. To do this with the mouse, position the arrow pointer on the Position text box, hold down the left mouse button, drag the arrow pointer to Bottom Center, then release the mouse button. If you are using the keyboard, press Alt + P, press the space bar, then key the letter **o** (for Bottom Center).
   c. Choose OK or press Enter.
6. Save the report again with the same name (c12ex05).
7. Print c12ex05.
8. Close c12ex05.

Selective Page Numbering

Page numbering can be turned off in a document where page numbering exists. To do this, you would change the Position option at the Page Numbering dialog box to No Page Numbering.

Page numbering will remain off from the page where the insertion point is located to the end of the document or until a page numbering code is encountered.

You can also suppress page numbering on specific pages. This is useful, for example, in a document where you want page numbering to print in the upper right corner of each page, except the first page. Insert the page numbering code at the beginning of the document, then insert a suppress page numbering code on the first page. To suppress a page number on a specific page, position the insertion point on the page, then display the Suppress dialog box by choosing Format,

Page, then Suppress; or clicking on the Suppress button on the Page Toolbar. At the Suppress dialog box, choose Page Numbering, then choose OK to close the dialog box.

Exercise 6 Numbering Specific Pages

1. At a clear editing window, open report02.
2. Save the report with Save As and name it c12ex06.
3. With the insertion point positioned anywhere in page 1, change the left and right margins to 1.5 inches and turn on the Widow/Orphan feature.
4. With the insertion point located somewhere on page 1, turn page numbering on and number pages at the top right corner of the page.
5. Suppress page numbering on the first page by completing the following steps:
   a. Choose Format, Page, then Suppress; or click on the Suppress button on the Page Toolbar.
   b. At the Suppress dialog box, choose Page Numbering.
   c. Choose OK to close the dialog box.
6. Save the report again with the same name (c12ex06).
7. Print c12ex06.
8. Close c12ex06.

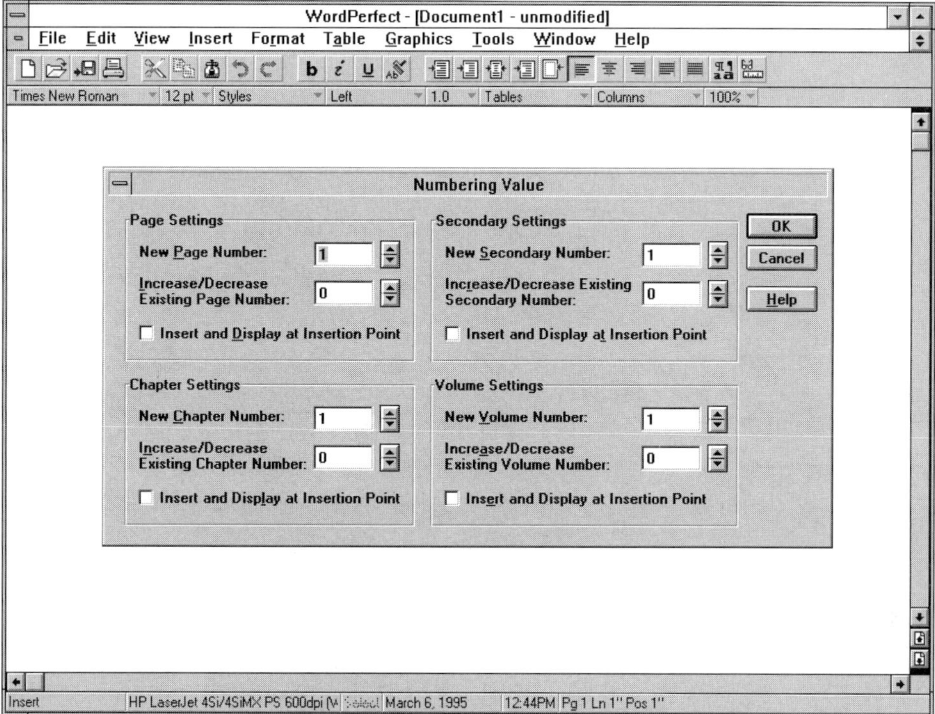

Figure 12.5 **Numbering Value Dialog Box**

Changing the Page Number

When page numbering is turned on, pages are numbered beginning with 1 and incremented. You can change the beginning page number at the Numbering Value dialog box shown in figure 12.5.

To change the default page number, increase or decrease the number in the New Page Number text box.

When you change the default page number, a code is inserted in the document that can be seen in Reveal Codes. For example, if you changed the page number on page 5 to page 8, the code Pg Num Set;Start Lev 1;8 would display in Reveal Codes at the beginning of page 5 (now page 8).

Exercise 7 Changing the Default Page Number

1. At a clear editing window, open report02.
2. Save the report with Save As and name it c12ex07.
3. With the insertion point positioned at the beginning of the document, change the left and right margins to 1.5 inches and turn on the Widow/Orphan feature.
4. With the insertion point positioned anywhere on page 1, turn on page numbering and number pages at the bottom of the page, alternating.
5. With the insertion point positioned anywhere on page 1, change the beginning page number to 9 by completing the following steps:
   a. Choose Format, Page, then Numbering; or click on the Page Numbering button on the Page Toolbar.
   b. At the Page Numbering dialog box, choose Value.
   c. At the Numbering Value dialog box key **9**. (The New Page Number option is already selected.)
   d. Choose OK or press Enter.
   e. At the Page Numbering dialog box, choose Close or press Enter.
6. Save the report with the same name (c12ex07).
7. Print c12ex07.
8. Close c12ex07.

Changing the Page Numbering Method

When page numbering is turned on in a document, WordPerfect uses Arabic numbers (1, 2, 3, etc.). This numbering method can be changed to lowercase letters (a, b, c, etc.), uppercase letters (A, B, C, etc.), lowercase Roman numerals (i, ii, iii, etc.), or uppercase Roman numerals (I, II, III, etc.). When the numbering method is changed, a code is inserted at the beginning of the page where the insertion point is located.

Exercise 8 Numbering Pages with Roman Numerals

1. At a clear editing window, open report02.
2. Save the report with Save As and name it c12ex08.
3. With the insertion point positioned at the beginning of the document, change the left and right margins to 1.5 inches and turn on the Widow/Orphan feature.
4. With the insertion point positioned anywhere on page 1, turn on page numbering and number pages at the bottom center.
5. Change the page numbering method to lowercase Roman numerals by completing the following steps:
   a. Choose Format, Page, then Numbering; or click on the Page Numbering button on the Page Toolbar.
   b. At the Page Numbering dialog box, choose Options.
   c. At the Page Numbering Options dialog box, choose Page, then Lowercase Roman. To do this with the mouse, position the arrow pointer in the Page text box, hold down the left mouse button, drag the arrow pointer to Lowercase Roman, then release the mouse button. If you are using the keyboard, press Alt + P, press the space bar, then key **o** (for Lowercase Roman).
   d. Choose OK or press Enter.
   e. At the Page Numbering dialog box, choose OK.
6. Save the report with the same name (c12ex08).
7. Print c12ex08.
8. Close c12ex08.

Keying Flush Right Text

With the Flush Right command, you can create text aligned at the right margin. To key text aligned at the right margin, choose Format, Line, then Flush Right; or press Alt + F7. This causes the insertion point to move to the right margin. As text is keyed, the insertion point moves to the left. The Flush Right command is ended when you press the Enter key. To align the next line at the right margin, choose Format, Line, then Flush Right; or press Alt + F7 again.

Exercise 9 Creating a Letterhead with Flush Right Text

1. At a clear editing window, create the letterhead shown in figure 12.6 by completing the following steps:
   a. Change the font to 14-point Arrus BT Bold.
   b. Key the hospital name, **DENVER MEMORIAL HOSPITAL**, in all capital letters.
   c. Press Enter, then access the Flush Right command by choosing Format, Line, then Flush Right; or pressing Alt + F7.
   d. Hold the Shift key down, then press the hyphen key (-) 30 times to create the line.
   e. Press Enter, then access the Flush Right command.
   f. Key the street address, then press Enter.
   g. Access the Flush Right command, key the city, state, and ZIP Code, then press Enter.
   h. Access the Flush right command, key the telephone number, then press Enter.
2. Save the letterhead and name it c12ex09.
3. Print c12ex09.
4. Close c12ex09.

Figure 12.6

DENVER MEMORIAL HOSPITAL

---

900 Colorado Boulevard
Denver, CO 86530
(303) 555-4400

CHAPTER SUMMARY

- WordPerfect inserts a page break at approximately 10 inches from the top of the page. With the default 1-inch top and bottom margins, this allows a total of 9 inches of text to be printed on a standard page.
- The default 1-inch top and bottom margins can be changed at the Margins dialog box. No matter where the insertion point is positioned when the margins are changed, the top and bottom margin will appear in Reveal Codes at the top of that page. These codes will affect the remainder of the document unless a new code is inserted.
- In addition to the margin codes at the top of the page where the insertion point was located when margins were changed, a Delay code will appear at the beginning of the document as Delay Codes: [Bot Mar][Top Mar].
- Turn on the Widow/Orphan feature to avoid having the first or last line of a paragraph printed at the bottom or top of the page.

- If an automatic page break (soft page break) occurs in an undesirable location, a page break can be forced above it. The new page break is called a hard page break and appears in Draft mode as a double line across the screen.
- To center text vertically on one page or on all pages in a document, use the Current Page or Current and Subsequent Pages option at the Center Page(s) dialog box. The text will not look centered in the Draft viewing mode.
- WordPerfect includes several options at the Page Numbering dialog box. The page numbers in a document can be placed in different locations on the page, turned on and off, and the page numbering method can also be changed.
- Use the Flush Right command to create text aligned at the right margin.

Commands Review

	Mouse	**Keyboard**
Margins dialog box	Format, Margins; or click on the Page Margins button on the Format Toolbar	Format, Margins
Keep Text Together dialog box	Format, Page, Keep Text Together; or click on the Keep Together button on the Page Toolbar	Format, Page, Keep Text Together
Format Toolbar	Click the right mouse button on the current Toolbar, then click on Format	
Page Toolbar	Click the right mouse button on the current Toolbar, then click on Page	
Hard page break	Insert, Page Break	CTRL + ENTER
Center Page(s) dialog box	Format, Page, Center; or click on the Center Page button on the Page Toolbar	Format, Page, Center
Page Numbering dialog box	Format, Page, Numbering; or click on Page Numbering button on the Page Toolbar	Format, Page, Numbering
Suppress dialog box	Format, Page, Suppress; or click on Suppress button on the Page Toolbar	Format, Page, Suppress
Flush Right	Format, Line, Flush Right	Alt + F7

CHECK YOUR UNDERSTANDING

True/False: Circle the letter T if the statement is true; circle the letter F if the statement is false.

T **F** 1. The code indicating a change to a 2-inch top margin is Top Mar: 2".

T **F** 2. The top/bottom margin codes will always appear at the bottom of the page where the insertion point was located when the margins were changed.

T **F** 3. If top/bottom margins are changed when the insertion point is on page 4, a Delay code will be inserted at the beginning of the document.

T **F** 4. A widow or an orphan is one line that appears alone on a page.

T **F** 5. The keyboard command to insert a hard page break is Shift + Enter.

T **F** 6. Two lines of text are subtracted from the total lines that are printed on each page when page numbering is turned on.

T **F** 7. For page numbering to begin on page 1, the insertion point must be placed at the very top of page 1 before inserting the page numbering code.

T **F** 8. The keyboard command for Flush Right is Alt + F7.

Matching: In the space provided at the right, indicate the correct letter that matches each description.

A.	1 inch	E.	7.5 inches
B.	8.5 inches	F.	10 inches
C.	9 inches	G.	11 inches
D.	11.5 inches	H.	9.5 inches

1. Length of a standard piece of paper. ____________
2. Default top and bottom margins. ____________
3. Total inches of printed vertical text on a page. ____________
4. Approximate measurement at which the automatic page break occurs on a page. ____________
5. Width of a standard piece of paper. ____________

SKILL ASSESSMENTS

Assessment 1

1. At a clear editing window, open report04.
2. Save the report with Save As and name it c12sa01.
3. With the insertion point positioned at the beginning of the document, make the following changes:
   a. Change the top, left, and right margins to 1.5 inches.
   b. Turn on the Widow/Orphan feature.
   c. Number pages at the top left side of each page except the first page.
4. Save the report again with the same name (c12sa01).
5. Print c12sa01.
6. Close c12sa01.

Assessment 2

1. At a clear editing window, change the font to 24-point Onyx BT, then key the notice shown in figure 12.7 centered and bolded.
2. Center the notice vertically on the page.
3. Save the document and name it c12sa02.
4. Print c12sa02.
5. Close c12sa02.

Figure 12.7

DRYER ELEMENTARY SCHOOL

Winter Program

Performing Arts Center

Tuesday, December 10, 1996

7:30 p.m.

Assessment 3

1. At a clear editing window, open report04.
2. Save the report with Save As and name it c12sa03.
3. With the insertion point positioned at the beginning of the document, make the following changes:
   a. Change the left margin to 1.5 inches.
   b. Turn on the Widow/Orphan feature.
   c. Insert a page break at the heading, *CHAPTER 4: DEVELOPMENT OF TECHNOLOGY, 1950 - 1960.*
   d. Number pages at the bottom right corner of each page.
4. Check page breaks. If necessary insert your own.
5. Save the report again with the same name (c12sa03).
6. Print c12sa03.
7. Close c12sa03.

Creating Document References 13

Upon successful completion of chapter 13, you will be able to finish multiple-paged reports with specific page characteristics including headers, footers, footnotes, and endnotes.

In a WordPerfect document, you can create document references such as headers, footers, footnotes, and endnotes. Text that appears at the top of pages is called a *header*, and text that appears at the bottom of pages is called a *footer*. A *footnote* is an explanatory note that is printed at the bottom of the page. An *endnote* is an explanatory note printed at the end of a document.

Creating Headers and Footers

A maximum of two headers and/or two footers can be created in a WordPerfect document. WordPerfect refers to them as Header A, Header B, Footer A, and Footer B. A header or footer can contain as many lines as needed, up to one page. Generally, however, most headers and footers are only a few lines in length.

Headers and footers can be created in various forms. They can appear on every page or can be identified as alternating headers or footers. With alternating headers or footers, text is printed only on even-numbered or odd-numbered pages.

A header or footer can be turned off or discontinued in a document. For example, you can have a header printed on the first and second pages of a document and not printed on the remaining pages. You can also turn a header or footer off on specific pages.

A header or footer can be created in any of the viewing modes. However, you may find it useful to have the Page viewing mode selected. In this viewing mode, you will see the header or footer displayed in the document.

When a header or footer is created, the header or footer code is inserted at the beginning of the page where the insertion point is positioned. For example, if you want a header to begin printing on page 1, make sure the insertion point is positioned somewhere in the first page.

To create a header or footer, choose Format, then Header/Footer. At the Headers/Footers dialog box, shown in figure 13.1, choose the desired header or footer, then choose Create. At the Header window shown in figure 13.2, key the header or footer, then choose Close.

Figure 13.1
Headers/Footers Dialog Box

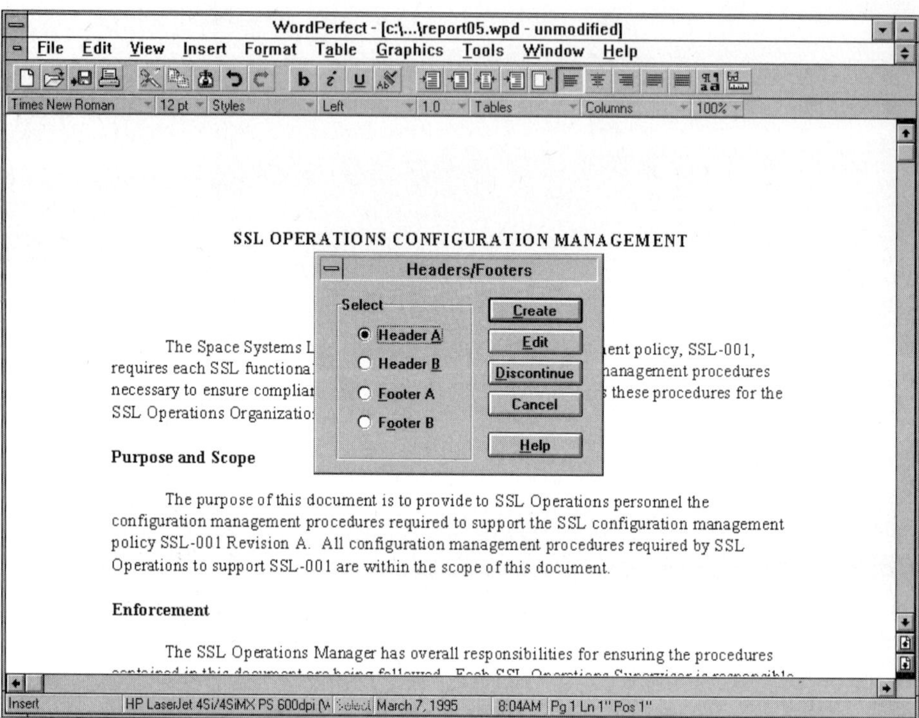

Figure 13.2
Header Window

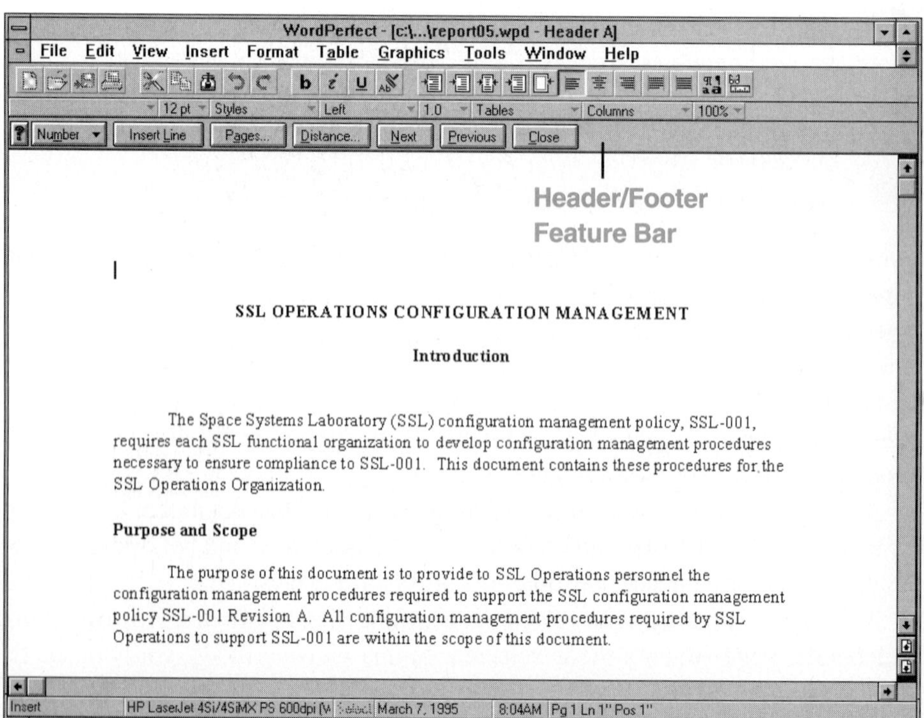

When a Header or Footer window is displayed, a bar is inserted in the document window below the Power Bar (or the Ruler Bar). This bar is called the Header/Footer Feature Bar and is identified in figure 13.2. Use options on this feature bar to insert page numbering, specify the pages and location of headers or footers, and close the Header or Footer window.

To choose options from the Header/Footer Feature Bar with the mouse, click on the desired option. To choose options with the keyboard, hold down the Alt key, the Shift key, then press the underlined letter of the desired option. For example, to choose the Close option on the Header/Footer Feature Bar, press Alt + Shift + C.

Exercise 1 Creating a Footer

1. At a clear editing window, open report01.
2. Save the report with Save As and name it c13ex01.
3. Change the left and right margins to 1.5 inches and turn on the Widow/Orphan feature.
4. Create Footer A that prints at the bottom of every page, is bolded, and reads *Trends in Telecommunications* by completing the following steps:
   a. Position the insertion point anywhere in the first page of the report.
   b. Choose Format, then Header/Footer.
   c. At the Headers/Footers dialog box, choose Footer A.
   d. Choose Create.
   e. At the Footer window, press Ctrl + B, then key **Trends in Telecommunications**.
   f. Choose Close.
5. Save the report again with the same name (c13ex01).
6. Print c13ex01.
7. Close c13ex01.

Beginning Headers or Footers on Specific Pages

If the insertion point is positioned in the first page when the header or footer is created, the header or footer code is inserted at the beginning of the document. With the code at the beginning of the document, the header or footer will print on every page in the document.

To specify on what page a header or footer should begin printing, position the insertion point in the page where you want the header or footer to begin, then create the header or footer. For example, if you want a header or footer to print in a document beginning with page 2, position the insertion point anywhere in page 2, then create the header or footer.

Exercise 2 Creating a Header

1. At a clear editing window, open report02.
2. Save the report with Save As and name it c13ex02.
3. Turn on the Widow/Orphan feature.
4. Create Header A that prints at the right margin of all pages except the first page, is bolded, and reads *Telecommunications Technology* by completing the following steps:
   a. Position the insertion point in the second page.
   b. Choose Format, then Header/Footer.
   c. At the Headers/Footers dialog box, Header A should already be selected so choose Create.
   d. At the Header window, choose Format, Line, then Flush Right; or press Alt + F7.
   e. Press Ctrl + B, then key **Telecommunications Technology**.
   f. Choose Close.
5. Save the report again with the same name (c13ex02).
6. Print c13ex02.
7. Close c13ex02.

You can also print headers or footers on only even-numbered or only odd-numbered pages by choosing the Placement option on the Header/Footer Feature Bar.

Exercise 3 Printing a Header on Even-Numbered Pages

1. At a clear editing window, open report02.
2. Save the report with Save As and name it c13ex03.
3. Turn on the Widow/Orphan feature.
4. Create Header A that prints at the top of all even-numbered pages, is bolded, and reads *Telecommunications Technology* by completing the following steps:
   a. Position the insertion point on the line containing the title of the report.
   b. Choose Format, then Header/Footer.
   c. At the Headers/Footers dialog box, Header A should already be selected so choose Create.
   d. At the Header window, choose Pages. (If you are using the keyboard, press Alt + Shift + A.)
   e. At the Pages dialog box, choose Even Pages.
   f. Choose OK or press Enter.
   g. Press Ctrl + B, then key **Telecommunications Technology**.
   h. Choose Close.
5. Save the report again with the same name (c13ex03).
6. Print c13ex03.
7. Close c13ex03.

Printing Headers or Footers

A header in a document with default top and bottom margins will print an inch from the top of the page with a blank line separating the header from the text. Unless the bottom margin is changed, the last line of a footer prints an inch from the bottom of the page with a blank line separating the text in the document from the footer. If you want a header or footer to print closer to the top or bottom of the page, change the top and/or bottom margins.

Headers and footers take the place of regular text lines. By default, 9 inches of text are printed on a standard piece of paper. WordPerfect automatically assigns a blank line after a header or a blank line before a footer. Therefore, if you create a header of two lines, WordPerfect prints the header (two lines), leaves one line blank, and then prints 8.5 inches of text. A footer prints in a similar manner.

Exercise 4 Printing a Footer One-Half Inch from Bottom of Page

1. At a clear editing window, open report01.
2. Save the report with Save As and name it c13ex04.
3. Change the bottom margin to 0.5 inches.
4. Turn on the Widow/Orphan feature.
5. Create Footer A that prints bolded and centered at the bottom of all pages and reads *Telecommunications Trends.*
6. Save the document again with the same name (c13ex04).
7. Print c13ex04.
8. Close c13ex04.

Editing Headers or Footers

A header or footer can be edited. To edit a header or footer, choose Format, then Header/Footer. At the Headers/Footers dialog box, select the header or footer to be edited, then choose Edit. At the Header or Footer window, make any necessary changes, then choose Close.

Exercise 5 Creating Two Footers and Editing One Footer

1. At a clear editing window, open report03.
2. Save the report with Save As and name it c13ex05.
3. Change the bottom margin to 0.5 inches.
4. Turn on the Widow/Orphan feature.
5. Create Footer A that prints at the right margin of odd-numbered pages, is bolded, and reads *Development of Technology*.
6. Create Footer B that prints at the left margin of all even-numbered pages, is bolded, and reads *Telecommunications*.
7. Save the report again with the same name (c13ex05).
8. Print c13ex05.
9. Edit Footer A so that it reads *History from 1800 - 1900* by completing the following steps:
   a. Choose Format, then Header/Footer.
   b. At the Headers/Footers dialog box, choose Footer A, then choose Edit.
   c. At the Footer window, delete the existing text, then key **History from 1800 - 1900** bolded.
   d. Choose Close.
10. Save the report again with the same name (c13ex05).
11. Print c13ex05.
12. Close c13ex05.

Discontinuing Headers and Footers

Header or footer text can appear at the top or bottom of each page, or it can appear on certain pages and be turned off on others. For example, you can create Header A that prints on the first three pages of a document, then turn off Header A for the remaining pages of the document. You can do the same for footers.

Exercise 6 Turning Off the Printing of a Header

1. At a clear editing window, open c13ex03.
2. Save the report with Save As and name it c13ex06.
3. Discontinue Header A at page 4 by completing the following steps:
   a. Position the insertion point in page 4.
   b. Choose Format, then Header/Footer.
   c. At the Headers/Footers dialog box, choose Header A, then Discontinue.
4. Save the report again with the same name (c13ex06).
5. Print c13ex06.
6. Close c13ex06.

Creating a Footnote or Endnote

A research paper or report contains information from a variety of sources. To give credit to those sources, a footnote can be inserted in the document. A *footnote* is an explanatory note or reference that is printed at the bottom of the page.

A footnote notation appears in the body of the document as a superscripted number. This number identifies the footnote at the bottom of the page that contains information identifying the source.

When footnotes are created in a document, WordPerfect determines the number of lines needed at the bottom of the page for the footnote information and adjusts the page endings accordingly.

An *endnote* is similar to a footnote, except that endnote reference information appears at the end of a document rather than on the page where the reference was made.

Footnotes and endnotes are created in a similar manner with WordPerfect. To create a footnote in a document, move the insertion point to the location in the document where the notation is to appear, then choose Insert, Footnote, then Create. At the Footnote window, shown in figure 13.3, key the footnote reference information, then choose Close.

To create an endnote, move the insertion point to the location in the document where the notation is to appear, then choose Insert, Endnote, then Create. At the Endnote window, shown in figure 13.4, access the Indent command, key the endnote reference information, then choose Close.

Figure 13.3
Footnote Window

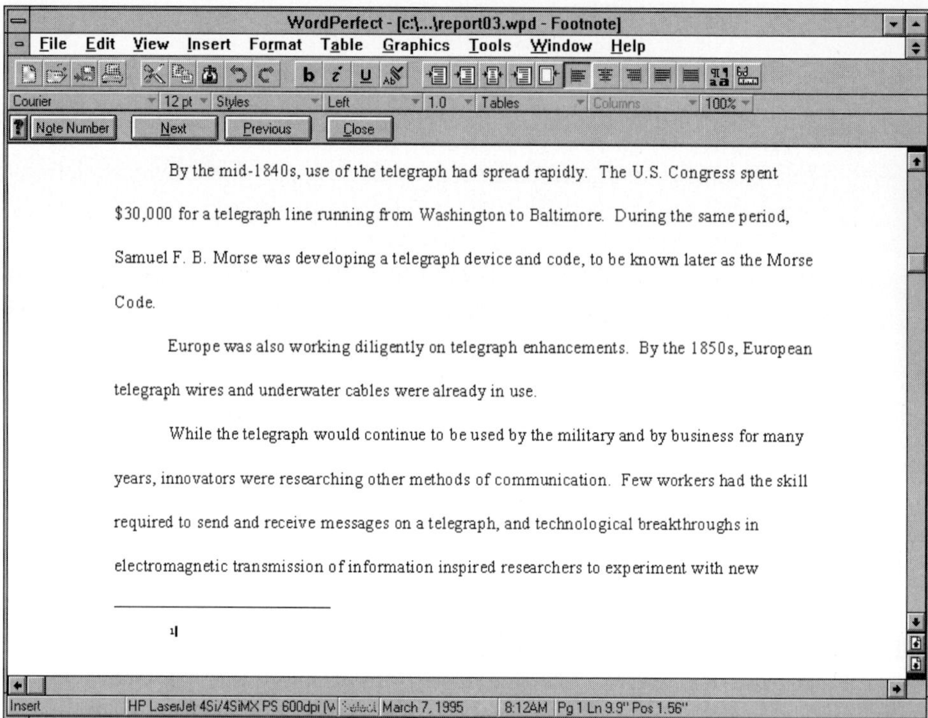

Figure 13.4
Endnote Window

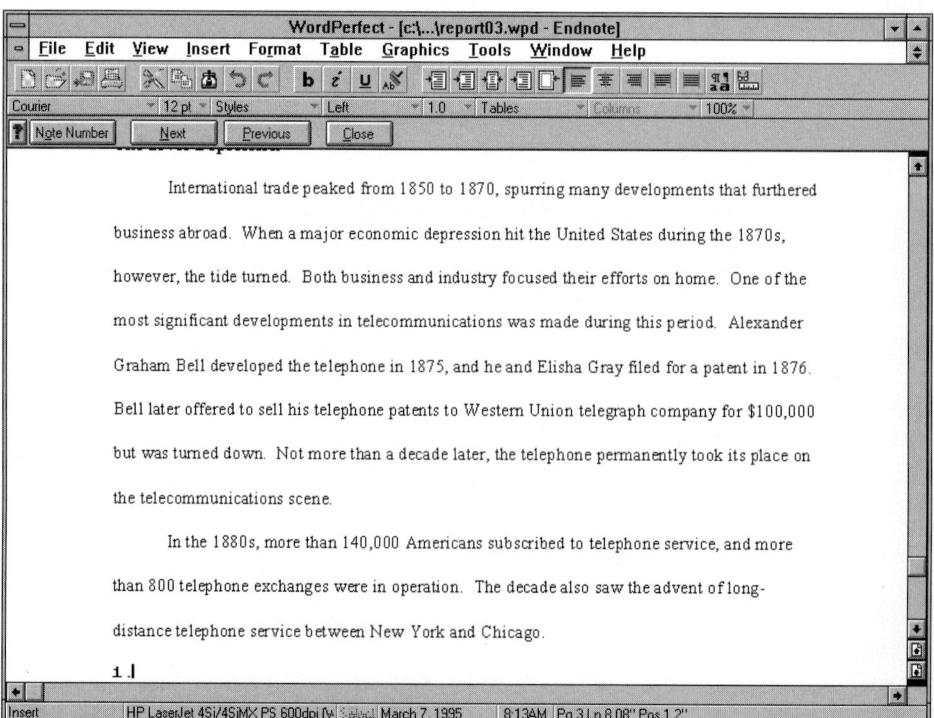

After keying the footnote or endnote reference text, *do not* press the Enter key. By default, WordPerfect separates footnotes and endnotes by a blank line. If you press the Enter key after keying the footnote or endnote reference text, an extra blank line is inserted between the notes.

At the Footnote or Endnote window, choose options with the keyboard by holding down the Alt key, the Shift key, then pressing the underlined letter of the desired option. For example, to close the Footnote window, press Alt + Shift + C for Close.

Exercise 7 Creating Footnotes

1. At a clear editing window, open report01.
2. Save the report with Save As and name it c13ex07.
3. Create the first footnote shown in figure 13.5 at the end of the first paragraph in the *Continued Growth of Photonics (Fiber Optics)* section by completing the following steps:
   a. Position the insertion point at the end of the first paragraph in the *Continued Growth of Photonics (Fiber Optics)* section.
   b. Choose Insert, Footnote, then Create.
   c. At the Footnote window, key the first footnote reference information shown in figure 13.5.
   d. Choose Close.
4. Move the insertion point to the end of the second paragraph in the *Continued Growth of Photonics (Fiber Optics)* section, then create the second footnote shown in figure 13.5 by completing steps similar to those in 3.
5. Move the insertion point to the end of the last paragraph in the *Continued Growth of Photonics (Fiber Optics)* section, then create the third footnote shown in figure 13.5 by completing steps similar to those in 3.
6. Move the insertion point to the end of the last paragraph in the report, then create the fourth footnote shown in figure 13.5.
7. Save the report again with the same name (c13ex07).
8. Print c13ex07.
9. Close c13ex07.

Figure 13.5

[1]Mitchell, William, Robert Hendricks and Leonard Sterry, *Telecommunications: Systems and Applications*, Paradigm Publishing, 1993, pages 39-41.

[2]Weik, Robert, "History of Light Wave Technology," *Computer Technologies*, May/June 1994, pages 9-12.

[3]Griffith, Kathleen, "The Importance of Fiber Optics," *Computing in the 90's*, April 1993, pages 2-6.

[4]McKenna, Kelly A., *Telecommunications Innovations*, Princetown Publishing, 1993, pages 44-48.

Printing Footnotes and Endnotes

When a document containing footnotes is printed, WordPerfect automatically reduces the number of text lines on a page by the number of lines in the footnote plus two lines for spacing between the text and the footnote. WordPerfect keeps at least 0.5 inches of footnote text together. If there is not enough room on the page for the 0.5 inches of footnote text, the footnote number and footnote are taken to the next page. WordPerfect separates the footnotes from the text with a 2-inch separator line that begins at the left margin. The footnote number in the document and the footnote number before the reference information print as a superscripted number above the text line.

When endnotes are created in a document, WordPerfect prints all endnote references at the end of the document. If you want the endnotes printed on a separate page at the end of the document, move the insertion point to the end of the document, then insert a hard page break by choosing Insert, then Page Break; or by pressing Ctrl + Enter.

Exercise 8 Creating Endnotes

1. At a clear editing window, open report02.
2. Save the report with Save As and name it c13ex08.
3. Move the insertion point to the end of the document, then insert a hard page break by choosing Insert, then Page Break; or pressing Ctrl + Enter.
4. Key **ENDNOTES**, bold and centered, then press the Enter key once. (This will cause the endnotes to print on a separate page with the heading *ENDNOTES*.)
5. Create the first endnote shown in figure 13.6 at the end of the first paragraph by completing the following steps:
   a. Position the insertion point at the end of the first paragraph.
   b. Choose Insert, Endnote, then Create.
   c. At the Endnote window, press F7 to access the Indent command, then key the first endnote reference information shown in figure 13.6.
   d. Choose Close.
6. Move the insertion point to the end of the first paragraph in the *Contributions of Major Historical Events* section, then create the second endnote shown in figure 13.6 by completing steps similar to those in 5.
7. Move the insertion point to the end of the last paragraph in the *Contributions of Major Historical Events* section, then create the third endnote shown in figure 13.6 by completing steps similar to those in 5.
8. Move the insertion point to the end of the last paragraph in the document, then create the fourth endnote shown in figure 13.6 by completing steps similar to those in step 5.
9. Save the report with the same name (c13ex08).
10. Print c13ex08.
11. Close c13ex08.

Figure 13.6

1. Mitchell, William, Robert Hendricks and Leonard Sterry, *Telecommunications: Systems and Applications*, Paradigm Publishing, 1993, pages 16-19.

2. Brewer, Ilene, *Industrialization in the U.S.*, City Publishing Services, 1992, pages 43-45.

3.	Morrell, Ashley, *History of Computing*, G. Hardy Publishing, 1994, pages 12-20.
4.	Pang, Yi, *Computing in the 1880s*, Pacific Coast Publishing, Inc., 1994, pages 7-13.

Editing a Footnote or Endnote

Changes can be made to a footnote or endnote that was previously created in a document. To edit an existing footnote in a document, choose Insert, Footnote, then Edit. At the Edit Footnote dialog box, key the footnote number to be edited, then choose OK or press Enter. WordPerfect displays the footnote reference text in the Footnote window. At this window make any necessary changes, then choose Close. You would follow similar steps to edit an endnote in a document.

Exercise 9 Editing Endnotes

1. At a clear editing window, open c13ex08.
2. Save the document with Save As and name it c13ex09.
3. Make the following changes to the document:
   a. Number pages in the document at the bottom center of each page.
   b. Edit the second endnote, changing the year from *1992* to *1994* and changing the page numbers from *43-45* to *21-24*, by completing the following steps:
      (1) Choose Insert, Endnote, then Edit.
      (2) At the Edit Endnote dialog box, key **2**, then choose OK or press Enter.
      (3) With the reference text for the endnote displayed in the Endnote window, change the year from *1992* to *1994* and the pages from *43-45* to *21-24*.
      (4) Choose Close.
   c. Edit the fourth endnote, changing the title from *Computing in the 1880s* to *Perspectives in Telecommunications*.
4. Save the document again with the same name (c13ex09).
5. Print c13ex09.
6. Close c13ex09.

Deleting a Footnote or Endnote

A footnote or endnote can be deleted from a document by positioning the insertion point immediately left of the footnote or endnote number, then pressing the Delete key. You can also position the insertion point immediately to the right of the footnote or endnote number, then press the Backspace key. Or, you can use the mouse to drag the footnote or endnote code out of the Reveal Codes window.

When a footnote or endnote is deleted from a document, WordPerfect automatically renumbers any remaining footnotes or endnotes.

Exercise 10 Editing and Deleting Footnotes

1. At a clear editing window, open c13ex07.
2. Save the document with Save As and name it c13ex10.
   a. Select the title, *TRENDS IN TELECOMMUNICATIONS*, then change the relative size to Very Large.
   b. Select the heading *Continued Growth of Photonics (Fiber Optics)*, then change the relative size to Large.
   c. Select the heading *Microcomputer Trends in the Nineties*, then change the

relative size to Large.

3. Move the insertion point to the end of the second paragraph in the *Continued Growth of Photonics (Fiber Optics)* section, then delete the footnote number.
4. Save the document again with the same name (c13ex10).
5. Print c13ex10.
6. Close c13ex10.

Changing the Beginning Number

When a footnote or endnote is created in a document, the numbering begins with 1 and continues sequentially. The beginning footnote or endnote number can be changed as well as the numbering style. To change the beginning number, choose Insert, Footnote, then New Number. At the Footnote Number dialog box, choose New Number, key the desired number, then choose OK or press Enter.

You would complete similar steps to change the beginning endnote number. The Endnote Number dialog box contains the same options as the Footnote Number dialog box.

Exercise 11 Renumbering Footnotes

1. At a clear editing window, open c13ex07.
2. Save the document with Save As and name it c13ex11.
3. Make the following changes to the document:
   a. Change the top margin to 1.5 inches.
   b. With the insertion point located at the beginning of the document, change the beginning footnote number to 5 by completing the following steps:
      (1) Choose Insert, Footnote, then New Number.
      (2) At the Footnote Number dialog box, choose New Number.
      (3) Key **5**.
      (4) Choose OK or press Enter.
   c. Number each page except the first page in the upper right corner of the page.
4. Save the document again with the same name (c13ex11).
5. Print c13ex11.
6. Close c13ex11.

Formatting Headers/Footers and Footnotes/Endnotes

Headers, footers, footnotes, and endnotes that are created in a document do not take on any formatting applied to the document. For example, if the margins and justification are changed in the document, headers, footers, footnotes, or endnotes text do not conform to these changes.

If you want formatting changes in a document to also affect headers, footers, footnotes, and endnotes, insert the formatting codes at the Styles Editor dialog box. To display the Styles Editor dialog box, shown in figure 13.7, choose Format, Document, then Initial Codes Style. Insert formatting codes in this dialog box in the normal manner.

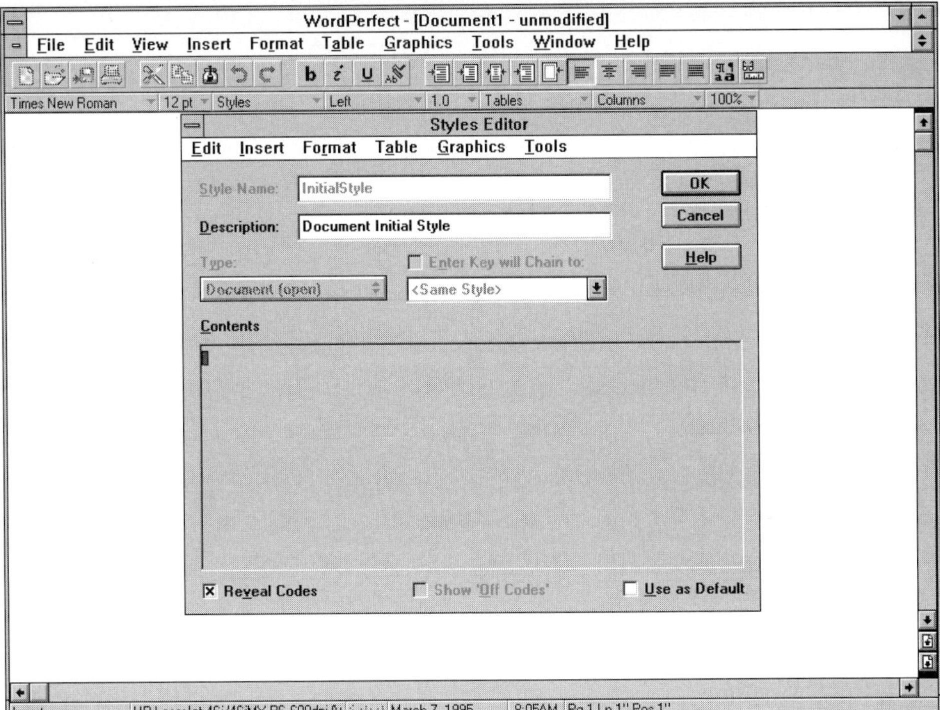

Figure 13.7
Styles Editor Dialog Box

Exercise 12 Changing Format at the Styles Editor Dialog Box

1. At a clear editing window, open report02.
2. Save the report and name it c13ex12.
3. Turn on the Widow/Orphan feature.
4. Change the left and right margins to 1.5 inches, the bottom margin to 0.5 inches, and the justification to Full at the Styles Editor dialog box by completing the following steps:
   a. Choose Format, Document, then Initial Codes Style.
   b. At the Styles Editor dialog box, complete the following steps to change the margins:
      (1) Choose Format, then Margins. (Be sure to choose the Format option at the top of the Styles Editor dialog box, not the Format option on the Menu Bar.)
      (2) At the Margins dialog box, change the left and right margins to 1.5 inches and the bottom margin to 0.5 inches.
      (3) Choose OK or press Enter to close the Margins dialog box.
      (4) Press Ctrl + J to change the justification to Full.
   c. Choose OK or press Enter to close the Styles Editor dialog box.
5. Create Footer A that prints at the right margin of each page, is bolded, and reads *Telecommunications Development*.
6. Save the report again with the same name (c13ex12).
7. Print c13ex12.
8. Close c13ex12.

If you want to change the font for a document and you want the font to also affect headers, footers, footnotes, and endnotes, change the font at the Document Initial Font dialog box. To display the Document Initial Font dialog box, choose Format, Document, then Initial Font.

Exercise 13 Creating and Formatting Footnotes

1. At a clear editing window, open c13ex07.
2. Save the document with Save As and name it c13ex13.
3. Make the following changes to the document:
   a. Display the Styles Editor dialog box, change the left and right margins to 1.5 inches and the justification to Full, then choose OK to close the Styles Editor dialog box.
   b. Change the font at the Document Initial Font dialog box by completing the following steps:
      (1) Choose Format, Document, then Initial Font.
      (2) At the Document Initial Font dialog box, change the Font Face to GeoSlab703 Lt BT. (Make sure the Font Size is 12.)
      (3) Choose OK to close the Document Initial Font dialog box.
   c. Select the title, *TRENDS IN TELECOMMUNICATIONS*, then change the font to 14-point Arial.
   d. Select the heading *Continued Growth of Photonics (Fiber Optics)*, then change the font to 12-point Arial.
   e. Select the heading *Microcomputer Trends in the Nineties*, then change the font to 12-point Arial.
4. Save the document again with the same name (c13ex13).
5. Print c13ex13.
6. Close c13ex13.

Any changes you make to the Styles Editor dialog box affect only the document in which you are working. Any changes you make at the Document Initial Font dialog box affect only the document in which you are working. If you want the font change to affect all new documents, select the Set as Printer Initial Font option at the Document Initial Font dialog box.

CHAPTER SUMMARY

- Text that appears at the top of pages is called a header; text that appears at the bottom of pages is called a footer. Header/footer text will display on the screen in the Page and Two Page viewing modes but not the Draft mode.
- A maximum of two headers and/or two footers can be created in one document. WordPerfect calls them Header A, Header B, Footer A, and Footer B.
- A header or footer can contain up to one page of text.
- A header or footer is created and/or edited at a separate screen called the Header/ Footer window.
- WordPerfect inserts the header code at the beginning of the page where the insertion point is positioned. If the code is positioned in the first page of the document, the header/footer will print on every page.
- When the Header or Footer window is displayed, the Header/Footer Feature Bar is inserted in the document window below the Power Bar (or Ruler Bar if it is displayed).
- When a document is printed, header or footer text occupies the place of regular text lines. By default, a blank line separates the header or footer from the main text.
- Header or footer text can be edited by choosing Edit at the Headers/Footers dialog box.
- A footnote is an explanatory note or reference that is printed at the bottom of a page. An endnote is a note or reference printed at the end of a document.
- When a footnote or endnote is created, a superscripted number is inserted in the document where the insertion point is located.
- Before the footnote/endnote is created at the Footnote/Endnote window, position the insertion point in the document where the notation (superscripted number) is to appear.

- A footnote prints at the bottom of the page where the text is referenced; footnotes are separated from the text by a 2-inch line that begins at the left margin.
- Endnotes print at the end of the last text in the document. To print the endnotes on a separate page, insert a hard page break at the end of the document.
- Footnotes/endnotes can be edited.
- A footnote/endnote can be removed by deleting the superscripted number in the document. WordPerfect will automatically renumber any remaining footnotes/endnotes.
- Headers/footers and footnotes/endnotes do not take on any formatting applied to the document. If you want formatting changes in a document to apply to headers/footers and footnotes/endnotes, insert the formatting codes at the Styles Editor dialog box.
- If you use a font in a document other than the default and want this font to apply to headers/footers and footnotes/endnotes, change the font at the Document Initial Font dialog box.

Commands Review

	Mouse/Keyboard
Headers/Footers dialog box	Format, Header/Footer
Footnote window	Insert, Footnote, Create
Endnote window	Insert, Endnote, Create
Edit Footnote dialog box	Insert, Footnote, Edit
Edit Endnote dialog box	Insert, Endnote, Edit
Styles Editor dialog box	Format, Document, Initial Codes Style
Document Initial Font dialog box	Format, Document, Initial Font

CHECK YOUR UNDERSTANDING

True/False: Circle the letter T if the statement is true; circle the letter F if the statement is false.

T F 1. Text that appears at the top of every page is called a header.
T F 2. A header or footer can contain a maximum of two lines.
T F 3. When a document is printed, header or footer text occupies the place of regular text lines.
T F 4. Header or footer text is separated from regular text by two blank lines.
T F 5. No matter where the insertion point is located in the document when the header/footer code is inserted, the code will appear at the beginning of the document.
T F 6. Any formatting that is applied to a document will automatically be applied to all headers/footers in the document.
T F 7. Headers can be edited but footers cannot.
T F 8. Footnote numbering starts with 1 at the beginning of each page.
T F 9. All footnotes in a document are printed on the last page.
T F 10. When an endnote is deleted, WordPerfect automatically renumbers the remaining endnotes.
T F 11. By default, WordPerfect separates footnotes from the text by a 2-inch line.

Completion: In the space provided at the right, indicate the correct term, command, or number.

1. Maximum number of headers that can be created in the same document. ____________________
2. Text that appears at the bottom of every page is referred to as this. ____________________
3. You can see how headers/footers will look on the page when you print in this viewing mode. ____________________

4. To print endnotes on a separate page, insert this code at the end of the document. ____________
5. By default, each footnote is single spaced and separated by this number of blank lines. ____________
6. If you want formatting changes to affect footnotes or endnotes, insert the formatting codes here. ____________

SKILL ASSESSMENTS

Assessment 1

1. At a clear editing window, open report02.
2. Save the report with Save As and name it c13sa01.
3. Make the following changes to the report:
   a. Turn on the Widow/Orphan feature.
   b. Change the top and bottom margins to 0.5 inches.
   c. Press the Enter key three times to move the title of the report down to approximately Line 1.7".
   d. Display the Styles Editor dialog box, then change the left and right margins to 1.5 inches and the justification to Full.
   e. Display the Document Initial Font dialog box, then change the font to 12-point GeoSlab703 Lt BT.
   f. Create Header A that prints at the right margin on every page except the first, is bolded, and reads *Development of Technology.*
   g. Create Footer A that prints centered and bolded at the bottom of every page and reads *Telecommunications.*
4. Save the report again with the same name (c13sa01).
5. Print c13sa01.
6. Close c13sa01.

Assessment 2

1. At a clear editing window, open report07.
2. Save the document with Save As and name it c13sa02.
3. Make the following changes to the report:
   a. Change the line spacing to double (2) and turn on the Widow/Orphan feature.
   b. Number each page except the first page at the upper right corner of the page.
   c. Create the first footnote shown in figure 13.8 at the end of the last paragraph in the *Industrialization* section of the report.
   d. Create the second footnote shown in figure 13.8 at the end of the last paragraph in the *Development of a World Market* section of the report.
   e. Create the third footnote shown in figure 13.8 at the end of the last paragraph in the report.
4. Save the document again with the same name (c13sa02).
5. Print c13sa02.
6. Close c13sa02.

Figure 13.8

[1]Mitchell, William, Robert Hendricks and Leonard Sterry, "Contributions of Major Historical Events," *Telecommunications: Systems and Applications*, Paradigm Publishing, 1993, pages 16-17.

[2]Reynolds, Susan, "The World Market in the 1850s," *Communicating in the World Market*, Lowell & Howe Publishing, 1993, pages 25-28.

[3]Boronat, Walter, "Impact of the 1870s Depression on Technology," *Computer Technology*, Holstein/Mann Publishing, 1994, pages 55-78.

Assessment 3

1. At a clear editing window, open c13sa02.
2. Save the document with Save As and name it c13sa03.
3. Make the following changes to the report:
   a. Display the Document Initial Font dialog box, then change the font to 12-point GeoSlab703 Lt BT.
   b. Display the Styles Editor dialog box, then change the left and right margins to 1.5 inches and the justification to Full.
   c. Select the title, then change the relative size to Large.
   d. Add the footnote shown in figure 13.9 at the end of the paragraph in the *Colonization* section of the report.
4. Save the document again with the same name (c13sa03).
5. Print c13sa03.
6. Close c13sa03.

Figure 13.9

[3]Champoux, Daniel, *Historical Perspectives in Computing*, Ashford Mountain Publishing Company, 1994, pages 75-87.

Cutting & Pasting Text

Upon successful completion of chapter 14, you will be able to manipulate blocks of text between areas of different business documents.

Some documents may need to be heavily revised, and these revisions may include deleting, moving, or copying blocks of text. This kind of editing is generally referred to as *cut and paste*.

Working with Blocks of Text

When cutting and pasting, you work with blocks of text. A block of text is a portion of text that you have selected. (Chapter 2 explained the various methods for selecting text.) A block of text can be as small as one character or as large as an entire page or document.

Once a block of text has been selected, it can be:

- deleted,
- moved to a new location, or
- copied and placed in a certain location within a document.

The last two operations involve using WordPerfect's Cut, Copy, and Paste features.

Moving Blocks of Text

After a block of text has been selected, it can be moved using the Cut and Paste options from the Edit menu, or the Cut and Paste buttons on the Toolbar. The Cut option from the Edit menu and the Cut button on the Toolbar delete text to temporary memory. The text in temporary memory can be inserted in a document with the Paste option from the Edit menu, or the Paste button on the Toolbar. The Cut button on the Toolbar is the fifth button from the left containing the image of a pair of scissors. The Paste button is the seventh button from the left containing the image of a bottle of paste.

In addition to the methods just described, a block of selected text can also be moved with the mouse. To do this you would select the text, then move the I-beam pointer inside the selected text until it becomes an arrow pointer. Hold down the left mouse button, drag the arrow pointer to the location where you want the selected text inserted, then release the button. Turn off Select by clicking anywhere in the editing window (outside the selected text) or pressing F8.

When you hold down the left mouse button and drag the arrow pointer, the arrow pointer turns into an arrow connected to a three-dimensional box. This box represents the text that is being moved. When you move the arrow pointer to the desired location and release the mouse button, the selected text is removed from its original position and inserted in the new location.

Exercise 1 Selecting and Moving Text

1. At a clear editing window, open para03.
2. Save the document with Save As and name it c14ex01.
3. Move the following text in the document:
   a. Move the second paragraph above the first paragraph by completing the following steps:
      (1) Select the second paragraph including the blank line below the paragraph.
      (2) Choose Edit, then Cut.
      (3) Position the insertion point at the beginning of the first paragraph.
      (4) Choose Edit, then Paste.
   b. Move the fourth paragraph above the third paragraph by completing the following steps:
      (1) Select the fourth paragraph including the blank line below the paragraph.
      (2) Click on the Cut button on the Toolbar.
      (3) Position the insertion point at the beginning of the third paragraph.
      (4) Click on the Paste button on the Toolbar.
   c. Move the fourth paragraph to the end of the document using the mouse by completing the following steps:
      (1) Select the fourth paragraph including the blank line below the paragraph.
      (2) Position the I-beam pointer inside the selected text area until it becomes an arrow.
      (3) Hold down the left mouse button, drag the arrow pointer a double space below the last paragraph, then release the mouse button.
      (4) Turn off Select.
4. Save the document again with the same name (c14ex01).
5. Print c14ex01.
6. Close c14ex01.

Copying a Block of Text

WordPerfect's Copy option can be useful in documents that contain repetitive portions of text. You can use this function to insert duplicate portions of text instead of rekeying the text. You can copy text in a document using the Copy and Paste options from the Edit menu or the Copy and Paste buttons on the Toolbar.

The mouse can also be used to copy a block of text in a document and insert the copy in a new location. To do this you would select the text, move the I-beam pointer inside the selected text until it becomes an arrow pointer, hold down the left mouse button and hold down the Ctrl key, drag the arrow pointer to the location where a copy of the selected text is to be inserted, then release the mouse button and then the Ctrl key. After copying text, deselect it.

With the Ctrl key down, the three-dimensional box with the arrow pointer displays with a black shadow (rather than a dotted shadow that displays when moving text).

When text is copied, the text remains in the editing window and a copy is inserted in temporary memory. Once text has been cut or copied to temporary memory, it can be inserted in a document any number of times without deleting or copying it again. The text will remain in temporary memory until other text is cut or copied to temporary memory or until you exit WordPerfect.

If you select a block of text and then decide you selected the wrong text or you do not want to do anything with the block, you can deselect it. If you are using the mouse, click the left mouse button outside the selected text. If you are using the keyboard, press F8 to turn Select off.

Exercise 2 Copying Selected Text

1. At a clear editing window, open block01.
2. Save the document with Save As and name it c14ex02.
3. Change the font to 18-point Brush738 BT.
4. Copy all the text to the end of the document by completing the following steps:
   a. Select the entire document (four lines of text plus two blank lines below the text) by choosing Edit, Select, then All.
   b. Choose Edit, then Copy.
   c. Turn off Select.
   d. Move the insertion point to the end of the document.
   e. Choose Edit, then Paste.
5. With the insertion point positioned at the end of the document, insert the text again by choosing Edit, then Paste.
6. Save the document with the same name (c14ex02).
7. Print c14ex02.
8. Close c14ex02.

Converting the Case of Letters

With the Convert Case option from the Edit drop-down menu, you can convert the case of selected letters to uppercase, lowercase, or initial caps. To convert the case of letters, select the text to be converted, then choose Edit, then Convert Case. At the submenu that displays, choose Uppercase to change selected letters to uppercase, Lowercase to change selected letters to lowercase, or Initial Capitals to capitalize the first letter of each word of selected text except words like *of*, *and*, and *a*.

When you choose Lowercase, WordPerfect changes selected letters to lowercase except the word *I*, words starting with *I* followed by an apostrophe such as *I've* and *I'm*, and the first letter of the first word of a sentence.

Exercise 3 Changing Case

1. At a clear editing window, open report04.
2. Save the document with Save As and name it c14ex03.
3. Convert the heading, *World War I*, to uppercase letters by completing the following steps:
   a. Select *World War I.*
   b. Choose Edit, Convert Case, then Uppercase.
   c. Turn off Select.
4. Convert the case of each of the following headings to uppercase:
   World War II
   Korean War
   Cold War and Vietnam
5. Save the document again with the same name (c14ex03).
6. Print c14ex03.
7. Close c14ex03.

Working with Documents

Some documents may contain standard information—information that remains the same. For example, a legal document, such as a will, may contain text that is standard and appears in all wills. Repetitive text can be saved as a separate document and then retrieved into an existing document whenever needed.

There are two methods that can be used for saving text into a separate document. The first is to save a document just as you have been doing. The other method is to select standard text within a document and save it as a separate document.

Saving Standard Text

If you know in advance what information or text is standard and will be used again, you can save it as a separate document. You should determine how to break down the information based on how it will be used. After deciding how to break down the information, key the text at a clear editing window, then save it with the Save option or Save As option from the File menu.

Saving Selected Text

When you create a document and then realize that a portion of the text in the document will be needed for future documents, you can save it as a separate document by selecting the text first. To save a paragraph as a separate document, select the paragraph, then choose File, then Save or click on the Save button on the Toolbar. At the Save dialog box shown in figure 14.1, choose Selected Text, then choose OK or press Enter. At the Save As dialog box, key a name for the document, then choose OK or press Enter.

This saves the paragraph as a separate document while retaining the paragraph in the original document.

Figure 14.1
Save Dialog Box

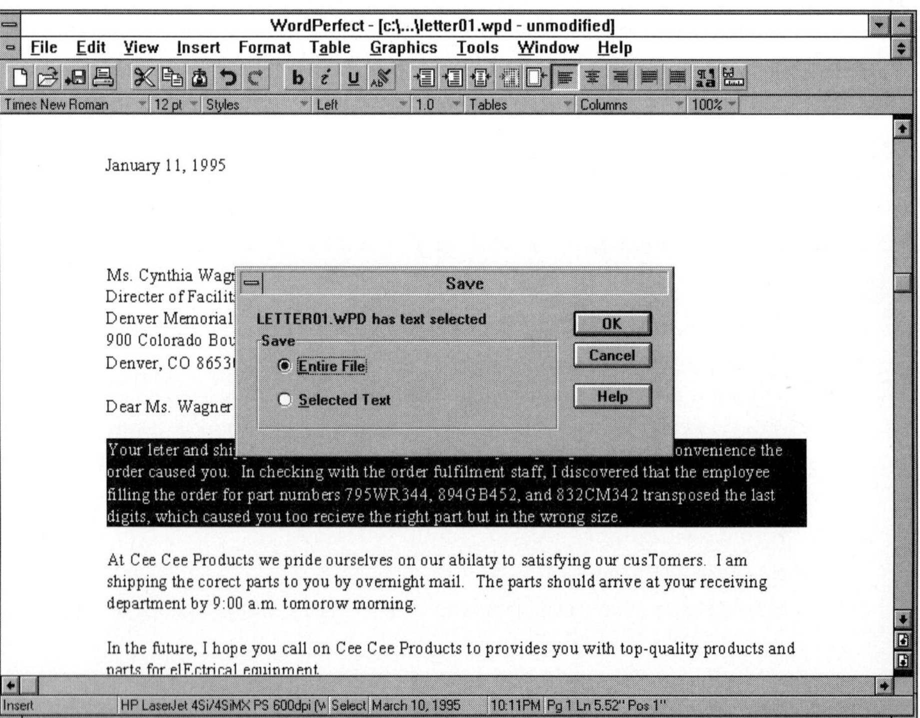

Inserting a Document

A document containing standard text can be inserted into an existing document with the File option from the Insert menu. To do this, position the insertion point in the document at the location where you want the standard text. Choose Insert, then File. At the Insert File dialog box, double-click on the document name to be inserted, or key the document name, then press Enter or choose Insert. At the query box containing the question *Insert file into current document?*, choose Yes or press Enter.

WordPerfect brings the entire document to the screen including any formatting codes. If you want standard text to conform to the formatting of the current document, do not insert any formatting codes in the standard document.

Exercise 4 Inserting a File into Another Document

1. At a clear editing window, open report01.
2. Select the bulleted items on the second page, then save them to a separate document named *hardware* by completing the following steps:
   a. Select the six bulleted items on the second page.
   b. Choose File, then Save; or click on the Save button on the Toolbar.
   c. At the Save dialog box, choose Selected Text, then choose OK or press Enter.
   d. At the Save As dialog box, key **hardware**.
   e. Choose OK or press Enter.
   f. Turn off Select.
3. Close report01.
4. At a clear editing window, key the memorandum headings and the first paragraph of the text shown in figure 14.2. Use an appropriate memorandum format. After keying the first paragraph, press Enter twice, then insert the *hardware* document by completing the following steps:
   a. Choose Insert, then File.
   b. At the Insert File dialog box, key **hardware**, then press Enter or choose Insert.
   c. At the query box containing the question *Insert file into current document?*, choose Yes or press Enter.
5. Move the insertion point a double space below the bulleted items, then key the last paragraph. Include your initials and the document name a double space below the last line of the paragraph.
6. Save the memorandum and name it c14ex04.
7. Print c14ex04.
8. Close c14ex04.

Figure 14.2

DATE: March 20, 1997; TO: Heath Brewer; FROM: Sonya Roth; SUBJECT: HARDWARE

The microcomputers at the two high schools need to be upgraded or replaced. This past quarter, I completed a telecommunications class at the local community college. During this class, I learned that new hardware should include the following:

[Insert hardware document here.]

We need to get together in the next week or so to put together our equipment request for the next school year. Please call me to schedule a meeting.

xx:c14ex04

Working with Windows

WordPerfect for Windows operates within the Windows environment created by the Windows program. However, when working in WordPerfect, a *window* refers to the editing window plus the scroll bars.

The Windows program creates an environment in which various software programs are used with menu bars, scroll bars, and icons to represent programs and files. With the Windows program, you can load several different software programs and move between them quickly. Similarly, using windows in WordPerfect, you can load several different documents and move between them quickly.

With multiple documents open, you can move between them, move or copy information between documents, or compare the contents of several documents.

Opening Windows

The maximum number of documents that you can have open at one time is nine. When you open a new window, it is placed on top of the original window. Once multiple windows are opened, you can resize the windows to see all or a portion of them on the screen.

A new window can be opened at the Open File dialog box, with the New option from the File menu, or with the New Blank Document button on the Toolbar. If you use the New option from the File menu or the New Blank Document button on the Toolbar, the document window is empty. The title bar displays *WordPerfect - [Document# - unmodified]*. (The document number will vary.)

When you are working in a document, the document fills the entire editing window. If you open another document without closing the first, the newly opened document will fill the editing window. The first document is still open, but it is covered by the new one. To see what documents are currently open, choose Window from the Menu Bar. When you choose Window, the Window drop-down menu shown in figure 14.3 displays. (The number of documents and document names displayed at the bottom of the menu will vary.)

Figure 14.3
Window Menu

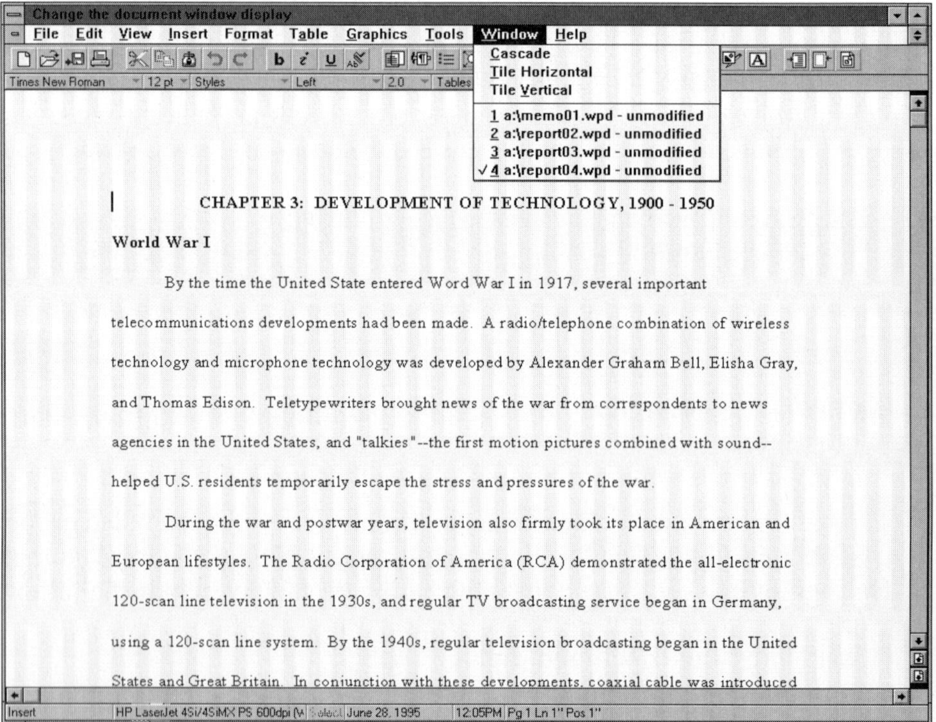

The open document names are displayed at the bottom of the menu. The document name with the check mark in front of it is the *active* document. The active document is the document containing the insertion point.

To make one of the other documents active, move the arrow pointer to the desired document, then click the left mouse button. If you are using the keyboard, key the number shown in front of the desired document. When you change the active document, the Window menu is removed from the screen and the new active document is displayed.

To close an open document, make the document active, then choose File, then Close. To close the other open documents, repeat these steps.

Exercise 5 Opening Multiple Documents

1. At a clear editing window, open column01.
2. Open memo05.
3. Open letter01.
4. Make memo05 the active document by choosing Window, then 2.
5. Make column01 the active document by choosing Window, then 1.
6. Close column01.
7. Close memo05.
8. Close letter01.

Cascading Windows

When you have more than one open document, you can use the Cascade option from the Window menu to view portions of all open documents. If your computer has enough memory, you can have up to nine documents open at one time. When open documents are cascaded, they overlap down the window, leaving the Title Bar of each open document visible.

For example, suppose you have three open documents named *memo08*, *letter04*, and *report04*. To cascade these three open documents, you would choose Window, then Cascade. The documents are arranged and displayed as shown in figure 14.4.

By default, the document closest to the front is the active document. The document name (along with drive and path) is displayed at the top of each open document. The Title Bar of the active document displays with a blue background. The Title Bar of the inactive document displays with a white background.

To change the active window with the mouse, position the arrow pointer on the Title Bar, then click the left button. This causes the open document to move to the front and become active. If you are using the keyboard, choose Window, then key the number of the desired document.

Exercise 6 Cascading Open Files

1. At a clear editing window, open para01.
2. Open memo01.
3. Open letter01.
4. Open report01.
5. Cascade the windows by choosing Window, then Cascade.
6. Make letter01 the active document by positioning the arrow pointer on the Title Bar for letter01, then clicking the left mouse button.
7. Close letter01.
8. Make para01 active, then close it.
9. Make memo01 active, then close it.
10. Close report01.

Figure 14.4 **Cascaded Windows**

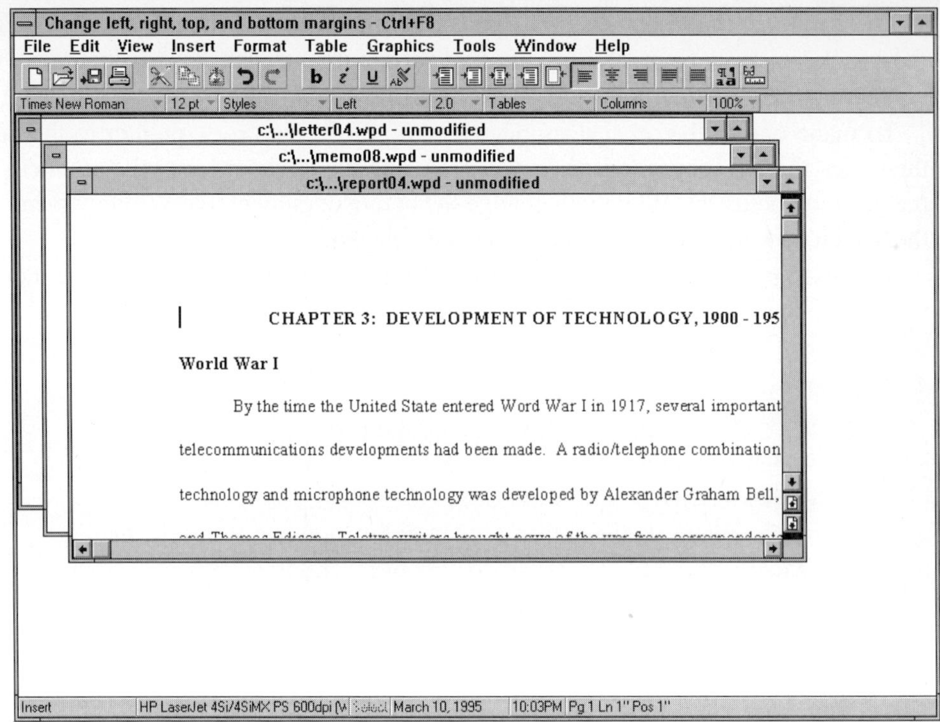

Tiling Windows

The Tile Horizontal and Tile Vertical options from the Window menu cause each open document to appear in a separate window with no windows overlapping. For example, suppose you have the three documents named *memo08*, *letter04*, and *report04* opened. To tile these three open documents horizontally, choose Window, then Tile Horizontal. The windows then display as shown in figure 14.5. Documents can also be tiled vertically as shown in figure 14.6 by choosing Window, then Tile Vertically.

The Title Bar in the active document is displayed with white characters on a blue background. The Title Bar for inactive documents displays with black characters on a white background.

To change the active window, move the arrow pointer to the document you want active, then click the left button. If you are using the keyboard, choose Window, then key the number of the desired document.

The ability to see more than one document on the screen at the same time can be useful in certain situations. For example, you can create an outline for a report in one window while you create the actual report in another.

Exercise 7 Tiling Open Documents

1. At a clear editing window, open memo01.
2. Open letter01.
3. Open report02.
4. Tile the windows horizontally by choosing Window, then Tile Horizontal.
5. Tile the windows vertically by choosing Windows, then Tile Vertical.
6. Make letter01 the active document.
7. Close letter01.
8. Make memo01 active, then close it.
9. Close report02.

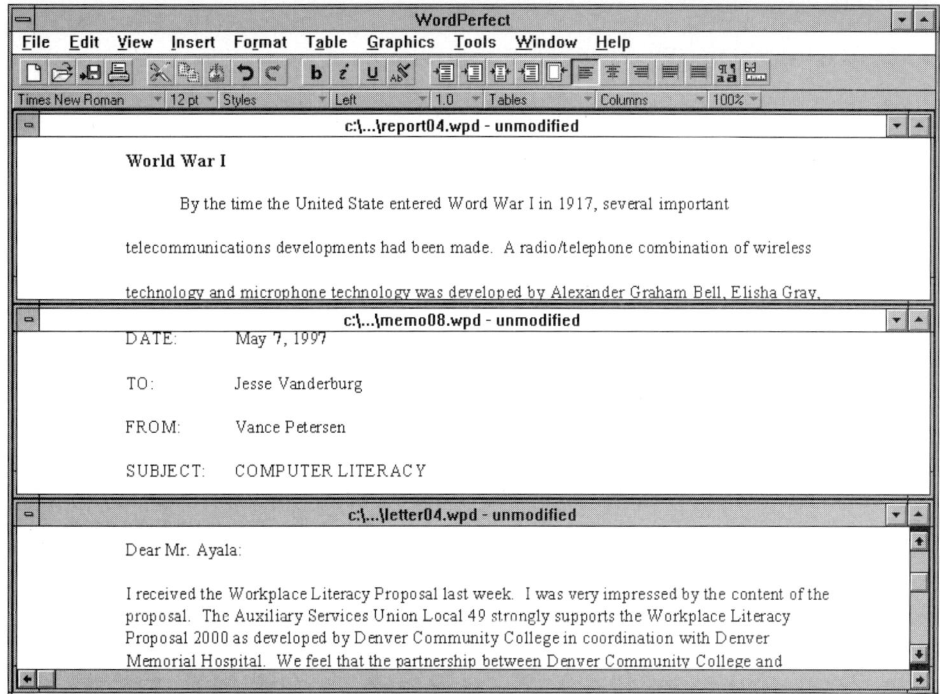

Figure 14.5
Horizontally Tiled Windows

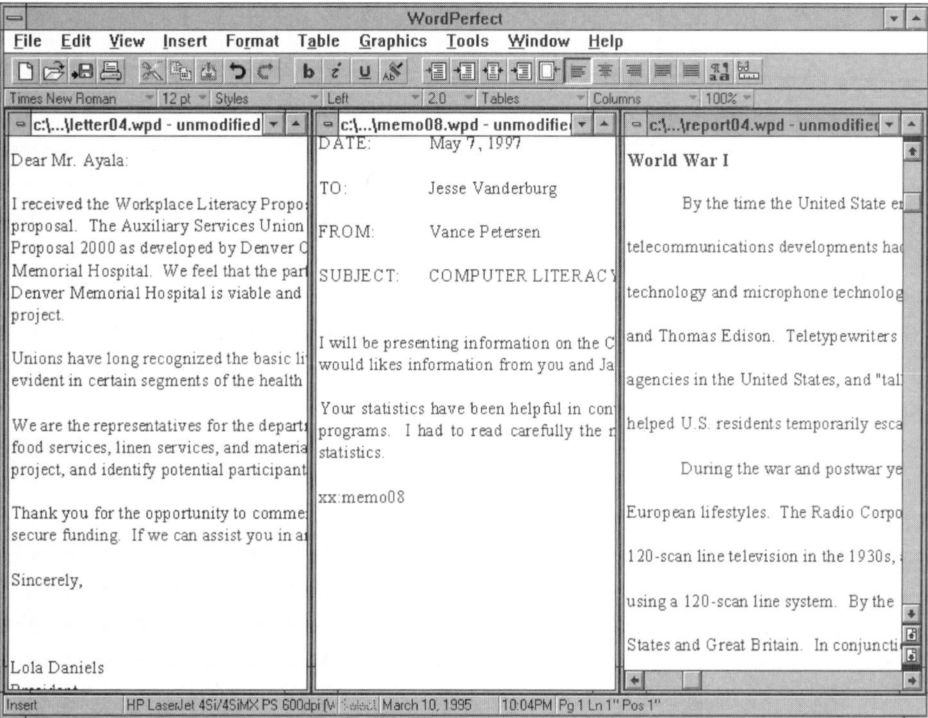

Figure 14.6
Vertically Tiled Windows

Sizing Windows

You can use the maximize, minimize, and restore buttons in the upper right corner of the window to reduce or increase the size of the active window. The maximize button is the button in the upper right corner of the active window with the up-pointing triangle. The minimize button is the button in the upper right corner with the down-pointing triangle. The restore button is the button in the upper right corner with up- and down-pointing triangles. The maximize and minimize buttons display in a document that has been tiled or cascaded.

For example, if you cascade or tile open documents, then click on the maximize button in the active document, the active document expands to fill the editing window. To return the active document back to its cascaded or tiled size, click on the restore button. If you click on the minimize button in the active document, the document is reduced to an icon that displays at the bottom of the document window. To restore a document that has been reduced to an icon, move the arrow pointer to the icon, then double-click the left mouse button. Figure 14.7 shows an example of a document named *report04* that has been minimized to an icon.

If only one document is open, two gray boxes display in the upper left corner of the document window. The top gray box is called the Application control button. It is used to change the size of the Windows application window. The second gray box is called the Document control button. The Document control button is used to change the size of the WordPerfect for Windows application window. When documents are tiled or cascaded, the Document control button displays at the left side of the Title Bar.

To minimize a document using the Document control button and the mouse, click on the Document control button (the second one in the upper left corner of the screen). At the Document control drop-down menu, click on Minimize.

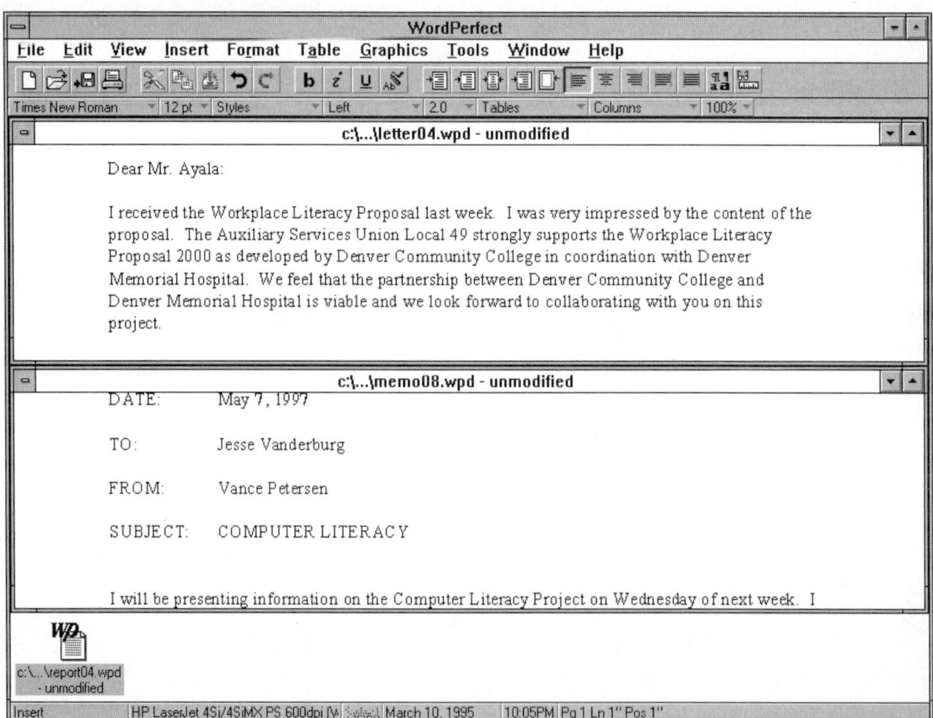

Figure 14.7
Minimized Document

To minimize a document using the Document control button with the keyboard, press Alt + hyphen (-), then at the Document control drop-down menu, key **N** for Minimize.

When a document has been minimized, it can be restored or maximized with the mouse or keyboard and the Document control button. To maximize a minimized document using the mouse, position the arrow pointer on the icon, then double-click the left mouse button.

The difference between the Maximize and Restore options is that Maximize increases the size of the document to fill the entire editing window, while Restore returns the icon to its previous size.

The size of documents that have been cascaded or tiled can be increased or decreased using the mouse. To increase or decrease the width of the active window, move the arrow pointer to the double line border at the right or left side of the window until the arrow pointer becomes a left- and right-pointing arrow. Hold down the left mouse button, then drag the border to the right or left. When the window is the desired size, release the mouse button.

To increase or decrease the height of the active window, move the arrow pointer to the double line border at the top or bottom of the window until the arrow pointer becomes an up- and down-pointing arrow. Hold down the left mouse button, then drag the arrow pointer up or down to increase or decrease the size. When the window is the desired size, release the mouse button.

A document window that has been tiled or cascaded can be moved. To move a document window, position the arrow pointer on the Title Bar of the tiled or cascaded window, hold down the left mouse button, drag the outline of the document window to the desired location, then release the mouse button.

Exercise 8 Changing the Size of Open Documents

1. At a clear editing window, open letter02.
2. Open memo02.
3. Open report02.
4. Tile the windows horizontally.
5. Make letter02 the active window.
6. Minimize letter02 to an icon using the mouse by clicking on the Minimize button at the right side of the Title Bar in the active window. (The Minimize button is the button with the down-pointing triangle.)
7. Make memo02 the active document, then minimize memo02 using the Document control button by completing the following steps:
   a. Click on the Document control button (the second gray button at the left side of the Title Bar in the active window).
   b. At the Document control drop-down menu, click on Minimize.
8. Restore the size of memo02 using the mouse by double-clicking on the memo02 icon.
9. Restore the size of letter02 using the mouse by double-clicking on the letter02 icon.
10. Make report02 the active document, then close it.
11. Close memo02.
12. Close letter02.

Cutting and Pasting Text between Windows

With several documents open, you can easily move, copy, and/or paste text from one document to another. To move, copy, and/or paste text between documents, use the cutting and pasting commands with text in open documents.

Exercise 9 Moving Text between Documents

1. At a clear editing window, key the memorandum shown in figure 14.8 in an appropriate memorandum format. (Press the Enter key four times after keying the first paragraph and before you key the second paragraph.)
2. Save the memorandum and name it c14ex09.
3. With c14ex09 still open in the editing window, open memo02.
4. With memo02 the active document, copy the first three books listed in the memorandum by completing the following steps:
   a. Select the three paragraphs containing the first three book titles (the paragraphs containing *The ABCs of Integrated Learning*, *Total Quality Management in the Education Environment*, and *Health Education for Today's Child*).
   b. Click on the Copy button on the Toolbar.
   c. Turn off Select.
   d. Make c14ex09 the active document.
   e. Position the insertion point a double space below the first paragraph, then click on the Paste button on the Toolbar.

5. Check the spacing of the memo and, if necessary, make corrections.
6. Save the memorandum again with the same name (c14ex09).
7. Print c14ex09.
8. Close c14ex09.
9. Close memo02.

Figure 14.8

DATE: October 23, 1996; TO: Carey Dearing, Librarian; FROM: Phillip Kainu, Assistant Librarian; SUBJECT: REFERENCE BOOKS

I found $62.40 in the library reference fund and $32.50 in the emergency fund. With these combined amounts, I was able to purchase the following books:

There were not enough funds to purchase the *Grant Writing* book. I contacted Anissa Jackson in the Human Resources Department and suggested they purchase the book out of their budget. I asked her to contact you directly.

xx:c14ex09

CHAPTER SUMMARY

- Moving or copying blocks of text within a document is generally referred to as *cutting and pasting*. A selected block of text can be as small as one character or as large as one page or one document.
- Selected text can be moved to a different location in the document.
- Selected text can be copied one or more times in a document.
- With the Convert Case option from the Edit drop-down menu, you have the options of converting the case of selected letters to uppercase, lowercase, or initial caps.
- Standard blocks of text that will be used repeatedly can be saved as separate documents, then inserted into existing documents. These blocks can be keyed separately, then saved. Or, sections of text within other documents can be selected then saved as separate documents.
- When working in WordPerfect for Windows, a window refers to the editing window plus the scroll bars.
- You can have from one to nine documents open at one time. With multiple documents open, you can copy or move text between documents or compare the contents of several documents.
- Each document you open will fill the entire editing window. Move among the open documents by choosing Window, then clicking the left mouse button on the desired document name or keying the number in front of that document name.
- Open documents can be cascaded, one over the top of the other; or they can be tiled, each arranged next to the other.
- Use the maximize, minimize, and restore buttons in the upper right corner of the window to reduce or increase the size of the active window.
- The minimize button will reduce the document to an icon that displays at the bottom of the document window. Restore the icon to a normal document by double-clicking on the icon.

- The Application control button, the top gray box in the upper left corner of the document window, is used to change the size of the Windows application window.
- The Document control button, the second gray box in the upper left corner of the document window, is used to change the size of the WordPerfect for Windows application window.
- Use the mouse on the border of the window to increase or decrease the width or height of the window.

Commands Review

	Mouse/Keyboard
Move text to temporary memory	Edit, Cut; or Cut button on Toolbar
Paste selected text from temporary memory	Edit, Paste; or Paste button on Toolbar
Move selected text using the mouse	With arrow pointer inside block of selected text, hold down the left mouse button, drag arrow pointer to desired location, release button
Copy selected text	Edit, Copy; or Copy button on Toolbar
Copy selected text using the mouse	With arrow pointer inside block of selected text, hold down left mouse button *and* the Ctrl key, drag arrow pointer to desired location, release button, then Ctrl key
Convert case of selected letters	Edit, Convert Case
Saving selected text as separate document	File, Save; or click on Save button on Toolbar
Insert saved document into current document	Insert, File, then double-click on the document you want opened
Open a new (empty) document	File, New; or New Blank Document button on Toolbar
Close a document	File, Close
Cascade Windows	Window, Cascade
Tile Windows Horizontally	Window, Tile Horizontal
Tile Windows Vertically	Window, Tile Vertical
Minimize a document	Click on Minimize button; or click on Document control button, then Minimize
Maximize a document	Click on Maximize button; or click on Document control button, then Maximize
Restore a document	Click on Restore button; or click on Document control button, then Restore
Size a document using the mouse	With mouse arrow pointer on double line border at right/left or top/bottom, hold left mouse button, drag the border

CHECK YOUR UNDERSTANDING

True/False: Circle the letter T if the statement is true; circle the letter F if the statement is false.

T **F** 1. One word could be considered a block of text.

T **F** 2. When text is copied, it remains in its original position, and a copy is inserted in a new location.

T **F** 3. Once text has been selected, it cannot be deselected.

T F 4. After text has been stored in temporary memory, it can be reinserted into a document only once.

T F 5. A document containing standard text can be inserted into an existing document.

T F 6. The Convert Case option will convert letters to uppercase, lowercase, or italics.

T F 7. When closing all the documents in the window, make sure each document is inactive before you close it the usual way.

T F 8. Documents displayed in a tiled or cascaded window can be increased or decreased to any size, vertically and/or horizontally, using the mouse.

T F 9. When a document is minimized, it is shrunk to an icon that displays at the bottom of the window.

T F 10. The Restore button is the top gray box in the upper left corner of an open document.

Completion: In the space provided at the right, indicate the correct term, command, or number.

1. The maximum number of documents that can be open at one time. ____________
2. The name of the feature that causes each open document to appear in a separate window with no windows overlapping. ____________
3. A document is reduced to this when it is minimized. ____________
4. The word that describes the document where the insertion point is located. ____________
5. Do this if you want a previously minimized document to fill the editing window. ____________
6. This is the second gray box in the upper left corner of an open document. ____________
7. This is the button in the upper right corner of a tiled or cascaded window with the down-pointing triangle. ____________
8. When documents are cascaded, this is all that is visible of the inactive documents. ____________

SKILL ASSESSMENTS

Assessment 1

1. At a clear editing window, open report06.
2. Save the document with Save As and name it c14sa01.
3. Make the following changes to the report:
   a. Insert a bullet before the last six items (you determine the type of bullet).
   b. Move the section titled *Continued Growth of Photonics (Fiber Optics)* below the section titled *Microcomputer Trends in the Nineties.*
   c. Delete the first sentence of the last paragraph in the *Continued Growth of Photonics (Fiber Optics)* section (the sentence that begins *The growth of fiber optics has other...*).
   d. Select the heading *Continued Growth of Photonics (Fiber Optics)*, then convert the case to uppercase.
   e. Select the heading *Microcomputer Trends in the Nineties*, then convert the case to uppercase.
   f. Change the relative size of the title to Large.
   g. Change the line spacing to double (2).
   h. Delete extra blank lines so there is only a double space between all lines in the document.
   i. Number pages at the bottom center of each page.

4. Save the document again with the same name (c14sa01).
5. Print c14sa01.
6. Close c14sa01.

Assessment 2

1. At a clear editing window, create the document shown in figure 14.9. Triple space after the last line in the document.
2. Select and copy the text a triple space below the original text.
3. Copy the text two more times. (There should be a total of four forms when you are done and they should fit on one page.)
4. Save the document and name it c14sa02.
5. Print c14sa02.
6. Close c14sa02.

Figure 14.9

COURSE REGISTRATION

Name: ____

Title: ______________________ Department: ______________________

Course: ____

Days: ____________________________ Times: ________________

Assessment 3

1. At a clear editing window, open policy01.
2. Select the first paragraph, then save it as a separate document named pol01.
3. Select the second paragraph, then save it as a separate document named pol02.
4. Select the third paragraph, then save it as a separate document named pol03.
5. Select the fourth paragraph, then save it as a separate document named pol04.
6. Select the fifth paragraph, then save it as a separate document named pol05.
7. Select the sixth paragraph, then save it as a separate document named pol06.
8. Close policy01.
9. At a clear editing window, make the following changes:
   a. Change the top margin to 1.5 inches.
   b. Change the line spacing to double (2).
10. Key the information shown in figure 14.10 with the following specifications:
    a. Key the document to the first bracketed item.
    b. Insert the documents as indicated in the brackets.
    c. After inserting pol06, move the insertion point to the end of the paragraph, make sure there is a double space after the paragraph, then change the line spacing back to single.
    d. Key the remaining text as indicated in figure 14.10.
    e. Move the insertion point to the beginning of the document, then create Footer A that prints *Automobile Insurance Policy* at the right side of each page.
11. Save the document and name it c14sa03.
12. Print c14sa03.
13. Close c14sa03.

Figure 14.10

AUTOMOBILE INSURANCE POLICY

Policy #: CR321-03

Name of Insured: Karen Heaberlin

Address of Insured: 1302 Second Street, Vancouver, WA 98022

[Insert pol01 here.]

[Insert pol02 here.]

[Insert pol03 here.]

[Insert pol04 here.]

[Insert pol06 here.]

____

KAREN HEABERLIN, Insured

____

Authorized Representative

Assessment 4

1. Open memo03, quote, and biblio01.
2. Make quote the active document.
3. Cascade the windows.
4. Tile the windows horizontally.
5. Make memo03 the active document, then minimize it.
6. Minimize the remaining documents.
7. Make quote active, then restore it.
8. Restore biblio01.
9. Restore memo03.
10. Close all documents.

Assessment 5

1. At a clear editing window, key the letter shown in figure 14.11 in an appropriate letter format through the first paragraph (to the location where the bolded message is displayed).
2. Save the letter and name it c14sa05.
3. With c14sa05 still open, open report01.
4. Tile the windows.
5. With report01 the active document, copy the first paragraph (do *not* include the Tab code) below the heading *Microcomputer Trends in the Nineties* and the six bulleted items that follow at the end of the first paragraph in the letter.

6. Make report01 the active document, then close it.
7. Maximize c14sa05. (Check spacing and, if necessary, make adjustments.)
8. Key the remaining text in the letter.
9. Save the letter again with the same name (c14sa05).
10. Print c14sa05.
11. Close c14sa05.

Figure 14.11

June 4, 1997

Mr. Vance Petersen
Director of Computer Services
Denver Memorial Hospital
900 Colorado Boulevard
Denver, CO 86530

Dear Mr. Petersen:

At Quality Systems, we maintain computer hardware and software that keeps us on the cutting edge of technology. **[Insert copied text here.]**

Quality Systems is offering a free assessment of the computer systems operating at Denver Memorial Hospital. Please contact me at 555-3422 to schedule a time for a visitation.

Very truly yours,

QUALITY SYSTEMS

Megan MacDougal
System Analyst
xx:c14sa05

Conducting a Find and Replace 15

Upon successful completion of chapter 15, you will be able to revise text and codes in standard business letters and reports by using WordPerfect's Find and Replace feature.

With WordPerfect's Find and Replace feature, you can look for a specific word(s) or code(s) within a document. When WordPerfect finds the word(s) or code(s), you can replace, edit, or delete the word(s) or code(s). With Find and Replace, you can:

- Correct a misspelled word by searching for it and replacing it throughout a document with the correct spelling.
- Use abbreviations for common phrases when entering text, then replace the abbreviations with the actual text later.
- Set up standard documents with generic names and replace them with other names to make personalized documents.
- Find and replace format codes.

This is just a short list of how the Find and Replace feature can make your keyboarding job easier. As you use the Find and Replace feature, you may find more ways that it can benefit you.

Finding and Replacing Text

When you choose Edit, then Find and Replace, the Find and Replace Text dialog box shown in figure 15.1 displays.

Figure 15.1
Find and Replace Text Dialog Box

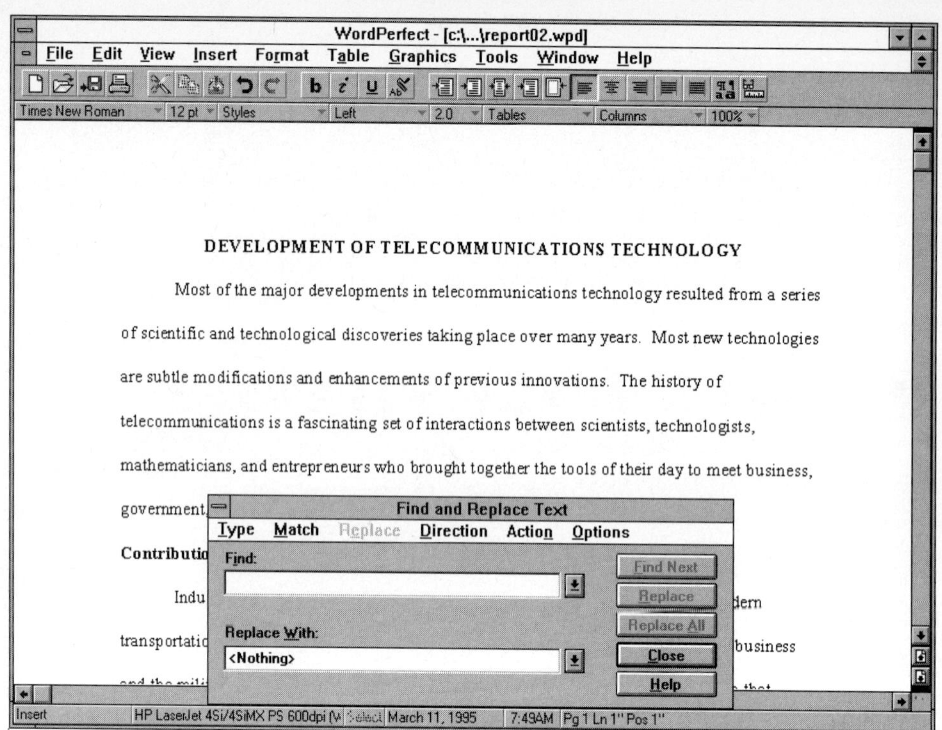

In the text box below the Find option, enter the string for which you are searching. A search string can be up to 80 characters in length and can include spaces.

Choose Replace With to move the insertion point to the text box below the Replace With option. In this text box, enter the string with which you want the search string replaced.

A find and replace begins at the position of the insertion point. You can find and replace a search string from the location of the insertion point to the beginning of the document or from the insertion point to the end of the document.

The Find and Replace Text dialog box contains five command buttons at the right side. Choose the Find button to tell WordPerfect to find the next occurrence of the search string. Choose the Replace button to replace the search string and find the next occurrence of the string. If you know that you want all occurrences of the search string replaced in the document, choose Replace All. This replaces every occurrence of the search string from the location of the insertion point to the beginning or end of the document (depending on the search direction). Choose Close to close the Find and Replace Text dialog box.

If you choose Help, WordPerfect will display information about the Find and Replace feature.

Exercise 1 Using Find and Replace

1. At a clear editing window, open report08.
2. Save the document with Save As and name it c15ex01.
3. Find all occurrences of SSL and replace with Space Systems Laboratory by completing the following steps:
   a. Position the insertion point at the beginning of the document.
   b. Choose Edit, then Find and Replace.
   c. At the Find and Replace Text dialog box, key **SSL**.
   d. Choose Replace With.
   e. Key **Space Systems Laboratory**.
   f. Choose Replace All.
   g. Choose Close to close the Find and Replace Text dialog box.

4. Save the document again with the same name (c15ex01).
5. Print c15ex01.
6. Close c15ex01.

In exercise 1, WordPerfect makes all replacements without getting confirmation from you. If you want to confirm each replacement before it is made, choose Find. When WordPerfect stops at the first occurrence of the search string, choose Replace if you want to replace the search string, or choose Find if you want WordPerfect to find the next occurrence of the search string without replacing the current occurrence.

Customizing Find and Replace

The Find and Replace Text dialog box contains a Menu Bar with six options—Type, Match, Replace, Direction, Action, and Options. Use options from this menu bar to customize a find and replace.

Changing Type Options

If you choose Type from the Find and Replace Text dialog box, the options Text, Word Forms, and Specific Codes display in a drop-down menu. The default setting is Text. Use this setting when searching for text.

Choose the Word Forms option to find and replace words based on the root form of the word. For example, you can search for the word form *buy* and WordPerfect will find words that match the root form such as *buys*, *buying*, and *bought* and replace them with the correct tense of the root form of the replace word.

Exercise 2 Using the Word Forms Option

1. At a clear editing window, open para05.
2. Save the document with Save As and name it c15ex02.
3. Find all word forms of *prepare* and replace with *create* by completing the following steps:
   a. With the insertion point positioned at the beginning of the document, choose Edit, then Find and Replace.
   b. At the Find and Replace Text dialog box, choose Replace With, then delete any text in the Replace With text box.
   c. Choose Type, then Word Forms. (This inserts a check mark before the option.)
   d. Choose Find, then key **prepare** in the Find text box.
   e. Choose Replace With, then key **create** in the Replace With text box.
   f. Choose Replace All.
   g. Choose Type, then Word Forms. (This removes the check mark before the option.)
   h. Choose Close to close the Find and Replace Text dialog box.
4. Save the document again with the same name (c15ex02).
5. Print c15ex02.
6. Close c15ex02.

Use the Specific Codes option from the Type drop-down menu to find a code that has been assigned a specific value. For example, instead of searching for a [Ln Spacing] code which would find any line spacing code, you can find a 1.5 line spacing code.

When you choose Specific Codes, the Specific Codes dialog box shown in figure 15.2 displays.

Figure 15.2
Specific Codes Dialog Box

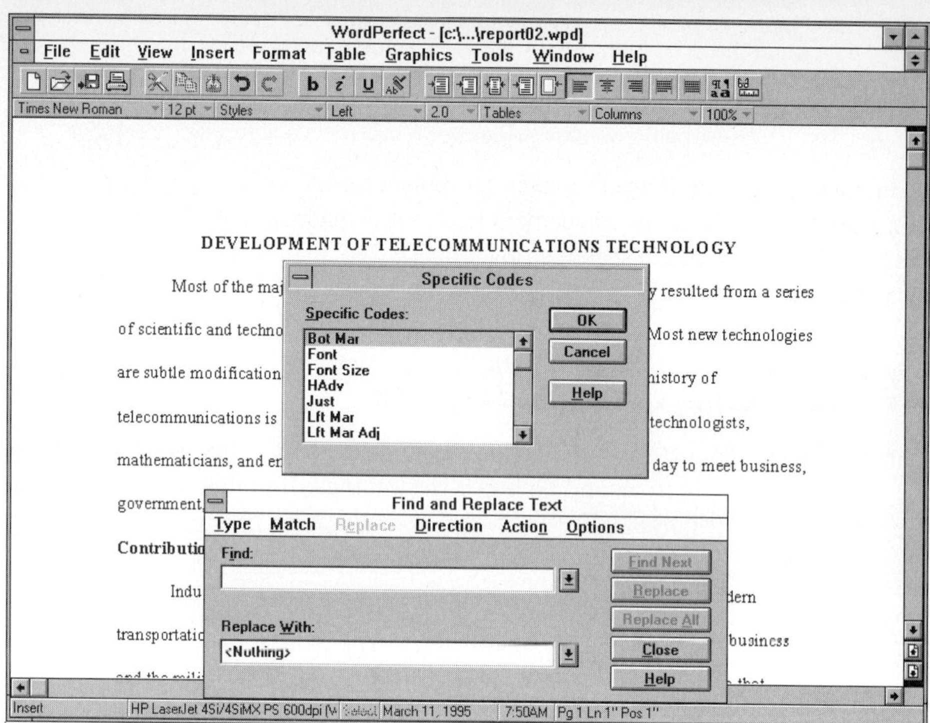

This dialog box contains a list of specific codes. To choose a specific code, position the insertion point on the desired code, then choose OK or press Enter. When you make a choice from this dialog box, WordPerfect then displays a dialog box where you enter the value. For example, to find all 1.5 line spacing codes, you would complete the following steps:

1. Position the insertion point at the beginning of the document.
2. Choose Edit, then Find and Replace.
3. At the Find and Replace Text dialog box, choose Type, then Specific Codes.
4. At the Specific Codes dialog box, position the insertion point on *Ln Spacing*. To do this with the mouse, click on the down-pointing arrow in the vertical scroll bar until *Ln Spacing* is visible, then click on *Ln Spacing*. If you are using the keyboard, press the down arrow key until the insertion point is positioned on *Ln Spacing*.
5. Choose OK or press Enter.
6. At the Find and Replace Line Spacing dialog box, key **1.5**.
7. Choose Find Next.
8. Continue choosing Find Next until WordPerfect displays the Find Not Found dialog box. At this dialog box, choose OK or press Enter.
9. Choose Close to close the Find and Replace Line Spacing dialog box.

Changing Match Options

With the Match drop-down menu options shown in figure 15.3, you can specify what you want WordPerfect to match.

When finding a search string, WordPerfect will stop at occurrences that match the search string. For example, if you enter the string *her* in the Find text box, WordPerfect stops at t*her*e, *her*s, rat*her*, and so on. If you want to find a specific word such as *her*, choose Whole Word at the Match drop-down menu. With this option selected, WordPerfect will stop at any occurrence of the word *her*. This includes any occurrence of *her* that ends in punctuation. You can also tell WordPerfect to find a whole word by keying a space followed by the word, then another space in the Find text box. This, however, causes WordPerfect to skip any word that is followed by punctuation.

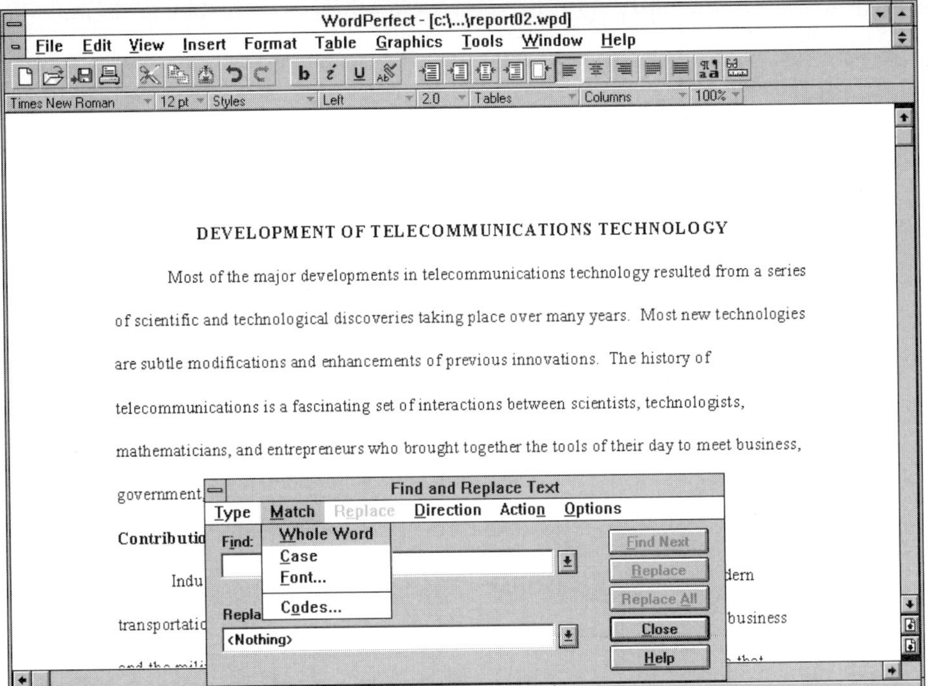

Figure 15.3
Match Drop-Down Menu

If you enter text as the search string, WordPerfect will match any case of the text. For example, if you enter *robin* as the search string, WordPerfect will find *robin*, *Robin*, or *ROBIN* (or any other combination of uppercase and/or lowercase letters). If you want WordPerfect to find only those occurrences that exactly match the search string, choose Case at the Match drop-down menu.

With the Font option from the Match drop-down menu, you can find a specific typeface, type size, or type style. When you choose Font from the Match drop-down menu, the Match Font dialog box shown in figure 15.4 displays.

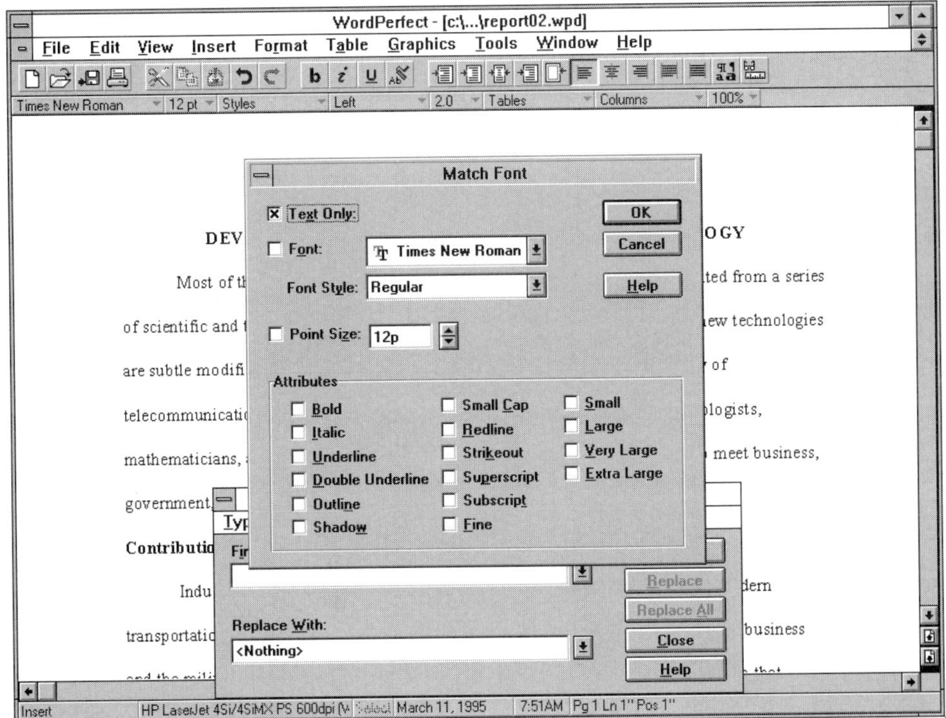

Figure 15.4
Match Font Dialog Box

At the Match Font dialog box, identify the font, font style, point size, and/or attributes, then choose OK or press Enter.

With the Codes option from the Match drop-down menu, you can find codes within a document. When you choose Codes, the Codes dialog box shown in figure 15.5 displays in the upper right corner of the editing window.

Figure 15.5
Codes Dialog Box

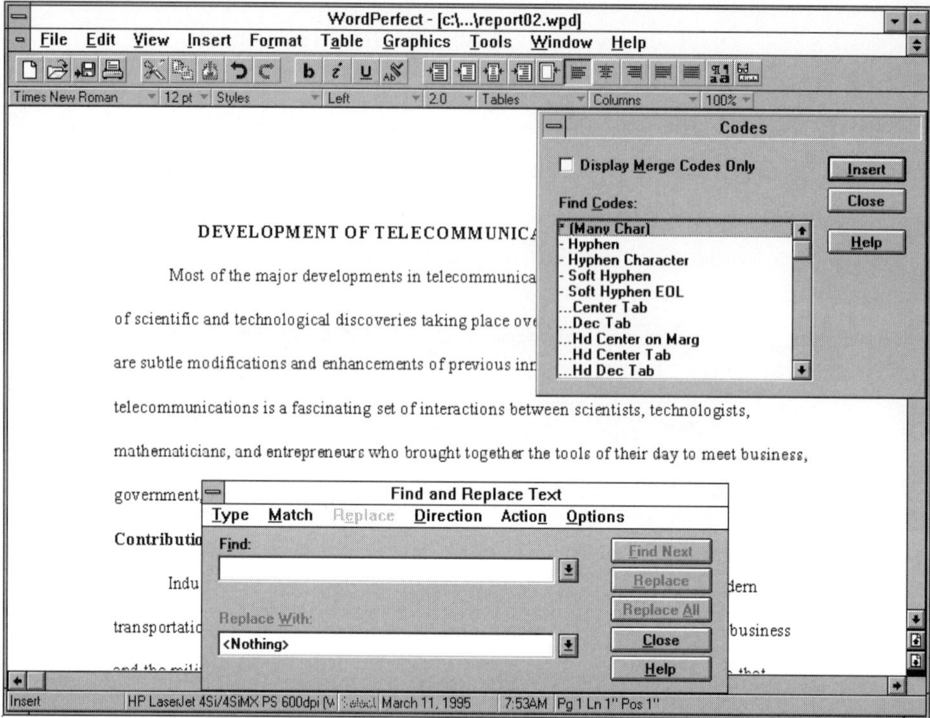

The Codes dialog box contains an extensive list of codes. Position the insertion point on the desired code, then choose Insert. This inserts the code in the Find text box. If you are using the mouse, you can also position the arrow pointer on the desired code, then double-click the left mouse button. More than one code can be inserted in the Find text box. When the code or codes have been inserted in the Find text box, you can close the Codes dialog box by clicking on the Close button or you can begin the search. (The Codes dialog box will disappear when the search begins.) As an example of how to search a document for codes, complete exercise 3.

Exercise 3 Searching a Document for Codes

1. At a clear editing window, open report03.
2. Save the document with Save As and name it c15ex03.
3. Find all bold codes and delete them by completing the following steps:
   a. With the insertion point positioned at the beginning of the document, choose Edit, then Find and Replace.
   b. At the Find and Replace Text dialog box, choose Match, then Codes.
   c. At the Codes dialog box, position the insertion point on *Bold On*. To do this with the mouse, click on the down-pointing arrow in the vertical scroll bar until *Bold On* is visible, then click on *Bold On*. If you are using the keyboard, press the down arrow key until the insertion point is positioned on *Bold On*.
   d. Choose Insert.
   e. Make sure there is nothing in the Replace With text box. If there is, select it, then delete it.
   f. Choose Replace All.
   g. Choose Close to close the Find and Replace Text dialog box.
4. Save the document again with the same name (c15ex03).

5. Print c15ex03.
6. Close c15ex03.

With the Find and Replace feature, you can also find codes and replace codes with other codes. For example, you can search for all double indent codes and replace them with hanging indent codes. For an example of how to find and replace codes, complete exercise 4.

Exercise 4 Finding and Replacing Codes

1. At a clear editing window, open report08.
2. Save the document with Save As and name it c15ex04.
3. Find all [Hd Left Ind] codes and replace with [Hd LeftRight Ind] codes by completing the following steps:
   a. Position the insertion point at the beginning of the document.
   b. Choose Edit, then Find and Replace.
   c. At the Find and Replace Text dialog box, choose Match, then Codes.
   d. At the Codes dialog box, position the insertion point on [Hd Left Ind], then choose Insert. (You must scroll down through the list to find the [Hd Left Ind] code.)
   e. Choose Replace With.
   f. Position the insertion point on the [Hd LeftRight Ind] code in the Codes dialog box, then choose Insert.
   g. Choose Replace All.
   h. Choose Close to close the Find and Replace Text dialog box.
4. Save the document again with the same name (c15ex04).
5. Print c15ex04.
6. Close c15ex04.

Changing Replace Options

When the Find and Replace Text dialog box is first displayed, the Replace option on the Menu Bar displays in gray. This option will become available and display in black when you choose Replace With. When you choose Replace, a drop-down menu displays with the options Case, Font, and Codes. These are the same options available at the Match drop-down menu.

Changing Direction Options

If you choose Direction from the Find and Replace Text dialog box Menu Bar, a drop-down menu displays with the options Backward and Forward. The default setting is Forward. At this setting, WordPerfect searches the document from the location of the insertion point to the end of the document. If you want to search from the location of the insertion point to the beginning of the document, choose Backward.

Changing Action Options

When WordPerfect finds text, it selects text that matches the search string. This is because the default setting at the Action drop-down menu at the Find and Replace Text dialog box is Select Match.

If you choose the Position Before option, WordPerfect will position the insertion point in front of the text. If you choose the Position After option, WordPerfect will position the insertion point after the text. You can choose Extend Selection to tell WordPerfect to select text from the insertion point to a specific word in the document.

Exercise 5 Using Find and Replace Options

1. At a clear editing window, open report04.
2. Select the text from the title, *CHAPTER 4: DEVELOPMENT OF TECHNOLOGY, 1950 – 1960*, to the end of the document.
3. Find *telecommunications* in the selected text and tell WordPerfect to position the insertion point before the text (rather than selecting it) by completing the following steps:
   a. Choose Edit, then Find and Replace.
   b. At the Find and Replace Text dialog box, key *telecommunications*.
   c. If there is any text in the Replace With text box, select it and then delete it.
   d. Choose Action, then Position Before.
   e. Choose Find Next.
   f. Continue choosing Find Next until WordPerfect displays the Find and Replace Not Found dialog box. At this dialog box choose OK or press Enter.
   g. Choose Close to close the Find and Replace Text dialog box.
4. Change Action back to the default of Select Match by completing the following steps:
   a. Choose Edit, then Find and Replace.
   b. At the Find and Replace Text dialog box, choose Action, then Select Match.
   c. Choose Close.
5. Close report04.

Changing Options

If you choose Options from the Menu Bar, the drop-down menu shown in figure 15.6 displays.

Figure 15.6
Options Drop-Down Menu

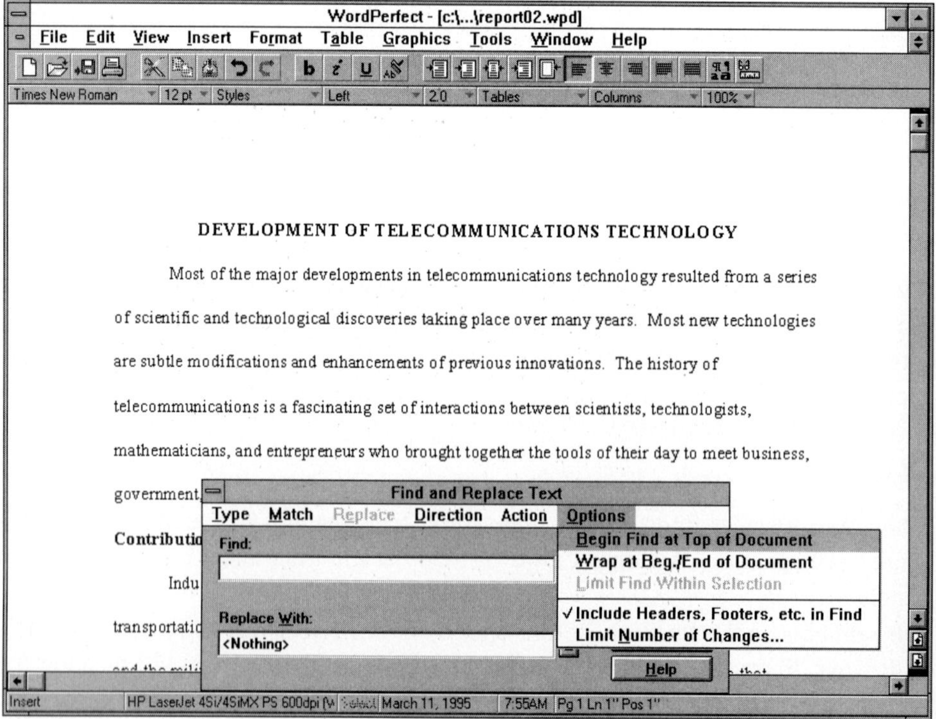

The default setting is *Include Headers, Footers, etc. in Find.* At this setting, WordPerfect searches all parts of a document for the search string including such features as headers, footers, footnotes, endnotes, and graphic elements.

If you choose *Begin Find at Top of Document*, WordPerfect will begin the search at the beginning of the document no matter where the insertion point is positioned.

At the *Wrap at Beg./End of Document* setting, WordPerfect will search from the position of the insertion point to the end of the document, then search from the beginning of the document to the position of the insertion point.

If you select text and then display the Find and Replace Text dialog box, the Limit Find Within Selection option is automatically selected. At this setting, WordPerfect will only search the selected text.

Use the Limit Number of Changes option to tell WordPerfect that you want only an *x* number of changes made. For example, if you know you only want the first four occurrences of the search text replaced with the replacement text, you would choose Options, then Limit Number of Changes. This causes the Limit Number of Changes dialog box to display. At this dialog box, you would key **4**, then choose OK or press Enter. When you complete the find and replace, WordPerfect only replaces the first four occurrences.

Exercise 6 Conducting a Find and Replace

1. At a clear editing window, open report08.
2. Save the document with Save As and name it c15ex06.
3. Find the [Ln Spacing: 2.0] code and replace it with [Ln Spacing: 1.5] using the mouse by completing the following steps:
   a. Click on Edit, then Find and Replace.
   b. At the Find and Replace Text dialog box, click on Direction, then Backward. (The line spacing code is positioned before the location of the insertion point.)
   c. Click on Type, then Specific Codes.
   d. At the Specific Codes dialog box, click on the down-pointing arrow at the right side of the Specific Codes list box until *Ln Spacing* is visible, then click on *Ln Spacing*.
   e. Click on OK.
   f. At the Find and Replace Line Spacing dialog box, click on the down-pointing triangle after the Replace With option box until the number in the option box displays as *1.5*.
   g. Click on Replace All.
   h. Click on Close.
4. Find and delete all bold codes except the bold codes around the title, *IDENTIFICATION OF CI*, and the subheadings, *Requirements During Development and Requirements for Operations/Maintenance*, by completing the following steps:
   a. Position the insertion point at the beginning of the document.
   b. Choose Edit, then Find and Replace.
   c. At the Find and Replace Text dialog box, choose Match, then Codes.
   d. At the Codes dialog box, position the insertion point on *Bold On*, then choose Insert.
   e. Choose Close to close the Codes dialog box.
   f. Make sure there is no text or codes in the text box below the Replace With option. If there is, select it, then delete it.
   g. Choose Find Next.
   h. WordPerfect stops at the first [Bold] code at the beginning of the title. You do not want to delete this code, so choose Find Next.

i. WordPerfect stops at the next occurrence of the [Bold] code (at the heading, *Introduction*). You want this code removed so choose Replace.
j. Continue finding [Bold] codes. Choose Find Next if you do not want to delete the code or choose Replace if you do.
k. Choose Close to close the Find and Replace Text dialog box.

5. Save the document again with the same name (c15ex06).
6. Print c15ex06.
7. Close c15ex06.

CHAPTER SUMMARY

- Use the Find and Replace feature to quickly locate a search string such as word(s) and/or code(s) and replace the search string with other words or codes.
- The text and/or codes you search for is called a search string and can be up to 80 characters in length.
- The Find and Replace Text dialog box contains a Menu Bar with six options—Type, Match, Replace, Direction, Action, and Options. Each option has a drop-down menu which allows you to customize your search.
- WordPerfect will search for specific formatting codes and replace them with other codes. Codes that are turned on and off, such as bold and underline, can be deleted in this manner but cannot be replaced with another code.
- If the search string is entered in lowercase letters, WordPerfect will find all occurrences of the string that contain lowercase or uppercase letters. If you want WordPerfect to find only those occurrences that exactly match the search string, choose Case at the Match drop-down menu.
- To search for format codes, use the Codes option from the Match drop-down menu or the Specific Codes option from the Type drop-down menu.
- By default, a search begins from the location of the insertion point forward through a document, unless another option is chosen at the Find and Replace Text dialog box.

Commands Review

	Mouse/Keyboard
Find and Replace Text dialog box	Edit, Find and Replace
Codes dialog box	Edit, Find and Replace, Match, Codes
Specific Codes dialog box	Edit, Find and Replace, Type, Specific Codes

CHECK YOUR UNDERSTANDING

True/False: Circle the letter T if the statement is true; circle the letter F if the statement is false.

T F 1. A search string can be no longer than 60 characters in length.
T F 2. A search string can contain spaces.
T F 3. By default, WordPerfect will search through the entire document, no matter where the insertion point is located.
T F 4. By default, WordPerfect will search through all footnotes in a document.
T F 5. To find all of the bold codes in a document, display the Specific Codes dialog box.
T F 6. WordPerfect always matches the case of the replacement text with the case of the find text, unless otherwise specified.
T F 7. With the Font option from the Match drop-down menu, you can find a specific font and font size.

T F 8. The Find and Replace feature can be used to find all bold codes in a document and replace them with italic codes.

T F 9. When using the Find and Replace feature, WordPerfect will find and replace words based on the root form of the word.

SKILL ASSESSMENTS

Assessment 1

1. At a clear editing window, open report08.
2. Save the document with Save As and name it c15sa01.
3. With the insertion point positioned at the beginning of the document, find all occurrences of *configuration item* and replace with *design unit.*
4. Move the insertion point to the end of the document, then complete a backward search for all occurrences of *CI* and replace with *DU.*
5. Save the document again with the same name (c15sa01).
6. Print c15sa01.
7. Close c15sa01.

Assessment 2

1. At a clear editing window, open legal01.
2. Save the document with Save As and name it c15sa02.
3. Complete the following find and replaces:
   a. Find all occurrences of *NAME1* and replace with *ALAN C. HOLMES.*
   b. Find all occurrences of *NAME2* and replace with *LOREN M. GUILL.*
   c. Find the one occurrence of *NUMBER* and replace with C-54327.
4. Find and delete all bold codes, except the bold codes around the document title and the word *DATED.*
5. Save the document again with the same name (c15sa02).
6. Print c15sa02.
7. Close c15sa02.

Assessment 3

1. At a clear editing window, open legal02.
2. Save the document with Save As and name it c15sa03.
3. Complete the following find and replaces:
   a. Find all occurrences of *NAME1* and replace with *ELENA C. TREECE.*
   b. Fine the one occurrence of *NUMBER* and replace with *D-4311.*
   c. Find all [Bold] codes and delete them *except* the following:
      (1) IN DISTRICT COURT NO. 4, PIERCE COUNTY
      (2) DATED
      (3) LESLIE COBURN
   d. Find all [Hd LeftRight Ind] indent codes and rcplace with [Hd Left Ind] codes.
4. Save the document again with the same name (c15sa03).
5. Print c15sa03.
6. Close c15sa03.

Creating Newspaper & Parallel Columns

16

Upon successful completion of chapter 16, you will be able to create business documents, such as newsletters, agendas, and résumés, with different column styles.

When creating some business documents, you may want to establish the text in columns. In WordPerfect, you can create newspaper columns and parallel columns.

Newspaper columns contain text that flows up and down in the document. When the first column on the page is filled with text, the insertion point wraps to the top of the next column on the same page. When the last column on the page is filled with text, the insertion point wraps to the beginning of the first column on the next page.

Parallel columns contain text that is grouped across the page in rows. The next row begins a double space below the longest column entry of the previous row.

Creating Newspaper Columns

Newspaper columns can be created with the Columns button on the Power Bar or with the Columns option from the Format menu. From two to five columns can be created with the Columns button on the Power Bar. Figure 16.1 shows text formatted in newspaper columns.

Creating Newspaper Columns with the Columns Button

The Columns button on the Power Bar is the seventh button from the left. When you click on the Columns button, the drop-down menu, shown in figure 16.2, displays. To create columns with the Columns button, click on the desired number of columns.

Figure 16.1
Newspaper Columns

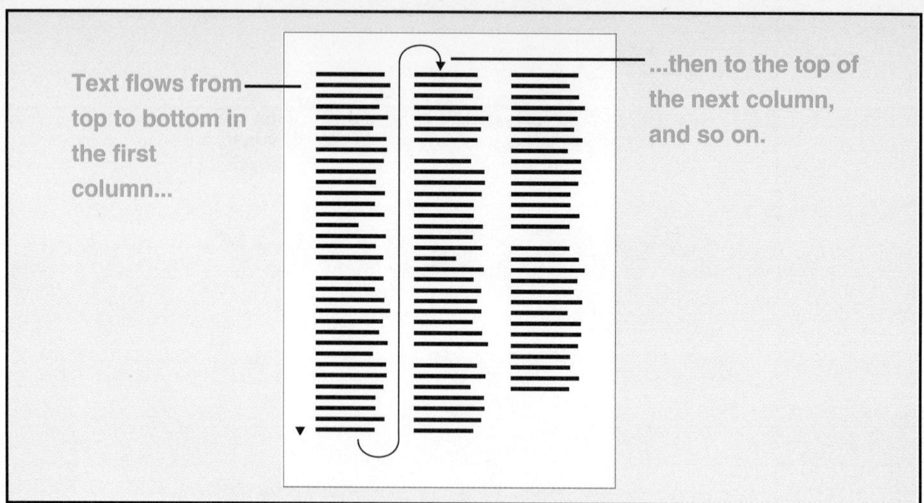

Figure 16.2
Columns Button Drop-Down Menu

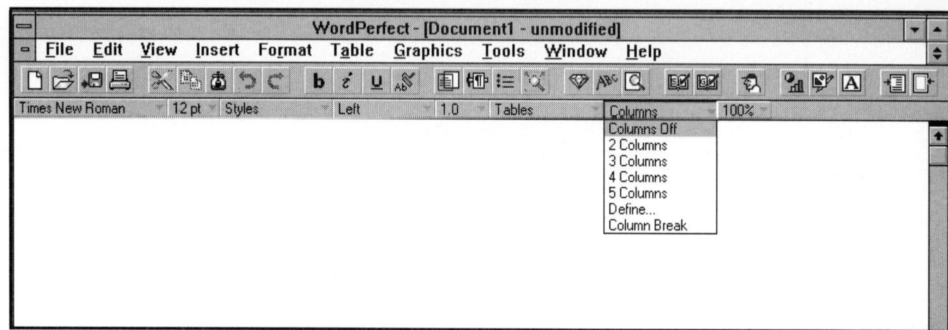

If you define three columns at a clear editing window, the column definition code Col Def: Newspaper, Total: 3, Col[Adj], Gut[0.5"], Col[Adj], Gut[0.5"]... is inserted in the document. If three columns are defined in a document containing text, the column definition code is inserted in the document and the text is automatically formatted into the columns.

Exercise 1 Formatting Text into Two Columns

1. At a clear editing window, open report07.
2. Save the document with Save As and name it c16ex01.
3. Insert a hard return above and below the following headings in the document:
   Industrialization
   Development of a World Market
   The American Civil War
   Colonization
   The 1870s Depression
4. Position the insertion point at the beginning of the line containing the heading *Industrialization*, then define two evenly spaced newspaper columns using the Power Bar by completing the following steps:
   a. Position the arrow pointer on the Columns button on the Power Bar, then click the left mouse button.
   b. Click on the 2 Columns option.
5. Save the document again with the same name (c16ex01).
6. Print c16ex01.
7. Close c16ex01.

The columns you create with the Columns button on the Power Bar are evenly spaced newspaper columns. This means that each column will contain the same amount of space. To create unevenly spaced newspaper columns you must use the Columns option from the Format menu.

Creating Newspaper Columns with the Columns Dialog Box

The Columns dialog box can be used to create newspaper columns that are evenly or unevenly spaced. To display the Columns dialog box, shown in figure 16.3, choose Format, Columns, then Define.

The Columns option in the Number of Columns section has a default setting of 2. This number can be changed by keying a new number or clicking on the up- or down-pointing triangle after the Columns text box. The number of columns is only limited to the space available on the page.

The Type section of the dialog box contains four options: Newspaper, Balanced Newspaper, Parallel, and Parallel w/ Block Protect. The default setting is Newspaper. The Balanced Newspaper option is like the Newspaper option, except each column is adjusted on the page to be as equal in length as possible, as shown in figure 16.4.

To change the Type using the mouse, position the arrow pointer on the radio button before the desired option, then click the left button. To change the Type with the keyboard, press Alt + the underlined letter of the desired option.

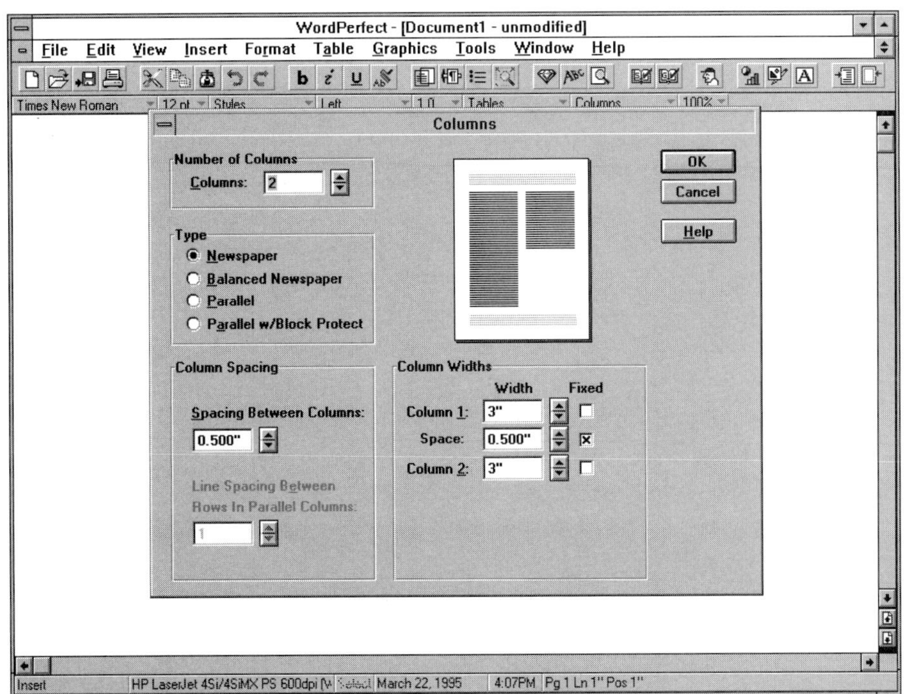

Figure 16.3
Columns Dialog Box

By default, columns are separated by 0.5 inches of space. This space between columns is referred to as the *gutter*. The amount of space between columns can be increased or decreased with the Spacing Between Columns option. At this option, you can key a new measurement for the amount of spacing between columns, or you can click on the up- or down-pointing triangle after the text box to increase or decrease the measurement.

If you create parallel columns, WordPerfect automatically inserts a blank line between the longest entry in a row and the first entry of the next row. With the Line Spacing Between Rows in Parallel Columns option, you can increase or decrease this number.

WordPerfect automatically determines column widths for the number of columns specified. By default, column widths are the same. If you want to enter your own column widths or change the amount of space between columns, choose the desired column, then key a measurement in the text box or click on the up- or down-pointing triangles after the column text box.

Figure 16.4
Newspaper Columns

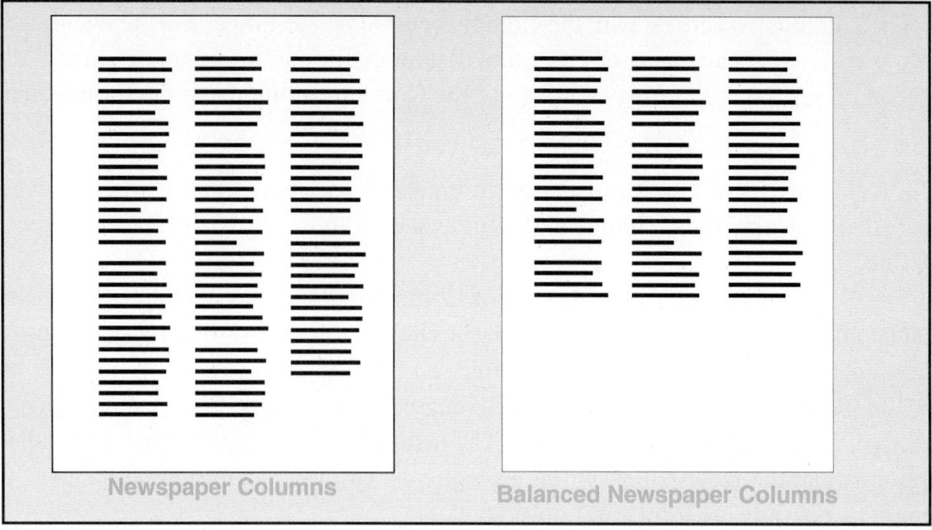

To the right side of the Column Widths options are Fixed check boxes. Insert an X in a Fixed check box if you want the width of the columns or space between columns to remain fixed regardless of what changes are made to the document margins or other column widths.

As an example of how to use the Columns dialog box, complete exercise 2.

Exercise 2 Creating Balanced Newspaper Columns

1. At a clear editing window, open report08.
2. Save the document with Save As and name it c16ex02.
3. Make the following changes to the document:
   a. Display Reveal Codes, then delete the [Ln Spacing: 2.0] code.
   b. Insert a hard return above and below the following headings in the document:
      Introduction
      Purpose and Scope
      Application
      Requirements
   c. Move the insertion point to the beginning of the document, display the Tab Set dialog box, clear all tabs, then set left tabs at +0.2 and +0.4 inches.
   d. With the insertion point still positioned at the beginning of the document, change the font to 11.5 GeoSlab703 Lt BT.
   e. Position the insertion point at the left margin of the line containing *Introduction*, then define three balanced newspaper columns by completing the following steps:
      (1) Choose Format, Columns, then Define.
      (2) At the Columns dialog box, key **3**.
      (3) Choose Balanced Newspaper.
      (4) Change the measurement in the Spacing Between Columns text box to 0.300" using the mouse by clicking on the down-pointing triangle after the Spacing Between Columns text box until *0.300"* displays.
      (5) Choose OK or press Enter.
   f. Select the title, *IDENTIFICATION OF CI*, then change the Relative Size to Large.
4. Save the document again with the same name (c16ex02).
5. Print c16ex02.
6. Close c16ex02.

WordPerfect inserts the column definition code at the beginning of the paragraph where the insertion point is located. Once columns have been defined, the columns can be turned off or on as many times as needed in a document. To turn off columns, position the insertion point where columns are to be turned off, then choose Format, Columns, then Off. If columns have been turned off in a document, they can be turned back on by choosing Format, Columns, then Define. At the Columns dialog box, you would choose OK or press Enter.

Newspaper columns can be defined before keying the text, or the columns can be defined in existing text. If you are defining newspaper columns in existing text, position the insertion point at the location where the columns are to begin, then define the columns.

If you want to end a newspaper column before the end of the page, insert a hard page break by pressing Ctrl + Enter or choosing Format, Columns, then Column Break. When a hard page break or column break is inserted, the insertion point moves to the beginning of the next column on the same page. If the hard page break is inserted in the last column on the page, the insertion point moves to the first column on the next page. When the insertion point is located in a newspaper column, the column number displays at the left side of the Status Bar.

Editing Text in Columns

To edit text established in columns, move the insertion point with the mouse or insertion point movement keys and commands either within columns or between columns.

Moving the Insertion Point within Columns

To move the insertion point in a document using the mouse, position the I-beam pointer where desired, then click the left button. If you are using the keyboard, the insertion point movement keys—up, down, left, and right arrows—cause the insertion point to move in the direction indicated. If you press the up or down arrow key, the insertion point moves up or down within the column. If the insertion point is located on the last line of a column on a page, the down arrow will cause the insertion point to move to the beginning of the same column on the next page. If the insertion point is located on the first line of text in a column, pressing the up arrow key will cause the insertion point to move to the end of the same column on the previous page.

The left and right arrow keys move the insertion point in the direction indicated within the column. When the insertion point gets to the end of the line within the column, it moves down to the beginning of the next line within the same column.

Moving the Insertion Point between Columns

You can use the mouse or the keyboard to move the insertion point between columns. If you are using the mouse, position the I-beam pointer where desired, then click the left button. If you are using the keyboard, use the insertion point movement commands shown in figure 16.5 to move the insertion point between columns.

Move insertion point to next column	ALT + →
Move insertion point to previous column	ALT + ←
Move insertion point to last line of column	ALT + END
Move insertion point to top of column	ALT + HOME

Figure 16.5
Insertion Point Movement between Columns

Exercise 3 Creating a Newsletter with Two Columns

1. At a clear editing window, create the heading for a newsletter shown in figure 16.6 by completing the following steps:
   a. Change the font to 14-point Swis721 BlkEx BT.
   b. Key **DISTRICT HAPPENINGS** centered.
   c. Change the font to 12-point Swis721 BlkEx BT.
   d. Press Enter.
   e. Key **April Newsletter** centered.
   f. Key **Joni Kapshaw, Editor** centered.
   g. Change the font to 12-point GeoSlab703 Lt BT.
   h. Press the Enter key twice.
2. Insert the document news01 into the current document. (Use the File command from the Insert menu.)
3. Bold the headings *Recreation Program*, *Sixth Grade Camp*, and *Library News*.
4. Position the insertion point at the left margin of the line containing *Recreation Program*, then define two newspaper columns using the Columns dialog box by completing the following steps:
   a. Choose Format, Columns, then Define.
   b. At the Columns dialog box, make sure the Type is Newspaper and the Number of Columns is 2.
   c. Choose OK or press Enter.
5. With the insertion point still positioned on the line containing *Recreation Program*, display the Tab Set dialog box, delete previous tabs, then set one tab at +0.25 inches.
6. Save the newsletter and name it c16ex03.
7. Print c16ex03.
8. Close c16ex03.

Figure 16.6

DISTRICT HAPPENINGS
April Newsletter
Joni Kapshaw, Editor

Creating Parallel Columns

Parallel columns contain text that is grouped to be read across the page in rows as shown in figure 16.7. The next row begins a double space below the longest column of the previous row. Parallel columns can be used to create documents such as agendas, itineraries, résumés, or address lists.

Parallel columns cannot be defined with the Columns button on the Power Bar. They must be defined at the Columns dialog box. After parallel columns have been defined, key the text for the first column, then insert a hard page or column break. The hard page or column break moves the insertion point to the next column. To insert a hard page break, press Ctrl + Enter. To insert a column break, choose Format, Column, then Column Break.

When a hard page or column break is inserted in the last column in a document, the insertion point moves to the left margin a double space below the longest column entry. When keying the text in each column, the Enter key does not have to be pressed to end each line. WordPerfect's word wrap feature will wrap text to the next line within the column.

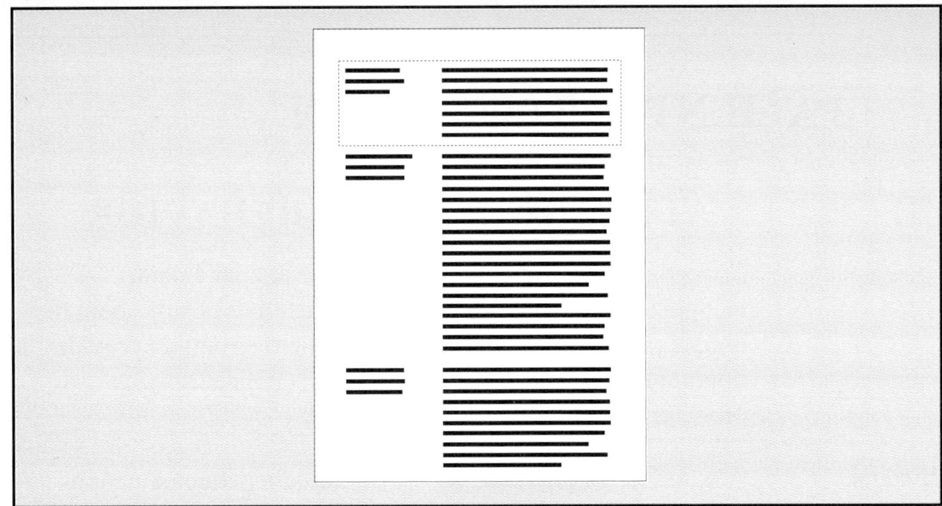

Figure 16.7
Parallel Columns

At the Columns dialog box, parallel columns can be created with block protect. If you choose Parallel w/Block Protect at the Columns dialog box, WordPerfect keeps all columns in a row together. If one column is too long to fit on a page, all the columns in the row are moved to the next page. If you define parallel columns without block protect, a row of columns may be divided between two pages.

As with newspaper columns, the parallel column number where the insertion point is located displays in the Status Bar.

Exercise 4 Creating Parallel Columns

1. At a clear editing window, create the document shown in figure 16.8 by completing the following steps:
   a. Key the title, **PATIENT SATISFACTION**, then press the Enter key three times.
   b. Define three parallel columns by completing the following steps:
      (1) Choose Format, Columns, then Define.
      (2) At the Columns dialog box, key **3**. (This changes the number of columns to three.)
      (3) Choose Parallel.
      (4) Choose OK or press Enter.
   c. Center and bold the heading *VALUE*. Press Ctrl + Enter to move the insertion point to the next column. Continue keying the text in figure 16.8. Use Ctrl + Enter to end a column and move the insertion point to the next column.
   d. Select the title, *PATIENT SATISFACTION*, then change the font to 18-point Times New Roman.
   e. Select the following text then change the font to 14-point Times New Roman:
      VALUE
      ATTITUDE
      BEHAVIOR
2. Save the document and name it c16ex04.
3. Print c16ex04.
4. Close c16ex04.

Figure 16.8

PATIENT SATISFACTION

VALUE	ATTITUDE	BEHAVIOR
Individualized patient care	Concern for the person; recognize that everyone is a unique person; recognize importance of patient's problem	Use patient's name; remember details about the patient's routine; provide personalized service
Respect for individual	Acceptance of physical disabilities, personalities, and cultural differences; tolerance and appreciation of differences	Handle patient situations with respect and tact; prepare personalized care plan; make sure they know you and you know them; provide for patient's individual needs for privacy and respect
Need for control and freedom of choice	Respect for patient competence; understanding; patients can take care of themselves	Explain environment; give choices; explain what is happening; involve patient in scheduling when possible
Being treated like a guest—respect and courtesy	Understand and respect that patient has fear; care for the whole person; treat people as guests	Respond to nonverbal cues; talk about fears; ask patient's opinion; do not rush treatment; maintain respect for family interaction; take time to allow patient to adjust

Changing Column Widths with the Ruler Bar

The options in the Column Widths section of the Columns dialog box can be used to change the width of columns as well as determine the space between columns. You can also change the width and size of columns and the space between columns using the Ruler Bar. To display the Ruler Bar, choose View, then Ruler Bar. When the Ruler Bar is displayed in a document set in newspaper or parallel columns, column width and column markers display as shown in figure 16.9.

Use the column margin markers shown in figure 16.9 to change left and right column margins. Use the column width markers to change column width. When changing column margins or widths, the insertion point must be positioned on the line where the column definition code is located. When changes are made to column widths, the changes affect the column definition code.

To change the column margin or width, position the insertion point on the line where the column definition code is located. Position the arrow pointer on the desired marker, then hold down the left mouse button, drag the marker to the desired position, then release the mouse button.

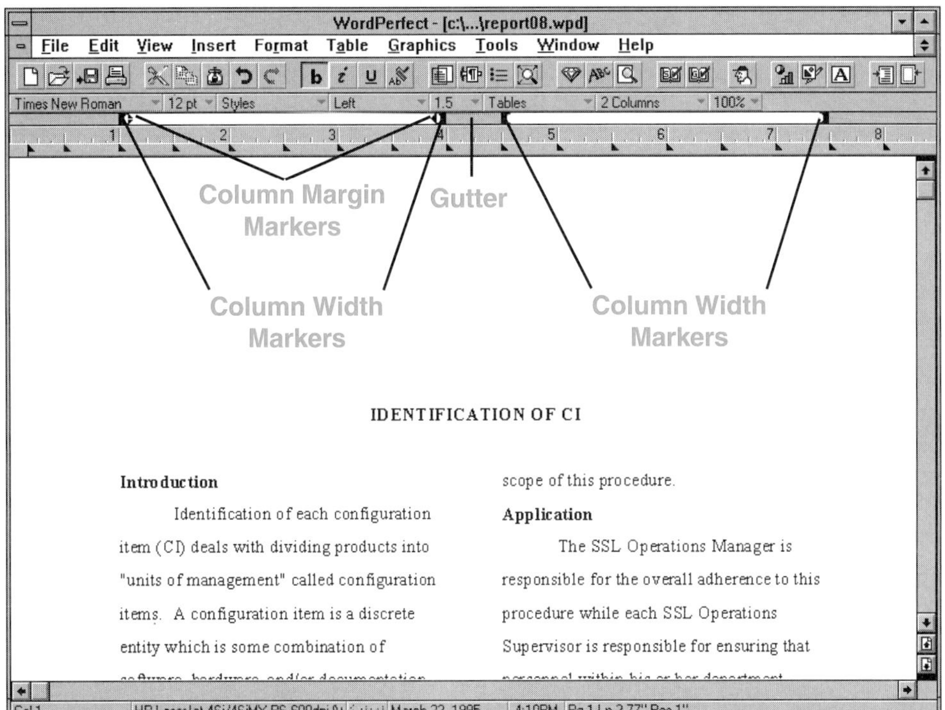

Figure 16.9
Column Markers on the Ruler Bar

When you position the arrow pointer on a column marker, then hold down the left mouse button, a dashed vertical line displays down the editing window. This dashed vertical line is referred to as the Ruler Bar Guide. This guide can help you visually determine the correct position for the marker.

The gray space on the Ruler Bar between column markers is referred to as the *gutter*. You can move the gutter along the Ruler Bar. To move a gutter, position the arrow pointer in the gray area of the gutter, hold down the left mouse button, drag the gutter to the desired position, then release the mouse button.

The tab markers on the Ruler Bar can be moved to different locations. Move a tab marker in the same manner as a column marker.

Exercise 5 Changing Column Widths

1. At a clear editing window, open c16ex01.
2. Save the document with Save As and name it c16ex05.
3. Change the widths of the columns by completing the following steps:
   a. Position the insertion point at the left margin of the line containing *Industrialization*. (The insertion point must be positioned *after* the column definition code. If necessary, display Reveal Codes to determine if the insertion point is in the correct location.)
   b. Turn on the display of the Ruler Bar.
   c. Move the left column marker for the first column by completing the following steps:
      (1) Position the arrow pointer on the left column marker for the first column (located at the 1-inch mark).
      (2) Hold down the left mouse button, drag the arrow pointer to the 1.5-inch mark, then release the mouse button.
   d. Move the right column marker for the first column to the 4 1/8-inch mark by completing steps similar to those in 3c(1) and 3c(2).
   e. Move the left column marker for the second column to the 4 3/8-inch mark.
   f. Move the right column marker for the second column to the 7-inch mark. (You may need to move the scroll box to the right on the vertical scroll bar to be able to see the right column marker for the second column.)
4. Save the document again with the same name (c16ex05).
5. Print c16ex05.
6. Close c16ex05.

CHAPTER SUMMARY

- Two types of text columns can be created with WordPerfect's columns feature: newspaper and parallel.
- Newspaper columns contain text that flows up and down in the document.
- Text keyed into parallel columns flows horizontally across the page in rows.
- Create from two to five evenly spaced newspaper columns with the Columns button on the Power Bar.
- Create any number of newspaper or parallel columns at the Columns dialog box.
- The space between columns or rows and the column width can be customized at the Columns dialog box or the Ruler Bar.
- The Type section of the Columns dialog box contains four options: Newspaper, Balanced Newspaper, Parallel, and Parallel w/Block Protect. The last option keeps all columns in a row together on one page.
- Newspaper columns can be defined before keying the text, or the columns can be defined in existing text.

Commands Review

	Mouse	Keyboard
Columns drop-down menu	Click on Columns button on the Power Bar (7th button from left)	
Columns dialog box	Format, Columns, Define	Format, Columns, Define

End a parallel column	Format, Columns, Column Break; or Insert, Page Break	CTRL + ENTER
Move insertion point between columns	Position I-beam pointer where desired, click left mouse button	
Move insertion point to		
—next column		ALT + →
—previous column		ALT + ←
—last line of column		ALT + END
—top of column		ALT + HOME
Ruler Bar	View, Ruler Bar	View, Ruler Bar

CHECK YOUR UNDERSTANDING

True/False: Circle the letter T if the statement is true; circle the letter F if the statement is false.

T F 1. Use the Columns button on the Power Bar to create two, three, four, or five evenly spaced newspaper columns.

T F 2. The space between columns is called the gutter.

T F 3. The Columns option at the Columns dialog box has a default setting of 3.

T F 4. The maximum number of columns that can be defined in a document is eight.

T F 5. The Type section of the Columns dialog box contains four options: Newspaper, Parallel, Balanced Parallel, and Parallel with Block Protect.

T F 6. By default, columns are separated by 0.5 inches.

T F 7. You can turn columns on and off as many times as necessary within a document.

T F 8. After parallel columns have been defined, key the text for the first column, then press the Enter key to move to the second column.

Completion: In the space provided at the right, indicate the correct term, command, or number.

1. This type of column is best suited for creating an agenda, an itinerary, a résumé, or an address list. ____________________
2. The only type of column that can be created with the Columns button on the Power Bar is this. ____________________
3. To ensure that all columns in a row are kept together and not divided between two pages, choose this type of column. ____________________
4. When creating parallel columns, use this command after keying the text for each column. ____________________
5. To create newspaper columns that are approximately equal in length, choose this Type at the Columns dialog box. ____________________

SKILL ASSESSMENTS

Assessment 1

1. At a clear editing window, open report02.
2. Save the document with Save As and name it c16sa01.
3. Make the following changes to the document:
   a. Delete the [Ln Spacing: 2.0] code.
   b. Insert a hard return above and below the headings in the document (*Contributions of Major Historical Events*, *Development of a World Market*, *The American Civil War*, *Colonization*, and *The 1870s Depression*).

c. Select the title and change the Relative Size to Large.
d. Position the insertion point at the left margin of the line that begins *Most of the major developments...*, then define two evenly spaced newspaper columns.

4. Save the document again with the same name (c16sa01).
5. Print c16sa01.
6. Close c16sa01.

Assessment 2

1. At a clear editing window, create the document shown in figure 16.10 by completing the following steps:
   a. Change the font to 14-point GeoSlab703 Lt BT.
   b. Key the title, **PROJECT TIMELINES**, centered and bolded.
   c. Change the font to 12-point GeoSlab703 Lt BT.
   d. Press Enter three times, then define three spaced parallel columns.
   e. Key the text in columns as shown in figure 16.10. Center and bold the column headings *Project*, *Completion*, and *Update*.
2. Save the document and name it c16sa02.
3. Print c16sa02.
4. Close c16sa02.

Figure 16.10

PROJECT TIMELINES

Project	**Completion**	**Update**
Engineering building	September - December, 1997	Framing underway, roofing begun, masonry going up
Administration annex	October, 1997	Expected bid date early spring, permit hearing scheduled
Remodeling of personnel offices	June - September, 1998	Mechanical and electrical beginning
East parking lot	September, 1998	Soil testing completed, preliminary plans completed

Assessment 3

1. At a clear editing window, create the résumé shown in figure 16.11 by completing the following steps:
   a. Change the font to 18-point Arrus BT Bold, then key **ANDREA BOWEN** centered.
   b. Press Enter once, then change the font to 14-point Arrus BT Bold.
   c. Key the address and telephone number centered as shown in figure 16.11.
   d. After keying the telephone number, change the font to 12-point Times New Roman.

e. Press Enter twice, then define two parallel columns. Set the width for the first column at 1.5 inches and the width for the second column at 4.5 inches.
f. Key the remainder of the résumé shown in figure 16.11. Bold the headings *OBJECTIVE*, *EDUCATION*, *SKILLS*, *EMPLOYMENT*, and *ORGANIZATIONS*. Press Ctrl + Enter to end a column and move the insertion point to the next column.

2. Save the résumé and name it c16sa03.
3. Print c16sa03.
4. Close c16sa03.

Figure 16.11

ANDREA BOWEN
1302 South 43rd Street
Tampa, FL 33643
(813) 555-9604

OBJECTIVE A position as a legal secretary in a company that provides opportunity for growth and advancement.

EDUCATION Bayside Community College—Associates of Arts and Sciences, Legal Secretary, June 1997

Wallace High School—Honor Graduate, 1995

SKILLS

Keyboarding (70+ wpm)	Legal theory
Legal terminology	Word processing
Desktop publishing	Machine transcription
Accounting	10-key calculator
Database management	Spreadsheet
Employee training	Supervision

EMPLOYMENT Legal Secretary, Galvin & Jacobs, 833 Riverside Drive, Tampa, FL 33641. Duties include answering the telephone, taking messages, scheduling appointments, filing manually and electronically, and transcribing and preparing legal documents.

Assistant Manager, Sportland, 1200 East 32nd, Tampa, FL 33460. Duties included supervising employees, training new employees, taking inventory, customer service, sales, and operating and cashing out till.

Food Server, Bluewater's, 220 North Second, Tampa, FL 33659. Duties included customer service, hosting birthday parties, cooking, operating cash registers and drive-through window, and taking and filling customer orders.

ORGANIZATIONS Treasurer, Student Government, Wallace High School, 1994-95
Member, Phi Beta Lambda, 1992-95

Unit 3 Performance Assessment

In this unit, you have learned to prepare multi-paged documents with specific formatting including page numbering, headers/footers, footnotes/endnotes, and newspaper and parallel columns.

PROBLEM-SOLVING AND DECISION-MAKING

Assessment 1

1. At a clear editing window, open report06.
2. Save the document with Save As and name it u03pa01.
3. Make the following changes to the report:
   a. Change the line spacing to double (2). Delete all extra lines in the report so there is only a double space between all lines.
   b. Turn on the Widow/Orphan feature.
   c. Create Footer A that prints *Telecommunications Trends* bolded at the right margin.
   d. Number all pages in the document, except the first page, in the upper right corner of the page.
4. Save the document and name it u03pa01.
5. Print u03pa01.
6. Close u03pa01.

Optional: Rewrite the report in one page or less for a nontechnical audience (parents and community members).

Assessment 2

1. At a clear editing window, open loandoc.
2. Select the first paragraph and save it as a separate document named loanpr01. Select the second paragraph and save it as a separate document named loanpr02. Do the same with the other paragraphs and name them loanpr03, loanpr04, and loanpr05.
3. Close loandoc.

4. At a clear editing window, create the document shown in figure U3.1 with the following specifications:
   a. Change the top margin to 1.5 inches.
   b. Turn on the Widow/Orphan feature.
   c. Change the line spacing to double (2) for the body of the document. Change the line spacing back to single (1) for the signature lines.
   d. Insert the documents as indicated by the bracketed items.
   e. After inserting the documents, renumber the paragraphs.
   f. Insert page numbering at the bottom center of each page.
5. Complete a spell check on the document.
6. Save the document and name it u03pa02.
7. Print u03pa02.
8. Close u03pa02.

Optional: Think of a different method for copying the paragraphs in step 2 to the new document you create. Use this method and then write a paragraph discussing which method is more efficient.

Figure U3.1

CONSUMER LOAN AGREEMENT

This Consumer Loan Agreement governs the open-end consumer loan plan issued through State Employees Credit Union. EDWARD G. WALLACE and TARA L. WALLACE, applicants, agree jointly to follow the terms and conditions and all other loan documents related to this Account including any Loan Advance Voucher, Loan Proceeds Check, Power of Attorney, if applicable, given when a loan is made, which collectively shall govern this account.

[Retrieve loanpr03 here.]

[Retrieve loanpr01 here.]

[Retrieve loanpr04 here.]

[Retrieve loanpr02 here.]

5. **Finance Charge.** When finance charges accrue, EDWARD G. WALLACE and TARA L. WALLACE will pay a finance charge calculated on the daily unpaid balance of all loans under this Account and any loan fee applicable to the Account. The finance charges will begin to accrue as of the date each loan advance is made. The finance charge is based on the outstanding balance.

____

EDWARD G. WALLACE, Applicant

____

TARA L. WALLACE, Applicant

Assessment 3

1. At a clear editing window, open u03pa02.
2. Save the document with Save As and name it u03pa03.
3. Make the following changes to the document:
   a. Change the font to 12-point GeoSlab703 Lt BT.
   b. Delete the top margin code.
   c. Delete the page numbering code.

d. Insert page numbering at the top right of every page except the first page.
e. Complete the following search and replaces:
   (1) Search for *EDWARD G. WALLACE* and replace with *BARRY C. NOLLAN*.
   (2) Search for *TARA L. WALLACE* and replace with *MELISSA A. NOLLAN*.
4. Save the document with the same name (u03pa03).
5. Print u03pa03.
6. Close u03pa03.

Optional: Research and define these terms: Power of Attorney, accrue, overdraft, and deposit share account.

Assessment 4

1. At a clear editing window, open report01.
2. Save the document with Save As and name it u03pa04.
3. Make the following changes to the document:
   a. Delete the [Ln Spacing: 2.0] code.
   b. Change the font to 12-point BernhardMod BT.
   c. Insert a hard return below the title, *TRENDS IN TELECOMMUNICATIONS*.
   d. Change the first heading in the document so it displays as *Continued Growth of Photonics* rather than *Continued Growth of Photonics (Fiber Optics)*.
   e. Change the second heading in the document so it displays as *Microcomputer Trends* rather than *Microcomputer Trends in the Nineties*.
   f. Insert a hard return above and below the headings *Continued Growth of Photonics* and *Microcomputer Trends*.
   g. Select the title and change the relative size to Large.
   h. Position the insertion point at the left margin of the line that begins *Several trends are occurring in the field...*, then define two balanced newspaper columns with 0.3 inches of space between columns.
   i. With the insertion point still positioned at the left margin of the line that begins *Several trends are occurring in the field ...*, delete all previous tabs then set a left tab 0.25 inches from the left margin and another 0.5 inches from the left margin.
4. Save the document again with the same name (u03pa04).
5. Print u03pa04.
6. Close u03pa04.

Assessment 5

1. At a clear editing window, create the list of medical suppliers shown in figure U3.2 with the following specifications:
   a. Change the font to 12-point GeoSlab703 Lt BT.
   b. With the insertion point a triple space below the title, define three parallel columns with 0.4 inches of space between the columns.
   c. Change the relative size of the title to Large.
2. Save the document and name it u03pa05.
3. Print u03pa05.
4. Close u03pa05.

Optional: Redesign the document by adding boldface column headings and by using a different font for the first column.

Figure U3.2

MEDICAL EQUIPMENT SUPPLIERS

Arthur Perella Office Manager	International Autoclave 32445 Ninth Avenue Denver, CO 86431	(303) 555-3049 Extension 43
Debra Faaborg Director of Personnel	Ryan Pharmaceuticals 2119 Mountain Avenue Denver, CO 86320	(303) 555-5544
Randy O'Connor Vice President	Bennett Medical 4032 North Fourth Street Denver, CO 86402	(303) 555-0098 Extension 122
Janet Zenor District Manager	A-1 Medical Suppliers 535 Pontiac Boulevard Denver, CO 86332	(303) 555-6675 Extension 20
Elena Torres-Wheeler Manager	Quality Care Products 12914 South 56th Denver, CO 86553	(303) 555-2200

WRITING

The following activities give you the opportunity to practice your writing skills along with demonstrating an understanding of some of the important WordPerfect features you have mastered in this unit. In planning the documents, remember to shape the information according to the writing purpose and the audience. Use correct grammar, appropriate word choices, and clear sentence constructions.

Activity 1

Situation: You are responsible for formatting the report in the document named *report05* on your student data disk. This report should include page numbers and headers and/or footers. Change to a serif typeface for the body of the report and a sans serif typeface for the title and headings. Correct the spelling in the document.

After formatting the report, create an appropriate title page for the report. Include your name as the author of the report. Save the document and name it u03act01. Print and then close u03act01.

Activity 2

Situation: You are responsible for creating an outline based on the information contained in *report03* and *report04* on your student data disk. The outline should contain the title and headings within each report. (*Hint: Try using multiple windows to complete this activity.*) Save the outline document and name it u03act02. Print and then close u03act02.

RESEARCH

Review Chapter 13, "Creating Document References." Then outline the information on headers, adding additional points offered in the Help feature or appropriate facts from other sources.

Creating Documents with Graphics Elements

In this unit, you will learn to enhance the visual display of documents with graphics elements, add visual enhancements to documents with WordPerfect Draw and TextArt, and display numerical data in a chart.

SCANS

Technology

- Design creative page layouts
- Modify and enhance graphics and text
- Communicate complex ideas
- Create tables and charts

Inserting Graphics Images 17

Upon successful completion of chapter 17, you will be able to insert graphics images in a document and insert tables, text, or art images inside boxes.

With WordPerfect's Graphics feature, you can insert graphics images into a document as well as create eight different graphics boxes including text, figure, table, user, equation, button, watermark, and inline equations. In each of these boxes, you can insert such items as graphics elements, equations, text, or statistical data. Each graphics box has a different border style. You can insert anything in any graphics box. Generally, however, insert text or quotes in a text box; an image, logo, or drawing in a figure box; a table, spreadsheet, or statistical data in a table box; whatever is not addressed by the other seven in a user box; mathematical, scientific, or business equations in an equation box; a keystroke, function key, or icon in a button box; an image that is printed behind text in the watermark box; and an equation or expression in a line of text in an inline equation box.

In this chapter, you will learn how to create text, figure, table, user, and button boxes as well as watermark images. For information on equation and inline equation boxes, please refer to the WordPerfect reference manual.

Inserting an Image into a Document

The WordPerfect program includes approximately 81 predesigned graphics images that are included when WordPerfect is installed. Some of the images and their names are displayed in Appendix D. You will be using some of these predesigned images in this chapter.

You can insert one of the 81 graphics images into a document, or you can retrieve a graphics image created in a different program. In this chapter, you will be using the images provided by WordPerfect.

WordPerfect provides a Graphics Toolbar that contains buttons for creating and editing graphics elements. To display the Graphics Toolbar, position the arrow pointer on the current Toolbar, click the right mouse button, then click on Graphics at the drop-down menu.

An image can be inserted in a document. To do this, position the insertion point where you want the image to appear, then choose Graphics, then Image; or click on the Image button on the Graphics Toolbar. At the Insert Image dialog box shown in figure 17.1, select the image document name in the Filename list box, then choose OK or press Enter. (You can also double-click on the desired image document name.) When the image is inserted in the document, choose Close to close the Graphics Box Feature Bar.

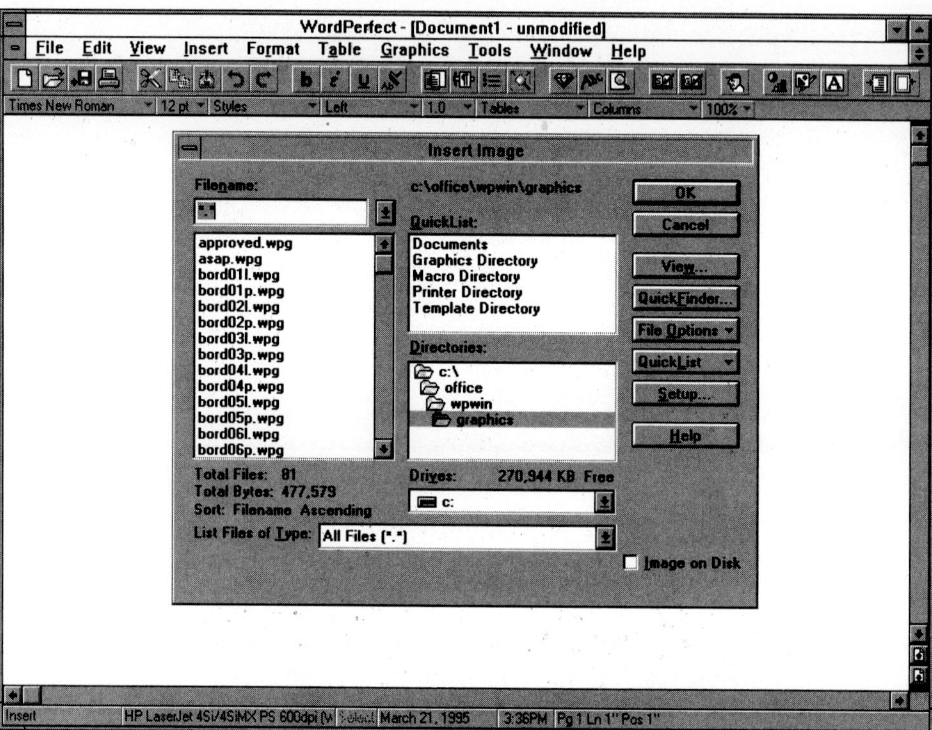

Figure 17.1
Insert Image Dialog Box

When the image is inserted in the document, the Graphics Box Feature Bar displays immediately below the Power Bar (or the Ruler Bar, if it is displayed). You will learn about the features on the Graphics Box Feature Bar later in this chapter.

When a graphics image is inserted in a document, it displays at the left margin. The width and the height of the image will vary depending on the image. An image does not contain a border.

Exercise 1 Inserting a Predesigned Image

1. At a clear editing window, display the Graphics Toolbar by completing the following steps. (If the Graphics Toolbar is already displayed, skip this step.)
   a. Position the arrow pointer on the current Toolbar, then click the right mouse button.
   b. At the drop-down menu that displays, click on Graphics.
2. At a clear editing window, insert the image named **ender01.wpg** by completing the following steps.

a. Choose Graphics, then Image; or click on the Image button on the Graphics Toolbar.
b. At the Insert Image dialog box, click on the down-pointing arrow in the Filename list box until *ender01.wpg* is visible, then double-click on *ender01.wpg*.
c. Choose Close at the Graphics Box Feature Bar.

3. Save the document and name it c17ex01.
4. Print c17ex01.
5. Close c17ex01.

Creating a Text Box

Generally, you create a text box for quotes or other special text to be set off. When a text box is created, it displays with a border with thick top and bottom lines and no left or right lines. Graphics boxes display with different borders. For example, a figure box displays with a single line border on all sides while a user box displays with no border lines. To create a text box, position the insertion point where the text box is to appear, then choose Graphics, then Text Box; or click on the Text Box button on the Graphics Toolbar. This causes a text box to be inserted in the document with the insertion point positioned inside the box. The Graphics Box Feature Bar displays below the Power Bar. Key the text to be included in the box, then choose Close to remove the Graphics Box Feature Bar. When a text box is created, it will display in the editing window as shown in figure 17.2.

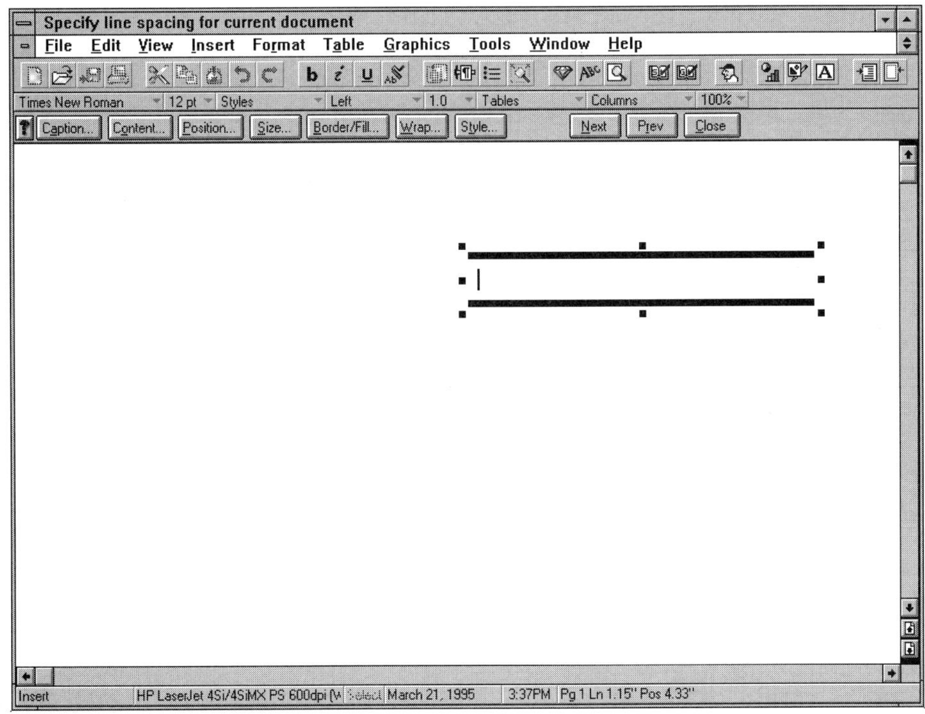

Figure 17.2
Text Box

You can key up to one page of text in a text box and format the text in the normal manner. For example, you can turn on bold or underlining, change the font, or change the justification of paragraphs. A text box is inserted at the right margin at the location of the insertion point. The width of the text box is approximately one-half the distance between the left and right margins. If the left and right margins are set at the default of 1 inch, the text box will be 3.25 inches wide. The height of the text box depends on the amount of text entered in the box. The box expands to include the text (up to one page).

Exercise 2 Creating a Text Box

1. At a clear editing window, create a text box containing the text *DENVER MEMORIAL HOSPITAL*, bold and centered, by completing the following steps:
   a. Choose Graphics, then Text Box; or click on the Text Box button on the Graphics Toolbar.
   b. With the insertion point inside the text box, complete the following steps:
      (1) Press Enter three times.
      (2) Press Shift + F7 to center.
      (3) Press Ctrl + B to turn on bold.
      (4) Key **DENVER MEMORIAL HOSPITAL**.
      (5) Press Ctrl + B to turn off bold.
      (6) Press Enter three times.
      (7) Choose Close at the Graphics Box Feature Bar.
2. Save the document and name it c17ex02.
3. Print c17ex02.
4. Close c17ex02.

Creating a Figure Box

A figure box is generally created for an image, logo, or drawing. To create a figure box with a graphics image inside, you would complete the following steps:

1 Position the insertion point where the figure box is to appear.
2 Choose Graphics, then Custom Box; or click on the Custom Box button on the Graphics Toolbar.
3 At the Custom Box dialog box shown in figure 17.3, select *Figure* in the Style Name list box.
4 Choose OK or press Enter.
5 Choose Content from the Graphics Box Feature Bar.
6 At the Box Content dialog box, click on the folder icon to the right of the Filename text box.
7 At the Select File dialog box, double-click on the desired image document name in the Filename list box.
8 At the Box Content dialog box, choose OK.
9 Choose Close to close the Graphics Box Feature Bar.

The default border for a figure box is a single line on each side of the box. The figure box is inserted in the document at the right margin and at the vertical location of the insertion point. If the left and right margins are set at the default of 1 inch, a figure box will be 3.25 inches wide. The height of the figure box will vary depending on what is inserted inside the box and how far down the page the insertion point is located.

Exercise 3 Creating a Figure Box

1. At a clear editing window, insert the graphics image named **crane_j.wpg** in a figure box by completing the following steps:
   a. Choose Graphics, then Custom Box; or click on the Custom Box button on the Graphics Toolbar.

b. At the Custom Box dialog box shown, select *Figure* in the Style Name list box.
c. Choose OK or press Enter.
d. Choose Content from the Graphics Box Feature Bar.
e. At the Box Content dialog box, click on the folder icon to the right of the Filename text box.
f. At the Select File dialog box, click on the down-pointing arrow in the Filename list box until *crane_j.wpg* is displayed, then double-click on *crane_j.wpg*.
g. At the Box Content dialog box, choose OK.
h. Choose Close to close the Graphics Box Feature Bar.

2. After the image is inserted in the document, press the Enter key until the insertion point reaches approximately Line 3.75", then insert the graphics image named **hotair.wpg** in a figure box by completing steps similar to those in steps 1a through 1h.
3. After the image is inserted in the document, press the Enter key until the insertion point reaches approximately Line 6.51", then insert the graphics image named **dragn.wpg** in a figure box by completing steps similar to those in steps 1a through 1h.
4. Change the viewing mode to Two Page to see how the document displays on the entire page, then change the viewing mode back to Page.
5. Save the document and name it c17ex03.
6. Print c17ex03.
7. Close c17ex03.

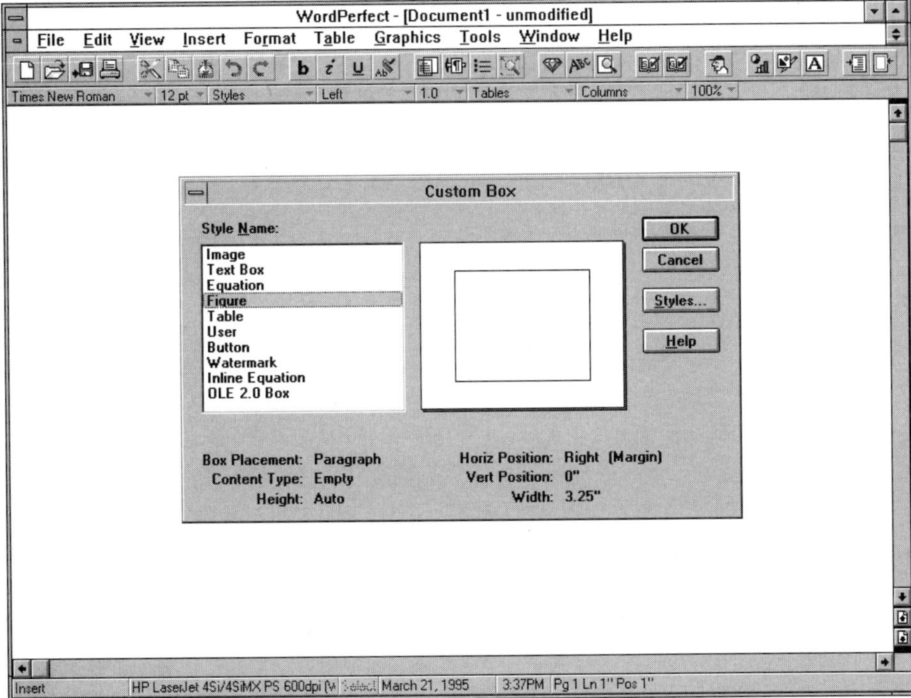

Figure 17.3
Custom Box Dialog Box

Creating a Table Box

A table box is generally created for a table, spreadsheet, or statistical data. You can insert a previously created document into a table box or key text directly into the table box. To create a table box and insert the contents of a previously created document into the box, you would complete the following steps:

1. Position the insertion point where the table box is to appear.
2. Choose Graphics, then Custom Box; or click on the Custom Box button on the Graphics Toolbar.

3 At the Custom Box dialog box, select Table in the Style Name list box.
4 Choose OK or press Enter.
5 Choose Content from the Graphics Box Feature Bar.
6 At the Box Content dialog box, choose Filename, then key the name of the document you want inserted into the table box.
7 Choose OK or press Enter.

Exercise 4 Inserting a Document into a Table Box

1. At a clear editing window, create a table box and insert the document *block01.wpd* into the box by completing the following steps:
    a. Choose Graphics, then Custom Box; or click on the Custom Box button on the Graphics Toolbar.
    b. At the Custom Box dialog box, select *Table* in the Style Name list box.
    c. Choose OK or press Enter.
    d. Choose Content from the Graphics Box Feature Bar.
    e. At the Box Content dialog box, choose Filename, then key **block01.wpd** (you may need to include the disk drive letter and path).
    f. Choose OK or press Enter.
    g. Choose Close at the Graphics Box Feature Bar.
2. Change the viewing mode to Two Page to see how the document displays on the entire page, then change the viewing mode back to Page.
3. Save the document and name it c17ex04.
4. Print c17ex04.
5. Close c17ex04.

Like a text box, a table box has thick top and bottom borders and no left or right borders. A table box is one-half the distance between the left and right margins and is inserted at the right margin. If the left and right margins are set at the default of 1 inch, the table box will be 3.25 inches wide. The height of the table box depends on what is inserted in the table.

Creating a User Box

A variety of boxes can be created for different situations. It does not matter what you insert inside a box. You can insert text in a figure box, or a graphics image in a text box. The reason WordPerfect offers the variety of boxes it does is to provide different border and fill styles. Additionally, you can use different boxes within the same document to keep information organized.

A user box can be created for any particular situation. A user box has no borders. It is inserted at the right margin and is 3.25 inches wide. You can insert a previously created document into a user box or key text directly into the box.

Exercise 5 Inserting a Document into a User Box

1. At a clear editing window, create a user box and insert the document *notice01.wpd* into the box by completing the following steps:
    a. Choose Graphics, then Custom Box; or click on the Custom Box button on the Graphics Toolbar.
    b. At the Custom Box dialog box, select *User* in the Style Name list box.
    c. Choose OK or press Enter.
    d. Choose Content from the Graphics Box Feature Bar.
    e. At the Box Content dialog box, choose Filename, then key **notice01.wpd** (you may need to include the disk drive letter and path).

f. Choose OK or press Enter.
g. Choose Close at the Graphics Box Feature Bar.
2. Save the document and name it c17ex05.
3. Print c17ex05.
4. Close c17ex05.

Creating a Button Box

A button box can be created for items such as a keystroke, function key, or an icon. Unlike text, figure, table, and user boxes, a button box is inserted at the left margin at the location where the insertion point is positioned and is approximately 1 inch wide. Figure 17.4 displays a sample button box.

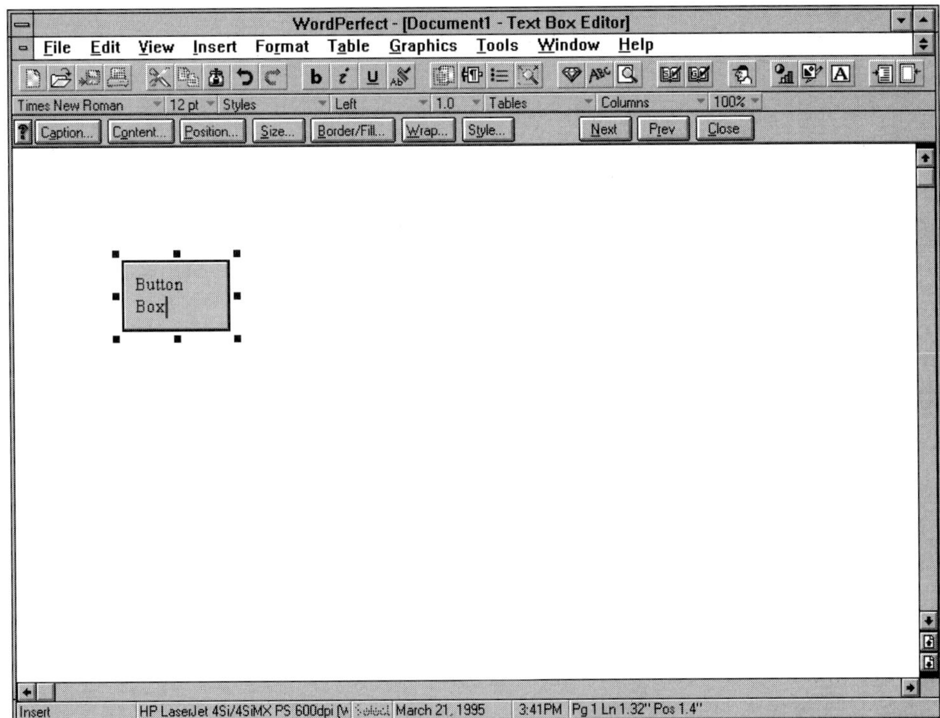

Figure 17.4
Button Box

To create a button box containing text inside, you would complete the following steps:

1. Position the insertion point where the button box is to appear.
2. Choose Graphics, then Custom Box; or click on the Custom Box button on the Graphics Toolbar.
3. At the Custom Box dialog box, select *Button* in the Style Name list box.
4. Choose OK or press Enter.
5. Choose Content from the Graphics Box Feature Bar.
6. At the Box Content dialog box, choose Content, then Text.
7. Choose Edit. (This causes the insertion point to move into the button box.)
8. Key the text you want in the button box.
9. After keying the text, choose Close.

Exercise 6 Adding Button Boxes to a Memo

1. At a clear editing window, key the top portion of the memo shown in figure 17.5 in an appropriate memorandum format. After keying the first paragraph of the memo, press Enter twice, then create the button boxes and text by completing the following steps:
   a. Press the Tab key once.
   b. Choose Graphics, then Custom Box; or click on the Custom Box button on the Graphics Toolbar.
   c. At the Custom Box dialog box, select *Button* in the Style Name list box.
   d. Choose OK or press Enter.
   e. Choose Content from the Graphics Box Feature Bar.
   f. At the Box Content dialog box, choose Content, then Text.
   g. Choose Edit. (This causes the insertion point to move into the button box.)
   h. With the insertion point positioned in the button box, complete the following steps:
      (1) Change the font size to 10 points.
      (2) Press Shift + F7 to move the insertion point to the horizontal center of the button box.
      (3) Key **Caption.**
   i. Choose Close to close the Graphics Box Feature Bar.
   j. Press the Tab key once, then key the equal sign (=).
   k. Press the Tab key once, then key the text after the Caption button as shown in figure 17.5.
   l. Press Enter twice, then create the remaining buttons and text following steps similar to those in 1a through 1k.
2. After creating the last button box and the text after the button box, press Enter twice, then key the last paragraph, reference initials, and document name for the memo.
3. When the memo is completed, save it and name it c17ex06.
4. Print c17ex06.
5. Close c17ex06.

Figure 17.5

DATE: April 3, 1997; TO: Newsletter Staff; FROM: Tonya Lowe, Editor; SUBJECT: GRAPHICS IN WORDPERFECT

One of the reasons we upgraded to WordPerfect 6.1 for Windows was for the expanded graphics capabilities. As we learn to use this new version, I would encourage you all to experiment with buttons on the Graphics Box Feature Bar. Some of the buttons available on the Graphics Box Feature Bar include the following:

= Create a caption for the box.

= Determine the contents of the box.

= Position the box horizontally and vertically.

= Determine width and height of the box.

A training session has been planned for early next month. I will contact all of you before the training to find out your specific needs.

xx:c17ex06

Creating a Watermark

A watermark is a lightened image that displays on the entire page. Text can be inserted over the watermark creating a document with a foreground and a background. The foreground is the text and the background is the watermark image. Figure 17.6 shows an example of a document containing a watermark image.

Important!!
All First-Year Residents
Operating Room Protocol
May 6, 1997
1:00 p.m. to 4:30 p.m.
Operating Room 3

Figure 17.6
Watermark Image

To create a watermark, you would complete the following steps:

1. Choose Graphics, then Custom Box; or click on the Custom Box button on the Graphics Toolbar.
2. At the Custom Box dialog box, select *Watermark* in the Style Name list box.
3. Choose OK or press Enter.
4. Choose Content from the Graphics Box Feature Bar.
5. At the Box Content dialog box, click on the file folder icon to the right of the Filename text box. This causes the Select File dialog box to display.
6. At the Select File dialog box, double-click on the desired image document name.
7. At the Box Content dialog box, choose OK or press Enter.
8. Choose Close to remove the Graphics Box Feature Bar.

Exercise 7 Inserting a Watermark Image

1. At a clear editing window, open letter04.
2. Save the document with Save As and name it c17ex07.
3. Create a watermark image with the document named **tiger_j.wpg** by completing the following steps:
   a. Choose Graphics, then Custom Box; or click on the Custom Box button on the Graphics Button Bar.
   b. At the Custom Box dialog box, select *Watermark* in the Style Name list box.
   c. Choose OK or press Enter.
   d. Choose Content from the Graphics Box Feature Bar.
   e. At the Box Content dialog box, click on the file folder icon to the right of the Filename text box. This causes the Select File dialog box to display.
   f. At the Select File dialog box, click on the down-pointing arrow in the Filename list box until *tiger_j.wpg* is visible, then double-click on *tiger_j.wpg*.
   g. At the Box Content dialog box, choose OK.
   h. Choose Close to remove the Graphics Box Feature Bar.
4. Save the document again with the same name (c17ex07).
5. Change the viewing mode to Two Page to see how the document displays on the entire page, then change the viewing mode back to Page.
6. Print c17ex07.
7. Close c17ex07.

Editing a Box

When a box is inserted in a document, the Graphics Box Feature Bar is displayed. If you have closed the Graphics Box Feature Bar and then want to redisplay it, position the arrow pointer inside a box, then click the *right* mouse button. From the drop-down menu that displays, click on Feature Bar.

The options available at the Graphics Box Feature Bar can be used to edit the box. The same editing options are available when you click the *right* mouse button inside an image or a box. To access options from the Graphics Box Feature Bar with the mouse, click on the desired option. If you are using the keyboard, press Alt + Shift + *x* (where *x* represents the underlined letter of the desired option).

Creating a Caption

A caption can be created for a box that displays information such as the box number and description of the box contents. WordPerfect includes a default caption for each type of box as shown in figure 17.7.

Text box	=	1
Figure box	=	**Figure 1**
Table box	=	**Table 1**
User box	=	1
Button box	=	(Not applicable)
Watermark	=	(Not applicable)

Figure 17.7
Default Box Captions

To create a caption, choose Caption from the Graphics Box Feature Bar. To do this with the mouse, click on Caption. If you are using the keyboard, press Alt + Shift + A. When you choose Caption, the Box Caption dialog box shown in figure 17.8 displays. Use options at this dialog box to customize a caption. You can also create a caption by positioning the arrow pointer inside a graphics box, clicking the right mouse button, then clicking on Create Caption at the pop-up QuickMenu™. If you want to display the Box Caption dialog box, choose Caption instead of Create Caption.

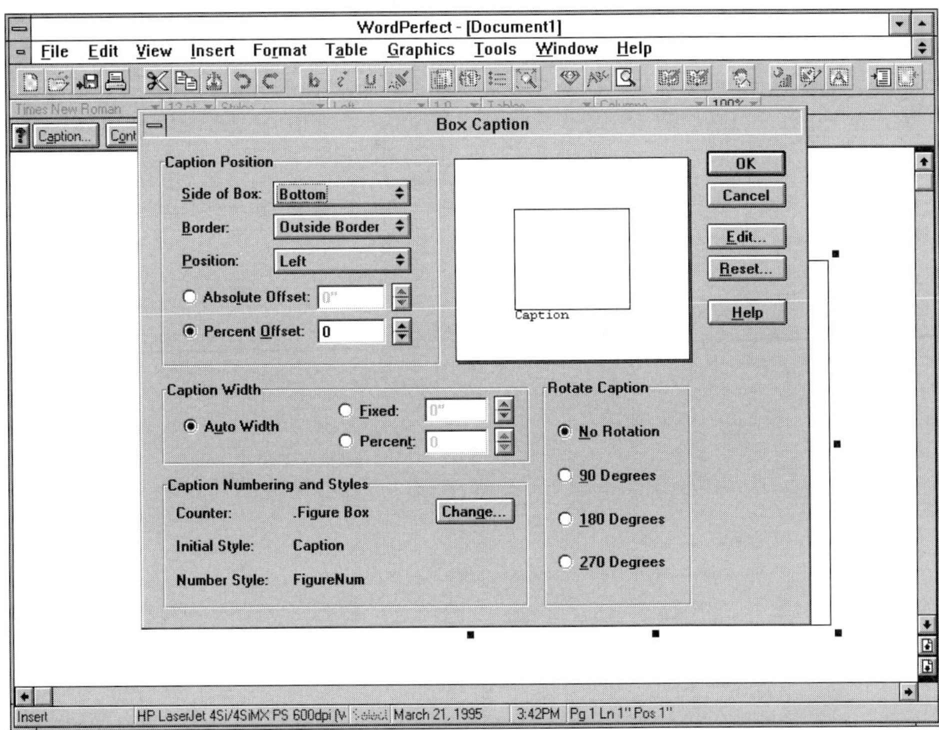

Figure 17.8
Box Caption Dialog Box

Exercise 8 Creating Captions for Figure Boxes

1. At a clear editing window, open c17ex03.
2. Save the document with Save As and name it c17ex08.
3. Create a caption for the figure box containing the image of the crane that is positioned at the left side of the box and rotated 90 degrees by completing the following steps:
   a. Position the arrow pointer inside the figure box containing the image of the crane, click the right mouse button, then choose Caption.
   b. At the Box Caption dialog box, choose Side of Box, then Left.
   c. Choose 90 Degrees in the Rotate Caption section.
   d. Choose Edit.
   e. At the caption editing window, complete the following steps:
      (1) Press Ctrl + B to turn on bold.
      (2) Key a colon (:).
      (3) Press the space bar twice.
      (4) Key **Crane.**

(5) Choose Close to close the Box Caption editing window.

4. Create a caption for the second figure box (the one containing the image of the hot air balloons) that reads **Balloons** by completing steps similar to those in steps 3a through 3g.
5. Create a caption for the third figure box (the one containing the image of the dragon) that reads **Dragon** by completing steps similar to those in steps 3a through 3g.
6. Save the document again with the same name (c17ex08).
7. Print c17ex08.
8. Close c17ex08.

Changing Content Options

If you choose Content from the Graphics Box Feature Bar, the Box Content dialog box shown in figure 17.9 displays. At this dialog box you can change the box contents. For example, you can specify the contents of the box such as an image, text, equation, image on disk, or empty. At the Box Content dialog box you can also specify the horizontal position of the contents of the box (left, right, or centered within the box) and the vertical position of the contents of the box (top, bottom, or centered within the box). You can also rotate the contents of the box.

Figure 17.9
Box Content Dialog Box

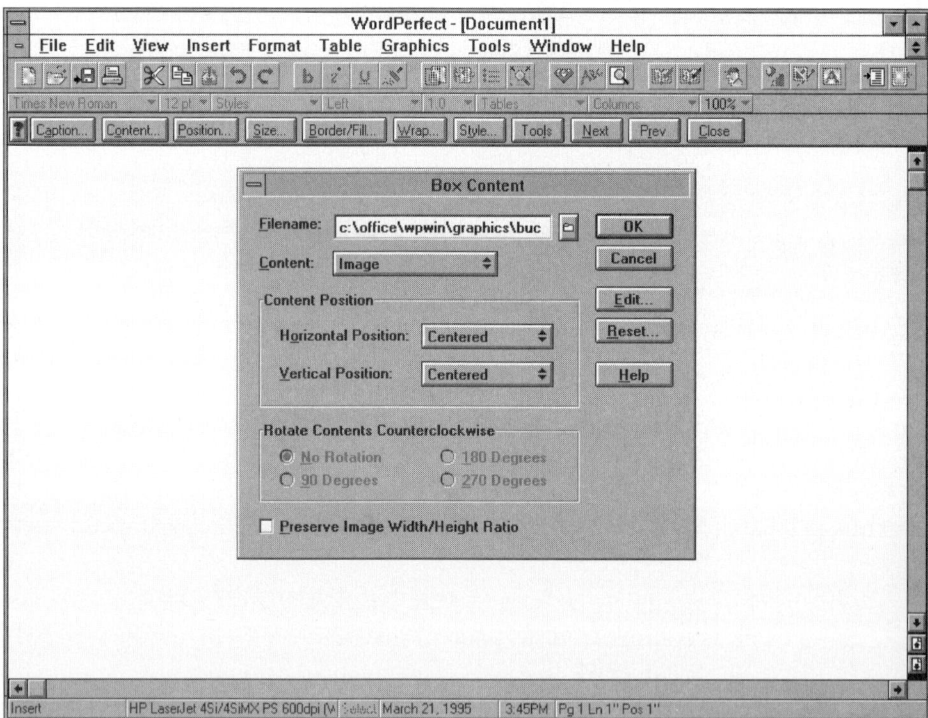

Changing the Box Position

If you choose Position from the Graphics Box Feature Bar, the Box Position dialog box shown in figure 17.10 displays. With options in the Box Placement section of the Box Position dialog box, you can determine where the box is anchored. The default option is determined by the type of box. For example, a figure box is anchored in the current paragraph. The default setting for a figure box is Put Box in Current Paragraph. Table, text, and user boxes are also anchored to the current paragraph.

At the Box Position dialog box you can also change the horizontal and vertical placement of the box. The horizontal and vertical options vary depending on the type of box and the type of anchor.

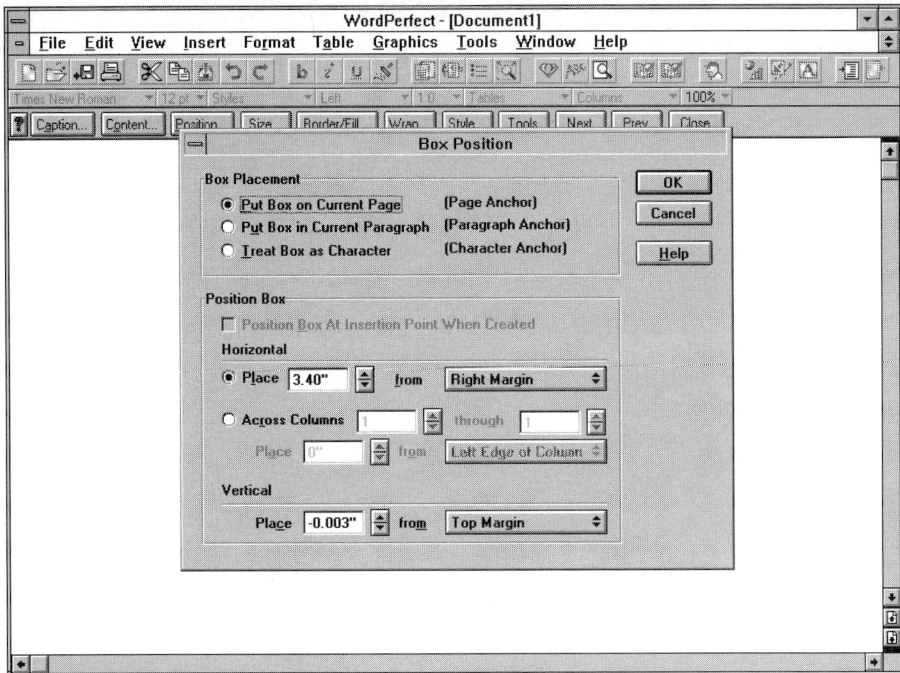

Figure 17.10
Box Position Dialog Box

Exercise 9 Manipulating Text Box Elements

1. At a clear editing window, create a text box centered on the page using the mouse by completing the following steps:
   a. Click on the Text Box button on the Graphics Toolbar.
   b. Click on the Content button on the Graphics Box Feature Bar.
   c. At the Box Content dialog box, position the insertion point inside the Filename text box, then click the left mouse button.
   d. Key **block02.wpd** (you may need to include the disk drive letter and path), then click on OK.
   e. At the question, *Insert file into box?*, click on Yes.
   f. Click on the Position button on the Graphics Box Feature Bar.
   g. At the Box Position dialog box, position the tip of the arrow pointer inside the radio button before the Put Box on Current Page, then click the left mouse button.
   h. Position the arrow pointer in the box to the right of the Horizontal Place text box (the box containing *Right Margin*), hold down the left mouse button, drag the arrow pointer to Center of Paragraph, then release the mouse button.
   i. Position the arrow pointer in the box to the right of the Vertical Place text box (the box containing *Top Margin*), hold down the left mouse button, drag the arrow pointer to Center of Margins, then release the mouse button.
   j. Click on the OK button at the upper right side of the dialog box.
   k. Click on the Close button on the Graphics Box Feature Bar.
2. Save the document and name it c17ex09.
3. Print c17ex09.
4. Close c17ex09.

Changing the Box Size

By default, a graphics box is one-half the width of the text line. For example, if the left and right margins are set at 1 inch, the graphics box is 3.25 inches wide (one-half the measurement of the text line). The height of the graphics box is automatically determined by WordPerfect. The height changes depending on what is inserted in the box.

The box size can be changed with the Size option from the Graphics Box Feature Bar. When you choose Size from the Graphics Box Feature Bar, the Box Size dialog box shown in figure 17.11 displays. Make any desired changes to the width and/or height of the box, then choose OK. In exercise 10 you will be changing the width and height of a box.

Figure 17.11
Box Size Dialog Box

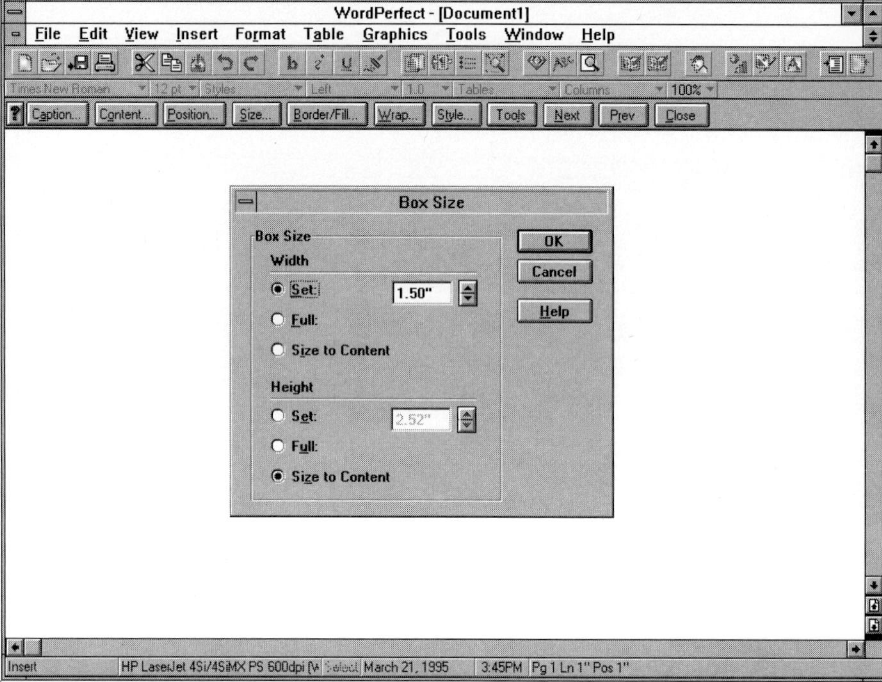

Exercise 10 Creating and Editing a Figure Box

1. At a clear editing window, create a figure box with the image *buck.wpg* inserted, change the size of the box, and add a caption by completing the following steps:
   a. Click on the Custom Box button on the Graphics Toolbar.
   b. At the Custom Box dialog box, double-click on *Figure* in the Style Name list box.
   c. Choose Content from the Graphics Box Feature Bar.
   d. At the Box Content dialog box, click on the file folder icon to the right of Filename text box.
   e. At the Select File dialog box, click on the down-pointing arrow in the Filename list box until the image document named *buck.wpg* is visible, then double-click on *buck.wpg*.
   f. Click on OK at the Box Content dialog box.
   g. Click on the Position button on the Graphics Box Feature Bar.
   h. At the Box Position dialog box, position the tip of the arrow pointer in the radio button before Put Box on Current Page, then click the left mouse button.
   i. Click on OK.
   j. Click on the Size button on the Graphics Box Feature Bar.
   k. At the Box Size dialog box, position the tip of the arrow pointer in the radio button before the Full option in the Width section, then click the left mouse button.
   l. Position the tip of the arrow pointer in the radio button before the Full option in the Height section, then click the left mouse button.
   m. Click on OK.
   n. Click on the Caption button on the Graphics Box Feature Bar.
   o. At the Box Caption dialog box, click on Edit.

   p. Key **Deer** bolded and separated from **Figure 1** by two spaces.
   q. Click on the Close button on the Graphics Box Feature Bar.
2. Save the document and name it c17ex10.
3. Print c17ex10.
4. Close c17ex10.

Exercise 11 Creating and Editing a User Box

1. At a clear editing window, create a user box containing a border image, then change the box anchor and size using the mouse by completing the following steps:
   a. Click on the Custom Box button on the Graphics Toolbar.
   b. At the Custom Box dialog box, double-click on *User* in the Style Name list box.
   c. Click on the Content button on the Graphics Box Feature Bar.
   d. At the Box Content dialog box, position the arrow pointer in the Content list box (containing the word *Empty*), hold down the left mouse button, drag the arrow pointer to Image, then release the mouse button.
   e. Position the arrow pointer on the file folder icon to the right of the Filename text box, then click the left mouse button.
   f. At the Select File dialog box, position the arrow pointer on the document named *bord01p.wpg* in the Filename list box, then double-click the left mouse button.
   g. At the Box Content dialog box, click on OK.
   h. Click on the Position button on the Graphics Box Feature Bar.
   i. At the Box Position dialog box, position the tip of the arrow pointer in the radio button before Put Box on Current Page, then click the left mouse button.
   j. Click on OK.
   k. Click on the Size button on the Graphics Box Feature Bar.
   l. At the Box Size dialog box, position the tip of the arrow pointer in the radio button before the Full option in the Width section, then click the left mouse button.
   m. Position the tip of the arrow pointer in the radio button before the Full option in the Height section, then click the left mouse button.
   n. Click on OK.
   o. Click on the Close button on the Graphics Box Feature Bar.
2. Change the viewing mode to Two Page to see how the border image displays on the entire page, then change the viewing mode back to Page. (At the Two Page view, you may need to press Alt + Pg Up to move the insertion point to page 1.)
3. Save the document and name it c17ex11.
4. Print c17ex11.
5. Close c17ex11.

Changing Box Border and Fill Styles

Graphics boxes have varying borders. For example, a figure box has a border of a single line on all sides. A text box has thick top and bottom borders and no left or right border. If you choose the Border/Fill button from the Graphics Box Feature Bar, the Box Border/Fill Styles dialog box shown in figure 17.12 displays. At this dialog box, you can customize the border and the fill of a box. When a change is made, the change is reflected in the Preview Box at the right side of the dialog box. You can also display this dialog box by positioning the arrow pointer in a box, clicking the right mouse button, then clicking on Border/Fill at the pop-up QuickMenu.

Figure 17.12
Box Border/Fill Styles Dialog Box

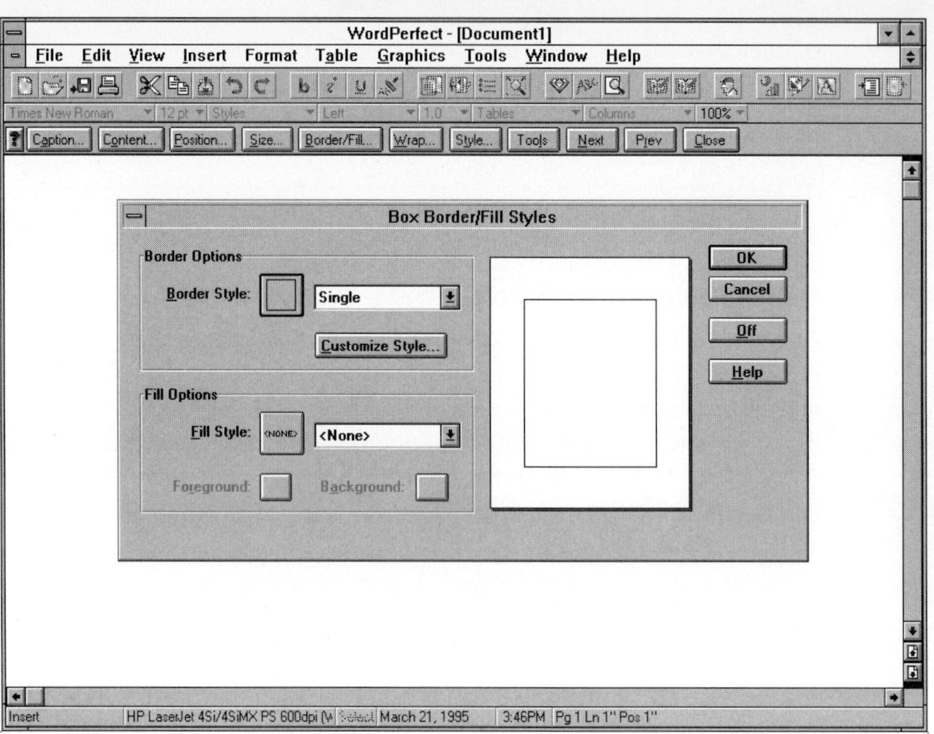

Exercise 12 Changing Box Border Styles

1. At a clear editing window, open c17ex03.
2. Save the document with Save As and name it c17ex12.
3. Change the border style to Double for the first figure box by completing the following steps:
   a. Position the arrow pointer inside the first figure box, hold down the right mouse button, drag the arrow pointer to Border/Fill, then release the mouse button.
   b. At the Box Border/Fill Styles dialog box, position the arrow pointer on the button after the Border Style, then click the left mouse button.
   c. Position the arrow pointer on the Double option (the first option from the left in the third row), then click the left mouse button.
   d. Click on OK.
   e. Click outside the box to deselect it.
4. Change the border style to Thick Top/Bottom for the second figure box by completing steps similar to those in steps 3a through 3e. (The Thick Top/Bottom option is the sixth option from the left in the second row.)
5. Change the border style to Shadow for the third figure box by completing steps similar to those in steps 3a through 3e. (The Shadow option is the sixth option from the left in the first row.)
6. Save the document again with the same name (c17ex12).
7. Print c17ex12.
8. Close c17ex12.

Exercise 13 Changing Box Border Style and Fill

1. At a clear editing window, open c17ex10.
2. Save the document with Save As and name it c17ex13.
3. Change the border style to Thick/Thin 2 and insert 20% fill in the figure box by completing the following steps:
   a. Position the arrow pointer inside the figure box, click the right mouse button, position the arrow pointer on Feature Bar, then click the left mouse button.
   b. At the Graphics Box Feature Bar, click on the Border/Fill button.
   c. At the Box Border/Fill Styles dialog box, position the arrow pointer on the button after the Border Style option, then click the left mouse button.
   d. Position the arrow pointer on the Thick/Thin 2 option (the fourth option from the left in the third row), then click the left mouse button.
   e. Position the arrow pointer on the button after the Fill Style option, then click the left mouse button.
   f. Position the arrow pointer on the 20% Fill option (the fourth option from the left in the first row), then click the left mouse button.
   g. Click on OK.
   h. Click on the Close button on the Graphics Box Feature Bar.
4. Save the document with the same name (c17ex13).
5. Print c17ex13.
6. Close c17ex13.

Changing Foreground and Background Color

If fill has been added to a box, the foreground and/or background color of the box can be changed. When you add a fill, then choose Foreground or Background, a box of color options displays.

The foreground and background color will display in the editing window, but will not print unless you are using a color printer. To display the Foreground box of color options with the mouse, click on the button immediately right of the Foreground option. If you are using the keyboard, press Alt + R, then press the space bar. At the box of color options, select the desired color. To do this with the mouse, position the arrow pointer on the desired color option, then click the left mouse button. If you are using the keyboard, move the insertion point to the desired color, then press Enter. When a change is made to the Foreground or Background options, the change is reflected in the Preview Box at the right side of the dialog box.

Exercise 14 Changing Foreground Color

1. At a clear editing window, open c17ex11.
2. Save the document with Save As and name it c17ex14.
3. Change the foreground color of the user box to blue by completing the following steps:
   a. Position the arrow pointer inside the user box, click the right mouse button, position the arrow pointer on Border/Fill, then click the left mouse button.
   b. At the Box Border/Fill Styles dialog box, click on the box to the right of the Fill Style option.
   c. At the list of Fill Style options, position the arrow pointer on the 10% Fill option (the third option from the left in the top row), then click the left mouse button.
   d. Click on the box to the right of the Foreground option.
   e. At the box of color options, position the arrow pointer on the tenth option from the left side in the top row (the blue color), then click the left mouse button.

f. Click on the OK button at the right side of the Box Border/Fill Styles dialog box.
g. Click outside the box to deselect it.

4. Save the document again with the same name (c17ex14).
5. Print c17ex14. (If you are not printing with a color printer, this step may be optional. Check with your instructor.)
6. Close c17ex14.

Wrapping Text Around a Box

Choose the Wrap button from the Graphics Box Feature Bar to specify how text flows around a box. When you choose Wrap, the Wrap Text dialog box shown in figure 17.13 displays. You can also display the Wrap Text dialog box by positioning the arrow pointer in a box, clicking the right mouse button, then clicking on Wrap at the pop-up QuickMenu. With the options in the Wrapping Type section of the Wrap Text dialog box, you can specify whether text in a document wraps around the side of the box (Square), wraps around the contours of the image (Contour), does not wrap on either side of the box (Neither Side), or wraps through the box (No wrap [through]). WordPerfect provides a visual representation of each of these options. Figure 17.14 also shows an example of wrapping text. The first image in the figure wraps text around the square. The second image contours the text around the image.

Figure 17.13
Wrap Text Dialog Box

Figure 17.14
Text Flow Around Graphics Images

This is a sample paragraph with a graphics image positioned within the paragraph. The first example displays with the text contoured around the borders of the box. The second example displays with text contoured around the image. With the Wrapping Type and Wrap Text Around options, you can also change the flow of text on the left side, right side, both sides, neither side, or through the box.

This is a sample paragraph with a graphics image positioned within the paragraph. The first example displays with the text contoured around the borders of the box. The second example displays with text contoured around the image. With the Wrapping Type and Wrap Text Around options, you can also change the flow of text on the left side, right side, both sides, neither side, or through the box.

The options in the Wrap Text Around section of the Wrap Text dialog box are used to specify where you want text wrapped in relation to the box. You can choose to wrap text around the largest side of the box, the left side, the right side, or both sides of the box. These options are also visually represented in the dialog box.

Exercise 15 Using the Wrap Text Option

1. At a clear editing window, open c17ex11.
2. Save the document with Save As and name it c17ex15.
3. Change the flow of text through the user box by completing the following steps:
   a. Position the arrow pointer inside the user box, click the right mouse button, position the arrow pointer on Wrap, then click the left mouse button.
   b. At the Wrap Text dialog box, click on No Wrap (through). (To do this, position the tip of the arrow pointer in the No Wrap (through) radio button, then click the left mouse button.)
   c. Click on the OK button at the right side of the dialog box.
   d. Click outside the user box to deselect it.
4. Key text that will print inside the border image by completing the following steps:
   a. Insert a code to center text on the current page.
   b. Change the font to 24-point Ribbon131 Bd BT.
   c. Press Shift + F7, then key **Denver Memorial Hospital Gift Shop**.
   d. Press Enter twice.
   e. Press Shift + F7, then key **New Hours**.
   f. Press Enter twice.
   g. Press Shift + F7, then key **8:00 a.m. to 8:30 p.m.**.
   h. Press Enter twice.
   i. Press Shift + F7, then key **Monday through Saturday**.
   j. Press Enter twice.
   k. Press Shift + F7, then key **Stop by to see all our new items!**
5. Save the document again with the same name (c17ex15).
6. Change the viewing mode to Two Page to make sure the text is inside the border and centered on the page, then change the viewing mode back to Page.
7. Print c17ex15.
8. Close c17ex15.

Changing the Box Style

You can change the style of box with the Style button from the Graphics Box Feature Bar. When you choose Style, the Box Style dialog box shown in figure 17.15 displays. Changing a box style changes the box size and border.

Figure 17.15
Box Style Dialog Box

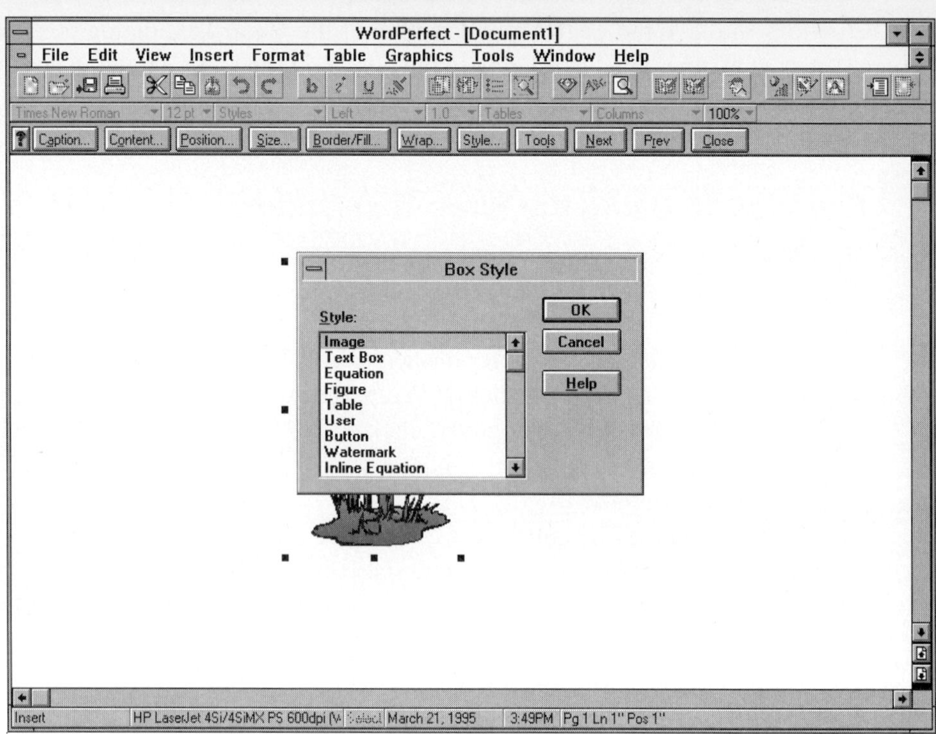

Editing with the Image Tool Palette

WordPerfect provides an Image Tool palette that contains a variety of tools you can use to edit or customize the contents of a figure box or a watermark image box. The Image Tool palette is not available for text, table, or button boxes. It is available for a watermark box and also for a figure box and user box containing a graphics image. To display the Image Tool palette as shown in figure 17.16, choose Tools from the Graphics Box Feature Bar. You can also display the Image Tool palette by positioning the arrow pointer in a box, clicking the right mouse button, then clicking on Image Tools at the pop-up QuickMenu.

Figure 17.16
Image Tool Palette

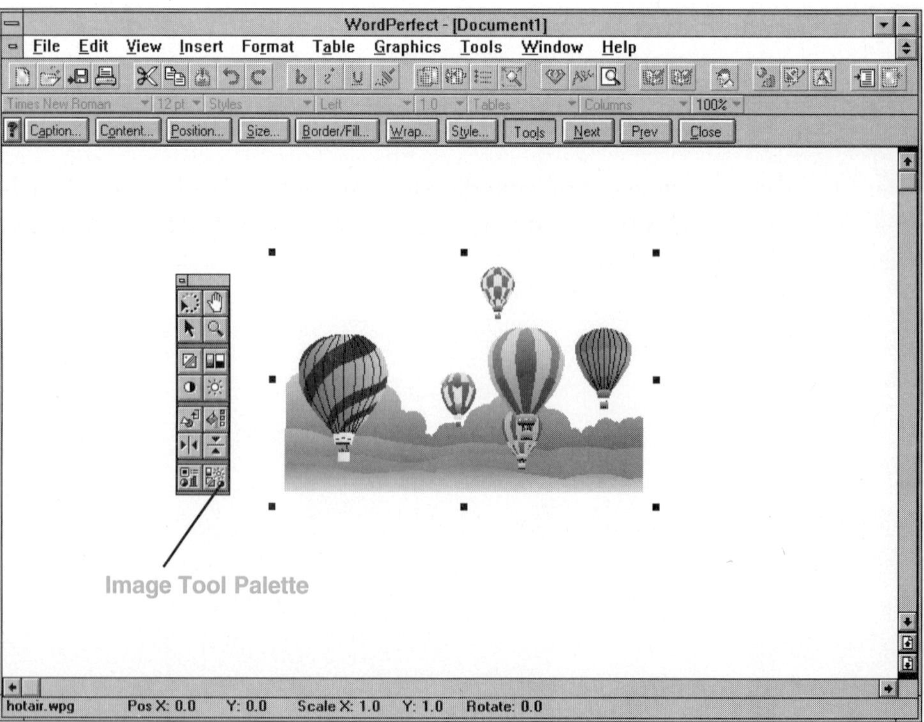

When you position the arrow pointer on a tool on the Image Tool palette, information about the tool displays in the Title Bar at the top of the document window. Figure 17.17 identifies each tool, what will display in the Title Bar when the arrow pointer is positioned on the tool, and a brief description of the tool.

Tool	Name	Tool Description
	Rotate	Rotate the image around a selected point. To do this, click on the tool. This causes a point of rotation to display at the middle of the graphics box. Move the point of rotation by dragging it to a new location with the mouse.
	Move	Move the image within the box. To do this, click on the tool. This causes the arrow pointer to turn into a hand. Position the hand on the box image, hold down the left mouse button, then drag the mouse.
	Select	Re-enable the mouse pointer for box movement. Choose this tool to move or resize the graphics box. When you click on this tool and then move the arrow pointer inside the graphics box, the arrow pointer turns into a four-headed arrow. To move a graphics box, hold down the left mouse button, drag the arrow pointer to the desired position, then release the mouse button.
	Scale	Scale the image (selected area, about image center, or reset). Use this tool to zoom in and out of an entire image or part of an image. When you click on the tool, three options display to the right of the palette. Use the magnifying glass icon to scale a specific area of an image. Use the icon containing the up- and down-pointing arrow to scale the entire image. The option containing **1:1** will return the image to its original size.
	Invert	Change the colors in the image to their complementary colors.
	B&W Attributes	Display the image in black and white only, and set threshold for blackness. When you click on the tool, a list of options displays. Use these options to set the blackness of the image. The darker the option, the darker the image.

Figure 17.17
Image Tool Palette Tools

Figure 17.17
Image Tool Palette Tools (cont.)

Tool	Name	Tool Description
	Contrast	Set the contrast level for the image. Use this tool to change the appearance between light and dark areas of a color. When you click on the Contrast tool, a list of contrast options displays. Choose one of the earlier options to decrease the contrast; choose one of the later options to increase the contrast.
	Brightness	Set the brightness level for the image. When you click on the tool a list of options displays. Choose one of the earlier options to increase the brightness; choose one of the later options to decrease the brightness.
	Reset All	Reset all image attributes. This returns the image to its original settings.
	Fill Attributes	Select normal, no fill, or white fill. Use this tool to make an image transparent or convert the image to an outline with a white fill. When you click on the tool a list of options displays. The first option will maintain the normal fill. Click on the second option to make the image transparent. Click on the third to convert the image to an outline with white fill.
	Mirror Vertical	Mirror the image around its vertical axis.
	Mirror Horizontal	Mirror the image around its horizontal axis.
	Image Edit	Edit the object with OLE server. Click on this tool to display the WordPerfect Draw™ program. (The WordPerfect Draw program is covered in chapter 18.)
	Image Settings	Move, scale, rotate, set color and fill attributes, etc. Click on this tool to display the Image Settings dialog box. At this dialog box, you can edit all image settings. The options available at this dialog box are the same options available with the tools from the Image Tool palette.

Exercise 16 Working with Contrast, Color, and Rotation

1. At a clear editing window, open c17ex03.
2. Save the document with Save As and name it c17ex16.
3. Flip the crane image on its vertical axis inside the first figure box and change the contrast of the image by completing the following steps:
   a. Position the arrow pointer inside the crane figure box, click the right mouse button, position the arrow pointer on Image Tools, then click the left mouse button.
   b. Click on the Contrast tool in the Image Tool palette. (The Contrast tool is the fourth option from the top of the palette in the first column.)
   c. At the list of Contrast options, click on the last option (butterfly) in the bottom row.
   d. Click on the Mirror Vertical tool on the Image Tool palette. (The Mirror Vertical tool is the second tool from the bottom in the first column.)
   e. Click outside the box to deselect it. This also removes the Image Tool palette.
4. Change to the complementary colors for the hot air balloon image in the second figure box by completing the following steps:
   a. Position the arrow pointer inside the hot air balloon figure box, click the right mouse button, position the arrow pointer on Image Tools, then click the left mouse button.
   b. Click on the Invert tool on the Image Tool palette. (The Invert tool is the third tool from the top of the palette in the first column.)
   c. Click outside the box to deselect it and remove the Image Tool palette.
5. Change the rotation of the dragon in the third figure box by completing the following steps:
   a. Position the arrow pointer inside the dragon figure box, click the right mouse button, position the arrow pointer on Image Tools, then click the left mouse button.
   b. Click on the Rotate tool on the Image Tool palette. (The Rotate tool is the first tool from the top of the palette in the first column.)
   c. Position the arrow pointer on the rotation handle in the upper left corner of the figure box until it turns into a double-headed arrow pointing diagonally, hold down the left mouse button, drag the arrow pointer down, then release the mouse button. (The dragon should be angled down and to the left.)
   d. Click outside the box to deselect it and remove the Image Tool palette.
6. Save the document again with the same name (c17ex16).
7. Change the viewing mode to Two Page to see how the images display on the entire page, then change the viewing mode back to Page.
8. Print c17ex16.
9. Close c17ex16.

Finding the Next or Previous Box

If you click on the Next button on the Graphics Box Feature Bar, WordPerfect will search and then display the next graphics box in the document. If there is no other graphics box, WordPerfect will display a not found message. Click on the Prev button on the Graphics Box Feature Bar to display the previous graphics box in the document.

Editing an Existing Box

A graphics box that has been inserted in a document can be edited. To edit an existing box, choose Graphics, then Edit Box; or click on the Edit Button on the Graphics Toolbar. At the Edit Box dialog box, enter the number of the box you want to edit in the Document Box Number text box, then choose OK or press Enter. WordPerfect finds the box and displays the graphics box in the editing window with the Graphics Box Feature Bar displayed. Edit the graphics box as desired, then close the Graphics Box Feature Bar. If there is only one graphics box in the document, the Box Find dialog box will not display. WordPerfect will automatically display this box and the Graphics Box Feature Bar.

Dragging a Box with the Mouse

When a graphics box is inserted in a document, the box can be moved to a different location using the mouse. To move a graphics box with the mouse, position the arrow pointer inside the graphics box, then click the left mouse button. This causes the mouse to turn into a four-headed arrow and sizing handles to appear as shown in figure 17.18.

Figure 17.18
Graphics Box with Sizing Handles

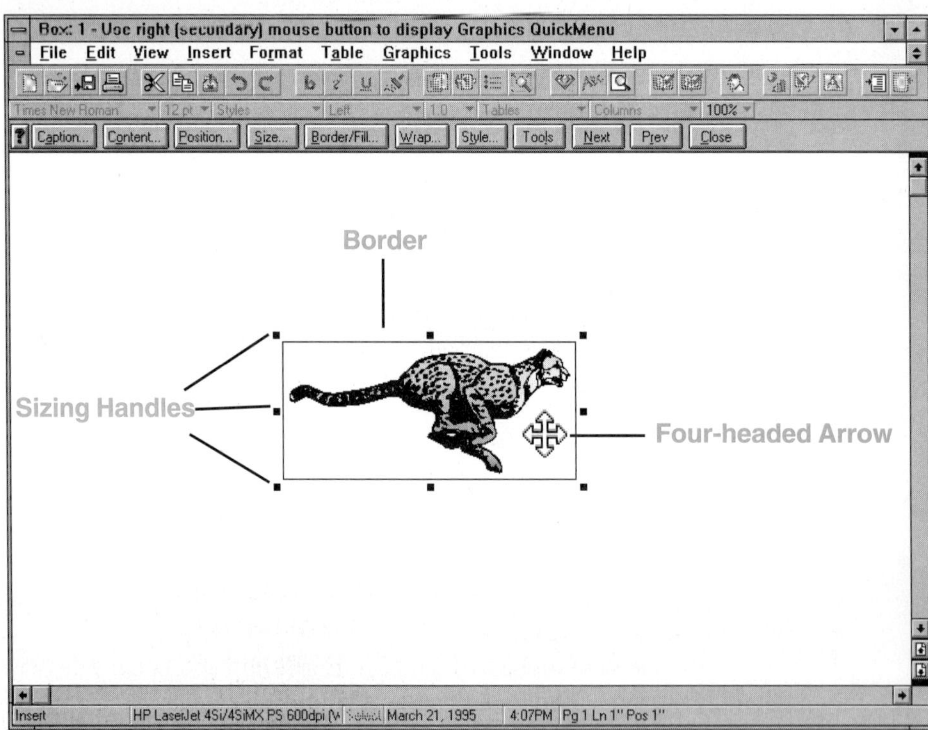

To move the box, hold down the left mouse button, then drag the four-headed arrow. As you drag the four-headed arrow, an outline border of the box follows. When the outline border is in the desired position in the document, release the mouse button. This causes the graphics box to display in the location of the outline border.

Using the mouse with the sizing handles, you can change the size of the graphics box. For example, to widen the graphics box, position the arrow pointer inside the graphics box, then click the left mouse button. Position the four-headed arrow on the sizing handle in the middle of the box at the left border until it turns into a double-headed horizontal arrow. Hold down the left mouse button, drag the double-headed arrow to the left, then release the button.

You can also widen the graphics box on the right side by completing similar steps. Make sure, however, that there is room at the right to widen the box. To make the box narrower, complete similar steps except drag the mouse into the box.

To make the box taller or shorter, position the four-headed arrow on the sizing handle at the top or bottom center of the box until the arrow pointer becomes a double-headed vertical arrow. Hold down the left mouse button, drag the double-headed arrow up or down, then release the mouse button.

If you position the four-headed arrow on any of the sizing handles at the corners of the border, the four-headed arrow becomes a double-headed arrow pointing diagonally. When it becomes a diagonally pointing double arrow, you can increase or decrease the width as well as the height of the box at the same time.

Exercise 17 Moving Figure Boxes

1. At a clear editing window, open c17ex03.
2. Save the document with Save As and name it c17ex17.
3. Move the first figure box to the middle of the editing window by completing the following steps:
   a. Position the arrow pointer inside the first figure box (the one containing the crane), then click the left button.
   b. Hold down the left mouse button, drag the border outline to approximately the middle of the left and right margins, then release the mouse button.
   c. Move the arrow pointer outside the figure box, then click the left mouse button. This deselects the figure box.
4. Move the second figure box to the middle of the editing window by completing steps similar to those in steps 3a through 3c.
5. Move the third figure box to the middle of the editing window by completing steps similar to those in steps 3a through 3c.
6. Save the document again with the same name (c17ex17).
7. Print c17ex17.
8. Close c17ex17.

Creating Horizontal and Vertical Lines

You can create horizontal and vertical lines in a document and adjust the width and shading of the lines. Horizontal and vertical lines can be used in a document to create lines in a document, separate sections, create a focal point, or add visual appeal.

Creating a Horizontal Line

To insert a horizontal line in a document, choose Graphics, then Horizontal Line; or click on the Horizontal Line button on the Graphics Toolbar. This inserts a horizontal line in the document at the location of the insertion point from the left margin to the right margin.

Creating a Vertical Line

Insert a vertical line in a document by choosing Graphics, then Vertical Line; or clicking on the Vertical Line button on the Graphics Toolbar. This inserts a vertical line in the document that extends from the top margin to the bottom margin and is positioned at the left margin.

Creating Customized Lines

If you use the Horizontal Line or Vertical Line button on the Graphics Toolbar, or the Horizontal Line or Vertical Line option from the Graphics drop-down menu, a default line is inserted in the document. If you want to create a customized horizontal or vertical line, click on the Custom Line button on the Graphics Toolbar or use the Custom Line option from the Graphics drop-down menu. When you click on the Custom Line button or choose Graphics, then Custom Line, the Create Graphics Line dialog box displays as shown in figure 17.19.

Figure 17.19
Create Graphics Line Dialog Box

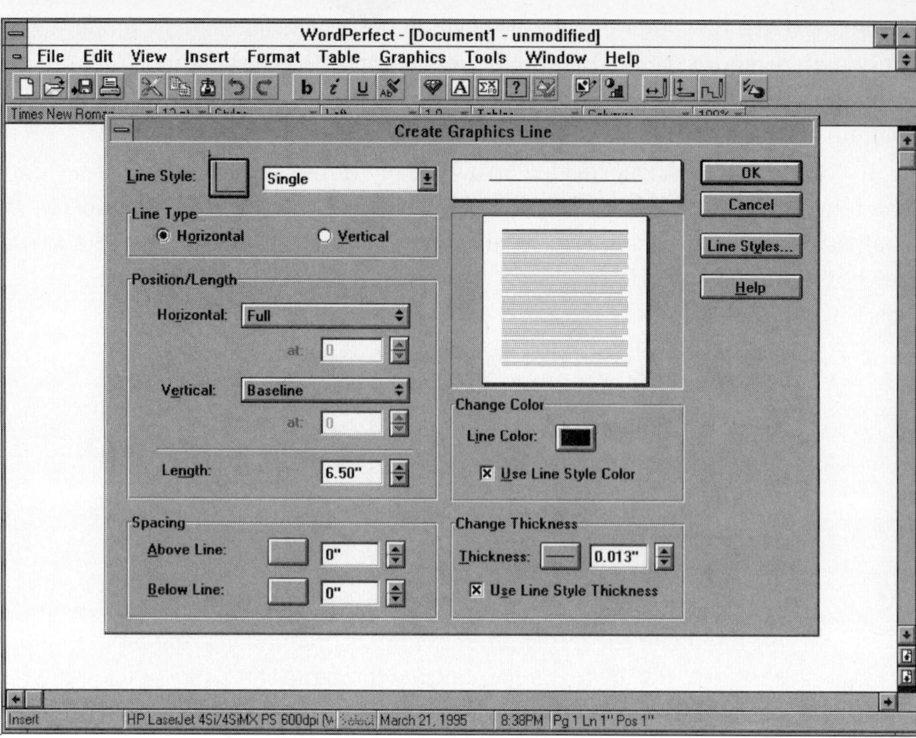

At the Create Graphics Line dialog box, specify the type of line desired in the document. The options available at this dialog box are explained in figure 17.20.

Figure 17.20
Create Graphics Line Dialog Box Options

Line Style	Change the line style for a horizontal or vertical line from the default of Single to one of the numerous style options available such as Double, Triple, Thick, Heavy, etc., with the Line Style option.
Line Type	Specify the type of line desired—Horizontal or Vertical—in the Line Type section. The default is Horizontal.
Position/Length	With the options from the Position/Length section, specify the horizontal and vertical position of the line as well as the length.
Spacing	Specify the spacing above and/or below a horizontal line or specify an offset measurement from a vertical line with options in the Spacing section.
Change Color	Change the line color with options from the Line Color option in the Change Color section.
Change Thickness	Specify the thickness of a horizontal or vertical line with the Thickness option in the Change Thickness section.

Exercise 18 Creating a Letterhead with Horizontal Lines

1. At a clear editing window, create the letterhead shown in figure 17.21 (the bottom line and the address and phone number will display in your document and print at the bottom of the page) by completing the following steps:
   a. Change the font to 18-point Arrus BT.
   b. Create a user box with the image **medical1.wpg** inserted with the following specifications:
      (1) Display the Box Position dialog box, select Put Box on Current Page, then choose OK to close the dialog box.
      (2) Display the Box Size dialog box, change the Width to Set at 1.5 inches, then choose OK to close the dialog box.
      (3) Choose Close to close the Graphics Box Feature Bar.
   c. Press Enter once, then key **DENVER MEMORIAL HOSPITAL**.
   d. Press Enter once, then create the horizontal line with a thickness of 4 points by completing the following steps:
      (1) Choose Graphics, then Custom Line.
      (2) At the Create Graphics Line dialog box, select the measurement currently displayed in the Thickness text box, then key **4p**. (The *p* specifies that the measurement is a point, rather than an inch.)
      (3) Choose OK to close the Create Graphics Line dialog box.
   e. Change the type size to 12 points.
   f. Press the Enter key until the insertion point is positioned at approximately Line 9.16".
   g. Create a horizontal line with a thickness of 2 points by completing steps similar to those in d(1) through d(3). (Key **2p** in the Thickness text box.)
   h. Press Enter once, press Alt + F7, then key **900 Colorado Boulevard**.
   i. Press Enter once, press Alt + F7, then key **Denver, CO 86530**.
   j. Press Enter once, press Alt + F7, then key **(303) 555-4400**.
2. Save the letterhead and name it c17ex18.
3. Print c17ex18.
4. Close c17ex18.

Figure 17.21

DENVER MEMORIAL HOSPITAL

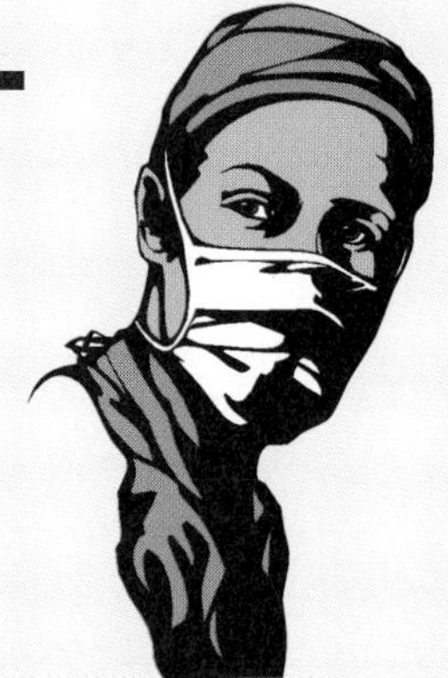

900 Colorado Boulevard
Denver, CO 86530
(303) 555-4400

Exercise 19 Creating Letterhead with Vertical and Horizontal Lines

1. At a clear editing window, create the letterhead shown in figure 17.22 (the vertical line in your letterhead will extend to the bottom margin) by completing the following steps:
   a. Create the vertical line by completing the following steps:
      (1) Choose Graphics, then Custom Line.
      (2) At the Create Graphics Line dialog box, choose Vertical in the Line Type section.
      (3) Click on the down-pointing arrow after the Line Style text box (the one containing the word *Single*), click on the down scroll arrow in the list box until *Thin/Thick 2* is visible, then click on *Thin/Thick 2*.
      (4) Choose OK to close the dialog box.
   b. Change the font to 18-point BernhardMod BT.
   c. Turn on bold, press Alt + F7, then key **LINCOLN HIGH SCHOOL**.
   d. Press Enter, then press the Tab key until the insertion point is positioned at 4".
   e. Create the short horizontal graphics line by completing the following steps:
      (1) Choose Graphics, then Custom Line.
      (2) At the Create Graphics Line dialog box, position the arrow pointer in the Horizontal text box (in the Position/Length section), hold down the left mouse button, drag the arrow pointer to Set in the pop-up menu, then release the mouse button.
      (3) Change the Line Style to Thin/Thick 2. (For assistance, refer to step a(3).)
      (4) Choose OK to close the dialog box.
   f. Press Enter, change the type size to 16 points, press Alt + F7, then key **345 North Baker Street**.
   g. Press Enter, press Alt + F7, then key **Salem, OR 97034**.
   h. Press Enter, press Alt + F7, then key **(509) 555-4566**.
2. Save the document and name it c17ex19.
3. Print c17ex19.
4. Close c17ex19.

Figure 17.22

LINCOLN HIGH SCHOOL

345 North Baker Street
Salem, OR 97034
(509) 555-4566

CHAPTER SUMMARY

- With WordPerfect's Graphics feature, you can insert a graphics image into a document and also create eight different graphics boxes including text, figure, table, user, button, watermark, equation, and inline equation.

Assessment 2

1. At a clear editing window, create the document shown in figure 17.23 by completing the following steps:
   a. Insert the graphics image named **medical1.wpg** in a user box. Change the Horizontal position of the box to Left Margin at the Box Position dialog box. Close the Graphics Box Feature Bar.
   b. At the editing window, complete the following steps:
      (1) Change the font to 12-point Arrus BT.
      (2) Press Enter five times, access the Center command, then key **IMPORTANT!!**.
      (3) Press Enter three times, access the Center command, then key **ALL FIRST-YEAR RESIDENTS**.
      (4) Continue until all text has been keyed.
2. Save the document and name it c17sa02.
3. Print c17sa02.
4. Close c17sa02.

Figure 17.23

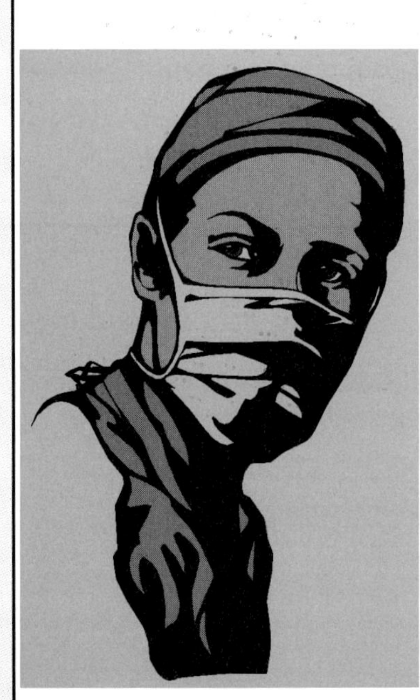

IMPORTANT!!

ALL FIRST-YEAR RESIDENTS

OPERATING ROOM PROTOCOL

MAY 6, 1997

1:00 p.m. to 4:30 p.m.

Operating Room 3

Assessment 3

1. At a clear editing window, key the memo shown in figure 17.24 in an appropriate memo format through the first paragraph. Create the text boxes by completing the following steps:
   a. Create a text box. Change the position of the text box to Center of Paragraph at the Box Position dialog box. Key the text in the text box as indicated in figure 17.24.
   b. After creating the first text box, press Enter eight times to move the insertion point below the first box.

c. Create the second text box with the same specifications as the first box.
d. After creating the second text box, press Enter seven times to move the insertion point below the second box.
e. Create the third text box with the same specifications as the first box.

2. After creating the third text box, press Enter eight times to move the insertion point a double space below the third box, then key the remaining text in the memo.
3. Save the memo and name it c17sa03.
4. Print c17sa03.
5. Close c17sa03.

Figure 17.24

DATE: May 15, 1997; TO: Joni Paulsen; FROM: Anne Maeda; SUBJECT: NEW EMPLOYEE BOOKLET

Thank you for letting me know about the next printing date for the New Employee Booklet. I have received recommendations from various employees to include the following additional items in the Caring Actions section of the booklet.

Listen actively:

Take time to listen. Give the person your full attention.

Be timely:

Respond quickly. Explain delays.

Explain what you are doing:

Make explanations brief and easy to understand. Answer questions honestly and kindly.

The sample typeset pages of the New Employee Booklet look very professional. I look forward to using the new booklet at orientations.

xx:c17sa03

Assessment 4

1. At a clear editing window, create the **dragn.wpg** image over the **windmill.wpg** image by completing the following steps:
   a. Insert the image named *windmill.wpg* into a user box. (Hint: To insert the **windmill.wpg** image into the user box, create a user box, display the Box Content dialog box, display the filenames, then double-click on *windmill.wpg*.)
   b. Change the anchor to Put Box on Current Page at the Box Position dialog box.
   c. Change the box width to Full and the height to Size to Content at the Box Size dialog box.
   d. Display the Wrap Text dialog box, then choose No Wrap (through).
   e. Close the Graphics Box Feature Bar.
   f. Insert the graphics image named **dragn.wpg** into a user box.
   g. Change the anchor to Put Box on Current Page at the Box Position dialog box.
   h. Change the box width to 2 inches and the height to Size to Content.
   i. Display the Wrap Text dialog box, then choose No Wrap (through).
   j. Close the Graphics Box Feature Bar.
2. Save the document and name it c17sa04.
3. Change the viewing mode to Two Page to see how the images display on the entire page, then change the viewing mode back to Page.
4. Print c17sa04.
5. Close c17sa04.

Assessment 5

1. At a clear editing window, create the letterhead shown in figure 17.25 by completing the following steps:
   a. Create a user box with the following specifications:
      (1) Insert the image named **crest.wpg**.
      (2) Display the Box Position dialog box, choose Put Box on Current Page, change the Horizontal position to Left Margin, then close the dialog box.
      (3) Display the Box Size dialog box, change the Width to Set at 1.5 inches, then close the dialog box.
   b. At the editing window, change the font to 14-point Humanst521 Lt BT.
   c. Turn on bold, press Enter once, press Alt + F7, then key **BLUE RIBBON PRODUCTS**.
   d. Key the address and telephone number at the right margin as shown in the figure.
   e. After keying the telephone number, press Enter, then create a horizontal line at the default settings except change the Thickness to 3 points.
2. Save the letterhead and name it c17sa05.
3. Print c17sa05.
4. Close c17sa05.

Figure 17.25

BLUE RIBBON PRODUCTS
4300 South Palm Drive
Mesa, AZ 85733
(602) 555-9776

Using WordPerfect Draw & TextArt 18

Upon successful completion of chapter 18, you will be able to enhance documents by creating shapes, images, or text in WordPerfect Draw and TextArt.

WordPerfect for Windows, version 6.1 provides many predesigned graphics images. You used some of these graphics images in exercises in chapter 17. If you would like to create your own graphics images, you can do so with WordPerfect Draw. This program was included with WordPerfect for Windows and provides many of the features of a standalone draw program. With TextArt®, you distort and modify text so it conforms to a variety of shapes.

In this chapter, you will learn the basic functions of WordPerfect Draw. For additional, more sophisticated ideas on how to use this program, please refer to the WordPerfect reference manual. With WordPerfect Draw, you can draw shapes, draw freehand, insert graphics images, and create and customize text.

Drawing Shapes

You can use WordPerfect Draw to draw a variety of shapes such as circles, squares, rectangles, ellipses, ovals, and much more. When using WordPerfect Draw to draw shapes, you would follow these basic steps:

1. Open WordPerfect Draw. To do this, choose Graphics, then Draw; or click on the Draw button on the Graphics Toolbar.
2. Draw the shape in the drawing area.
3. When you are done drawing, click on the Close button on the Draw Toolbar or click in the editing window outside the drawing area.
4. Deselect the box containing the draw objects. To do this, position the I-beam pointer in the editing window outside the box, then click the left mouse button.

When you click on the Close button on the Draw Toolbar, the shape you drew displays in the editing window and WordPerfect Draw is closed. What you drew is inserted in a box with no borders. This box is inserted at the left margin of the document and is approximately 5 inches wide and 4.5 inches tall. You can also close WordPerfect Draw by clicking in the editing window outside the draw area.

When you choose Graphics, then Draw; or click on the Draw button on the Graphics Toolbar, the Draw window shown in figure 18.1 displays.

Figure 18.1
Draw Window

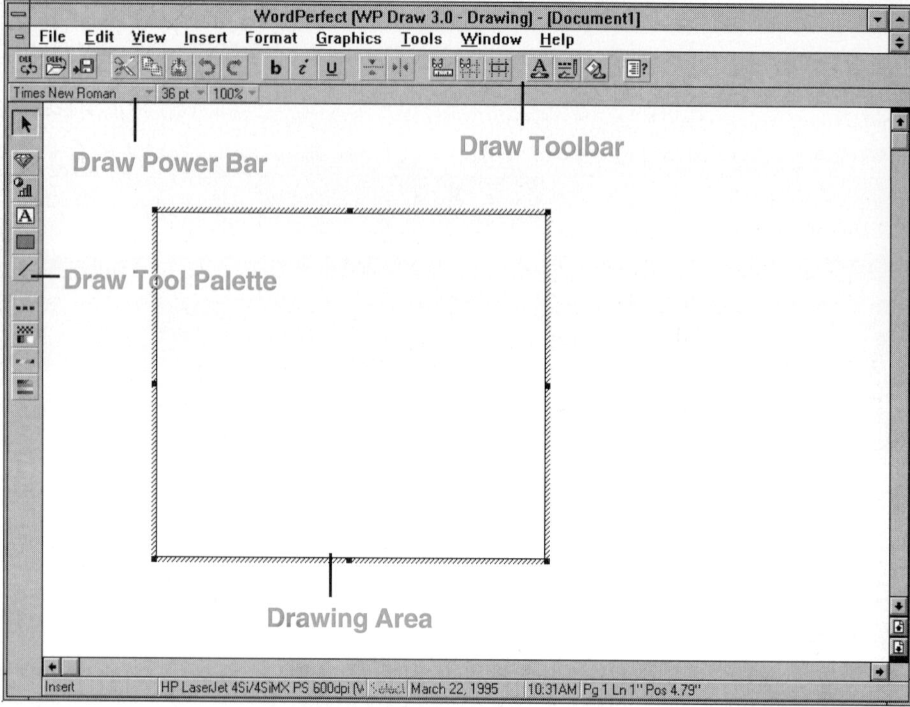

At the left side of the Draw window, the Draw Tool palette is displayed. This palette includes a variety of tools for selecting, drawing, and changing the fill and attributes of objects. The names of the tools are shown in figure 18.2. Two tools on the Draw Tool palette, Closed Object Tools and Line Object Tools, contain options for drawing closed shapes and line shapes.

Figure 18.2
Draw Tool Palette Tools

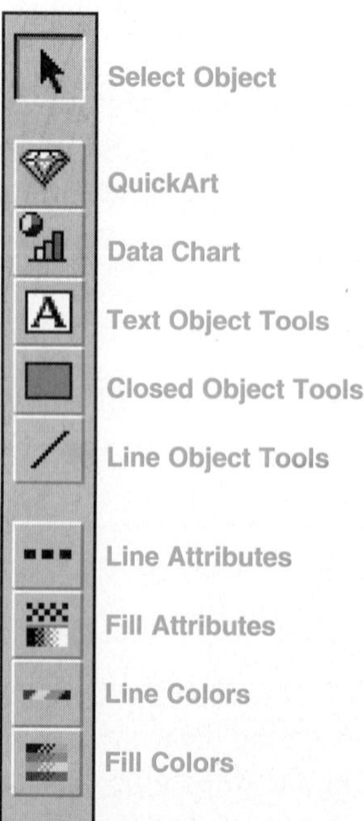

If you click on the Closed Object Tools tool, six shape options display as shown in figure 18.3. Click on the Line Object Tools tool and four line options display as shown in figure 18.3.

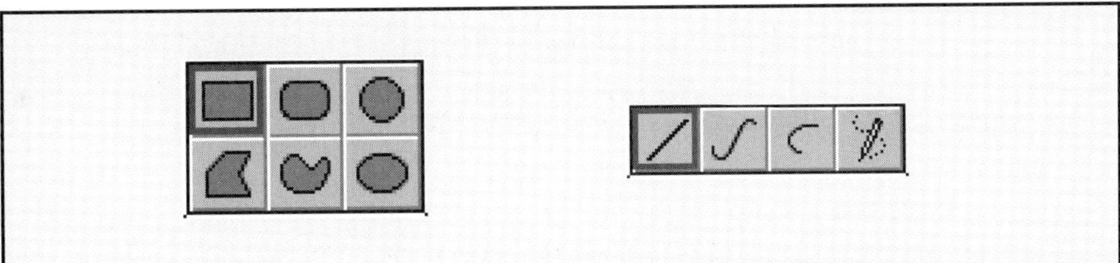

Figure 18.3
Closed Object Tools and Line Object Tools Options

With options from the Closed Object Tools tool, you can draw closed shapes. WordPerfect Draw will fill a closed object with blue color. Use the options from the Line Object Tools tool to draw lines. Shapes you draw with line tools are not considered closed objects and will not display with blue color.

With the options from the Closed Object Tools tool, you can draw a rectangle, a rectangle with rounded corners, a circle, a polygon, a closed curve, and an ellipse. The shape is depicted as an icon on each tool. Use options from the Line Object Tools tool to draw a line, a curved line, sections of an ellipse, or to draw freehand.

To draw a line drawing, you would complete the following steps:

1. Position the arrow pointer on the Line Object Tools tool, hold down the left mouse button, drag the arrow pointer to the desired line tool, then release the mouse button.
2. Position the mouse pointer inside the drawing area. When the mouse pointer is positioned in the drawing area, it displays as crosshairs.
3. Position the crosshairs at the location in the drawing area where the object is to begin, then click the left mouse button. Continue to click to add points, and double-click to end the drawing of the object. For some line tools such as the freehand tool, you may need to hold down the left mouse button as you draw.

To draw a shape, you would complete the following steps:

1. Position the arrow pointer on the Closed Object Tools tool, hold down the left mouse button, drag the arrow pointer to the desired shape tool, then release the mouse button.
2. Position the mouse pointer (crosshairs) inside the drawing area.
3. Position the crosshairs at the position where the object is to begin, hold down the left mouse button, drag the crosshairs up, down, left, or right, to draw the shape, then release the mouse button when the desired shape displays.

You can use the rectangle tool to draw a square. To draw a square, hold down the Shift key as you draw the shape in the drawing area.

Exercise 1 Creating a Circle and a Square

1. At a clear editing window, draw a circle and square using WordPerfect Draw by completing the following steps:
   a. Open WordPerfect Draw. To do this, choose Graphics, then Draw; or click on the Draw button on the Graphics Toolbar.
   b. Position the arrow pointer on the Closed Object Tools tool, hold down the left mouse button, drag the arrow pointer to the circle tool, then release the mouse button. (The circle tool is the last tool to the right in the top row.)

c. Position the mouse pointer (crosshairs) in the drawing area.
d. Hold down the left mouse button, drag the crosshairs down until the outline image displays as a circle, then release the mouse button.
e. Position the arrow pointer on the Closed Object Tools tool, hold down the left mouse button, drag the arrow pointer to the rectangle tool, then release the mouse button. (The rectangle tool is the first tool at the left in the first row.)
f. Position the crosshairs in the drawing area toward the right side.
g. Hold down the Shift key and the left mouse button, drag the crosshairs down and to the right (or left) until the outline image displays as a square, then release the mouse button and the Shift key.
h. Click on the Close button on the Draw Toolbar; or click in the editing window outside the box containing the circle.
i. Deselect the box containing the circle. To do this, click in the editing window outside the box.

2. Save the document and name it c18ex01.
3. Print c18ex01.
4. Close c18ex01.

Clearing a Shape

A shape you have drawn can be cleared from the drawing area. To clear a shape, choose Edit, then Clear; or press Ctrl + Shift + F4 at the Draw window. WordPerfect Draw inserts a confirmation prompt asking if you want to clear all objects. At this box, choose OK. This clears the drawing area and keeps the Draw window open.

Exercise 2 Drawing a Diamond Shape

1. At a clear editing window, draw a diamond shape using WordPerfect Draw by completing the following steps:
   a. Open WordPerfect Draw.
   b. Position the arrow pointer on the Line Object Tools tool, hold down the left mouse button, drag the arrow pointer to the line tool (the first tool), then release the mouse button.
   c. Position the crosshairs approximately in the middle of the drawing area between the left and right edges and toward the top of the drawing area.
   d. Click the left mouse button once. This adds a point.
   e. Move the crosshairs down and to the right approximately 1 inch, then click the left mouse button. This adds another point.
   f. Move the crosshairs down and to the left approximately 1 inch, then click the left mouse button. This adds another point.
   g. Move the crosshairs up and to the left approximately 1 inch, then click the left mouse button. This adds another point.
   h. Position the arrow pointer on the first point, then double-click the left mouse button. This completes the diamond shape.
   i. If you are not satisfied with the way the diamond shape looks, you can clear the current shape, and redraw another by completing the following steps:
      (1) Choose Edit, then Clear; or press Ctrl + Shift + F4.
      (2) At the confirmation prompt asking if you want to clear all objects, choose OK.
   j. When the diamond is the desired shape, click on the Close button on the Draw Toolbar; or click in the editing window outside the drawing area.

k. Deselect the box containing the diamond shape. To do this, click in the editing window outside the box.

2. Save the document and name it c18ex02.
3. Print c18ex02.
4. Close c18ex02.

Displaying the Ruler and Grid

WordPerfect Draw includes a ruler and grid that you can use to draw shapes or position images at specific locations in the drawing area. To turn on the display of the Ruler, choose View, then Ruler; or click on the Ruler button on the Draw Toolbar. This causes a horizontal ruler to display at the top of the drawing area and a vertical ruler to display at the left side of the drawing area as shown in figure 18.4. If you choose View, Grid/Snap, then Grid; or click on the Grid button on the Draw Toolbar, a grid pattern displays in the drawing area as shown in figure 18.4.

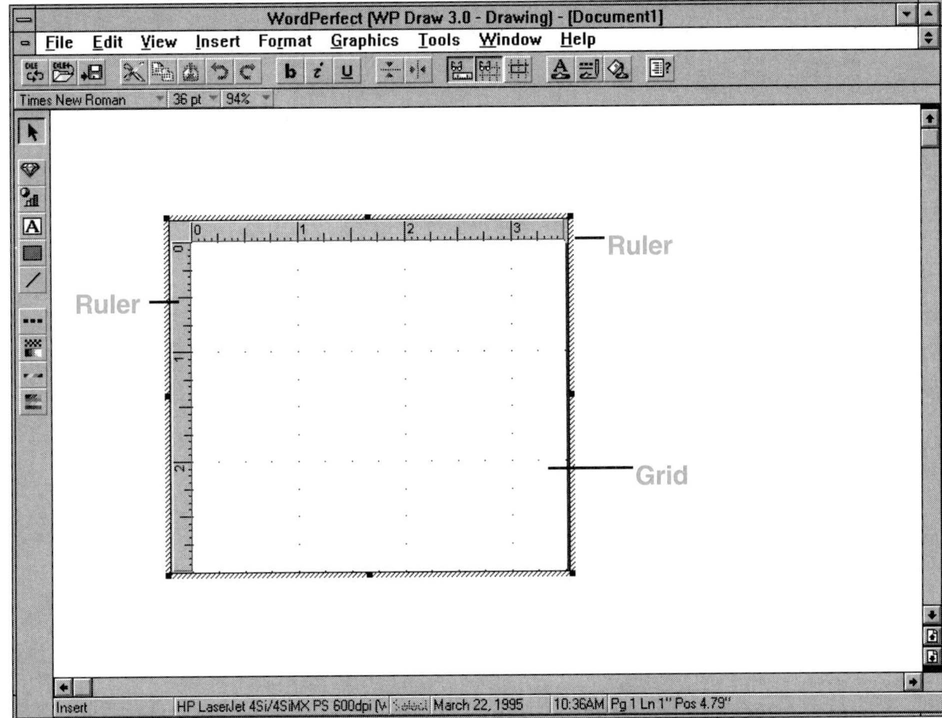

Figure 18.4
Ruler and Grid in WordPerfect Draw

With the Ruler displayed, a drawing tool selected, and the crosshairs positioned inside the drawing area, red marks display on the horizontal ruler and vertical ruler identifying the position of the crosshairs. If the crosshairs are positioned precisely on a whole number measurement, the red marker turns turquoise.

Exercise 3 Drawing a Square on the Grid

1. At a clear editing window, create a square using WordPerfect Draw by completing the following steps:
   a. Open WordPerfect Draw.
   b. Click on the Ruler button, then click on the Grid button on the Draw Toolbar.
   c. Position the arrow pointer on the Closed Object Tools tool, hold down the left mouse button, drag the arrow pointer to the rectangle tool, then release the mouse button.

d. Position the crosshairs in the drawing area until the red markers are positioned on the 1-inch mark on the horizontal ruler and the 1-inch mark on the vertical ruler and the markers turn turquoise.
e. Hold down the left mouse button, drag the crosshairs down and to the right until the red markers appear on the 2-inch mark on the horizontal and vertical rulers and the markers turn turquoise, then release the mouse button.
f. Close WordPerfect Draw.
g. At the editing window, deselect the box containing the square.

2. Save the document and name it c18ex03.
3. Print c18ex03.
4. Close c18ex03.

Editing a Box

When you close WordPerfect Draw, what you drew is inserted in a box with no borders. This box is inserted at the left margin of the document and is approximately 5 inches wide and 4.5 inches tall. The box that is inserted in the document when you close WordPerfect Draw is the same type of box you learned to create in chapter 17. All the same editing options are available. You can display the Graphics Box Feature Bar for the box, then choose options from the bar. To display the Graphics Box Feature Bar for a drawing box, position the arrow pointer on the shape in the box, then click the *right* mouse button. At the drop-down menu that displays, click on Feature Bar. At the Graphics Box Feature Bar, you can make changes to the box containing the drawn shapes just as you learned to edit graphics boxes in chapter 17.

You can also move the box containing the drawn shape with the mouse. To do this, position the arrow pointer on the shape, then click the left mouse button. This causes the box containing the shape to be selected. Position the arrow pointer (displays as a four-headed arrow) inside the selected area, hold down the left mouse button, drag the outline to the desired location, then release the mouse button.

Exercise 4 Editing a Drawing

1. At a clear editing window, open c18ex03.
2. Save the document with Save As and name it c18ex04.
3. Change the position and size of the box containing the square by completing the following steps:
   a. Position the arrow pointer on the square shape, click the *right* mouse button, then click on Feature Bar at the drop-down menu.
   b. With the Graphics Box Feature Bar displayed, change the box size width to Full and the height to Size to Content at the Box Size dialog box.
   c. Choose Close to close the Graphics Box Feature Bar.
4. Change the viewing mode to Two Page to see how the box displays on the page, then change the viewing mode back to Page.
5. Save the document again with the same name (c18ex04).
6. Print c18ex04.
7. Close c18ex04.

Deleting a Box

If you insert a box in the editing window, a Box code is inserted in the document. If you decide you want to delete the box from the editing window, display Reveal Codes then delete the Box code.

Creating Text in WordPerfect Draw

In WordPerfect Draw, you can create, customize, and edit text. You can perform such activities as inserting text inside a graphics image, scaling text, contouring text, inserting text inside shapes, and much more.

To insert text with WordPerfect Draw, you would complete the following steps:

1. Open WordPerfect Draw.
2. Position the arrow pointer on the Text Object Tools tool, hold down the left mouse button, drag the arrow pointer to the first text tool (the one with an A on a white background), then release the mouse button.
3. Position the mouse pointer (hand holding a square) in the drawing area where you want the text to appear. Hold down the left mouse button, drag the mouse pointer (hand holding a square) down and to the right to draw a box for the text, then release the mouse button. This causes a blue box to appear in the drawing area as shown in figure 18.5.
4. Key the text in the blue box. If the text you key fills more than the first line in the box, the text wraps to the next line.
5. After keying the text, position the arrow pointer outside the blue box, then click the left mouse button.

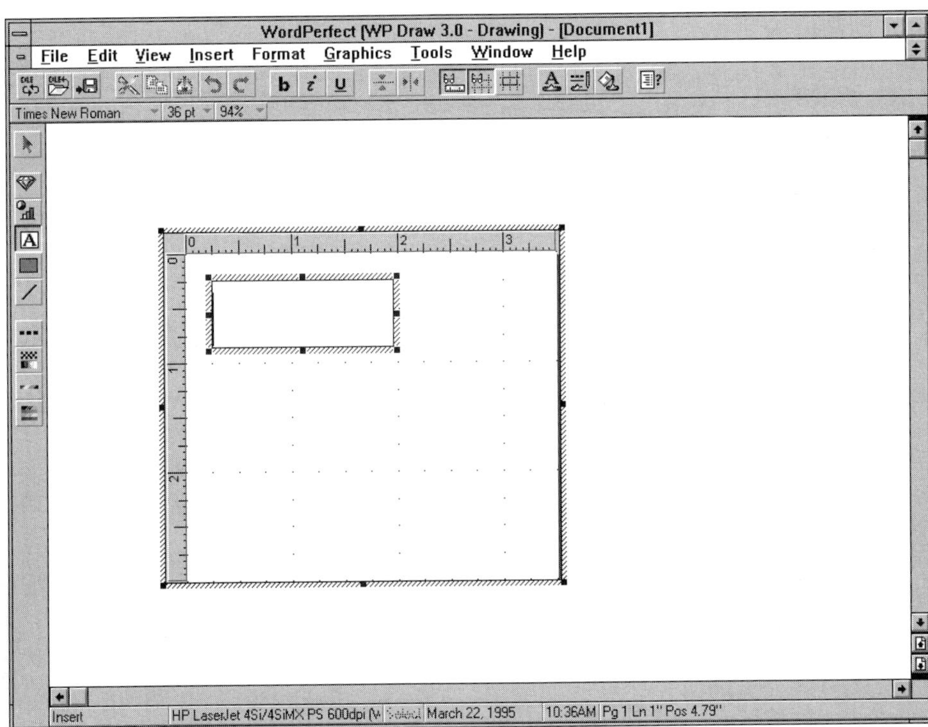

Figure 18.5
Text Box in Drawing Area

You can also draw a box for text using the Insert option from the Draw Menu Bar. To do this, choose Insert, then Text Area. Position the mouse pointer in the drawing area and it turns into a hand holding a square. To draw an area for text and insert text, complete steps 3 through 5 listed above.

You can also key text directly into the drawing area. To do this, position the arrow pointer on the Text Object Tools tool, hold down the left mouse button, drag the arrow pointer to the second text tool (the A on a gray background), then release the mouse button. You can also choose Insert, then Text Line. Move the crosshairs in the drawing area to the location where you want the text to appear, then click the left mouse button. This causes the insertion point to display in the drawing area.

The default font for text in the drawing area is 36-point Times New Roman. This information displays in the Draw Power Bar. You can change the typeface by clicking on the Font Selection button on the Draw Power Bar, then clicking on the desired typeface at the drop-down menu. Use the Font Sizes button on the Draw Power Bar to change the size of text in the drawing area. You can also change the font for text in the drawing area at the Font dialog box. To display the Font dialog box, choose Format, then Font.

Exercise 5 Creating a Shape Containing Text

1. At a clear editing window, create an oval with the words *Ramona Sampson* and *Vice Principal* inside using WordPerfect Draw by completing the following steps:
   a. Open WordPerfect Draw.
   b. At the Draw window, turn on the display of the Ruler and the Grid.
   c. Position the arrow pointer on the Closed Object Tools tool, hold down the left mouse button, drag the arrow pointer to the ellipse tool (the last tool at the right in the bottom row), then release the mouse button.
   d. Position the crosshairs in the drawing area until the red markers are positioned on the 0.5-inch mark on the horizontal and vertical ruler (the markers will turn turquoise when positioned properly).
   e. Hold down the left mouse button, drag the crosshairs down and to the right until the red markers display on the 3-inch mark on the horizontal ruler and the 2.5-inch mark on the vertical ruler. (When positioned properly, the red markers will turn turquoise.)
   f. Release the mouse button.
   g. Change the font size to 14 points. To do this, click on the Font Sizes button on the Draw Power Bar, then click on *14*. (You will need to scroll up the list to see 14.)
   h. Position the arrow pointer on the Text Object Tools tool, hold down the left mouse button, drag the arrow pointer to the right to the first text tool (the one with the A on a white background), then release the mouse button.
   i. Position the crosshairs inside the oval until the red markers are positioned on the 0.75-inch mark on the horizontal ruler and the 1.25-inch mark on the vertical ruler (and the markers turn to turquoise).
   j. Hold down the left mouse button, drag the mouse pointer (hand holding a square) down and to the right until the red markers are positioned on the 2.75-inch mark on the horizontal ruler and the 1.75-inch mark on the vertical ruler, then release the mouse button.
   k. Press Shift + F7, turn on bold, then key **Ramona Sampson**.
   l. Press Enter, press Shift + F7, then key **Vice Principal**.
   m. Click in the blue area of the oval, outside the name and title. (This deselects the text box.)
   n. Close WordPerfect Draw.
   o. Deselect the box containing the oval.
2. Save the document and name it c18ex05.
3. Print c18ex05.
4. Close c18ex05.

Changing the Drawing Area Size

When you open WordPerfect Draw, the drawing area displays with sizing handles. Use these sizing handles to change the size of the drawing area. Use the sizing handles in the middle of the sides to change the width of the drawing area. Use the sizing handles in the middle at the top and bottom to change the height. The sizing handles in the corners are used to change both the width and height of the drawing area at the same time.

The Draw Power Bar contains a Zoom Options button with options for changing the display of text in the drawing area. These options, displayed in figure 18.6, change the viewing size but do not change the actual size of the objects. Use the Zoom To Area option to view a specific area. When you click on Zoom To Area, the mouse pointer displays as a magnifying glass. Position the magnifying glass in the drawing area, hold down the mouse button, draw a box around the area you want to view, then release the mouse button. When you release the mouse button, the area inside the box fills the drawing area.

If you have zoomed in on an area, you can return to the default view by clicking on the Zoom Options button, then clicking on Zoom To Drawing. Use the percentages in the Zoom Options drop-down menu to change the percentage of the viewing size in the drawing area. Zoom options are also available by choosing View, then Zoom.

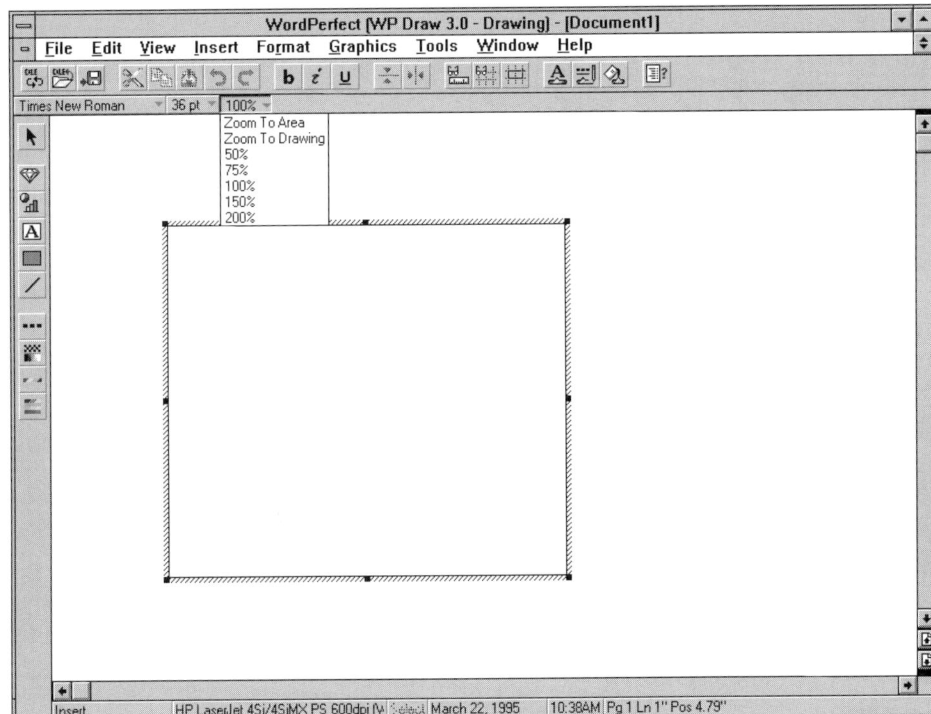

Figure 18.6
Draw Zoom Options

Exercise 6 Creating and Editing a Shape and Text

1. At a clear editing window, create a rounded rectangle with the words COMMITTED and CONCERNED inside by completing the following steps:
   a. Change the viewing mode to Draft.
   b. Open WordPerfect Draw.
   c. Turn on the display of the Ruler and the Grid.
   d. Change the size of the drawing area by completing the following steps:
      (1) Position the arrow pointer on the sizing handle in the middle of the bottom border until it turns into a double-headed arrow pointing up and down.
      (2) Hold down the left mouse button, drag the double-headed arrow down to the bottom of the editing window, then release the mouse button.
      (3) Position the arrow pointer on the sizing handle in the middle of the right border until it turns into a double-headed arrow pointing left and right.
      (4) Hold down the left mouse button, drag the double-headed arrow to the right side of the editing window, then release the mouse button.

e. Position the arrow pointer on the Closed Object Tools tool, hold down the left mouse button, drag the arrow pointer to the rounded rectangle tool (second tool from the left in the top row), then release the mouse button.
f. Draw a rounded rectangle from the 1-inch mark on the horizontal and vertical rulers to the 5-inch mark on the horizontal ruler and the 3.5-inch mark on the vertical ruler.
g. Position the arrow pointer on the Text Object Tools tool, drag the arrow pointer to the second tool (the A on a gray background), then release the mouse button.
h. Position the crosshairs in the rounded rectangle at the 1.5-inch mark on the horizontal ruler and the 2-inch mark on the vertical ruler, then click the left mouse button.
i. Key the word **COMMITTED**, then press the Enter key.
j. Position the crosshairs in the rounded rectangle at the 1.5-inch mark on the horizontal ruler and the 2.75-inch mark on the vertical ruler, then click the left mouse button.
k. Key the word **CONCERNED**, then press the Enter key.
l. Change the viewing area by completing the following steps:
   (1) Click on the Zoom Options button on the Power Bar, then click on 50%.
   (2) Click on the Zoom Options button on the Power Bar, then click on 150%.
   (3) Choose View, Zoom, then Drawing Area. (This returns the view to the default.)
m. Close WordPerfect Draw by clicking on the Close button on the Draw Toolbar.

2. At the editing window, change the position and size of the box containing the shapes and text by completing the following steps:
   a. Position the arrow pointer on the rounded rectangle, click the *right* mouse button, then click on Feature Bar.
   b. With the Graphics Box Feature Bar displayed, change the box size width to Full and the height to Size to Contents at the Box Size dialog box.
   c. Choose Close to close the Graphics Box Feature Bar.
3. Change the viewing mode to Two Page to see how the rounded rectangle displays on the page, then change the viewing mode back to Page.
4. Save the document and name it c18ex06.
5. Print c18ex06.
6. Close c18ex06.

Editing an Object

Once you have inserted an object, such as a shape or text, in the drawing area you may want to edit the object. For example, you may want to move, copy, or delete an object or sections of an object.

Selecting an Object

If you want to move, copy, or delete an object or a part of an object, it needs to be selected. To select an object in the drawing area, click on the Select Object tool on the Draw Tool palette. Position the arrow pointer on the object to be selected, then click the left mouse button. When you select an object in the drawing area, sizing handles surround the image as shown in figure 18.7.

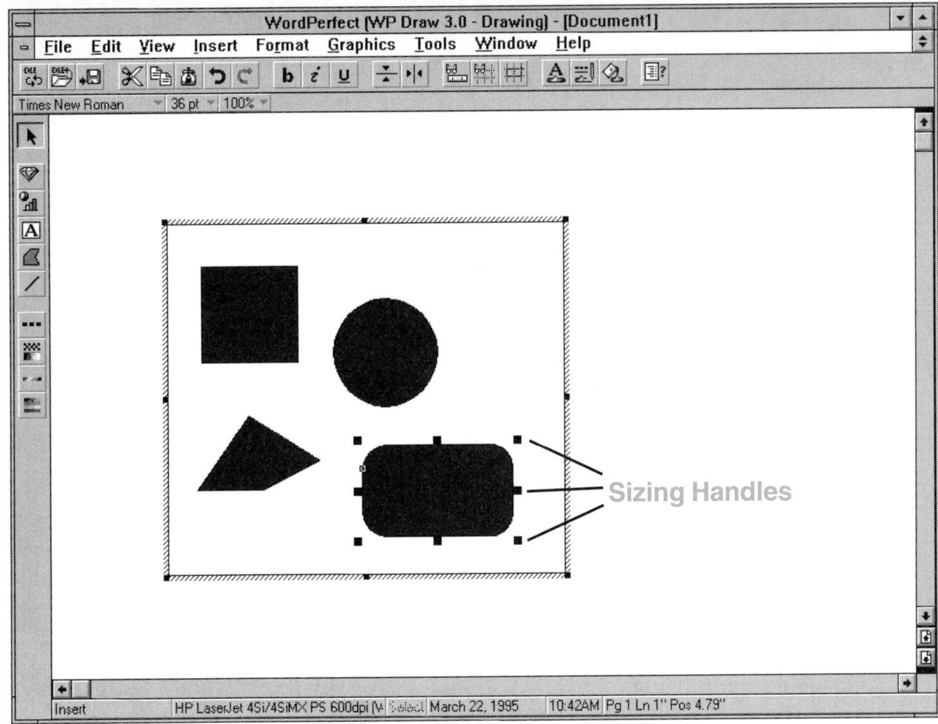

Figure 18.7
Selected Object

You can also select an object with the Edit menu option at the Draw window. To do this, choose Edit, Select, then Object(s). Position the arrow pointer on the item in the drawing area you want to select, then click the left mouse button.

The methods described above select just one image. You can also select several objects in the drawing area. To select several objects using the mouse, you would complete the following steps:

1. At the Draw window, click on the Select Object tool on the Draw Tool palette.
2. Position the arrow pointer on the object in the drawing area to be selected, hold down the Ctrl key, then click the left mouse button.
3. Position the arrow pointer on the next object to be included, hold down the Ctrl key, then click the left mouse button.
4. Continue holding down the Ctrl key and clicking on objects until you have selected all desired objects.

When you use the Ctrl key plus the Select Object tool, the sizing handles include all selected images. For example, if you use the Ctrl key plus the Select Object tool to select all the objects in figure 18.7, the sizing handles will appear as shown in figure 18.8. All objects in the drawing area can be selected with options from the Edit menu. To select all objects in the drawing area, choose Edit, Select, then All.

Moving a Selected Object

Once an object (or objects) has been selected, it can be moved. To do this, position the arrow pointer in the selected area, hold down the left mouse button, drag the outline of the object to the desired location in the drawing area, then release the mouse button. When you release the mouse button, the selected object(s) is inserted at the location of the outline.

Figure 18.8
Selected Objects

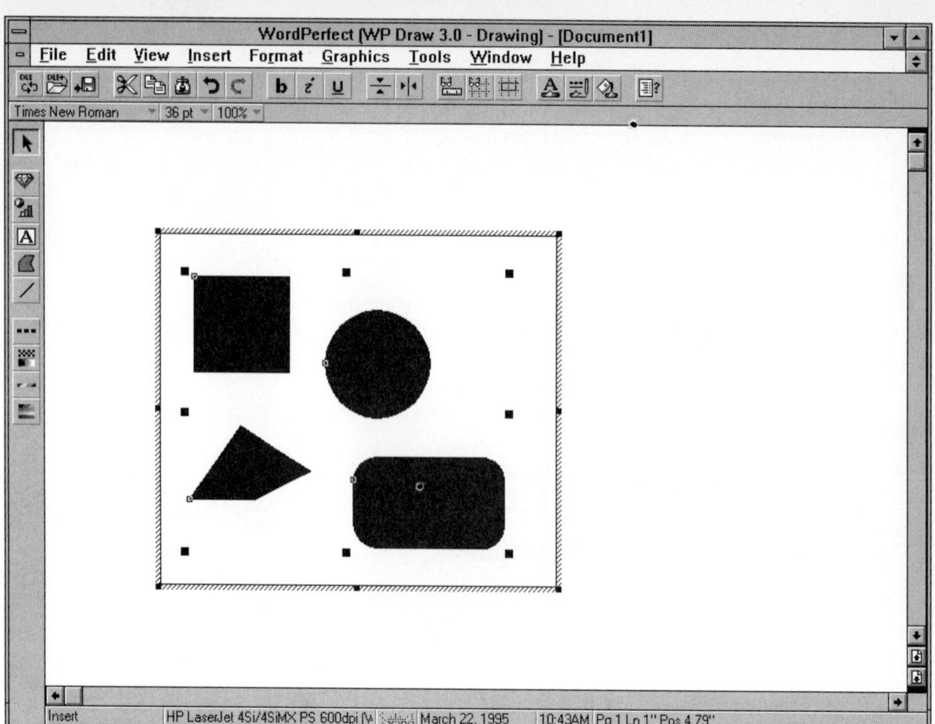

Exercise 7 Editing a Selected Object

1. At a clear editing window, open c18ex01.
2. Save the document with Save As and name it c18ex07.
3. Position the arrow pointer on the circle shape, then double-click the left mouse button. This opens WordPerfect Draw.
4. At the Draw window, make the following changes:
   a. Click on the Closed Object Tools tool, then click on the polygon tool. (This is the first tool from the left in the bottom row.)
   b. With the polygon drawing tool selected, draw a triangle in a free area in the drawing area.
   c. Select and move the circle you drew earlier by completing the following steps:
      (1) Click on the Select Object tool.
      (2) Position the arrow pointer on the circle, then click the left mouse button. (This selects the circle.)
      (3) Position the arrow pointer inside the selected area, hold down the left mouse button, drag the circle outline so it slightly overlaps the square, then release the button.
      (4) Select the triangle, then move it so it slightly overlaps the circle and the square.
   d. When all changes are made, close WordPerfect Draw.
   e. At the editing window, deselect the box containing the shapes.
5. Save the document again with the same name (c18ex07).
6. Print c18ex07.
7. Close c18ex07.

Copying a Selected Object

Moving a selected object removes the object from its original position and inserts it into a new location. You can also copy an object into a new location in the drawing area. To do this, position the arrow pointer in the selected area, hold down the Ctrl key and the left mouse button, drag the outline of the shape to the new location, then release the left mouse button and then the Ctrl key.

Exercise 8 Copying and Editing Squares

1. At a clear editing window, create the squares shown in figure 18.9 by completing the following steps:
   a. Change the viewing mode to Draft.
   b. Open WordPerfect Draw.
   c. Increase the size of the drawing area by completing the following steps:
      (1) Position the arrow pointer on the sizing handle at the bottom right corner of the drawing area until it turns into a diagonally pointing arrow.
      (2) Hold down the left mouse button, drag the outline of the drawing area down and to the right so the outline displays near the bottom of the editing window and near the right side of the editing window, then release the mouse button.
   d. Turn on the display of the Ruler and the Grid.
   e. Select the rectangle tool, then draw a square from the 2-inch mark on the horizontal ruler and the 1-inch mark on the vertical ruler to the 3-inch mark on the horizontal ruler and the 2-inch mark on the vertical ruler.
   f. Copy the square by completing the following steps:
      (1) Click on the Select Object tool.
      (2) Position the arrow pointer inside the square, then click the left mouse button.
      (3) With the arrow pointer still positioned inside the square, hold down the Ctrl key and the left mouse button.
      (4) Drag the outline of the square down and to the left so the left side is positioned at the 1.25-inch mark on the horizontal ruler and the 3-inch mark on the vertical ruler and the right side is positioned on the 2.25-inch mark on the horizontal ruler and the 3-inch mark on the vertical ruler.
      (5) When the outline is in the desired position, release the mouse button, then release the Ctrl key.
   g. Copy the square again so that the left side of the square is positioned on the 2.75-inch mark on the horizontal ruler and the 3-inch mark on the vertical ruler and the right side is positioned at the 3.75-inch mark on the horizontal ruler and the 3-inch mark on the vertical ruler.
   h. Position the arrow pointer on the Text Object Tools tool, hold down the left mouse button, drag the arrow pointer to the second text tool (the A on a gray background), then release the mouse button.
   i. Position the arrow pointer inside the top square, click the left mouse button, key the letter **A**, then press Enter.
   j. Complete steps similar to those in 1i to insert the letter **B** in the square at the left and the letter **C** in the square at the right.
   k. After keying the letters in the squares, you may need to adjust the letters so they are centered within the squares. To do this, complete the following steps:
      (1) Click on the Select Object tool.
      (2) Position the arrow pointer on the letter, then click the left mouse button.
      (3) Position the arrow pointer inside the selected area, hold down the left

mouse button, drag the outline of the box containing the letter to the desired position in the square, then release the mouse button.

l. When the letters are in the correct position in the squares, close WordPerfect Draw.

m. At the editing window, change the position and size of the box containing the squares by completing the following steps:
   (1) Position the arrow pointer on one of the squares, click the *right* mouse button, then click on Feature Bar.
   (2) With the Graphics Box Feature Bar displayed, display the Box Position dialog box, then change the Horizontal option from Right Margin to Center of Paragraph.
   (3) Choose Close to close the Graphics Box Feature Bar.

2. Change the viewing mode to Two Page to see how the squares display on the page then change the viewing mode back to Page.
3. Save the document and name it c18ex08.
4. Print c18ex08.
5. Close c18ex08.

Figure 18.9

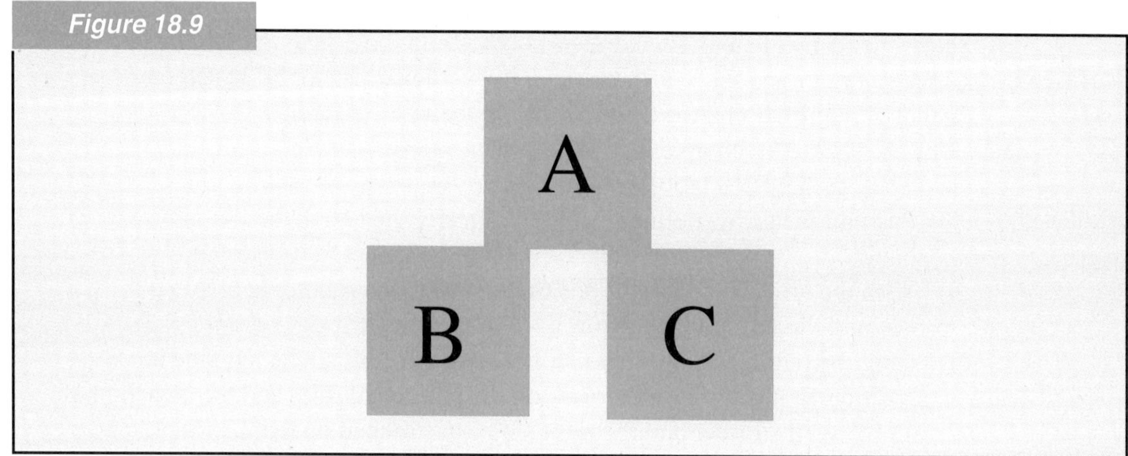

Deleting a Selected Object

After an object (or objects) has been selected, it can be deleted by pressing the Delete key. You can also delete everything in the drawing area by choosing Edit, then Clear; or pressing Ctrl + Shift + F4. At the Clear Drawing dialog box, choose OK or press Enter.

Changing the Size of a Selected Object

When an object (or objects) is selected, sizing handles display at the left, right, and middle of the image. You can use these sizing handles to change the size and/or shape of the selected object. Use the sizing handles in the middle of the sides to change the width of the object. Use the sizing handles in the middle at the top and bottom to change the height of the object. The sizing handles in the corners are used to change both the width and height of the object at the same time.

 Exercise 9 Using the Sizing Handles

1. At a clear editing window, open c18ex03.
2. Save the document with Save As and name it c18ex09.
3. Make the following changes to the document:
   a. Change the viewing mode to Draft.
   b. Position the arrow pointer inside the square, then double-click the left mouse button. This opens WordPerfect Draw with the square displayed in the drawing area.

c. Make sure the Ruler and the Grid are displayed. If not, click on the Ruler button and the Grid button on the Draw Toolbar.
d. Increase the size of the drawing area by completing the following steps:
   (1) Position the arrow pointer on the sizing handle at the bottom right corner of the drawing area until it turns into a diagonally pointing arrow.
   (2) Hold down the left mouse button, drag the outline of the drawing area down and to the right so the outline displays near the bottom of the editing window and near the right side of the editing window, then release the mouse button.
e. Change the size of the square by completing the following steps:
   (1) Click on the Select Object tool.
   (2) Position the arrow pointer inside the square, then click the left mouse button. (This selects the square.)
   (3) Position the arrow pointer on the middle sizing handle at the right side of the square until it turns into a double-headed arrow pointing left and right.
   (4) Hold down the left mouse button, drag the double-headed arrow to the right to the 5-inch mark on the horizontal ruler, then release the mouse button.
   (5) Position the arrow pointer on the middle sizing handle at the bottom of the square until it turns into a double-headed arrow pointing up and down.
   (6) Hold down the left mouse button, drag the double-headed arrow down to the 3-inch mark on the vertical ruler, then release the mouse button.
f. Deselect the rectangle (previously a square).
g. Draw a text box inside the rectangle from the 1.5-inch mark on the horizontal ruler to the 4.5-inch marker on the horizontal ruler. (Use the tool containing an A on a white background to do this.)
h. Change the font to 16-point Swis721 BlkEx BT. To do this, complete the following steps:
   (1) Click on the Font Selection button on the Draw Power Bar, then click on *Swis721 BlkEx BT.*
   (2) Click on the Font Sizes button on the Draw Power Bar, then click on *16.* (You may need to scroll up the list to see 16.)
i. With the insertion point positioned inside the text box, press Shift + F7, then key **Word Processing.**
j. Press Enter twice, press Shift + F7, then key **Room 244**.
k. Click on the Close button on the Draw Toolbar.

4. At the editing window, make the following changes:
   a. Display the Graphics Box Feature Bar for the rectangle.
   b. Display the Box Position dialog box, then change the Horizontal option from Right Margin to Center of Paragraph.
   c. Change the box size width to Full and the height to Size to Content at the Box Size dialog box.
   d. Close the Graphics Box Feature Bar.
5. Save the document again with the same name (c18ex09).
6. Print c18ex09.
7. Close c18ex09.

Contouring Text

At the drawing area, you can insert text, draw a curved line, and then contour the text on the curved line. To do this, you would complete the following steps:

1. Open WordPerfect Draw.
2. Position the arrow pointer on the Line Object Tools tool, hold down the left mouse button, drag the arrow pointer to the curved tool (second tool from the left), then release the mouse button.
3. Draw a curved line in the drawing area.
4. Position the arrow pointer on the Text Object Tools tool, hold down the left mouse button, drag the arrow pointer to the second text tool (the A on a gray background), then release the mouse button.
5. Position the crosshairs in the drawing area, click the left mouse button, then key the text.
6. Select the curved line and the text by completing the following steps:
   - **a** Choose the Select Object tool.
   - **b** Position the arrow pointer on the curved line in the drawing area, hold down the Ctrl key, then click the left mouse button. (This selects the curved line.)
   - **c** Position the arrow pointer on the text, hold down the Ctrl key, then click the left mouse button. (This selects the curved line and the text as shown in figure 18.10.)
7. With the curved line and the text selected, choose Graphics, then Contour Text.
8. At the Contour Text dialog box, determine the text position in relation to the curve, then choose OK or press Enter.
9. Click outside the selected area.

Figure 18.10
Selected Line and Text

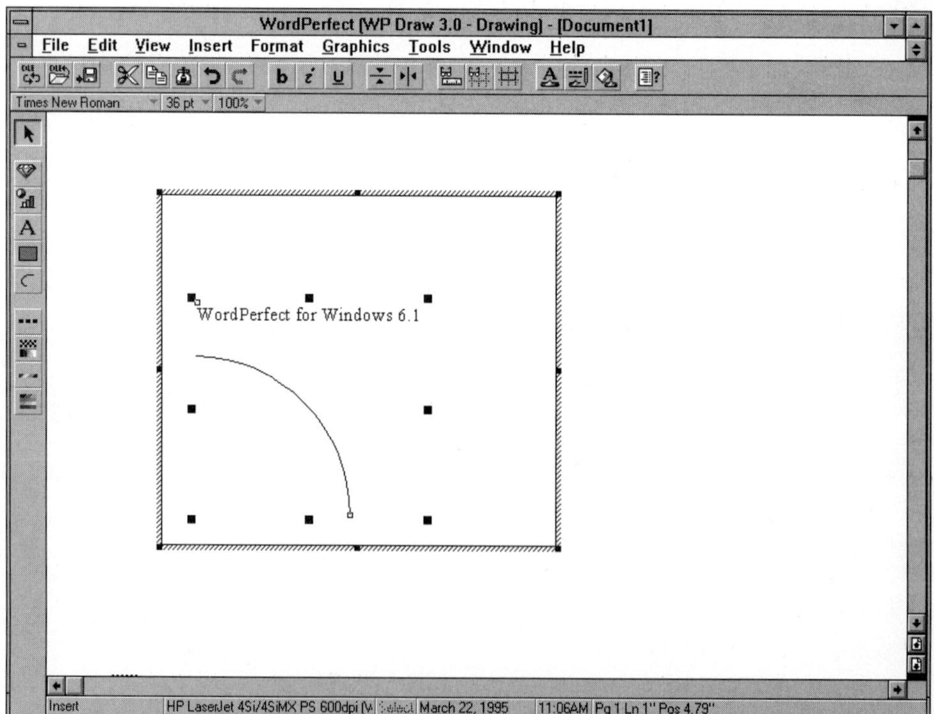

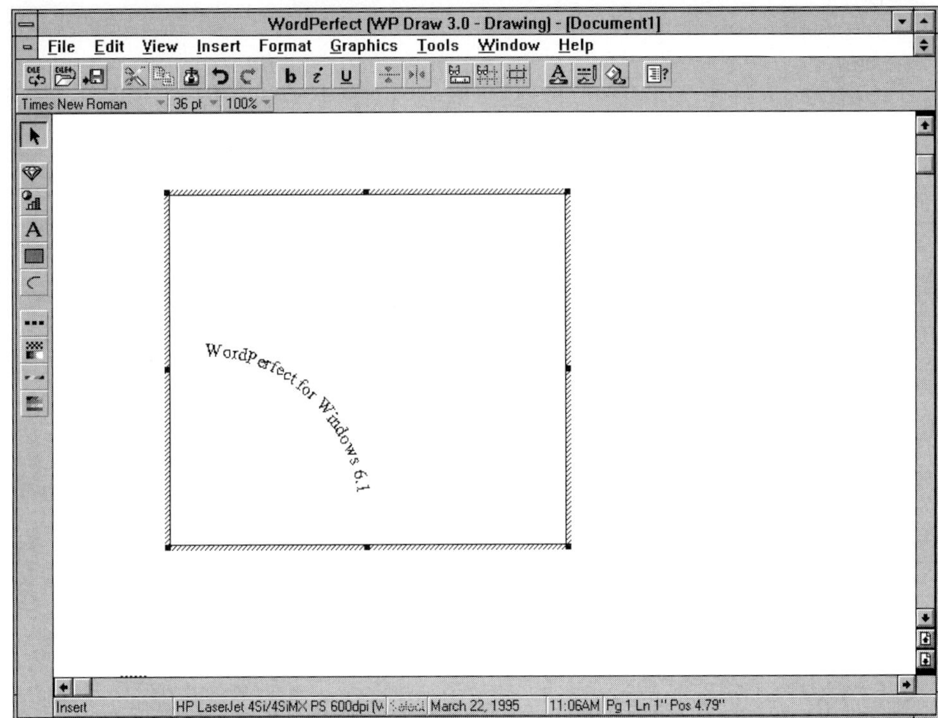

Figure 18.11
Contoured Text

If you do not change the settings at the Contour Text dialog box, the text will be contoured as shown in figure 18.11. By default, WordPerfect Draw will contour text at the top left of the curved line. The Position option at the Contour Text dialog box lets you specify whether you want the text at the Top Left (the default), Top Center, Top Right, Bottom Left, Bottom Center, or Bottom Right of the curved line.

When text is contoured, the curved line does not display. If you want the contoured text and the curved line to display, remove the X from the Display Text Only check box at the Contour Text dialog box. If you contour text, then want to separate the text from the line, select the contoured text, then choose Graphics, then Separate.

Exercise 10 Creating a Letterhead with the Contoured Text

1. At a clear editing window, create the letterhead shown in figure 18.12 by completing the following steps:
   a. Change the viewing mode to Draft.
   b. Open WordPerfect Draw.
   c. Turn on the display of the Ruler and Grid.
   d. Expand the size of the drawing area so the 4.5-inch mark on the horizontal ruler is visible and the 3-inch mark on the vertical ruler is visible.
   e. Select the circle tool.
   f. Position the crosshairs at the 1-inch mark on the horizontal ruler and the 1.75-inch mark on the vertical ruler, hold down the left mouse button, drag the crosshairs down to the 2.5-inch mark on the vertical ruler (remain at the 1-inch mark on the horizontal ruler), then release the mouse button.
   g. Select the rectangle tool.
   h. Position the crosshairs at the 1.25-inch mark on the horizontal ruler and the 2-inch mark on the vertical ruler, hold down the Shift key and the left mouse button. Drag the crosshairs to the 2.5-inch mark on the horizontal ruler and the 3.25-inch mark on the vertical ruler, then release the mouse button.

i. Position the arrow pointer on the Line Object Tools tool, hold down the left mouse button, drag the arrow pointer to the ellipse tool, then release the mouse button.
j. Position the crosshairs at the 0.75-inch mark on the horizontal and the vertical rulers, then hold down the left mouse button. Drag the crosshairs to the 3.25-inch marks on the horizontal and vertical rulers, then release the mouse button. (This causes a curved line to display.)
k. Position the arrow pointer on the Text Object Tools tool, hold down the left mouse button, drag the arrow pointer to the last option (the A on a gray background), then release the mouse button.
l. Change the font to 30-point ShelleyVolante BT.
m. Position the crosshairs at the 0.5-inch mark on the horizontal ruler and the 0.5-inch mark on the vertical ruler, then click the left mouse button.
n. Key **Shapes by Sarah and Sam**, then press Enter.
o. Click on the Select Object tool.
p. Position the arrow pointer on the text you just keyed, hold down the Ctrl key, then click the left mouse button.
q. Position the arrow pointer on the curved line, hold down the Ctrl key, then click the left mouse button.
r. Choose Graphics, then Contour Text.
s. At the Contour Text dialog box, choose OK or press Enter.
t. Click outside the selected area.
u. Close WordPerfect Draw.

2. At the editing window, display the Graphics Box Feature Bar for the objects you just created. With the Graphics Box Feature Bar displayed, make the following changes:
   a. Display the Box Position dialog box, then change the horizontal position to Left Margin. (Do this in the Position Box section.)
   b. Display the Box Size dialog box, then change the width to 3 inches and the height to Size to Content.
   c. Close the Graphics Box Feature Bar.
3. Save the document and name it c18ex10.
4. Print c18ex10.
5. Close c18ex10.

Figure 18.12

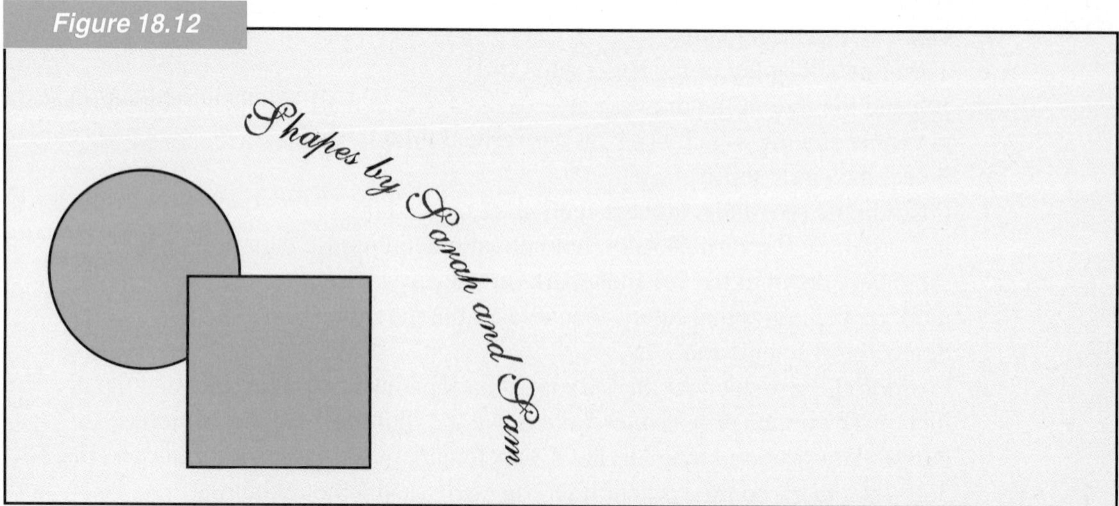

Changing Attributes

You can change attributes such as color and fill patterns. You can change the attribute, then draw the object, or you can draw the object, then select the object and change attributes. If you change attributes before drawing an object, these attributes will apply to all subsequent objects. If you want attributes to apply to only specific objects, draw the objects first, select them, then change attributes.

Changing Line Attributes

WordPerfect Draw uses a thin black line when drawing shapes. You can customize this line by clicking on the Line Attributes tool on the Draw Tool palette. This causes a list of options to display. Use these options to select a thicker or thinner line, turn off the border line, and change from a solid line to a line with varying patterns.

Line Attributes can also be changed at the Line Attributes dialog box. To display this dialog box, click on the Line button on the Draw Toolbar, or choose Format, then Line Attributes. At the Line Attributes dialog box, you can specify line color, line thickness, and line style. You can also add an arrowhead to a line.

Changing Fill Attributes

When you draw a shape, the shape is filled with a solid pattern. If you click on the Fill Attributes tool on the Draw Tool palette, a wide variety of fill patterns display. For example, you can choose a honeycomb pattern, diamond pattern, wave pattern, and much more. You can also choose a gradient pattern. A gradient pattern shades the object in varying degrees. For example, an object can be shaded darker at the left side and then gradually lighten toward the right side.

Fill Attributes can also be changed at the Fill Attributes dialog box. To display this dialog box, click on the Fill button on the Draw Toolbar, or choose Format, then Fill Attributes. At the Fill Attributes dialog box, you can specify a fill pattern, a fill gradient, and specify a foreground and background color for the pattern.

Changing Line Color

In WordPerfect Draw, you can change the color of the line used to draw an object with the Line Colors tool on the Draw Tool palette, or with an option at the Line Attributes dialog box. To change the line color using the tool palette, click on the Line Colors tool, then click on the desired color at the variety of colors that display. The color you select will be used to draw the lines for shapes.

You can also change the line color at the Line Attributes dialog box. To display this dialog box, click on the Line button on the Draw Toolbar or choose Format, then Line Attributes.

Changing Fill Color

By default, WordPerfect fills a shape with the color blue. You can change this fill color by clicking on the Fill Colors tool on the Draw Tool palette or at the Fill Attributes dialog box. When you click on the Fill Colors tool, a variety of color options displays. At this list of colors, click on the desired color.

Fill color can also be changed at the Fill Attributes dialog box. To display this dialog box, click on the Fill button on the Draw Toolbar; or choose Format, then Fill Attributes.

Exercise 11 Changing Shape Attributes

1. At a clear editing window, open c18ex08.
2. Save the document with Save As and name it c18ex11.
3. Change the border, fill, and pattern of the squares by completing the following steps:
   a. Change the viewing mode to Draft.
   b. Position the arrow pointer on one of the shapes, then double-click the left mouse button. This causes the Draw window to display with the shapes and text displayed.

c. Change the line, fill, and pattern of the square containing the A by completing the following steps:
   (1) Select the square containing the A.
   (2) Click on the Line Attributes tool on the Draw Tool palette. From the line options that display, select the sixth line option from the top in the first column (a thick line).
   (3) Click on the Fill Colors tool on the Draw Tool palette. From the color options that display, click on the bright pink color in the first row.
   (4) Click on the Fill Attributes tool on the Draw Tool palette. From the pattern options that display, select the third pattern from the left in the third row (vertical lines).

d. Change the line, fill, and pattern of the square containing the B by completing the following steps:
   (1) Select the square containing the B.
   (2) Click on the Line Attributes tool on the Draw Tool palette. From the line options that display, select the sixth line option from the top (a thick line).
   (3) Click on the Fill Colors tool on the Draw Tool palette. From the color options that display, click on the turquoise (light blue) color in the first row.
   (4) Click on the Fill Attributes tool on the Draw Tool palette. From the pattern options that display, select the fourth pattern from the left in the first row (diagonal lines).

e. Change the line, fill, and pattern of the square containing the C by completing the following steps:
   (1) Select the square containing the C.
   (2) Click on the Line Attributes tool on the Draw Tool palette. From the line options that display, select the sixth line option from the top (a thick line).
   (3) Click on the Fill Colors tool on the Draw Tool palette. From the color options that display, click on the yellow color in the first row.
   (4) Click on the Fill Attributes tool on the Draw Tool palette. From the pattern options that display, select the fourth pattern from the left in the third row (diagonal lines).

f. Close WordPerfect Draw.

4. Save the document again with the same name (c18ex11).
5. Print c18ex11. (Unless you are using a color printer, the colors will print in shades of gray.)
6. Close c18ex11.

WordPerfect Draw is a powerful mini-application that contains tools for creating professional-looking graphics. You have learned many of the basic options in WordPerfect Draw. There are additional features you may want to try when creating graphics. When using some of the more advanced features in WordPerfect Draw, refer to the on-line help screens for information relating to specific features. You can also refer to the WordPerfect reference manual for information.

Using TextArt

With WordPerfect TextArt, you can distort or modify text to conform to a variety of shapes. This is useful for creating company logos and headings. With TextArt, you can change the font, style, and justification of text. You can also add a shadow to the text, use different fills and outlines, and resize the text. To enter TextArt, choose Graphics, then TextArt; or click on the TextArt button on the 6.1 WordPerfect Toolbar. This causes the TextArt window shown in figure 18.13 to display.

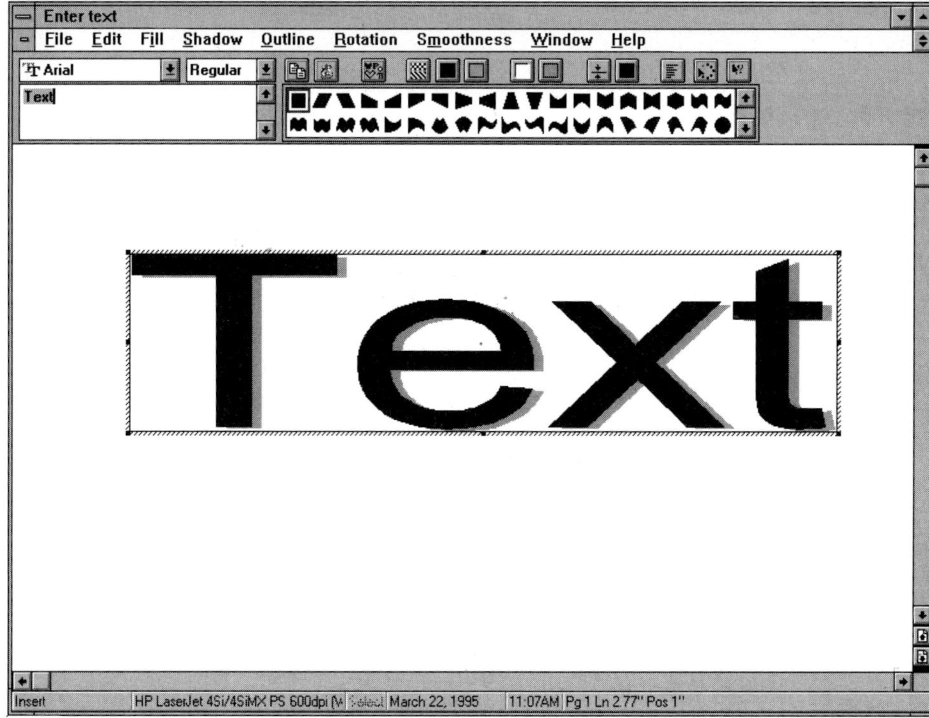

Figure 18.13
TextArt Window

Entering Text

When the TextArt window is displayed, the word *Text* displays in the box in the upper left corner of the TextArt window. The word *Text* also displays in the sample box. (This is the box that displays the word *Text* in large blue letters.) With the word *Text* selected in the box in the upper left corner of the TextArt window, key the text you want inserted as TextArt. The text you key is automatically displayed in the preview box. The maximum number of characters that can be entered in the text box varies depending on the size of characters entered. Up to three lines of characters can be entered. Press the Enter key to move the insertion point to the next line.

Exercise 12 Creating a Letterhead with TextArt

1. At a clear editing window, create the letterhead shown in figure 18.14 by completing the following steps:
   a. Create the NAN text using TextArt by completing the following steps:
      (1) Choose Graphics, then TextArt; or click on the TextArt button on the 6.1 WordPerfect Toolbar.
      (2) At the TextArt window, key **NAN.**
      (3) Position the I-beam pointer anywhere in the editing window outside the TextArt window, then click the left mouse button. (This removes the TextArt window.)
   b. At the editing window, display the Graphics Box Feature Bar for NAN. To do this, position the arrow pointer anywhere on NAN, click the *right* mouse button, then click on Feature Bar.
   c. With the Graphics Box Feature Bar displayed, change the box size width and height to 1 inch at the Box Size dialog box.
   d. Close the Graphics Box Feature Bar.

e. Change the font to 14-point Arial Bold.
f. Key **NATIONAL ASSOCIATION OF NURSES**.
g. Press Enter, then create a horizontal line with the default settings except change the Thickness to 4 points.
h. Key the address and telephone number as shown in figure 18.14.

2. Save the document and name it c18ex12.
3. Print c18ex12.
4. Close c18ex12.

Figure 18.14

NATIONAL ASSOCIATION OF NURSES

1211 Kinsington Drive
Kansas City, MO 84320
(314) 555-6700

Changing Fonts

By default, TextArt uses the Arial font (this may vary depending on the selected printer). You can change to a different font with options from the Font drop-down menu. To display this menu, click on the down-pointing arrow to the right of the Font button that displays just above the TextArt text box. To change the font, click on the desired font in the drop-down menu. When you change to a different font, the text in the sample box reflects the new font.

Change the type style with options from the Style drop-down menu. To display this menu, click on the down-pointing arrow to the right of the Style button that displays above the TextArt text box. By default, the style is Regular. This will change depending on the font you have selected. For many fonts, you may have only one choice of style.

Modifying TextArt

The TextArt window contains a toolbar with options for modifying text. With buttons on the TextArt Toolbar, you can perform such actions as changing text pattern, foreground and background color, adding shadow, changing the justification of text, and rotating text. Figure 18.15 describes the functions of the TextArt Toolbar buttons.

Figure 18.15
TextArt Toolbar Buttons

Press this button	Named	To do this...
	Copy	Copy TextArt image to the Windows Clipboard. The image can then be pasted into another Windows application.
	Paste	Paste text from the Windows Clipboard into TextArt.
	Character select	Display the Characters dialog box containing a variety of characters that can be inserted in TextArt.
	Text pattern	Choose a pattern for the TextArt characters.
	Text pattern foreground color	Choose the foreground color for a pattern.
	Text pattern background color	Choose the background color for the spaces in a pattern.
	Shadow position	Choose a shadow type. Choosing the center box will turn off the shadow.
	Shadow color	Choose a shadow color.
	Text outline width	Choose the line width around characters. Choose the single line with the X through it to turn off the outline.
	Text outline color	Choose the line color around characters.
	Justification	Choose left, right, or center justification for the text.
	Rotate	Drag a rotation handle to rotate TextArt.
	Help	Click on this button, then position arrow pointer on an item in the TextArt window to view help about that item.

Exercise 13 Creating a Newsletter Heading with TextArt

1. At a clear editing window, create the top part of a newsletter as shown in figure 18.16 by completing the following steps:
   a. Choose Graphics, then TextArt; or click on the TextArt button on the Toolbar.
   b. At the TextArt window, key **THE ST. C**.
   c. Create **Ô** by completing the following steps:
      (1) Click on the Character select button on the TextArt Toolbar.
      (2) At the Characters dialog box that displays at the left side of the editing window, click on the down-pointing arrow in the vertical scroll bar in the Characters list box until *Ô* is visible. (This is the first character in the nineteenth row.) When *Ô* is visible, click on it.
      (3) Click on Insert and Close.
   d. Position the insertion point in the text box (not the Preview Box) immediately after the *Ô*. To do this, position the I-beam pointer immediately right of the *Ô*, then click the left mouse button.
   e. Key **ME VOICE** (to complete the name).
   f. Change the text pattern. To do this, click on the Text pattern button on the TextArt Toolbar, then click on the fourth pattern option in the third row.
   g. Change the text outline width. To do this, click on the Text outline width button on the TextArt Toolbar, then click on the first line option in the second column.
   h. Click in the editing window outside the TextArt window. (This removes the TextArt window.)
   i. Deselect the TextArt box.
2. Save the document and name it c18ex13.
3. Print c18ex13.
4. Close c18ex13.

Figure 18.16

THE ST. CÔME VOICE

Changing Text Shape

With the shape options that display below the TextArt Toolbar, you can conform text to a variety of shapes. To select a shape, position the arrow pointer on the desired shape, then click the left mouse button. This causes the text in the sample box to conform to the selected shape. If you want to return the shape to the default of a rectangle, click on the first shape in the first row.

A vertical scroll bar displays to the right of the shapes. To view additional shapes, click on the down-pointing arrow in the vertical scroll bar. To scroll back up through the shapes, click on the up-pointing arrow.

Exercise 14 Changing the Shape of a Logo

1. At a clear editing window, create the logo shown in figure 18.17 by completing the following steps:
   a. Choose Graphics, then TextArt; or click on the TextArt button on the Toolbar.
   b. At the TextArt window, change the font to Arrus BT.
   c. Select the word *Text* in the text box, then key **Visual Expressions**.
   d. Change the shape by clicking on the eleventh shape in the third row. (To display the third row of shapes, click on the down-pointing arrow in the vertical scroll bar at the right side of the shapes.)
   e. Change the text pattern foreground color to light blue. To do this, click on the Text pattern foreground color button on the TextArt Toolbar, then click on the light blue color in the first row.
   f. Add a shadow to the text. To do this, click on the Shadow position button on the TextArt Toolbar, then click on the last option in the last row.
   g. Change the shadow color to blue. To do this, click on the Shadow color button on the TextArt Toolbar, then click on the blue color in the first row.
   h. Change the text outline width. To do this, click on the Text outline width button on the TextArt Toolbar, then click on the fourth option in the first column.
   i. Click in the editing window outside the TextArt window. (This removes the TextArt window.)
   j. Deselect the TextArt box.
2. Save the document and name it c18ex14.
3. Print c18ex14.
4. Close c18ex14.

Figure 18.17

Using the Menu Bar

The TextArt window contains a Menu Bar that displays at the top of the window below the Title Bar. Options from this Menu Bar include many of the same features as the buttons on the TextArt Toolbar. For example, you can add a shadow to TextArt with options from the Shadow drop-down menu; or you can add a pattern and change the foreground and background color of text with options from the Fill drop-down menu.

The Menu Bar contains a Smoothness drop-down menu with options that are not available from the TextArt Toolbar. When you choose Smoothness from the TextArt Menu Bar, a drop-down menu displays with the following options: Normal, High, and Very High. The default setting is Normal. Choose a higher smoothness to increase the roundness of lines in the characters and make the image more distinguishable. Changing to a higher smoothness will increase the time it takes for TextArt to redraw the image.

Editing a TextArt Image in the Editing Window

When a TextArt image is inserted in the document, it is inserted in a box. This box can be edited in the same manner as the graphics boxes you learned to create in chapter 17. For example, you can select the box and then move it to a different location in the document, or change the size of the box. You can also display the Graphics Box Feature Bar for the box containing the TextArt, then choose any of the editing options.

Exercise 15 Editing a TextArt Image Box

1. At a clear editing window, create the sign shown in figure 18.18 by completing the following steps:
   a. Choose Graphics, then TextArt; or click on the TextArt button on the Toolbar.
   b. At the TextArt window, key **The Red Circle Restaurant**, then press the space bar once.
   c. Increase the size of the TextArt Preview Box. To do this, complete the following steps:
      (1) Position the arrow pointer on the middle sizing handle at the bottom of the Preview Box until it turns into a double-headed arrow pointing up and down, hold down the left mouse button, drag the double-headed arrow close to the bottom of the editing window, then release the mouse button.
      (2) Position the arrow pointer on the middle sizing handle at the top of the sample box until it turns into a double-headed arrow pointing up and down, hold down the left mouse button, drag the double-headed arrow close to the top of the editing window, then release the mouse button.
   d. Change the shape by clicking on the thirteenth shape in the third row. (To display the third row of shapes, click on the down-pointing arrow in the vertical scroll bar at the right side of the shapes.)
   e. Rotate the text 180 degrees by completing the following steps:
      (1) Click on Rotation on the TextArt Menu Bar.
      (2) At the Rotation drop-down menu, click on Rotation.
      (3) At the Rotation dialog box, position the tip of the arrow pointer in the radio button before 180 Degrees, then click the left mouse button. (This rotates the text in the Preview Box.)
      (4) Click on the Close button at the Rotation dialog box.
   f. Change the smoothness to very high by completing the following steps:
      (1) Click on Smoothness.
      (2) At the Smoothness drop-down menu, click on Very High.
   g. Change the text pattern foreground color to red. To do this, click on the Text pattern foreground color button on the TextArt Toolbar, then click on the red color in the first row.
   h. Click in the editing window outside the TextArt window. (There is not much free editing window area.)
2. At the editing window (with TextArt closed), make the following changes:
   a. Deselect the TextArt image. To do this, position the arrow pointer in the editing window outside the image, then click the left mouse button.
   b. Click on the Page/Zoom Full button on the Toolbar. (This displays the entire page.)
   c. Select the TextArt image. To do this, position the arrow pointer inside the image, then click the left mouse button.
   d. Increase the size of the TextArt image. To do this, position the arrow pointer on the middle sizing handle at the bottom of the TextArt image box until it turns

into a double-headed arrow pointing up and down. (The arrow pointer must be precisely positioned for it to turn into a double-headed arrow.) When the arrow pointer turns into a double-headed arrow, hold down the left mouse button, drag the outline down approximately one inch, then release the mouse button. (Drag the image down enough so the text appears in a more perfect circle.)

e. Drag the image to the middle of the page. To do this, position the mouse pointer inside the image and it displays as a four-headed arrow. Hold down the left mouse button, drag the outline of the TextArt image box to the middle of the page, then release the mouse button.
f. Deselect the box containing the TextArt.
g. Click on the Page/Zoom Full button. (This returns the viewing mode back to Page.)

3. Save the document and name it c18ex15.
4. Print c18ex15.
5. Close c18ex15.

Figure 18.18

CHAPTER SUMMARY

- With WordPerfect Draw, you can draw shapes, draw freehand, insert graphics images, and create and customize text.
- An object created in the drawing area can be cleared with the Clear option from the Edit drop-down menu or with Ctrl + Shift + F4.
- Whatever you create at the Draw window is inserted in the document in a box without borders that is approximately 5 inches wide and 4.5 inches tall.
- A graphics image can be inserted in the drawing area where it can be customized. The graphics image can then be inserted in the document.
- WordPerfect Draw includes a ruler and grid that you can use to draw shapes or position objects at specific locations in the drawing area.
- A box containing drawn objects can be edited using options from the Graphics Box Feature Bar. The box can also be sized and/or relocated in the document using the mouse.

- The Draw Tool palette is available at the Draw window and includes a variety of tools for selecting, drawing, and changing the fill and attributes of objects.
- At the Draw window, a drawn object can be moved, copied, or deleted. An object can also be made wider/narrower or taller/shorter.
- At the Draw window, you can create text, create a curved line, and then contour the text on the curved line.
- With WordPerfect TextArt, you can distort or modify characters of text to conform to a variety of shapes.
- Other options available with TextArt include the following: changing fonts, adding pattern, changing the foreground and background color, adding shadow, changing the outline width, changing the justification, and rotating text.

Commands Review

	Mouse/Keyboard
Draw	Graphics, Draw; or click on the Draw button on the Graphics Toolbar
Graphics Box Feature Bar	Position arrow pointer on drawn shape, hold down right mouse button, drag the arrow pointer to Feature Bar, then release the mouse button
TextArt	Graphics, then TextArt; or click on the TextArt button on the Toolbar

CHECK YOUR UNDERSTANDING

True/False: Circle the letter T if the statement is true; circle the letter F if the statement is false.

T F 1. You can display the Draw window by choosing Draw from the Tools drop-down menu.

T F 2. At the Draw window, a closed shape will be filled with the color blue.

T F 3. Use the Line Object Tools tool to draw a line, curved line, sections of an ellipse, or draw freehand.

T F 4. To clear objects from the drawing area, choose Clear from the File drop-down menu.

T F 5. When WordPerfect Draw is closed, the drawn object(s) is inserted in a box with a single line border.

T F 6. At the editing window, a box containing a drawn shape can be moved using the mouse.

T F 7. Text cannot be keyed in the drawing area.

T F 8. To select more than one object in the drawing area, hold down the Ctrl key as you click the left mouse button.

T F 9. Text can be contoured on a curved line at the drawing area.

T F 10. Shadow can be added to text in TextArt.

Completion: In the space provided at the right, indicate the correct term, command, or number.

1. This displays at the left side of the Draw window and contains tools for selecting, drawing, and changing the fill and attributes of objects. ____________________
2. With this tool, you can draw closed shapes. ____________________
3. To draw a square, choose the rectangle tool, then hold down this key while drawing the square. ____________________

4. This is the default font at the drawing area. ____________________
5. This button on the Draw Power Bar contains options for changing the display of text in the drawing area. ____________________
6. To select an object in the drawing area, click on this tool on the Draw Tool palette, then click on the object. ____________________
7. When an object is selected in the drawing area, these display around the object. ____________________
8. You can customize the black line used to draw shapes with this button on the Draw Tool palette. ____________________
9. By default, a shape is filled with this color. ____________________
10. Click on this button on the TextArt Toolbar to choose a foreground color for a pattern. ____________________

SKILL ASSESSMENTS

Assessment 1

1. At a clear editing window, use WordPerfect Draw to create the rounded rectangles containing text shown in figure 18.19 with the following specifications:
   a. Create the rounded rectangles at the Draw window. (*Hint: Create the first rounded rectangle, then copy it.*)
   b. After creating the rounded rectangles and the text inside, select each rounded rectangle individually, then change the fill color to yellow.
   c. At the editing window, display the Graphics Box Feature Bar for the box containing the rounded rectangles, then change the horizontal position to Center of Paragraph at the Box Position dialog box.
2. Save the document and name it c18sa01.
3. Print c18sa01.
4. Close c18sa01.

Figure 18.19

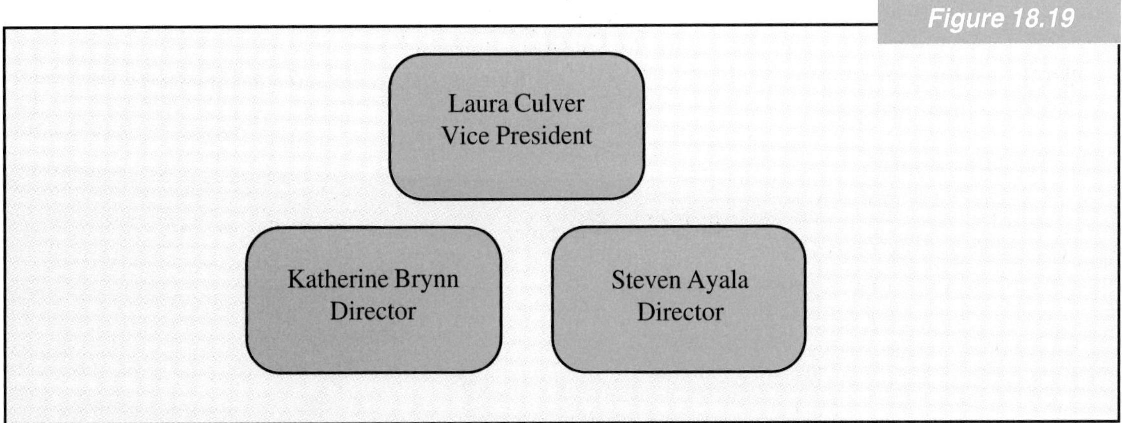

Assessment 2

1. At a clear editing window, create the letterhead shown in figure 18.20 using WordPerfect Draw with the following specifications:
   a. Change to the Draft viewing mode.
   b. Create the circles at the Draw window. Make the circles approximately 1.5 inches in diameter. After creating the circles, move the draw border close to the circles on all sides.

c. At the editing window, display the Graphics Box Feature Bar for the circles, then change the horizontal position to Left Margin and the Vertical Place to 0 inches from the Top Margin at the Box Position dialog box and change the width to Set at 2 inches at the Box Size dialog box.
d. Close the Graphics Box Feature Bar.
e. Change the font to 18-point Swis721 BlkEx BT.
f. Press Enter once, then key **FLOW SYSTEMS LIMITED**.
g. Press Enter once, then create the horizontal line with a thickness of 10 points.

2. Save the document and name it c18sa02.
3. Print c18sa02.
4. Close c18sa02.

Figure 18.20

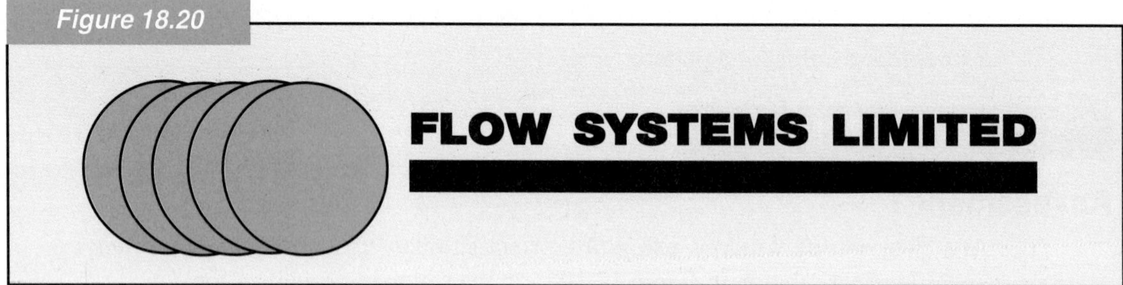

Assessment 3

1. At a clear editing window, create the document shown in figure 18.21 with the following specifications:
   a. At the Draw window, create the shapes, the curve, and the text. (Before keying the text, change the font to Brush738 BT. You determine the point size.) Select the text and the curve, then contour the text around the curve.
   b. At the editing window, display the Graphics Box Feature Bar, then change the anchor to Put Box on Current Page at the Box Position dialog box and the Horizontal placement to Center of Paragraph. Change the box size width to Full and the height to Size to Content. (Be sure to close the Graphics Box Feature Bar when you are done.)
2. Save the document and name it c18sa03.
3. Print c18sa03. (Your document will print larger than what you see in figure 18.21.)
4. Close c18sa03.

Figure 18.21

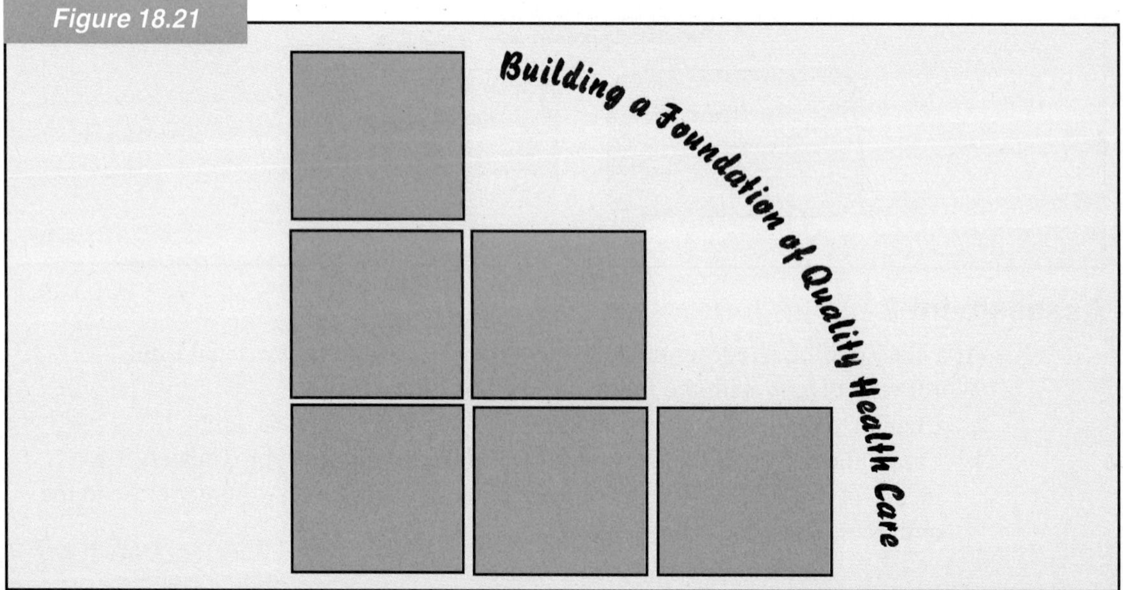

Assessment 4

1. At a clear editing window, create the sale notice shown in figure 18.22 at the TextArt window with the following specifications:
   a. At the TextArt window, change the font to CaslonOpnface BT.
   b. Select the word *Text* in the text box, then key **30% Off Sale!**.
   c. Change the shape to match what you see in the figure.
   d. Add a shadow to the lower right side of the text.
   e. Add a fill pattern and change the fill color. (You determine the fill and the color.)
   f. Close the TextArt window.
   g. At the editing window, display the Graphics Box Feature Bar, then change the anchor to Put Box on Current Page at the Box Position dialog box and the Horizontal placement to Center of Paragraph. Change the box size width to Full and the height to Size to Content. (Be sure to close the Graphics Box Feature Bar when you are done.)
2. Save the document and name it c18sa04.
3. Print c18sa04. (Your document will print larger than what you see in figure 18.22.)
4. Close c18sa04.

Figure 18.22

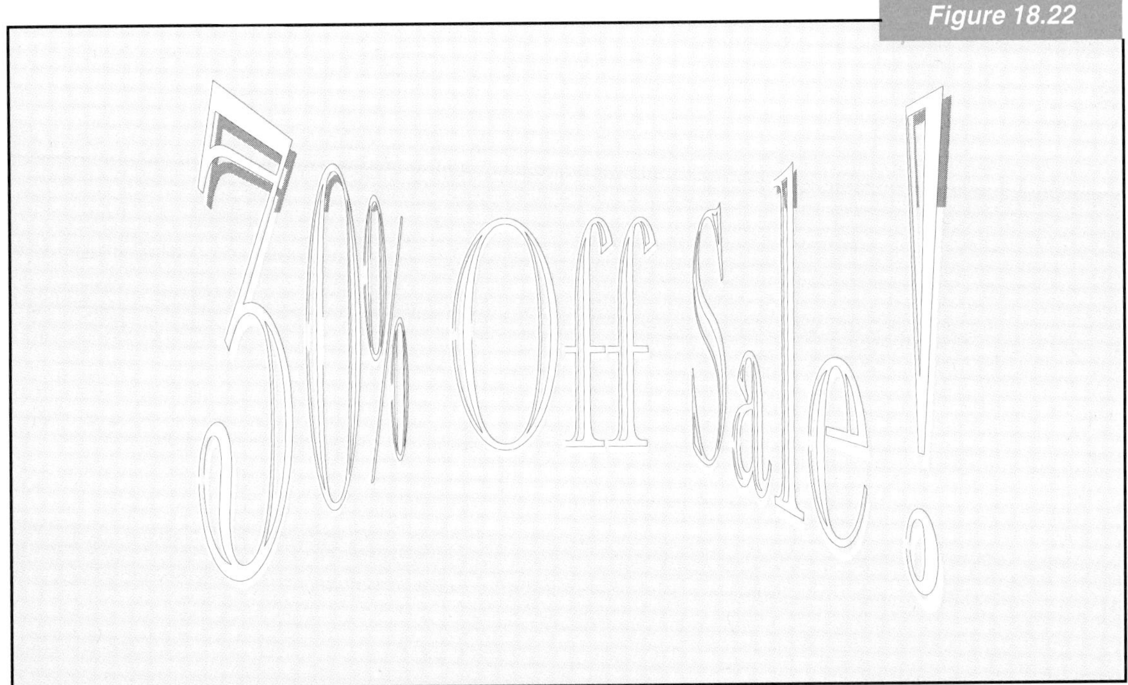

Creating Tables 19

Upon successful completion of chapter 19, you will be able to define and adjust structures for business tables according to a variety of format and size considerations.

WordPerfect's Tables feature can be used to create columns and rows of information that are surrounded by horizontal and vertical lines. The boxes created by the intersection of rows and columns are called cells.

A cell can contain text, characters, numbers, data, or formulas. Text within a cell can be formatted to display left, right, center, or decimal aligned and can include character formatting such as bold, italics, and underlining. The formatting choices available with Tables are quite extensive and allow flexibility in creating a variety of tables.

Creating a Table

A table can be created with the Table option from the Menu Bar or the Tables button on the Power Bar (the sixth button from the left). To create a table with the Tables button on the Power Bar, position the arrow pointer on the Tables button, then hold down the left mouse button. This causes a grid to appear as shown in figure 19.1. Drag the arrow pointer down and to the right until the correct number of rows and columns displays above the grid, then release the mouse button. As you drag the arrow pointer, selected columns and rows are displayed in black, and the number of rows and columns displays above the grid.

Figure 19.1
Table Grid

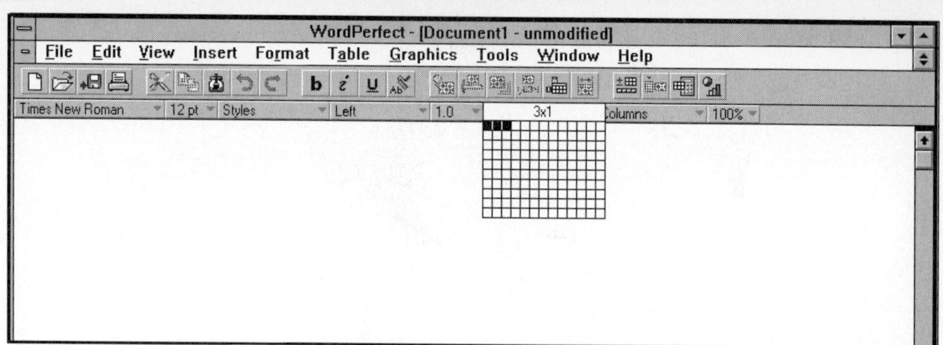

Figure 19.2
Create Table Dialog Box

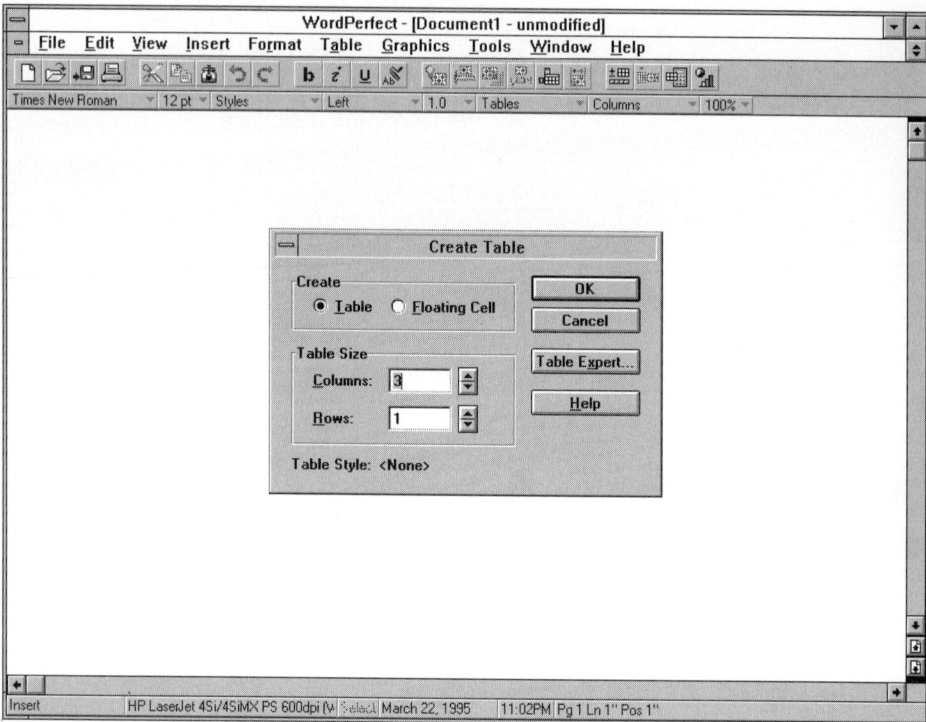

A table can also be created at the Create Table dialog box, shown in figure 19.2. Display the Create Table dialog box by choosing Table, then Create. At the Create Table dialog box, specify the number of columns and rows, then choose OK or press Enter. When you choose OK or press Enter at the Create Table dialog box, a table similar to the one shown in figure 19.3 is inserted in the document at the location of the insertion point.

The insertion point is located in the upper left corner of the table in cell A1. Columns are lettered from left to right, beginning with A. The cell to the right of A1 is B1, the cell to the right of B1 is C1, and so on. Rows in a table are numbered. The cells below A1 are A2, A3, and so on.

WordPerfect provides a Tables Toolbar containing buttons for formatting and customizing a table. To display the Tables Toolbar, position the arrow pointer on the current toolbar, click the right mouse button, then click on Tables. The Tables Toolbar automatically displays when a table is created. The Tables Toolbar contains a button that will identify columns and rows. To display column letters and row numbers, click on the Row/Column Indicators button on the Tables Toolbar (the eighteenth button from the left). This causes the column letters and row numbers to display as shown in figure 19.4. The cell name in which the insertion point is located is displayed at the left side of the Status Bar.

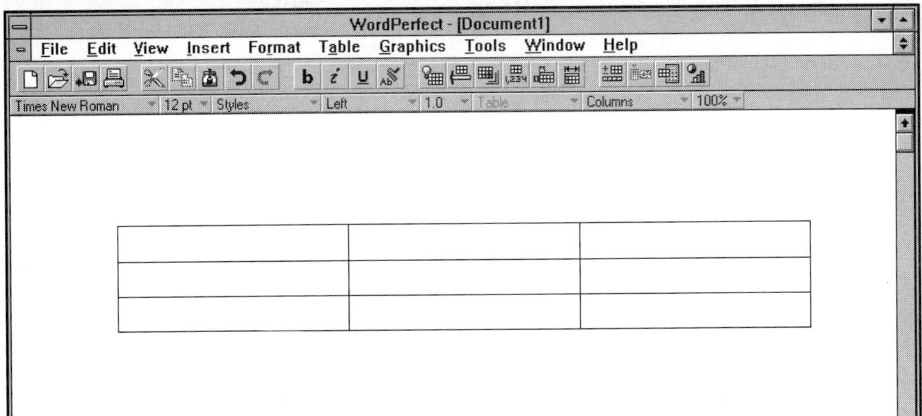

Figure 19.3
Table

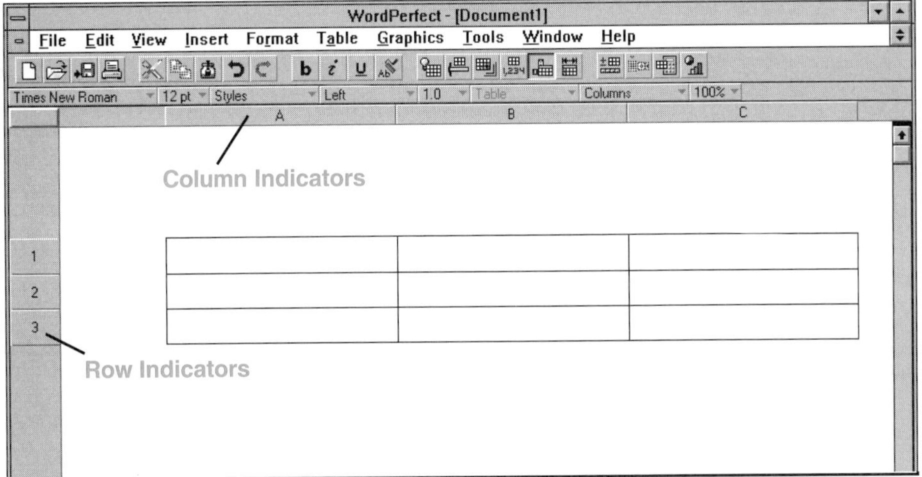

Figure 19.4
Table with Row/ Column Indicators

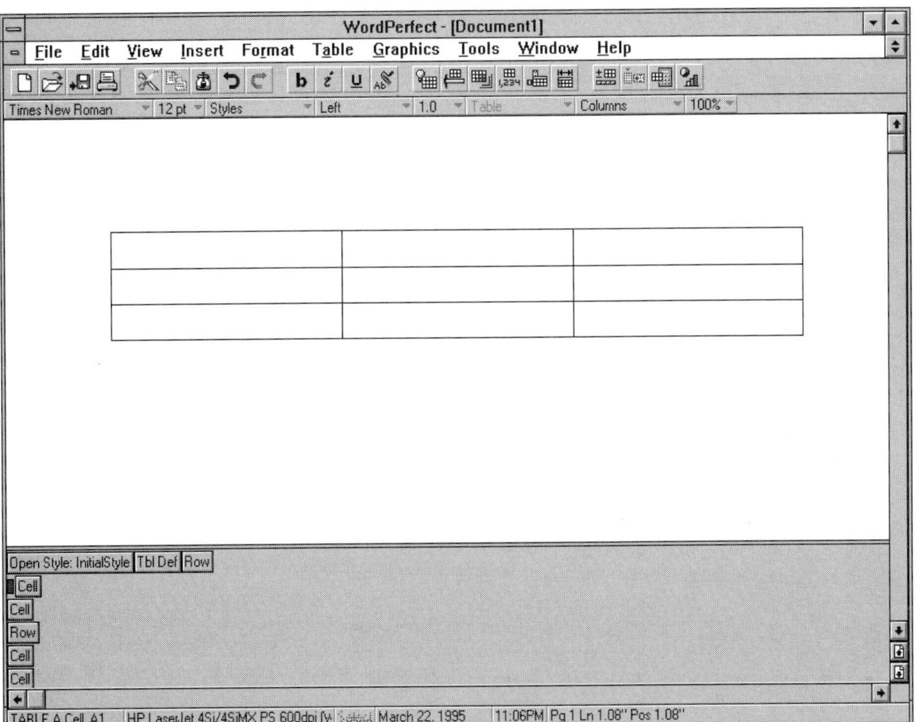

Figure 19.5
Table Codes in Reveal Codes

When the insertion point is positioned in a table, the Table button on the Power Bar and the Create option from the Table drop-down menu are grayed (dimmed) because a table cannot be created within a table. When a table is created, codes are inserted in the document that can be seen in Reveal Codes. For example, the codes for the table shown in figure 19.4 will display as shown in figure 19.5.

Entering Text in Cells

With the insertion point positioned in a cell, key or edit text as you would normal text. Move the insertion point to other cells with the mouse by positioning the I-beam pointer in the desired cell, then clicking the left mouse button. If you are using the keyboard, press Tab to move the insertion point to the next cell or press Shift + Tab to move the insertion point to the previous cell.

If the text you key does not fit on one line, it wraps to the next line within the same cell. Or, if you press Enter within a cell, the insertion point is moved to the next line within the same cell. The cell vertically lengthens to accommodate the text, and all cells in that row also lengthen.

Pressing the Tab key in a table causes the insertion point to move to the next cell in the table. If you want to insert a tab *within* a cell, use one of the commands shown in figure 19.6.

Figure 19.6 Commands to Insert Tabs in Cells

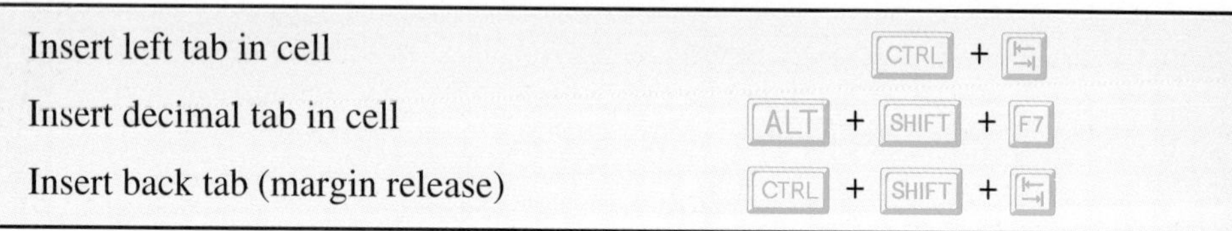

Insert left tab in cell	CTRL + TAB
Insert decimal tab in cell	ALT + SHIFT + F7
Insert back tab (margin release)	CTRL + SHIFT + TAB

If the insertion point is located in the last cell of the table and you press the Tab key, WordPerfect adds another row to the table. To avoid this situation, make sure you do not press the Tab key after entering text in the last cell.

You can insert a page break within a table by pressing Ctrl + Enter. The page break is inserted between rows, not within.

When all information has been entered in the cells, move the insertion point below the table and, if necessary, continue keying the document, or save the document in the normal manner.

Moving the Insertion Point within a Table

To move the insertion point to different cells within the table using the mouse, position the I-beam pointer in the desired cell, then click the left button.

To move the insertion point to different cells within the table using the keyboard, refer to the information shown in figure 19.7.

Figure 19.7 Insertion Point Movement within a Table

Move insertion point within cell in direction indicated	↑, ←, ↓, and →
Move insertion point to next cell	TAB
Move insertion point to previous cell	SHIFT + TAB
Move insertion point one cell down	ALT + ↓
Move insertion point one cell up	ALT + ↑
Move insertion point to first cell in row	HOME, HOME
Move insertion point to last cell in row	END, END

Move insertion point to top line of multi-line cell	ALT + HOME
Move insertion point to bottom line of multi-line cell	ALT + END

Exercise 1 Creating a Table with the Tables Button

1. At a clear editing window, create the table shown in figure 19.8 by completing the following steps:
   a. Center and bold the title, *WORDPERFECT CLASS.*
   b. Press Enter twice.
   c. Create the table by completing the following steps:
      (1) Position the arrow pointer on the Tables button on the Power Bar.
      (2) Hold down the left mouse button. This causes a grid to appear.
      (3) Drag the arrow pointer down and to the right until the number above the grid displays as *2x10*, then release the mouse button.
   d. Key the heading, *Employee*, in cell A1 by completing the following steps:
      (1) Make sure the insertion point is positioned in cell A1.
      (2) Press Shift + F7; or choose Format, Line, then Center.
      (3) Click on the Bold button on the Toolbar; or press Ctrl + B.
      (4) Key **Employee**.
      (5) Press the Tab key to move the insertion point to cell B1.
      (6) Complete similar steps to insert *Department* in cell B1.
2. Save the table and name it c19ex01.
3. Print c19ex01.
4. Close c19ex01.

Figure 19.8

WORDPERFECT CLASS

Employee	**Department**

Exercise 2 Creating a Table at the Create Table Dialog Box

1. At a clear editing window, create the table shown in figure 19.9 by completing the following steps:
   a. Center and bold *DENVER MEMORIAL HOSPITAL.*
   b. Press Enter twice, then center and bold *Executive Officers.*
   c. Press Enter three times, then create a table with two columns and five rows by completing the following steps:
      (1) Choose Table, then Create; or double-click on the Tables button on the Power Bar.
      (2) At the Create Table dialog box, key **2**.
      (3) Choose Rows.
      (4) Key **5**.
      (5) Choose OK or press Enter.
   d. Key the text in the cells as shown in figure 19.9. To indent the text within cells, press Ctrl + Tab to insert a tab within the cell. (Do this for each cell.)
2. Save the table and name it c19ex02.
3. Print c19ex02.
4. Close c19ex02.

Figure 19.9

DENVER MEMORIAL HOSPITAL

Executive Officers

President	Chris Hedegaard
Vice President	Robert Freitas
Vice President	Richard Dudley
Vice President	Glenna Wykoff
Vice President	Laura Culver

Changing the Column Width of a Table

When a table is created, the columns are the same width. The width of the columns depends on the number of columns as well as the document margins. In some tables, you may want to change the width of certain columns to accommodate more or less text. You can change the width of columns using the mouse, the Ruler Bar, or the Format dialog box.

Changing Column Width with the Mouse

To change column widths using the mouse, position the I-beam pointer on the line separating columns until it turns into a left- and right-pointing arrow with a vertical line between. Hold down the left mouse button, drag the column line to the desired location, then release the mouse button. This moves only the column line where the double-headed arrow is positioned. If you hold down the Shift key while you drag a column line, all columns to the right are also moved.

Changing Column Width with the Ruler Bar

When the insertion point is positioned in a table, the column widths are displayed on the Ruler Bar above the ruler numbers as down-pointing triangles. (To display the Ruler Bar, choose View, then Ruler Bar.) These down-pointing triangles are called *column width markers*. Other table markers display on the Ruler Bar, including the *table sizing marker*, the *right column margins marker*, and the *left column margins marker*. These markers are identified in figure 19.10.

To change the column width with the Ruler Bar, position the arrow pointer on the column width marker to be moved, hold down the left mouse button, then drag the marker to widen or narrow the columns. (As you drag the marker, the column width marker in the original location displays in blue, and the column marker being moved displays in black, with a vertical guide showing the position.) When the column width marker is in the new position, release the mouse button.

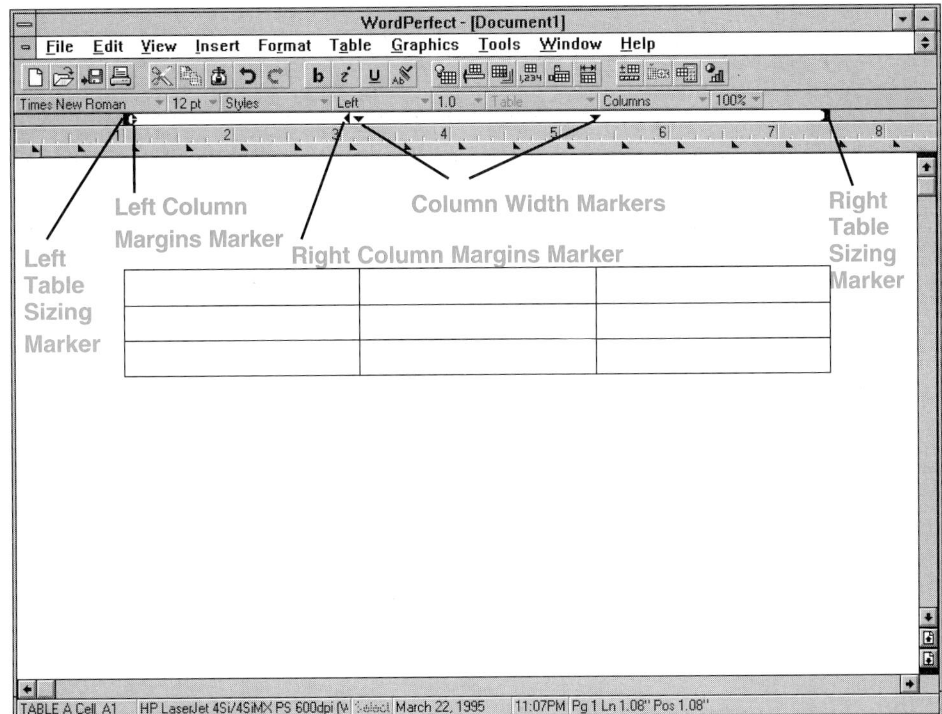

Figure 19.10
Table Markers on the Ruler Bar

When you move a column width marker in this manner, only the column width marker on which the arrow pointer is positioned is moved. Any other column width markers in the table stay in their original position. If you want to move a column width marker and any other column width markers to the right the same distance, hold down the Shift key when dragging the mouse.

When you are dragging the column width marker, the Status Bar displays the position of the marker on the Ruler Bar. Use this position measurement to move the column width marker to the desired measurement on the Ruler Bar.

The left column margins marker and the right column margins marker can be used to adjust the left or right column margins in all columns. To do this, drag the marker to the desired location on the Ruler Bar. When you change the left margin or right margin, the margin is changed for all columns in the table.

Use the table sizing marker to increase or decrease the overall size of a table. This does not affect the number of columns or rows, it only affects the width of the table. To change the width of a table, drag the left and/or right table sizing marker to the desired location on the Ruler Bar.

If the right table sizing marker is not visible, you can make it visible by dragging the scroll box on the horizontal scroll bar to the right. When you drag the scroll box to the right, the display of text is shifted to the left in the editing window. Continue to do this until the right table sizing marker is visible.

Exercise 3 Creating and Editing a Table

1. At a clear editing window, create the memo shown in figure 19.11 by completing the following steps:
   a. Change the font to 12-point Courier New.
   b. Key the headings and the first paragraph of the memo.
   c. With the insertion point a double space below the first paragraph, create a table that contains three columns and eight rows.
   d. Change the width of the first column by completing the following steps:
      (1) Display the Ruler Bar.
      (2) Position the arrow pointer on the column width marker between the 3-inch and the 3.25-inch marks on the Ruler Bar.
      (3) Hold down the left mouse button.
      (4) Drag the marker to the 4.5-inch mark on the Ruler Bar, then release the mouse button. (Check the right side of the Status Bar. The Position measurement should display as *4.5"* before releasing the left mouse button.)
   e. Change the width of the second column by completing the following steps:
      (1) Position the arrow pointer on the column width marker between the 5-inch and the 5.5-inch marks on the Ruler Bar.
      (2) Hold down the left mouse button.
      (3) Drag the marker to the 6-inch mark on the Ruler Bar, then release the mouse button. (The Position measurement in the Status Bar should display as *6"* before releasing the left mouse button.)
   f. Key the text in the cells as indicated in figure 19.11. Center the text in cells A1, B1, and C1. Use Ctrl + Tab to indent the text in cells A2 through A8.
   g. Move the insertion point a double space below the table, then key the last paragraph and reference line shown in figure 19.11.
2. Save the memo and name it c19ex03.
3. Print c19ex03.
4. Close c19ex03.

Figure 19.11

```
DATE:    February 4, 1997

TO:      Paula Kerns

FROM:    Steven Ayala

SUBJECT: WORDPERFECT CLASS

The deadline for enrolling in the WordPerfect class was
January 31.  A total of seven employees registered for
the class.  The list of employees and their status is
displayed below.
```

Name	Hospital #	Department
Arnold Koch	523-44-0944	Med. Records
Margaret Williamson	312-33-0393	Finances
Karyn Thomas-Briggs	128-03-3372	Pediatrics
Lillian Smith	329-55-4964	Payroll
Raymond Ottmar	543-34-7751	Med. Records
Leonard Strickertz	243-09-5943	Finances
Elizabeth Landes	423-43-2009	Payroll

I have reserved Room 102 for the class. Please let me know what special equipment you will need. There will be eight computers available in the room.

xx:c19ex03

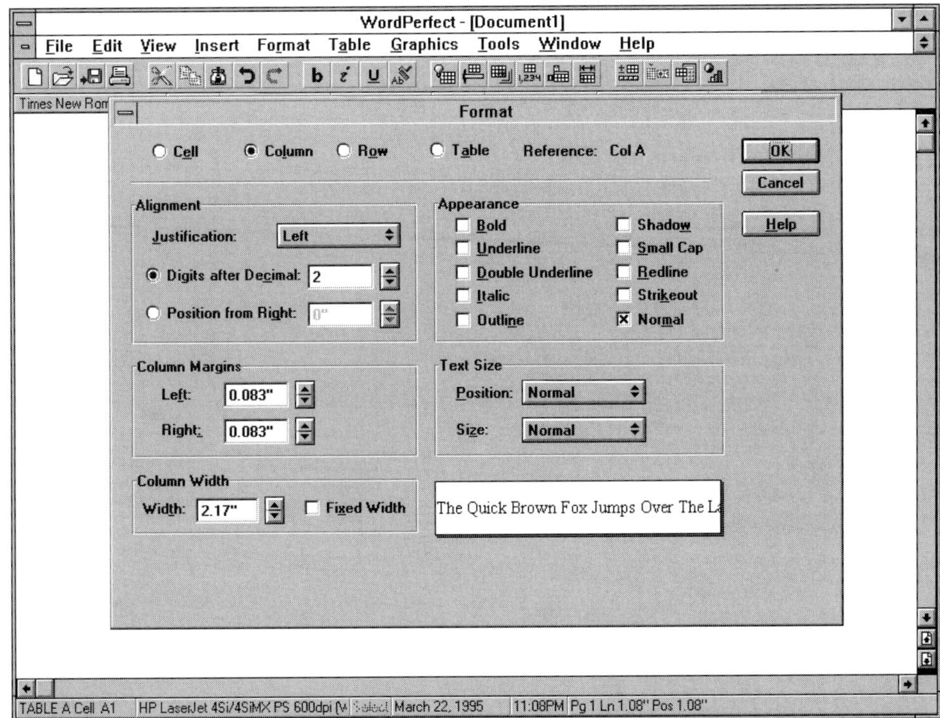

Figure 19.12
Format Dialog Box

Changing Column Width with the Format Dialog Box

To change the column width with the Format dialog box, choose Table, then Format. At the Format dialog box, choose Column. To do this with the mouse, click on the radio button before the Column option at the top of the dialog box. If you are using the keyboard, press Alt + L. At the Format dialog box, shown in figure 19.12, choose Width. To do this, with the mouse, select the current number displayed in the Width text box. If you are using the keyboard, press Alt + T. Key the desired column measurement, then choose OK or press Enter.

Exercise 4 Changing Column Widths

1. At a clear editing window, create the table shown in figure 19.13 by completing the following steps:
   a. Change the font to 12-point GeoSlab703 Lt BT.
   b. Center and bold *CARIBBEAN CRUISE.*
   c. Press Enter twice, then center and bold *Dining Room Reservations.*
   d. Press Enter three times, then create a table with three columns and five rows.
   e. Change the width of the first column to 2 inches by completing the following steps:
      (1) Position the insertion point in any cell in the first column.
      (2) Choose Table, then Format.
      (3) At the Format dialog box, choose Column. To do this with the mouse, click on the radio button before the Column option at the top of the dialog box. If you are using the keyboard, press Alt + L.
      (4) At the Format dialog box, choose Width. To do this with the mouse, select the current number displayed in the Width text box. If you are using the keyboard, press Alt + T.
      (5) Key **2**.
      (6) Choose OK or press Enter.
   f. Change the width of the second column to 1.5 inches by completing steps similar to those in 1e(1) through 1e(6).
   g. Change the width of the third column to 1.5 inches by completing steps similar to those in 1e(1) through 1e(6).
   h. Key the text in the cells as indicated in figure 19.13. Center the text in the second and third columns.
2. Change the size of the table with the table sizing marker by completing the following steps:
   a. Position the insertion point inside the table.
   b. Display the Ruler Bar.
   c. Position the arrow pointer on the left table sizing marker.
   d. Hold down the Shift key, then hold down the left mouse button.
   e. Drag the arrow pointer to the 2-inch mark on the Ruler Bar. (Check the Status Bar for the Position measurement.)
   f. Release the mouse button and the Shift key.
3. Save the table and name it c19ex04.
4. Print c19ex04.
5. Close c19ex04.

Figure 19.13

CARIBBEAN CRUISE

Dining Room Reservations

	Early	Late
Breakfast (in port)	6:45 a.m.	8:00 a.m.
Breakfast (at sea)	7:45 a.m.	9:00 a.m.
Luncheon	12:00 noon	1:30 p.m.
Dinner	6:00 p.m.	8:00 p.m.

Selecting Cells

A table can be formatted in special ways. For example, the alignment or margins of text in cells or rows can be changed or character formatting can be added. To identify the cells that are to be affected by the formatting, the specific cells need to be selected.

Selecting Cells with the Mouse

The mouse pointer can be used to select a cell, row, column, or an entire table. The table selection arrows are used to select specific cells in a table. There is a left-pointing arrow called the *horizontal selection arrow* and an up-pointing arrow called the *vertical selection arrow*.

To display the horizontal selection arrow, move the I-beam pointer to the left border of any cell until it turns into a left-pointing arrow. This arrow is the horizontal selection arrow. To display the vertical selection arrow, move the I-beam pointer to the top border of any cell until it turns into an up-pointing arrow. This arrow is the vertical selection arrow.

To select one cell in a table, position the I-beam pointer in the cell to be selected so that either the horizontal or the vertical selection arrow is displayed, then click the left mouse button. When you click the left mouse button, the selected cell displays in black and any text within the cell displays in white.

To select a row in a table, position the I-beam pointer in any cell in the row until the horizontal selection arrow is displayed, then double-click the left mouse button.

To select a column in a table, position the I-beam pointer in any cell in the column at the top border of the cell until the vertical selection arrow is displayed, then double-click the left mouse button.

To select all cells within a table, position the insertion point in any cell in the table until either the horizontal or the vertical selection arrow is displayed, then click the left mouse button quickly three times.

If you want to select the text within a cell rather than the entire cell, select the text in the normal manner.

If you click on the Row/Column Indicators button on the Tables Toolbar, letters display identifying columns and numbers display identifying rows. These column and row indicators can be used to select cells within a table. To select a row, click on the row indicator number next to the row to be selected. To select a column, click on the column letter above the column to be selected. When column and row indicators are displayed, a square displays in the top left corner of the row and column indicators. Click on this button to select the entire table.

Selecting Text with the Keyboard

The keyboard can be used to select specific cells within a table. Figure 19.14 displays the commands for selecting specific amounts of a table.

Amount of the Table	Command
Current cell	SHIFT + F8
Current row	SHIFT + CTRL + →
Current column	SHIFT + CTRL + ↑
One cell, row, or column at a time	SHIFT + →
Beginning of current row	SHIFT + HOME
End of current row	SHIFT + END

Figure 19.14
Selecting Commands

Current table to beginning of document	SHIFT + CTRL + HOME
Current table to end of document	SHIFT + CTRL + END

If you want to select only text within cells, rather than the entire cell, press F8 to turn on the Select mode, then move the insertion point with the insertion point movement commands.

When a cell is selected, the entire cell is changed to black. When text within a cell is selected, only those lines containing text are selected.

Exercise 5 Selecting Cells and Changing the Text Appearance

1. At a clear editing window, open c19ex03.
2. Save the document with Save As and name it c19ex05.
3. Select and bold cells A1, B1, and C1 using the mouse by completing the following steps:
   a. Position the I-beam pointer in cell A1 at the left border of the cell until the horizontal selection arrow is displayed.
   b. Double-click the left mouse button.
   c. With the first row selected, click on the Bold button on the Toolbar.
   d. Turn off Select by clicking the I-beam pointer anywhere outside the selected area.
4. Select and italicize the text in cells B2 through B8 using the keyboard by completing the following steps:
   a. Position the insertion point in cell B2.
   b. Hold down the Shift key and press the down arrow key until the insertion point reaches cell B8, then release the Shift key and the down arrow key.
   c. With cells B2 through B8 selected, press Ctrl + I.
   d. Press F8 to turn off Select.
5. Select and italicize the text in cells C2 through C8 by completing steps similar to those in 4a through 4d.
6. Save the document again with the same name (c19ex05).
7. Print c19ex05.
8. Close c19ex05.

Editing a Table

A table that has been created with WordPerfect's Tables feature can be edited in a variety of ways. For example, text within cells can be inserted or deleted; columns or rows can be copied or moved; or rows and columns can be inserted or deleted.

Inserting Rows or Columns

With the Insert option from the Table drop-down menu, you can insert rows or columns in a table. By default, a row is inserted above the row where the insertion point is positioned and a column is inserted to the left of the column where the insertion point is positioned.

To insert a row in a table, position the insertion point in the row below where the row is to be inserted, then choose Table, then Insert. At the Insert Columns/Rows dialog box, shown in figure 19.15, choose OK or press Enter.

To insert a column, position the insertion point in the column immediately right of where the column is to be inserted, then choose Table, then Insert. At the Insert Columns/Rows dialog box, choose Columns, then choose OK or press Enter.

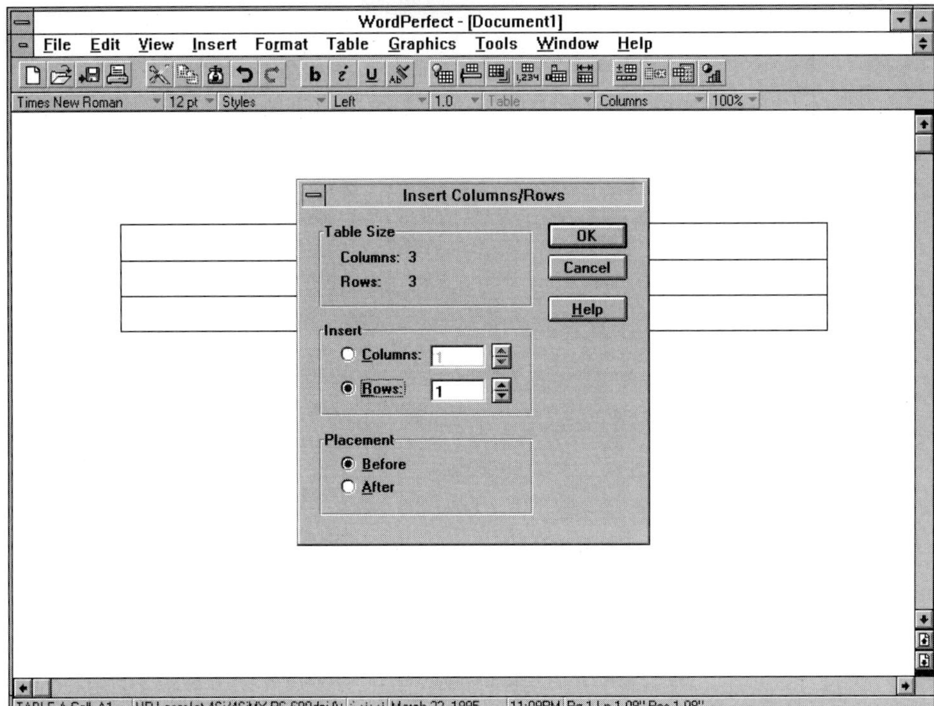

Figure 19.15
Insert Columns/Rows Dialog Box

More than one column or row can be inserted at the Insert Columns/Rows dialog box. To insert more than one, choose Rows or Columns at the Insert Columns/Rows dialog box, then key the number to be inserted.

The Insert Columns/Rows dialog box contains a Placement section with two options—Before and After. The Before option is selected by default. This causes a row to be inserted above the position of the insertion point or a column to be inserted to the left of the position of the insertion point. If you choose After, a row is inserted below the position of the insertion point and a column is inserted to the right of the position of the insertion point.

Exercise 6 Inserting a Row in a Table

1. At a clear editing window, open c19ex03.
2. Save the document with Save As and name it c19ex06.
3. Select cells A1 through C1, then turn on bold.
4. Add a row in the table between Lillian Smith and Raymond Ottmar by completing the following steps:
   a. Position the insertion point in any cell in the row for Raymond Ottmar.
   b. Choose Table, then Insert.
   c. At the Insert Columns/Rows dialog box, choose OK or press Enter.
5. Key the following text in the new cells:
   A6 = **Lena McCaw**
   B6 = **423-07-4534**
   C6 = **Finances**
6. Save the document again with the same name (c19ex06).
7. Print c19ex06.
8. Close c19ex06.

Deleting Rows or Columns

Rows or columns in a document can be deleted with the Delete option from the Table drop-down menu. To delete a row in a table, position the insertion point in any cell in the row to be deleted, then choose Table, then Delete. At the Delete dialog box, shown in figure 19.16, choose OK or press Enter.

To delete a column, position the insertion point in any cell in the column to be deleted, then choose Table, then Delete. At the Delete dialog box, choose Columns, then choose OK or press Enter.

More than one column or row can be deleted at the Delete dialog box. To delete more than one, choose Rows or Columns at the Delete dialog box, then key the number to be deleted.

Figure 19.16
Delete Dialog Box

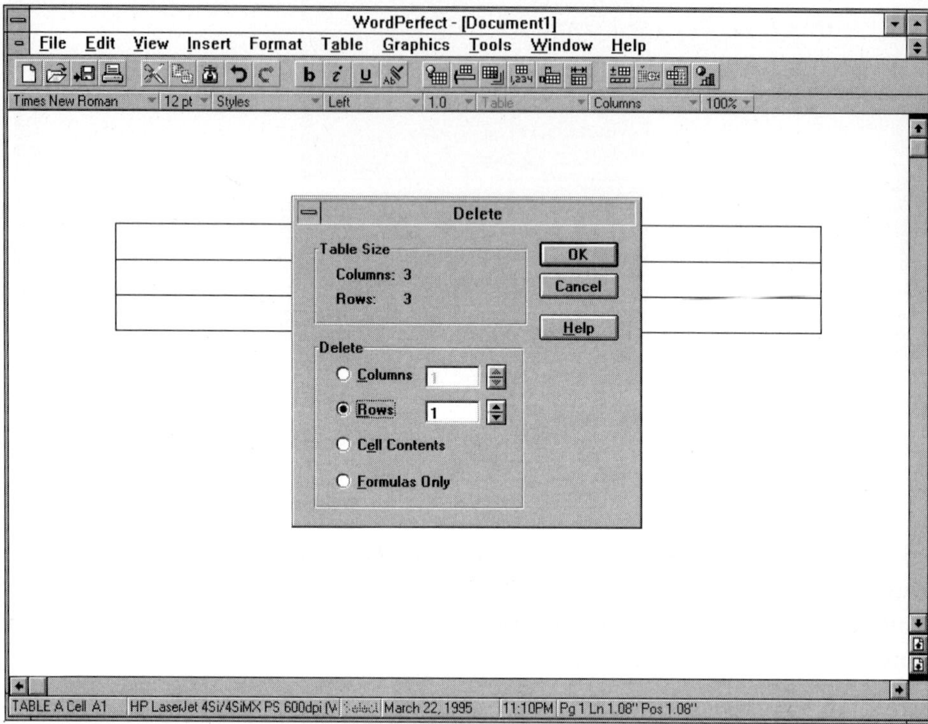

Text in cells can also be deleted without removing the table structure. You can delete text within one cell or select several cells, then delete all the text in the selected cells. To do this, select the cells, display the Delete dialog box, choose Cell Contents, then choose OK or press Enter.

Exercise 7 Inserting and Deleting Rows

1. At a clear editing window, open c19ex03.
2. Save the document with Save As and name it c19ex07.
3. Delete rows 3 and 4 by completing the following steps:
   a. Position the insertion point in cell A3.
   b. Choose Table, then Delete.
   c. At the Delete dialog box, key **2** in the Rows text box. To do this with the mouse, select the *1* in the Rows text box, then key **2**. If you are using the keyboard, press Tab, then key **2**.
   d. Choose OK or press Enter.
4. Insert two rows above the sixth row by completing the following steps:
   a. Position the insertion point in cell A6.
   b. Choose Table, then Insert.

c. At the Insert Columns/Rows dialog box, key **2** in the Rows text box. To do this with the mouse, select the *1* in the Rows text box, then key **2**. If you are using the keyboard, press Tab, then key **2**.
d. Choose OK or press Enter.

5. Key the following text in the identified cells:
   A6 = **Jon LaMarr**
   B6 = **542-20-5483**
   C6 = **Med. Records**
   A7 = **Marcia O'Neill**
   B7 = **231-29-3827**
   C7 = **Payroll**
6. Save the document again with the same name (c19ex07).
7. Print c19ex07.
8. Close c19ex07.

Joining Cells

Cells can be joined with the Join option from the Table drop-down menu. Before joining cells, the cells to be joined need to be selected. With the cells selected, choose Table, then Join. At the Join drop-down menu, choose Cell.

Exercise 8 Joining Cells

1. At a clear editing window, create the table shown in figure 19.17 by completing the following steps:
   a. Create a table with three columns and ten rows.
   b. Join cells A1 through C1 by completing the following steps:
      (1) Select cells A1 through C1.
      (2) Choose Table, Join, then Cell.
   c. Join cells A2 through C2 by completing steps similar to those in 1b(1) and 1b(2).
   d. Key the text in the table as shown in figure 19.17. Center and bold the text as indicated. (Press Enter once after keying **ACTIVITY LOG**. Press Enter once after keying **Training and Education Department**.)
2. Save the document and name it c19ex08.
3. Print c19ex08.
4. Close c19ex08.

Figure 19.17

ACTIVITY LOG		
Training and Education Department		
Client	**Activity**	**Date**

Splitting Cells

With the Split option from the Table drop-down menu, you can split a cell, a row, or a column of cells. To do this, choose Table, then Split. At the Split Cell dialog box, shown in figure 19.18, specify whether the cell is to be split into columns or rows, then choose OK or press Enter.

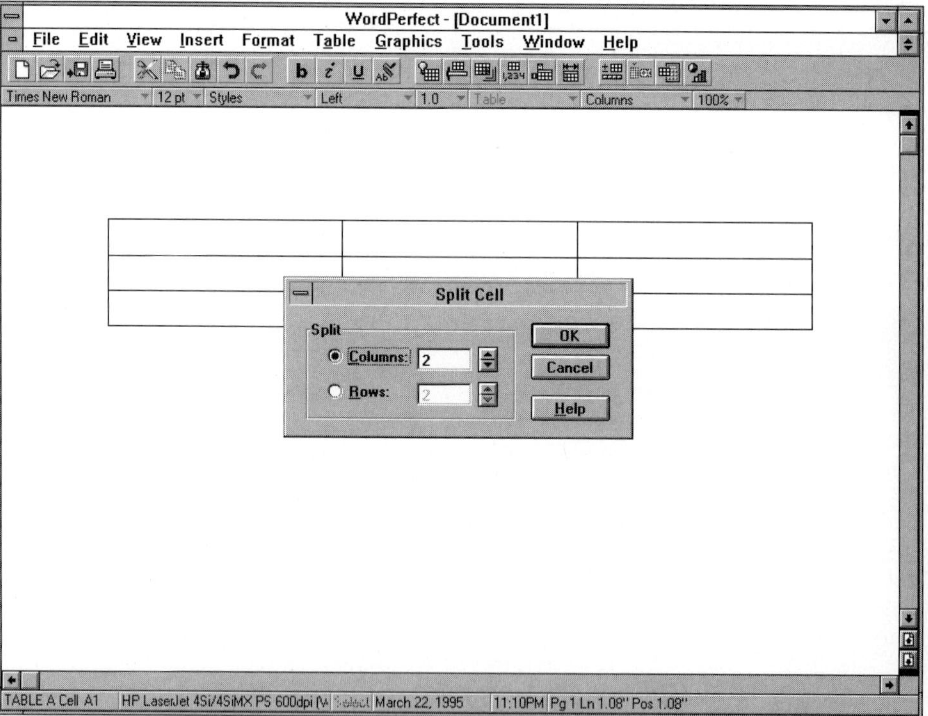

Figure 19.18
Split Cell Dialog Box

Exercise 9 Splitting Cells into Two Columns

1. At a clear editing window, open c19ex08.
2. Save the document with Save As and name it c19ex09.
3. Split cells C3 through C10 into two columns by completing the following steps:
   a. Select cells C3 through C10.
   b. Choose Table, Split, then Cell.
   c. At the Split Cell dialog box, choose OK or press Enter.
4. Bold and center the word *Time* in cell D3.
5. Save the document again with the same name (c19ex09).
6. Print c19ex09.
7. Close c19ex09.

Deleting Text

After text has been inserted in a cell, it can be deleted in the normal manner. For example, press Delete to delete the text immediately to the right of the insertion point; press Backspace to delete the character to the left of the insertion point; or press Ctrl + Backspace to delete the word in which the insertion point is positioned.

You can delete a row or column by selecting the row or column, then pressing Backspace. When you press Backspace, the Delete dialog box, shown in figure 19.16, displays on the screen. If you want to delete the row or column, choose OK or press Enter. If you want to delete the text within the cell as well as the cell in the column, make sure Columns is selected at the Delete dialog box, then choose OK or press Enter.

Exercise 10 Deleting Cell Contents

1. At a clear editing window, open c19ex03.
2. Save the document with Save As and name it c19ex10.
3. Delete the contents of cells A4 through C5 by completing the following steps:
   a. Select cells A4 through C5.
   b. Press Backspace.
   c. At the Delete dialog box, choose Cell Contents.
   d. Choose OK or press Enter.
4. Key the following text in the identified cell:
   A4 = **Toni Velluci**
   B4 = **490-43-9283**
   C4 = **Payroll**
   A5 = **Kenneth Barret**
   B5 = **865-04-3822**
   C5 = **Finance**
5. Save the document again with the same name (c19ex10).
6. Print c19ex10.
7. Close c19ex10.

Changing Cell/Column Justification

By default, text in a cell aligns at the left margin. This alignment can be changed with the Justification option from the Format dialog box shown in figure 19.12. Cell justification can be changed from left to right, center, full, all, or decimal align. The Right setting aligns text within a cell at the right margin of the cell. At the Center setting, text within a cell will be centered between the left and right margins of the cell. At Full, text will be aligned at the left and right margins within the cell. The All setting aligns all lines within a cell at the left and right margins (including short lines). The Decimal Align setting aligns numbers in a cell at the decimal point.

Cell justification can be changed for a specific cell, selected cells, or all cells within a column. To change the justification of one cell, position the insertion point in the desired cell, then choose Table, then Format. At the Format dialog box, choose Justification, then choose the desired justification from the drop-down menu. To change the justification for several cells, select the cells first and then display the Format dialog box. To change justification of all cells within a column, position the insertion point in any cell in the column, then choose Table, then Format. At the Format dialog box, choose Column. At the Format dialog box for columns, choose Justification, then choose the desired justification.

Changing Table Position

By default, a table is positioned at the left margin. This can be changed to right, center, full, or a specific distance from the left edge of the paper. To change table position, position the insertion point in the table, then choose Table, then Format. At the Format dialog box, select Table at the top of the dialog box. Position the arrow pointer in the Table Position text box in the lower left corner of the dialog box (contains the word *Left*), hold down the left mouse button, drag the arrow pointer to the desired option, then release the mouse button. Choose OK to close the Format dialog box.

Exercise 11 Changing Cell Justification

1. At a clear editing window, create the document shown in figure 19.19 by completing the following steps:
   a. Create a table with three columns and ten rows.
   b. Change the column width of the first column to 2 inches, the second column to 2.5 inches, and the third column to 1 inch..
   c. Join cells A1 through C1.
   d. Join cells A2 through C2.
   e. Change the justification to Center for cell A1 by completing the following steps:
      (1) Position the insertion point in cell A1 (do not select the cell).
      (2) Choose Table, then Format.
      (3) At the Format dialog box, change the Justification to Center. To do this with the mouse, position the arrow pointer in the Justification text box, hold down the left mouse button, drag the arrow pointer to the Center option, then release the mouse button.
      (4) Choose OK or press Enter.
   f. Change the justification to Center for cell A2 by completing steps similar to those in step e.
   g. Change the justification to Center for cells A3 through C3 by completing the following steps:
      (1) Select cells A3 through C3.
      (2) Choose Table, then Format.
      (3) At the Format dialog box, choose Cell. (By default, WordPerfect displays the Format dialog box for rows.)
      (4) Change the Justification to Center.
      (5) Choose OK or press Enter.
   h. Select cells C4 through C10, then change the justification to Center by completing steps similar to step g.
   i. Change the table position to center by completing the following steps:
      (1) With the insertion point in any cell in the table, choose Table, then Format.
      (2) At the Format dialog box choose Table at the top of the dialog box.
      (3) Position the arrow pointer in the Table Position text box in the lower left corner of the dialog box (contains the word *Left*), hold down the left mouse button, drag the arrow pointer to Center, then release the mouse button.
      (4) Choose OK to close the dialog box.

j. Key the text in the cells as shown in figure 19.19. Bold the text as indicated.
2. Save the document and name it c19ex11.
3. Print c19ex11.
4. Close c19ex11.

Figure 19.19

OMAHA CITY SCHOOL DISTRICT		
Technology Advisory Committee		
Name	**Organization**	**Phone**
Barry Vialle	Horizon Broadcasting Company	555-3209
Colonel Gerry Lund	Satler Air Force Base	555-3321
Dr. Jeremy Needham	Omaha Community College	555-4332
Arlene Tommaney	Midwest Banking Institution	555-0091
Kathy Hemphill	Omaha Economic Development	555-8327
Lyle McKeller	Nebraska Health Council	555-1225
Roberta Hughes	Sampson/Kraft Corporation	555-3123

Exercise 12 Changing Column Width and Justification

1. At a clear editing window, create the memo shown in figure 19.20 by completing the following steps:
   a. Change the font to 12-point GeoSlab703 Lt BT.
   b. Key the headings and the first paragraph of the memo.
   c. With the insertion point a double space below the first paragraph, create the table by completing the following steps:
      (1) Create a table with three columns and six rows.
      (2) Change the width of the first column to 2.5 inches, the width of the second column to 1.8 inches, and the width of the third column to 2.2 inches.
      (3) Change the justification of the second column to Center by completing the following steps:
         (a) Position the insertion point in any cell in the second column.
         (b) Choose Table, then Format.
         (c) At the Format dialog box, choose Column.
         (d) At the Format dialog box for columns, choose Justification, then Center.
         (e) Choose OK or press Enter.
      (4) Change the justification of the third column to Right by completing steps similar to those in step (3).
      (5) Key the text in the columns as indicated.
   d. After keying the text in the columns, position the insertion point a double space below the table, then key the remainder of the memo.
2. Save the document and name it c19ex12.
3. Print c19ex12.
4. Close c19ex12.

Figure 19.20

DATE: February 6, 1997

TO: Jack Eismann

FROM: Joni Kapshaw

SUBJECT: MARCH NEWSLETTER

The following information needs to be included in the March newsletter under the heading "Newsletter Resources."

Superintendent	Pat Windslow	Administrative Offices
Assistant Superintendent	Jocelyn Cook	Administrative Offices
Director, Human Resources	Cheryl Woodburn	District Headquarters
Director, Curriculum Develop.	William Cho	District Headquarters
Newsletter Editor	Joni Kapshaw	Nyland High School
Newsletter Assistant Editor	Jack Eismann	Leland Elementary School

Please include instructions on how employees can submit articles or items of interest to be published in the newsletter.

xx:c19ex12

Deleting a Table

An entire table, including cell entries, can be deleted; you can delete the structure of the table, leaving the cell entries; or you can delete the cell entries, leaving the table structure. To delete the entire table, including cell entries, select the entire table, then press the Backspace key. At the Delete Table dialog box, shown in figure 19.21, make sure Entire Table is selected, then choose OK or press Enter.

Figure 19.21
Delete Table Dialog Box

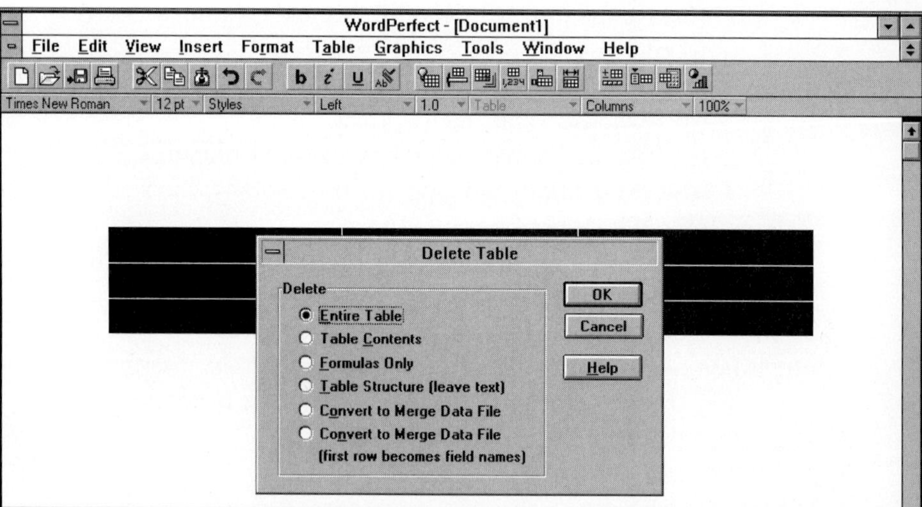

To delete the table contents, leaving the table structure, select the entire table, display the Delete Table dialog box, then choose Table Contents. If you want to delete the table structure and leave the text within cells, choose Table Structure (leave text) at the Delete Table dialog box.

Another method for displaying the Delete Table dialog box is to display Reveal Codes, position the insertion point immediately left of the table definition code, then press the Delete key. This displays the Delete Table dialog box where you can choose to delete the entire table, the cell contents only, or just the table structure, leaving the cell contents.

Exercise 13 Deleting a Table Structure

1. At a clear editing window, open c19ex02.
2. Save the document with Save As and name it c19ex13.
3. Delete the table structure but leave the text by completing the following steps:
   a. Select the entire table.
   b. Press Backspace.
   c. At the Delete Table dialog box, choose Table Structure (leave text).
   d. Choose OK or press Enter.
4. With the insertion point on the line containing *President* and *Chris Hedegaard*, use the mouse on the Ruler Bar to clear all tabs, then set left tabs at the 2.5-inch mark, 4-inch mark, and the 4.75-inch mark.
5. Save the document again with the same name (c19ex13).
6. Print c19ex13.
7. Close c19ex13.

Formatting with the Table Expert

WordPerfect has created a variety of table formatting options that can be applied to a table. This table formatting feature is called the *Table Expert*. The various formatting options are available at the Table Expert dialog box shown in figure 19.22. To display this dialog box, position the insertion point in a table, then choose Table, then Expert.

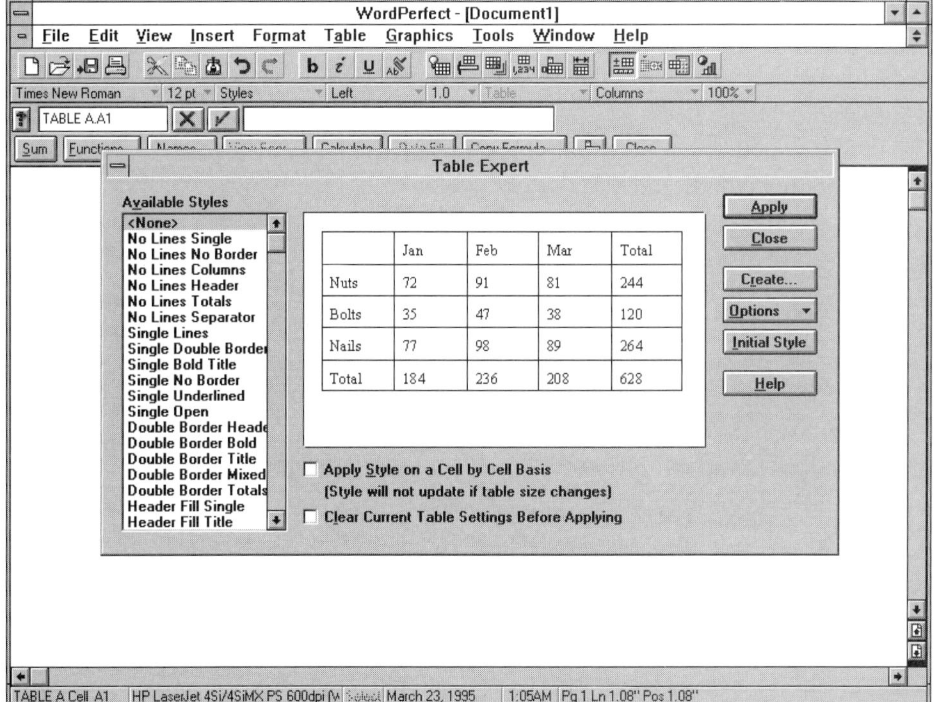

Figure 19.22
Table Expert Dialog Box

The list of formatting options displays in the Available Styles list box. Click on an option from this list and the preview table in the middle of the dialog box will display the formatting contained in the option. In this way, you can view the various options to find the one that contains the table formatting desired.

If you want to apply formatting to an individual cell, insert an X in the Apply Style on a Cell by Cell Basis check box. Insert an X in the Clear Current Table Settings Before Applying check box if you want any previous formatting contained by the table to be removed.

Exercise 14 Formatting with the Table Expert

1. At a clear editing window, open table01.
2. Save the document with Save As and name it c19ex14.
3. Apply formatting to the table at the Table Expert dialog box by completing the following steps:
   a. With the insertion point positioned in any cell in the table, choose Table, then Expert.
   b. At the Table Expert dialog box, select *Row Fill Columns* in the Available Styles list box. To do this, click on the *Row Fill Columns* option in the Available Styles list box. (This option is quite far down on the list.)
   c. Choose Apply.
4. Save the document again with the same name (c19ex14).
5. Print then close c19ex14.

CHAPTER SUMMARY

- With WordPerfect's Tables feature, a form can be created that has boxes of information, called *cells*, with customized lines surrounding each cell.
- A table can be created with the Tables button on the Power Bar or at the Create Table dialog box.
- Columns in a table are lettered from left to right, beginning with A. Rows in a table are numbered from top to bottom beginning with 1.
- Change the width of columns with the mouse in the table, the Ruler Bar, or at the Format dialog box.
- The mouse pointer or the keyboard can be used to select a cell, row, column, or an entire table. After cells are selected, alignment or margins can be changed or character formatting can be added.
- Insert rows or columns in a table with the Insert option from the Table drop-down menu.
- Delete rows or columns in a table with the Delete option from the Table drop-down menu.
- Two or more cells can be joined with the Join option from the Table drop-down menu. Or, a cell or a row or column of cells can be split with the Split option from the Table drop-down menu.
- Text in a cell aligns at the left margin. This alignment can be changed with the Justification option from the Format dialog box.
- The position of a table can be changed from the default of left to right, center, full, or a specific measurement from the left edge of the paper.
- An entire table, including cell entries, can be deleted; you can delete the structure of the table, leaving the cell entries; or you can delete the cell entries, leaving the table structure.
- Use the Table Expert to apply formatting to a table.

Commands Review

	Mouse	Keyboard
Create table with Tables button	With arrow pointer on Tables button on Power Bar (sixth from left) hold down left mouse button, drag arrow pointer down and right to create table of desired size, then release mouse button	
Create Table dialog box	Table, Create	Table, Create
Ruler Bar	View, Ruler Bar	View, Ruler Bar
Format dialog box	Table, Format	Table, Format
Move insertion point to next cell	With I-beam pointer in desired cell, click left mouse button	Tab
Move insertion point to previous cell	With I-beam pointer in desired cell, click left mouse button	SHIFT + Tab
Insert left tab in cell		CTRL + Tab
Insert decimal tab in cell		ALT + SHIFT + F7
Insert back tab (margin release)		CTRL + SHIFT + Tab

CHECK YOUR UNDERSTANDING

True/False: Circle the letter T if the statement is true; circle the letter F if the statement is false.

T F 1. Press the Enter key to move the insertion point to the next cell in a table.

T F 2. When a table is created, the columns are the same width.

T F 3. When adding rows or columns, by default a row is inserted above the insertion point and a column is inserted to the left of the insertion point.

T F 4. Columns in a table are numbered from left to right.

T F 5. To display the horizontal selection arrow, move the I-beam pointer to the top border of any cell until it turns into a left-pointing arrow.

Completion: In the space provided at the right, indicate the correct term, command, or number.

1. You can change the column width at the table with the mouse, at the Format dialog box, or here. ____________________
2. The quickest method for creating a table with the mouse is to use this button on the Power Bar. ____________________
3. Before joining cells, you need to first do this. ____________________
4. This is the default justification for text in a cell. ____________________
5. To delete the table structure and leave the text within cells, choose this at the Delete Table dialog box. ____________________

SKILL ASSESSMENTS

Assessment 1

1. At a clear editing window, create the document shown in figure 19.23.
2. Save the document and name it c19sa01.
3. Print c19sa01.
4. Close c19sa01.

Figure 19.23

BUILDING A NETWORK

Contact six people working in the field of interest to you. Find out what they like about their job, what they do not like, how they obtained their position, and the skills and qualifications required for the position. Fill in the form below.

Name	Phone Number	Company	Comments

Assessment 2

1. At a clear editing window, create the letter shown in figure 19.24.
2. Save the document and name it c19sa02.
3. Print c19sa02.
4. Close c19sa02.

Figure 19.24

January 8, 1997

Mr. and Mrs. Phillip Hunter
3120 South 32nd Avenue
Seattle, WA 98104

Dear Mr. and Mrs. Hunter:

The final arrangements have been made for your cruise to the Caribbean. The airfare has been charged to your account. A receipt of this transaction is included in your travel packet. Your itinerary for the cruise is described below:

Day	Port	Arrive	Depart
Sat., 03/04/96	Miami		4:00 p.m.
Sun., 03/05/96	At sea		
Mon., 03/06/96	San Juan	6:00 p.m.	
Tue., 03/07/96	San Juan		2:00 a.m.
Tue., 03/07/96	St. Thomas	8:00 a.m.	5:30 p.m.
Wed., 03/08/96	St. Maarten	7:00 a.m.	5:00 p.m.
Thu., 03/09/96	At sea		
Fri., 03/10/96	At sea		
Sat., 03/11/96	Miami	8:00 a.m.	

I'm sure you will have a wonderful time on the cruise. Please stop by our office to pick up your travel packet before the end of the week.

Sincerely,

Judy Peterson

xx:c19sa02

Assessment 3

1. At a clear editing window, open c19sa02.
2. Save the document with Save As and name it c19sa03.
3. Select cells B2 through B10, then change the justification to center.
4. Select and center the text in cells C2 through C10.
5. Select and center the text in cells D2 through D10.
6. Save the document again with the same name (c19sa03).
7. Print c19sa03.
8. Close c19sa03.

Assessment 4

1. At a clear editing window, create the table shown in figure 19.25 with the following specifications:
   a. Create a table with three columns and eight rows.
   b. Change the width of the first column to 3.5 inches.
   c. Join cells A1 through C1.
   d. Join cells A2 through C2.
   e. Key the text in the cells as indicated. Bold and center text as shown. Use Indent (F7) to indent the text after the numbers in the first column. When keying the text in the cells in the first column, do not press Enter. Let word wrap take text to the next line within the cell.
2. Save the table and name it c19sa04.
3. Print c19sa04.
4. Close c19sa04.

Figure 19.25

ACTIVITY DIRECTOR		
Rating Form for Candidates		
Rating Category	**Pts. Allowed**	**Pts. Awarded**
1. Experience managing a program designed to provide services for unemployed.	25	
2. Experience working with others as the chair of a committee or other group.	15	
3. Experience developing, maintaining, and evaluating adult education program.	15	
4. Communicates experience working with multiple agencies.	10	
5. Experience developing and maintaining budgets.	10	

Assessment 5

1. At a clear editing window, create the table shown in figure 19.26 with the following specifications:
   a. Create a table with three columns and ten rows.
   b. Change the width of the first column to 1.8 inches, the second column to 2.5 inches, and the third column to 1 inch.
   c. Join cells A1 through C1.
   d. Join cells A2 through C2.
   e. Bold and center the text as indicated.
   f. Center the table horizontally. (Do this at the Format dialog box with Table selected at the top.)
2. Save the table and name it c19sa05.
3. Print c19sa05.
4. Close c19sa05.

Figure 19.26

EMERGENCY PREPAREDNESS COMMITTEE MEMBERS		
STEERING COMMITTEE		
Employee	**Position**	**Extension**
Sally Chapman	Chair, Emergency Prep.	3410
Charlene Knudtsen	Medical Director	1023
Suzanna Childers	Associate Administrator	4311
Joseph Washington	Pharmacy Services	2019
Benjamin Lindler	Administrative Services	9422
Judith Krandall	Head Nurse, Emergency Room	6223
Montgomery Brooks	Director, Ambulatory Care	3492

Assessment 6

1. At a clear editing window, open c19sa05.
2. Save the document with Save As and name it c19sa06.
3. Delete rows 5 and 6.
4. Add two rows between the third and fourth rows.
5. Key the text in the identified cells.
   A4 = **Tina Boyer**
   B4 = **Safety Services**
   C4 = **3055**
   A5 = **Glen Maloney**
   B5 = **Nurse Manager**

Creating Charts 20

Upon successful completion of chapter 20, you will be able to enhance and improve the clarity of data by creating a chart with the data.

In chapter 19 you learned to create data in tables. While this does an adequate job of representing data, a chart can be created from data in a table that provides a more visual presentation of the data.

A chart is sometimes referred to as a *graph* and is a picture of numeric data. A chart can be created in the Chart Editor or from data in a table. In this chapter you will learn how to create a chart from data in a table. For information on how to create charts in the Chart Editor, please refer to the WordPerfect reference manual and the on-screen help guide.

Creating a Chart

A chart is created using data in a table. For example, the data shown in the table in figure 20.1 can be created as a chart.

Salesperson	January	February	March
T. Langford	$54,540	$48,300	$59,800
S. Eckhardt	45,200	39,780	48,550
G. Owens	35,100	29,480	41,320

Figure 20.1
Table

To insert the data shown in the table in figure 20.1 into a Bar chart (the default), position the insertion point in any cell in the table, then choose Graphics, then Chart; or click on the Chart button on the Graphics Toolbar. (To display the Graphics Toolbar, position the arrow pointer on the current toolbar, click the right mouse button, then click on Graphics.) At the Chart Editor shown in figure 20.2, click on the Close button on the Chart Toolbar (the second button from the left) or click in the editing window outside the chart area.

Figure 20.2
Chart Editor

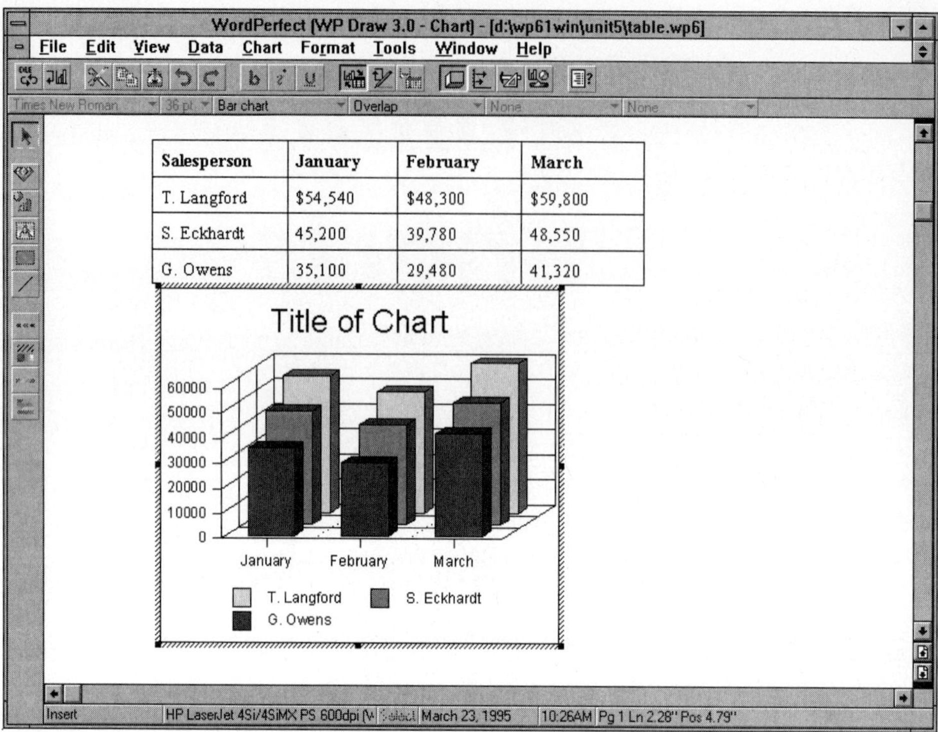

Salesperson	January	February	March
T. Langford	$54,540	$48,300	$59,800
S. Eckhardt	45,200	39,780	48,550
G. Owens	35,100	29,480	41,320

Figure 20.3
Chart Based on Table

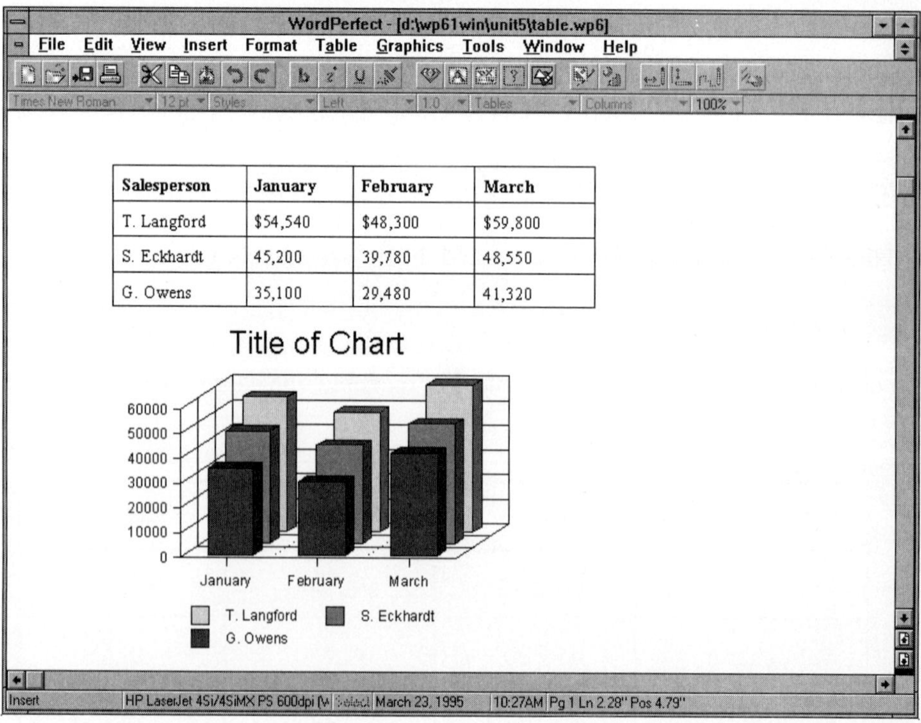

Salesperson	January	February	March
T. Langford	$54,540	$48,300	$59,800
S. Eckhardt	45,200	39,780	48,550
G. Owens	35,100	29,480	41,320

When you click on the Close button on the Chart Toolbar, or click in the editing window outside the chart area, the chart is inserted in the document at the left margin and appears as shown in figure 20.3. Like other graphics boxes, a box containing a chart is inserted at the left margin and is approximately 3.25 inches wide. A box containing a chart contains no border lines.

The left side of a chart is the vertical y-axis. The y-axis is marked like a ruler and is broken into units by marks called *ticks*. Next to each tick mark is the amount of the value at that particular point on the axis. In figure 20.3, the y-axis is displayed in numbers by ten thousands beginning with zero and continuing to 60,000.

The x-axis is the bottom of the chart. The names of items in the chart generally display along the x-axis. In the chart shown in figure 20.3, the bars are identified along the x-axis as **January**, **February**, and **March**.

Exercise 1 Creating a Bar Chart

1. At a clear editing window, open table02.
2. Save the document with Save As and name it c20ex01.
3. Create a Bar chart for the table by completing the following steps:
   a. Position the insertion point in any cell in the table.
   b. Choose Graphics, then Chart; or click on the Chart button on the Graphics Toolbar.
   c. At the Chart Editor, click on the Close button on the Chart Toolbar (the second button from the left).
   d. At the editing window, click outside the chart to deselect it.
4. Save the document again with the same name (c20ex01).
5. Print c20ex01.
6. Close c20ex01.

Creating a Title

The chart shown in figure 20.3 displays with the default title of *Title of Chart*. A title can be added to a chart at the Chart Editor. To create a title, you must display the chart in the Chart Editor. To display the Chart Editor for an existing chart using the mouse, position the arrow pointer inside the chart, then double-click the left mouse button.

To create a title in the Chart Editor, choose Chart, then Titles; or double-click on the title. This causes the Titles dialog box to display as shown in figure 20.4.

Figure 20.4
Titles Dialog Box

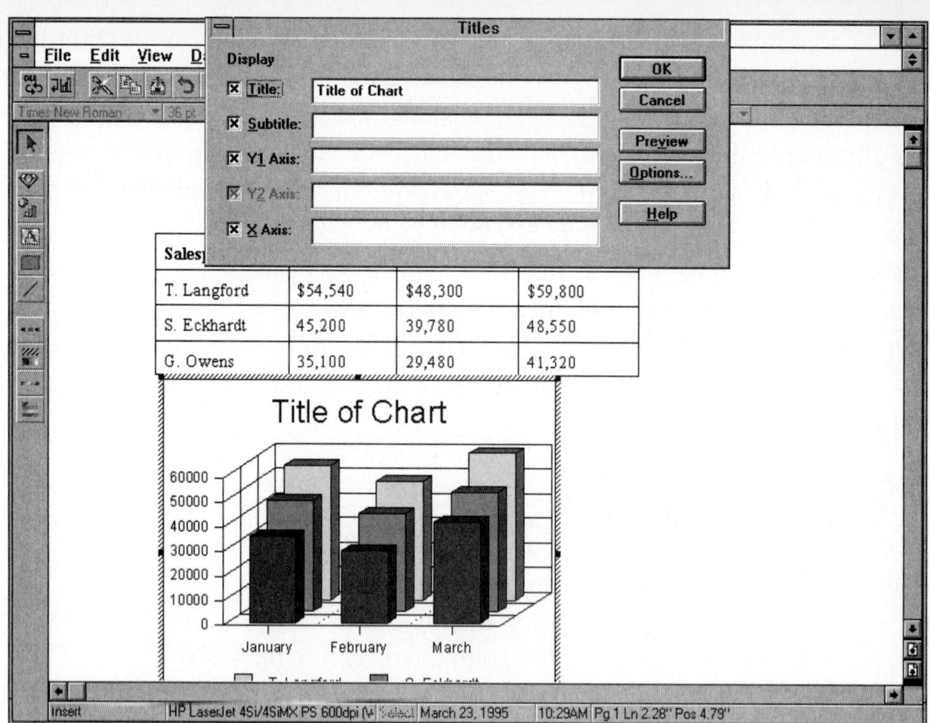

At the Titles dialog box, you can create a title or a subtitle for a chart. You can also identify the y-axis and the x-axis. You can further customize the title with options from the Titles Options dialog box. To display this dialog box, choose Options at the Titles dialog box. By default, the title or subtitle of a chart is centered at the top of the chart. This can be changed to Left or Right with the Position option from the Titles Options dialog box.

You can change the font used for the title, subtitle, x-axis, or y-axis at the Font dialog box. Display the Font dialog box by choosing Font from the Titles Options dialog box.

If you choose Attributes from the Titles Options dialog box, the Box Attributes dialog box shown in figure 20.5 displays.

Figure 20.5
Box Attributes Dialog Box

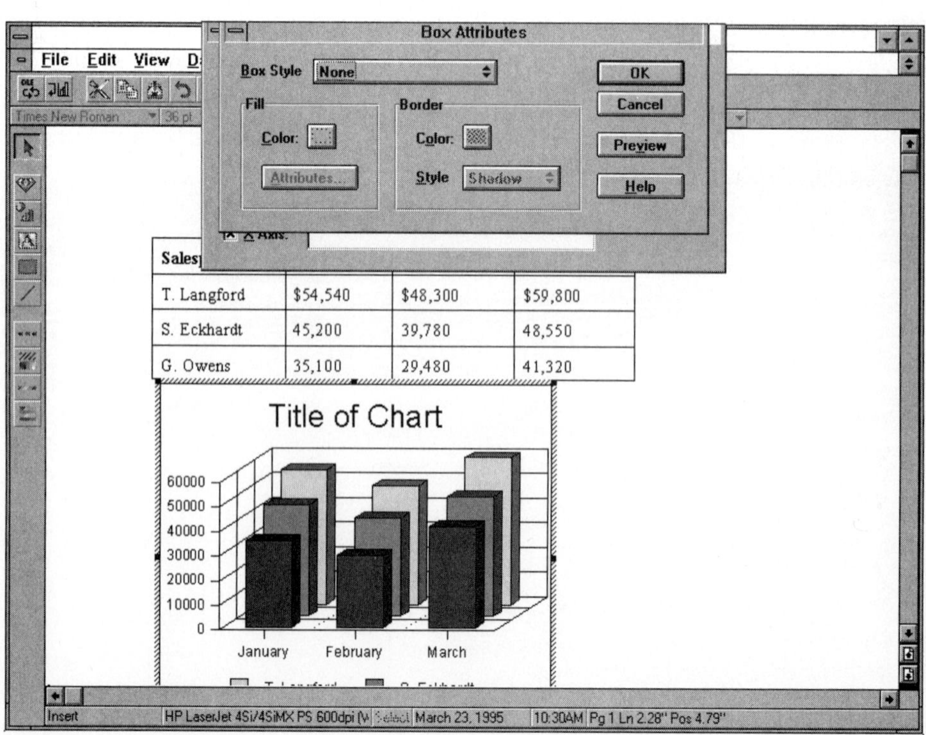

With the Box Style option, you can create a box for the title or subtitle. You can choose Rectangle, Rounded Rectangle, Octagon, or the default of None at the Box Style drop-down menu.

Change the fill color of the box for the title or subtitle with the Color option from the Box Attributes dialog box. Change the border color of the box with the Color option.

The Style option lets you change the border style of a box around the title or subtitle. The choices are None (the default), Single, Double, Dotted, Dashed, Thick, Shadow, or Beveled.

Exercise 2 Adding a Title and Formatting a Chart

1. At a clear editing window, open c20ex01.
2. Save the document with Save As and name it c20ex02.
3. Create a title for the chart as well as a name for the y-axis, add a double line border around the title, and change the font of the title by completing the following steps:
   a. Open the Chart Editor. To do this with the mouse, position the arrow pointer inside the chart, then double-click the left mouse button.
   b. At the Chart Editor, double-click on the title.
   c. At the Titles dialog box, key **UNITED FOODS** in the Title text box.
   d. Choose Options.
   e. At the Titles Options dialog box, choose Attributes.
   f. At the Box Attributes dialog box, choose Box Style, then Rectangle.
   g. At the Box Attributes dialog box, choose Style, then Double.
   h. Choose OK or press Enter.
   i. At the Titles Options dialog box, choose Font.
   j. At the Font dialog box, select Arrus BT in the Font Face list box, then choose OK.
   k. At the Titles Option dialog box, choose OK or press Enter.
   l. At the Titles dialog box, choose Y1, then key **Net Sales**.
   m. Choose OK or press Enter.
   n. Click on the Close button on the Chart Toolbar; or click in the editing window outside the chart.
   o. At the editing window, click outside the chart to deselect it.
4. Save the document again with the same name (c20ex02).
5. Print c20ex02.
6. Close c20ex02.

Customizing a Legend

When a chart is created from data in a table, a legend is automatically created. A legend identifies the bars in the chart. For example, the legend in figure 20.3 specifies the salesperson for each bar in the chart. The legend displays outside and below the chart. This can be changed at the Legend dialog box shown in figure 20.6.

By default, a legend is displayed with the chart. If you do not want a legend displayed, remove the X from the Display Legend check box. If the X is removed, many of the options at the dialog box become dimmed.

A legend displays outside and at the bottom of the chart. The legend can be placed inside the chart by choosing Inside Chart. The legend position is Bottom Center. If you choose Position, the position of the legend can be changed to Top Left, Top Center, Top Right, Middle Left, Middle Right, Bottom Left, or Bottom Right.

If you choose Attributes from the Legend dialog box, the Box Attributes dialog box shown in figure 20.5 displays. At this dialog box, you can create a border for the legend and customize the border style, color, and fill.

Choosing Series font causes the Font dialog box to display. At this dialog box, you can change the font for the legend series (the text identifying the bar colors).

By default, a legend displays in a horizontal position. If you want the legend to display in a vertical position, choose Vertical from the Legend dialog box.

With the Display Name option, you can create a name for the legend. The default name is Legend. You can key your own name in the Display Name text box. You can change the font of the legend name by choosing Font.

Figure 20.6
Legend Dialog Box

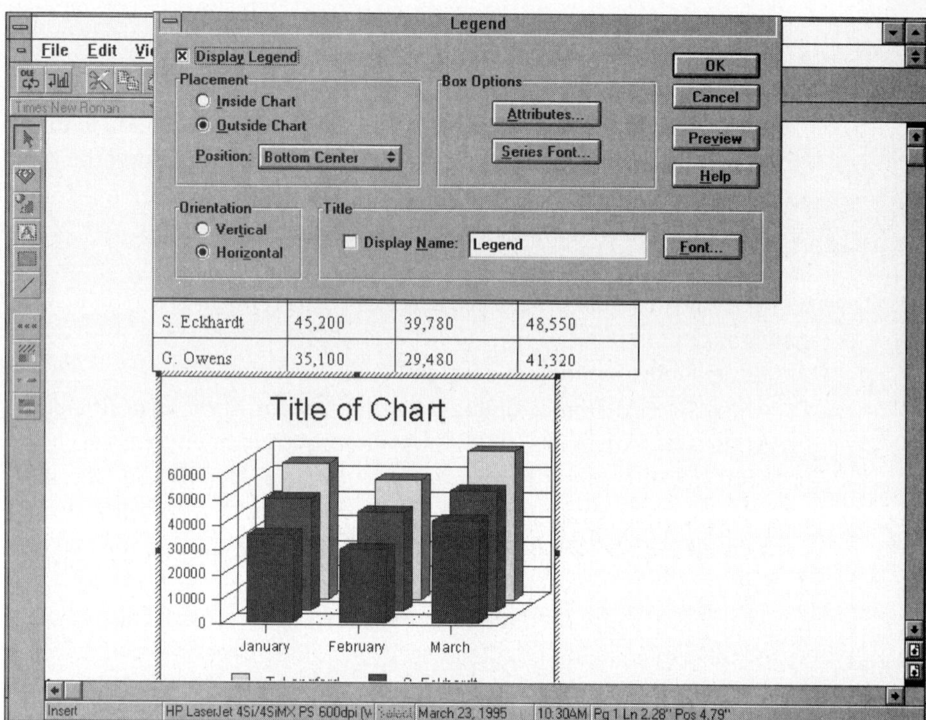

Exercise 3 Formatting a Chart Legend

1. At a clear editing window, open c20ex02.
2. Save the document with Save As and name it c20ex03.
3. Customize the legend for the chart by completing the following steps:
   a. Position the insertion point in the chart, then double-click the left mouse button. This opens the Chart Editor.
   b. At the Chart Editor, choose Chart, then Legend.
   c. At the Legend dialog box, choose Attributes.
   d. At the Box Attributes dialog box, choose Box Style, then Octagon.
   e. Choose Style, then Double.
   f. Choose OK or press Enter.
   g. At the Legend dialog box, choose Position, then Bottom Left.
   h. Choose OK or press Enter.
   i. Click on the Close button on the Chart Toolbar; or click in the editing window outside the chart area.
   j. At the editing window, deselect the chart.
4. Save the document again with the same name (c20ex03).
5. Print c20ex03.
6. Close c20ex03.

Deleting a Chart

When a chart is inserted in the editing window, a Box code is inserted in the document. To delete the chart, display Reveal Codes, then delete the Box code. You can also delete the chart by selecting it, then pressing the Delete key. To select the chart, position the arrow pointer inside the chart, then click the left mouse button. This causes sizing handles to display around the chart.

As mentioned at the beginning of this chapter, you are learning how to create charts based on a table. If you create a chart based on a table, and then make changes to the data in the table, you must delete the first chart and then create another chart based on the table. You cannot update a chart that was created from a table.

Exercise 4 Deleting a Chart and Creating a New Chart

1. At a clear editing window, open c20ex03.
2. Save the document with Save As and name it c20ex04.
3. Delete the chart by completing the following steps:
   a. Position the arrow pointer inside the chart, then click the left mouse button.
   b. With the chart selected, press the Delete key.
4. Make the following changes to the data in the table:
   a. Change the number in cell B2 from 120205 to 100500.
   b. Change the number in cell C3 from 115460 to 97800.
5. Create a chart based on the table by completing the following steps:
   a. Position the insertion point in any cell in the table, then choose Graphics, then Chart; or click on the Chart button on the Graphics Toolbar.
   b. At the Chart Editor, click on the Close button on the Chart Toolbar.
6. Save the document with the same name (c20ex04).
7. Print c20ex04.
8. Close c20ex04.

Editing a Chart Box

When a chart is inserted in a document, it is inserted in a graphics box. This is the same type of box you learned to create and edit in chapter 17. All the same editing options are available to you. For example, you can display the Graphics Box Feature Bar for a chart box and then change the contents, size, position, and much more of the box. To display the Graphics Box Feature Bar, position the arrow pointer inside the chart in the editing window (*not* the Chart Editor), hold down the *right* mouse button, drag the arrow pointer to Feature Bar, then release the mouse button.

A box containing a chart can be moved and sized. To move a box containing a chart, position the arrow pointer inside the chart, then click the left mouse button. This selects the box and inserts sizing handles around the box. Position the arrow pointer inside the chart and it turns into a four-headed arrow. Hold down the left mouse button, drag the outline of the box to the desired location, then release the mouse button.

A selected box containing a chart can also be sized. To size the box, use the sizing handles that display in the corners and in the middle of the box surrounding the chart. Size the box in the same manner as you learned to size graphics boxes in chapter 17.

Exercise 5 Sizing and Positioning a Chart

1. At a clear editing window, open c20ex03.
2. Save the document with Save As and name it c20ex05.
3. Delete the table in the document (not the chart) by completing the following steps:
   a. Position the I-beam pointer in any cell in the table until it turns into the horizontal or vertical selection arrow, then triple-click the left mouse button. (Make sure all cells in the table are selected.)

b. Press the Delete key.
c. At the Delete Table dialog box, make sure Entire Table is selected, then choose OK or press Enter.

4. Click on the Page/Zoom Full button on the 6.1 WordPerfect Toolbar (not the Graphics Toolbar).
5. Change the position and size of the chart by completing the following steps:
   a. Select the chart. To do this, position the arrow pointer inside the chart, then click the left mouse button.
   b. Position the arrow pointer inside the chart until it turns into a four-headed arrow. With the four-headed arrow inside the chart, hold down the left mouse button, drag the outline of the box to the middle of the page, then release the mouse button.
   c. Increase the height of the chart box by approximately one-half inch. To do this, position the arrow pointer on the middle sizing handle at the top of the box until it turns into a double-headed arrow pointing up and down. Hold down the left mouse button, drag up approximately one-half inch, then release the mouse button.
   d. Increase the width of the chart box by approximately one-half inch. To do this, position the arrow pointer on the middle sizing handle at the right side of the box until it turns into a double-headed arrow pointing left and right. Hold down the left mouse button, drag to the right approximately one-half inch, then release the mouse button.
   e. If necessary, reposition the chart box so it is in the middle of the page.
   f. Click in the editing window outside the chart to deselect the chart box.
6. Save the document with the same name (c20ex05).
7. Print c20ex05.
8. With the chart still open in the editing window, change the size of the chart by completing the following steps:
   a. Position the arrow pointer inside the chart, hold down the *right* mouse button, drag the arrow pointer to Feature Bar, then release the mouse button. (This displays the Graphics Box Feature Bar.)
   b. Display the Box Size dialog box, then change the box width to Full and the height to Size to Content.
   c. Close the Graphics Box Feature Bar.
9. Save the document again with the same name (c20ex05).
10. Print c20ex05.
11. Close c20ex05.

Changing Chart Type

In the Chart Editor, you can create seven different types of charts. Figure 20.7 shows an illustration and explanation of each type.

Figure 20.7
Types of Charts

Area	An Area chart shows trends and the amount of change over time. 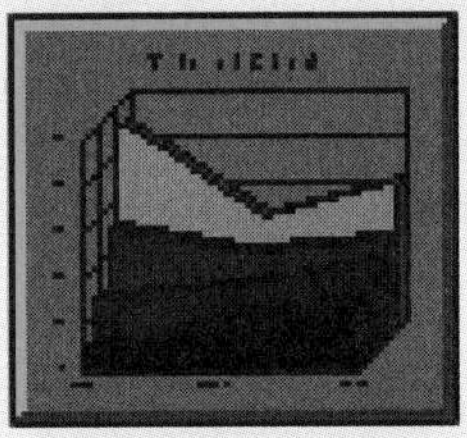
Bar	A Bar chart shows variations between components but not in relationship to the whole. Horizontal and vertical bar charts are available 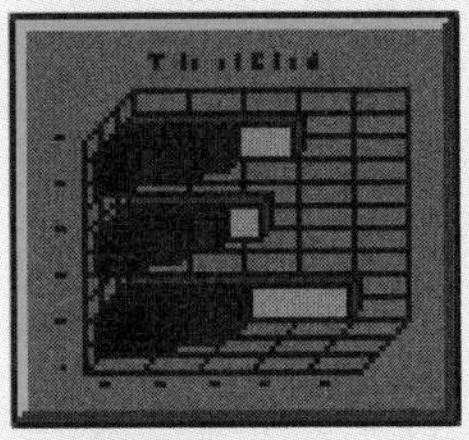
High/Low	A High/Low chart shows the high, low, open, and close quotes for a stock. 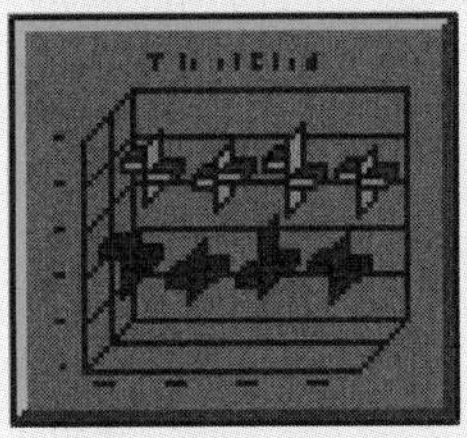
Line	A Line chart shows trends and change over time. 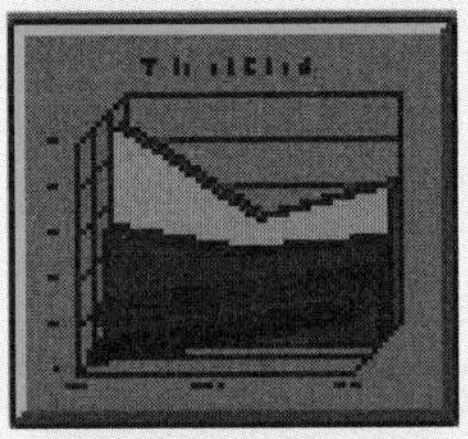
Pie	A Pie chart shows proportions and relationships of parts to the whole 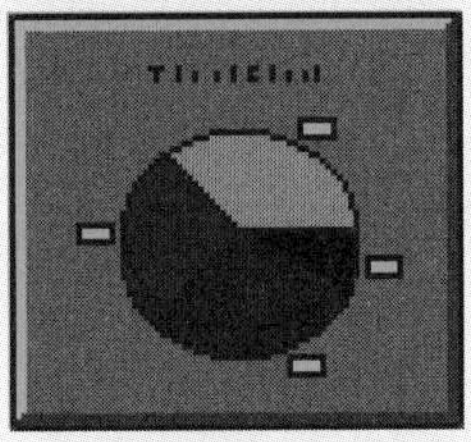
Radar	A Radar chart shows data over time and displays variations and trends. 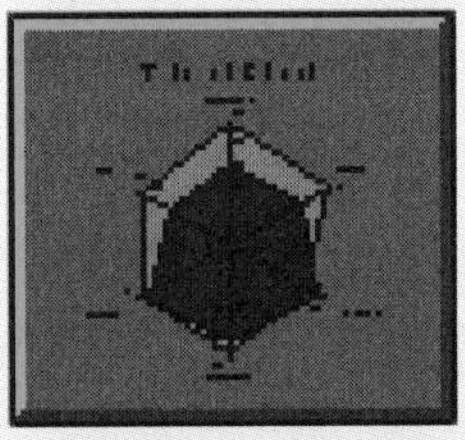
Scatter	A Scatter chart shows the interception points between x and y values. 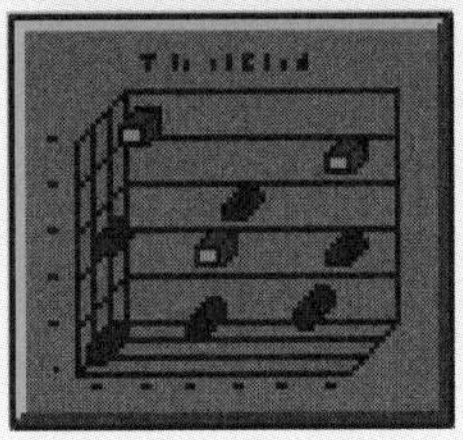

To change to a different chart type, choose Chart, then Type. At the drop-down menu that displays, select the desired chart type. You can also change the chart type at the Data Chart dialog box shown in figure 20.8. To display this dialog box, choose Chart, then Gallery.

The seven chart types are displayed in the Chart Type list box. To the right, the formatting for the highlighted chart displays. For each chart, WordPerfect provides variations containing different combinations of enhancements. You can choose a variation without having to customize the chart yourself. As you choose a chart type from the Chart Type list box, various chart formatting displays to the right. In figure 20.8, various formatting of bar charts displays.

Figure 20.8
Data Chart Dialog Box

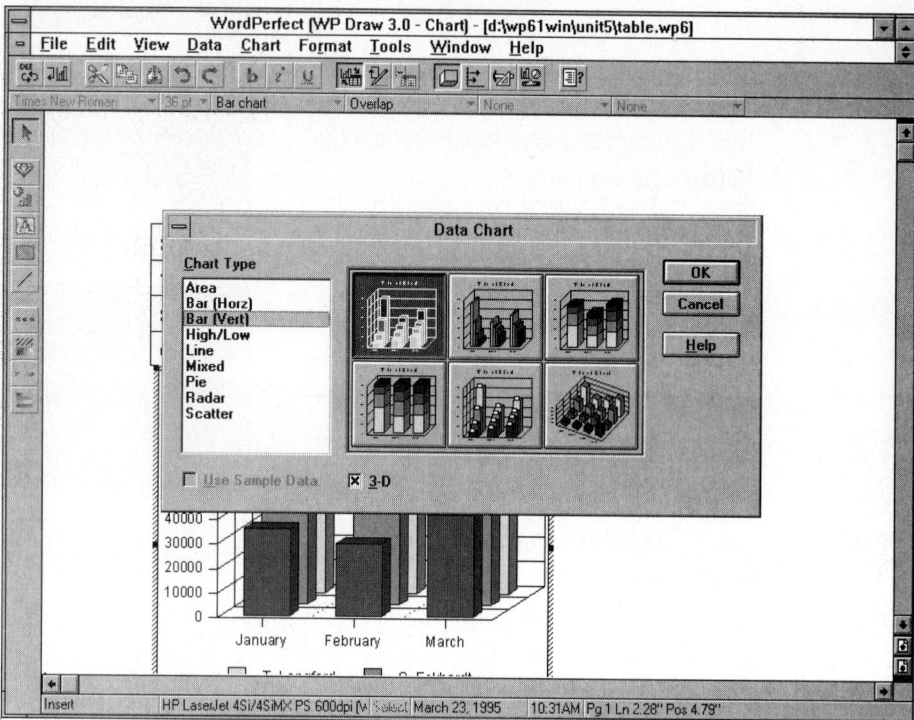

Exercise 6 Creating a Pie Chart

1. At a clear editing window, create the table shown in figure 20.9. (The middle column must be blank for the data to display in the proper locations in the chart.)
2. Create a Pie chart for the table by completing the following steps:
   a. Position the insertion point inside the table, then display the Chart Editor.
   b. At the Chart Editor, choose Chart, Type, then Pie.
   c. Create the title, **VISION ASSOCIATION**, for the chart and the subtitle, **Donation Dollars at Work**.
   d. Close the Chart Editor.
3. At the table editing window, delete the table.
4. Display the Graphics Box Feature Bar for the chart, then change the box width to Full and the height to Size to Content at the Box Size dialog box. Close the Graphics Box Feature Bar.
5. Save the document and name it c20ex06.
6. Print c20ex06.
7. Close c20ex06.

Figure 20.9

Category		Percentage
Research		37.5
Community Service		24.7
Management		5.5
Fund Raising		15
Education		17.3

Exercise 7 Creating a Line Chart

1. At a clear editing window, create the table shown in figure 20.10.
2. Create a Line chart for the table by completing the following steps:
   a. Position the insertion point inside the table, then display the Chart Editor.
   b. At the Chart Editor, choose Chart, Type, then Line.
   c. Create a title for the chart and change the font size for the title by completing the following steps:
      (1) Choose Chart, then Titles.
      (2) At the Titles dialog box, press Tab, then key **Benefit of Tax-Free Compounding**.
      (3) Choose Options.
      (4) At the Titles Options dialog box, choose Font.
      (5) At the Font dialog box, change the size to 36, then choose OK.
      (6) At the Titles Options dialog box, choose OK or press Enter.
      (7) At the Titles dialog box, choose OK or press Enter.
   d. Close the Chart Editor.
3. At the editing window, delete the table.
4. Display the Graphics Box Feature Bar for the chart, then change the box width to Set at 5 inches and the height to Set at 4.5 at the Box Size dialog box. Close the Graphics Box Feature Bar.
5. Move the chart to the middle of the page by completing the following steps:
   a. Click on the Page/Zoom Full button on the Toolbar.
   b. Position the arrow pointer inside the chart, then click the left mouse button. (This selects the chart.)
   c. Position the arrow pointer (four-headed arrow) inside the chart, hold down the left mouse button, drag the outline of the chart box to the middle of the page, then release the mouse button.
   d. Deselect the chart, then click on the Page/Zoom Full button.
6. Save the document and name it c20ex07.
7. Print c20ex07.
8. Close c20ex07.

Figure 20.10

Years	10	20	30
Taxable Account	15000	22000	34000
Tax-Free Account	17000	32000	58000

Exercise 8 Creating a High/Low Chart

1. At a clear editing window, create the table shown in figure 20.11.
2. Create a High/Low chart for the table by completing the following steps:
   a. Position the insertion point inside the table, then display the Chart Editor.
   b. At the Chart Editor, choose Chart, Type, then High/Low.
   c. Create the title **STOCKS** for the chart.
   d. Close the Chart Editor.
3. At the editing window, delete the table.
4. Display the Graphics Box Feature Bar for the chart, then change the box width to Full and the height to Size to Content at the Box Size dialog box. Close the Graphics Box Feature Bar.
5. Save the document and name it c20ex08.
6. Print c20ex08.
7. Close c20ex08.

Figure 20.11

Stock	High	Low	Open	Close
United Foods	48	22.5	33.5	34
Milton Electric	74	45	71	70.25
SL Products	14	5	11.5	9.5
Lanson, Inc.	22	9	19.5	19.25

Exercise 9 Changing the Line Chart Type

1. At a clear editing window, open c20ex07.
2. Save the document with Save As and name it c20ex09.
3. Change the type of Line chart by completing the following steps:
   a. Position the insertion point inside the chart, then display the Chart Editor.
   b. Choose Chart, then Gallery.
   c. At the Data Chart dialog box, click on the second Line chart option in the bottom row in the middle of the dialog box.
   d. Choose OK or press Enter.
4. Close the Chart Editor.
5. Save the document again with the same name (c20ex09).
6. Print c20ex09.
7. Close c20ex09.

CHAPTER SUMMARY

- A chart, sometimes referred to as a *graph*, can be created from data in a table. A chart provides a more visual presentation of the data.
- A Bar chart is the default style and is created at the Chart Editor.
- By default, a chart is approximately 3.25 inches wide and is inserted in a box at the left margin with no border lines.
- In a chart, the left side of the chart is the vertical y-axis. The x-axis is the bottom of the chart.
- A title or subtitle or identification for the x and y axes can be added to a chart at the Titles dialog box.
- At the Graphics Box Feature Bar, you can make changes to the box containing the chart just as you can for other graphics boxes. You can also use the mouse to drag the chart in the document.
- The types of charts available include Area, Bar, High/Low, Line, Pie, Radar, and Scatter. Change the type of chart by choosing Chart, then Type at the Chart Editor.

Commands Review

	Mouse/Keyboard
Chart Editor	With insertion point in any cell in a table, choose Graphics, then Chart; or click on the Chart button on the Graphics Toolbar
Close Chart Editor	Click on Close button on Chart Toolbar; or click in the editing window, outside the chart
Titles dialog box	Chart, Titles; or double-click on title
Legend dialog box	Chart, Legend
Graphics Box Feature Bar	With arrow pointer in a chart at the editing window, hold down *right* mouse button, drag the arrow pointer to Feature Bar, then release mouse button

CHECK YOUR UNDERSTANDING

True/False: Circle the letter T if the statement is true; circle the letter F if the statement is false.

T **F** 1. The Pie chart is the default chart type.
T **F** 2. After a chart is created, it is inserted in a box that displays at the left margin of the document and measures about 3.25 inches wide.
T **F** 3. The x-axis runs horizontally across the bottom of a chart.
T **F** 4. A Line chart shows the high, low, open, and close quotes for a stock.
T **F** 5. By default, a legend is not created with the chart.

Completion: In the space provided at the right, indicate the correct term, command, or number.

1. The y-axis is marked like a ruler and is broken into units by marks called these. ____________
2. To create a title, the chart must be displayed here. ____________
3. This appears in a chart and shows which colors correspond with which series of data. ____________
4. This type of chart shows proportions and relationship of parts to the whole. ____________

5. This type of chart shows the interception points between x and y values. ______________
6. This type of chart shows trends and the amount of change over time. ______________

SKILL ASSESSMENTS

Assessment 1

1. At a clear editing window, create the table shown in figure 20.12.
2. Create a Bar chart with the table with the following elements:
   a. Create the title, **Estimated Living Expenses**.
   b. Create the subtitle, **Retirement**.
3. At the editing window, delete the table.
4. Display the Graphics Box Feature Bar for the chart, change the box width to Full and the height to Size to Content at the Box Size dialog box, then close the Graphics Box Feature Bar.
5. Save the document and name it c20sa01.
6. Print c20sa01.
7. Close c20sa01.

Figure 20.12

Expense	Current Cost	Retirement Cost
Housing	14080	4570
Food & Household	5800	4000
Clothing	2800	1800
Transportation	3600	3000
Medical & Dental	2360	2700
Entertainment	3920	6750

Assessment 2

1. At a clear editing window, create the table shown in figure 20.13.
2. Create a Line chart for the table with the following elements:
   a. At the Chart Editor, choose Chart, Type, then Line.
   b. Choose Chart, then Gallery. At the Data Chart dialog box, choose the fifth line chart in the middle of the dialog box (middle chart, bottom row).
   c. Create the title, **CITY OF WESTON**.
   d. Create the subtitle, **Population Growth**.
3. At the editing window, delete the table.
4. Display the Graphics Box Feature Bar for the chart, change the box width to Full and the height to Size to Content, then close the Graphics Box Feature Bar.
5. Save the document and name it c20sa02.
6. Print c20sa02.
7. Close c20sa02.

Figure 20.13

Year	1950	1960	1970	1980	1990
Population	9073	15218	28122	43932	48309

Assessment 3

1. At a clear editing window, key the headings and first paragraph of the memo in figure 20.20 in an appropriate memo format.
2. Create the table as shown in figure 20.14.
3. Create a Pie chart for the table with the following specifications:
   a. At the Chart Editor, change the type of chart to Pie.
   b. Create the title, **PTO FUND RAISING EVENTS**.
4. At the editing window, delete the table.
5. Move and/or size the Pie chart so it appears centered below the first paragraph of the memo.
6. Press Enter until the insertion point is positioned below the chart, then key the remaining text of the memo as shown in figure 20.14.
7. Save the document and name it c20sa03.
8. Print c20sa03.
9. Close c20sa03.

Figure 20.14

DATE: June 8, 1996
TO: Elizabeth White
FROM: Michelle Wong
SUBJECT: PTO FUNDS

The treasurer of the PTO, Leigh Gantz, presented the following information at the meeting on how the yearly PTO funds were raised.

Activity		Net Profit
Walk-a-thon		5800
Gift wrap		1130
Candy sale		570
Spring carnival		1450
Bake sale		150

The activity that provided the largest amount of money was one of the least time-consuming. After careful consideration of the various fund-raising activities, the PTO members voted to discontinue the bake sale and gift wrap for next year. Members will invest more time helping students get sponsors for the Walk-a-thon.

xx:c20sa03

Assessment 4

1. At a clear editing window, create a High/Low chart with the information shown in figure 20.15. (*Hint:* Create a table for the information but do not include the title in the table. Create the title in the Chart Editor.) You determine the following:
   a. Elements to include in the chart.
   b. Position and size of the chart in the editing window. (Delete the table at the editing window after creating the chart.)
2. Save the document and name it c20sa04.
3. Print c20sa04.
4. Close c20sa04.

Figure 20.15

MAINLINE STOCKS

	High	Low	Open	Close
Calform Corporation	46	21	45.5	46.25
Packston Printing	14	6	11.5	10
Ehli Electronics	70	38	65.5	66
Meyers, Inc.	25	11	22	24.5

Unit 4 Performance Assessment

In this unit, you have learned to enhance the visual display of documents with graphics elements, add visual enhancements to documents with WordPerfect Draw and TextArt, and display numerical data in a chart.

PROBLEM-SOLVING AND DECISION-MAKING

Assessment 1

1. At a clear editing window, insert the graphics image named **hotair.wpg** into a figure box with the following specifications:
   a. Change the anchor to Put Box on Current Page at the Box Position dialog box.
   b. Change the box width and height to Full at the Box Size dialog box.
   c. Create a caption that reads *Figure 1 Hot Air Balloons*.
   d. Move the caption to the outside of the top border.
   e. Change the figure box border to Triple and add 10% fill.
2. Save the document and name it u04pa01.
3. Print u04pa01.
4. Close u04pa01.

Optional: Experiment with different fill gradations and image sizes. Print your favorite variation.

Assessment 2

1. At a clear editing window, create the document shown in figure U4.1 by completing the following steps:
   a. Create a user box with the following specifications:
      (1) Insert the image named **winrace.wpg** in the user box.
      (2) Change the anchor to Put Box on Current Page at the Box Position dialog box.
      (3) Change the horizontal position to Left Margin.
      (4) Change the width to 2 inches.

b. Change the font to 14-point Arrus BT Bold.
c. Press Enter twice, then key the text shown in figure U4.1.
d. Create the horizontal line at the default settings except change the Horizontal option to Set.
e. Change the font to 12-point Arrus BT Bold for the text *Sponsored by Denver Memorial Hospital*.

2. Save the document and name it u04pa02.
3. Print u04pa02.
4. Close u04pa02.

Optional: Recreate the document in a different font. Add information about the length of the race and where it starts and finishes.

Figure U4.1

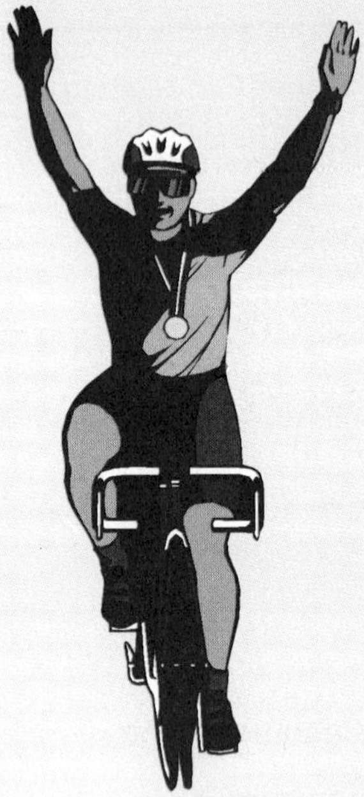

COME JOIN IN THE FUN!!

Parkside Bicycle Race

Saturday, August 9, 1997

Starting time: 9:00 a.m.

Registration fee: $20

Sponsored by Denver Memorial Hospital

Assessment 3

1. At a clear editing window, create a letterhead for the organization WILDLIFE RESTORATION LEAGUE. Include the following information in the letterhead:

   WILDLIFE RESTORATION LEAGUE
   P.O. Box 345
   Bismarck, ND 74523
   (701) 555-2309

   Include a user box in the letterhead with the image **buck.wpg** inserted in the user box. Also, include at least one horizontal or vertical line.
2. Save the letterhead and name it u04pa03.
3. Print u04pa03.
4. Close u04pa03.

Assessment 4

1. At a clear editing window, create the table shown in figure U4.2.
2. Save the table and name it u04pa04.
3. Print u04pa04.
4. Close u04pa04.

Figure U4.2

ARMSTRONG ELEMENTARY SCHOOL			
READING INCENTIVE PROGRAM			
NAME:		GRADE:	ROOM:
Min.	**Book Title**	**Min.**	**Book Title**

Assessment 5

1. At a clear editing window, create the table shown in figure U4.3.
2. Save the table and name it u04pa05.
3. Print u04pa05.
4. Close u04pa05.

Optional: Analyze the patterns and trends in the data and write a two paragraph report comparing the needs of elementary and secondary teachers. What technology improvements would benefit you the most? Why?

Figure U4.3

OMAHA CITY SCHOOL DISTRICT			
Technology Study Question, #4			
What forms of technology would improve your job?	**H.S.**	**J.H.**	**E.S.**
1. Networking of computers.	3	2	2
2. Computers in the classroom for student use.	2	1	1
3. Adequate access to phones, intercoms, and FAX.	1	5	4
4. Systematic upgrading of hardware/software.	6	4	7
5. Computer in every classroom for teacher use.	4	9	5
6. Improved access to student information.	7	7	4
7. District-wide technology plan.	9	5	3
8. More frequent maintenance cycles.	3	5	3

Assessment 6

1. At a clear editing window, create the table shown in figure U4.4.
2. Create a Line chart with the table and include the following:
   a. Add the title, *EFFECT OF 5% INFLATION.*
   b. Add the subtitle, *ON $100,000 POLICY.*
   c. Change the chart type to Line.
   d. Display the Data Chart dialog box (Chart, Gallery) for Line charts, then choose the middle box in the bottom row.
   e. After creating the chart, delete the table from the editing window.
   f. Change the size of the chart to 5.5 inches wide and 4.5 inches high.
   g. Move the chart to the middle of the page.
3. Save the chart and name it u04pa06.
4. Print u04pa06.
5. Close u04pa06.

Optional: In one paragraph, explain what the data in U4.4 means.

Figure U4.4

Year	0	5	10	15	20
Amount	100,000	78,350	61,390	48,100	37,690

Assessment 7

1. At a clear editing window, create the table shown in figure U4.5.
2. Create a Pie chart with the table and include the following:
   a. Add the title, *SOURCES OF.*
   b. Add the subtitle, *RETIREMENT INCOME.*
   c. After creating the chart, delete the table from the editing window.
   d. Change the horizontal position to Center of Paragraph at the Box Position dialog box.
   e. Change the width of the chart to 5.5 inches and the height to Size to Content.

3. Save the chart and name it u04pa07.
4. Print u04pa07.
5. Close u04pa07.

Optional: Personalize this chart for your anticipated or planned retirement source.

Figure U4.5

Income Source		Percentage
Social Security		32.5
Retirement Plan		24.4
SRAs, IRAs, etc.		18.8
Interest, Dividends		14.6
Savings		9.7

WRITING

The following activities give you the opportunity to practice your writing skills along with demonstrating an understanding of some of the important WordPerfect features you have mastered in this unit. In planning the documents, remember to shape the information according to the writing purpose and the audience. Use correct grammar, appropriate word choices, and clear sentence constructions.

Activity 1

Situation: You work for CYCLE CITY, a store that sells bicycles and bicycling gear. You have been asked to design a letterhead for the store. When designing this letterhead, include the image *winrace.wpg* along with this information:

CYCLE CITY
2305 Benson Highway
Kent, WA 98033
(206) 555-4422

Save the letterhead and name it u04act01. Print and then close u04act01.

Activity 2

Situation: You are Cynthia Lakeland, assistant manager for CYCLE CITY. Write a letter to R & L Suppliers, 903 North Union Street, Seattle, WA 98049, using the letterhead you created in Activity 1. In the letter, request information on a new ultra light bicycling helmet you saw advertised in the R & L Suppliers catalog. Ask that a representative of the company visit the store and bring a sample of the helmet. You are also interested in any bicycling safety goggles manufactured by the company. Save the letter and name it u04act02. Print and then close u04act02.

Activity 3

Situation: You are Jenna McCormick, financial advisor for the Omaha City School District. You have been asked by Pat Windslow, the superintendent for the school district, to prepare a table showing computer expenditures for each school and write a one page report using the data that follows:

OMAHA CITY SCHOOL DISTRICT

Computer Expenditures, 1996-97

School	**Amount**
Leland Elementary School	$59,060
Carr Elementary School	43,230
Sahala Elementary School	15,304
Young Elementary School	20,430
Armstrong Elementary School	39,390
Grant Junior High School	68,405
Washington Junior High School	55,304
Roosevelt Junior High School	49,300
Nylan High School	89,000
Cleveland High School	100,230
Total Amount	(calculate total)

Create a table with the data and insert a formula to calculate the total. Save this document and name it u04act03. Print and then close u04act03.

Appendix A • Formatting Disks

Before a disk can be used to save WordPerfect documents, it must be formatted. (If you are using the student data disk that comes with this textbook, the disk has already been formatted. Do not format it again since formatting erases everything on the disk.) Formatting is a process that prepares the surface of a disk for receiving data from the particular disk operating system that you are using. A disk can be formatted using the Format command from the Disk Operating System (DOS).

During the formatting process, any information on the disk is erased. Before formatting, make sure you do not have anything on the disk that you want to keep.

Complete the following steps to format a disk:

1. Turn on the computer.
2. At the C:\> prompt, key **format a:** (or format b: depending on where the disk is located), then press Enter.
3. The message *Insert new diskette for drive A: and press Enter when ready...* appears on the screen. Insert a blank disk in drive a, close the disk drive door, then press Enter.
4. When you press Enter, the formatting process begins and the disk light comes on. Do not remove the disk while the disk is being formatted.
5. When the disk is formatted, you will see the message *Format another (Y/N)?*. If you do not want to format another disk, key **N**, then press Enter. The C:\> appears on the screen. (Depending on the version of DOS you are using, you may see the message, *Volume label (11 characters, Enter for none)?*. At this message, press Enter; or key your name, then press Enter.)
6. Take the disk out and turn off the computer.

Appendix B • Proofreaders' Marks

Proofreaders' Mark		Example	Revised
#	Insert space	lettertothe	letter to the
℘	Delete	the commands is	the command is
lc /	Lowercase	lc he is Branch Manager	he is branch manager
(cap) or uc ≡	Uppercase	(cap) Margaret simpson	Margaret Simpson
¶	New paragraph	¶ The new product	The new product
no ¶	No paragraph	the meeting. no ¶ Bring the	the meeting. Bring the
^	Insert	pens, clips (and)	pens, and clips
⊙	Insert period	a global search	a global search.
⊐	Move right	⊐ With the papers	With the papers
⊏	Move left	⊏ access the code	access the code
⊐ ⊏	Center	⊐ Chapter Six ⊏	Chapter Six
∽	Transpose	It is raesonable	It is reasonable
(sp)	Spell out	(sp) 475 Mill Ave.	475 Mill Avenue
. . .	Stet (do not delete)	I am very pleased	I am very pleased
⁀	Close up	regret fully	regretfully
ss	Single-space	The margin top ss is 1 inch.	The margin top is 1 inch.
ds	Double-space	ds Paper length is set for 11 inches.	Paper length is set for 11 inches.
ts	Triple-space	ts The F8 function key contains commands	The F8 function key contains commands
bf	Boldface	bf Boldface type provides emphasis.	**Boldface** type provides emphasis.
(ital)	Italics	(ital) Use italics for terms to be defined.	Use *italics* for terms to be defined.

Appendix C • Formatting Business Documents

There are many memorandum and business letter styles. This appendix includes one memorandum and two business letter styles.

At the end of a memorandum or business letter, the initials of the person keying the document appear. In exercises in this textbook, insert your initials where you see the *xx* at the end of a document. The name of the document is included after the initials.

Both business letters in this appendix were created with standard punctuation. Standard punctuation includes a colon after the salutation and a comma after the complimentary close.

A business letter can be printed on letterhead stationery, or the company name and address can be keyed at the top of the letter. For the examples in this text, assume that all business letters you create will be printed on letterhead stationery.

1-inch top margin

DATE: September 23, 1997

ds

TO: Adam Mukai, Vice President

ds

FROM: Carol Jenovich, Director

ds

SUBJECT: NEW EMPLOYEES

ts

Two new employees have been hired to work in the Human Resources Department. Lola Henderson will begin work on October 1 and Daniel Schriver will begin October 14.

ds

Ms. Henderson has worked for three years as an administrative assistant for another company. Due to her previous experience, she was hired as a Program Assistant.

ds

Mr. Schriver has just completed a one-year training program at Gulf Community College. He was hired as an Administrative Assistant I.

ds

I would like to introduce you to the new employees. Please schedule a time for a short visit.

ds

xx:memo

Traditional Memo Style

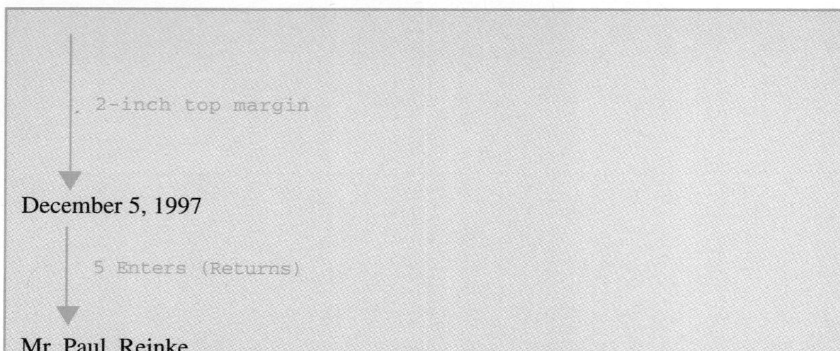

2-inch top margin

December 5, 1997

5 Enters (Returns)

Mr. Paul. Reinke
Iverson Medical Center
1290 South 43rd Street
Houston, TX 77348

ds

Dear Mr. Reinke:

ds

During the entire month of January, our laser printer, Model No. 34-454, will be on sale. We are cutting the original price by 33 percent!

ds

When you purchased your computer system from our store last month, you indicated an interest in a laser printer. Now is your chance, Mr. Reinke, to purchase a high-quality laser printer at a rock-bottom price. Once you have seen the quality of print produced by a laser printer, you will not be satisfied with any other type of printer.

ds

Visit our store at your convenience and see a demonstration of this incredible printer. We are so confident you will purchase the printer that we are enclosing a coupon for a free printer cartridge worth over $100.

ds

Very truly yours,

4 Enters (Returns)

Gina Cerazzo, Manager

ds

xx:blockltr

ds

Enclosure

Block-style Letter

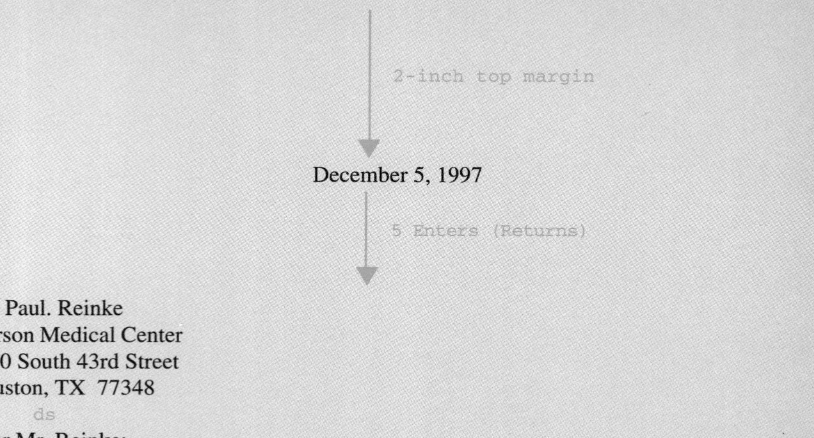

2-inch top margin

December 5, 1997

5 Enters (Returns)

Mr. Paul. Reinke
Iverson Medical Center
1290 South 43rd Street
Houston, TX 77348

ds

Dear Mr. Reinke:

ds

During the entire month of January, our laser printer, Model No. 34-454, will be on sale. We are cutting the original price by 33 percent!

ds

When you purchased your computer system from our store last month, you indicated an interest in a laser printer. Now is your chance, Mr. Reinke, to purchase a high-quality laser printer at a rock-bottom price. Once you have seen the quality of print produced by a laser printer, you will not be satisfied with any other type of printer.

ds

Visit our store at your convenience and see a demonstration of this incredible printer. We are so confident you will purchase the printer that we are enclosing a coupon for a free printer cartridge worth over $100.

ds

Very truly yours,

ds

HOUSTON COMPUTING

4 Enters (Returns)

Gina Cerazzo, Manager

ds

xx:blockltr

ds

Enclosure

Modified Block-style Letter

Appendix D • Graphics Images

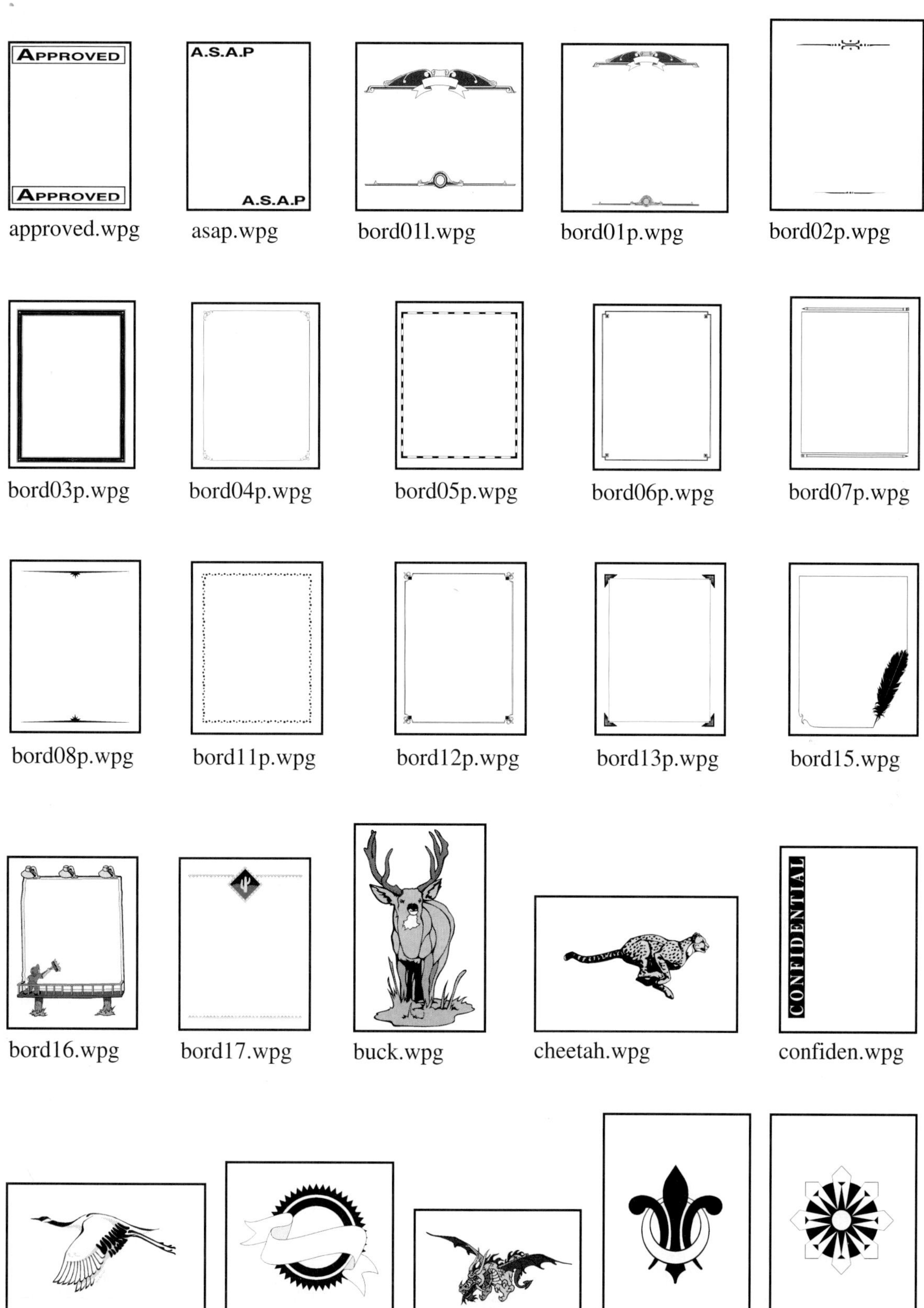

approved.wpg asap.wpg bord01l.wpg bord01p.wpg bord02p.wpg

bord03p.wpg bord04p.wpg bord05p.wpg bord06p.wpg bord07p.wpg

bord08p.wpg bord11p.wpg bord12p.wpg bord13p.wpg bord15.wpg

bord16.wpg bord17.wpg buck.wpg cheetah.wpg confiden.wpg

crane_j.wpg crest.wpg dragn.wpg ender01.wpg ender02.wpg

ender03.wpg

ender04.wpg

ender05.wpg

ender06.wpg

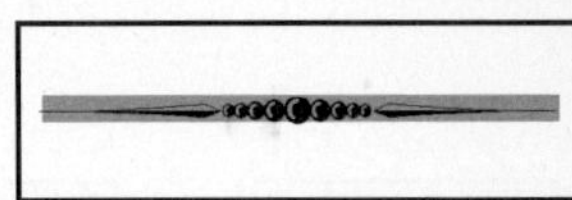
ender07.wpg

horse_j.wpg

hotair.wpg

importnt.wpg

invitatn.wpg

marsh.wpg

medical1.wpg

past_due.wpg

prohibit.wpg

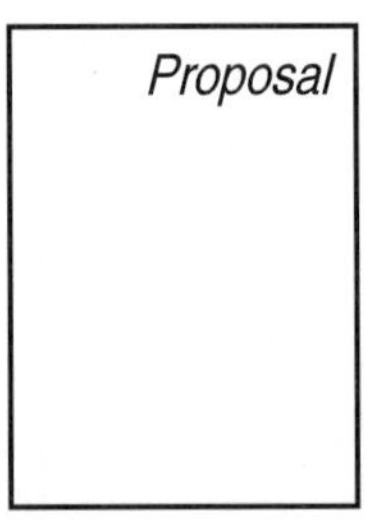

proposal.wpg

rose.wpg

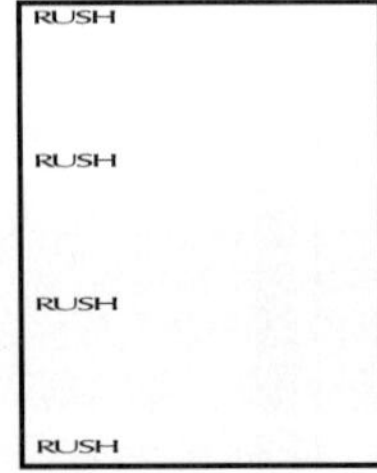

rush.wpg

rsvp.wpg

sil02.wpg

sil03.wpg

thanks.wpg

tiger_j.wpg

topsecrt.wpg

windmill.wpg

winrace.wpg

world.wpg

Index

A

Absolute tabs, 161
Active document or window, 223
All Caps, 31
Antonyms, 76, 77
Application control button, 226
Area charts, 369
Arrow pointer. *See* Mouse pointer

B

Balanced newspaper columns, 250
Bar charts, 361-63, 369
Block protect, parallel columns, 253
Blocks of text, 217. *See also* Selecting text
  copying, 218-19
  moving, 217-18
Block-style letter, 386
Bolding text, 32
Borders, graphics boxes, 281-83
Box Border/Fill Styles dialog box, 282
Box Caption dialog box, 277
Box Content dialog box, 278
Boxes. *See* Graphics boxes
Brightness, Image Tool palette, 288
Bullets, inserting, 107-8
Business documents, formatting, 385-86
Button boxes, 273-74

C

Calendars, 122-23
Canceling a merge, 146
Canceling commands, 10
Captions, graphics boxes, 276-78
Cascading document windows, 223-24
Cascading submenu, xii
Case of letters, changing, 219
Cells, 333. *See also* Tables
  deleting contents, 349
  joining, 347
  justification, 349-50
  selecting, 343-44
  splitting, 348-49
Centering text, 45-46
Centering text vertically on page, 192-93
Character sets, 105-8
Chart boxes, editing, 367-68
Chart button, Graphics Toolbar, 362
Chart Editor, 361, 362, 363
Charts, 361
  based on tables, 361-62
  deleting, 367
  legends, 365-66
  positioning, 367-68
  sizing, 367-68
  titles, 363
  types, 368-70
Chart Toolbar, 362, 363
Check boxes, xiii-xiv
Checking style, in Grammatik, 80, 81-82
Clearing shapes, 304
Closed Object tools, 302-4
Closing documents, 10
Coaches, 39, 40
Codes, Find and Replace, 237-38, 240-41
Color
  graphics boxes, 283
  graphics images, 289
  shapes, 319, 320
Column markers, 255
Columns. *See also* Tables
  changing widths, 249-50, 251
  defining in existing text, 251
  editing text, 251
  justification, 349-50
  moving insertion point in, 251
  newspaper, 247-52
  page breaks, 251, 252
  parallel, 247, 252-53
  turning off or on, 251
Columns button, Power Bar, 247-49
Command buttons, xiv
Commands
  canceling, 10
  executing, xii-xiv
  keyboard, xii-xiv
Computer hardware, vii
Computer systems, vii
Contouring text, 316-18
Contrast, Image Tool palette, 288
Converting case of letters, 219
Copying
  blocks of text, 218-19
  documents, 171-72
  objects, 313-14
Corrections, automatic. *See* QuickCorrect
Corrections in Grammatik, 80-81
cpi (characters per inch), 98
CPU (Central Processing Unit), vii
Create Data File dialog box, 141
Create Graphics Line dialog box, 292
Create Table dialog box, 334
Cursor. *See* Insertion point
Cutting text, 217, 218

D

Data Chart dialog box, 370
Data files
  creating, 137-42
  fields, 138-39, 142, 145
Data File Feature Bar, 141
Date, inserting, 105
Deleting
  cell contents, 349
  charts, 367
  documents, 173-74
  endnotes and footnotes, 209
  graphics boxes, 306
  macros, 121
  selected objects, 314
  table contents, 353
  tables, 352-53
  table structures, 353
  text, 19, 22. *See also* Undelete; Undo
Deletion commands, 19
Dialog boxes, xii-xiv
Dialog boxes, removing, 10
Dictionaries, Spell Checker, 73
Disk Drives, vii, viii-ix. *See also* Drives
Disks
  formatting, x, 383
  handling, ix-x
Document control button, xii, 226
Document icons, 226
Document information, 79
Document Initial Font dialog box, 105
Documents
  closing, 10
  copying, 171-72
  creating, 3
  deleting, 173-74
  inserting, 221
  inserting into boxes, 272-73
  maintaining, 170
  moving, 172-73
  moving text between, 227
  naming, 9-10
  opening, 11, 13, 175-76
  page numbering, 193-94
  printing, 26, 27, 167, 174, 175
  renaming, 173
  saving, 7-8, 13, 25
  selecting, 174-75
  viewing, 176-77
Document windows, 5-6, 222
  cascading, 223-24
  moving, 227
  moving text between, 227
  opening, 222-23

sizing, 225-27
tiling, 224-25
Draft viewing mode, 52, 53
Draw
closing, 302
drawing shapes, 301-6
editing and moving drawings, 306
editing objects, 310-20
font, 308
inserting text, 307-8
opening, 301
Ruler and grid, 305-6
sizing drawing area, 308-10
zooming, 309
Draw Power Bar, 302, 308
Draw Toolbar, 302
Draw Tool palette, 302
Draw window, 302
Drives, changing default, 9. *See also* Disk drives
Drop-down menus, xii, xiii

E

Editing
chart boxes, 367-68
documents, 15-25
drawings, 306
endnotes and footnotes, 209
graphics boxes, 290
headers and footers, 204-5
macros, 117-18
objects in Draw, 310-20
tables, 344-45, 346-47
TextArt images, 326-27
text in columns, 251
Editing window. *See* Document windows
Endnotes, 201, 205
creating, 206-7, 208
deleting, 209
editing, 209
formatting, 210, 211
printing, 208
renumbering, 210
Endnote window, 206
Envelopes
addressed during a merge, 147-48
creating, 124-26
form files, 147
Exiting
Windows program, 11, 13
WordPerfect, 11, 13
Extension, 9, 10

F

Figure boxes, 270-71, 277-78, 280
Fields
in data files, 138-39, 142, 145
in form files, 144
File information, 170
Files. *See* Documents
Fill, changing in shapes, 319, 320
Fill attributes, Image Tool palette, 288
Fill styles, graphics boxes, 281, 283
Find and Replace, 235-37
Action options, 241-42
direction of search, 241
codes, 237-38, 240-41
customizing, 237-43
Match options, 238-41
replacing, 241
search options, 242-43
specific codes, 237-38
word forms, 237
Flush Right command, 197
Font cartridge, 99
Font face. *See* Typefaces
Fonts, 99-104
changing for entire document, 211-12
default, 104-5
in Draw, 308
in TextArt, 322
Font sizes. *See* Type sizes
Font Style list box, Power Bar, 102-3
Font style. *See* Type styles
Footers. *See* Headers and footers
Footnotes, 205
creating, 206-7
deleting, 209
editing, 209
formatting, 210, 211-12
printing, 208
renumbering, 210
Footnote window, 206
Formatting, 31
business documents, 385-86
characters, 32-36
disks, 383
endnotes and footnotes, 210, 211, 212
headers and footers, 210-11
lines, 45
with Table Expert, 353-54
Format Toolbar, 51
Form files, 143-44
defined, 137
for envelopes, 147
for labels, 148
Function keys, viii

G

Grammatik, 79-84
Graphics boxes. *See also* Button boxes; Figure boxes; Table boxes; Text boxes; Userboxes; Watermarks
borders and fill styles, 281-83
captions, 276-78
changing contents, 278
changing styles, 285-86
deleting, 306
editing existing boxes, 290
fill styles, 281, 283
finding next or previous, 289
foreground and background color, 283
Image Tool palette, 286-89
moving, 290-91
position, 278-79, 280
sizing, 279-80, 290-91
wrapping text, 284-85
Graphics Box Feature Bar, 268
Graphics images
inserting into documents, 267-68, 280
rotation, 289
text flow around, 284-85
WordPerfect files, 387-88
Graphics lines. *See* Lines
Graphics Toolbar, 268
Chart button, 362
Horizontal Line button, 291
Vertical Line button, 291
Grid in Draw, 305
Gutter, 249, 255

H

Hanging indents, 66-67
Hard copy, ix
Hard page breaks, 191-92
Hardware, 3, 10
Header/Footer Feature Bar, 202-3
Headers and footers, 201-5
discontinuing, 205
editing, 204-5
formatting, 210-11
printing, 204
on specific pages, 203-4
viewing, 201
Header window, 202
Headwords, in Thesaurus, 76
Help template, x
Help menu options, 38-39
High/Low charts, 369, 372

I

I-beam pointer. *See* Mouse pointer
Icons, 5, 17, 226
Image Tool palette, 286-88
Indenting text, 62-67
hanging indents, 66-67
from margins, 63, 64, 65
Inserting
date, 105
documents, 221

documents in graphics boxes, 272-73
graphics images, 267-68, 280
rows or columns into tables, 344-45, 346-47
text, 19
Insertion point, 6
moving, 15-18
moving between fields, 141
moving in labels, 127
moving in tables, 336-37
Insert mode, 6
Italicizing text, 35

J

Joining
cells in tables, 347
paragraphs, 19-20
Justification. *See also* Flush Right command
changing, 48-51
changing in cells, 349-50

K

Keep Text Together dialog box, 191
Keyboard, vii, viii

L

Labels, 126-28
creating, 126-28
moving insertion point, 127
viewing, 127
Label form files, 148
Legends, charts, 365-66
Letter styles, 386
Letter template, 123-24
Line charts, 369, 371, 372
Line Object tools, 302-4
Lines
changing in shapes, 319, 320
creating, 291-93, 294
Line spacing, 47-48
List boxes, xiii
Loading WordPerfect, 4, 13
Logical page, 127

M

Macros, 113
deleting, 121
editing, 117-18
location, 114
naming, 115
pausing, 119-21
playing, 116-17
recording, 114-15
Macro Tools Toolbar, 114
Mailing labels. *See* Labels
Maintaining documents, 170
Margin markers, 61
Margins
changing, 59-61, 189-90
defaults, 59, 189
Marquee, xiii
Matching, in Find and Replace, 239-41
Maximizing document windows, 225-27
Memo style, 385
Menu Bar, xii, 5
Merge dialog box, 140
Merge Feature Bar, 144
Merges, canceling, 146
Merging files, 144-45, 146
Microcomputers. *See* Computer systems
Minimizing document windows, 225-27
Modified block-style letter, 386
Monitor, vii
Monospaced typefaces, 97
Moving
blocks of text, 217-18, 227
documents, 172-73
between document windows, 227
drawings, 306
graphics boxes, 290-91
objects, 311-12
Moving insertion point
in columns, 251
with keyboard, 17-18
with mouse, 15-17
in tables, 336-37
Mouse, vii, ix, xi, xii, 15-17
Mouse pointer, ix, xi, 6

N

Naming,
documents, 9-10
macros, 115
New Blank Document button, 122
New Document button, 122
Newspaper columns
balanced, 250
creating with Columns button, 247-49
creating with Columns dialog box, 249-50, 252
Numbering. *See* Page numbering
Numbers, inserting, 107-8

O

Objects in Draw
copying, 313-14
deleting, 314
editing, 310-20
moving, 311-12
selecting, 310-11
sizing, 314-15
Open As Copy, 175-76
Opening
documents, 11, 13, 175-76
multiple documents or windows, 222-23
Option buttons, xiv

P

Page breaks, 189, 191-92
in columns, 251, 252
in tables, 336
viewing, 189, 192
Page icons, 17
Page numbering, 193-96
changing beginning page number, 195-96
changing method, 196
selective, 194-95
viewing, 193
Pages, printing, 167-69
Page viewing mode, 52, 53
Paragraph adjustment marker, 61
Paragraphs
indenting, 62-66
splitting and joining, 19-20
Parallel columns, 247, 249
with Block Protect, 253
creating, 252-53
Pasting text, 217, 218
Pausing macros, 119-21
Physical page, 127
Pie charts, 369, 370
Pitch, 98
Playing macros, 116-17
Pointer. *See* Mouse pointer
Pop-up lists. *See* Drop-down menus
Position
of charts, 367-68
of graphics boxes, 278-79, 280
of tables, 350
POSTNET Bar Code, 126
Power Bar, 5, 6
Columns button, 247-49
Font Face button, 101
Font Size button, 102
Justification button, 50
Table button, 336
Point size, 98
Printer, vii, ix
Printer fonts, 100
Printing, 167-70
documents, 26, 27, 167, 174, 175
endnotes and footnotes, 208
headers and footers, 203-4
multiple copies, 169-70
pages, 167-69
selected text, 169
Proofreaders' marks, 384
Proportional typefaces, 97

Q

QuickCorrect, 7, 128-30
Quick Data Entry dialog box, 141
QuickTip, 5-6

R

Radar charts, 369
Radio buttons, xiv
Recording macros, 114-15
Redo, 23-24, 27
References, in Thesaurus, 76
Relative Size, 103-4
Relative tabs, 161
Renaming documents, 173
Replacements in Grammatik, 80-81
Replacing in Find and Replace, 241
Restoring document windows, 225-27
Reveal Codes, 33-34
Rotation of graphics images, 289
Rows, inserting in tables, 344-45, 346-47
Rule class in Grammatik, 83-84
Ruler Bar, 61, 154, 255
  changing tabs with, 153-57
  table markers, 339
Ruler Bar Guide, 255
Ruler in Draw, 305

S

San serif typefaces, 97-98
Saving
  documents, 7-8, 13, 25
  selected text, 220
  standard text, 220
Scatter chart, 369
Scroll bars, xiii, 5, 6, 16-17
Scrolling, 15-17
Searching. *See* Find and Replace
Selecting, 6
  cells, 343-44
  documents, 174-75
  objects, 310-11
  text, 20-22, 27
Selection bar, 21
Select mode, 21-22
Serif typefaces, 97-98
Shapes
  changing attributes, 319-20
  clearing, 304
  drawing, 301-6
Sizing
  charts, 367-68
  document windows, 226-27
  drawing area, 308-10
  graphics boxes, 279-80, 290-91
  objects, 314-15
Sizing handles, 290, 308, 311, 314-15
Small Caps, 103
Soft copy, ix
Soft fonts, 99, 100
Soft page breaks, 192
Software, 3
Specific Codes dialog box, 238
Spell Checker, 73-75
Spell Checker dictionaries, 73
Splitting cells, 348-49
Splitting paragraphs, 19-20
Standard text, 220
Statistics, document, 79
Status bar, 5, 6, 251, 253
Subgroups, in Thesaurus, 76
Symbols, inserting, 105-7
Synonyms, 76-77

T

Tab key, 31
Table boxes, 271-72
Table button, Power Bar, 336
Table column indicators, 335
Table data files, 145-46
Table Expert, 353-54
Table grid, 333-334
Table row indicators, 335
Tables
  changing position, 350
  column widths, 338-42
  creating, 333-36, 337, 338
  deleting, 352-53
  deleting cell contents, 349
  deleting table contents, 353
  deleting table structure, 353
  entering text, 336
  inserting rows or columns, 344-45, 346-47
  joining cells, 347
  moving insertion point, 336-37
  page breaks, 336
  selecting cells, 343-44
  splitting cells, 348-49
  tabs, 336
Tables Toolbar, 334
Tabs
  absolute, 161
  changing with Ruler Bar, 153-57
  changing with Tab Set dialog box, 157-61
  clearing, 155, 158
  default, 153, 161
  evenly spaced, 161
  moving, 157
  relative, 161
  in tables, 336
  types, 153-55, 161
Templates, 113, 122-24
TextArt, 301, 320
  changing text shape, 324-25
  editing images, 326-27
  entering text, 321-22
  Menu Bar, 325
  modifying, 322-23
TextArt Toolbar, 323
Text
  changing shape in TextArt, 324-25
  contouring in Draw, 316-18
  entering in TextArt, 321-22
  inserting in Draw, 307-8
  selecting, 20-22, 27
Text boxes, xiii, 269-70
Text flow around graphics images, 284-85
Thesaurus, 76-78
Tiling windows, 224-25
Title Bar, 5
Titles for charts, 363-65
Toolbar, 5-6
Traditional memo style, 385
True Type fonts, 100, 124
Two-Page viewing mode, 52
Typefaces, 97-98, 100, 101
Type sizes, 98, 101-2, 103-4
Type styles, 99, 102-3

U

Undelete, 23-24, 27
Underlining text, 36
Undo, 23-24, 27
User boxes, 272-73, 281

V

Viewing documents, 176-77
Viewing mode, 52, 53

W

Watermarks, 275-76
Widow/Orphan feature, 190-91
Windows, document. *See* Document windows
Windows program, 222
  exiting, 11, 13
  Program Manager screen, 4
Word forms, Find and Replace, 237
WordPerfect
  exiting, 11, 13
  loading, 4, 13
WordPerfect Help template, x
Word wrap, 7
Wrapping text, in graphics boxes, 284-85

XYZ

Zooming, 53, 309